The
Edinburgh
Companion
to the
History of
Democracy

The Edinburgh Companion to the History of Democracy

From Pre-history to Future Possibilities

Edited by
Benjamin Isakhan and Stephen Stockwell

EDINBURGH
University Press

© editorial matter and organisation Benjamin Isakhan and Stephen Stockwell, 2012, 2015
© the chapters their several authors, 2012

Edinburgh University Press Ltd
The Tun - Holyrood Road,
12(2f) Jackson's Entry,
Edinburgh EH8 8PJ
www.euppublishing.com

First published in hardback by Edinburgh University Press 2012
This paperback edition 2015

Typeset in 11 on 13 Ehrhardt by
Iolaire Typesetting, Newtonmore, and
printed and bound in Great Britain by
CPI Group (UK) Ltd, Croydon CR0 4YY

A CIP record for this book is available from the British Library

ISBN 978 0 7486 4075 1 (hardback)
ISBN 978 1 4744 0014 5 (paperback)
ISBN 978 0 7486 5366 9 (webready PDF)
ISBN 978 0 7486 5368 3 (epub)

Contents

Acknowledgements

More than eighty years ago, a distinguished professor of history by the name of Alan F. Hattersley set out on an ambitious project to write a history of democracy. However, in his Preface, Hattersley acknowledged that to 'attempt a comprehensive and unprejudiced examination of the forms of democracy in the past, and of the principles upon which they have rested, would be to undertake the task of a lifetime' (Hattersley 1930: vii). We can certainly relate to Hattersley's problem. While this volume did not take a lifetime, it is the result of several years of joint scholarly enquiry into democracy and its complex and contested history. In fact, we have probed much further and deeper into human history than Hattersley and many other scholars concerned with democracy's past. This volume therefore sets a benchmark as the first collection on the history of democracy to present lesser known examples, such as those of ancient China, medieval Islam, colonial Africa or today's Burma, alongside more familiar cases like Athens, the English Parliament, the French Revolution and Women's Suffrage. Overall, we have attempted to move debate and discussion one step closer to Hattersley's goal of a history of democracy that is both comprehensive and unprejudiced.

However, we have not undertaken this task alone. Foremost mention must go to our collection of distinguished contributors who produced such insightful and detailed chapters. They were as enthusiastic as we were about the history of democracy and responded to various editorial requests with acuity and celerity. We also owe thanks to Anne Richards for her initial research assistance and for making first contact with many of our contributors. We are likewise indebted to Jennifer Kloester for her thoughtful editing of the chapters; her commitment to clear and precise style has made a major contribution to this volume. Also worthy of mentioning are the staff of Edinburgh University Press, especially Nicola Ramsey, who took an initial interest in the scope and content of the volume and was both patient and professional as it came to fruition.

Throughout the completion of this volume and the associated project on the history of democracy, Benjamin Isakhan has been privileged enough to hold four consecutive research fellowships. He is indebted to his colleagues and friends at Griffith University's Islamic Research Unit and La Trobe University's Centre for Dialogue. However, foremost mention must go to Deakin University's Centre for Citizenship and Globalisation, and especially to the centre's director, Fethi Mansouri, who recognised the importance of this volume and supported its completion. Most recently,

Ben has been fortunate enough to receive an Australian Research Council Discovery Early Career Researcher Award (DE120100315), a fellowship which has allowed him to complete this volume. On a personal level, Ben thanks his family and friends for their encouragement, understanding and support, and his wife, Lyndal, for her patience and love.

Stephen Stockwell would like to thank the School of Humanities at Griffith University and the Griffith Centre for Cultural Research for the time and support to complete his contribution to this book. In particular, he would like to thank Kay Ferres, former Dean of Humanities and Social Sciences, who supplied the seed funding for this project. He thanks all those friends and opponents in politics, journalism and academia who have taught him so much about democracy. Finally, he thanks his parents and his son for their support and dedicates his contribution to his patient and understanding partner, Ann Baillie.

Preface

Jack Goody

It used to be thought that democracy was invented in ancient Greece. The Greeks were certainly the first to use the word, but this book helps us see that the practice of coming to decisions only after consulting those involved was much more widely known. It also shows that the will of the people can be ascertained in a variety of ways. In small groups, it is possible to have direct democracy by means of a meeting of all the members. In larger groups, one has to have representation, perhaps by heads of households in the simplest case. But such a system of 'automatic representation' may clearly fail to embody the voice of the young, or of women. Any form of representation involves a system of selection of the representative, either by a show of hands or, in a 'literate' society, by the vote, by marking a paper or a potsherd with that of the candidate of one's choice. Such a type of universal democracy did not exist in Greece where women, slaves and non-citizens were excluded from the vote.

To study the history of democracy is to trace the story of organised human society. The simplest human community consists of a clan, as recently among the aboriginal inhabitants of Australia. Such units display little delegation of authority, so that the question of representation and authority hardly exists. Decisions were taken by consultation among heads of families, who had the responsibility of discussing issues with their respective families, otherwise there was minimal coordination of a deliberate kind. The idea of coming to decisions without consulting those involved was practically unheard of.

The next level of complexity beyond the horde has been seen, in political anthropology, as the acephalous society, which again has no overall leadership, and so little call for delegation or for 'rule'. Typical of such societies are lineage systems in the African model where authority and decision making take place in the segments of society. There is thus no overall authority or system of governance that can be subject to the rule of the people; each individual being represented in every collective decision by a household or lineage head in a manner of 'automatic representation'. In such systems, individuals do not generally have a choice of their representative, who is born into the role. But not in every case. Among the LoDagaa of northern Ghana, a leader for joint farming activities is needed, especially when marriages take place, and an exceptional farmer (*kukuor na*) emerges for the occasion. More lasting is the role of 'chief of the bow' (*taamyuur na*), who leads the community in hunting and possibly in war. He is known as a practised hunter or warrior and is called upon to take the initiative. Another example exists among the nomadic Bakhtiari of Iran today. When they decide to move camp, each major tent is approached for its views. Only then do they start, with one man designated to carry out the collective decision. But this leadership is context specific, is often temporary and is achievement oriented. When the crop is harvested, the hunting successful or the camp relocated, such leadership is suspended and 'automatic representation' returns.

It is at the third level, that of centralised government, that the question of representation arises most critically. Even in highly centralised and autocratic societies, decision making may involve consultation and leadership can be representative. For instance, an Asante chief in West Africa would have his council of elders representing the constituent lineages. Each of his councillors would express their opinion on a current issue and this would be summed up by the chief, known as 'the man who speaks last'. His role was not to make a decision on his own but to incorporate the opinion of others, who would themselves have been in touch with their own lineage members. Not all of these decisions were taken 'democratically' after consulting all members, but, on the other hand, they were taken responsibly, not arbitrarily.

Moreover, even where centralised states are governed 'despotically', the decisions at a local level may be subject to such consultation, if not to election. It has often been alleged that the early Near Eastern and Asian city-states and empires were so-called despotisms at a national level, but much evidence has emerged about the important role of assemblies in local decision making. The invention of writing in the Bronze Age created not only a new dimension of stratification, but permitted the growth of knowledge, thought and action, what is often referred to as 'civilisation'. Voting as we know it was part of that written culture in that it involved inscribing one's name on a potsherd to ensure that one's choice was recorded. In Greece not everyone was eligible to vote; women, slaves and foreigners were excluded and the privilege was tied to participation in the army. Nonetheless, it is unclear whether such early civilisations should be judged in terms of their autocratic governments or their local democratic dimensions.

Equally, it is difficult to characterise monarchical societies as these may also be democratic lower down. Monarchies are *ipso facto* non-democratic, since they do not allow for the choice and therefore the change of leader – the position is ascribed by heredity rather than achieved by actions. In Europe democracy was forced on monarchs by the necessity of getting their subjects' consent to engage in war and to the financial contributions it required for the exchequer; the Crown was forced to pay attention to the opinion of the multitude. In England the monarch's prime minister took over more and more responsibility and became responsible to an elected Parliament that could raise taxes from the bourgeoisie not simply from the aristocracy, thus giving birth to a 'constitutional monarchy', which we refer to as a democracy. But although this particular form is peculiar to Europe, the consultation or even the rule of the people is evidently not.

A republic, on the other hand, does away entirely with the hereditary monarch, giving formal responsibility to elected representatives, that is, to a democracy; the head and others being chosen by popular vote. What has become critical for procedures of representative democracy is how often the selection is carried out and for how long a representative's mandate is valid. In the best of all possible worlds, the voter would be consulted on every issue, but that is clearly impractical except by way of on-going referendums. In most cases we have to accept that our representative thinks on roughly the same lines as we do, and hence the importance of political parties to reflect one's views. The mandate usually lasts about four years, but in Carthage and Phoenicia a new representative was elected every year, ensuring that he was in closer touch with his constituency. Another problem confronting representative democracy is the extent of consultation. In the United Kingdom, universal suffrage, which we now think of as intrinsic to the concept of democracy, was instituted only in 1928. It is a concept that is often linked to the notion of military service. Today, debates continue about how and to whom the franchise can be further extended. Also an issue is the fact that even in modern republics, there is a tendency for the voter to opt for a measure of continuity of leadership (as with the Kennedys), which is the opposite of what should take place in an elective democracy. Power holders often try to retain their position within the family, even when they have attained it by the ballot box or by a coup followed by popular confirmation, so that democracy gradually slips into dictatorship or oligarchy. There is often some conflict between the continuity of kinship and elites, and the alternation or choice intrinsic to democracy.

These issues, and a great many more, are comprehensively treated in this en-cyclopaedic work, which presents a very different view of democracy's history than that normally held in the West. Although many claim democracy is peculiar to Europe and its offshoots (the United States, Australia, etc.), consultation and the rule of the people are evidentially not. Indeed, the intent of this book is to show the worldwide extent of democracy, which over the last couple of centuries has been erroneously regarded as a distinct feature of Europe. Democracy may be a characteristic of our way of life, but it is certainly not confined to the West. As democracy spreads out across the world and gains both advocates and opponents in every corner, it is worth remembering its deep and universal roots.

Introduction:

The Complex and Contested History of Democracy

Benjamin Isakhan

The twentieth century was a great success for democracy, but every victory was hard won. On the world stage, democracies had to fend off credible threats from various forms of fascism before 1945 and then communism until 1989. Inside each democracy, a myriad of civil society actors and peoples' movements struggled for every gain of liberty, for every civil right and for an ever widening franchise. During the twentieth century, in countries all over the world, people took risks, pushed old laws and entrenched elites to their limits, and put their lives on the line in order to claim their sovereignty. In 1900, barely twenty counties would have qualified as a democracy even on the broadest criteria, and if we use universal suffrage as the measure the number would dwindle to but a handful. At the end of the Second World War, things were little better: universal suffrage had been achieved sporadically, but there were fewer than a dozen functional or provisional democracies. Since then the efficiency of democracy and its effectiveness in providing strong, stable government became more apparent and democratic experiments gradually succeeded. By the mid-1970s, the world had about 40 democracies, mostly in the West but also in Japan and India. In 1990, there were 76 electoral democracies, by 1995 that number had shot up to 117, and in 1999 it had reached 119 of the world's 192 countries (*Freedom in the World* 1991, 1996, 2000). At the close of the twentieth century and for the first time in human history, the majority of the world's population lived under one form or another of democracy.

This was great cause for celebration. Various pundits pointed to the end of the Cold War as the ultimate victory of the Western liberal model of democracy. In the most pronounced example, Francis Fukuyama declared that we were in fact witnessing the *End of History*; the death knell had rung on any credible alternative to democracy and the struggle of people everywhere towards liberty and justice was coming to a close (Fukuyama 1992). As the number of democracies continued to grow throughout the 1990s, such notions became increasingly popular. While some warned that there were still many threats to democracy and that there may yet be a 'reverse wave', most were enthusiastic that democracy had gone through a global resurgence (Diamond and Plattner 1996). As 'Democracy's Century' wound down, humankind was said to be 'rejecting oppression and opting for greater openness and freedom'; the battles and struggles of the twentieth century had been worthwhile, the Western liberal model of democracy had succeeded and the world could look forward to a new millennium of stability, prosperity and 'the prospect of a more peaceful world' (*Democracy's Century* 1999: 2).

This new era was still in its infancy when disaster struck. The attacks in the United States on 11 September 2001 – as tragic as they were – brought several key challenges to democracy. First, they were a graphic reminder that freedom had not triumphed everywhere, that ideological rivals certainly remain and that the more extreme among them are prepared to use devastating violence in the name of their fatally flawed visions. Secondly, 9/11 also saw a significant setback for hard-won civil liberties as democratic governments across the world assumed unprecedented rights to monitor the actions of their own citizens and to detain and torture terror suspects without trial. Thirdly, 9/11 ushered in two protracted and largely unsuccessful wars in which US-led coalitions of mostly democratic countries invaded first Afghanistan (2001) and then Iraq (2003). These interventions were followed by an ambitious, and as yet inconclusive, project that sought to implant obedient models of democracy as part of an aggressive democracy promotion agenda.

This led to a sudden flurry of democratic activity across parts of Asia, the Middle East, Latin America and in sub-Saharan Africa. Modest political gains were made and reforms implemented, people took to the streets in unprecedented numbers and relatively free and fair elections were held in places previously thought inhospitable to democracy. In the former USSR, three long-held dictatorships were toppled as the 'Colour Revolutions' swept across Georgia, the Ukraine and Kyrgyzstan between 2003 and 2005 (Beachain and Polese 2010). In the Middle East, there were a number of positive, if inconclusive, democratic developments: in Lebanon the 'Cedar Revolution' led to the ousting of Syrian troops and national elections; Egypt amended its constitution to enable a multi-candidate popular vote; Saudi Arabia held municipal elections; and the Palestinian territories held its first ever election leading to the ascension of Hamas. By 2005, the number of electoral democracies had reached an all-time high of 123 out of 192 countries – almost 65 per cent (*Freedom in the World* 2006).

However, as people watched the failure of democracy to meet the needs of the average Iraqi or Afghani, and the tragedies of Abu Ghraib and Guantanamo Bay unfolded, the Western liberal model began to lose some of its shine. Many of the gains of the early 2000s proved to be remarkably shallow: revolutions were followed by new elites with a similar thirst for power; electoral openings and media freedoms were gradually reversed; hard-won reforms were overturned; and recently written constitutions were ignored. US democracy promotion had led to the emergence of several hybrid 'semi-authoritarian' regimes that were able to utilise the mechanisms and discourses of democracy to further tighten their grip on power (Ottaway 2003). Then there were those who simply ignored the call for more democracy, ranging from some of the world's most powerful states, such as Russia and China, to bastions of a bygone era in which power is centred around a cult of personality and a stranglehold on opposition, such as in North Korea, Belarus or Sudan. Elsewhere, attempts at democratisation were quashed by violence: Burma's Saffron Revolution (2007), Zimbabwean elections (2008) and Iran's Green Revolution (2009) all ended in disaster; the mass protests in Thailand (2009–10) saw little more than the rotation of power from one elite faction to another.

Even the world's best democracies were struggling. While positive moments like the grass-roots movement that catapulted Barack Obama to power gave many hope, others would point to the struggle of the Western liberal model to deal effectively with many of the major global issues of our time: climate change, disease pandemics, transnational migration and refugee crises, and the growing inequity between the global haves and have nots. Of these, the marriage between Western liberal democracy and the global capitalist free market system became a central focus. Towards the end of the first decade of the new millennium the world slipped into a financial crisis comparable to the Great Depression. As major financial institutions collapsed and governments took unprecedented steps to bail them out, even the strongest economies began to feel the strain and many citizens who had gambled their wealth on an expanding economy walked away empty-handed. The crisis of faith that followed was compounded by an increasing sense that politics was a distant and impenetrable discourse that really had little to do with the everyday lives of ordinary people. Almost overnight, a series of popular grassroots movements and protests emerged across both sides of the Atlantic. In the United Kingdom, the London riots brought violence and chaos to normally peaceful streets, as did many of the protests against austerity measures in Greece and other European Union countries. In the United States, the Occupy Wall Street movement was a broader attempt to rethink power relations and wealth distribution in advanced democracies. Its message and strategy spread rapidly across the world, even to far-flung corners barely affected by the financial crisis, like Melbourne, Australia.

The celebrations and self-congratulatory rhetoric of the 1990s had come too early. Across the world, democracy was stumbling. In 2011, Freedom House pointed out that global freedom suffered the sixth consecutive year in which countries with declines outnumbered those with improvements, the longest continuous downturn since the survey was launched in the 1970s. The number of electoral democracies had dropped from the 2005 peak of 123 down to 117, a significant step backwards to the 1995 figure (*Freedom in the World* 2012). Their report makes several grave assessments about the prospect of a more democratic world. It asserts that 'The continued pattern of global backsliding – especially in such critical areas as press freedom, the rule of law, and the rights of civil society' are both a sobering reminder that the institutions that anchor democratic governance are difficult to achieve and sustain, and that democracy has an uncertain future (*Freedom in the World* 2012: 1).

While both the reduction of democracy and its uncertain future must be taken seriously, what is interesting here is that Freedom House misses two important facts about the state of democracy in our times. First, it overlooks the variety and vibrancy of democracy today. Among the countries that meet their criteria for an electoral democracy are those on every inhabited continent: Asia, Africa, North America, South America, Europe and Australia. It includes countries that have majorities of Catholics (Malta), Protestants (Denmark), Muslims (Indonesia), Hindus (India), Buddhists (Taiwan), Jews (Israel) and those with a rich mixture of religious affiliations (Mauritius). It also includes counties that are relatively homogeneous (Japan), and those that are culturally, religiously, linguistically and/or ethnically diverse (Suriname). In terms of geographical size it includes tiny countries like Monaco and entire continents like Australia, while in terms of population size it includes the world's second most populated country with 1.2 billion (India) down to tiny islands like Tuvalu or Nauru each with around 10,000 people. It includes some of the world's newest countries, such as Montenegro and Palau, and some of the oldest, including France and Portugal. There are those that have recently emerged from conflict (Croatia and Serbia), those that have long been neutral/peaceful (Switzerland), and those that face ongoing civil dispute over territory (Cyprus). It includes those among the richest (Luxembourg and Norway) and the poorest (Mali and Benin) of nations, as well as the world's last remaining superpower (the United States) and two rapidly emerging powerbrokers (Brazil and India).

Secondly, Freedom House also misses the point that while the actual number of democracies may be slipping, democracy itself has never been more popular. For those who have it, democracy offers a grab-bag of freedoms and rights that are routinely celebrated and defended. They are free to form political parties, protest key decisions and criticise their government; they have equal access to information and equality before the law; and they are vested with the power to choose and hold to account those who would rule on their behalf. Arguably, democracy is even more popular among those who do not have it. While no one could have predicted the as yet inconclusive mass protests that constituted the 2010–11 'Arab Revolutions', these events are indicative of a much broader phenomenon: people everywhere are prepared to take grave risks in order to topple dictators and tyrants, and to agitate for a more democratic order. For the people who set themselves alight in Tunisia, for the protestors who took control of Tahrir Square in Egypt, for the rebels who fought in Libya and for those demonstrating across the region, it is democracy they want and it is democracy that they assume will solve their problems (Isakhan *et al.* 2012).

What is interesting, however, is that the more popular democracy becomes and the more vibrant and various it is, the less we know about it. When democracy was being practised by a small handful of states at the start of the twentieth century, it seemed a relatively easy thing to define because there was much in common between those who had it and sharp differences with those who did not. Today, there are a plethora of different democracies. Mongolian democracy is very different to that practised in Samoa, Argentina, Canada or Ghana. The German system is nothing like that found in South Africa, or in Jamaica, Iceland, Chile or the United Kingdom. Democracy also means different things to those who do not have it: the democracy that the Tunisians desire is very different from the one the Thais, Iranians or Zimbabweans want.

The spread, popularity and variety of democracy has therefore raised a significant problem: how can democracy be defined in a way that is relevant and meaningful in all of these different contexts and – most importantly for this volume – how can it be defined in a way that captures its historical development? In other words, the more democracy we have, the more we are confronted with two highly contested and notoriously difficult questions: 'What is democracy?' and 'Where does democracy come from?' While this volume is primarily concerned with the second question, any attempt to capture the history of democracy must be preceded by an attempt to define it.

What is Democracy?

Defining democracy is a difficult and perhaps ultimately futile exercise that has achieved a kind of grandeur in recent years with many political scientists fumbling and

INTRODUCTION 5

debating over the precise wording of a definition: whether it should be minimalist or robust, procedural and scientific or abstract and esoteric. For all their efforts, such scholars have not been able to assert one agreed definition, one standard way of measuring which societies – both contemporary and historical – ought to be ranked among the pantheon of democracies. As Larry Diamond conceded a decade ago, the rapid uptake of democracy in the twentieth century and 'the renaissance it brought in comparative democracy studies' has left us very far 'from consensus on what constitutes "democracy"' (Diamond 2002: 22).

However, this lack of consensus ought to be celebrated, not lamented; such debates and disagreements themselves represent a microcosm of the democratic ethos. In a democracy, diversity of opinion is to be respected and celebrated, and it is in the aggregate of difference (rather than in the tyranny of forced consensus) that democracy is at its best. To impose one standard definition of democracy is to restrict its ability to resonate with different people and adapt to different conditions. If democracy does not change over time, if it does not defy stagnant definitions or break with long-held assumptions, how can it respond to the ever-changing needs of the people? At one level, democracy, like justice or freedom, is more of an ideal than a cold, hard reality. No society has ever been fully democratic (or just or free) and no two attempts to approximate democracy have ever been the same. The ancient Greeks could not have imagined representative democracy in the way that it was practised in the late eighteenth century, just as eighteenth-century democrats had no way of imagining the ways in which democracy is evolving today in the light of new media technologies. If the Greeks had agreed on a definition 2,500 years ago, or if the Paris Commune had done so more than two centuries ago, what use would it be to us today? Such a definition would not only be irrelevant, but it would limit democracy, make it prone to misuse, and more difficult to understand, promote or achieve.

Another problem that confronts any attempt to define democracy is the fact that much ink has been spilt describing democracy by those who were, ironically, adamantly opposed to it. Plato despised democracy and argued in favour of rule by a wise and benevolent *philosopher-king*, who had the training, expertise and moral valour to mould the opinions of the people rather than being guided by them (Plato [380 BCE] 1975). Many centuries later, Thomas Hobbes argued that democracy was divisive because politicians were motivated by power and used demagogy to manipulate the masses away from virtue (Hobbes [1651] 2002). Similarly, Louis de Bonald detested the French Revolution because it usurped the natural position of the aristocracy and gave rise to mob rule (Bonald [1818] 2004). James Madison, one of America's Founding Fathers, favoured a strong and highly centralised republic because: 'democracies have ever been spectacles of turbulence and contention . . . and have in general been as short in their lives as they have been violent in their deaths' (Madison [1788] 1981: 20). With the rise of fascism in the early twentieth century, scholars such as Carl Schmitt preferred a streamlined and efficient dictatorship to the sluggish and cumbersome nature of democracy (Schmitt [1923] 1988).

And yet, the tide has slowly and steadily turned against those who despise democracy. Today, most would agree with Winston Churchill that 'democracy is the worst form of government except all those other forms that have been tried from time to time' (Churchill 1947: 207). But what is democracy? Despite the many significant difficulties facing any attempt to define democracy, for the purposes of this volume some guidelines are needed in order to measure the degree to which past and present societies have practised it.

First and foremost, a democracy must have citizens. While all manner of regimes have leaders and a broader general populace, only democracies have citizens in the full sense of the term: that is, a group of equal individuals who are vested with sufficient power to determine how and by whom they are governed. In many definitions of democracy, these citizens are both central and ill-defined. This is as true in Antoine Furetière's posthumous universal dictionary in which democracy is a '*Sorte de gouvernement où le peuple a toute l'autorité*' (Form of government in which the people have all authority) (Furetière [1690] 1978), as it is for Abraham Lincoln for whom 'Democracy is the government of the people, by the people, for the people' (Lincoln 1863: 210). But which people are citizens? For most of democracy's history women, minorities, foreigners, slaves and others have been routinely disenfranchised. In the nineteenth and twentieth centuries, however, the hard-won battles of various civil rights movements have gradually expanded our definition of citizenship.

To those who qualify as citizens, democracy brings a host of rights, freedoms, privileges and responsibilities. Paramount among these, for Aristotle and others, was the personal freedom and unquestioned equality of all citizens, as well as a long list of inalienable rights: to run for office, to have a fair trial, to assemble and speak freely (Aristotle [350 BCE] 1962: IV:4, VI:2). In more recent times, this collection of rights has expanded. Widely cited benchmarks include the American *Declaration of Independence* and its *First Amendment*, which ensure rights such as freedom of religion as well as 'freedom of speech, or of the press; or the right of the people peaceably to assemble, and to petition the Government for a redress of grievances' (*Amendment the First* 1791; *Declaration of Independence* [1776] 1997). However, with each new set of rights came parallel responsibilities. The Athenians were expected to participate in the courts and assemblies, respect the opinions of others, submit to the rule of law and stand aside when their term in office had expired. In modern representative democracy 'active citizenship' has added things such as bettering one's community through economic participation and civic engagement, and seeking to create and re-create democratic institutions and practices that meet the needs of the people (Crick and Lockyer 2010).

Secondly, and for democracy to work, the citizens must be governed by a set of laws or socio-political norms that uphold their rights, protect them from injustice and detail their responsibilities. To have legitimacy, these laws and the government that enforces them, must have at least the tacit consent, if not the full support, of the citizens. The laws must also be independent of the government of the day and capable of holding it to account. As Pericles revealed in a funeral speech recorded by Thucydides, in a democracy 'everyone is equal before the law . . . we keep to the law . . . because it commands our deepest respect' (Thucydides [410 BCE] 1972: II:37). The radical eighteenth-century British thinker, Thomas Paine, agreed that the law was central to a functioning democracy: 'The Law is King. For as in absolute government the king is law, so in free countries the law ought to be king; and there ought to be no other' (Paine

[1776] 1986: 98). In the best examples, the spirit of these laws is generally enshrined in a written constitution, tabled in a parliament or congress that can balance the power of the executive branch of government, enacted with the oversight of a neutral public bureaucracy and enforced by an independent judiciary.

Finally, beyond the citizen body and the rule of law, democracies must have equal parts of three fundamental elements: contestation, cooperation and participation. In a democracy, contestation is critical to the very health and vitality of the system. Without competition democracy is just a façade for those in power. There have to be opposing points of view, alternative arguments and proposals for different ways of doing things. So important is the need for competition in a democracy that for some it has become the defining characteristic. In Joseph Schumpeter's minimalist empirical definition, democracy 'is that institutional arrangement for arriving at political decisions in which individuals acquire the power to decide by means of a competitive struggle for the people's vote' (Schumpeter [1947] 2011: 269). Such 'a competitive struggle for the people's vote' usually means the presence of oppositional entities, who must be as free to run for office as those in power. While in classical participatory democracies the opposition was loose and individuals could switch sides often and decide which policies to oppose and which to accept, today the competition between the government and its opposition has become more rigidly formalised via political parties. While this may have taken some of the liveliness out of political contestation, the presence of opposition politics does provide alternative voices and remains central to any legitimate claim to democracy.

However, there comes a time in every democracy when contestation must be put aside and cooperation must take precedence. When the election cycle is over and a new government assumes office the citizen is required to submit to the incumbent while retaining the right to work towards ousting them at the next election. Democracy also asks that citizens cooperate to form political parties and voluntary associations, and to debate and discuss the major issues of the time. Alexis de Tocqueville argued that America was the 'most democratic country on the face of the earth' in part because the people had 'carried to the highest perfection the art of pursuing in common the object of their common desires, and have applied this new science to the greatest number of purposes' (Tocqueville [1835] 2008: II:5). In order to do so, the people formed 'associations' and, while he understood that each such association sought to impose their views on society, the aggregate effect was an increase in tolerance and an acceptance of differences of opinion. In today's democracies, such associations are usually referred to as civil society: that is, the set of social and civic institutions that are distinct from the state. For Jürgen Habermas, civil society is part of a broader 'public sphere' where citizens engage in debate and deliberation that 'connects society with the state and thus has a function in the political realm' (Habermas [1989] 1996: 28).

Habermas' work here points to a final and very important element central to any genuine democracy, that of participation. If the citizens do not want democracy, if they are not prepared to fulfil their rights and responsibilities, to uphold the rule of law and to contest and cooperate towards the common good, then democracy simply cannot succeed. This is startlingly obvious in direct democracies like that of ancient Greece: if the amphitheatres of Athens had been empty so too would have been its claim to democracy. Modern representative democracy often reduces participation to the sole requirement of casting a ballot on election day (which may not even be mandatory). After the election, even the world's best democracies struggle to engage their citizens in a continuing system of participation and decision making (Khan 1999). As Carole Pateman pointed out in her ambitious critique, many scholars of democracy in fact prefer such restricted degrees of participation (Pateman [1970] 1999: 3–13). Pateman challenged such notions by calling for a revitalisation of democracy via 'Full participation . . . a process where each individual member of a decision-making body has equal power to determine the outcome of decisions' (Pateman [1970] 1999: 71). While the practicality of such degrees of participation in large complex states, let alone on a global scale, remains contentious, such calls only emphasise the centrality of citizen participation to any claim to democratic legitimacy.

For the purposes of this volume, democracy can therefore be seen as a system of governance in which the citizens are: invested with the full rights and responsibilities of citizenship; governed by a set of laws or norms that both protect their citizenship and hold to account those in power; and actively encouraged to contest, cooperate and participate in political life. This definition is particularly useful because it is broad enough to permit a consideration of the many different ways in which democracy has been practised both historically and currently. It is also specific enough to establish a set of criteria by which democracies can be judged, including the rights and responsibilities of citizens, the strength of the rule of law and the levels of actual citizen engagement. By applying these criteria to human history, a surprising catalogue of democratic practice emerges in which, at various times and in various ways, people all over the world have come close to the democratic ideal. Thus, this definition enables new insights into the second of our two highly contested and notoriously difficult questions: 'Where does democracy come from?'

Where does Democracy come From?

Until very recently, the standard answer to this question was so widely accepted that few bothered to ask it. Mostly, scholars of democracy and its history have been content to rattle off a familiar catalogue of events that emphasise the key moments of Western civilisation: the achievements of the ancient Greeks and Romans; the development of the British Parliament; the American Declaration of Independence; the French Revolution; and the gradual spread of democracy across the globe since the end of the Cold War. While each of these epochs has made an important contribution to our understanding of democracy and must be included in any robust history on the subject, they do not tell the whole story. Histories of democracy that focus exclusively on these events not only privilege Europe and its successful colonies, but also miss the broader human story of the struggle for and achievement of democracy.

There are several key reasons why the history of democracy has been so persistently Eurocentric. One is simply that the vast majority of people who have practised or lived under or fought for democracy have not used the Greek-derived word 'democracy' to describe their government. It is little wonder that ancient Assyrians or Israelites, medieval Muslims or Scandinavians, or pre-colonial Africans or Maoris did not use a Greek word to describe their best governmental arrangements. This does not mean that these people did not practise democracy, only that they did not use the word. Just as we acknowledge that the ancient Chinese practised and contributed greatly to the discipline of philosophy (another Greek word), they never used the word 'philosophy' to describe their most profound cogitations. In answering the question of where democracy might come from, it is important to focus on the approximation of best practice rather than the employment of particular nomenclature to describe it.

This points to a further problem: virtually every attempt to define and understand the word 'democracy' has occurred within a small circle of largely white, wealthy Anglo-American men. This is, of course, very undemocratic. An ideal history of democracy would be broad enough to include the experiences of women, minorities and subalterns who have lived under one type or another of democracy. Given this Anglo-American patriarchal heritage, it is little wonder that democracy has so often been considered a unique trait of Western civilisation. Although the ancient Greeks made many great contributions to our understanding of democracy, figures such as Aristotle also believed that Grecian *dēmokratia* distinguished them from other cultures, barbarians and Asiatics, who he considered more servile and deficient in character than his countrymen and therefore more prone to despotism (Aristotle [350 BCE] 1962: I.9). Such ideas about the democratic distinctiveness of the Greeks persist today (Finley 1973; Pritchard 2010), with authors such as Cynthia Farrar going as far as to argue that not only did the Athenians of the fifth century BCE invent politics, they also invented democracy and were the first to have ever thought about how collective and inclusive forms of government might work (Farrar 1988).

Such notions of democracy as a uniquely Western proclivity achieved renewed momentum after the tumultuous events in Europe and America during the late eighteenth century and the gradual emergence of modern representative democracy. There was an enormous intellectual effort to connect European experiments with democracy to those of Athens, even though modern Central European Christians had little in common with the ancient pagan Greeks other than the vague notion that they were both 'Europeans' (Bernal [1987] 1991). A virtual consensus emerged that because democracy had succeeded among the Greeks and was being practised by the British or French, democracy and its history were inexorably tied to Western civilisation (Bryce 1921a, 1921b; Goodwin 1864; Maine [1885] 1976; Norcross 1883). For Lord Acton, 'Liberty . . . has been the motive of good deeds . . . from the sowing of the seed at Athens . . . until the ripened harvest was gathered by men of our race' (Acton [1907] 2005: 1). While the non-European was prone to slavery under forms of 'Asiatic despotism':

> Wherever we can trace the earlier life of the Aryan nations we discover germs which favouring circumstances and assiduous culture might have developed into free societies. They exhibit some sense of common interest in common concerns, little reverence for external authority, and an imperfect sense of the function and supremacy of the state. (Acton [1907] 2005: 5)

As democracy triumphed largely under US tutelage after the Second World War and the Cold War, it continued to be seen as most at home in the Western world or in places most heavily influence by it. Anglo-Saxon Protestantism was held up as being most conducive to democracy, while other cultural lineages such as Islam and Confucianism, came to be seen as profoundly anti-democratic (Almond and Verba [1963] 1989; Huntington 1991). Unfortunately, few contemporary scholars concerned with the history of democracy challenged this intellectual orthodoxy, preferring to recycle the Eurocentric story (Arblaster 2002; DeWiel 2000; Dunn 1992; Lakoff 1996; Stromberg 1996). While examples abound of this kind of reductive historical analysis, it is worth citing John Dunn's *Democracy: A History* at length. For Dunn and those of his ilk, democracy:

> began as an improvised remedy for a very local Greek difficulty two and a half thousand years ago, flourished briefly but scintillatingly, and then faded away almost everywhere for all but two thousand years. It . . . came back to life as a real modern political option . . . in the struggle for American independence and with the founding of the new American republic. It . . . then returned, almost immediately . . . if far more erratically, amid the struggles of France's Revolution. It . . . [had a] slow but insistent rise over the next century and a half, and . . . triumph[ed] in the years since 1945 . . . Within the last three-quarters of a century democracy has become the political core of the civilization which the West offers to the rest of the world. (Dunn 2005: 13–14)

It is this standard answer to the question of where democracy comes from that is taught in classrooms across the globe, endlessly recycled in the mass media, and which informs much of the policy making that governs the world in which we live. In recent years, however, a number of scholars have begun to question this traditional history of democracy, and many books and articles have appeared offering detailed accounts of democracy at work in surprising locations and across various eras.

The earliest traces of this alternative approach to democracy's history can be found in Nahum Capen's *The History of Democracy* and Alan Hattersley's *A Short History of Democracy*. Writing in the late nineteenth and early twentieth centuries, both scholars swam against the intellectual tide of their time by making a number of bold assertions about the history of democracy and its broader human ancestry. Indeed, Capen took his contemporaries to task for their short-sightedness in a critique that still resonates today: 'It is not a little remarkable that while democratic principles have been recognised, more or less, during all ages of the world, intelligent thinkers approach the inquiry respecting the tendencies of democracy as if its mission were of recent origin' (Capen 1875: 26). Although Capen admits the Eurocentric limits of his own study, he nonetheless sees democracy as part of the broader human mosaic and argues that future investigations should acknowledge the significant contributions made by the Israelites, the Chinese and the Egyptians, for example (Capen 1875: 31–2). Hattersley takes this alternative approach to democracy's history a step further in a collection of chapters that consider topics such as: the prehistoric origins of democracy among the earliest hunters and gatherers; the medieval roots of the British Parliament; democratic thought in the Middle Ages; and the influence of the Reformation on the rise of modern representative democracy (Hattersley 1930: 15–21, 76–119). While scholars such as Capen and

Hattersley have to be admired for their prescience and intellectual bravery, their early nods to the broader history of democracy soon give way to a focus on the gradual development of democracy in European and American history.

This is not the case in more recent writing on other potential histories of democracy. John Markoff, for example, moves beyond the overwhelming emphasis on 'great powers', such as England, France and the United States, to focus on smaller, less powerful states where many of the actual innovations in the recent history of democracy have taken place. Among the many examples he provides is the fact that Mexico (1812) was among the first to extend the suffrage to propertyless non-black men; then Argentina (1821), Uruguay (1823) and Brazil (1824) extended it to all freemen, albeit temporarily (Markoff 1999: 678–9). Steven Muhlberger and Phillipe Paine expand the argument by investigating a series of non-Western examples of democracy in traditional Chinese village life, African tribal moots, ancient Indian republics and Native American societies. They find that, contrary to the concept of democracy as a Western invention, humanity itself 'possesses a long history of government by discussion, in which groups of people sharing common interests make decisions that affect their lives through debate and consultation, and often enough by voting' (Muhlberger and Paine 1993: 26). Similarly, Amartya Sen rallies against the widespread presumption 'that democracy is an idea of which the roots can be found exclusively in some distinctly Western thought that has flourished uniquely in Europe – and nowhere else' (Sen 2003: 29).

Along similar lines, scholars such as Jack Goody, John Keane, John Hobson and Larbi Sadiki have asked important questions about democracy's origins, its gradual spread and its uncertain future (Goody 2006; J. M. Hobson 2004; Keane 2009; Sadiki 2004). Central to their work is a critique of the assumption embedded into traditional accounts that democracy is of exclusively Anglo-American stock. As Hobson explains:

> Eurocentrism typically extrapolates backwards the modern conception of political democracy all the way to Ancient Greece. It then fabricates a permanent picture of Western democracy by tracing this conception forwards to Magna Carta in England (1215), then to England's Glorious Revolution (1688/9), and then on to the American Constitution (1787/9) and the French Revolution (1789). In this way, Europe and the West is (re)presented as democratic throughout its long rise to power. (J. M. Hobson 2004: 290)

Thus, the history of democracy, once thought to be complete, has become a contested field and the question of democracy's origins has become increasingly contentious. In *The Secret History of Democracy*, the editors sought to capture the fundamental rupture that is currently taking place in the study of democracy and its history (Isakhan and Stockwell 2011). It set out an ambitious critique of those who were not only content to reiterate the standard narrative of democracy and its history, but who also failed to recognise that democracy has roots and relevance beyond the West. The book also outlined many fundamental problems evident in traditional thinking, including its inherent racism and hubris, its historical inaccuracies, and its tendency to make democracy an exclusive doctrine that has little relevance to the peoples and histories outside the Anglo-American sphere. It then demonstrated that by applying any standard definition of democracy to the political past or present, one would inevitably unearth a whole collection of democratic stories beyond those captured in the typical Western account.

The Edinburgh Companion to the History of Democracy

This volume seeks to build upon this earlier work to provide a broader and deeper account of the history of democracy than has generally been conceded. It moves beyond the erroneous assumption that democracy has occurred in only a handful of isolated contexts to suggest instead the breadth and depth of democracy's place in human history. To do this, this book brings together leading experts on a wide range of epochs, peoples and places, together demonstrating the rich variety of ways in which democracy has formed part of the common history of human civilisation. It seeks to set a benchmark as the first collection on the history of democracy to present lesser known examples of democracy, including ancient China, medieval Islam, colonial Africa or today's Burma alongside more familiar cases like Athens, the English Parliament, the French Revolution and Women's Suffrage. In this way, the chapters that follow allow for the history of democracy to be put on trial. Readers are invited to pass judgement on how democracy in ancient Athens compares with developments in ancient India, how medieval Islam compared with the Catholic Church, how the systems of governance among Native Americans compared with those of the Founding Fathers, and how the Arabs and Burmese can learn from each other's democratic movements today.

Putting the history of democracy on trial in this way is not just of interest to historians and political scientists concerned with the political past, it is central to democracy's collective project of inventing and reinventing ways to address the need of people everywhere to live in peace, freedom and with a say in the decisions affecting their livelihood. Understanding where democracy comes from, where its greatest successes and most dismal failures lie, is central to striving towards greater democracy today and overcoming the many challenges that lie ahead. With this in mind, this volume takes us one step further towards an articulation of democracy's past that is free of old prejudices and out-dated historical models. It is a fresh attempt to shed light on the two questions underpinning this volume: 'What is democracy?' and 'Where does democracy come from?'

The book's first section, *Part I: Pre-Classical Democracy*, finds answers to these question long before the traditional date for the invention of democracy by the Greeks. In the opening chapter, Christopher Boehm uses behavioural phylogenetics to uncover the building blocks of both despotism and democracy among the Common Ancestor of the primate 7–9 million years ago. In terms of nascent democratic practices, primates developed social norms which resisted alpha male domination by forming coalitions, protecting the weak and encouraging the equitable distribution of resources (Boehm [1999] 2001). As human beings evolved into hunter-gatherers, the tendency for communities to oscillate between despotism and democracy continued in 'tribal' or 'band' societies. Individuals could dominate, but so too could the will of the many, honed in mass hunting operations, sometimes developing into 'kinship democracy' where an entire clan made decisions in a tribal moot or council (Glassman 1986a, 1986b).

There is now also substantial evidence to suggest that, as human beings settled in the world's first city-states across the Middle East, the Indus valley and China, democratic tendencies formed part of their central administration. In the case of Mesopotamia, archaeological excavations have revealed more political complexity than previously assumed (Jacobsen [1943] 1970). Focusing here on the case of the Assyrians, Benjamin Isakhan argues that Mesopotamian civilisations had participatory elements with checks and balances on absolute power, people's assemblies and the rule of law. Similarly, the ancient practice of 'government by discussion' across the Indian subcontinent has real significance for the history of democracy (Sharma 1968). In his chapter, Steven Muhlberger draws on both Greek and Roman descriptions of the political landscape of India as well as the religious literature of Brahmanism, Buddhism and Jainism to paint a nuanced picture of political practices in the Vedic period, where forums of people with great oratorical skill engaged in complex debates, careful counsel and met to plan wars and pass laws. In ancient China, Confucianism seeded an ideological opposition to its own hierarchy, patriarchy and authoritarianism (Keating 2011), and in her chapter, Victoria Tin-bor Hui argues that, during times of division, the state made concessions on citizenship rights in return for military service. This gave former soldiers access to the justice system, freedom of expression and the ability to criticise their government. In the final chapter in this section, Stephen Stockwell examines the relationship between two Semitic peoples, the Israelites and the Phoenicians. While important scholarship has already documented the democratic tendencies in both ancient Israel and Phoenicia (Bernal [1987] 1991; Wolf 1947), Stockwell focuses on the implications of the negotiations between monarchies and citizens in these two societies as demonstrated by the power of the assemblies, the elders' and the people's participation in the covenant.

While the developments of Greece and Rome have some precedent in the prehistoric and ancient world, *Part II: Classical Democracy* discusses the defining contributions of the Greeks and Romans to the history of democracy, contributions which have had a profound influence on our understanding of democracy today. While much of the focus on the democratic practices of ancient Greece tends to emphasise the developments of Athens, there is a growing body of literature which has sought to examine the earliest forms of collective governance in Greece, evident in the Homeric epics and the functioning of earlier city-states (Raaflaub *et al.* 2007; Robinson 1997). This is the topic of Kurt Raaflaub's chapter for this volume with particular focus on pre-Athenian steps towards democracy in early Greece and Sparta.

David J. Phillips follows this trajectory to examine the rise of the Athenian *polis* and the important reforms of Kleisthenes which made democracy the official governmental system of the city-state, providing a constitution where political authority rested with the people. Over two centuries, Athenian democracy set a standard for democracy that had never been realised. Although it had many flaws and faults, Athenian democracy granted participation to the citizen via popular assembly, it protected rights and freedoms, it was premised on equal measures of contestation and cooperation and it held that all citizens had liberty and equality before the law (Ober 1996). Parallel to the development of democracy in ancient Athens was the experience of Rome, where their bureaucratic-judicial system of governance had egalitarian elements even though it limited popular involvement in politics and privileged the wealthy and elite (Matyszak 2003). In his chapter, Philip Matyszak examines the various dimensions of the republic to examine the degree to which the people were included or excluded in the exercise of power. He shows that while the patrician Senate dominated the Republic, the military, the magistrates and the consuls were countervailing influences on their power.

Part III: Medieval Democracy considers another neglected epoch in most accounts of democracy's history to date, that from the fall of Rome to the start of the Renaissance. While often denigrated as the 'dark ages', this period provides evidence of the persistence of democratic tendencies in a variety of historical niches. For example, there is now growing appreciation that some of the medieval Islamic empires used political systems remarkably similar to what we have come to term democracy. Underneath the rule of the caliphs and sultans, there existed mechanisms for the peaceful transfer of power and decision making via consultation (Esposito and Voll 1996; Sachedina 2001; Soroush 2000). In this section Larbi Sadiki delves into the work of medieval Islamic scholars to examine their engagement with Grecian notions of *dēmokratia* and to argue that Islam played a crucial role in preserving democratic ideals in an era when much of feudal Europe cared little for the rights of its subjects.

But medieval Europe did have its democratic moments. In the case of Venice, this important trading hub between western Europe and the rest of the world developed a republic based on large, sovereign assemblies (Muir 1999). The significance of medieval Venice is discussed here by Stephen Stockwell, who argues that it fostered a democratic culture that engendered debate, allowed for innovation and invention and encouraged human endeavour. In the far north of Europe, the Nordic countries were also convening assemblies, or *Things*. In medieval Iceland, the *Althing* was a two-week long annual general assembly that served as the central legal and administrative decision-making body, presided over by the elected law-speaker (Byock 2002). In his chapter, Frode Hervik finds that the Nordic countries of the medieval period contained proto-democratic features and that, while they were never fully fledged democracies, they did protect the rights of the citizen and restrain the power of the monarchy. In Europe, the Christian church often defended the rights of the people against the excesses of feudalism, arguing *vox populi vox Dei* ('the voice of the people is the voice of God'). Thomas Aquinas argued that authorities should not interfere in popular customary law, and William of Ockham held that justice, truth and beauty were decided by common consent (Hittinger 2003; Kilcullen 1999). Here, John Hittinger argues that many aspects of modern representative democracy have their origins in the beliefs and practices of the medieval Christian church, which pursued political representation, a written constitution and opposition to forms of oppression.

The next section, *Part IV: Early Modern Democracy*, addresses a significant era in the history of democracy, the birth of the modern representative form in Europe and America. Initially, democracy emerged as a concession to the masses and as a strategy to protect white, male-dominated class interests, but it soon brought to the fore issues such as women's role in politics, human rights, justice, liberty, personal freedoms and minority representation. In her chapter on the rise of the English Parliament, Ann Lyon probes into British history to discover the origins of British assemblies and their gradual emergence as a fully-fledged parliament that served as a counterweight to the throne, to the point where it deposed Edward II in 1327 (Lyon 2003). In 1649, during the English Civil War, a union of agricultural workers known as 'The Diggers' and 'The True Levellers' fought against the privatisation of land in England and for Parliament to democratise the state (Bradstock 2000). In his chapter, Andrew Bradstock discusses their short and rebellious history, and how they were the first modern political movement to suggest that a fully representative government could govern an entire nation-state. While such ideals never became a reality in their lifetime, the Diggers and the Levellers had a profound impact on the spread of democratic ideals across England in the ensuing centuries (Wootton 1992).

In Central Europe, the Old Swiss Confederacy was constituted by six rural cantons that functioned as democratic republics, and seven urban cantons governed by wealthy oligarchs. The successes of the democratic systems employed by the rural cantons gradually impressed their urban neighbours and, as Thomas Lau explains, by the time the Swiss federal state was created in 1848, each canton had adopted a nominally democratic system of government with a constitution, legislature, judiciary and parliament (Lau 2008). The next chapter moves from Europe to the British colonies of North America. With the catch-cry 'no taxation without representation', the thirteen American colonies issued the *Declaration of Independence* in 1776, retaining elements of British democracy, but transforming it to avoid the monarchical system of Britain (Shankman 2004). Andrew Shankman discusses the framing of the *Constitution of the United States* and the forming of representative democracy in America. In 1789, as America was emerging as a democracy, France's Third Estate announced itself to be the National Assembly and an unprecedented popular revolt swept away the monarchy (Markoff 1997). In his chapter for this volume, John Markoff documents how the French Revolution developed the new French Constituent Assembly, which issued *The Declaration of the Rights of Man and of the Citizen* that, in 1791, formed the preamble for a constitution that set in place a representative democracy with near universal male suffrage.

The questions of what democracy is and where it comes from are also explored throughout *Part V: Colonialism and Democracy* by focusing on the experience of democracy in traditional societies before and after colonial contact. The indigenous people of Africa, North America and Australasia are seen to have had their own distinctive, democratic tendencies in the consultation, deliberation and debate exercised in their own communities. Europeans typically assumed that their colonial subjects were without a tradition of collective governance or egalitarian politics; that they were beyond democracy. In Africa, the colonial administrations erased many elements of indigenous culture, including centuries of tribal- and village-based governments with democratic tendencies (Ejiofor 1981; Fortes and Evans-Pritchard [1940] 1987; Legesse 2001). In his chapter, Maxwell Owusu confronts the myth that African chiefs and kings were despots and reveals the various restraints on power exerted by the people over their leaders. He demonstrates the significance of indigenous African democracy, not just for historical purposes, but also for promoting and legitimising democracy across the continent today. Along similar lines, Bruce E. Johansen was among the first to argue that Native Americans had their own democratic traditions (Johansen 1982). Here he examines the political practices of these remarkably egalitarian communities, which accepted debate and protected the rights of their citizens. He joins others in asserting that the democratic tendencies of the Native Americans had an important but undervalued impact on the thinking of the Founding Fathers (Weatherford 1988).

In his contribution Timothy Rowse analyses the rarely acknowledged, proto-democratic cultural practices of the many indigenous peoples of Australasia. For example, indigenous Australians and Maoris have both made use of inclusive debate, the rule of law and participation in political decision making. This democratic culture was obvious to early colonialists, who negotiated sophisticated treaties between tribes and with the British Empire in the case of New Zealand's 1840 Treaty of Waitangi, or witnessed the formation of early Indigenous Australian political organisations, members of which signed petitions and composed letters that even reached Queen Victoria (Bowden 1979; Reynolds 1995). In the final chapter in this section, Christine Doran extends the discussion to focus on the work of Chinese intellectuals in southeast Asia who opposed colonial rule and called for a more democratic order in various cultural and political movements of the late nineteenth and twentieth centuries (Doran 1998, 2006). She relates how Chinese Singaporean intellectuals like Tan Teck Soon and Lim Boon Keng found a powerful democratic tradition in Chinese history and political philosophy that they saw as central to their political strategy to advocate a more democratic future for both China and Singapore.

The next section of this volume, *Part VI: National Movements*, focuses on the important sequence of national movements that occurred throughout the nineteenth and twentieth centuries, bringing democracy to places as diverse as South America, Japan and Eastern Europe. In the first chapter, John Fisher focuses on South American liberation post-1808. Influenced by the French and Scottish Enlightenment, as well classical Greek and Roman thinkers, figures such as Simon Bolivar and José de San Martín personified the liberal, avowedly South American, spirit of this movement as first Venezuela and Colombia were liberated, followed by Panama, Ecuador, Peru, Bolivia, Argentina and Chile (Lynch 1986). This rapid sequence of national liberation movements was mostly premised on a democratic ethos that not only called for independence, but also for a more active involvement of the Latin American people in politics. This same spirit is evident in the national movements that spread across Europe after 1848. Beginning in France, where the uprising ended the constitutional monarchy of Louis-Philippe and led to the creation of the French Second Republic, the liberalising wave then spread to the Italian and German states (foreshadowing their unification), to Hungary where the aftershocks spread through the Habsburg Empire, and on to Switzerland, Poland and Britain (Rapport 2008). Mike Rapport outlines in his chapter the key events of the period and the degree to which they were based on calls for civil rights and parliamentary government. He also argues that while the developments of 1848 were short-lived – all the revolutions having collapsed by the end of 1849 – they nonetheless carry an important legacy for all those interested in the history of democracy.

Of similar interest is the spread of democracy following the First and Second World Wars and the Cold War. Dealing with the first of these, Conan Fischer addresses the 1919 Treaty of Versailles, which provided for degrees of democratisation in parts of the former German, Austro-Hungarian, Ottoman and Russian empires, and which saw the introduction of varieties of democracy in the Baltic countries, Finland, Poland and Czechoslovakia (Graebner and Bennett 2011). Fischer concludes that, while the Treaty of Versailles was a brittle and contrived solution to the many ethnic problems of Europe and beyond, the arrangements gave many citizens their first taste of democracy. Similar degrees of democratisation followed the conclusion of the Second World War, with US-sponsored democracy introduced in Germany, Italy and Japan (Coyne 2008). In his chapter, Takashi Inoguchi focuses on the Japanese experience with democracy after 1945. Tracing the ongoing influence of the United States in the formation of this democracy and the ways in which democratic aspirations were both encouraged and hampered by US occupation and interference. He also examines the regional and ideological constraints that emerged from the Cold War (Ruoff 2002). As the Cold War was coming to an end, another democratic transformation was taking place, this time in the socialist republics of the Eastern Bloc (Volten 1990). Here, Peter Volten discusses the experiences of Czechoslovakia, Poland and Hungary (with some mention of Bulgaria and Romania) and the diverse ways in which these nations, previously in the grip of communism, gradually shifted towards democracy.

Part VII: Peoples' Movements also focuses on the events of the nineteenth and twentieth centuries, but from the perspective of the various popular movements where people rather than governments have used democratic tactics to improve the quality of democracy. The first chapter in this section from Seymour Drescher concerns the end of human enslavement. By the close of the eighteenth century, anti-slavery movements and protests were being organised across Europe and Britain leading to the official abolition of slavery in Europe by the mid-nineteenth century. In America, early lobbying gave way to a fiery grassroots movement of black activists, female reformers and working-class elites (Drescher 2009). Drescher points out that the anti-slavery movement was decidedly democratic in spirit, mobilising mass demonstrations, publishing graphic reports on human rights abuses and organising sophisticated grassroots campaigns. It also brought to the fore a host of questions about who did – and who did not – constitute the citizen body of a democracy. It was not long before this question was being discussed in relation to gender, leading to a series of dramatic changes as women all over the world demanded their basic civil rights. First in New Zealand in 1893, then in parts of Australia and the United States, and then in places as diverse as the Corsican Republic, the Isle of Man, Britain, Scandinavia and France, women's suffrage began to garner considerable momentum (Grimshaw 1972; Sowerwine 1982). In their chapter here, Patricia Grimshaw and Charles Sowerwine note cautiously that while the issue of women's marginalisation from politics remains a problem across the world, the women's suffrage movements brought unprecedented rights to women in some parts of the world.

From the mid-nineteenth century, socialism and communism emerged as credible social and economic models arguing that, as the majority, the working classes should control the state and the means of production (Marx and Engels [1848] 1990). Out of these ideas came the more radical notion of anarchism where the state is regarded as a hindrance to the creation of a society which is democratically self-managed by the workers (Proudhon [1849] 1927). These ideas opened up new pathways for democratic action in which various intellectual, working–class, soldier and peasant movements criticised the dehumanising effects of industrialisation and private ownership. In his chapter on socialism, communism and anarchism, Barry Hindess documents the ideological differences between these three models, especially on the issue of democracy, and traces the influence such debates have had on peoples' movements and global politics into the modern era. One such influence has been the rise of various political movements, often with communist or socialist leanings, which have demanded equal rights for disenfranchised or marginalised minorities in countries such as Northern Ireland, Canada, Germany, France, Mexico, Czechoslovakia and Japan. The most well known of these was the Civil Rights movement that occurred in the United States and concerned the racially discriminatory laws and racial violence directed towards African Americans (Morris 1984). Michael L. Ondaatje discusses the events that led up to the Civil Rights movement and reviews its greatest challenges and most significant achievements. The political ascendancy of US President Barack Obama is an indicator of progress towards a more inclusive and democratic world, though there is still a long way to go.

The penultimate section of this volume, *Part VIII: Democracy Today*, looks at a range of recent democratic moments. The late twentieth and the early twenty-first centuries have witnessed a massive upsurge in the number of democracies across the globe, but the path to meaningful popular government has not been easy. There have been many successes, but also many problems, reversals, failures and innovative attempts to include democratic mechanisms under authoritarian rule. While there are too many to include in a single volume, a sample of examples have been selected for their significance in the history of democracy and their representation of broader trends. The first two chapters in this section focus on examples of initial success that have more recently been troubled, and even paralysed, by a number of deeply rooted problems. In the case of the anti-Apartheid movement in South Africa, Roger Southall reviews the eventual success of the African National Congress (ANC) over the white supremacist National Party, ranking it as a major victory for democracy against intractable social inequalities and the political power of an authoritarian state (Bonner *et al.* 1993). However, Southall also balances his assessment with an acknowledgement of the ANC's subsequent electoral dominance and its emphasis on ethnic (rather than policy) differences between them and their political opponents (Southall and Daniel 2009). Similarly, the success of a young indigenous Bolivian man, Evo Morales, in bringing together groups such as coca farmers, indigenous people and political activists saw him win the 2006 presidential election (Sivak 2008). As Juan Manuel Arbona and Carmen Medeiros explain in their chapter, however, while this has seen Bolivia transformed into a equitable and democratic state, the ousting of the former ruling minority has created a political vacuum that is generating a new set of obstacles and problems for the nation.

The next two chapters focus on reversals of democracy following mass social upheavals and US democracy promotion efforts. The first of these, by Lincoln A.

Mitchell, documents the events of the 'Rose Revolution' in Georgia in which 100,000 Georgians celebrated the fall of President Eduard Shevardnadze and his autocratic government. However, as Mitchell points out in his contribution to this volume, despite the best efforts to 'spin' the Rose Revolution as a story of democratic success, it should be viewed with caution. For Mitchell, it is a case of 'semi-authoritarianism' where democratic elements co-exist with a continued centralisation of power, a weakened media and parliament, and faltering judicial independence (Mitchell 2009; Wheatley 2005). Although it came about through very different circumstances, Benjamin Isakhan makes a similar point in his discussion of Iraqi democracy since 2003. He explains that, while the US invasion did lead to an initial uptake of media freedoms and political parties, after the 2005 elections power was increasingly centralised in the hands of the Iraqi elite and there was an upsurge in ethno-religious sectarian violence. Although the Iraqi people continue to struggle towards democracy, as demonstrated by recent mass protests especially in the wake of the Arab Revolutions (2010–11), a number of alarming counter-democratic developments are on the rise, including spikes in violence and the increasingly authoritarian nature of Iraq's government (Isakhan 2012).

This section also includes a discussion of the failure of democracy to emerge in Burma despite the best efforts of various student protests, monastic movements and the work of pro-democracy activists such as Aung San Suu Kyi (Lintner 2011). Here, Donald M. Seekins details the events that led up to the unsuccessful 'Saffron Revolution' of 2007. As with earlier exercises in popular protest in Burma, the junta immediately cracked down, arresting and detaining dozens of protestors and leaving countless dead and wounded (Seekins 2002). While it may seem strange to include the unsuccessful 'Saffron Revolution' in an edited volume on democracy, the events nonetheless indicate that the spirit of democracy is alive even in the most isolated states, for around the world people continue to struggle against oppression and dictatorship and towards democracy and inclusion.

The final two chapters in this section consider grassroots initiatives to build democracy in two unexpected arenas: China since Tiananmen Square and Islam since 9/11. In the wake of the 1989 Tiananmen Square massacre, China has reaffirmed its authoritarian rule while introducing a variety of local mini-democratisation practices. Baogang He's chapter provides a critical overview of these practices, including village and township elections, intra-party democracy, participatory budgeting and deliberative forums (He 1996, 1997). This is followed by Nader Hashemi's discussion of the post-9/11 epoch and the various Muslim responses to the argument that Islam is antithetical to democracy. As he demonstrates, Muslims both in the West and in the Islamic sphere of influence have adopted beliefs, practices and institutions of democracy, with little indication that they see any inherent contradiction between their faith and democratic politics (Hashemi 2009; Sadiki 2004). The cases of China and the Muslim world are particularly interesting because, on the one hand, many advances towards democracy have been manufactured by authoritarian states, while, on the other hand, they force us to re-think democracy in Chinese or Islamic, rather than purely Western, terms.

Finally, *Part IX: Futures and Possibilities*, contains a collection of essays which consider the present and future of democracy, in terms of its advocacy as part of foreign policy, its changes due to globalisation and mass communications technology, and its quest to become more democratic via different normative models. In his chapter, Christopher Hobson examines the post-Cold War promotion of the Western liberal model of democracy and the largely US-led project to advocate and install democracies since the end of the Second World War. While the most recent attempts, those in Afghanistan and Iraq, are far from conclusive, these instances of democracy promotion have drawn vitriolic critique that America's stated desire to spread democracy is actually more directly connected to their geo-strategic agenda and the spread of free market economies under US control (C. Hobson 2005; C. Hobson and Kurki 2011). Hobson concludes by suggesting that, while democracy's appeal may wane, it is likely that democracy promotion practices will continue to be an important dimension of international politics and democracy's future development.

Another dimension central to the present and future of democracy is the advent of globalisation in the late twentieth century. In this context, many have asked whether democracy can adapt to work in a pan-regional, transnational or even global context (Anderson 2002). James Anderson reviews the desirability and possibility of transnational democracy, and argues that it may well be the only way to deal with the problems and challenges that exist beyond the traditional confines of the state, such as climate change, global poverty and disease pandemics. Globalisation has in part been brought about by the proliferation and affordability of mass communications technologies that have themselves been adapted for political purposes in numerous ways (Loader 2008). In his contribution to this volume, Brian Loader outlines the various ways in which democracy interacts with new technologies and how these are used by citizens to access information and communicate with politicians, interest groups and each other; and how these same technologies increase the government's capabilities for surveillance, command and control in ways that undermine the sovereignty of its citizenry.

Changes in our understanding of the potential of transnational democracy and communications technologies have led to new normative models, which seek to understand democracy in the era of globalisation and information. In his chapter, Lincoln Dahlberg explores the notion of radical democracy first proposed by Ernesto Laclau and Chantelle Mouffe (Laclau and Mouffe 1985; Mouffe 1992). Radical democracy is a means to challenge the hegemony of the liberal model and its tendency to build consensus at the expense of difference. To counter this, radical democrats are called upon to broaden and deepen democratic engagement to embrace those with differing opinions and those of different race, class, gender, religion and so on. Another approach, by John Dryzek and others, has been to point out that power-free communication can lead to wide participation in decision making, which in turn serves as a mechanism for determining popular sentiment beyond the ballot box (Dryzek 2000, 2010). In their chapter for this volume Kasper Moller Hansen and Christian Rostbøll explore this model of deliberative democracy and its potential for creating more robust platforms for various civil society, international organisations and governmental apparatus.

Finally, John Keane underlines the unfinished nature of the democratic project and the importance of, and possibilities in, basing new thinking firmly on the everyday experience of people and their hopes, aspirations and visions for the future (Keane 2009). His chapter proposes fresh ways of addressing the 'wicked problems' facing democratic ideals and institutions in the twenty-first century. He outlines new directions for research into democracy, including the indigenisation of democracy, the political anthropology of democracy, the attractions of unelected representatives, the potential for monitory democracy, the possibilities of political markets and the need to prepare for democracy's possible failure.

Together, the essays collected here provide a rich and diverse insight into democracy and its history. From its earliest iterations among our Common Ancestors, down through humankind's first societies and grandest civilisations, democracy has been present at those moments when people came together to fight for their rights, to develop a society which protected their interests, and to have a say in their immediate political environment. This has included loose tribal moots that met sporadically, formal assemblies that served as the heart of a city-state's administration, sophisticated legal and bureaucratic mechanisms that governed great empires, and recent attempts to effect democracy on a transnational or global scale. Democracy has appeared in some form on all of the inhabited continents on earth and in conjunction with every major religious belief or set of cultural customs. There were brief moments of democracy that were snuffed out by moguls and tyrants, extended periods of creeping authoritarianism and oligarchy, and great democratic waves in which country after country threw off the mantle of oppression. Democracies have been destroyed by war, proliferated by war and wars have been fought in the name of democracy. There have also been times when democracy was the result of peaceful grassroots political activism and times when it was imposed by a pro-democracy elite or foreign power.

What all of this reveals is that the history of democracy is a complex field, far too large ever to be captured comprehensively in a single volume. Inevitably, this book excludes several notable moments in global democratic history. The tribal democracies of the earliest hunters and gatherers are not adequately explored, nor are the sophisticated bureaucracies of the ancient Egyptians or the Byzantines; the moots of the Huns or Goths are left out, as are the successes of democracy following major post-colonial independence movements, such as those in Haiti or India; the Machnovist movement in Russia is absent, as is the Green movement of more recent times; while many contemporary stories of democracy's successes (Bhutan), problems and reversals (Russia) and failures (Afghanistan) are also missing, along with other normative models (associative and social democracy). Future investigations of these other histories of democracy, and a great many more, are urgently needed and certainly encouraged.

Nonetheless, the chapters that are collected here provide an unprecedented snapshot of the democratic vista through time. They shift debate from out-dated analyses of democracy and its history as an exclusively Western ideal, towards a new framework in which the multiple origins and complex trajectories of democracy are appreciated in a broader, more nuanced and less prejudiced fashion. The chapters provide rich historical detail, empirical analysis and normative ideals that converge to offer new insights to the age-old questions, 'What is democracy?' and 'Where does democracy come from?' What they reveal is that democracy is not 'ours' to give to the world. It is a dynamic system of governance underpinned by virtues and practices that have legitimate ancestry in every corner and culture of the globe. Scholars, democrats and citizens alike would do well to remember this as democracy is strived for, achieved, overturned and strived for again through the twenty-first century and beyond.

References

Acton, J. E. E. D. ([1907] 2005), *The History of Freedom and Other Essays*, New York: Cosimo.

Almond, G. A. and S. Verba ([1963] 1989), *The Civic Culture: Political Attitudes and Democracy in Five Nations*, Newbury Park, CA: Sage.

Amendment the First of the United States Constitution (1791), The Bill of Rights: A Transcription, Washington, DC: US National Archives and Records Administration.

Anderson, J. (ed.) (2002), *Transnational Democracy: Political Spaces and Border Crossings*, London: Routledge.

Arblaster, A. (2002), *Democracy*, 3rd edn, Buckingham: Open University Press.

Aristotle ([350 BCE] 1962), *The Politics*, trans. T. A. Sinclair, London: Penguin Classics.

Beachain, D. O. and A. Polese (eds) (2010), *The Colour Revolutions in the Former Soviet Republics: Successes and Failures*, London: Routledge.

Bernal, M. ([1987] 1991), *Black Athena: The Afroasiatic Roots of Classical Civilisation, vol. I: The Fabrication of Ancient Greece 1785–1985*, London: Vintage.

Boehm, C. H. ([1999] 2001), *Hierarchy in the Forest: The Evolution of Egalitarian Behavior*, Cambridge, MA: Harvard University Press.

Bonald, L. G. A. de ([1818] 2004), 'Observations on Madame de Stael's Considerations on the Principal Events of the French Revolution', in O. C. Blum (ed.), *Critics of the Enlightenment: Readings in the French Counter-Revolutionary Tradition*, Wilmington, NC: ISI Books, pp. 81–106.

Bonner, P., P. Delius and D. Posel (eds) (1993), *Apartheid's Genesis, 1935–1962*, Johannesburg: Raven Press.

Bowden, R. (1979), '*Tapu* and *Mana*: Ritual Authority and Political Power in Traditional Maori Society', *Journal of Pacific History*, 14(1), 50–61.

Bradstock, A. (2000), *Winstanley and the Diggers 1649–1999*, Portland, OR: Frank Cass.

Bryce, J. (1921a), *Modern Democracies*, vol. I, London: Macmillan.

Bryce, J. (1921b), *Modern Democracies*, vol. II, London: Macmillan.

Byock, J. (2002), 'The Icelandic Althing: Dawn of Parliamentary Democracy', in J. M. Fladmark (ed.), *Heritage and Identity: Shaping the Nations of the North*, Shaftesbury: Donhead, pp. 1–17.

Capen, N. (1875), *The History of Democracy: Or, Political Progress, Historically Illustrated, from the Earliest to the Latest Periods*, New York: American Publishing Co.

Churchill, W. (1947), 'British Parliament Bill', *Hansard*, 444, 206–7.

Coyne, C. J. (2008), *After War: The Political Economy of Exporting Democracy*, Stanford, CA: Stanford University Press.

Crick, B. and A. Lockyer (eds) (2010), *Active Citizenship: What Could it Achieve and How?*, Edinburgh: Edinburgh University Press.

Declaration of Independence, The ([1776] 1997), in S. M. Cahn (ed.), *Classics of Modern Political Theory: Machiavelli to Mill*, Oxford: Oxford University Press, pp. 601–3.

Democracy's Century: A Survey of Global Political Change in the 20th Century (1999), New York: Freedom House.

DeWiel, B. (2000), *Democracy: A History of Ideas*, Vancouver: University of British Columbia Press.

Diamond, L. J. (2002), 'Thinking about Hybrid Regimes', *Journal of Democracy*, 13(2), 21–35.

Diamond, L. J. and M. Plattner (eds) (1996), *The Global Resurgence of Democracy*, 2nd edn, Baltimore, MD: Johns Hopkins University Press.

Doran, C. (1998), 'Confucianism, Cultural Reform and the Politics of Identity in Singapore', *ASEAN Forum*, 2(3), 18–27.

Doran, C. (2006), 'Bright Celestial: Progress in the Political Thought of Tan Teck Soon', *SOJOURN: Journal of Social Issues in Southeast Asia*, 21(1), 46–67.

Drescher, S. (2009), *Abolition: A History of Slavery and Antislavery*, Cambridge: Cambridge University Press.

Dryzek, J. S. (2000), *Deliberative Democracy and Beyond: Liberals, Critics, Contestations*, Oxford: Oxford University Press.

Dryzek, J. S. (2010), *Foundations and Frontiers of Deliberative Governance*, Oxford: Oxford University Press.

Dunn, J. (ed.) (1992), *Democracy: The Unfinished Journey, 508 BC to AD 1993*, Oxford: Oxford University Press.

Dunn, J. (2005), *Democracy: A History*, New York: Atlantic Monthly.

Ejiofor, L. U. (1981), *Dynamics of Igbo Democracy: A Behavioural Analysis of Igbo Politics in Aguinyi Clan*, Ibadan: University of Nigeria Press.

Esposito, J. L. and J. O. Voll (1996), *Islam and Democracy*, New York: Oxford University Press.

Farrar, C. (1988), *The Origins of Democratic Thinking: The Invention of Politics in Classical Athens*, Cambridge: Cambridge University Press.

Finley, M. I. (1973), *Democracy Ancient and Modern*, New Brunswick, NJ: Rutgers University Press.

Fortes, M. and E. E. Evans-Pritchard (eds) ([1940] 1987), *African Political Systems*, London: KPI.

Freedom in the World (1991), New York: Freedom House.

Freedom in the World (1996), New York: Freedom House.

Freedom in the World (2000), New York: Freedom House.

Freedom in the World (2006), New York: Freedom House.

Freedom in the World: The Arab Uprisings and their Global Repercussions (2012), New York: Freedom House.

Fukuyama, F. (1992), *The End of History and the Last Man*, London: Penguin.

Furetière, A. ([1690] 1978), *Dictionnaire universel*, Paris: SNL – Le Robert.

Glassman, R. M. (1986a), *Democracy and Despotism in Primitive Societies: A Neo-Weberian Approach to Political Theory, vol. I: Primitive Democracy*, Millwood, NY: Associated Faculty Press.

Glassman, R. M. (1986b), *Democracy and Despotism in Primitive Societies: A Neo-Weberian Approach to Political Theory, vol. II: Primitive Despotism*, Millwood, NY: Associated Faculty Press.

Goodwin, T. S. (1864), *The Natural History of Secession: Despotism and Democracy at Necessary, Eternal, Exterminating War*, New York: John Bradburn.

Goody, J. (2006), *The Theft of History*. Cambridge: Cambridge University Press,

Graebner, N. A. and E. M. Bennett (2011), *The Versailles Treaty and its Legacy: The Failure of the Wilsonian Vision*, Cambridge: Cambridge University Press.

Grimshaw, P. (1972), *Women's Suffrage in New Zealand*, Auckland: Auckland University Press.

Habermas, J. ([1989] 1996), 'The Transformation of the Public Sphere's Political Function', in W. Outhwaite (ed.), *The Habermas Reader*, Cambridge: Polity, pp. 28–31.

Hashemi, N. (2009), *Islam, Secularism and Liberal Democracy: Toward a Democratic Theory for Muslim Societies*, Oxford: Oxford University Press.

Hattersley, A. F. (1930), *A Short History of Democracy*, Cambridge: Cambridge University Press.

He, B. (1996), *The Democratization of China*, New York: Routledge.

He, B. (1997), *The Democratic Implication of Civil Society in China*, London: Macmillan.

Hittinger, J. (2003), *Liberty, Wisdom and Grace: Thomism and Modern Democratic Theory*, Lanham, MD: Lexington Books.

Hobbes, T. ([1651] 2002), *Leviathan*: Project Gutenberg.

Hobson, C. (2005), 'A Forward Strategy of Freedom in the Middle East: US Democracy Promotion and the "War on Terror"', *Australian Journal of International Affairs*, 59(1), 39–53.

Hobson, C. and M. Kurki (eds) (2011), *The Conceptual Politics of Democracy Promotion*, London: Routledge.

Hobson, J. M. (2004), *The Eastern Origins of Western Civilisation*, Cambridge: Cambridge University Press.

Huntington, S. P. (1991), *The Third Wave: Democratization in the Late Twentieth Century*, Norman, OK: University of Oklahoma Press.

Isakhan, B. (2012), *Democracy in Iraq: History, Politics and Discourse*, London: Ashgate.

Isakhan, B., F. Mansouri and S. Akbarzadeh (eds) (2012), *The Arab Revolutions in Context: Civil Society and Democracy in a Changing Middle East*, Melbourne: Melbourne University Press.

Isakhan, B. and S. Stockwell (eds) (2011), *The Secret History of Democracy*, London: Palgrave Macmillan.

Jacobsen, T. ([1943] 1970), 'Primitive Democracy in Ancient Mesopotamia', in W. L. Moran (ed.), *Toward the Image of Tammuz and Other Essays on Mesopotamian History and Culture*, Cambridge, MA: Harvard University Press, pp. 157–70.

Johansen, B. E. (1982), *Forgotten Founders: How the American Indian Helped Shape Democracy*, Boston, MA: Harvard Common Press.

Keane, J. (2009), *The Life and Death of Democracy*, New York: Simon & Schuster.

Keating, P. (2011), 'Digging for Democracy in China', in B. Isakhan and S. Stockwell (eds), *The Secret History of Democracy*, London: Palgrave Macmillan, pp. 60–75.

Khan, U. (ed.) (1999), *Participation Beyond the Ballot Box: European Case Studies in State–Citizen Political Dialogue*, London: UCL Press.

Kilcullen, J. (1999), 'Ockham's Political Writings', in P. V. Spade (ed.), *The Cambridge Companion to Ockham*, Cambridge: Cambridge University Press.

Laclau, E. and C. Mouffe (1985), *Hegemony and Socialist Strategy: Towards a Radical Democratic Politics*, London: Verso.

Lakoff, S. (1996), *Democracy: History, Theory, Practice*, Boulder, CO: Westview Press.

Lau, T. (2008), *Stiefbrüder: Nation und Konfession in der Schweiz und in Europa (1656–1712)*, Köln: Böhlau.

Legesse, A. (2001), *Oromo Democracy: An Indigenous Political System*, Trenton, NJ: Red Sea Press.

Lincoln, A. ([1863] 1953), 'The Gettysburg Address', in R. B. Basler (ed.), *The Collected Works of Abraham Lincoln*, New Brunswick, NJ: Rutgers University Press, pp. 234–8.

Lintner, B. (2011), *Aung San Suu Kyi and Burma's Struggle for Democracy*, Chiang Mai: Silkworm Publisher.

Loader, B. (2008), *Beyond e-Government: New Media, Market Liberalism and Democratic Governance*, London: Routledge.

Lynch, J. (1986), *The Spanish American Revolutions 1808–1826*, 2nd edn, New York: W. W. Norton.

Lyon, A. (2003), *The Constitutional History of the United Kingdom*, London: Cavendish.

Madison, J. ([1788] 1981), 'The Federalist No. 10', in R. P. Fairfield (ed.), *The Federalist Papers: A Collection of Essays Written in Support of the Constitution of the United States, from the Original Text of Alexander Hamilton, James Madison, John Jay*, 2nd edn, Baltimore, MD: Johns Hopkins University Press.

Maine, H. S. ([1885] 1976), *Popular Government: Four Essays*, Indianapolis, IN: Liberty Classics.

Markoff, J. (1997), *The Abolition of Feudalism: Peasants, Lords and Legislators in the French Revolution*, University Park, PA: Pennsylvania State University Press.

Markoff, J. (1999), 'Where and When Was Democracy Invented?', *Comparative Studies in Society and History*, 41(4), 660–90.

Marx, K. and F. Engels ([1848] 1990), 'Manifesto of the Communist Party', in L. S. Feuer (ed.), *Karl Marx and Friedrich Engels: Basic Writings on Politics and Philosophy*, Glasgow: Fontana, pp. 43–82.

Matyszak, P. (2003), *Chronicle of the Roman Republic: The Rulers of Ancient Rome from Romulus to Augustus*, London: Thames & Hudson.

Mitchell, L. A. (2009), *Uncertain Democracy: U.S. Foreign Policy and Georgia's Rose Revolution*, Philadelphia, PA: University of Pennsylvania Press.

Morris, A. D. (1984), *Origins of the Civil Rights Movements: Black Communities Organizing for Change*, New York: Free Press.

Mouffe, C. (ed.) (1992), *Dimensions of Radical Democracy: Pluralism, Citizenship, Community*, London: Verso.

Muhlberger, S. and P. Paine (1993), 'Democracy's Place in World History', *Journal of World History*, 4(1), 23–47.

Muir, E. (1999), 'The Sources of Civil Society in Italy', *Journal of Interdisciplinary History*, 29(3), 379–406.

Norcross, J. (1883), *The History of Democracy: Considered as a Party Name and as a Political Organization*, New York: G. P. Putnam.

Ober, J. (1996), *The Athenian Revolution: Essays on Ancient Greek Democracy and Political Theory*, Princeton, NJ: Princeton University Press.

Ottaway, M. (2003), *Democracy Challenged: The Rise of Semi-Authoritarianism*, Washington, DC: Carnegie Endowment for International Peace.

Paine, T. ([1776] 1986), *Common Sense*, London: Penguin.

Pateman, C. ([1970] 1999), *Participation and Democratic Theory*, Cambridge: Cambridge University Press.

Plato ([380 BCE] 1975), *The Republic*, trans. D. Lee, 2nd edn, London: Penguin.

Pritchard, D. (2010), 'The Symbiosis between Democracy and War: The Case of Ancient Athens', in D. Pritchard (ed.), *War, Democracy and Culture in Classical Athens*, Cambridge: Cambridge University Press, pp. 1–62.

Proudhon, P.-J. ([1849] 1927), *Solution of the Social Problem*, ed. H. Cohen, New York: Vanguard.

Raaflaub, K., J. Ober and R. Wallace (2007), *Origins of Democracy in Ancient Greece*, trans. R. Franciscono, Berkeley, CA: University of California Press.

Rapport, M. (2008), *1848: Year of Revolution*, New York: Basic Books.

Reynolds, H. (1995), *Fate of a Free People: A Radical Re-Examination of the Tasmanian Wars*, Ringwood: Penguin Australia.

Robinson, E. W. (1997), *The First Democracies: Early Popular Government Outside Athens*, Stuttgart: Steiner.

Ruoff, K. J. (2002), *The People's Emperor: Democracy and the Japanese Monarchy, 1945–1995*, Cambridge, MA: Harvard University Asia Center.

Sachedina, A. (2001), *The Islamic Roots of Democratic Pluralism*, New York: Oxford University Press.

Sadiki, L. (2004), *The Search for Arab Democracy: Discourses and Counter-Discourses*, New York: Columbia University Press.

Schmitt, C. ([1923] 1988), *The Crisis of Parliamentary Democracy*, trans. E. Kennedy, Boston, MA: MIT Press.

Schumpeter, J. ([1947] 2011), *Capitalism, Socialism, and Democracy*, 2nd edn, Mansfield, CT: Martino.

Seekins, D. M. (2002), *The Disorder in Order: the Army-State in Burma since 1962*, Bangkok: White Lotus.

Sen, A. (2003), 'Democracy and its Global Roots: Why Democratisation is Not the Same as Westernisation', *The New Republic*, 229(14), 28–35.

Shankman, A. (2004), *Crucible of American Democracy: The Struggle to Fuse Egalitarianism and Capitalism in Jeffersonian Pennsylvania*, Lawrence, KS: University Press of Kansas.

Sharma, R. S. (1968), *Aspects of Political Ideas in Ancient India*, 2nd edn, Delhi: Motilal Barnarsidass.

Sivak, M. (2008), *Evo Morales: The Extraordinary Rise of the First Indigenous President of Bolivia*, London: Palgrave Macmillan.

Soroush, A. (2000), *Reason, Freedom, and Democracy in Islam*, trans. M. Sadri and A. Sadri, Oxford: Oxford University Press.

Southall, R. and J. Daniel (eds) (2009), *Zunami! The 2009 South African Elections*, Pretoria: Jacana Media.

Sowerwine, C. (1982), *Sisters or Citizens?: Women and Socialism in France since 1876*, Cambridge: Cambridge University Press.

Stromberg, R. N. (1996), *Democracy: A Short, Analytical History*, Armonk, NY: M. E. Sharpe.

Thucydides ([410 BCE] 1972), *History of the Peloponnesian War*, trans. R. Warner, Harmondsworth: Penguin.

Tocqueville, A. de ([1835] 2008), *Democracy in America*, vol. II, Charleston, SC: BiblioBazaar.

Volten, P. M. E. (ed.) (1990), *Uncertain Futures: Eastern Europe and Democracy*, New York: Institute for EastWest Studies.

Weatherford, J. (1988), *Indian Givers: How the Indians of the Americas Transformed the World*, New York: Fawcett Columbine.

Wheatley, J. (2005), *Georgia from National Awakening to Rose Revolution: Delayed Transition in the Former Soviet Union*, London: Ashgate.

Wolf, C. U. (1947), 'Traces of Primitive Democracy in Ancient Israel', *Journal of Near Eastern Studies*, 6(2), 98–108.

Wootton, D. (1992), 'The Levellers', in J. Dunn (ed.), *Democracy: The Unfinished Journey 508 BC to AD 1993*, Oxford: Oxford University Press, pp. 71–89.

Part I

Pre-Classical Democracy

Chapter 1

Prehistory

Christopher Boehm[1]

Democracy is a political system that allows the will of the rank and file to be expressed in arriving at and executing policies that affect the group. A prerequisite for this sharing of power is a set of political institutions that prevent those in higher positions from increasing their power in ways that encroach on the autonomy of those below them; and while we think of these checks and balances mainly in the context of constitutional democracies, they were present less formally in egalitarian agricultural tribes (Fried 1967) and in egalitarian hunting bands (Glassman 1986). Because some obvious parallels were present also in our ape ancestors, the natural history of democracy has some antiquity, and here its evolutionary trajectory will be traced by means of behavioural phylogenetics (Brosnan 2006), a field of study that has risen in the wake of our capacity to describe and compare genomes.

Richard Wrangham pioneered an approach that permits many behaviours of the Common Ancestor of chimpanzees, gorillas, humans, and bonobos to be reconstructed with a high degree of reliability, and a rule of thumb is that any major behaviour shared by all four of these African species will have been present in the ancestor – whereas less than unanimity results in a question mark (Wrangham 1987). On the basis of the conservative 'parsimony' principle from biology (Cavalli-Sforza and Edwards 1967), Wrangham determined that 7–9 million years ago the Common Ancestor would have lived in closed groups, and that it was capable of stalking and attacking members of the same species. That was just the beginning of an ancestral politics that was extended when dispositions to hierarchical behaviour were added to this ancient political repertoire, even though for much of their more recent evolutionary past human foragers have been egalitarian (Boehm 1991, 1994, 1999; Knauft 1991).

Despotism and Democracy have the Same Roots

This Common Ancestor was followed by a more recent ape-precursor, the direct ancestor of humans, bonobos, and chimpanzees. This quadrupedal ape lived about 6 million years ago, and many of this ancestor's political patterns can also be reliably reconstructed (Boehm 1997, 2000; Ghiglieri 1988; Wrangham and Peterson 1996). Unlike the Common Ancestor, Ancestral *Pan* lived in groups that behaved territorially, hunted some small game, and, to a limited degree, shared the meat (Boehm 1999). All three living species exhibit not only a mixture of individual dominance and submission

dispositions, but noteworthy tendencies for subordinates concerned with their autonomy to form defiant coalitions, which can reduce the power of dominants. It is here
that we see a major link with democracy, in terms of pre-existing 'building blocks' that
were able to provide evolutionary continuity.

In further reconstructing this ancestral pattern, a number of details about power
relationships are of interest (Boehm and Flack 2010). Today's chimpanzees have linear
male hierarchies with pronounced dominance by alpha males, while subordinate males
routinely form dyadic coalitions to try to usurp alpha power – and once in a while a
large group of subordinates will actually eject a high-ranking dominator from the
group, with possibly lethal consequences (Goodall 1992; Nishida 1996). While females
in the wild form few coalitions and wield little power, in captivity they form permanent
coalitions that sharply limit the power of alphas, particularly with respect to their
physically attacking the females (Goodall 1986; Waal 1996).

Bonobos are different, yet similar. They, too, have male hierarchies, but the males
gain power by forming coalitions not with other males, but with their mothers. Thus, a
male whose mother is the top female will become alpha, but when his mother dies his
social dominance position among the males will weaken (Kano 1992). Unlike
chimpanzees, in the wild female bonobos form coalitions all the time as they compete
with males for food, and quite often they win such contests. In fact, sizable coalitions of
female bonobos have been known to attack, wound, and very likely kill an intimidating
male that aroused their strong hostility.

There is no African great-ape equivalent of a democratic society, although bonobos
would come closer than chimpanzees because their social hierarchies seem to be less
pronounced, and because female coalitions work so continuously as a serious check on
the power of alpha males. On the other hand, human hunter-gatherer subordinate
coalitions suppress alpha behaviour quite definitively, and by carrying their 'counter-
domination' (Erdal and Whiten 1994) so far they do not merely attenuate the
expression of political dominance, rather, they actively reverse the dominance process
(Boehm 1984, 1993, 1994, 1997). Basically, as with human egalitarians it is the
subordinates who are in charge, all the time, routinely, and they are determined to
keep things that way.

The evolutionary roots of despotism and democracy are very much the same.
Ancestral *Pan* had strong individual tendencies to dominate and submit, which are the
building blocks of any social dominance hierarchy, and these provide a ready avenue
for tyranny to develop. Far less recognised is the fact that subordinates so regularly
resented being dominated, and that there were two outlets for their frustration (Boehm
1999). One was simply to bide one's time, in hopes of overwhelming today's dominator
and becoming dominant oneself. The other was to join in a subordinate coalition, and
at least partially undermine the authority of a dominator, who was too strong to be
wholly displaced (Boehm 1997). Ancestral *Pan* did both, but humans found a radical
solution for the subordination problem. This was to both forcefully eliminate the alpha
male's control role, and, more generally, to neutralise the hegemony of higher-ranking
males. If we wish to explain any modern case of despotism in terms of its evolutionary
background, the strong tendencies to dominate and submit we have identified in
Ancestral *Pan* provided major building blocks, or pre-adaptations, that make such

cultural developments likely. But at the same time, that same ancestor's rebellious subordinate coalitions provided a major pre-adaptation for democracy to develop, in terms of 'control from below' that becomes culturally institutionalised.

The Effect of Large-game Hunting

At the latest, people probably became egalitarian 250,000 years ago. Rather surprisingly, the decisive evolutionary catalyst for this development was likely to have been a new twist in our subsistence pursuits. Archaic humans did not hunt large game actively, regularly, and effectively until a quarter of a million years BP, when large ungulates became a staple food (Stiner 2002). Based on some highly predictive assumptions from human behavioural ecology, this would have been a signal development with respect to the prehistoric evolution of political democracy (Winterhalder 2001).

For any social carnivore that depends on unpredictably acquired large prey for its subsistence, there have to be enough hunters in its groups to ensure that 'variance reduction' takes place: that is, the variance in the amount of meat an individual eats weekly must become low enough, over time, so that steady, effective nutrition is possible (Kaplan and Hill 1985). From this theory we can derive two rules of thumb. First, if hunting is to be efficient, at least half a dozen hunters must pool their efforts if the meat is to come in often enough to significantly reduce this unwanted variance. And second, this meat has to be shared among all the individuals in the group so that the entire hunting team can be well nourished, healthy and vigorous enough to keep on hunting efficiently as a cooperative unit.

Both of these principles apply to social carnivores in general, such as lions, dolphins or wolves. These animals are hierarchical, but the dominant individuals are tolerant enough so that the carcasses are shared reasonably well. They also apply to humans, to the extent that recently we have been large-game hunters. It is the sheer size of the game, combined with the unpredictability of bringing it in, that gives rise to the need to reduce variance in meat intake. And with the help of culture, humans – and only humans – evolved a unique way of dealing with this problem. Before this major hunting career began, with archaic humans we may assume that basically some kind of a pronounced political hierarchy was still the order of the day, in spite of a continuation of the ancestral pattern of resistance by subordinate coalitions. Such moderate degrees of counter-domination would have been insufficient to facilitate really effective large-game hunting; indeed, still-powerful alpha males would have made the equalised distribution of meat impossible, as is the case today with chimpanzees and bonobos (Boehm and Flack 2010; Whallon 1989). What was needed was a necessarily violent abolition of the ancestral-type alpha male system so that a subsistence based on regular intake of large game could work efficiently.

A quarter of a million years ago, the African humans whose interest in intensive hunting set off this chain of ecological and political events were archaic *Homo sapiens*, who had brains approaching the size of ours but whose Middle Paleolithic cultural traditions were far less inventive (Klein 1999). Within another 50,000 years they had become anatomically modern, and after another 150,000 years they had become culturally modern (McBrearty and Brooks 2000). During this transitional period an important evolutionary transformation can be hypothesised, as forceful group social control, heavily escalated from the ancestral level, continued to systematically and violently quash alpha-type behaviour so as to permit an equalised meat distribution (Boehm 2004). In terms of gene selection, this led to moral origins because individuals with better self-control gained fitness advantages, and eventually this led to the evolution of a conscience (Boehm 2008, 2012). This vigilant counter-domination by subordinates involved raw political dynamics similar to those seen in democracies today, and we may assume that as humans became moral, the control of dominants by subordinates became less bloody, better strategised, ideologically well defined by symbolic language, and in general more like what we see today.

Central Tendencies in Hunter-gatherer Egalitarianism

Influential anthropologists have tacitly assumed that contemporary hunting societies are 'just naturally' egalitarian, noting that ideologically the people were actively defining themselves as equals in this context (Fried 1967; Service 1975). Subsequently, in an analysis of forty-eight non-literate groups the present author was able to identify in fine detail the political basis of such band or tribal egalitarianism, and what was found was that much more than ideology and public disapproval were needed to keep such societies devoid of domination among the adult hunters or farmers (Boehm 1993). The advantage of using a sizable ethnographic sample was that eventually some rare episodes of tyrants emerging and their execution came to light. Out of forty-eight egalitarian societies for which information on counter-domination was available, there were ten executions of males who seriously violated the 'rights' of their egalitarian colleagues in these bands or tribes.

However, with respect to reporting such executions accurately, anthropologists often fail to gain information if their study is made after the arrival of either a colonial order or missionaries, for indigenous people are quick to learn that such authorities will treat their moralistic use of capital punishment as an instance of murder that brings outside condemnation and requires incarceration. For instance, Bushman specialist Richard Lee at first could get no good information on homicide, but once he was able to verify a few cases, people let their guard down and for a number of bands surveyed he verified a total of twenty-two killings, which provided an overall homicide rate comparable to that of a dangerous American city like New York or Los Angeles (Knauft 1991; Lee 1979). Of these killings, several would appear to be ones decided upon by groups no longer willing to deal with overbearing males, ones who were prone to express their dominance homicidally.

In the above-mentioned survey, nine of the forty-eight societies were hunter-gatherers of the mobile egalitarian type that evolved most of our genes for us, and they accounted for half of the ten executions of political upstarts (Boehm 1993). Thus, it is safe to say that such Pleistocene-style foraging societies were characterised by strong political tensions between the more powerful males and the rank-and-file, and that such tensions sometimes had to be resolved by killing self-aggrandisers who violated the egalitarian ethos by intimidating others or trying to boss them around. While

serious would-be self-aggrandisers who cannot control themselves have to be eliminated if an egalitarian order is to be preserved, the majority of political upstarts can be
held down by lesser measures. Indeed, small-scale egalitarian societies exhibit a wide
range of sanctions that are used to curb 'abuse of power' by ordinary males, such as
criticism, ridicule, disobedience, desertion and banishment. These counter-domination measures are directly analogous to checks and balances built into the constitutions
of modern democracies, so our presumptively long prehistory as egalitarians did not
mean that humans were 'just naturally' egalitarian (Glassman 1986; Knauft 1991).
Rather, some individuals were so strongly inclined to personal despotism that it was
necessary for the rest to be quite vigilant in keeping their 'mini-democracies'
equalised, and sometimes the only means to this end was homicide.

The reason that such checks and balances are needed in any type of democratic
organisation goes right to the competitive, self-aggrandising side of our political
nature. Of course, independent of personal ambition any leader will realise that gaining
more authority is useful to the job of keeping the peace, and will tend to aggrandise
power for that reason. But it is the unusually dominant outliers who are most likely to
require stern measures to keep them in line, and as we've seen, both the dominance
tendencies that pose the problem – and the predictable tendencies to resist being
dominated – can be traced back to Ancestral *Pan*.

Moral Origins

An evolutionary trajectory has been revealed. First, came an innately despotic ancestor
that was resentful of being dominated and bossed around (Boehm 1999; Wrangham
and Peterson 1996). Next came a large-brained early human, a serious hunter that was
intelligent enough to tailor its political system to its subsistence needs. The result was
the first egalitarian societies, in which male domination was definitively curbed
through checks on power that consisted of raw physical attacks or threats thereof.
Once such regimes were in place, morality began to evolve in the sense that free-riding
bullies who were better able to restrain themselves gained fitness due to their superior
self-control (Boehm 2008, 2012). The result, eventually, was a socially strategising
conscience that permitted people to internalise the rules of their groups, while having a
conscience transformed the nature of group social control. It became imbued with a
moralistic sense of right and wrong, and a judgemental rank-and-file was able to move
from physical attacks that were likely to quickly cost a deviant his life, to morally-based
sanctions that included ostracism and shaming, and permitted deviants to reform.
Thus, as of 45,000 years ago, when humans had definitely become culturally modern,
we had evolved a 'modern' way of keeping our potential 'alphas' in line that was
decisive, quite efficient and involved increasingly less lethal checks on the growth of
personal power.

Primitive Democracy 45,000 BP

If we ask what political life was like just as humans became culturally modern, this can
be approximated by looking for strong central tendencies in how independent

egalitarian hunting nomads behave today (Boehm 2002). The methodology for cultural reconstruction is straightforward. Any feature that is universal or very widespread in an appropriate contemporary sample is assumed to have been universal or very widespread among Late Pleistocene humans, after they became culturally modern.

With respect to democracy, there were small local groups with 'reversed' hierarchies, while the guiding ethos of each group was egalitarian: all adult hunters, at least, were deemed to be equal. This did not mean that individual differences and competition were not tolerated. Rather, it meant that no hunter could actively self-aggrandise, try to boss others around or seek to monopolise large carcasses that were, in effect, the property of the group, and that subordinate coalitional power would be used physically, when needed, to curb such attempts at dominance (Boehm 2004). More generally, very limited and sometimes ephemeral leadership roles were informal, and acceptable leaders had to be self-effacing and generous, while group decisions were made by using symbolic communication to find a band-wide consensus. These features are widespread and probably universal among today's independent, egalitarian hunting nomads, and in them we can see some major cultural roots of democracy as we know it today (Boehm 1999). For instance, there is an ideology of individual political parity that allows all the main political actors to contribute to decisions that affect the group as a whole – and at the same time keeps them from being bossed around personally (Boehm 1993). There is also a set of informal checks and balances that are designed to pre-emptively keep both legitimate leaders and self-aggrandising males from turning into tyrants. One is the equalised meat-sharing system. Another is the pre-emptive use of ridicule to keep individual egos in line, or use of any of the other counter-dominance measures (Lee 1979). This social arsenal of checks on power is formidable. The ideological definition of hunters as political equals can be seen as a means of power equalisation.

Further Political Evolution

Just after 10,000 BP the warmer, more stable Holocene Epoch began and egalitarian foragers had the opportunity to create changes in their subsistence economy. One such change was that sometimes resources became so rich that year-round foraging settlements became possible. The other was that domestication of plants and animals began to pay off for people who were able to pursue a sedentary lifestyle and store their food, so they left the foraging way of life. Initially, settling down in one place had little effect on politics, aside from the fact that somewhat stronger leadership roles emerged as a response to the needs of these larger communities for better conflict management. The egalitarian ethos persisted strongly, as did a consensual style of decision making. It was only when such agricultural societies became quite sizable, that the need for greater command and control led to the development of chiefly 'perks' and a moderate degree of centralised authority that saw the end of egalitarianism in various parts of the world. In this transition, the ethos moved from egalitarian to hierarchical and social classes emerged even though chiefs would be opposed if they tried to act as tyrants.

Most sedentary tribesmen who live by agriculture have remained fiercely egalitarian right down to the present (Boehm 1993). It has been where population densities increased that hereditary chiefdoms arose with their enhanced centralised command

and control of definitive social classes (Service 1975). Chiefdoms led eventually to early states, which were uniform in having very powerful leadership roles, bureaucrats, economic division of labour, formalised legal systems, taxation and standing armies, while all these political transformations took place in short periods of evolutionary time because they were cultural; no genetic change was needed. The underlying basics provided by Ancestral *Pan*'s primitive political propensities were there, of course, and in fact the return to hierarchy was quite consistent with Ancestral *Pan*'s despotic political lifestyle.

It would appear that one thing that led to the loss of an ancient and once universal democratic egalitarianism was the indigenous view of tradeoffs involved in having more powerful leaders. Hunter-gatherers had been extreme in their dislike of allowing authority to develop; they simply could not countenance a leader who was strong enough to step in effectively and arrest a conflict that could seriously disrupt a local group. Today's mobile hunter-gatherers sometimes try to act in this role, but they are likely to be killed while trying to stop a physical conflict. Indeed, out of twenty-two homicides recorded for the !Kung bushman, anthropologist Richard Lee counted several instances of would-be peacemakers losing their lives (Lee 1979). Tribal egalitarians who farm also value personal autonomy, and they too are very suspicious of power as they resist the development of social classes, strong leaders or political dynasties. When chiefdoms began to form, it was because this strict egalitarian ethos was set aside that chiefs were able to develop considerable personal influence and some limited but effective peace-making authority, and create leadership dynasties. But as these dynasties led to the existence of nobles and commoners the result was far from tyranny, for these economically privileged hereditary chiefs were not in a position to hire full-time enforcers (Service 1975). Thus, they had to govern primarily by means of influence, even though people looked up to them and made them customary gifts. This income made a chiefly standard of living possible, but chiefs were expected to help out those in need.

Formal taxation and standing armies were only on the horizon. It was as primitive kingdoms and then states arose that wealth accruing to centralised leaders led to the paying of professional bureaucrats and soldiers, and it was the soldiers who finally provided the basis for despotic power to develop at the political centre (Service 1975). However, even in autocratic military states there is always the possibility of a generalised subordinate rebellion. If one considers both uprisings and coups, there is no form of government in which substantial subordinate control of leaders is totally impossible, although military dictatorships have always headed the list of those that are least vulnerable.

This evolutionary scenario makes it clear that over time there has existed a political continuum, with egalitarian bands (and tribes) at one end and despotic states at the other. One has only to look at the patterns of Ancestral *Pan* to see where the behavioural potential for both outcomes came from, and a modern (or ancient) democracy is easy enough to fit into this evolutionary picture. In today's nations, or in elite-run Greek city-states, requirements for centralised command and control have been significant because large populations require an organised social order if they are to flourish – especially if they go to war. This means that, above all, internal conflicts must be minimised, for they can lead to civil war. Some kind of consensualised group decision process aids in keeping internal conflict to a minimum. It is because people rightly fear the human tendency to aggrandise power, which stems from evolved political dispositions that are so clearly identifiable in Ancestral *Pan*, that we create the sometimes elaborate sets of checks and balances found in constitutional democracies, which permit a carefully restrained type of centralised command and control. What these checks and balances do is to elaborate and formalise what is done on a much smaller scale by egalitarian hunter-gatherers.

The argument has been that we humans are innately set up to be social and political animals. We are geared to dominate and submit, but we dislike being submissive because this encroaches on our personal autonomy. Obviously, the safest route to personal autonomy for the citizens is simply to outlaw all alpha behaviour. The problem is that this leaves local groups with no one powerful enough to step in and stop conflicts as alpha chimpanzees and bonobos do, as chiefs do in chiefdoms and as absolute rulers so readily did in early civilisations. There are three conditions under which we give up control from below, and thereby give up on the guarantee of local democracy. We may do so willingly because a trusted altruistic leader is so good at leading that the perceived advantages of letting this role develop outweigh the loss of autonomy. With far less calculation, we may do the same thing simply because a leader is so charismatic that the people identify with him or her and thereby lose sight of their need for autonomy (Weber 1947). Finally, despotic leadership may be imposed in a draconian fashion through application of coercive force from the political centre.

Democracy and Political Evolution

First, surely, came egalitarian bands followed by egalitarian tribes; next came chiefdoms, with their social classes and their real but limited chiefly authority; and next came despotic leaders, with standing armies whose power was limited only by the spectre of major popular revolts. Each is a direct outgrowth of our original hunter-gatherer local democracies, but with the equalised political system, which was, in effect, guided by an egalitarian ethos writ much larger. The resentment and suspicion of leadership that led primitive democracies to invent and maintain strong checks and balances stemmed from a human political nature that resented authority – unless the advantages were obvious and overwhelming. At the base, of course, is the competitive human proclivity to dominantly self-aggrandise, which stirs this suspicion in the first place. All of these proclivities go back for at least 6 million years, and in combination these ingredients are the basis for any democracy.

Democracy predictably involves a rank-and-file mistrust of what individuals in leadership positions are likely to do – once they taste some personal power. Thus, culturally imposed checks and balances are set up to cope with an ever-present contingency, for eventually some leader will try to become unduly dominant. This is what must be prevented – even as the benefits of leadership are exploited by groups that are shrewd enough to keep their leaders on a leash. Often the checks and balances that go with modern political democracy are traced back to the Magna Carta, which was the result of anti-hierarchical tendencies of the peasants, not tribesmen. But the basic political dynamics are of the same type that we have seen in zealously egalitarian hunter-gatherers and can be traced back to our earliest ancestors.

Conclusion

This chapter has combined phylogenetics, prehistory, ethnography and ethno-history to present an anthropological analysis of group political dynamics which underlies the existence of democracies everywhere, at all times in history. The hypothesis is that every democracy has involved similar political dynamics because our genetic nature interacts with our remarkable cultural problem-solving capacity and steers us in this direction. Clearly, we are not speaking the language of genetic determinism here, for the innate dispositions and social forces that make for egalitarianism and democratic rule from below are far from being inexorable. What can be predicted, however, is that unless a despotism is either extremely benign or kept in place by political charisma, a resistant populace will at least want to create checks and balances so as to reduce their vulnerability to power from above. They can thereby increase their personal freedom of action as autonomy-loving individuals, but whether they are in a position to accomplish this is a different matter.

Democracy is basically a *cultural* solution to a practical problem that stems from our multifaceted genetic nature and everyday political situations. The underlying problem is that human individuals are likely to aggrandise their power whenever they are established at the political centre, and, because individuals are variable both in their genetic make-up and in their life experience, some leaders will exhibit a compulsion in this direction and others may not. It has been our counter-dominant tendencies, shared with the other African great apes, that have helped to engender pre-emptive democratic checks and balances wherever we find them. Tens of millennia ago, culturally modern egalitarian hunter-gatherers were the first people to develop philosophies of equality, and were the first to set up some informal, but highly effective, constraints on the development of leadership, which in fact became quite definitive. Thus, our capacity for self-governance took on new, cultural dimensions of power-sharing – and today, the underlying basics remain very similar. This is still the case, whether we are thinking of the few remaining egalitarian forager groups that pre-emptively ridicule their most successful hunters or ignore the 'commands' of an upstart who would see himself in charge, or whether we are looking at a written constitution that has the power to send a Richard Nixon into political exile at the zenith of his power. The phylogenetic roots of democracy are ancient and understanding them can assist us in understanding its more recent history.

Note

1. The author wishes to thank Kristin Howard for editorial comments.

References

Boehm, C. (1984), 'Can Hierarchy and Egalitarianism Both be Ascribed to the Same Causal Forces?', *Politics and the Life Sciences*, 1, 34–7.

Boehm, C. (1991), 'Response to Knauft, Violence and Sociality in Human Evolution', *Current Anthropology*, 32(4), 411–12.

Boehm, C. (1993), 'Egalitarian Behavior and Reverse Dominance Hierarchy', *Current Anthropology*, 34(3), 227–54.

Boehm, C. (1994), 'Pacifying Interventions at Arnhem Zoo and Gombe', in R. W. Wrangham, W. C. McGrew, F. B. M. de Waal and P. G. Heltne (eds), *Chimpanzee Cultures*, Cambridge, MA: Harvard University Press, pp. 211–26.

Boehm, C. (1997), 'Impact of the Human Egalitarian Syndrome on Darwinian Selection Mechanics', *American Naturalist*, 150, Supplement, 100–21.

Boehm, C. (1999), *Hierarchy in the Forest: The Evolution of Egalitarian Behavior*, Cambridge, MA: Harvard University Press.

Boehm, C. (2000), 'Conflict and the Evolution of Social Control', *Journal of Consciousness Studies*, 7(1–2), 79–183.

Boehm, C. (2002), 'Variance Reduction and the Evolution of Social Control', Paper presented at Santa Fe Institute, 5th Annual Workshop on the Co-Evolution of Behaviors and Institutions, November 2002, Santa Fe.

Boehm, C. (2004), 'What makes Humans Economically Distinctive? A Three-species Evolutionary Comparison and Historical Analysis', *Journal of Bioeconomics*, 6(2), 109–35.

Boehm, C. (2008), 'Purposive Social Selection and the Evolution of Human Altruism', *Cross-Cultural Research*, 42(4), 319–52.

Boehm, C. (2012), *Moral Origins: The Evolution of Virtue, Altruism and Shame*, New York: Basic Books.

Boehm, C. and J. Flack (2010), 'The Emergence of Simple and Complex Power Structures through Social Niche Construction', in A. Guinote (ed.), *The Social Psychology of Power*, New York: Guilford Press.

Brosnan, S. F. (2006), 'Nonhuman Species' Reactions to Inequity and their Implications for Fairness', *Social Justice Research*, 19(2), 153–85.

Cavalli-Sforza, L. L. and A. W. F. Edwards (1967), 'Phylogenetic Analysis: Models and Estimation Procedures', *Evolution*, 32(3), 550–70.

Erdal, D. and A. Whiten (1994), 'On Human Egalitarianism: An Evolutionary Product of Machiavellian Status Escalation?', *Current Anthropology*, 35(2), 175–84.

Fried, M. H. (1967), *The Evolution of Political Society*, New York: Random House.

Ghiglieri, M. (1988), *East of the Mountains of the Moon: Chimpanzee Society in the African Rain Forest*, New York: Free Press.

Glassman, R. A. (1986), *Democracy and Despotism in Primitive Societies*, vol. I, Port Washington, NY: Associated Faculty Press.

Goodall, J. (1986), *The Chimpanzees of Gombe: Patterns of Behavior*, Cambridge, MA: Belknap Press.

Goodall, J. (1992), 'Unusual Violence in the Overthrow of an Alpha Male Chimpanzee at Gombe', in T. Nishida, W. C. McGrew, P. Marler, M. Pickford and F. B. M. de Waal (eds), *Topics in Primatology, vol. 1: Human Origins*, Tokyo: University of Tokyo Press, pp. 131–42.

Kano, T. (1992), *The Last Ape: Pygmy Chimpanzee Behavior and Ecology*, Stanford, CA: Stanford University Press.

Kaplan, H. and K. Hill (1985), 'Food Sharing among Aché Foragers: Tests of Explanatory Hypotheses', *Current Anthropology*, 26(2), 223–46.

Klein, R. G. (1999), *The Human Career: Human Biological and Cultural Origins*, Chicago, IL: University of Chicago Press.

Knauft, B. M. (1991), 'Violence and Sociality in Human Evolution', *Current Anthropology*, 32(4), 391–428.

Lee, R. B. (1979), *The !Kung San: Men, Women, and Work in a Foraging Society*, Cambridge: Cambridge University Press.

McBrearty, S. and A. Brooks (2000), 'The Revolution that Wasn't: A New Interpretation of the Origin of Modern Human Behavior', *Journal of Human Evolution*, 39(5), 453–563.

Nishida, T. (1996), 'The Death of Ntologi, the Unparalleled Leader of M Group', *Pan Africa News*, 3, 4.

Service, E. R. (1975), *Origin of the State and Civilization: The Process of Cultural Evolution*, New York: W. W. Norton.

Stiner, M. C. (2002), 'Carnivory, Coevolution, and the Geographic Spread of the Genus *Homo*', *Journal of Archaeological Research*, 10(1), 1–63.

Waal, F. B. M. de (1996), *Good Natured: The Origins of Right and Wrong in Humans and Other Animals*, Cambridge, MA: Harvard University Press.

Weber, M. (1947), *The Theory of Social and Economic Organization*, trans. T. Parsons, New York: Free Press.

Whallon, R. (1989), 'Elements of Cultural Change in the Later Paleolithic', in P. Mellars and C. Stringer (eds), *The Human Revolution: Behavioural and Biological Perspectives on the Origins of Modern Humans*, vol. 1, Edinburgh: Edinburgh University Press, pp. 433–54.

Winterhalder, B. (2001), 'Intragroup Resource Transfers: Comparative Evidence, Models, and Implications for Human Evolution', in C. B. Stanford and H. T. Bunn (eds), *Meat-Eating and Human Evolution*, New York: Oxford University Press, pp. 279–301.

Wrangham, R. W. (1987), 'African Apes: The Significance of African Apes for Reconstructing Social Evolution', in W. G. Kinzey (ed.), *The Evolution of Human Behavior: Primate Models*, Albany, NY: SUNY Press, pp. 51–71.

Wrangham, R. and D. Peterson (1996), *Demonic Males: Apes and the Origins of Human Violence*, New York: Houghton Mifflin.

Chapter 2

The Assyrians

Benjamin Isakhan

In the fertile floodplains that stretch between the Tigris and Euphrates rivers, humankind settled to form perhaps the earliest organised and permanent settlements anywhere in the world. By around 3500 BCE, these relatively simple agricultural societies had evolved into city-states, the first of which was Uruk (modern Al-Warka, Iraq), centred around a temple complex and populated by traders, merchants, farmers and the temple bureaucracy. The need for a sophisticated accounting system led to the development of the world's first written language, which itself evolved into a rich corpus of literary and bureaucratic texts. However, in order to compete for and control the scarce resources, these early city-states also developed standing armies. Success on the battlefield led to the emergence of empires and dynasties, which accumulated enough wealth to erect impressive architectural wonders and extraordinary works of art.

Today, these ancient societies are increasingly acknowledged for their enormous contribution to human civilisation, but many questions remain as to the precise nature of their government. Conventional wisdom would have us believe that cruel tyrants with a penchant for bloodshed and terror ruled over Mesopotamia. However, the archaeological work conducted during the nineteenth and twentieth centuries began to unearth a more sophisticated political landscape, leading the renowned Danish Assyriologist Thorkild Jacobsen to conclude that many of the city-states and empires of ancient Mesopotamia were in fact governed by what he referred to as 'Primitive Democracy' (Jacobsen [1943] 1970). Since Jacobsen's not uncontroversial thesis was first asserted some seventy years ago, both the volume of evidence and the number of scholars who more or less agree with him has increased to the point where it would be difficult for any serious scholar of the history of democracy to ignore the Mesopotamian developments (Barjamovic 2004; Fleming 2004; Isakhan 2007; Keane 2009). Taking this even further, recent work by the author has argued that, when compared with the Athenian experiment with democracy from around the fifth century onwards, the democracies of ancient Mesopotamia can in no measurable way be considered more 'primitive' (Isakhan 2011).

This chapter seeks to extend this earlier work to a particular Mesopotamian civilisation that is not only typically excluded from such discussions of democracy in the ancient Near East, but generally considered to be among the region's most bloodthirsty and bellicose: the Assyrians. On the one hand, it cannot be denied that the

Assyrians went through periods of aggressive expansion, that they were cruel to at least some of their enemies and that the more militant Assyrian kings struck fear into the hearts of men and women across the region (I:106–10, 113; II:1, 54–6 in Grayson 1991: 201). On the other hand, however, it is peculiar that the intermittent warmongering of the Assyrians is seen not only as 'a modern myth exaggerated beyond all proportion' (Parpola 2003: 1060), but also seen to exclude them from practicing any form of democracy. This is starkly inconsistent with the contemporary assessment of other societies of the ancient world, such as the Greeks or Romans, who were both belligerent and at least nominally democratic. To give one example of this double standard, Jana Pecirkova argues that while the Greek *polis* enabled the birth of science, philosophy and the rule of law, the Assyrians were not able to distinguish 'between the rational and the irrational, between reality and illusion' (Pecirkova 1985: 155). The reason for this, according to Pecirkova, is simple: their 'only alternative to monarchy . . . was anarchy . . . Political decisions were arbitrary in character and not governed by any laws or generally acknowledged and accepted rules' and the 'people were the passive subjects of political decision making' (Pecirkova 1985: 166–8). This chapter, while cautious not to overstate the democratic tendencies of the Assyrians, takes Pecirkova's argument to task by examining the complex functioning of power and politics, the checks and balances on monarchical authority, the rule of law and the sophisticated intellectual scene of the three key epochs of ancient Assyrian civilisation.

The Old Assyrian Empire: Ashur is King but his Sons must be Governed

Under the reign of the Akkadian Empire (2334–2154 BCE), the northern Assyrians controlled the powerful city-state of Ashur (modern Qalat Sherqat, Iraq). However, with the rapid decline of the Akkadians, came the rise of what is commonly referred to as the Old Assyrian Empire (OAE 2025–1765 BCE) in which the Assyrians extended their dominion over much of northern Mesopotamia and waged regular attacks on their southern neighbours (especially their long-time rivals, the Babylonians). The city-state of Ashur was unique in that it was named after a god (Ashur) and because the citizens were named after both their god and city, literally, the 'sons of Ashur' (Assyrians). Ultimate power rested with the god Ashur; his will was divine law, his blessings coveted and his wrath feared. But the Assyrians had to govern the temporal world, coordinate their complex society and win their many battles. Underneath the authority of the god Ashur, therefore, extended a series of complex and overlapping institutions that governed in his name: the king, the elders, the citizen assembly and the merchant-eponym. Collectively, this network of institutions and the citizens they served constituted what the Assyrians called 'the City' (Larsen 2000: 85; Veenhof 2010: 53).

The king was therefore the first among the sons of Ashur and was expected to play two key roles. First, to be Ashur's 'steward', his earthly representative in both a political sense (as a divinely appointed subject of Ashur's will and legitimate representative of the sons of Ashur) and in a spiritual sense (as chief priest, in consultation with the clergy). Secondly, he was the 'executive officer' of the state in that one of his key responsibilities was to implement the political and legal decisions made by the other institutions (Larsen 2000: 82–3). Although they retained a great deal of power, it would be wrong to assume that the Assyrian kings held it absolutely or indefinitely. Instead, the king carried the rather unenviable burden of being subject to a canon of spiritual and civil laws, and a complex array of duties and political institutions.

Perhaps the strongest counter-balance to any abuse of power by the king was the assembly of elders, usually the heads of wealthy or privileged families, but also including significant and senior bureaucratic, scholarly and military figures. This was the central political and judicial institution in Ashur and, because of their prominent role in public life, many elders achieved a degree of power, prestige and popularity. Indeed, the kings knew all too well the ability of the elders to influence the wider community of citizens and were always careful not to offend them. When differences of opinion between the king and the elders did occur, they 'were quite ready to revolt against the king if they did not approve of his policies' (Oppenheim 1964: 103). In addition, the power of the Assyrian elders can be seen in the fact that the king was not able to directly appoint his own successor, but instead nominated a potential heir who was then subject to the consent of the council. The primary function of the elders, however, was to uphold the law and exact justice in their court. In the event that the elders were confronted with a particularly challenging case or if they reached some type of stalemate, they would set up specially appointed subcommittees that would investigate and deliberate further before reporting back to the full assembly of elders (Larsen 2000: 83–4).

When the case was particularly serious, however, or had aroused popular attention, the elders would convene a citizen assembly, which would reach agreement under the guidance of the elders. At every stage, these assemblies appear to have been lively places, with participants openly pointing out the contradictions and inconsistencies in their opponents' arguments. Freedom of speech was paramount and, when each of the participants had been given a chance to state their case at least once, the proceedings ended before debate became cyclical, emotional or counter-productive. Beyond this, the citizen assembly also had the power to make recommendations to the king, particularly when there was popular agreement that the king needed to alter some aspect of his policy or implement new laws. In such an instance, the elders would work with the citizen assembly to write a letter addressed to the king. In this way, the citizens of Ashur were able to fight for exemptions and privileges, 'make legal decisions, sell real estate within the city that had no private owner, and assume corporate responsibility in cases of murder or robbery' (Oppenheim 1964: 112).

The power of the state was also mitigated by a thriving private sector as the merchants of the Assyrian empire grew in wealth and, subsequently, in influence. From among this body of merchants, one member was chosen by lot annually to serve as the chairman of the board, the merchant-eponym who gave his name to the year in which he governed. This individual was conferred with the highest honours underneath the authority of the king and 'was responsible for public works, for overseeing the judiciary, and took a leading part in the city's religious and ceremonial rites' (Leick 2001: 203). His foremost duty, however, was as 'chief financial officer'; his office was the central economic institution of Ashur. Unlike other Mesopotamian states of the time where the economy was controlled by the palace, the Assyrians seem to have encouraged a freer market with trade and tax controlled by the merchant-eponym, the head of an independent financial collective (Larsen 2000: 84–5).

In addition to these examples where democratic practices formed part of the governing structures at the heart of the Assyrian empire, one also finds examples in Assyrian colonies such as Kanesh (modern Kultepe, Turkey). This important economic and trading hub flourished from around 2000–1800 BCE and while, in many significant ways, its political system mirrored that of Ashur, its status as a trading rather than a politico-religious centre and its smaller population, meant that Kanesh also developed its own brand of political participation. The assembly of elders at Kanesh appears to have wielded a great deal more power than their brethren in Ashur. The elders not only presided over many domestic issues, including both political and judicial decision making, they also took many significant decisions independent of the king and his court (Veenhof 2010: 45). Also different was the citizen assembly. Although, as in Ashur, it was usually convened when the elders failed to agree, it appears to have been governed by more formal and sophisticated protocols. First, it could be called into session only by a secretary (high official) of Kanesh under the direct instructions of the majority of the elders. Strict punishments were handed out to anyone – even a wealthy merchant – who tried to circumvent this process and call a full assembly for his own purposes (Larsen 1976: 284). Once convened, the citizen assembly was governed by a statute that prescribed the specific protocols of the body: a type of formal constitution that set the parameters of power for the assembly and dictated its rights and responsibilities (Larsen 2000: 84–5).

The Middle Assyrian Empire: The Rule of Law and the Bureaucracy

In 1765 BCE the Babylonians, under the leadership of the 'King of Justice', King Hammurabi (1792–1750 BCE), conquered Ashur and brought to an end the OAE. However, the Assyrian monarchy survived the conquest and when Hammurabi's successors gradually lost control of the north, the Assyrians re-emerged as a credible force in Mesopotamia during the Middle Assyrian Empire (MAE 1813–1076 BCE). It is during this time that the Assyrians emerged onto the international stage, playing an increasingly significant role in regional politics and asserting themselves as a force to be reckoned with, as is attested by the so-called 'Amarna Letters' sent by King Ashur-Uballit I (1365–1330 BCE) to his Egyptian counterpart, Amenhotep IV (1353–1336 BCE) (IX, XV–XVI in Moran 1992: 9–10, 15–17).

One significant development of this epoch was the sophisticated legal system that emerged in both Babylon and Assyria, the former had the famed Hammurabi Code and the latter had the so-called Assyrian Code (Roth 1997). These complex legal and judicial prescriptions were designed, among other things, to protect the rights of the individual, to protect private property, to bring swift justice to perpetrators of crimes (such as theft, violence, slander or lying, various perversions and sorcery) and to ensure that an appropriate support network existed for the less fortunate, aggrieved and ill-treated. While the Assyrian Code certainly reflects a cruder form of judicial procedure and a more bellicose society than the picture of Babylon we glean from the Hammurabi Code, it nonetheless held the same importance in the north as the Hammurabi Code held in the south. In addition, the Assyrian Code also serves as one of the most important sources we have regarding the proto-democratic functioning of social institutions, the protection of civilian rights and the rule of law in the time of the MAE.

Of foremost relevance here is the fact that the Assyrian Code makes frequent reference to an assembly of judges – a court of law – who preside over complicated legal issues, interpret the law and apply it to complex scenarios. This is evidenced by a phrase repeated throughout the laws: 'they seize him (or her) and determine his (or her) guilt and then issue him (or her) a sentence'. Certain laws reveal that the 'they' referred to here is in fact the plural 'judges' who were vested with the power to summon people to court, presided over their public trial and issued appropriate punishments (I:14, 17 in Jastrow 1921: 18, 20). We also know that the judges had the responsibility of drawing up complex civil contracts between various stakeholders. For example, the judges often had to design irrigation contracts for farmers who had adjacent properties, water being such a precious commodity. However, when the farmers failed to adhere to these contracts, the judges would summon them to court, listen to the case put forward by each of them and review their contracts before reaching a decision. If no solution could be found, the court could threaten to renege the contract and force the farmers to organise their own water supply (II:17–18 in Jastrow 1921: 57–8), a likely failsafe designed to prompt otherwise stubborn individuals to come to an agreement.

The court of judges of the MAE did much more than punish crime or resolve contractual disputes, however. In some cases legal matters were extremely complex and sensitive, involving a great deal of political and bureaucratic negotiation. For example, one particular law, which stipulates the correct legal process for disposing of the estate of a wealthy citizen after his (or her) death, though convoluted, is worth citing in full:

The [surrogate] within the city of Ashur shall cause proclamation to be made three times. Three times, he shall cause the field and house which is to be acquired to be proclaimed in the city, to wit: 'the field and house which belongs to . . . [this one, son of this one] within the confines of this city, I wish to acquire [for silver]'. Whatever their demands and [whatever] claims there may be, let them draw up their documents and in the presence of the recorder let them deposit them, and let them put in a claim so as to make it free to be disposed of. If within this month, fixed as the time limit, they have not neglected to produce their documents and in the presence of the recorder have deposited them, then the man shall take to the full extent of his field. On the day that the surrogate makes proclamation within the city of Ashur, one as a secretary in place of the king, the city scribe, the surrogate and the recorder of the king shall assemble to dispose of the field and house within the city. [With] the prefect and three magistrates of the city standing by, the surrogate shall make the announcement. They shall hand over the documents that have been drawn up. But if within this month, the surrogate three times makes proclamation, and within this month any one's document was not brought, [and] in the presence of the recorder was not deposited, then on the field and house he lays his hand. The one who caused the proclamation of the surrogate to be made is free to act. Three documents of the proclamation of the surrogate which the judges shall draw up [are to be deposited in the presence of the recorder]. (II:6 in Jastrow 1921: 52–4)

This law is particularly interesting for several key reasons. The first thing to notice is the transparency of the transaction and the fact that it is made known to the wider citizenship. The surrogate (a high official and representative of the king) instructs the prospective landowner to announce his intention to purchase the property in public three times. If his or her bid is successful, the surrogate must then inform the people by making a further public announcement within an assembly held in the city of Ashur. Such freedom of information surely served as a counter-balance to the possibility of corruption and nepotism in the transfer of large estates. Secondly, the law gives us an insight into the sophisticated process that must be followed in order to secure such an estate. Within one month of making an initial public proclamation the interested party must submit a legally binding written bid (in triplicate), the writing and submission of which must be witnessed by the recorder (official state archivist). If successful, the bid is then transcribed into a contract by the judges, who again produce the document in triplicate and write and submit it in the presence of the recorder. Finally, it is important to point out that, in order for the transfer of an estate to be completed, it had to be confirmed in a public assembly, attended by some of the most important bureaucrats and dignitaries of the state. On the same day that the sale was finalised, the surrogate would convene a public assembly that included a secretary (another high official and representative of the king), the city-scribe (an esteemed official scholar), another recorder (also from the king's coterie), a prefect (a high-ranked bureaucrat) and three magistrates (Judges). In front of this esteemed crowd, the surrogate then made the final public proclamation with the assembly serving as legal witness.

The Neo-Assyrian Empire: International Law, Citizen Rights and the Power of Knowledge

With the death of King Tiglath-Pileser I in 1076 BCE, the MAE came to an end as much of ancient Mesopotamia descended into what is often described as the ancient 'Dark Ages' (1200–900 BCE), marked by inter-tribal warfare and brutality. However, shortly after the turn of the tenth century the political landscape of the ancient Near East shifted rapidly from one dominated by factionalism and violence to one governed and united under a single ruling power: the Neo-Assyrian Empire (NAE, 911–609 BCE). From their new capital of Nineveh (modern Kouyunjik, Iraq), the Assyrians set out on a series of military campaigns that saw them re-capture those parts of northern Mesopotamia they had formerly controlled. Over the next 300 years, they marched through the rest of Mesopotamia, Syria, the Levant, Egypt, Armenia and Cyprus as well as parts of Anatolia and Persia to become the largest empire the world had yet seen.

Among the many challenges that came with such rapid expansion was the urgent need to develop an appropriate legal framework. As the empire expanded, the Assyrian legal system evolved from one that catered mostly for domestic issues, to one that included what can only be described as a sophisticated corpus of 'international law' (Altman 2010). While it cannot be denied that the bulk of these laws concerned war-making, they nonetheless reveal a complex system of jurisprudence, and the application of abstract thought and juridical reasoning to intractable problems and complex scenarios. War was not just a demonstration of brawn and barbarousness, it was governed by a strict set of legal prescriptions in which the antagonist must first establish a 'just cause for war' (Oded 1992). Once a war began the Assyrian army was expected to adhere to a specific set of rules of engagement, including protocols for parley and surrender, the capture and treatment of prisoners, and the conquest or annexation of foreign territories.

International law in the NAE also concerned the rights of the many different citizens that now made up the empire. The people of sacred and/or politically valuable cities, such as their former capital Ashur, as well as Harrun, Babylon, Sippar, Nippur, Ur, Uruk, Borsipa and others were all extended the same rights and privileges as those in Nineveh (Altman 2010: 126). These citizens were 'free'; they were not obliged to perform corvee work or military service, they received tax exemptions and they could not be fined or imprisoned – even by the king – without due process in the courts of their city of origin (Lambert [1960] 1996). While those who lived outside these privileged cities were never accorded the same status, they were, at least theoretically, on equal footing with each other, subject to the same laws and responsibilities and were not actively discriminated against based on their wealth, class, status, colour or creed (Oded 1979: 81–6, 115; Parpola 2003: 1061). More to the point, the citizens of the NAE, whether in the central cities or in peripheral towns, played a crucial role in local governance and had a degree of political influence via the citizen assemblies that were similar to those of earlier periods and convened at least as often (Barjamovic 2004: 55–84).

To manage such a large and diverse empire, the Assyrian palace hosted an increasing number of bureaucrats, merchants, physicians, clergymen, judges, poets and military leaders, who played a key role in decision making and in influencing the king. Foremost among these were a group of what are sometimes erroneously referred to as 'scribes' and who might better be understood as 'scholars'. These scholars were made up of the diviners and astrologers who constituted a well-established political institution in their own right and whose members were the esteemed practitioners of a refined and specific set of disciplines (Oppenheim 1969; Parpola 1993). Their role was to interpret various divine omens in order to understand the will of the gods and communicate this to their fellow humans. There were two fundamental ways in which this could be done: 'extispicy' in which the diviners examined the entrails of a sacrificial sheep; and what is sometimes mistakenly called 'astrology' in which they observed various natural phenomena, primarily cosmological mechanics but also other unexplained events such as the unusual behavior of animals or earthquakes. They compiled lengthy compendia, wrote detailed omen reports, penned letters to kings and officials, and authored complex commentaries that were designed to facilitate the interpretation of omens (Parpola [1970] 2007a, [1970] 2007b).

At all times, the diviners and astrologers appear to have been encouraged to engage in lengthy and complex scholarly debates, employing rhetorical devices, dialectics, analogies and abstract reasoning to illustrate their points. The fact that such debates were often hosted by the palace indicates that the king not only had a very strong faith in the omens of the divine and the ability of the scholars to interpret them, but also that he was open to conflicting opinions, to rigorous discussion and to due deliberation. In fact, the diviners and astrologers served both a religious and a political purpose. They were often presented with political problems and required to come up with pragmatic solutions (Frahm 2004: 45–50). They also served as a kind of check on the power of the king; he could not easily ignore their advice and he was routinely forced to navigate between the will of the gods (and their earthly interpreters) and his own personal ambition (Star 1990: xxx, xxxv). Perhaps the most significant indication of the power of the diviners and astrologers of the NAE lies in the fact that they could force the king to temporarily abdicate the throne. To do so, they could argue that a particularly inauspicious sign had been interpreted and that the king may have been in danger or may have suffered some misfortune if he was not immediately replaced by a substitute king who would reign on his behalf until the omen had passed (279 in Parpola [1970] 2007a: 226–7). In such an environment, it is likely that certain scholars conspired to temporarily have the king removed from office in order to take a particular decision or pass a piece of legislation to which the king had proved resistant, all in the name of the divine.

However, there are a handful of examples that reveal that the kings were all too aware of the potential for conspiracy and corruption among the scholars and developed their own ways of curtailing such abuses of power. For example, both King Sennarcherib (705–681) and his son and heir King Esarhaddon (680–669) divided the scholars into different groups and then put their predicaments before each of them. The groups were asked to provide their own interpretation and the king would listen to their arguments and cross-examine them for consistency. This played to the king's advantage: where the scholars agreed, the king could be certain of the correct course of action, but when they disagreed the king could choose the interpretation that best suited his own agenda (Lieberman 1990: 327–8).

Esharaddon's son went a step further. King Ashurbanipal (668–626 BCE) assembled a Great Library at Nineveh composed of thousands of Babylonian and Assyrian texts as well as others from across the empire (Parpola 1987–2003). Ashurbanipal appears to have had two key motivations for setting up such a vast library. First, there was his apparent thirst for knowledge. Records reveal him to have been a very intelligent king who considered himself to be educated to the highest standards of his time, while letters addressed to him attest to his keen interest in a wide array of issues and disciplines (Lieberman 1990: 319). It is also known that Ashurbanipal took part in the 'assembly of scholars' in which he studied astrology and deliberated over extispicy with his colleagues (L4 I:13–18 in Streck 1916: 255). It seems more than likely that on these occasions Ashurbanipal was little more than the first among equals and that his interpretations and methods – and the advice he gleaned from them – were subject to the same hermeneutic enquiry and robust interrogation as that of his fellow academicians. Secondly Ashurbanipal had political reasons for compiling his vast library. While he certainly placed a lot of faith in the work of the diviners and astrologers, he was also determined to understand their methods and the reasons why they made their recommendations. Learning from his father and grandfather, Ashurbanipal realised that only a strong education and a vast collection of both primary texts and associated commentaries would permit him to be certain that the omen interpretation and subsequent advice he received were accurate and would protect him from those scholars who would conspire against him. Even in the time of the NAE, knowledge was power.

Conclusion

Unfortunately, the NAE did not long outlast Ashurbanipal's passing. Having peaked under his reign it ended abruptly when a combined force of Babylonians and Medes conquered Nineveh in 612 BCE. While much about the political machinations of the Assyrians remains opaque, the stereotypical image of them as being ruled by violent conquerors reveals only part of the picture. Even the worst Assyrian kings had to contend with a complex array of political institutions, a sophisticated legal system, an ever-increasing number of 'free' citizens, and the rise of powerful elders, merchants and scholars. While this cannot be taken in lieu of a robust democracy in which the entire body of citizens plays an active role in decision making, the case of the Assyrians forces us to consider that the will towards democracy and the institutions that make that will a reality are more common in the ancient world than is generally acknowledged. When the politics of the various Assyrian empires are considered in this light, a picture emerges of a system of government that was concerned with keeping a check on the power vested in the king and diffusing that same power outward; first, to the wealthy and elite, but also to the ordinary citizens whose rights were often respected and protected.

References

Altman, A. (2010), 'Tracing the Earliest Recorded Concepts of International Law. Part V: The Near East 1200–330 BCE', *Journal of the History of International Law*, 12, 101–53.

Barjamovic, G. (2004), 'Civic Institutions and Self-Government in Southern Mesopotamia in the mid-first Millennium BCE', in J. G. Dercksen (ed.), *Assyria and Beyond: Studies Presented to Mogens Trolle Larsen*, Leiden: Nederlands Anstituut voor heir Nabije Oosten, pp. 47–98.

Fleming, D. E. (2004), *Democracy's Ancient Ancestors: Mari and Early Collective Governance*, Cambridge: Cambridge University Press.

Frahm, E. (2004), 'Royal Hermeneutics: Observations on the Commentaries from Ashurbanipal's Libraries at Nineveh', *Iraq*, 66, 45–50.

Grayson, A. K. (ed.) (1991), *Assyrian Rulers of the Early First Millennium BC (1114–859 BC)*, vol. I: *The Royal Inscriptions of Mesopotamia: Assyrian Periods*, Toronto: University of Toronto Press.

Isakhan, B. (2007), 'Engaging "Primitive Democracy": Mideast Roots of Collective Governance', *Middle East Policy*, 14(3), 97–117.

Isakhan, B. (2011), 'What is so "Primitive" about "Primitive Democracy"? Comparing the Ancient Middle East and Classical Athens', in B. Isakhan and S. Stockwell (eds), *The Secret History of Democracy*, London: Palgrave Macmillan, pp. 19–34.

Jacobsen, T. ([1943] 1970), 'Primitive Democracy in Ancient Mesopotamia', in W. L. Moran (ed.), *Toward the Image of Tammuz and Other Essays on Mesopotamian History and Culture*, Cambridge, MA: Harvard University Press, pp. 157–70.

Jastrow, M. (1921), 'An Assyrian Law Code', *Journal of the American Oriental Society*, 41, 1–59.

Keane, J. (2009), *The Life and Death of Democracy*, New York: Simon & Schuster.

Lambert, W. G. ([1960] 1996), 'Advice to a Prince', in *Babylonian Wisdom Literature*, Oxford: Oxford University Press, pp. 110–15.

Larsen, M. T. (1976), *The Old Assyrian City-State and its Colonies*, Copenhagen: Akademisk Forlag.

Larsen, M. T. (2000), 'The Old Assyrian City-State', in M. H. Hansen (ed.), *A Comparative Study of Thirty City-State Cultures*, Copenhagen: Copenhagen Polis Centre, pp. 77–88.

Leick, G. (2001), *Mesopotamia: The Invention of the City*, London: Penguin.

Lieberman, S. J. (1990), 'Canonical and Official Cuneiform Texts: Towards an Understanding of Assurbanipal's Personal Tablet Collection', in T. Abusch, J. Huehnergard and P. Steinkeller (eds), *Lingering Over Words: Studies in Ancient Near Eastern Literature in Honor of William L. Moran*, Atlanta, GA: Scholars Press, pp. 305–36.

Moran, W. L. (ed.) (1992), *The Amarna Letters*, Baltimore, MD: Johns Hopkins University Press.

Oded, B. (1979), *Mass Deportations and Deportees in the Neo-Assyrian Empire*, Wiesbaden: Reichert Verlag.

Oded, B. (1992), *War, Peace and Empire: Justifications for War in Assyrian Royal Inscriptions*, Wiesbaden: Reichert Verlag.

Oppenheim, A. L. (1964), *Ancient Mesopotamia: Portrait of a Dead Civilization*, Chicago, IL: University of Chicago Press.

Oppenheim, A. L. (1969), 'Divination and Celestial Observation in the Last Assyrian Empire', *Centaurus*, 14, 97–135.

Parpola, S. (1993), 'Mesopotamian Astrology and Astronomy as Domains of the Mesopotamian "Wisdom"', in H. D. Galter (ed.), *Die Rolle der Astronomie in den Kulturen Mesopotamiens*, Graz: rm-Druck- & Verlaggesellschaft mbH, pp. 47–59.

Parpola, S. (ed.) (1987–2003), *State Archives of Assyria*, vols I–XVIII, Helsinki: University of Helsinki Press.

Parpola, S. (2003), 'International law in the First Millennium', in R. Westbrook (ed.), *A History of Ancient Near Eastern Law*, vol. II, Leiden: Brill, pp. 1047–66.

Parpola, S. (ed.) ([1970] 2007a), *Letters from Assyrian Scholars to the Kings Esarhaddon and Assurbanipal, vol. I: Texts*, Winona Lake, IN: Eisenbrauns.

Parpola, S. (ed.) ([1970] 2007b), *Letters from Assyrian Scholars to the Kings Esarhaddon and Assurbanipal, vol. II: Commentary and Appendices*, Winona Lake, IN: Eisenbrauns.

Pecirkova, J. (1985), 'Divination and Politics in the Late Assyrian Empire', *Archiv Orientalni*, 53, 155–68.

Roth, M. T. (1997), *Law Collections from Mesopotamia and Asia Minor*, 2nd edn, Atlanta, GA: Scholars.

Starr, I. (ed.) (1990), *Queries to the Sungod: Divination and Politics in Sargonid Assyria, vol. IV: State Archives of Assyria*, Helsinki: University of Helsinki Press.

Streck, M. (1916), *Assurbanipal und die letzten Assyrischen Könige bis zum Untergange Niniveh's*, Leipzig: Hinrichs.

Veenhof, K. R. (2010), 'Ancient Assur: The City, its Traders, and its Commercial Network', *Journal of the Economic and Social History of the Orient*, 53, 39–82.

Chapter 3

Ancient India

Steven Muhlberger

In the period before CE 400, ancient India was home to a variety of self-governing polities using quasi-democratic institutions comparable with those of the Greek city-states of the same era. Indeed, Greek and Roman historians, relying on the reports of Greek visitors, did not hesitate to say that the India they knew was largely democratic. But although the evidence has been carefully analysed and the existence of a multitude of republics has long been established, these republics and the political culture that they represent are little known to anyone but specialists. The purpose of this chapter is to set forth a brief summary of the history of republicanism in ancient India.

There are good reasons for the obscurity of this Indian story. The ancient sources for the life of the subcontinent are particularly difficult. Nearly all of them that survive exist because they were religiously significant to some organised community. There is no ancient historiography. The discovery of the ancient republican tradition of India was a product of the late nineteenth and the early twentieth centuries. Both foreign and Indian scholars were systematically reading, translating and publishing ancient sources. Research slowly revealed that the Indian past held more than passive subjects ruled by absolute monarchs. At the turn of the twentieth century the British expert, T. W. Rhys Davids, argued that the earliest Buddhist scriptures depicted north India as a country in which there were many clans, dominating extensive and populous territories, who made their public decisions in popular assemblies (Rhys Davids 1903). This claim was all the more credible because investigation of contemporary Indian village life by British officials had revealed an unanticipated degree of popular government; at the same time early anthropologists had documented village self-government around the world (Maine [1889] 1974). The history and nature of self-government in ancient India became a hot topic, with implications not just for the subcontinent, but the entire world: the unchanging East was more adaptable than it had been given credit for. For the next three decades, nationalist historians and political scientists revisited and analysed the ancient sources and even discovered new material. This effort did not result in consensus about the nature of early Indian government, but has provided us with the bulk of our knowledge of India's republics and other manifestations of a strong non-monarchical tradition (R. S. Sharma 1991: 1–13).

Vedic Councils and Post-Vedic Republics

It remains impossible to write a continuous history of the ancient subcontinent; whatever aspect of Indian life we make our focus, we are dependent on difficult sources that do not even provide a secure chronology. For instance, one relevant and very ancient body of texts, Vedic literature, was created at various times over a thousand-year span, c. 1500–500 BCE. Vedic literature speaks directly only about the prayers, rituals, incantations and sacrifices of the lost cultures of that vast period. Unsurprisingly, scholars have come up with quite different reconstructions of 'Vedic society'. The most obvious political figures who emerge from the Vedas are *rajas*, who can be seen as kings or (taking a less lofty view) elected war chieftains. Yet re-examination of Vedic literature in the early twentieth century led some scholars to argue that Vedic India was characterised by tribal societies which, like Greek, Roman or Iroquoian societies, possessed a variety of assemblies and councils that not only expressed the popular will, but also exercised a certain amount of authority in religion, war and justice (R. S. Sharma 1991: 89–90). Experts have debated the definition and functions of these bodies, notably those called the *vidatha*, the *sabha* and the *samiti*, but it seems clear that even in monarchical communities, it was common enough to have a council or an assembly or both. J. P. Sharma has argued that some non-monarchical communities were led by a multitude of *rajas* instead of just one (J. P. Sharma 1968: 15–80). Today's reader may not find these conclusions particularly exciting, but in the 1910s this hint of self-government in the past was a subject for celebration. India, even at a very early time, had participated in the common human pattern of small-scale governance, what Walter Bagehot aptly called 'government by discussion' (Bagehot 1873: 158).

Between about 600 and 300 BCE, sometimes called the post-Vedic period, sources proliferate and we are much better informed about the politics and political geography of the country. Unlike the kingdoms/chieftainships of early Vedic society, which give the impression of being primitive, tribal, even nomadic, the post-Vedic kingdoms seem much more substantial, with definite territories and rulers making claims to universal domination. Important religious developments were underway. The theory of *varna* (caste) had emerged, which gave divine endorsement to the position of the Brahmanas (priests), Kshatriyas (warriors) and *rajas* drawn from the ranks of the Kshatriyas. *Varna* asserted that Brahmanas and Kshatriyas were entitled to a hereditary lordship over the Vaishyas (farmers, artisans and merchants) and the Shudras (labourers). At the same time, there was a strong counter-current resisting this construct. There were religious teachers who disputed the teachings of *varna* and the religious leadership of the Brahmanas, and who preached equality before the divine. The most successful movements of this sort evolved into Buddhism and Jainism (Wagle 1966).

Similarly, some communities rejected the claims of monarchy and its religious justification. One manifestation of this opposition were the many corporate bodies whose members enjoyed a certain equality and who governed themselves through discussion and voting, in other words organisations that manifested varying degrees of democratic practice. Panini's Sanskrit grammar, an irreplaceable window into ancient Indian life, indicates that there was at the dawn of the post-Vedic period a well-known terminology for the process of corporate decision making: Panini gives us the terms for vote, decisions reached by voting and the completion of a quorum. Another cluster of words indicates that the division of assemblies into political parties was well known. Further, Panini and his commentators show that sometimes select groups within a *sangha* had special functions: acting as an executive or perhaps as committees for defined purposes. A specialised vocabulary described groups that ran their own affairs: warrior bands, guilds and religious brotherhoods. The words *gana* and *sangha* were the most important terms for such groups. Both words originally meant 'multitude', but by the sixth century BCE, they meant both a self-governing multitude in which decisions were made by the members working in common, and the style of government characteristic of such groups. The strongest of such groups, which acted as sovereign governments, were the equivalent of the republics of the contemporaneous Mediterranean (Agrawala 1963: 426–44; A. K. Majumdar 1980: 131; J. P. Sharma 1968: 8–14).

The Buddhist Evidence

The best account of the workings of quasi-democratic republics and other corporations of this era concern the Buddhist monastic brotherhood, also called the *sangha*. The earliest parts of the Buddhist scriptures, known as the Pali Canon, show us in detail how the founder of this particular *sangha* was believed to have organised his followers when he was preparing to die. The key organisational virtue was the full participation of all the monks in the ritual and disciplinary acts of their group. To ensure that this would be remembered, detailed rules concerning the voting in monastic assemblies, their memberships and their quorums, were set down in the scriptures known as the *Mahavagga* and the *Kullavagga*.

Business could be transacted legitimately only in a full assembly, by a vote of all the members. If, for example, a candidate wanted the *upasampada* ordination, the question (*ñatti*) was put to the *sangha* by a learned and competent member, and the other members asked three times to indicate dissent. If there was none, the *sangha* was taken to be in agreement with the *ñatti* (Rhys Davids and Oldenberg 1881: 169–70).

Of course, unanimity was not always possible. The *Kullavagga* provides other techniques that were used in disputes especially dangerous to the unity of the *sangha*, those which concerned interpretation of the monastic rule itself. If such a dispute proved to be bitterly divisive, it could be decided by majority vote, or referred to a jury or committee specially elected by the *sangha* to treat the matter at hand. If the members of the *sangha* were concerned enough, the rules for taking votes sanctioned the disallowance by the vote-taker of results that threatened the essential law of the *sangha* or its unity (Rhys Davids and Oldenberg 1885: 20–65). Evidently, the usual principle of full participation and the equality of the membership had to be balanced against survival of the religious enterprise: disunity of the membership was the great fear of all Indian republics and corporations (Altekar 1958: 129–30; A. K. Majumdar 1980: 140). The rules of the Buddhist *sangha* are the best known of any *gana* or *sangha* of the period. The exact structure and procedures used by political *ganas* are irrecoverable. However, R. C. Majumdar's early judgement remains convincing: the techniques seen in the Buddhist *sangha* reflect a sophisticated and widespread political culture based on the popular assembly (R. C. Majumdar [1918] 1969: 233–4).

That the Buddhist sangha and political *gana* shared similar principles can be illustrated out of an important episode depicted in the early scriptures. The story that begins the *Maha-parinibbana-suttanta*, among the oldest of Buddhist texts, shows the Buddha outlining principles of measured self-government and how they applied to his brotherhood and to the *gana* of the Vajjis (Vaggis), a prominent republican confederation of northeast India. Asked by Vassakara the Brahmana, the envoy of King Ajasastru, how the Vajjis could be conquered, the Buddha answered indirectly, by discussing the strengths of their community with his disciple Ananda:

'Have you heard, Ananda, that the Vajjians hold full and frequent public assemblies?'
'Lord, so I have heard,' replied he.
'So long, Ananda', rejoined the Blessed One, 'as the Vajjians hold these full and frequent public assemblies; so long may they be expected not to decline, but to prosper.' (Rhys Davids 1881: 3)

In a series of rhetorical questions to Ananda, the Buddha outlines other requirements for the Vajjian prosperity:

So long, Ananda, as the Vajjians meet together in concord, and rise in concord, and carry out their undertakings in concord . . . so long as they enact nothing not already established, abrogate nothing that has been already enacted, and act in accordance with the ancient institutions of the Vajjians as established in former days . . . so long as they honour and esteem and revere and support the Vajjian elders, and hold it a point of duty to hearken to their words . . . so long as no women or girls belonging to their clans are detained among them by force or abduction . . . so long as they honour and esteem and revere and support the Vajjian shrines in town or country, and allow not the proper offerings and rites, as formerly given and performed, to fall into desuetude . . . so long as the rightful protection, defence and support shall be fully provided for the Arahats among them, so that Arahats from a distance may enter the realm, and the Arahats therein may live at ease – so long may the Vajjians be expected not to decline, but to prosper. (Rhys Davids 1881: 3–4)

We may reasonably take this as a list of ideal republican virtues. There are two important things about this list. First, the scripture writers not only have the Buddha endorse these virtues, but claim them for his own, as his own teachings:

Then the Blessed One addressed Vassakara the Brahman, and said, 'When I was once staying, O Brahman, at Vesali at the Sarandada Temple, I taught the Vajjians these conditions of welfare; and so long as those conditions shall continue to exist among the Vajjians, so long as the Vajjians shall be well instructed in those conditions, so long may we expect them not to decline, but to prosper.' (Rhys Davids 1881: 4)

Secondly, the same story tells us that these republican virtues were very close to the ideal organisational virtues applicable to the monastic life. Once the king's envoy had departed, the Buddha and Ananda went to meet the assembly of monks. The Buddha told the monks that they too must observe seven conditions if they were to prosper. Three of those conditions were specific to the monastic life, but the first four were identical to those Buddha had imposed on Vajji: full and frequent assemblies; concord; preserving and not abrogating established institutions; and honouring elders (Rhys Davids 1881: 5–7). The preservation of these precepts and other adjurations to monastic virtue that follow in further sets of seven, were the main point for the monks who composed and transmitted the *Maha-parinibbana-suttanta* to us. For students of Indian political thought of the time, it is striking that righteous and prosperous communities, whether secular or monastic, rested upon the holding of 'full and frequent assemblies'. That first virtue in particular, was not an innovation of the Buddhist tradition; rather it resembles and grew out of a pre-existing tradition of 'government by discussion', rather than by command and submission.

But *who* discussed? It has been argued elsewhere that it is logical and justifiable to consider any form of government by discussion a potential subject for historians of democracy (Muhlberger and Paine 1993). All historical democracies have grown from less inclusive roots. Students of the Indian republics, however, put off by the enthusiastic and extravagant claims to ancient democracy made by earlier nationalists still feel obliged today to deny that the ancient republics, some of which were highly oligarchic in structure and perhaps even in theory, have anything to do with democracy (Jayaswal [1911–13] 1943; Singh 2009: 267).

Democracies or Oligarchies?

The ancient republics were far from being lost utopian democracies; indeed, the most prominent in the sources can be classified as oligarchies dominated by the Kshatriyas, the warrior class or *varna*. Indeed, political participation was sometimes further restricted to a subset of all the Kshatriyas, to the members of a specific royal clan, the *rajanya* (Agrawala 1963: 430–2). Enfranchised members of such republics identified themselves with the slippery term *raja*, which suggests noble or even regal status, as well as (a share of) executive power. The *Lalitavistara*, in a satirical jab, depicts Vesali, the chief city of the Licchavi *gana* and of the Vajji confederacy of which it was part, as being full of Licchavi *rajans*, each one thinking, 'I am king, I am king' (A. K. Majumdar 1958: 140). In some places, it seems likely that political power was restricted to the heads of a restricted number of 'royal families' (*rajakulas*) among the ruling clans. The heads of these families were consecrated as *rajas*, and thereafter took part in deliberations of state.

The sources, however, permit another perspective. Both sympathetic and unsympathetic sources showed the republics as being characterised by inclusive, perhaps too inclusive, politics. The *Lalitavistara* in the passage just cited presented Vesali as a place where piety, age and rank were ignored; there were too many *rajas*, and the worthy few had been pushed aside by a mob of upstarts. Furthermore, power in some republics was vested in a large number of individuals. In a well-known *Jataka* tale we are told that in Vesali there were 7,707 kings (*rajas*), 7,707 viceroys, 7,707 generals and 7,707 treasurers (Cowell [1895] 1957: I:316. III:1). These figures, since they come from about half a millennium after the period they describe, have no precise evidentiary value, but confirm what we find elsewhere: the rulers were many, in some cases supposedly numbering in the tens of thousands (Agrawala 1963: 432; Cowell [1895] 1957: IV:94, VI:266; J. P. Sharma 1968: 99). One wonders that if these numbers were true, would the *rajas* be citizen/warriors? Certainly the memory of large *ganas* can be found in other sources critical of republicanism. The *Santi Parva* section of the *Mahabharata*, for instance, shows the participation of too many people in the affairs of state as being a great flaw in the republican polity (R. C. Majumdar [1918] 1969: 247–52).

Other evidence also suggests that in some states the enfranchised group was quite wide. Such a development is hinted at by Kautilya, who wrote a pioneering treatise in political science. According to him, there were two kinds of *janapadas* (traditional regions): *ayudhiya-praya*, those made up mostly of soldiers; and *sreni-praya*, those comprising guilds of craftsmen, traders and agriculturalists (Agrawala 1963: 436–9). The first were political entities where military tradition alone defined those worthy of power, while the second would seem to be communities where wealth derived from peaceful economic activity gave some access to the political process. Sometimes corporate organisation encouraged secession, so that a political community more responsive to the membership would be created. Panini's most thorough modern student believed that there was in the post-Vedic period 'a craze for constituting new republics', which 'had reached its climax in the *Vahika* country and northwest India where clans constituting of as many as one hundred families only organised themselves as *Ganas*' (Agrawala 1963: 432). There was, indeed, an interesting and various political tradition of self-government at work in post-Vedic north India, even if our sources give us a shadowy picture in most cases.

Judging whether the ancient Indian republics were democracies or, better, whether their history is relevant to the study of democracy depends on the definition of the crucial term. Scholars rejecting the label democracy as irrelevant to the Indian republics are engaging with Jayaswal's rhetoric of a century ago, not with the historiography of ancient democracy. What makes Indian republics look undemocratic to us is primarily the fact that the franchise – the right to participate – was so restricted by modern standards. No doubt the ruling group of most republics thought of their *gana* as a closed club – but so did the citizens of Athens, who also defined themselves as a hereditarily privileged group. We can interrogate the Greeks themselves as to the relationship between Greek and north Indian ideas of government. Alexander the Great invaded India in 326 BCE, and afterwards Greek monarchs ruled parts of the subcontinent and interacted with larger areas of it for centuries. As a result, quite a bit of the history and geography of India survives in Greek, mostly in accounts of Alexander's conquests. Alexander's historians mention a large number of republics of various sizes, but only a handful of kings (Altekar 1958: 111). Although Greek descriptions of India sometimes featured exotic races, animals and plants, Greek accounts of Indian politics lack exotic elements. Arrian's *Anabasis of Alexander*, which is derived from the eyewitness accounts of Alexander's companions, portrays him as meeting many 'free and independent' Indian communities. What 'free and independent' meant is illustrated from the case of Nysa, a city on the border of modern Afghanistan and Pakistan that was ruled by a president named Aculphis and a council of 300. After surrendering to Alexander, Aculphis used the city's supposed connection with the god Dionysus to seek lenient terms from the king:

> The Nysaeans beseech thee, O king out of respect for Dionysus, to allow them to remain free and independent; for when Dionysus had subjugated the nation of the Indians . . . he founded this city from the soldiers who had become unfit for military service . . . From that time we inhabit Nysa, a free city, and we ourselves are independent, conducting our government with constitutional order. (R. C. Majumdar 1960: 20)

Nysa was an oligarchy, as further discussion between Alexander and Aculphis reveals, and a single city-state; the set-up was familiar and the Nysaeans were distant cousins with comprehensible, Greek-like values. There were other Indian states that were both larger in area – confederations similar to those in fourth-century Greece – and wider in franchise (R. C. Majumdar 1960: 47, 64–75). Q. Curtius Rufus and Diodorus Siculus mention a people called the Sabarcae or Sambastai among whom 'the form of government was democratic and not regal' (R. C. Majumdar 1960: 151). The prevalence of republicanism and its democratic form is explicitly stated by Diodorus Siculus. After describing the mythical monarchs who succeeded the god Dionysus as rulers of India, he says: 'At last, however, after many years had gone, most of the cities adopted the democratic form of government, though some retained the kingly until the invasion of the country by Alexander' (R. C. Majumdar 1960: 180).

This statement seems to derive from a first-hand description of India by a Greek traveller named Megasthenes. Around 300 BCE, Megasthenes served as ambassador of the Greek king Seleucus Nicator to the Indian emperor Chandragupta Maurya, and in the course of his duties crossed northern India to the eastern city of Patna, where he lived for a while (Stein 1893: XV:1:232–3). His evaluation of the state of northern India, and the existence of democracy there, is the statement of an experienced and educated Greek politician. It is worth remembering that in the previous century the grammarian Panini attested to a special term for the *gana* where 'there was no distinction between high and low' (Agrawala 1963: 428).

The End of Ancient Republicanism

Scholars looking at the record as a whole have understandably been interested in the ultimate failure of the ancient republics. This is more complicated than a simple story of monarchical success. Comparison with recent scholarship on the Greek *poleis* is instructive. Traditionally the end of the *poleis* style of government has been identified with the defeat of Athens and its allies by the king of Macedon, Philip II, at Chaeronea

(338 BCE); after that, the vast majority of Greek city-states were subject to one or another Macedonian or Hellenistic king. Yet, as M. H. Hansen points out, the loss of sovereignty was not the crucial factor for ancient Greek citizens that it has been for modern historians. For the Greeks, as long as a *polis* enjoyed internal self-government, it could consider itself 'free and independent'. Hansen puts it this way:

> In the Hellenistic kingdoms all *poleis* were actually subordinate to the ruling monarch, but in different degrees. Many *poleis* were tribute-paying and so formally subordinate to the king, but many were formally free, independent states. The typical 'independent' *polis* was now a democracy (*dēmokratia*) that had its freedom (*eleutheria*) and self-government (*autonomia*) guaranteed by royal rescript published by the Hellenistic king in whose kingdom the city-state lay. (Hansen 2006: 50)

In contrast to our modern understanding of their situation, many Greeks of the Hellenistic and even the Roman period believed they lived under a regime of democracy. That local democracy was eroded over centuries as the imperial government became more bureaucratic and interventionist, until the reign of Justinian saw the last traces of what Hansen calls 'the Greek city-state culture' (Hansen 2006: 50).

There are some similarities in the evolution of the Indian republics. The Pali Canon shows that already in the time of the Buddha and Mahavira, even major republics like the Vajji were having a difficult time competing with monarchical warlords. The Vajji confederation, based on the populous city of Vesali and dominated by the Licchavis, seems to have attained for a short time hegemonic or imperial status like Sparta or Athens briefly did; similarly, after the Vajjis were defeated and their federation broken up, we hear of no more such hegemonic cities in northeastern India. There were large republican federations in northwestern India with tens of thousands of *rajas* at the time of Alexander, but, again, after his intervention we have no records of such. The larger polities of post-Alexandrian times seem to have been monarchies.

Ganas survived nevertheless, as coins and inscriptions attest. Ancient Indian empires were rather precarious, and the communities that they conquered revived after the empires fell apart. The process of competition with imperial monarchies, however, seems to have strengthened the always existing tendency towards oligarchy. We have seen that many republics were content even in the earliest post-Vedic era with a very exclusive definition of the political community. Intermarriage of leading members of *ganas* with the royal clans of monarchies, recounted in the stories of the Buddha's lifetime, can only have encouraged such exclusivity. Later, states known to be republics in earlier times were subject to hereditary executives. Like Medici Florence, eventually such republics became monarchies (Altekar 1958: 137–8; A. K. Majumdar 1980: 144). There should be no surprise that such a development was possible, or that leading families of powerful republics should adopt aristocratic habits and its scions pursue kingly or at the very least oligarchic ambitions. Not all citizens of democracies are democrats.

An evolution away from egalitarianism can also be seen in the literature of politics and religion. Later Brahmanical classics (300 BCE–CE 200) such as the *Mahabharata*, the writings of Kautilya and the *Manu-Smrti* opposed the *gana–sangha* type of government. Kautilya, who is traditionally identified with the chief minister of the Mauryan conqueror Chandragupta Maurya (300 BCE), is famous for advising monarchs on how to tame or destroy *ganas* through subterfuge; more importantly, he formulated a political science in which royalty was normal, even though his own text shows that *ganas* were very important factors in the politics of his time (Kautilya [300 BCE] 1951: 410). Similarly, the religious law book *Manu-Smrti* formulated a systematic view of society where human equality was non-existent and unthinkable (Manu [200 BCE–CE 200] 1886).

Members of *ganas* were encouraged to fit themselves into a hierarchical, monarchical framework by practical considerations, too. Warlord *rajas* with unique religious claims could not only inspire fear, but also offer a sometimes welcome court of last resort to competing *ganas*, whose claims to autonomy and self-determination must often have come into conflict (as we see in the Italian communes of the High Middle Ages). How were these claims to be sorted out other than by force? The king had an answer to this question: if he were acknowledged as 'the only monarch [i.e., *raja*, chief executive] of all the corporations' he would commit himself to preserving the legitimate privileges of each of them, and even protect the lesser members of each *gana* from abuse of power by their leaders (Kautilya [300 BCE] 1951: 410). It was a tempting offer, and it was slowly accepted, sometimes freely, sometimes under compulsion. The end result was the acceptance of a social order in which many *ganas* and *sanghas* existed, but none were sovereign and none were committed to any general egalitarian view of society. They were committed instead to a hierarchy in which they were promised a secure place (R. C. Majumdar [1918] 1969: 42–59). Such a notional hierarchy seems to have been constructed in north India by the fifth century CE. Even the Buddhist *sangha*, perhaps the greatest 'republican confederacy' of all, was chased out of the subcontinent.

Government by discussion must have continued within many *ganas* and *sanghas*, but the ideas of hierarchy and inequality of caste were increasingly dominant. The degree of corporate autonomy in later Indian society was considerable, but a corporation that accepts itself as a subcaste in a great divine hierarchy is different from the more pugnacious *ganas* and *sanghas* of the Pali Canon, Kautilya or even the *Jataka* stories.

Conclusion

The significance of the Indian republics and other forms of 'government by discussion' can be summed up in three points. First, there is enough information to show that even in the supposed home of oriental despotism, there were in ancient times institutions and practices that were created, named and commonly used to implement a degree of equality among the members of self-governing communities. The ancient subcontinent, with its documented councils and assemblies, voting procedures and constitutional awareness, shared in the worldwide human tendency to create quasi-democratic organisations at the local level. Secondly, there is also evidence for a degree of egalitarian doctrine associated with these practical developments. How many ancient Indians were sincerely moved by democratic principles is difficult to say; in the ancient subcontinent, as in ancient Greece, opponents of and sceptics about democracy dominate our sources. Thirdly, the republican and the quasi-democratic history of India, interesting in its own right, has had, like the history of classical Greece, a significant effect on modern history, in that it has challenged people to look into their historical experience and find in it inspiration for democratic change.

References

Agrawala, V. S. (1963), *India as Known to Panini: A Study of the Cultural Material in the Ashatadhyayi*, 2nd edn, Varanasi: Prithvi Prakashan.
Altekar, A. S. (1958), *State and Government in Ancient India*, 3rd edn, Delhi: Motilal Banarsidass.
Bagehot, W. (1873), *Physics and Politics*, New York: D. Appleton.
Cowell, E. B. (ed.) ([1895] 1957), *The Jataka, or Stories of the Buddha's Former Births*, [380 BCE], trans. Various, 6 vols, Oxford: Pali Text Society.
Hansen, M. H. (2006), *Polis: An Introduction to the Ancient Greek City-State*, Oxford: Oxford University Press.
Jayaswal, K. P. ([1911–13] 1943), *Hindu Polity: A Constitutional History of India in Hindu Times*, 2nd edn, Bangalore: Bangalore Printing & Publishing.
Kautilya ([300 BCE] 1951), *Kautilya's Arthasastra*, trans. R. Shamasastry, 4th edn, Mysore: Mysore Printing & Publishing House.
Maine, H. S. ([1889] 1974), *Village Communities in the East and West*, New York: Arno Press.
Majumdar, A. K. (1980), *Concise History of Ancient India, vol. 2: Political Theory, Administration, and Economic Life*, New Delhi: Munshiram Manoharlal.
Majumdar, R. C. (1960), *The Classical Accounts of India*, Calcutta: Firma K. L. Mukhopadhyay.
Majumdar, R. C. ([1918] 1969), *Corporate Life in Ancient India* 3rd edn, Calcutta: Firma K. L. Mukhopadhyay.
Manu ([200 BCE–CE 200] 1886), *The Laws of Manu*, in F. Max Müller (ed.), *Sacred Books of the East*, trans. G. Bühler, vol. 25, Oxford: Oxford University Press.
Muhlberger, S. and P. Paine (1993), 'Democracy's Place in World History', *Journal of World History*, 4(1), 23–47.
Rhys Davids, T. W. (trans.) ([post-480 BCE] 1881), *The Maha-parinibbana-suttanta: Buddhist Suttas vol. 1*, in F. Max Müller (ed.), *Sacred Books of the East*, Oxford: Oxford University Press.
Rhys Davids, T. W. (1903), *Buddhist India*, London: T. Fisher Unwin.
Rhys Davids, T. W. and H. Oldenberg (trans.) ([post-480 BCE] 1881, 1882, 1885), *Mahavagga, Kullavagga, and Pattimokkha: Vinaya Texts*, in F. Max Müller (ed.), *Sacred Books of the East*, vols 13, 17, 20, Oxford: Oxford University Press.
Sharma, J. P. (1968), *Republics in Ancient India, c. 1500 B.C.–500 B.C.*, Leiden: Brill.
Sharma, R. S. (1991), *Aspects of Political Ideas and Institutions in Ancient India*, 3rd edn, Delhi: Motilal Banarsidass.
Singh, U. (2009), *A History of Ancient and Early Medieval India: From the Stone Age to the 12th Century*, Englewood Cliffs, NJ: Prentice Hall.
Stein, O. (1893), *Megasthenes*, in A. von Pauly, G. Wissowa et al. (eds), *Real-Encyclopädie der classischen Altertumwissenschaft*, vol. 2, Stuttgart: J. B. Metzler.
Wagle, N. K. (1966), *Society at the Time of the Buddha*, Bombay: Popular Prakashan.

Chapter 4

Ancient China

Victoria Tin-bor Hui

Both Western and Chinese analysts often presume that democracy is unique to Western civilisation and alien to the Chinese. The roots of Western dynamism are, in turn, assumed to derive from the political complexity of Europe, whereas those of Chinese stagnation from political unity. However, as this chapter illustrates, China in fact experienced fluctuations between unification and division in history. Intense international competition in the classical era (770–221 BCE) gave rise to citizenship rights defined as state–society bargains over the means of war. Although the development of Chinese citizenship was aborted by Qin's successful unification of the Warring States system in 221 BCE, the classical legacy continued to live on in the rest of Chinese history, albeit in diminished forms. In subsequent eras of division, contending regimes would be compelled to make concessions to society. Even in eras of unification, formally unchecked emperors were subject to Confucian doctrines developed in the classical period.

The Military Basis of Citizenship Rights

There is a general consensus that China's political tradition is fundamentally anti-democratic. Although Karl Marx's notion of the 'Asiatic mode of production' and Karl Wittfogel's notion of 'hydraulic despotism' are no longer in vogue, most observers would agree with R. Bin Wong that citizenship is 'a culturally foreign concept' in China (Wong 1997: 93). Elizabeth Perry suggests that even if the classical concept of Mandate of Heaven (divine right) provides for socio-economic rights, there is no place for political rights or democracy in China's political tradition. She argues that even the recent explosion of rural and urban protests does not signify any new-found 'rights consciousness', because such protests are typically 'framed in a language more reminiscent of Mencius or Mao than of Locke or Jefferson (Perry 2008: 43). This understanding explains why generations of Chinese intellectuals have blamed the Chinese tradition as being the source of backwardness, and why the current government has promoted 'democracy with Chinese characteristics' in order to buttress one-party dictatorship.

What this mainstream view overlooks is that China shares with Europe crucial contingent developments conducive to the emergence of citizenship and democracy. The Chinese political tradition is often taken to be Confucian, and the Confucian tradition is taken to be fundamentally anti-democratic. However, as Chaibong Hahm points out:

> Confucianism was actually exceptional in the degree to which . . . it took a stand against absolutism and autocracy. Yet Confucianism never had much more than gossamer-thin institutional means with which to buttress principled opposition to monarchs who had armies of soldiers and legions of officials at their back. (Hahm 2004: 105)

Of course, political dissenters in Europe also faced monarchs who claimed the divine right to rule and who commanded enormous numbers of troops and bureaucrats. What made it so difficult for European kings and princes to subjugate their populations in the domestic realm was the fact that they had to fight other kings and princes in the international realm at the same time. Scholars of European state formation have highlighted the military basis of citizenship and democracy. Citizenship emerged in Europe not because European rulers were more benign or their subjects had high levels of 'rights consciousness', but because European rulers were compelled by fierce international competition to bargain with domestic resource-holders. When we examine historical trajectories, the focus should not be electoral democracy, a largely twentieth-century phenomenon even in the West, but citizenship rights, a more transhistorical development. If citizenship rights are defined as recognised enforceable claims on the state that are themselves by-products of state–society bargaining over the means of war (Tilly 1992: 101–2), then we can find both political and socio-economic rights in the Chinese tradition.

Rethinking Chinese Unity

In China, as in Europe, the overwhelming coercive power of the state was most effectively checked when a multitude of states competed against one another. This point is overlooked in mainstream Sinology because analysts have uncritically accepted the presumption of Chinese oneness. Instead, Chinese history books re-construct history through clean dynastic cycles, which begin with Xia (a mythical period), Shang (1600–1046 BCE), and Zhou (1045–256 BCE), through Qin (221–206 BCE), Han (202 BCE–CE 220), Jin (265–420), Sui (581–618), Tang (618–907), Song (960–1279), Yuan (1279–1368), Ming (1368–1644), Qing (1644–1911), ending with the Republic of China (1912–1949) and the People's Republic (1949–present). Such a presentation gives the impression of a linear history in which Chinese unity is the norm and division is a deviance that is destined to be corrected. Contrary to this received wisdom, a Chinese historical geographer Ge Jianxiong,[1] points out that the official founding of a new dynasty does not necessarily restore unification because transitional periods between two dynasties are uniformly marked by armed struggles. He suggests that there is no genuine unification whenever armed forces that fight for the previous dynasty or their own ambitions persist; whenever regional power-holders pledge nominal allegiance to the reigning dynasty, but assert semi-auton-omous status and maintain armed forces; and whenever scattered peasant rebellions become organised, armed rebellions (Ge 1994: 85–6). It is remarkable that Ge's conceptualisation is consistent with Weber's idea of the effective state as one 'that [successfully] claims the monopoly of the legitimate use of physical force within a given territory' (Weber 1991: 78).

If we follow this Weberian–Ge understanding of the state, we need also to outline what 'a given territory' means in the Chinese context. Historical China often refers to the maximum territorial reach achieved under the Qing dynasty – which includes both China Proper and the Periphery. While China Proper is roughly bounded by the Yellow River in the northwest, the Yin Shan and the lower Liao River in the northeast, the Sichuan basin in the west, the eastern edge of the Yunnan–Guizhou plateau in the southwest, the Guangdong and Guangxi regions in the south, and the coastline in the east, the Periphery refers to Manchuria, Mongolia, Xinjiang and Tibet (Tan 2000: 2–4). It is noteworthy that, if unification is defined as the establishment of effective central control over the Qing's maximum territorial reach as outlined, then historical China was unified for only eighty-one years from 1759 to 1840 (Ge 1994: 79). Ge thus suggests a more limited definition: the establishment of effective central control over China Proper without the Periphery. Even this narrower definition does not support the mainstream view that unity was the norm in Chinese history, as it yields only 991 years of unification throughout the long span of Chinese history up to 2000. The figure of 991 years represents 44.6 per cent of Chinese history if the baseline excludes the classical era (i.e., a total of 2,221 years from Qin's unification in 221 BCE to CE 2000), or a smaller fraction if the baseline includes the classical era, or an even smaller fraction if the baseline refers to China's supposed 5,000 years of civilisation. Indeed, it is often overlooked that the Chinese term for 'China' (*zhongguo*) does not always mean the unified and powerful 'central (or middle) kingdom'. The term *zhongguo* originally referred to 'central states' in the plural form during two periods of the Zhou Dynasty, the Spring and Autumn period (770–403 BCE) and the Warring States period (475–221 BCE). It acquired the meaning of 'central kingdom' in the singular form only long after Qin's successful unification. Because the Chinese language does not distinguish between the singular and plural forms, the initial meaning of *zhongguo* is easily lost in modern retrospective thinking. If Chinese history contains more duality and diversity than unity and uniformity, then the recurrence of war-induced state–society bargains should not be underestimated.

War and Citizenship Rights in the Classical Era

The military basis of citizenship was most pronounced in the pristine Spring and Autumn and Warring States periods. Ambitious Chinese rulers faced a daunting challenge familiar to European rulers: how to motivate the people to fight and die in war. International competition compelled three major state–society bargains (Hui 2005). The first bargain was peasant welfare. To mobilise resources for war, Chinese rulers introduced national conscription and national taxation. This development meant that the security of the state rested with the well-being of peasant soldiers who paid taxes and fought wars. As hungry peasants could not afford grain tax or military service, various states distributed land grants to ensure subsistence. To improve productivity, states introduced intensive farming methods. To stabilise the livelihood of peasants amid annual fluctuations in yields, states established grain stores, provided disaster relief and introduced a counter-cyclical policy. Confucian and Mencian thinkers of the time regarded the state's provision of material welfare as representing a conditional state–society relationship: if the basic economic needs of the people were met, loyalty would ensue, and the state would be strong; if not, resentment would ensue, and the state would be weakened (Brooks and Brooks 2002: 250, 259).

The second bargain was a justice-based definition of citizenship. As Xu Jinxiong observes:

> Rulers gradually promulgated laws which were meant to bind rulers and ruled alike . . . Laws were originally tools used by aristocrats to arbitrarily suppress the people. They gradually became the contractual basis on which the people would accept a given rulership. (Xu 1988: 543)

E. Bruce Brooks calls this development 'the new legal quid' in exchange for 'the new military quo' (Brooks 1998: 6). Transmitted texts and unearthed legal documents show that the right of access to justice and the right of redress before higher judges existed at least in the states of Qin, Chu and Qi by the late fourth century BCE.

International competition further nurtured the third bargain: freedom of expression akin to the Enlightenment, making classical thinkers, especially Mencius, closer to Locke than to Mao (in Perry's language). Ambitious rulers competed not just for the support of peasant soldiers, but also the assistance of talented generals and strategists. In the interest of the state, senior court ministers and free scholars were expected to freely criticise rulers' mistaken policies, an expectation that they met with little hesitation. Wong argues that the European phenomenon of popular sovereignty had no place in China's late imperial state dynamics (Wong 1997: 101). He overlooks that the Warring States era was a different world. The received wisdom that the Mandate of Heaven rested with the Son of Heaven (divinely appointed Emperor) was a post-unification construction by Han emperors. The Mandate of Heaven as originally articulated in the classical era insisted on the ultimate sovereignty of the people. Most notably, the *Mencius* unequivocally places the Mandate in the hands of the people because 'Heaven does not speak; it sees and hears as the people see and hear' (Pines 2009: 75). In discussing the last Shang ruler, Mencius is quoted as saying: 'I have heard about the killing of the ordinary fellow Zhou, but I have not heard of the assassination of any ruler' (Brooks and Brooks 2002: 254). This passage is reminiscent of Thomas Hobbes' complaint about resistance theorists: 'they say not regicide, that is, killing of a king, but tyrannicide, that is, killing of a tyrant, is lawful' (Hobbes [1651] 1992: 2.29). The *Zuo chuan* similarly remarks that if a ruler 'exhausts the people's livelihood . . . and betrays the hopes of the populace, then . . . what use is he? What can one do but expel him?' (Watson 1989: xv–xvi). Even the *Xunzi*, the classical text most supportive of strong central authority, states that 'the ruler is like a boat and the people are like the water. While the water can float the boat, it can also capsize it' (Pines 2009: 206). Classical Chinese thinkers thus preceded modern European resistance theorists in arguing that tyrants ceased to be rulers.

Together, the three bargains of material welfare, legal protection and freedom of expression marked the emergence of citizenship rights in classical China. Of course, the Warring States were not democracies, and many rulers remained abusive of the people (the same can be said of their European counterparts). Nevertheless, the very existence of a multi-state system necessarily gave rise to the fourth citizenship right: the 'right of exit', which made rulers aware of limits to repression lest the people move to competing states. Europeanists argue that the right of exit served as an implicit check on arbitrary power, and even a substitute for formal representation in modern European politics (Jones 1981: 118; Moravcsik 1997: 518). In the Chinese context, scholars, peasants and traders similarly could 'vote with their feet' and move to states with the most open policies. As population size was the basis of military power and economic wealth, the threat of talented citizens and peasant soldiers leaving for enemy states was not taken lightly. As another classic, the *Book of Odes*, says to uncaring rulers: 'Never have you cared for my welfare. I shall leave you and journey to that fortunate land' (Kuhn 2002: 118).

Unification and Erosion of Citizenship Rights

Unfortunately, Qin's unification of the Warring States system in 221 BCE fundamentally reversed state–society relations. Under the Qin dynasty (221–206 BCE), all elements of classical citizenship rights disappeared. Peasant welfare was abandoned and the imperial court increased tax burdens and further drafted over 800,000 men to expand to the northern and southern frontiers. The principle of justice was eroded, with punishments becoming so harsh that there were about 1.4 million convicts to provide forced labour to build the Emperor's palaces and tomb. Freedom of expression was similarly stifled, with all books, except Qin's court records and those on medicine and agriculture, were seized and burnt, and 460 scholars who expressed doubts about the Emperor's policies were persecuted. Beginning from 209 BCE, Qin's subjects turned to the ultimate right under tyranny: the right to rebel.

At the Qin's collapse, the most promising rebel leader, Xiang Yu, sought to revive the pre-Qin states. A Chinese historian Shi Shi suggests that if Xiang had succeeded, China could have developed a loose federal system more conducive to regional autonomy and political freedom (Shi 2007). But Xiang Yu was overtaken by Liu Bang, who established the Han dynasty (202 BCE–CE 220) on the model of the Qin dynasty. Chinese history books praise the Han for correcting Qin's excesses and promoting Confucianism. However, the imperial version of Confucianism advocated by Dong Zhongshu (179–104 BCE) for Emperor Wu (r. 141–87 BCE) involved important deviations from the classical version. Most of all, the Mandate of Heaven was now reinterpreted as resting with the 'Son of Heaven' instead of the people. And despite Confucianism's prescription for benevolent rule, the Han criminal code largely followed the harsh Qin code. As John K. Fairbank observed, although 'the first Han emperors took great pains to claim that their rule was based on the Confucian teachings of social order . . . they used the methods of the Legalists as the basis for their institutions and policy decisions' (Fairbank 1974: 11). Shi even remarks that the key difference between the Qin and the Han was pure coercion versus coercion masked by deception (Shi 2007). Subsequent dynasties followed the Han model of 'Legalism with a Confucian façade' (Hsiao 1977: 137).

The Legacy of Classical Citizenship Rights

The contrast between the Warring States period and the Qin–Han period leads Michael Loewe to ask 'to what extent the unified empires of Qin and Han maintained easier conditions of living or imposed harsher burdens on the population than the localised kingdoms of China that preceded or followed them' (Loewe 1987: 18). Gu Jiegang, a critical Chinese historian of the early twentieth century, once suggested that political unification by the centralised empire had led to constriction and, ultimately, decay, but the in-between periods of flux, chaos and competition were the most creative eras of Chinese history (Duara 1995: 42). Indeed, in eras of division after the Qin and Han, competing states would again be compelled by international competition to introduce more open policies to attract new talents and develop neglected regions to enlarge their tax bases. Of course, Chinese regimes remained autocratic – just as early modern European regimes were absolutist. But it is worth repeating that the very existence of a multi-state system always gave rise to the 'right of exit', which presented a formidable check against arbitrary power. This 'right of exit' has been overlooked in mainstream Sinology because analysts have uncritically accepted the presumption of Chinese oneness. While state–society bargains would always be revived to some extent in eras of division, they were not altogether lost in eras of unification. Most notably, the underlying principles were kept alive in Confucian rites and principles to which even all-powerful emperors were compelled to at least pay lip service. Though formally unchecked, emperors could be trapped by their own rhetoric. In seeking legitimacy in the Confucian tradition and the Mandate of Heaven, Chinese emperors also subjected themselves to the higher authority of Confucianism and Heaven. As Alan Wood observes: 'Confucianism may have been used to expand the power of the state, but it also provided moral limits to that power' (Wood 1995: 11). Chu Ron Guey points out that, when Han's first emperor Gaozu (r. 202–195 BCE) offered sacrifice to Confucius, he not only legitimised his claim to rule, but also 'exposed himself to being regulated by' the Confucian tradition (Chu 1998: 170). A number of historians have highlighted that, because Confucian rites fostered a 'constitutional culture limiting the exercise of dynastic rule' (Chu 1998: 174), and even 'set limits on the actions and decisions of both the emperor and the bureaucracy and ruled their relations with the population' (Will 2009: 262), they served a 'potentially constitutional function' (Brooks and Brooks 1998: 117) which 'occupie[d] much of the space that in the modern West would be identified with a constitutional order' (Bary 1998b: 43). Moreover, in the Confucian order, however elevated the Son of Heaven made himself, he was ultimately subordinate to Heaven. When Dong Zhongshu reinterpreted the Mandate of Heaven to rest with the Son of Heaven for Han's Emperor Wu, he also 'attempted to curb the arbitrary exercise of the ruler's power by threatening the intervention of Heaven in the form of natural portents and disasters' and by retaining the people's 'right to rebel' (Wood 1995: 13, 154). Pierre-Étienne Will calls this the idea of twin sovereignty: 'the ruler is the master of men, but the people are "the master of the master of men"': that is, 'the people's sovereignty is a *given*, whereas the ruler's sovereignty is *conditional*' (Will 2009: 273).

In the more open environment of the Song dynasty (960–1279) (which did not achieve unification of China Proper and faced intense international competition), neo-Confucian scholars further worked out a 'doctrine of political rights' (Wood 1995). Song neo-Confucian scholars such as Cheng Yi and Zhu Xi moved away from Han scholars' emphasis on rites towards 'heavenly principles', which 'transcended the ruler and therefore obliged him to obey them' (Wood 1995: xi). Alan Wood insists that the theory of 'heavenly principles' is strikingly similar to the European conception of natural law because both uphold the belief 'that there exist certain laws or rules of action that are inherent in human nature and that reflect the rationally apprehensible order of the universe' (Wood 1995: 136).

Such debates over Confucian rites and principles over the ages testify to the continued existence of the classical bargain of freedom of expression in imperial times, albeit in reduced form. Generations of Confucian scholars followed Xunzi's dictum: 'Follow the Way, do not follow the ruler' (Pines 2009: 179). Will defines 'freedom of expression' as 'the right to remonstrate and to denounce, in memorials sent to the throne, abuses of power' (Will 2009: 270–1). Theodore de Bary also highlights 'freedom of discussion', both in terms of 'the responsibility Confucian scholars felt to speak out against the abuse of power' and in terms of 'the increasing recognition by Neo-Confucians . . . of duly constituted institutions to protect this public discussion' (Bary 1998c: 109). This 'literati power' to criticise emperors was not buttressed, however, by the classical bargain of legal protection. As Will puts it: 'one could be brutally beaten on order of the emperor, thrown in one of the central governmental jails to die, or at a minimum lose all of one's ranks and titles. But, nevertheless, one *had* such a right and one could always choose to exercise it' (Will 2009: 271). In such a harsh institutional environment, the 'dissenting Confucian tradition' was 'unable historically to prevail over the politically more dominant dynastic tradition' (Bary 1998a: 22). Nevertheless, it does 'constitute a significant line of Confucian thought from Confucius and Mencius down through Song and Ming scholars to modern times (Bary 1998c: 109).

The classical bargain of peasant welfare likewise persisted in the imperial era, again in diminished form. Chinese emperors understood that political stability depended on whether or not the people could maintain a decent livelihood. From the Han on, emperors and officials would always profess to follow the Confucian policy of promoting peasant well-being and maintaining light taxation. And a key government function was to keep track of harvest conditions and grain prices so that famine relief could be efficiently delivered. Nevertheless, the prevalence of tax rebellions testifies to the fragility of this bargain in the imperial era.

A related Confucian ideal – that of local autonomy – was more consistently realised in Chinese history. According to Bary, 'From the Confucian viewpoint, a large sphere of social activity was rightly governed by voluntary adherence to traditional rites without the intervention of the state and its laws' (Bary 1998c: 31). As Ho-fung Hung explains, 'mass Confucianism,' as opposed to 'imperial Confucianism' was 'reflected in lineage organisations at the community level and also by pseudo-kinship or common-local-origin ties' (Hung 2009: 82). According to Will, Western visitors such as Father Évariste Huc had indeed observed how village mayors were elected by fellow citizens in the nineteenth century (Will 2005). Of course, such 'village democracy' was more pro forma than substantive because the votes were always decided behind the scenes by influential notables before the election dates – just as elections in the Western world were not exactly 'free and fair' in the nineteenth century. Nevertheless, the very existence of the electoral institution does attest to the relative autonomy of local governance. This particular Confucian ideal was more extensively implemented in imperial China partly because the imperial state had no capacity for direct rule at the village level. The central court appointed magistrates down to the department and county levels, but gave them such scanty resources that they had to rely on the cooperation of 'a range of extra-bureaucratic actors and groups, including local militias, clan and lineage associations, and members of the local gentry' (Thornton 2007: 24). Nor did the imperial state provide a budget for support staff so that magistrates had to rely on a sub-bureaucratic staff of clerks, secretaries and tax collectors who made their livings from imposing surtaxes and fees on local populations. Because centrally appointed magistrates relied on local authority and local resources they had to tolerate a certain degree of self-government. It was certainly not lost on imperial officials that most peasant rebellions were started at village levels and led by local notables.

Thus, the state–society bargains inherited from the classical era lingered on in the rest of Chinese history, though they were more theoretical than substantive in eras of unification. The bargain of peasant welfare was always upheld as a core ruling principle. But the prevalence of peasant rebellions suggests that this bargain could be readily discarded. The bargain of freedom of expression was sustained by generations of literati who gave primary loyalty to Confucian principles over the Son of Heaven. But because the right to criticise was not buttressed by another bargain of legal protection, Confucian scholars who exercised this right had to risk their lives. Sinologists often argue that Confucian moral restraints were so weak because they were not buttressed by any institutional support. However, as Bary points out, Huang Zongxi (1610–95) already understood that one could not count on the emperor's capacity for self-restraint and thus sought to 'limit the power of the ruler by defining legal constraints and incorporating them in the organizational structure of government' (Bary 1998b: 49–50). Like previous reformist Confucian ideas, Huang's 'constitutional programme' was not translated into policy.

Why did indigenous ideas of both natural law and constitutional constraints fail to take root in China? The development of local autonomy from the Han on suggests that the very emergence of checking institutions itself has to be explained – and that it was as much a function of the balance of power between the state and the society as it was the development of political ideas. This balance of forces could be altered only when an imperial court faced intense international competition with equally powerful regimes, as in the Song and other eras of division, or when a once powerful dynasty was in decline, as in the late Ming and late Qing.

The Chinese Enlightenment in the Civil War Era

China would experience an Enlightenment in the late Qing and Republican periods, 2,000 years after the classical era. In the Chinese nationalist narrative, modern Chinese history is an episode of national humiliation, chaos and sufferings. Nevertheless, as Stephen MacKinnon argues, fierce international competition 'also politicized the citizenry in a liberating sense' (MacKinnon 1996: 943). The decades from the 1890s to the 1930s represented a time when Chinese intellectuals openly debated the notions of constitutional monarchy, republicanism and democracy. Philip Kuhn points out that the first petition by the educated elite to the Qing court for popular representation in 1895 was 'only conceivable under the duress of imminent foreign conquest' (Kuhn 2002: 123). Orville Schell highlights that the May Fourth era (around 1919) was a great 'Chinese Enlightenment' (Schell 2004: 117). Arthur Waldron observes that the Republican period under the Northern government of 1912–28 was 'a period of professedly parliamentary rule', enjoying 'substantial economic growth . . . freedom of the press . . . and a flowering of culture' (Waldron 2003: 264). Likewise, MacKinnon points out that the short-lived Nationalist–Communist unity government at Hankou in 1938 was marked by power-sharing among rival militarists and thus witnessed 'the absence of the repressive power of the state' (MacKinnon 1996: 935). Against the backdrop of Japanese invasion, 'parliamentary-like debate', 'third-party movements' (independent of both the Nationalists and Communists), the free press and the arts flourished and 'reached a twentieth-century zenith' (MacKinnon 1996: 937). The conclusion of the civil war, unfortunately, again aborted China's democratic experiments. After 1949, totalitarian states emerged on both sides of the Taiwan Strait.

Conclusion

In short, the roots of democracy are not alien to the Chinese tradition. The classical Warring States period gave rise to citizenship rights defined as state–society bargains. After Qin's unification aborted the development of Chinese citizenship, classical bargains were preserved in classical texts, though more as moral doctrines than as actual policies. But the fact that China was more often divided than unified allowed periodic revival of state–society bargains, especially the right of exit. If China has not translated constitutional ideas and state–society bargains into democracy, it is not the fault of the Chinese tradition in general or Confucianism in particular. China's past in fact provides immense resources to build a future that is simultaneously Chinese and democratic. There is some hope that the twenty-first century will provide an opportunity for those resources to be utilised and China's democratic potential to be fulfilled.

Note

1. Following the Chinese convention, Chinese names begin with surnames unless the scholars in question publish in English and go by the English convention.

References

Bary, W. T. de (1998a), 'Introduction', in W. T. de Bary and T. Weiming (eds.), *Confucianism and Human Rights*, New York: Columbia University Press, pp. 1–26.

Bary, W. T. de (1998b), 'Confucianism and Human Rights in China', reprinted in L. Diamond and M. F. Plattner (eds), *Democracy in East Asia*, Baltimore, MD: Johns Hopkins University Press, pp. 42–54.

Bary, W. T. de (1998c), *Asian Values and Human Rights: A Confucian Communitarian Perspective*, Cambridge, MA: Harvard University Press.

Brooks, E. B. (1998), 'Evolution Toward Citizenship in Warring States China', paper presented at the European–North American Conference on 'The West and East Asian Values', Victoria College, University of Toronto.

Brooks, E. B. and A. T. Brooks (1998), *The Original Analects: Sayings of Confucius and His Successors*, New York: Columbia University Press.

Brooks, E. B. and A. T. Brooks (2002), 'The Nature and Historical Context of the *Mencius*', in A. K. L. Chan (ed.), *Mencius: Contexts and Interpretations*, Honolulu, HI: University of Hawaii Press, pp. 242–81.

Chu, R. G. (1998), 'Rites and Rights in Ming China', in W. T. de Bary and T. Weiming (eds), *Confucianism and Human Rights*, New York: Columbia University Press, pp. 169–78.

Duara, P. (1995), *Rescuing History from the Nation: Questioning Narratives of Modern China*, Chicago, IL: University of Chicago Press.

Fairbank, J. K. (1974), 'Introduction: Varieties of the Chinese Military Experience', in F. A. Kierman, Jr and J. K. Fairbank (eds), *Chinese Ways in Warfare*, Cambridge, MA: Harvard University Press, pp. 1–26.

Ge, J. X. (1994), *Tongyi yu fenlie: Zhongguo lishi de qishi* (*Unification and Division: Insights from Chinese History*), Beijing: Shenghuo, dushu, xinzhi sanlian shudian.

Hahm, C. (2004), 'The Ironies of Confucianism', *Journal of Democracy*, 15(3), 93–107.

Hobbes, T. ([1651] 1992), *Leviathan*, in *Classics of Moral and Political Theory*, ed. Michael Morgan, Indianapolis, IN: Hackett, pp. 571–732.

Hsiao, K. C. (1977), 'Legalism and Autocracy in Traditional China', in Yu-ming Li (ed.), *Shang Yang's Reform and State Control in China*, New York: M. E. Sharpe, pp. 125–43.

Hui, V. T. (2005), *War and State Formation in Ancient China and Early Modern Europe*, New York: Cambridge University Press.

Hung, H. F. (2009), 'Cultural Strategies and the Political Economy of Protest in Mid-Qing China, 1740–1839', *Social Science History*, 33(1), 75–115.

Jones, E. L. (1981), *Growth Recurring: Economic Change in World History*, New York: Oxford University Press.

Kuhn, P. A. (2002), *Origins of the Modern Chinese State*, Stanford, CA: Stanford University Press.

Loewe, M. (1987), 'Introduction', in D. Twitchett and M. Loewe (eds), *The Cambridge History of China, vol. 1: The Ch'in and Han Empires, 221 BCE–AD 220*, New York: Cambridge University Press, pp. 1–19.

MacKinnon, S. (1996), 'The Tragedy of Wuhan, 1938', *Modern Asian Studies*, Special Issue: *War in Modern China*, 30(4), 931–43.

Moravcsik, A. (1997), 'Taking Preferences Seriously: A Liberal Theory of International Politics', *International Organization*, 51(4), 513–53.

Perry, E. J. (2008), 'Chinese Conceptions of "Rights": From Mencius to Mao – and Now', *Perspectives on Politics*, 6(1), 37–50.

Pines, Y. (2009), *Envisioning Eternal Empire: Chinese Political Thought of the Warring States Era*, Honolulu, HI: University of Hawaii Press.

Schell, O. (2004), 'China's Hidden Democratic Legacy', *Foreign Affairs*, 83(4), 116–24.

Shi, S. (2007), 'Qin-Han zhijian weihe loudiao yige Chu wangchao?' ('Why is a Chu Dynasty Missing during the Qin-Han Transition?'), interview with Zhibo Lin, People Network.

Tan, Q. X. (2000), '*Lishishang de zhongguo (Historical China)*', in *Qiusuo shikong (An Exploration of Time and Space)*, Tianjin: Baihua wenyi.

Tilly, C. (1992), *Coercion, Capital, and European States, AD 990–1992*, Oxford: Blackwell.

Thornton, P. M. (2007), *Disciplining the State: Virtue, Violence, and State-Making in Modern China*, Cambridge, MA: Harvard University Asia Center.

Waldron, A. (2003), *From War to Nationalism: China's Turning Point, 1924–1925*, New York: Cambridge University Press.

Watson, B. (1989), *The Tso chuan [Zuo chuan]: Selections from China's Oldest Narrative History*, translation with a commentary, New York: Columbia University Press.

Weber, M. (1991), *From Max Weber*, H. H. Gerth and C. Wright Mills (eds), London: Routledge & Kegan Paul.

Will, P. (2005), '"Democratic China" in the 19th Century', speech delivered at St John's College, University of British Columbia, 24 October.

Will, P. (2009), 'Epilogue: Virtual Constitutionalism in the Late Ming Dynasty', in Stéphanie Balme and Michael W. Dowdle (eds), *Building Constitutionalism in China*, New York: Palgrave Macmillan, pp. 261–74.

Wood, A. (1995), *Limits to Autocracy: From Sung Neo-Confucianism to a Doctrine of Political Rights*, Honolulu, HI: University of Hawaii Press.

Wong, R. B. (1997), *China Transformed: Historical Change and the Limits of the European Experience*, Ithaca, NY: Cornell University Press.

Xu, J. X. (1988), *Zhongguo gudai shehui (Ancient Chinese Society)*, Taipei: Taipei shangwu.

Chapter 5

Israel and Phoenicia

Stephen Stockwell

The Greeks made major contributions to the development of democracy not only as an idea, but even more significantly as a set of practical laws and pragmatic institutions that evolved over centuries to translate the sovereignty of the people into a relatively stable and effective system of government. However, while the Greek invention of democracy is often treated as an indisputable truth, recent work suggests that democracy may have antecedents. Martin Bernal stirred a major controversy with his book, *Black Athena*, and its claims to establish the 'Afro-Asiatic' roots of classical Greek society (Bernal [1987] 1991). A later paper sought to extend the argument and establish the contribution of the Semitic Phoenician cities to the development of the Greek city-state with 'fundamental similarities between them . . . best explained as results of diffusion' (Bernal 2001: 346). Others would point to the archaeological and textual evidence of Phoenician experiments in democracy and their interaction with the Greeks to suggest that along with the phonetic alphabet and the rudiments of the scientific method, the Phoenicians may have brought the possibilities of popular government from east to west (Stockwell 2011).

The notion that the Phoenicians foreshadowed the Greek invention of the democratic *polis* raises the question as to where the Phoenicians found the inspiration for these experiments in democracy. The long tradition of proto-democracy from the earliest cities in Mesopotamia through Babylon and Assyria and across the Middle East has been discussed elsewhere (Isakhan 2011; Jacobsen [1943] 1970). One tradition that deserves particularly close scrutiny comes from one of Phoenicia's closest Semitic neighbours and trading partners, Israel. Martin Buber, modern Jewish theologian and anti-Nazi activist, points out that the ancient state of Israel depended not on the king's relationship with God, but with the people's participation in the covenant. Mosaic law created a leader constrained by the law of God, just as his people were, and that underwrote a sense of equality that informed an emerging democratic politics in ancient Israel (Buber 1967).

This chapter considers the available evidence to appreciate that, while the Semitic states of Israel and Phoenicia were predominantly governed by monarchies, those monarchies were limited and there were periods without the leadership of kings when the people had no choice but to exercise their own sovereignty. In both Israel and Phoenicia forms of popular government emerged that exhibited elements of democracy: equality, free speech, individual autonomy and the rule of law. The result is a broader view of the history of democracy and a wider appreciation of how democracy might work.

Popular Government in Ancient Israel

The tribal assembly was part of ancient Israeli politics from the time of Abraham's migration from Mesopotamia to Canaan in the early second millennia BCE. There may well have been historical figures cognate with Abraham, but contemporary scholars are only too aware that this story was first written down in the sixth century BCE by Israelis in Babylonian exile hoping to follow Abraham's putative footsteps back to Canaan (Blenkinsop 2009: 39). Traditionally, it was Abraham's grandson Jacob who first took the name Israel when he fathered the twelve sons who would each found one of the tribes of Israel. On his death-bed, Jacob-Israel calls his sons to give them frank assessments of their conduct. In particular, he is concerned that Simeon and Levi 'in their anger they slew a man and in their self-will they hamstrung an ox', so their father asks: 'Let not my soul enter their council, let not my honour be united to their assembly' (Genesis 49:6). Even if these lines were not written until the sixth century BCE, they attest to the centrality of deliberative councils and assemblies to Israeli nationhood and may have basis in earlier fact. Nevertheless, these ideas were clearly in circulation around the sixth century when they were being used in Phoenicia and introduced in Greece.

The assembly becomes more prevalent in biblical texts when the narrative turns to Moses and his travels in the Sinai desert with the people of Israel. It was Moses who made the covenant accepting the kingship of God so that the people did not require an earthly king. Moses himself accepted his own fallibility and equality with his brethren before God, a God who directed precisely how silver trumpets should be blown to call together the assembly (Numbers 8:10). The 'cosmic theme' of the kingship of God was an irresistible force operating on the political situation (Gray 1961: 5). The law ordained a limited monarch and that produced a social structure tending towards the egalitarian, with a citizenry that used the advantages of sovereignty so that they could participate in deliberations, challenge the authority of leaders and choose the judges to lead them in times of turmoil (Finer 1997: 238–44; Friedman 1962: 48–9; Wolf 1947).

The Hebrew word *mo'ed*, which is typically translated as 'assembly', has a broad meaning as 'congregation': 'The gathering . . . may be a special religious and educational meeting rather than a political assembly' (Wolf 1947: 100; Deuteronomy 31:10–12). However, the *mo'ed* is not the passive recipient of Moses', or God's, prescriptions and can take its own political position (Wilson 1945: 245). For example, when the people become disillusioned about escaping from the Sinai desert they ask: 'Why has the Lord brought us to this land to fall by the sword . . . Would it not be better for us to return to Egypt?' (Numbers 14:3). That leads to the particularly political suggestion, 'Let us select a leader and return to Egypt', which prompts Moses and his brother Aaron to show deference to the collective will when they 'fell on their faces before all the assembly of the congregation of the children of Israel' (Numbers 14:4–5). Debate continues until God intervenes to punish those without faith who would return to Egypt, but the assembly does not lose any of its political will. Shortly afterwards, when Moses and Aaron order the stoning of a man for gathering sticks on the Sabbath: 'two hundred and fifty leaders of the congregation, representatives of the congregation, men of renown' claim not only mercy for the law-breaker but also autonomy for the *mo'ed*. They say to Moses and Aaron: 'You take too much upon yourselves, for all the congregation is holy, every one of them, and the Lord is among them. Why then do you exalt yourselves above the assembly of the Lord?' (Numbers 16:2–3).

The view of the assembly that emerges is one of some breadth and tolerance. Of course, there are requirements for membership of the assembly: 'the man who is unclean and does not purify himself, that person shall be cut off from among the assembly' (Numbers 19:20). Further there are a variety of proscriptions: 'He who is emasculated by crushing or mutilation . . . of illegitimate birth . . . [or] Ammonite or Moabite shall not enter the assembly of the Lord' (Deuteronomy 23:1–3). However, on occasions the assembly does include women, children and foreigners who live with the Israelis (Deuteronomy 31:10–120; Wolf 1947: 100). The law applies equally to the children of Israel and outsiders alike: 'One law and one custom shall be for you and for the stranger who dwells with you' (Numbers 15:15). The 'readiness in accepting strangeness and the stranger' assisted in the shift from nomadic to agricultural enterprise and the 'development of an urban civilization' that transformed the Israeli 'pattern of social organization from a loose tribal democracy' to monarchy moderated by the assembly (Greifer 1945: 744).

The state of the assembly after Moses is evident when the new leader, Joshua, takes the people into Canaan and renews the covenant with God: 'There was not a word of all that Moses had commanded which Joshua did not read before all the assembly of Israel, with the women, the little ones, and the strangers who were living among them' (Joshua 8:35). Once in Canaan, the Israelis settle the land with a large degree of individual autonomy, dependent for collective decision making on the judges – arbiters rather than leaders – who gain their position by common acceptance rather than by formal process. This informal system can be seen at work during the Israeli's civil war with the Benjamites, when an aggrieved party summons the assembly to hear evidence and debate before deciding a course of action (Judges 20). Also, in the aftermath of the civil war, 'the whole congregation sent word to the children of Benjamin . . . and announced peace to them' (Judges 21:10–13). It is in this period that Gideon, a judge and a successful military leader, is offered the kingship after a particularly gruelling war: 'Then the men of Israel said to Gideon: "Rule over us, both you and your son, and your grandson also" . . . But Gideon said to them, "I will not rule over you, nor shall my son rule over you; the Lord shall rule over you"' (Judges 8:22–3). This refusal of hereditary monarchy is a striking example of the equality, fraternity and self-sufficiency of the Israeli people and their adherence as a collective group to the kingship of God.

Eventually, in the eleventh century BCE, with the ever-present threat of the warlike Philistines, the Israelis see the need for a permanent military leader. God warns them of the dangers, but the Israelis persuade Him to allow the Judge Samuel to appoint a leader by lot. Saul becomes the first Israeli king, but he appears resistant to the office. When Saul is named as leader, he cannot be found until God says: 'There he is, hidden among the equipment' (1 Samuel 10:22). Samuel produces a written guide concerning how the institution of royalty works, an early example of a written constitution (1 Samuel 10:23–5). Of course, if the Bible was written in chronological order, Samuel would have had clear precepts to work with because the principles of kingship appear to have been laid down in Moses' time: he should be an Israelite, not a foreigner; he should not seek to increase his wealth; nor should he cause the people to return to Egypt; he should read the law every day 'that he may . . . observe all the words of this law and these statutes, that his heart may not be lifted above his brethren' (Deuteronomy 17:19–20). Whatever the chronology, the Israeli kings were always constitutional monarchs. While kings around them declared their own divinity, the Israeli king was constrained by the law of God. As Samuel says at Saul's coronation: 'here is the king whom you have chosen . . . [but] do not rebel against the commandment of the Lord . . . [because] if you still do wickedly, you shall be swept away, both you and your king' (1 Samuel 12:13–17).

Saul eventually fell into excess, massacring populations and becoming paranoid about his most successful general, David. After Saul's suicide, David became king of Judah, anointed by the men of Judah (2 Samuel 2:4). For seven years David battled Saul's son, Ishbosheth, before his assassination left David as the only one with a claim to kingship. This claim was substantiated when 'all the tribes of Israel came to David at Hebron and spoke, saying, "Indeed we are your bone and your flesh"' (2 Samuel 5:1). Then the elders of Israel made a covenant with David before anointing him king of Israel. This established the constitutional constraints on David and his son, Solomon, who were advised by both a council of elders and an assembly of all the men of Israel (1 Kings 8:1–2). For example, when David wanted to move the Ark of the Covenant to Jerusalem, he first sought the support of the assembly (1 Chronicles 13:1–4). After David, constitutional constraints on the king weakened: Solomon took power by intrigue and was not approved by the assembly; Solomon's son, Rehoboam, responded to the threat of revolt in the assembly by ignoring the elder's council and increasing the burdens on the people – he then had to flee and lost control of the united Israel but maintained a hold on Judah (1 Kings 12:8–18).

As the kingdoms of Israel and Judah declined they became targets for nearby empires, but even after their decline and exile, the assembly had not lost its power to challenge authority. The prophets became the *de facto* leaders of the Israeli people and used assemblies to renew strict marriage laws, outlaw oppressive usury and decry folly (Ezra 10:1; Job 30: 28; Nehemiah 5:7–13). This period was described by the Jewish chronicler, Josephus, as both a democracy and an oligarchy, and the truth is no doubt somewhere between (Feldman 2000: 267; Josephus [97 CE] 1732). The prophets were unique in the ancient East in that they 'represented the common people [while] immune from royal punishment owing to their sanctity and maintained the strongly democratic spirit . . . and more than once their protest against tyranny and injustice proved effective' (Oesterley and Robinson 1932: I:272–3).

Thus, throughout the history of ancient Israel, the democratising influence of the kingship of God connected with assembly practicalities to produce relative equality and autonomy that allowed elements of the democratic approach to flourish: 'combining . . . an indissoluble sense of human solidarity and an equally indefeasible conviction of the worth of personality . . . together their peculiar combination produced . . . human brotherhood' (Hutchison 1947: 34–7). The ancient Israeli did not understand the term democracy, but he had 'an unconscious theory of life . . . which the free Athenian citizen of the fifth century BCE boasted as his highest achievement' (Oesterley and Robinson 1932: II:105). The rudiments of democracy were 'prevalent in the earliest times and . . . vestiges of democratic procedures may be discerned in both political and religious concepts throughout the later periods of Israelite history' (Wolf 1947: 98).

Popular Government in Phoenicia

The close links between ancient Israel and the sea-trading culture of what is now called Phoenicia are evident in the archaeological findings of early Canaanite literature in the ancient city of Ugarit. The city was laid waste by the so-called Sea People in 1200 BCE just as the Israeli tribes reached the promised land: '[i]n the *Psalms*, *Prophets*, and the *Book of Job* the legacy of Canaan is particularly apparent especially in poetic structure, vocabulary, and imagery' (Gray 1956: 269). This intercultural connection is confirmed by the genetic record that shows that the Phoenicians' descendants in Lebanon and Jewish Israelis were originally a single population and any differences are the result of later intermarriage with Arabs and Europeans, respectively (Hammer 2000; Nebel *et al.* 2001). Also the new phonetic alphabet that the Phoenicians popularised along their trading routes came from the Sinai via Israel, and the Phoenicians were close trading partners with Israel: Hiram of Tyre provided Solomon with the timber and craftsmen to build the Temple in return for grain (1 Kings 5–7; Logan 2004: 36–42).

While the Phoenicians, like the ancient Israelites, did not have a word for democracy, the remainder of this chapter examines the diffusion of political power in their city-states and how, from time to time, the people were intimately involved and even dominant in the political decision-making process. Our knowledge of the Phoenicians comes from Greek and Roman classical literature and is thus 'a somewhat partial historiography, for it was compiled by enemies who tended to cast shadows . . . stressing their cruelty and perfidy' (Karageorghis 2004: 86). However, there is a growing body of scholarship building on the work of Sabatino Moscati committed to dealing with the subtlety and complexity of the Phoenician contribution to the development of world historical forces (Karageorghis 2004; Moscati 2001).

Phoenicia was a maritime and mercantile culture based around city-states, such as Sidon, Tyre, Arwad, Byblos and Beirut, on the eastern edge of the Mediterranean between 1600 and 300 BCE. The Phoenicians had no national identity as such and identified with their city. It was the Greeks who called them *phoinikes*, meaning 'crimson people', most probably because of the purple cloth the Phoenicians dyed using extracts from *Murex* shells and then traded widely (Markoe 2005: xvii). Ugarit, in what is now northern Syria, is the source of much Phoenician culture and the Sea People's destruction of that city, their defeat of the Hittites and their destabilisation of Egypt produced a vacuum that allowed Phoenician towns to flourish as they traded wood, metal, glass and purple dye from the Far East to the Atlantic (Ezekiel 27; Markoe 2005: 15–19, 109–20).

The impact of Mosaic ideas on Phoenician political institutions and the contribution of those institutions to the development of democracy are vexed issues. The Phoenicians lived in city-states where kings had civic and commercial functions as well as ritual and religious responsibilities. The wealth and power of the Phoenician kings can be seen in the sarcophaguses now in the Istanbul Archaeological Museum and the National Museum of Beirut. The rise of the Phoenician cities depended to a large degree on the kings' coordination of independent sailors, who required autonomy to trade far from the kings' influence. These traders were the biblical 'merchant princes' and, while not necessarily of the royal line, these traders formed councils to assist the kings in the management of their cities and so accrued power (Isaiah 23:8). The interesting question is whether that power spread further than the councils of the oligarchic few to assemblies of citizens engaged in debate that we would recognise as nascent democracies.

Martin Bernal's *Black Athena* stirred debate about the Phoenician contribution to democracy, but it depends to a large extent on some finer points of Marxist theory: Bernal sees Phoenicia at the centre of the shift from the 'Asiatic mode of production' managed by the monarch, to a slave society where the excess production of slaves gave their owner-citizens time to participate in democracy (Bernal 1991, 2001). But evidence cited by Bernal from primary sources is slight, so he makes a far from compelling case. Nevertheless, his work drew attention to scholars connecting Greece with the East, and particularly via Phoenicia (Aubert 2001; Burkert 1992; Goody 1996; Morris 1992; West 1997). This work reveals that while Phoenician cities were mostly in the hands of kings, there were moments of alternative, non-monarchical constitutional arrangements that deserve closer inspection.

The earliest available material concerning Phoenician politics can be found among the Amarna Letters, Egyptian clay tablets containing many diplomatic reports and entreaties from the mid-fourteenth century BCE (Moran 1992). The Egyptian state was powerful in the Levant at this time, though their power was contested by the Hittites (Cohen and Westbrook 2000). The Amarna Letters contain references to councils of elders or influential citizens in Phoenician territory, with whom local kings had to consult regarding important matters of state and who could frustrate the local king's will. For example, one letter from Aziru, the Caananite ruler of Amurru, to the pharaoh reads: 'My lord, from the very first I have wanted to enter the service of the king but the magnates of Sumur do not permit me . . . The king, my lord, knows who the real rebels are' (Moran 1992: 243). It appears that rebellion was constantly on the minds of local rulers. In another letter, the king of Byblos complains: 'I am afraid the peasantry will strike me down . . . they became traitors to me. A man with a bronze dagger attacked me but I killed him . . . I was struck 9 times. Accordingly, I fear for my life' (Moran 1992: 148–50). These passages suggest an independent-minded citizenry with some degree of internal cohesion and organisation. Flinders Petrie even identifies 'people from Gubla [Byblos]' communicating directly with the pharaoh, but others consider that time and storage conditions have erased mention of the king of Byblos from the tablet in question (Moran 1992: 212–13; Petrie 1898: 99).

Further, councils could act on their own behalf as when 'Irqata and its elders' wrote to the pharaoh to profess their allegiance after the appointed local ruler had perished:

'This tablet is a tablet from Irqata. To the king, our lord [the pharaoh]: Message from Iraqata and its elders . . . May the heart of the king, our lord know that we guard Iraqata for him' (Moran 1992: 172). The council of Irqata was not afraid to justify their independent decisions and went on to explain a coalition of convenience they had made with one enemy of the pharaoh against another: 'When a tablet from the king arrived saying to raid the land that the Apiru had taken from the king, [these others] waged war with us against the enemy of the man whom you placed over us' (Moran 1992: 172).

There are also other examples of broader assemblies of citizens directly addressing the Egyptian pharaoh over long periods, even if there was no response from the pharaoh:

Message of the citizens of Tunip [Baalbek], your servant . . . for 20 years, we have gone on writing to the king . . . but our messengers have stayed on with the king . . . And now Tunip, your city weeps, and its tears flow and there is no grasping of our hand. (Moran 1992: 130–1)

Benno Landsberger suggests a level of 'republican' organisation within Tunip at that time (Landsberger 1954: 61). Cohesive organisation that sought to keep diplomatic contact with the Pharaoh indicates the likelihood of ongoing deliberative institutions. The 'men of Arwad' or the 'people of Arwad' are portrayed as engaged in action independent of royalty in a number of the Amarna tablets (Moran 1992: 174, 178). The most pronounced democratic moment is revealed when 'Zimredda of Sidon, the rebel against the king, and the men of Arwad have exchanged oaths among themselves, and they have assembled their ships, chariots and infantry, to capture Tyre, the maidservant of the [pharaoh]' (Moran 1992: 236). As Bernal points out, this rebellion against the pharaoh is evidence that sovereignty lay with 'the people, as opposed to the monarch' (Bernal 2001: 356–7). Further, one Egyptian official reveals a high level of deliberation within and among towns when he expresses his concerns about opposition to his position: 'my towns are threatening me [and] they have all agreed among themselves against me' (Moran 1992: 138). The weight of evidence in the Amarna Letters is convincing, as Flinders Petrie claimed more than a century ago, that municipalities with deliberative assemblies and citizen participation show some sort of democratic activity existed in Phoenicia in the fourteenth century BCE (Petrie 1898: 139).

The next significant primary source relating to constitutional arrangements in a Phoenician city is the *Report of Wenamun* (Goedicke 1975). This report dates from the early part of the eleventh century BCE, about 250 years after the Amarna Letters, and it confirms a deliberative municipal forum in Byblos. The *Report* follows the journey of an Egyptian priest to acquire timber to build a sacred barge. Egyptian influence in the Phoenician cities had waned since the Amarna Letters, leaving strong local monarchies. Wenamun meets Zakarbaal, the king of Byblos. Zakarbaal is advised by 'his assembly' with regard to state matters, in this case the extradition of Wenamun to another jurisdiction to answer charges of theft (Goedicke 1975: 123). This assembly is referred to by Ezekiel as 'the ancients of Gebal [Byblos] and the wise men thereof', but may have been something broader (Ezekiel 27:9). Initially Wenamun's hieroglyphic for assembly resisted translation, but it has now been transcribed as *mw'd*, which is close to the aforementioned Hebrew word for assembly *mo'ed* (Wilson 1945: 245). The *Report of Wenamun* establishes that the Phoenicians did have a word for assembly, even if it was borrowed from the Hebrew, and that it was broader than an elite, oligarchic council.

As trade increased, the power of the king became constrained by the wealth of a merchant middle class keen to influence public affairs: 'after Hiram in the tenth century [the kings of Tyre] are not imposing figures' (Drews 1979: 47; see also Markoe 2005: 105). By the late ninth century, Tyre had both aristocratic and democratic dimensions. The people exerted their influence when they proclaimed Pygmalion as king, forcing his aristocratically inclined sister into exile where, traditionally, she founded Carthage (Rawlinson 1889: 205). By the seventh century BCE, the treaty between Esarhaddon of Assyria and Baal of Tyre shows that the council of Tyre governed alongside the monarch: the relationship was 'in conjunction with you [Baal], in conjunction with the elders of your country' (Aubert 2001: 146; Markoe 2005: 101). After Nebuchadnezzar II's siege of Tyre (585–572 BCE), Josephus notes that Tyre was without a monarchy for seven years and the city was administered by suffetes (or judges): 'after [Ithobal] were judges appointed: Ecnibalus, the son of Baslacus, two months; Chelbes, the son of Abdeus, ten months; Abbar, the high priest, three months; Mitgonus and Gerastratus, the sons of Abdelemus, were judges six years' (Josephus [97 CE] 1732: 21; Markoe 2005: 46–7). Sandro Bondi, who is otherwise resistant to democratic interpretations of Phoenician constitutions, admits that Tyre was 'a republic headed by elective magistrates' during this period (Bondi 2001: 153).

Suffetes also governed the Tyrian colony of Carthage with the support of the senate and the people's assembly (Markoe 2005: 103–4). The Carthaginian constitution required two suffetes who were elected annually to govern on the advice of the senate. Where there was a lack of agreement between the suffetes and the senate, the popular assembly was called to decide the issue (Aristotle [350 BCE] 1981). The diffusion of power in Carthaginian society is apparent in a municipal inscription in the Carthage Museum commemorating the opening of a new street: where a similar inscription from a monarchical society would give all credit to the king, this inscription gives credit to the two suffetes, four construction experts and the traders and workers who had contributed to the project 'all together'. Checks and balances in the Carthaginian constitutional system included elections, trade guilds, town meetings and the citizenry as the final arbiters of political decision, all of which suggest equality and participation close to modern democratic standards.

Towards the end of the Phoenician period in the Levant there is evidence that the people eclipsed the monarchy. Later Roman sources suggest that 'the people of Sidon' were the ones who ruled (Rufus [40 CE] 2001: IV:1.16). As Alexander's army approached Tyre it was met by 'representatives' sent by the 'community'; it was 'the people' who refused Alexander entry (Arrian [145 CE] 1970: 81; Bondi 2001: 154).

It is clear from this historic arc that the Phoenician cities commenced with strong leadership and ended with relatively weak kings or no kings at all. It is also clear that, from the sixteenth to the fourth century BCE, the leaders were advised by councils and assemblies, which gradually allowed the people to take a greater share of power. There is a lack of evidence as to how broadly Phoenician institutions represented the populace and how free and unconstrained their deliberations were. However, it may be concluded from occasions when the people are visible that at some times Byblos, Sidon and Tyre had something more than an autocracy or oligarchy and something much closer to democracy.

Conclusion

The preceding discussion establishes significant democratic experimentation in Israel and Phoenicia in the late second and early first millennia BCE. In both societies we see forms of popular government emerging with elements of what was to become known as democracy. The two societies were intertwined not just through trade, but also via ideas: Moses and the other prophets are constantly fighting the influence of the Phoenician god, Baal, while the autonomy promised by the kingship of the Israeli god is a crucial element in the Phoenician's trading success. Israel and Phoenicia were neighbours with close trade links and literary interconnections dating back to 1200 BCE (Gray 1956). Their interactions deserve further scrutiny.

The Phoenicians brought more than just trade into the Greek sphere, they also brought the experience of people governing themselves and, on the balance of probabilities, they had a formative influence on the rise of democratic political institutions (Stockwell 2011). Kleisthenes' reforms in Athens of 508 BCE were vital in formalising democracy, but these ideas and institutional forms had already been tried and tested in Israel and Phoenicia. The Phoenician influence in Athens is attested by trade and taxation agreements, coins and various artistic motifs, and while there is little evidence of any direct Phoenician influence on Athenian political institutions, there can be no doubt that Phoenician and, by extension, Israeli ideas were in circulation (Markoe 2005: 52, 124, 219–20). Many contemporary US commentators have noted that the practices and institutions of ancient Israel provide striking precedents for their democracy: 'The founding of the nation has often been described in terms of a covenant with the Supreme Being' (Fairbanks 1981: 216). This chapter establishes that both ancient Israeli and Phoenician experiments with democracy provide useful lessons for all those interested in the origins and possibilities of democracy.

References

Aristotle ([350 BCE] (1981), *The Politics*, trans. T. A. Sinclair, London: Penguin.
Arrian ([145 CE] 1970), *The Life of Alexander the Great*, London: Folio Society.
Aubert, M. E. (2001), *The Phoenicians and the West*, Cambridge: Cambridge University Press.
Bernal, M. ([1987] 1991), *Black Athena: The Afroasiatic Roots of Classical Civilisation, vol. I: The Fabrication of Ancient Greece 1785–1985*, London: Vintage.
Bernal, M. (2001), 'Phoenician Politics and Egyptian Justice in Ancient Greece', in *Black Athena Writes Back*, Durham, NC: Duke University Press, pp. 345–71.
Blenkinsopp, J. (2009), *Judaism, the First Phase: The Place of Ezra and Nehemiah in the Origins of Judaism*, Grand Rapids, MI: Eerdmans.

Bondi, S. F. (2001), 'Political and Administrative Organization', in S. Moscati (ed.), *The Phoenicians*, London: I. B. Tauris.

Buber, M. (1967), *Kingship of God*, New York: Harper & Row.

Burkert, W. (1992), *The Orientalizing Revolution*, trans. M. E. Pinder and W. Burkert, Cambridge, MA: Harvard University Press.

Cohen, R. and R. Westbrook (eds) (2000), *Amarna Diplomacy*, Baltimore, MD: Johns Hopkins University Press.

Drews, R. (1979), 'Phoenicians, Carthage and the Spartan Eunomia', *American Journal of Philology*, 100(1), 45–58.

Fairbanks, J. D. (1981), 'The Priestly Functions of the Presidency', *Presidential Studies Quarterly*, 11(2), 214–32.

Feldman, L. H. (2000), ' "Josephus'" Portrayal of the Benjaminite Affair', *Jewish Quarterly Review*, New Series, 90(3/4), 255–92.

Finer, S. E. (1997), *The History of Government*, Oxford: Oxford University Press.

Friedman, M. (1962), 'Social Responsibility in Judaism', *Journal of Religion and Health*, 2(1), 42–60.

Goedicke, H. (1975), *The Report of Wenamun*, Baltimore, MD: Johns Hopkins University Press.

Goody, J. (1996), *The East in the West*, Cambridge: Cambridge University Press.

Gray, J. (1956), 'The Hebrew Conception of the Kingship of God', *Vetus Testamentum*, 6(3), 268–85.

Gray, J. (1961), 'The Kingship of God in the Prophets and Psalms', *Vetus Testamentum*, 11(1), 1–29.

Greifer, J. L. (1945), 'Attitudes to the Stranger: A Study of the Attitudes of Primitive Society and Early Hebrew Culture', *American Sociological Review*, 10(6), 739–45.

Hammer, M. F. (2000), 'Jewish and Middle Eastern non-Jewish populations Share a Common Pool of Y-chromosome Biallelic Haplotypes', *Proceedings of the National Academy of Sciences*, 97(12), 6769–74.

Hutchison, J. A. (1947), 'Biblical Foundations of Democracy', *Journal of Bible and Religion*, 15(1), 34–7.

Isakhan, B. (2011), 'What is so "Primitive" about "Primitive Democracy"? Comparing the Ancient Middle East and Classical Athens', in B. Isakhan and S. Stockwell (eds), *The Secret History of Democracy*, London: Palgrave Macmillan, pp. 19–34.

Jacobsen, T. ([1943] 1970), 'Primitive Democracy in Ancient Mesopotamia', in W. L. Moran (ed.), *Toward the Image of Tammuz and Other Essays on Mesopotamian History and Culture*, Cambridge, MA: Harvard University Press, pp. 157–70.

Josephus, F. ([97 CE] 1732), *Against Apion*, trans. W. Whiston, Project Gutenberg.

Karageorghis, V. (2004), 'Phoenician Studies in the Mediterranean: Looking Ahead', *Archaeology and History in Lebanon*, 20, 86–94.

Landsberger, B. (1954), 'Assyrische Königsliste und "Dunkles Zeitalter"', *Journal of Cuneiform Studies*, 8(2), 47–73.

Logan, R. K. (2004), *The Alphabet Effect*, Cresskill, NY: Hampton Press.

Markoe, G. (2005), *The Phoenicians*, London: Folio Society.

Moran, W. L. (ed.) (1992), *The Amarna Letters*, Baltimore, MD: Johns Hopkins University Press.

Morris, S. (1992), *Daidalos and the Origins of Greek Art*, Princeton, NJ: Princeton University Press.

Moscati S. (ed.) (2001), *The Phoenicians*, London: I. B. Tauris.

Nebel, A., D. Filon, B. Brinkmann, P. Majumder, M. Faerman and A. Oppenheim (2001), 'The Y Chromosome Pool of Jews as Part of the Genetic Landscape of the Middle East', *American Journal of Human Genetics*, 69(5), 1095–112.

Oesterley, T. H. and W. O. E. Robinson (1932), *History of Israel*, vol. I, Oxford: Clarendon Press.

Petrie, W. M. F. (1898), *Syria and Egypt*, London: Methuen.

Rawlinson, G. (1889), *History of Phoenicia*, London: Longmans, Green.

Rufus, Q. C. ([40 CE] 2001), *The History of Alexander*, trans. J. Yardley, London: Penguin.

Stockwell, S. (2011), 'Before Athens', in B. Isakhan and S. Stockwell (eds), *The Secret History of Democracy*, London: Palgrave Macmillan, pp. 35–48.

West, M. L. (1997), *The East Face of Helicon*, Oxford: Clarendon Press.

Wilson, J. A. (1945), 'The Assembly of a Phoenician City', *Journal of Near Eastern Studies*, 4(4), 245.

Wolf, C. U. (1947), 'Traces of Primitive Democracy in Ancient Israel', *Journal of Near Eastern Studies*, 6(2), 98–108.

Part II

Classical Democracy

Chapter 6
Early Greece

Kurt A. Raaflaub

Greek democracy emerged in either late sixth- or mid-fifth-century[1] Athens, with strong arguments supporting both dates (Raaflaub *et al.* 2007). However, *dēmokratia*, 'rule by the people', was the result of a long evolution that affected other communities as well (Robinson 1997). This chapter has two purposes. One is to trace the beginnings of this evolution from the earliest extant evidence on Greek communities, institutions and political reflection (in Homer's epics and early laws) to the enactment of the first known *polis* constitution in Sparta and the breakthrough of political and constitutional thought in Solonian Athens. The other purpose is to explain in what ways these really were steps towards democracy and why they were taken in archaic Greece, of all places.

Homer

Homer weaves into the *Iliad*'s dramatic narrative a series of political threads that focus on problems of leadership worked out in the interaction among leaders in the council and between leaders and community in the assembly (Homer [700 BCE] 1950: 2.252–335). The *Odyssey* explicitly addresses the importance of such institutions in the description of the Cyclopes' completely uncivilised 'non-society': they have 'no common norms, no meetings (*agorai*) for counsels'; they live independently in mountain caves, 'and each one is the law for his own wives and children, and cares nothing about the others' (Homer [700 BCE] 1965: 9.112–15). The Phaeacians, an ideal community, demonstrate that communal norms and meetings are typical of civilised society (Homer [700 BCE] 1965: 6–8, 13). They have a permanent assembly place: a paved *agora* with polished stones as seats for councillors; leader, council and assembly interact properly (Homer [700 BCE] 1965: 6.266–7).

The marvellous shield of Achilles shows the *agora* as the setting for judicial disputes and arbitration (Homer [700 BCE] 1950: 18.497–508). The elders, sitting in a circle, listen to two men who argue their case in turn, surrounded by a crowd of their supporters who speak up for them and are kept in check by heralds. In the conceptual design of the shield, this scene characterises a city in peace. Hence, in peace justice rules; conflicts are resolved through arbitration amid an assembly of people in the *agora*. The elders, 'who safeguard the norms on behalf of Zeus' (Homer [700 BCE] 1950: 1.238–39), propose verdicts on which ordinary people express their opinions.

Such cases of explicit conceptualisation are rare. The evidence the epics offer lies primarily in narrative and descriptive detail, and is often incidental – but plentiful. It is part of the poet's depiction of his actual social environment into which heroically elevated events and actions are embedded. The society is essentially realistic and historical, datable to around 700 BCE (Finkelberg 2011: 359–61, 810–13). The epic community is an early form of the *polis*, as yet without formalised institutions. The *polis* was not a 'city-state', but a small, independent, face-to-face community, encompassing settlements and territory, with its own customs, norms, cults and government. The community of citizens was primary: Athens was a town, Attica a territory; the *polis* was 'the Athenians'. 'The men are the polis', says Thucydides (Thucydides [400 BCE] 1972: 7.77.7). He was anticipated by the poet Alcaeus around 600 (Campbell 1982: 112.10, 426). Thus, the *polis* was a 'citizen-state' (Davies 1997; Hansen 1993: 7–29). Homer's *polis in nuce* represents this principle (Raaflaub 1993).

The institutional structure of the *polis* is clearly visible. The paramount leader is a *primus inter pares*; his position, based on household resources, personal qualities and achievement, is firmly embedded in the community. The privileges of office oblige the leaders to justify themselves through outstanding service (Homer [700 BCE] 1950: 12.310–21; 1.117; 2.233–4). Agamemnon and Hector illustrate success and failure in this respect. The dramatic narrative thus enables audiences to recognise good and bad leadership, the qualities and behaviours associated with it and the consequences. Here, and in the conceptualisations mentioned above, lie the beginnings of Greek political reflection that focuses not least on debates in council and assembly (Balot 2006: 16–47; Cartledge 2009: 29–40; Finkelberg 2011: 104, 143; Raaflaub 2000: 27–34). The men meeting in assembly also fight in the army, playing an indispensable role even in 'heroic' battles (Raaflaub 2008).

In the epic period the *agora* is the centre of the *polis* where communal activities take place, often legitimised by the presence of the *demos* (people). The assembly is an indispensable part of communal life: the men involved are convened whenever a decision needs to be made (Raaflaub 1997: 8–20). Detailed descriptions of meetings illustrates the procedures. There is neither general debate nor vote, and the assembly cannot take the initiative, but the men express their opinion unmistakably by voice or feet. The leader can ignore their opinion (as Agamemnon does), but if he then fails he is in trouble and in some situations it seems difficult to act against the firm will of council or assembly (Homer [700 BCE] 1950: 15.721–3; Homer [700 BCE] 1965: 13.239). A good leader listens to advice and follows the best proposal. Consensus and conflict resolution are crucial to maintaining communal peace, so the ideal leader is explicitly characterised as the best at fighting and in speaking (Homer [700 BCE] 1950: 1.274, 3.216–24, 9.440–3). Usually, it is the leaders who speak, but anyone who has good advice to offer can be heard. A lowly person, Thersites, is disciplined not for speaking out, but for doing so 'against the order or norms' (*kosmos*) (Homer [700 BCE] 1950: 2.213–14). Hence, there are norms to be observed.

The assembly deals with public matters (*dēmion*) (Homer [700 BCE] 1965: 2.32). Arguing that the woes of his household, though private, should be of concern to the community, Telemachus tries to mobilise public opinion against the suitors of his mother (Homer [700 BCE] 1965: 2.25–79). A friend blames the people for remaining silent and not restraining the few suitors, 'being yourselves so many' (Homer [700 BCE]

1965: 2.239–41). Indeed, after trying to murder Telemachus, the suitors fear that the people will expel them from the community (Homer [700 BCE] 1965: 16.376–82, 424–30). All this suggests that the assembly, and the people in general, might be (or become) forces to be reckoned with.

In epic society, institutions are firmly established, communally indispensable and function according to well-established norms. Politics is not institutionalised or guided by laws, but performed in the communal interaction among leaders and men (Hammer 2002). The epic *polis* is already a community of citizens whose communal importance is reflected in their roles as fighters and assemblymen. Although the poet usually focuses on the leaders' actions, these are embedded in and validated by the community. Political developments in subsequent centuries have their roots in the structures and relations fostered by the emerging *polis* as seen in Homer.

Hesiod (early seventh century) offers further valuable insights into the conceptualisation of political values and political reflection concerning the qualities of leadership and the crucial importance of justice for individual and communal well-being (Raaflaub 2000: 34–7). But he does not focus on the *polis* or institutions, and it is unclear whether the community has any influence. He can only urge both leaders and commoners to act justly and trust in the ultimate power of Zeus' justice. A century later, Solon will refute and transcend some of Hesiod's positions as is seen below.

Early Laws

Many of the laws the Greek *poleis* enact from the mid-seventh century deal with political issues and government, presumably reacting to negative experiences. They become more frequent in the sixth century and are important indicators for the process of formalising institutions and 'institutionalising' the *polis* (Farenga 2006; Gagarin 1986; Gehrke 2000; Hölkeskamp 1994). The earliest extant law, from Dreros on Crete dated about 650, begins with 'this was decided by the polis' (Fornara 1983: 11; Koerner 1993: 90; Meiggs and Lewis 1988: 2; van Effenterre and Ruzé 1994: 81). Decision by *polis* or *demos* recurs in several other laws. Hence, the collectivity of citizens takes action and enacts laws – sometimes in elaborate ways (Effenterre and Ruzé 1994: 41; Fornara 1983: 18; Herodotus [430 BCE] 1972: 4.150–3; Meiggs and Lewis 1988: 5). The Dreros law prohibits repetition within ten years of the chief office of *kosmos*, imposes on the violator a fine and loss of active citizenship, and lists as witnesses the *kosmos*, *damioi* and 'twenty of the polis'. By 650, therefore, this small *polis* had an apparatus of officials and regulated rotation in the chief office. Other laws differentiate between citizens and foreigners, mention a variety of officials, a council of elders, civic subdivisions, public funds and, by 550 on Chios, a 'popular council' with specific responsibilities and powers (Fornara 1983: 19; Koerner 1993: 61; Meiggs and Lewis 1988: 8; van Effenterre and Ruzé 1994: 62). Early lawgivers, sometimes enacting clusters of laws, are attested in several *poleis* (Hölkeskamp 1999). An inscribed collection of laws has survived in Gortyn, while much of Solon's comprehensive legislation is cited by later authors (Willetts 1967).

Early laws thus reflect *poleis* that acted with a communal will and voice, had a differentiated government apparatus which they tried to regulate, and defined their membership and relations with others. Laws were instruments to realise the community's collective will and to change its order and institutions. They presuppose political reflection and an awareness of the potential and consequences of thought and action in the political realm. Laws were inscribed, mostly on stone monuments and thus intended to be visible and last (Gagarin 2008). They were often placed in sanctuaries under divine protection. Perhaps more than instructing a (mostly illiterate) public, such monumentalisation demonstrated respect for the law and made it secure (Eder 2005; Thomas 1996; Whitley 1998). The law also became changeable. Greek law was not static but dynamic. Communities realised that they had control over their law and recognised its significance for communal stability. Accordingly, they expanded, refined and adapted it to changing needs. In contrast to Near Eastern antecedents, Greek legal culture – like Greek culture in general – was developed from the middle of citizen communities (Meier 2011; Raaflaub 2009: 41–8). This facilitated constitutional creativity and reform.

Sparta's 'Great Rhetra': The First *Polis* Constitution

Though later unique, seventh-century Sparta differed much less from other Greek *poleis* than had long been believed (Cartledge 2001: 21–38; Finley 1982: ch. 2). Its famous militarised system with its regimented education and lifestyle evolved in the sixth and fifth centuries to meet specific challenges (Plutarch [75 CE] 1914; Xenophon [380 BCE] 1925). The mid-seventh-century poet Tyrtaeus witnessed some of its causes: a crisis that was probably connected with a revolt of Messenia, a large territory Sparta had conquered earlier (Cartledge 2002; West 1992: 169–84, 1994: 23–7;). In an elegy entitled 'Eunomia', Tyrtaeus summarises a set of political regulations, cited also by Plutarch and referring to the 'Great Rhetra' (Effenterre and Ruzé 1994: 61; Fornara 1983: 12; Plutarch [75 CE] 1914: 6; West 1992: 4). Scholars agree on the essential authenticity of this account's, though not on the details. Plutarch mentions a new sanctuary, new civic subdivisions and a *gerousia* (council of elders) of thirty members, including the two 'kings'; assembly meetings are to be held regularly on the festival day of Apollo at a specified place, 'so as to propose and stand aside. But to the people shall belong the authority to respond and power (*kratos*)' (Plutarch [75 CE] 1914: 6). 'Making proposals' is unproblematic, while 'to stand aside' seems corrupted; perhaps the *demos* were entitled to respond to proposals made by others. *Kratos* is undisputed: power was in the hands of the *demos*. Tyrtaeus' summary of the Rhetra (West 1992: 4.3–10) defines a hierarchy of speaking: first, the 'kings'; second, the other members of the *gerousia*; last, the commoners. The *demos* have the final decision (*nikē*) *and in this sense power (kratos)*.

   The two documents complement each other, suggesting both civic/military and political reform. New civic subdivisions elsewhere reflect organisational adjustments necessitated by the formalisation of hoplite fighting (in a dense formation of heavily armed infantrymen). The reform's communal importance was emphasised by placing it under the protection of Zeus and Athena. The institutions and process of decision making were regulated. The *gerousia* now consisted specifically of thirty men, distinguished by age and experience. The fixed number implies an election; the method was collective shouting (Plutarch [75 CE] 1914: 26). Although the *demos* ultimately decided, the councillors spoke first and introduced proposals. Whether there was open discussion remains unclear. An additional clause gave councillors some kind of veto power (Plutarch [75 CE] 1914: 6.7–8). In addition, there were five ephors. When they were introduced is debated. Elected for one-year terms by the assembly, they somehow represented the *demos* and balanced the power of leaders and *gerousia*.

The Rhetra is the first *polis* constitution known from ancient Greece. The *demos* were the Spartiates, a few thousand full citizens defined by landed property, and the capacity to fight in the hoplite army that proved crucial in defeating the Messenians and controlling this territory with its large slave population (*helots*). This explains the formalisation of the Spartiates' decision-making power and the ensuing evolution of Sparta's peculiar system, based on an elite of citizen-soldiers known as *homoioi or* 'peers' (Cartledge 2001: 68–75). Although impulses for further innovation did not come from this *polis*, known for having few written laws and adhering to tradition, the Rhetra is a singularly important document because, despite all its restrictions, it sealed the *demos*' sovereignty.

Solon of Athens: 'Good Order' and Civic Responsibility

Athens, too, had a problem with dependent labour and internal crisis. Its lawgiver, Solon, left poetry that formulates his ideas and justifies his actions and laws (Ruschenbusch 1966, 2010; West 1992: 139–65, 1994: 74–83). Apparently, widespread social and economic crises and ruthless exploitation of debt resulted in social unrest, and in 594 prompted the Athenians to appoint Solon as chief magistrate and mediator and give him full power to enact necessary reforms (Blok and Lardinois 2006; Murray 1993; Wallace 2007). Such mediators played a crucial role at the time, offering a peaceful alternative to civil strife or tyranny (Wallace 2009). They were connected with the Delphic oracle (famous for advocating moderation); stood above the conflicting parties, thus representing a 'third position'; and as 'sages' they enjoyed far-reaching authority (Meier 1990: 40–52). Importantly, they were appointed by the community and acted on its behalf. Thus, Solon speaks as an Athenian and addresses his fellow citizens, standing between the conflicting parties and preventing either from hurting the other or profiting unjustly (West 1992: 4.1–8, 30; 36.1–2; 5; 36.20–7; 37).

In a programmatic elegy, later also entitled 'Eunomia', Solon establishes the theoretical foundation of his reforms (West 1992: 4). Like Homer and Hesiod, he emphasises that it is not the gods, but humans themselves that are responsible for their fate (Homer [700 BCE] 1965: 1.28–43; West 1992: 4.1–4). The citizens, particularly the elite, driven by greed, commit abuses that cause *stasis* with disastrous consequences for all (West 1992: 5–6, 18–25). Based on empirical observation, Solon constructs an inescapable chain of cause and effect, comparable with the laws of nature (such as thunder following upon lightning), that links socio-political wrongdoing by citizens with harm suffered by the community (West 1992: 9, 4.5–25). Unlike Homer and Hesiod, Solon places such consequences entirely on the socio-political level. In Hesiod's thought, justice is realised by the power of Zeus through whom his daughter, Dike, exacts her revenge (Hesiod [700 BCE] 1978: 256–62). Solon sees Dike as an independent demon of revenge, acting on her own, almost as an abstract principle: justice will prevail – with certainty (West 1992: 4.14–17). The entire city is affected; nobody can escape (West 1992: 26–9). Hesiod's advice, to avoid the public and focus on the private sphere, proves to be ineffective (Hesiod [700 BCE] 1978: 27–30, 299–354).

For the first time, a political process was analysed entirely on the political level. This represented a thrilling breakthrough in political thought (Meier 2011). Hesiod's appeals had been founded on myth, belief and hopes of divine intervention; Solon's proceeded from empirical knowledge, political analysis and theoretical understanding. Knowing the causes of the communal problems, he aimed at eliminating them and thus avoiding the aggravation or recurrence of the problem. The community, afflicted by 'bad order' (*dysnomia*) and 'taught' by the mediator (West 1992: 4.30), was enabled to re-establish 'good order' (*eunomia*) (West 1992: 4.30–9); the aristocracy, equally affected, found it in their own interest to collaborate (Eder 2005). Thus, in Hesiod, Tyrtaeus and Solon, *eunomia* appears as a central communal value: lawgiver and community, confronted with crisis and conflict (*dysnomia*), aimed at restoring *eunomia* and that was the focus of early constitutional thought (Meier 1990: 160). The combination of *eunomia* with 'equality' soon defined the key value characterising Kleisthenes' new constitution: *isonomia* (equal distribution, participation) (Raaflaub 1996).

Dealing with the immediate crisis, Solon cancelled debts and prohibited lending on the security of the borrower's person, thus abolishing debt bondage and guaranteeing the citizens' personal freedom (Raaflaub 2004: 45–53). Solon commented on his legislation: 'I wrote down ordinances for low and high alike, providing straight justice fitted for each man (or case)' (West 1992: 36.18–20). This approximates to the principle of equality before the law, fully expressed later by *isonomia*. His priority was to establish certainty of law, to give all citizens access to justice and to involve the citizens in the jurisdiction: a special assembly served as a court for communally important issues and any person who wished was empowered to take legal action on behalf of an injured third party.

In the political sphere, Solon expanded the division of the citizens into 'classes', which, based on military and economic capacity, determined their political status (Hansen 1999: 29–32). Henceforth, wealth, not birth, would determine political participation and access to political office. This made it more difficult for the aristocracy to monopolise power and introduced more openness into politics. A new council with 400 members, elected annually for one-year terms, was presumably charged with preparing the assembly's agenda (Rhodes 1981: 153–4). If authentic, this council balanced the power of the aristocratic 'Areopagus Council' and enhanced the role of the assembly. Some regulation of the assembly's meetings and procedures is thus likely. Finally, Solon protected the Athenian institutions from subversion, outlawing tyranny and making it mandatory for citizens to take sides in the event of *stasis*. All these measures served three purposes: to stabilise the community by eliminating abuses and establishing a firm system of justice; to balance elite power by creating avenues for political participation by non-elite citizens; and to prevent civil discord with the potential result of tyranny. They are the logical consequence of

Solon's understanding of civic responsibility: if every citizen was to suffer from political abuses, every citizen had to assume responsibility for the common good.

Early Constitutional Developments and Democracy

The juxtaposition, in Sparta's 'Rhetra,' of *demos* and *kratos* reminds us of *dēmokratia*. In both Sparta and Athens the assembly passed final decisions. Some scholars thus date the beginning of democracy in this early period (Hansen 1994: 33; Ruschenbusch 1995). This seems mistaken, especially for Sparta, because many Greeks later looked to Sparta as an ideal of oligarchy and because the assembly was severely constrained by the council's prerogatives (Raaflaub *et al.* 2007: 39–40; Rawson 1969). Although sovereign, the *demos* were far from ruling the *polis*. Although Solon urged his fellow citizens to assume political responsibility, his ideal was not democratic, but rather conservative (Raaflaub *et al.* 2007: 142–4; Wallace 2007). He differentiated political functions according to military and economic capacities, and endorsed the traditional distribution of roles: the aristocracy was to lead; the *demos*, clearly not considered capable of leading, was to follow (West 1992: 5–6). Whether or not active political participation was restricted *de facto* to the propertied classes who were eligible for service in the hoplite army, democracy in any meaningful sense was far beyond Solon's horizon (Raaflaub 2006: 404–23; Rhodes 1981: 140–1).

What matters, though, is that in a severe social crisis a person of exceptional political insight developed a political theory and a programme of reform, 'sold' it to his fellow citizens and, when endowed by them with full power, realised a broad and incisive legislative agenda to fix the problems. Although Solon was unable to prevent the recurrence of factional strife and eventually tyranny, he demonstrated what the individual laws discussed above only suggested: that the community had itself become the object of political action by the citizens. Through legislation enacted in the assembly or by the delegation of power to an elected lawgiver, the citizens were able to change and improve their communal order: they were in control of their community. Overall, Solon's accomplishment was huge: he provided protection to lower-class citizens, guaranteed citizens' rights to personal freedom, established the certainty of law, improved equality before the law, made the political process more transparent and involved the *demos* in communal responsibility. Some of his measures were crucial in setting Athens on a path that led eventually to democracy.

From its emergence in the early archaic period, Greek literature paid attention to politics and institutions and engaged in political reflection that focused, from a strongly communal perspective, on leadership, the role of institutions and justice. Early political laws and 'constitutions', decided upon or authorised by the assembly, concentrated on the same issues. Political reforms enacted by elected lawgivers aimed initially at restoring 'good order' based on justice, equitable distribution and popular participation. Some of the earliest stages of this development, reflected in the epics, have analogies in the ancient Near East. The next steps – formal legislation by communal decision (not royal decree), constitutionalisation (Sparta) and reform based on theoretical analysis (Solon) – lead beyond such analogies. Close comparison of collective forms of government in Greece and the ancient Near East is useful (Fleming

2004; Isakhan and Stockwell 2011; Oswald 2009; Raaflaub 2009). The explanation for the further Greek development lies in the conditions under which society and culture in archaic Greece were formed, and in the specific nature of the Greek *polis* (Hall 2007; Meier 2011; Osborne 1996; Snodgrass 1980; Starr 1977). Features typical of the ancient Near East, such as centralised states, strong and religiously sanctioned monarchies and vassal systems, were unknown in archaic Greece. Although the early *polis* was structurally similar to emerging Near Eastern city-states, it quickly developed in a different direction. Its paramount leader did not stand above the community, let alone 'rule' it. Members of an emerging aristocracy were essentially equal, separated by a relatively small gap from the majority of independent farmers who played an indispensable communal role in army and assembly. The elite's status and privileges were embedded in the community because elite and commoners depended on each other, hence, the *polis* rested on a strong egalitarian foundation (Morris 2000; Raaflaub *et al.* 2007).

The Aegean World developed outside the power sphere of major empires. *Poleis* developed in clusters, balancing each other. Some large *poleis* emerged, but were unable to create even proto-imperial power formations. Lack of external pressure and the limited role of war obviated the need for a strong and cohesive elite. Instead, elite competition was intense and often destructive; it mobilised resistance among the *demos* and often opened the way to tyranny: a weak and transient form of monarchy. In a period of rapid change, the communal element in the *polis* was strengthened at the expense of elite aspirations, as power and political procedures were formalised. Overseas trade and emigration offered opportunities for profit and social mobility, challenging traditional values and aristocratic leadership (Donlan 1999: 35–111). Social and economic crisis and often violent confrontations between elite and non-elite made it necessary to find new ways of resolving conflicts. In a striking move unique to Greece, in such situations many *poleis* turned to mediators and lawgivers. Although endowed with virtually autocratic power, they were appointed by the community and acted on its behalf. Differences among *poleis* encouraged comparison and reflection, and the foundation of new *poleis* abroad, with settlers of different origins, made it necessary to experiment with new institutional solutions that, in turn, influenced developments in the 'old world'. As a result, a sophisticated culture of political thinking emerged that generated remarkably complex and sometimes radical solutions.

Conclusion

Whatever they thought of the power of gods and fate, the Greeks understood early on that ultimately humans themselves were responsible for both their fortunes and misfortunes. As enforcers of justice, too, the gods were needed only as long as no sufficiently powerful human agency existed. Legislation, backed by communal enforcement, and Solon's understanding of justice as an autonomous factor, pushed the gods into the background in both the political and legal spheres – though not in that of popular morality. The citizens assumed control, especially as a community. Hence, the *polis* enacted laws – itself or through appointed lawgivers – not least in the political sphere, and engaged in comprehensive communal reform and rebuilding. Government in Greece was not a suffered reality, but a communal project, the object of political reflection, analysis and action. Homer suggests that the role of the *demos* was potentially powerful early on. Intercommunal wars enhanced the commoners' communal importance. This trend reached a climax in Sparta where extraordinary conditions – an enemy within the *polis'* own boundaries – required constant military preparation and facilitated the early enactment of a constitution that placed communal decisions formally in the hands of the citizens. Elsewhere, elite abuses resulted in *stasis*, which, in the interest of all, including the elite, could be resolved only by enhancing the citizens' communal responsibility, and formalising and adjusting the institutions. As a consequence, the *polis*, placed on a broader foundation, was institutionalised and stabilised.

Institutions and their interplay, and constitutions in a broader sense, even *politeia* as the entire way of life of a *polis*, thus became the focus of political thought and action, even of first attempts at theorisation, and of laws by which such ideas could be realised. Broad efforts in those directions were undertaken by Solon, whose work represents a first highlight in the interactive development of the *polis*: 'the political' and political thought (Cartledge 2009; Meier 1990). The next step, achieved decades later in many *poleis* (Robinson 1997), and culminating in a magnificent edifice of comprehensive and sophisticated structural reform in Kleisthenic Athens, aimed at fully integrating the *polis* and institutionalising the equal participation of the citizens – democracy or, perhaps rather, the last stage before it: 'isonomy'.

Note

1. All dates in this chapter are BCE.

References

Balot, R. K. (2006), *Greek Political Thought*, Malden, MA: Blackwell.
Blok, J. and A. Lardinois (eds) (2006), *Solon of Athens*, Leiden: Brill.
Campbell, D. A. (ed. and trans.) (1982), *Greek Lyric*, vol. I, Cambridge, MA: Harvard University Press.
Cartledge, P. (2001), *Spartan Reflections*, London: Duckworth.
Cartledge, P. (2002), *Sparta and Lakonia*, 2nd edn, London: Routledge.
Cartledge, P. (2009), *Ancient Greek Political Thought in Practice*, Cambridge: Cambridge University Press.
Davies, J. K. (1997), 'The "Origins of the Greek *Polis*": Where Should We be Looking?', in L. G. Mitchell and P. J. Rhodes (eds), *The Development of the* Polis *in Archaic Greece*, London: Routledge, pp. 24–38.
Donlan, W. (1999), *The Aristocratic Ideal and Selected Papers*, Wauconda, IL: Bolchazy-Carducci.
Eder, W. (2005), 'The Political Significance of the Codification of Law in Archaic Societies', in K. Raaflaub (ed.), *Social Struggles in Archaic Rome: New Perspectives on the Conflict of the Orders*, Malden, MA: Blackwell, pp. 239–67.
Effenterre, H. van and F. Ruzé (eds) (1994), *Nomima: Recueil d'inscriptions politiques et juridiques de l'archaïsme grec*, vol. I, Paris: École française de Rome.

Farenga, V. (2006), *Citizen and Self in Ancient Greece: Individuals Performing Justice and the Law*, Cambridge: Cambridge University Press.

Finkelberg, M. (ed.) (2011), *Homer Encyclopedia*, Malden, MA: Wiley-Blackwell.

Finley, M. I. (1982), *Economy and Society in Ancient Greece*, New York: Viking Press.

Fleming, D. (2004), *Democracy's Ancient Ancestors: Mari and Early Collective Governance*, Cambridge: Cambridge University Press.

Fornara, C. W. (ed. and trans.) (1983), *Archaic Times to the End of the Peloponnesian War*, 2nd edn, Cambridge: Cambridge University Press.

Gagarin, M. (1986), *Early Greek Law*, Berkeley, CA: University of California Press.

Gagarin, M. (2008), *Writing Greek Law*, Cambridge: Cambridge University Press.

Gehrke, H.-J. (2000), 'Verschriftung und Verschriftlichung sozialer Normen im archaischen und klassischen Griechenland', in E. Lévy (ed.), *La Codification des lois dans l'antiquité*, Paris: Boccard, pp. 141–59.

Hall, J. M. (2007), *A History of the Archaic Greek World ca. 1200–479* BCE, Malden, MA: Blackwell.

Hammer, D. (2002), *The* Iliad *as Politics: The Performance of Political Thought*, Norman, OK: University of Oklahoma Press.

Hansen, M. H. (ed.) (1993), *The Ancient Greek City-State*, Copenhagen: Royal Danish Academy of Sciences and Letters.

Hansen, M. H. (1994), 'The 2500th Anniversary of Cleisthenes' Reforms and the Tradition of Athenian Democracy', in R. Osborne and S. Hornblower (eds), *Ritual, Finance, Politics*, Oxford: Clarendon Press, pp. 25–37.

Hansen, M. H. (1999), *The Athenian Democracy in the Age of Demosthenes*, Norman, OK: University of Oklahoma Press.

Herodotus ([430 BCE] 1972), *The Histories*, Penguin: Harmondsworth.

Hesiod ([700 BCE] 1978), *Works & Days*, trans. M. L. West, Oxford: Oxford University Press.

Hölkeskamp, K.-J. (1994), 'Tempel, Agora und Alphabet. Die Entstehungsbedingungen von Gesetzgebung in der archaischen Polis', in H.-J. Gehrke (ed.), *Rechtskodifizierung und soziale Normen im interkulturellen Vergleich*, Tübingen: Narr, pp. 135–64.

Hölkeskamp, K.-J. (1999), *Schiedsrichter, Gesetzgeber und Gesetzgebung im archaischen Griechenland*, Stuttgart: Steiner.

Homer ([700 BCE] 1950), *The Iliad*, trans. E. V. Rieu, London: Penguin.

Homer ([700 BCE] 1965), *The Odyssey*, trans. R. Lattimore, New York: HarperCollins.

Isakhan, B. and S. Stockwell (eds) (2011), *The Secret History of Democracy*, London: Palgrave Macmillan.

Koerner, R. (1993), *Inschriftliche Gesetzestexte der frühen griechischen Polis*, ed. K. Hallof, Cologne: Böhlau.

Meier, C. (1990), *The Greek Discovery of Politics*, trans. D. McLintock, Cambridge, MA: Harvard University Press.

Meier, C. (2011), *A Culture Born in Freedom: Ancient Greece and the Origins of Europe*, Oxford: Oxford University Press.

Meiggs, R. and D. Lewis (eds) (1988), *A Selection of Greek Historical Inscriptions to the End of the Fifth Century b.c.*, rev. edn, Oxford: Clarendon Press.

Morris, I. (2000), *Archaeology as Cultural History*, Malden, MA: Blackwell.

Murray, O. (1993), *Early Greece*, 2nd edn, Cambridge, MA: Harvard University Press.

Osborne, R. (1996), *Greece in the Making, 1200–479 bc*, London: Routledge.

Oswald, W. (2009), *Staatstheorie im Alten Israel. Der politische Diskurs im Pentateuch und in den Geschichtsbüchern des Alten Testaments*, Stuttgart: Kohlhammer.

Plutarch ([75 ce] 1914), *Lives: Theseus and Romulus. Lycurgus and Numa. Solon and Publicola*, trans. B. Perrin, Cambridge: Loeb Classical Library.

Raaflaub, K. A. (1993), 'Homer to Solon: The Rise of the *Polis*. The Written Sources', in M. H. Hansen (ed.), *The Ancient Greek City-State*, Copenhagen: Royal Danish Academy of Sciences and Letters, pp. 41–105.

Raaflaub, K. A. (1996), 'Equalities and Inequalities in Athenian Democracy', in J. Ober and C. Hedrick (eds.), *Demokratia: A Conversation on Democracies, Ancient and Modern*, Princeton, NJ: Princeton University Press, pp. 129–74.

Raaflaub, K. A. (1997), 'Politics and Interstate Relations among Early Greek *Poleis*: Homer and Beyond', *Antichthon*, 31, 1–27.

Raaflaub, K. A. (2000), 'Poets, Lawgivers, and the Beginnings of Political Reflection in Archaic Greece', in C. Rowe and M. Schofield (eds), *The Cambridge History of Greek and Roman Political Thought*, Cambridge: Cambridge University Press, pp. 23–59.

Raaflaub, K. A. (2004), *The Discovery of Freedom in Ancient Greece*, Chicago, IL: University of Chicago Press.

Raaflaub, K. A. (2006), 'Athenian and Spartan *eunomia*, or: What to Do with Solon's Timocracy?', in J. Blok and A. Lardinois (eds), *Solon of Athens*, Leiden: Brill, pp. 390–428.

Raaflaub, K. A. (2008), 'Homeric Warriors and Battles: Trying to Resolve Old Problems', *Classical World*, 101, 469–83.

Raaflaub, K. A. (2009), 'Early Greek Political Thought in its Mediterranean Context', in R. Balot (ed.), *A Companion to Greek and Roman Political Thought*, Malden, MA: Wiley-Blackwell, pp. 37–56.

Raaflaub, K. A., J. Ober and R. W. Wallace (eds) (2007), *Origins of Democracy in Ancient Greece*, Berkeley, CA: University of California Press.

Rawson, E. (1969), *The Spartan Tradition in European Thought*, Oxford: Clarendon Press.

Rhodes, P. J. (1981), *A Commentary on the Aristotelian Athenaion Politeia*, Oxford: Clarendon Press.

Robinson, E. W. (1997), *The First Democracies: Early Popular Government Outside Athens*, Stuttgart: Steiner.

Ruschenbusch, E. (1966), *Solônos nomoi. Die Fragmente des solonischen Gesetzeswerkes mit einer Text- und Überlieferungsgeschichte*, Wiesbaden: Steiner.

Ruschenbusch, E. (1995), 'Zur Verfassungsgeschichte Griechenlands', in K. Kinzl (ed.), *Demokratia. Der Weg zur Demokratie bei den Griechen*, Darmstadt: Wissenschaftliche Buchgesellschaft, pp. 432–45.

Ruschenbusch, E. (2010), *Solon: Das Gesetzeswerk – Fragmente. Übersetzung und Kommentar*, Stuttgart: Steiner.

Snodgrass, A. (1980), *Archaic Greece: The Age of Experiment*, Berkeley, CA: University of California Press.

Starr, C. G. (1977), *The Economic and Social Growth of Early Greece, 800–500 B.C.*, New York: Oxford University Press.

Thomas, R. (1996), 'Written in Stone? Liberty, Equality, Orality, and the Codification of Law', in L. Foxhall and A. D. E. Lewis (eds), *Greek Law in its Political Setting: Justifications not Justice*, Oxford: Clarendon Press, pp. 9–31.

Thucydides ([400 BCE] 1972), *History of the Peloponnesian War*, trans. R. Warner, Harmondsworth: Penguin.

Wallace, R. W. (2007), 'Revolutions and a New Order in Solonian Athens and Archaic Greece', in K. A. Raaflaub, J. Ober and R. W. Wallace (eds), *Origins of Democracy in Ancient Greece*, Berkeley, CA: University of California Press, pp. 49–82.

Wallace, R. W. (2009), 'Charismatic Leaders', in K. A. Raaflaub and H. van Wees (eds), *A Companion to Archaic Greece*, Malden, MA: Wiley-Blackwell, pp. 411–26.

West, M. L. (ed.) (1992), *Iambi et Elegi Graeci ante Alexandrum Cantati*, vol. II, 2nd edn, Oxford: Clarendon Press.

West, M. L. (trans.) (1994), *Greek Lyric Poetry*, Oxford: Oxford University Press.

Whitley, J. (1998), 'Literacy and Law-Making: The Case of Archaic Crete', in N. Fisher and H. van Wees (eds), *Archaic Greece: New Approaches and New Evidence*, London: Duckworth, pp. 311–31.

Willetts, R. F. (ed.) (1967), *The Law Code of Gortyn*, Berlin: Gruyter.

Xenophon ([380 BCE] 1925), *Constitution of the Lacedaimonians*, trans. E. C. Marchant and G. W. Bowersock, Cambridge, MA: Harvard University Press.

Chapter 7

Athens

David J. Phillips

The term *dēmokratia* most probably dates back to 508/7[1] (Ehrenberg 1950; Hansen 1986, 1991: 69–71; Sealey 1973). At that time in the Athenian *polis* (city-state), the aristocratic Kleisthenes 'took the people (*demos*) into his faction' (Aristotle [332 BCE] 1984: 20.1; Herodotus [430 BCE] 1972: 5.66.2). He did so in order to gain the upper hand in his struggle for political power with the aristocratic and Spartan-backed Isagoras who had been elected as the eponymous *archon* for 508/7. These two men contested power in the aftermath of the tyranny of the Peisistratids (545–511/10), which had curbed the opportunities for aristocrats to seek honour through political leadership. After the expulsion of the last tyrant, Hippias, contests for leadership resumed in what was still an aristocratic *polis*. However, one of the consequences of the tyranny was the consolidation and growth of the *demos*, especially those living in and near the city (*asty*). Kleisthenes turned to this element of the population, promising to lead the Athenian *polis* to a constitution (*politeia*) in which ultimate authority rested with the *demos*. It would be *dēmokratia* – the rule of the people or as Thucydides defines it: 'Our constitution is called a democracy [*dēmokratia*] because power is the hands not of a minority but of the whole people' (Thucydides [400 BCE] 1972: 2.37.1).

But how do we know these particular details? The study of the Athenian democracy dates back to classical antiquity and the fifth and the fourth centuries during which democracy in one form or another prevailed in Athens. Our earliest source is Herodotus and his *Histories* which were written during the middle decades of the fifth century (Herodotus [430 BCE] 1972). He was primarily concerned with the wars between the Greeks and the Persians, but made numerous digressions, particularly on matters Athenian. Other ancient sources include historians such as Thucydides and Xenophon, playwrights such as Aeschylus, Euripides and Aristophanes, some mainly fourth-century Athenian orators and inscriptions (Aeschylus [463 BCE] 1930; Aristophanes [422 BCE] 1998; Euripides [423 BCE] 1995; Marr and Rhodes 2008; Ober 1989; Rhodes and Osborne 2003; Thucydides [400 BCE] 1972). Then, in the late nineteenth century, the British Museum acquired four papyrus rolls, which contained a near continuous text of *Athenaion Politeia*, the lost history of the Athenian Constitution (Aristotle [332 BCE] 1984; Fritz and Kapp 1950; Moore 1975; Rhodes 1981). Previously known from over 200 quotations in other works and from two small leaves of a papyrus codex, this history of the Athenian constitution was attributed to Aristotle and may be one of a collection of 158 histories of *polis* constitutions which supposedly formed the research for Aristotle's *Politics*. Several opening chapters dealing with the period of the Athenian kings and the early aristocratic Athenian *polis* are lost and some of the concluding chapters on the law courts (*dikasteria*) are damaged. Chapters 1–40 cover the history of the Athenian constitution and the emergence of democracy from the seventh century to the end of the fifth century. Chapter 41 summarises the changes in the constitution from its early 'tribal' days and monarchy to the restoration of the democracy in 403 after a nine-month period of extreme and violent oligarchy which had been established, with Spartan backing, following the defeat of Athens and her allies in the Peloponnesian War (Krentz 1982: 131–52). Chapters 42–69 give a detailed account of the workings of the Athenian democracy as it was in the 330s and 320s – the last two decades of fully functioning Athenian direct participatory democracy.

Modern Scholarship on Athenian Democracy

Significant modern scholarship on Athenian democracy begins with Charles Hignett, who adopts a very sceptical approach to the sources and provides a legalistic constitutional study of sixth- and fifth-century Athens devoid of political or social context (Hignett 1952). Arnold Jones addresses some of these omissions by examining the economic basis of the Athenian democracy, its social and political contexts, its ideology, its critics and its day-to-day operations (Jones 1957). In 1962, Moses Finley published a seminal paper on the Athenian demagogues in which he demonstrated that the *demagogoi* (leaders of the *demos*/people) were an essential factor in the functioning of the democracy (Finley 1962). *Demagogos* was a descriptive and neutral term that assumed pejorative overtones only when used by critics of democracy (Connor 1971; Ober 1989). A brief and sometimes overlooked study by William Forrest traced the emergence of democracy in Greece, and particularly Athens, in its broad socio-political and historical context (Forrest 1966). Inevitably, because the abundance of the evidence is for Athens, the history of Greek democracy tends to be the history of Athenian democracy, although evidence of democracies elsewhere in Greece grows (Brock 2009; Brock and Hodkinson 2000; Carlsson 2010; Hansen and Nielsen 2004; O'Neil 1995; Robinson 1997, 2011; Rutter 2000).

   In the mid-1970s, the Danish scholar Mögens Hansen began an extensive series of studies that culminated in 1991 with publication of *The Athenian Democracy in the Age of Demosthenes* (Hansen 1991). A second edition in 1999 includes an invaluable additional chapter: 'One Hundred and Sixty Theses about Athenian Democracy'. Hansen's study is definitive and the starting point for any study of Athenian democracy. Important further studies include monographs by Josiah Ober exploring political leadership and the relationship between the masses and the elite, drawing upon the evidence of the mainly fourth-century orators with a catalogue of extant speeches (Ober 1989). He also gives the most comprehensive account of the classical critics of Athenian democracy, pointing to the origins of Western political thought in the opposition to the ideology of Athenian democracy, and his latest book analyses Athenian political practice – what he calls democratic knowledge management – and demonstrates why Athens worked as a direct, participatory democracy (Ober 1998, 2008).

Three different accounts of how, when and why democracy began to emerge at Athens have been published together, reflecting the vital debate in this important area (Raaflaub et al. 2007). Robert Wallace focuses on the beginning of the sixth century when the crisis in the aristocratic *polis* resulted in the reforms of Solon (Aristotle [332 BCE] 1984: 5–12). This was the first of 'three rupture moments' identified by Kurt Raaflaub in his introduction. Ober focuses on the revolutionary actions of the *demos* and the reforms of Kleisthenes in 508/7 (Aristotle [332 BCE] 1984: 20.3; Ober 1993). Raaflaub develops his earlier work to view events after the Persian Wars, and specific changes to the constitution in 462/1 attributed to Ephialtes and his young supporter Pericles, as marking the final emergence of the radical, naval-based democracy of the later fifth and fourth centuries (Aristotle [332 BCE] 1984: 25; Morris and Raaflaub 1998). Since the mid-1980s the Cambridge scholar Robin Osborne has carried on Jones's tradition of exploring the contexts of Athenian democracy, including the religious and secular rituals which underpin it (Osborne 2010). In a similar vein are studies on democracy, empire and the arts, and on warfare and democracy (Boedeker and Raaflaub 1998; Pritchard 2010).

Beginning with Finley, there is a tradition in scholarship on Athenian democracy that seeks to contribute to debates about the nature and future of modern democracy (Finley 1985). These discussions have been particularly vigorous in the United States, with some scholars advocating the utility of studies of Athenian democracy for modern democracy, while others call for caution in the deployment of Athens in discussions of democracy in the United States, a representative republic with a democratic ideology and not a democracy *per se* (Ober and Hedrick 1996; Samons 2004). The two extremes reflect divergent modern ideologies, liberal and neo-conservative, with the latter following the anti-democratic tradition from Socrates, Plato and Aristotle through to the Republican fathers of the United States and beyond (Roberts 1994).

Direct Participatory Democracy at Athens

The Greek *polis* was characterised by its small size and by a town centre connected to its hinterland, which together constituted the *polis*-state. In terms of size and complexity, Athens was not a typical *polis* (Cohen 2000). Its territory covered the entire Attic peninsular, some 2,500 km^2, and its population peaked in 431 at around 300,000, of which about 60,000 were adult male citizens. However, following the losses of the Peloponnesian War (431–404) this number dropped to 25,000–30,000 citizens in a total population of about 250,000 (Hansen and Nielsen 2004: 627). The majority of the population were non-citizens: that is, women, children, foreign residents (*metics*) and slaves. A more typical *polis* was smaller with less than 100 km^2 and fewer than 1,000 adult males (Hansen 1991: 55–8).

The exclusions from citizenship which lead to negative judgements of Athenian democracy need to be seen in historical perspective. Democracy in the early United States co-existed with slavery. Nowhere, until the late nineteenth century, were women given the right to vote, and modern states do not grant citizenship rights to aliens unless they are naturalised (Kagan 2009: 98). It is the inclusions within Athenian, and Greek, democracy that are significant. The usual constitutions of Greek *poleis* were aristocratic or oligarchic: full participation and political power rested with a few based on birth (the *gennaioi*, the *aristoi*) or wealth (the *plousioi*, the *oligoi*). Democracy gave full political rights to the many (the *plethoi*, the *demos*) who were native to the land.

In 508/7, three years after the overthrow of the Peisistratid tyranny and the expulsion of Spartan-backed Isagoras and his supporters, Kleisthenes was recalled by the *demos* to lay the foundations of democracy by creating ten new tribes (Aristotle [332 BCE] 1984: 20–1; Herodotus [430 BCE] 1972: 5.69). While some see a popular uprising of the *demos* (Ober 1993), others view events more cynically and argue that Kleisthenes used the opportunity to manipulate the tribal reorganisation to advantage himself and his Alkmeonid *genos* or family (Bicknell 1972; Stanton 1984). All agree, however, that what Kleisthenes established with his tribal reorganisation was a democracy that embodied the principle of *isonomia*, that is, equality before the law (Ostwald 1986: 27). Apart from wanting to prevail over Isagoras, Kleisthenes' motives are not mentioned in any extant source. After the passage of his reforms through the assembly, he disappears from history. From the outset, the new system of popular government where the assembly of citizens (*ekklesia*) was sovereign was called *isonomia* as well as *dēmokratia* (Herodotus [430 BCE] 1972: 3.80.6, 6.131.1). The tribes formed the basis of the political and military organisation of the Athenian *polis*. Each tribe was composed of *demes* (villages and city districts), of which there were 139 (Bicknell 1972). Member-ship of a *deme* made one a citizen (Aristotle [332 BCE] 1984: 42.1–2). The *demes* were assigned by lot to a tribe with a selection from Attica's three regions – city, shore and inland – so the tribes were composed of a mix of citizens (Aristotle [332 BCE] 1984: 21.4). Each tribe supplied equal numbers to the council (*boule*) of 500 and the board of ten generals (*strategoi*), who were not only military leaders but also, by the 480s, political leaders. Kleisthenes also introduced the law of ostracism which allowed a leading Athenian politician to be banished for ten years, but without loss of citizenship or confiscation of property (Aristotle [332 BCE] 1984: 22.1; Phillips 1982). Ostensibly designed to prevent tyranny, it was used on at least nine occasions during the fifth century and possibly more (Aristotle [332 BCE] 1984: 22.3). A vote on ostracism (*ostrakophoria*) could be called only once a year and, although it remained on the statutes, it was not used during the fourth century (Aristotle [332 BCE] 1984: 43.5).

With adjustments over time, such as the appointment of the nine chief magistrates (*archons*) by lot rather than by popular vote, Athenian democracy may have remained essentially the same as it was at the beginning of the fifth century (Aristotle [332 BCE] 1984: 22.5; 487/6). But events, not necessarily of the Athenians own choosing, unfolded so that Athens became a naval power and the citizen rowers in the fleet became a significant voice in the assembly. Persia, the most powerful empire in the east, expanded westward in the 540s and gained control over Greek *poleis* in Asia Minor, the eastern Aegean and parts of northern Greece. In the 490s, during the reign of King Darius I (521–486), the Persians launched a large-scale invasion that saw the capture of *poleis* in Euboea and the Cycladic Islands. Aegina in the Saronic Gulf, almost within sight of Athens, had already gone over to the Persians. Athens' exiled tyrants, the Peistratidai, were with the Persians seeking to be installed once more (Herodotus [430 BCE] 1972: 6.94.1, 102, 107.1, 109.5). Against all odds the Athenians, with their neighbour, Plataia, defeated the Persians at Marathon on the east coast of Attica (Herodotus [430 BCE] 1972: 6.102–3). Because of their religious scruples the Spartans, the strongest force in the Greek world, did not join the Athenians at Marathon. The standing of the Athenians in the eyes of both themselves and other Greeks was greatly enhanced.

At the end of the 480s, after five ostracisms saw leaders exiled for supposed tyrannical or Persian sympathies, Athens was once again facing a massive Persian invasion by land and sea led by King Xerxes (Aristotle [332 bc] 1984: 22.5–7). This time, however, Athens was joined by Sparta and many other *poleis*, and she was prepared with a new navy of 200 triremes. The fleet was built with the income from silver mined in southern Attica (Aristotle [332 BCE] 1984: 22.7; Herodotus [430 BCE] 1972: 7.144.1). The Athenian general Themistokles, who had proposed the building of the ships, was able to deploy them at Salamis for a major victory against the Persian fleet in September 480. Believing the power of the Persians to be unstoppable, the Delphic oracle advised the Athenians to abandon Hellas (Herodotus [430 BCE] 1972: 7.139.6–140). However, in 479 the Greeks were victorious at Plataia and Mycale (Herodotus [430 BCE] 1972: 9.28–73, 96–105). The Persian defeat saw the creation in 478 of a defensive naval alliance, the Delian League, headed by Athens. Its aim was to prevent incursions of Persian forces into Greece, the Aegean and the *poleis* on the shores of Asia Minor. Athens had become a naval power and in due course, as a democracy, it headed an empire. The fleet became what has termed 'the trireme school of democracy' (Strauss 1996).

The 470s and 460s saw a consolidation of Athenian power abroad and an increased significance for the poorer (*thetic*) citizen rowers in the assembly. The *thetes* were the lowest property class and constituted about 60 per cent of the citizenry. It was a period when political leaders manoeuvred to win their support. The Areopagus, the tradi- tional council composed mostly of former *archons*, was pitted against generals who attacked its members and its powers (Aristotle [332 BCE] 1984: 23.1, 25.1). Matters came to a head in 462/1 when Ephialtes sponsored political reforms through the assembly which stripped the Areopagus of most of its powers and assigned them to the *boule* of 500, the assembly and the courts (Aristotle [332 BCE] 1984: 25.2–3). The Areopagus remained as a homicide court. The details of these changes are lost, but can be inferred from the subsequent powers of these institutions (Ostwald 1986: 47–83; Raaflaub *et al.* 2007: 105–54). At last Athens' radical democracy was in place.

Changes did take place; Athenian democracy was not static (Rhodes 1979/80). The late 450s saw the introduction of two significant new laws. First, Perikles confined citizenship to individuals where both parents were citizens and not just the father as had previously applied and, secondly, he introduced pay (*misthos*) for jurors (*dikastai*) (Aristotle [332 BCE] 1984: 26.1, 42.1, 27.3, 4). There were also changes after two brutal episodes of oligarchy (the 400 in 411 and the Thirty in 404/3) and after Athens was finally defeated by Sparta in the Peloponnesian War (431–404). After the restoration of the democracy in 410 and again in 403, commissions were set up to revise the laws and that produced the last stages in the passage from popular sovereignty to sovereignty of the law (Ostwald 1986; Sealey 1975). Mogens Herman Hansen too sees sovereignty within the democracy as finally residing in the law courts (Hansen 1991: 299–303).

While decrees (*psephismata*) were always decided by the assembly, after 403 voting on laws (*nomoi*) was handed to a panel appointed by lot from the annual pool of 6,000 *dikastai* (Jurors), which itself was appointed by sortition from the full citizenry. In 403/2 pay for attendance at the assembly was introduced (Aristotle [332 BCE] 1984: 41.3). Initially paid at a rate of 1 obol per meeting, it was increased in the late 390s to 3 obols (half a drachma), about one day's wages for an unskilled labourer or rower in the fleet (Phillips 1981: 30–1, 45–6).

Participatory Institutions and Practice

A number of scholars have investigated the workings of Athenian democracy with particular attention to participation and political leadership (Hansen 1991; Jones 1957: 99–133; Phillips 1981; Sinclair 1988). Aristotle's contemporaneous account begins with citizenship and then turns to magistracies (*archai*), who were mostly appointed by lot for one year while all military officers and some treasurers were appointed by show of hands (Aristotle [332 BCE] 1984: 42, 44.4, 61.1–7). The *Athenaion Politeia* then turns to the *boule* of 500, which oversaw the day-to-day operations of the democracy and was appointed by lot from the ten tribes, each tribe selecting fifty councillors over thirty years of age who also served together as *prytaneis*, members of the executive board for one-tenth of the year, a prytany. It appointed, also by lot, the *epistates ton prytaneion* who served as the 'president' of the Athenian *polis* for twenty-four hours (Aristotle [332 BCE] 1984: 44.1–3). In the fourth century, the 450 councillors who were not in prytany also selected by lot the *proedroi*, whose job it was to preside over meetings of the *boule* and the assembly. The *boule* drafted the agendas for meetings of the assembly, in the fourth century, four each prytany or forty each year (Aristotle [332 BCE] 1984: 43). The *boule* received ambassadors and was addressed by the generals. It attended to the commission and care of naval triremes and the welfare of the horses used by the cavalry (Aristotle [332 BCE] 1984: 46.1, 49.1). The *boule* also supervised magistrates, who served as members of boards of ten or multiples of ten so each tribe was represented (Aristotle [332 BCE] 1984: 46–9). The chief *archai* were the ten generals and the nine *archons* (Aristotle [332 BCE] 1984: 55–9, 61.1–2). With the exception of the generals and other military offices, a magistrate could only serve for one year in each office. *Bouleutai* could only serve twice, but never consecutively. According to *Athenaion Politeia* there were approximately seven hundred *archai* in the mid-fifth century (Aristotle [332 BCE] 1984: 24.3). There were also Athenian *archai* located in the *poleis* of the Athenian allies in the Delian League. Magistrates' duties ranged from *poletai*, who granted public contracts to *hodopoioi* (commissioners for roads), and *sitophylakes* (grain guards), who provided consumer protection (Aristotle [332 BCE] 1984: 47.2–5, 51.3). *Archai*, such as the *archon basileus* (the 'king' *archon*), and boards of *hieropoioi* ('makers of sacrifices') had major roles to play in the *polis* cult (Aristotle [332 BCE] 1984: 57). *Archai* also administered legal proceedings in the law courts (Aristotle [332 BCE] 1984: 63–9).

The assembly was open to any Athenian citizen to attend and, if so inclined, to address. It deliberated on all matters to do with foreign policy, declared wars, approved peace treaties, sent out ambassadors and received foreign ambassadors. It also ensured that the gods were honoured by the *polis* through the proper administration of ritual and cult. Many of its enactments were *leges sacrae*, that is, sacred laws. Religion and the *polis* were inextricably intertwined (Parker 1996, 2005). Epigraphically attested laws and decrees from the fourth century demonstrate a considerable attention to detail, division of responsibilities and the accountability of those administering laws and decrees (Rhodes and Osborne 2003). There was no aspect of *polis* life, secular or religious, that assembly, council or *archai* did not supervise. The Athenian democracy had built in checks and balances. Each magistrate, councillor or anyone who spoke in the assembly was held to account. Magistrates underwent an examination of their suitability (*dokimasia*) before assuming office and a scrutiny (*euthynai*) at the end of their term (Aristotle [332 BCE] 1984: 55.3, 48.3–5). Many misdeeds attracted fines. Generals were subject to scrutiny every prytany and could be impeached (*eisangelia*) (Aristotle [332 BCE] 1984: 61.2). Magistrates and citizens were subject to legal procedures, including the *graphe paranomon* where it could be alleged that a proposed new law or decree contravened an existing law (Phillips 1981: 31–2; Roberts 1982)

The people's courts (*dikasteria*) implemented and upheld the laws which were a cornerstone of the Athenian democracy (MacDowell 1978; Todd 1993). The courts were constituted from an annual panel of 6,000 *dikastai* (Jurors) who had been appointed by lot (Hansen 1991: 225–45). A complex ballot procedure assigned *dikastai* to juries and to specific courts (Aristotle [332 BCE] 1984: 63–9). Trials were presided over by an *archon* whose role was entirely administrative. He could not advise the court. Both plaintiff and defendant were given equal amounts of speaking time and large numbers of jurors (201, 401, 501 or more especially for political prosecutions) tried the case. Having heard the arguments the *dikastai* participated in a secret vote. A simple majority decided the case. Not every Athenian participated fully in the political life his *polis*. There were many factors influencing participation: ambition, wealth, leisure, education, military training and distance from the political centre (Phillips 1981; Sinclair 1988). Thucydides claims that in 411 'as many as 5,000 Athenians had never yet assembled' (Thucydides [400 BCE] 1972: 8.72.1). In the fourth century there was a quorum of 6,000 for the chief meeting of the assembly (*kuria ekklesia*) in each prytany. Six thousand was also the quorum required for ostracism to be effective. Probably most citizens attended some meetings of the assembly and served a term on the *boule*. Political leadership of the people (*prostasia tou demou*), *demagogia* or acting as a *rhetor kai strategos* (orator and general) was largely confined to the elite, although the nexus between aristocratic birth and political leadership began to break down by the last third of the fifth century.

Participatory Democracy and Ideology

The ideology of democracy was forged out of political practice and in response to contemporaneous critics. No single text survives with an account of Athenian democratic ideology. It needs to be inferred from the works of its critics such as Thucydides, Socrates, Plato, Aristotle and *The Old Oligarch* (Marr and Rhodes 2008). It can also be pieced together from favourable treatment in tragedies, such as the different versions of *The Suppliant Woman* (Aeschylus [463 BCE] 1930: 365–9, 397–9,

600–8, 946–9; Euripides [423 BCE] 1995: 399–441). Comedies such as Aristophanes' *Wasps* can also be helpful, as can funeral orations (*epitaphioi*) such as that given by Pericles during the Peloponnesian War (Aristophanes [422 BCE] 1998; Loraux 1986: 172–220; Thucydides [400 BCE] 1972: 2.35–46).

While Herodotus' 'debate on constitutions' was set in 521, it reflects the period 440–420 when Herodotus wrote (Connor 1971: 199–206). Otanes promotes democracy:

> The rule of the majority . . . not only has the most beautiful and powerful name of all, equality (*isonomia*), but in practice, the majority does not act at all like a monarch. Indeed, the majority chooses its magistrates by lot, it holds all of these officials accountable to an audit, and refers all resolutions to the authority of the public (*plethos* 'the many'). (Herodotus [430 BCE] 1972: 3.80–3)

Excellent discussions of Athenian democratic ideology are to be found in a number of works (Balot 2006; Farrar 1988; Ober 1998; Raaflaub 1989). Key democratic concepts include the sovereign assembly of citizens (*ekklesia*), equal legal rights (*isonomia*), equal right to speak (*isegoria*), individual freedom (*eleutheria*), freedom of speech (*parrhesia*), the power of the law, justice, accountability of magistrates, rotation of magistracies, sortition (drawing of lots) and the payment of citizens for some public services (Loraux 1986: 181; Ostwald 1969; Raaflaub 2004: 203–49). Democracy was cast as the antithesis of tyranny from early Athenian democracy when it dealt with the twin issues of Persian invasion and the return of the Peisistratid tyrants (Herodotus [430 BCE] 1972: 6.109.3–6).

Oligarchic criticisms of democracy are summarised in the pamphlet from around 420 known as *The Old Oligarch* attributed to pseudo-Xenophon (Marr and Rhodes 2008; Moore 1975). This brief work offers an elite, oligarchic discourse on democracy in Athens. The work uses negative designations to effect: *poneroi* (base men); *penetai* (the poor); *demotikos* (sympathetic to the common people); *amathes* (ignorant); *kakiston* (worst elements); and *kakoi* (bad, vile). In contrast the elite are called: *aristoi* (best men); *gennaioi* (noble); *kaloi k'agathoi* (beautiful/fair and good); *chrestoi* (good men); *eupatridae* (well born); *gnorimoi* (notable, wealthy); *dexiotatoi* (cleverest); and *dunatotatoi* (capable). Such men characterised themselves as having *arête* (virtue) and being *sophos* (wise). Their oligarchic polity was noted for its *eunomia* (good order), a term which oligarchic Sparta used to describe its constitution. By contrast, democracy was characterised by *dusnomia* (lawlessness), the result of a bad constitution. Thus, oligarchy was praised as the antithesis of democracy: 'the safe and sound government of the best men' (Thucydides [400 BCE] 1972: 3.82.8). Democracy, by contrast, provided equality for the masses (*to plethos*) and was thus morally base. From the eighteenth-century Enlightenment, whenever democracy has been debated, critics have turned to the negative, oligarchic characterisation of democracy as an unruly, lawless and destructive mob to undermine democracy as a preferred form of government. The Founding Fathers of the United States of America, for example, turned to a representative and collegial constitution that drew structurally more from the Roman Republic than it did from the direct participatory model of the Athenian democracy (Roberts 1994; Wood 1988).

Conclusion

Flawed it may have been, but the democracy created and maintained at Athens in the fifth and fourth centuries was, in the words of Donald Kagan, a unique 'flowering in the jungle of human experience' (Kagan 1991: 3). One of the benefits of democracy often overlooked by oligarchs is the way it promoted unity by limiting distinctions between wealthy and poor in Greece: 'Democracy played a vital part in the class struggle by mitigating the exploitation of poorer citizens by richer ones' (Ste. Croix 1981: 284). Traditionally, Athenian democracy was said to have lasted for less than two centuries (507/8–322), but it has been argued recently that their defeat in the Lamian War in 322 did not see the end of democracy at Athens and that it was restored on a number of occasions, most notably in 307, down to the end of the Chremonidean War in 262 (Bayliss 2011).

In that time Athenian democracy coined the term *dēmokratia*, worked out a practical set of institutions and procedures to allow for popular rule and direct, rather than representative, democracy, and articulated the ideology of such popular rule. The ideals of Athenian democracy and modern Western democracy remain in many ways similar, though citizenship is now more inclusive, direct participation has been replaced by representation and greater emphasis is placed on human rights. It is unlikely that debates about whether or not studies of Athenian democracy can inform and invigorate discussions about democracy in the twenty-first century will cease. Athenian democracy is still a useful tool with which to think about democracy today.

Note

1. All dates in this chapter are BCE.

References

Aeschylus ([463 BCE] 1930), *The Suppliant Women*, trans. G. Murray, London: George Allen & Unwin.

Aristophanes ([422 BCE] 1998), *The Clouds, Wasps, Birds*, trans. P. Meineck, Indianapolis, IN: Hackett.

Aristotle ([332 BCE] 1984), *The Athenian Constitution*, trans. P. J. Rhodes, Harmondswoth: Penguin.

Balot, R. (2006), *Greek Political Thought*, Oxford: Blackwell.

Bayliss, A. J. (2011), *After Demosthenes: The Politics of Early Hellenistic Athens*, London: Continuum.

Bicknell, P. J. (1972), 'Kleisthenes as a Politician: An Exploration', *Studies in Athenian Politics and Genealogy*, Historia Einzelschriften 19, Weisbaden: Steiner, pp. 1–53.

Boedeker, D. and K. Raaflaub (eds) (1998), *Democracy, Empire, and the Arts in Fifth-Century Athens*, Cambridge, MA: Harvard University Press.

Brock, R. (2009), 'Did the Athenian Empire Promote Democracy?', in J. Ma, J. Papazaradas and R. Parker (eds), *Interpreting the Athenian Empire*, London: Duckworth, pp. 149–66.

Brock, R. and S. Hodkinson (eds) (2000), *Alternatives to Athens: Varieties of Organization and Community in Ancient Greece*, Oxford: Oxford University Press.

Carlsson, S. (2010), *Hellenistic Democracies: Freedom, Independence and Political Procedure in some East Greek City-States*, Historia Einzelschriften 206, Stuttgart: Steiner.

Cohen, E. E. (2000), *The Athenian Nation*, Princeton, NJ: Princeton University Press.

Connor, W. R. (1971), *The New Politicians of Fifth Century Athens*, Princeton, NJ: Princeton University Press.

Ehrenberg, V. (1950), 'The Origins of Democracy', *Historia*, 1, 515–48.

Euripides ([423 BCE] 1995), *Suppliant Women*, trans. R. Warren and S. Scully, Oxford: Oxford University Press.

Farrar, C. (1988), *The Origins of Democratic Thinking: The Invention of Politics in Classical Athens*, Cambridge: Cambridge University Press.

Finley, M. I. (1962), 'Athenian Demagogues', *Past and Present*, 21, 3–24.

Finley, M. I. (1985), *Democracy Ancient and Modern*, 2nd edn, London: Hogarth Press.

Forrest, W. G. (1966), *The Emergence of Greek Democracy: The Character of Greek Politics, 800–400 BC*, London: Weidenfeld & Nicolson.

Fritz, K. von and E. Kapp (1950), *Aristotle's Constitution of the Athenians and Related Texts*, New York: Hafner.

Hansen, M. H. (1986), 'The Origin of the Word *Demokratia*', *Liverpool Classical Monthly*, 11, 35–6.

Hansen, M. H. (1991), *The Athenian Democracy in the Age of Demosthenes: Structure, Principles and Ideology*, trans. J. A. Crook, Oxford: Blackwell.

Hansen M. H. and T. H. Nielsen (eds) (2004), *An Inventory of Archaic and Classical Poleis*, Oxford: Oxford University Press.

Herodotus ([430 BCE] (1972), *The Histories*, Penguin: Harmondsworth.

Hignett, C. (1952), *A History of the Athenian Constitution to the End of the Fifth Century B.C.*, Oxford: Clarendon Press.

Jones, A. H. M. (1957), *The Athenian Democracy*, Oxford: Blackwell.

Kagan, D. (1991), *Pericles of Athens and the Birth of Democracy*, New York: Free Press.

Kagan, D. (2009), *Thucydides: The Reinvention of History*, New York: Viking Press.

Krentz, P. (1982), *The Thirty at Athens*, Ithaca, NY: Cornell University Press.

Loraux, N. (1986), *The Invention of Athens: The Funeral Oration in the Classical City*, trans. A. Sheridan, Cambridge, MA: Harvard University Press.

MacDowell, D. M. (1978), *The Law in Classical Athens*, London: Thames & Hudson.

Marr, J. L. and P. J. Rhodes (2008), *The 'Old Oligarch': The Constitution of the Athenians Attributed to Xenophon*, Oxford: Aris & Phillips/Oxbow.

Moore, J. M. (trans.) (1975), *Aristotle and Xenophon on Democracy and Oligarchy*, Berkeley, CA: University of California Press.

Morris, I. and K. A. Raaflaub (eds) (1998), *Democracy 2500? Questions and Challenges*, Dubuque, IA: Kendall & Hunt.

Ober, J. (1989), *Mass and Elite in Democratic Athens: Rhetoric, Ideology and the Power of the People*, Princeton, NJ: Princeton University Press.

Ober, J. (1993), 'The Athenian Revolution of 508/7 B.C.', in C. Dougherty and L. Kurke (eds), *Cultural Poetics in Ancient Greece*, Cambridge: Cambridge University Press, pp. 215–32.

Ober, J. (1998), *Political Dissent in Democratic Athens: Intellectual Critics of Popular Rule*, Princeton, NJ: Princeton University Press.

Ober, J. (2008), *Democracy and Knowledge: Innovation and Learning in Classical Athens*, Princeton, NJ: Princeton University Press.

Ober, J. and C. W. Hedrick (eds) (1996), *Demokratia: A Conversation on Democracies, Ancient and Modern*, Princeton, NJ: Princeton University Press.

O'Neil, J. L. (1995), *The Origin and Development of Greek Democracy*, Lanham, MD: Rowman & Littlefield.

Osborne, R. (2010), *Athens and Athenian Democracy*, Cambridge: Cambridge University Press.

Ostwald, R. (1969), *Nomos and the Beginnings of Athenian Democracy*, Oxford: Clarendon Press.

Ostwald, R. (1986), *From Popular Sovereignty to the Sovereignty of the Law*, Berkeley, CA: University of California Press.

Parker, R. (1996), *Athenian Religion: A History*, Oxford: Clarendon Press.

Parker, R. (2005), *Polytheism and Society in Athens*, Oxford: Oxford University Press.

Phillips, D. J. (1981), 'Participation in the Athenian Democracy', *Ancient Society: Resources for Teachers*, 11(1), 7–43.

Phillips, D. J. (1982), 'Athenian Ostracism', in G. H. R. Horsley (ed.), *Hellenika: Essays on Greek History and Politics*, North Ryde: Macquarie Ancient History Association, pp. 21–43.

Pritchard, D. (ed.) (2010), *War, Democracy and Culture in Classical Athens*, Cambridge: Cambridge University Press.

Raaflaub, K. A. (1989), 'Contemporary Perceptions of Democracy in Fifth-Century Athens', *Classica et Mediaevalia*, 40, 33–70.

Raaflaub, K. A. (2004), *The Discovery of Freedom in Ancient Greece*, trans. R. Franciscono, Chicago, IL: University of Chicago Press.

Raaflaub, K. A., J. Ober and R. W. Wallace (2007), *Origins of Democracy in Ancient Greece*, Berkeley, CA: University of California Press.

Rhodes, P. J. (1979/80), 'Athenian Democracy after 403 B.C.', *Classical Journal*, 75, 305–23.

Rhodes, P. J. (1981), *A Commentary on the Aristotelian Athenaion Politeia*, Oxford: Oxford University Press

Rhodes, P. J. and R. Osborne (2003), *Greek Historical Inscriptions 404–323 BC*, Oxford: Oxford University Press.

Roberts, J. T. (1982), *Accountability in Athenian Government*, Madison, WI: University of Wisconsin Press.

Roberts, J. T. (1994), *Athens on Trial: The Antidemocratic Tradition in Western Thought*, Princeton, NJ: Princeton University Press.

Robinson, E. W. (1997), *The First Democracies: Early Popular Government Outside Athens*, Historia Einzelschriften 107, Stuttgart: Steiner.

Robinson, E. W. (2011), *Democracy Beyond Athens: Popular Government in Classical Greece*, Cambridge: Cambridge University Press.

Rutter, N. K. (2000), 'Syracusan Democracy: "Most Like the Athenian"?', in R. Brock and S. Hodkinson (eds), *Alternatives to Athens: Varieties of Organization and Community in Ancient Greece*, Oxford: Oxford University Press, pp. 137–51.

Samons II, L. J. (2004), *What's Wrong with Democracy? From Athenian Practice to American Worship*, Berkeley, CA: University of California Press.

Sealey, R. (1973), 'The Origins of *Demokratia*', *Californian Studies in Classical Antiquity*, 6, 253–95.

Sealey, R. (1975), 'Constitutional Changes in Athens in 410 B.C.', *Californian Studies in Classical Antiquity*, 8, 271–95.

Sinclair, R. K. (1988), *Democracy and Participation in Athens*, Cambridge: Cambridge University Press.

Stanton, G. R. (1984), 'The Tribal Reforms of Kleisthenes the Alkmeonid', *Chiron* 14, 1–41.

Ste. Croix, G. E. M. de (1981), *The Class Struggle in the Ancient Greek World*, London: Duckworth.

Strauss, B. S. (1996), 'The Athenian Trireme School of Democracy', in J. Ober and C. W. Hedrick (eds), *Demokratia: A Conversation on Democracies, Ancient and Modern*, Princeton, NJ: Princeton University Press, pp. 313–25.

Thucydides ([400 BCE] 1972), *History of the Peloponnesian War*, trans. R. Warner, Harmondsworth: Penguin.

Todd, S. C. (1993), *The Shape of Athenian Law*, Oxford: Clarendon Press.

Wood, E. M. (1988), *Peasant-Citizen and Slave: The Foundations of Athenian Democracy*, London: Verso.

Chapter 8

Rome

Philip Matyszak

Although this chapter takes a broader view, democracy in Rome is generally considered in the context of the mid- to late Republic. The view that the oligarchy exercised *de facto* control of the voting process in this latter period has been challenged from the 1990s onward (Millar 2002). The ensuing debate has exposed extensive deficiencies in what is known about the democratic process in Rome (Sandberg 2001). Recently the focus has shifted to the role of the army, a focus which will be retained in this chapter (Southern 2007). It will also be stressed that throughout the history of Rome, voting rights were limited and biased in favour of the propertied class and there existed means – both constitutional and otherwise – of circumventing the popular will when it was democratically expressed.

Rome was not intended to be a democracy and was not a full democracy at any time. Instead, government was called the *res publica*, 'public thing'. The (unwritten) constitution of Rome was backed by the force of the *mos maiorum* or 'ancestral tradition', though the translation has little of the resonance of deep reverence and powerful authority of the Latin. Within very circumscribed limits, selection for office and passing legislation was by vote. Thus far, and no further, was Rome a democracy. Even this limited degree of commitment to democracy was only because Roman voters were originally also the Roman army. Social upheavals in early Rome demonstrated that the city could be governed only with the army's consent. To a large degree, the democratic institutions of Rome were the constitutional means by which the army could give that consent (Keppie 1998; Smith 2006). The failure of this mechanism (for reasons discussed below), led directly to the fall of the Roman Republic.

Whether or not Rome was founded on the morning of 7 April in the year 763 BCE, the first surviving discussions of Roman constitutional arrangements came half a millennium later. This is unfortunate, but the elite had no need to explain their constitution to themselves. The few written communications to the masses which survive as inscriptions are ambiguous and often unhelpful. Therefore, studies of constitutional matters in pre-imperial Rome rely strongly on surviving literary texts. The relationship of these texts to reality is the subject of heated debate (Wiseman 2004). It cannot be stated with absolute accuracy how the Roman constitution functioned at any given time. The historian of Roman democracy must discuss, for example, Rome's Servian constitution without any certainty as to whether King Servius (578–535 BCE) was a real or imagined figure, or whether any such constitution actually existed in his time. Fortunately, like many pre-literate societies, the Romans had an extraordinarily well-developed oral tradition. In addition, the elite were literate almost from the beginning so something of their traditions were preserved in family records. Thus, some grounds do exist for plausible conjecture, if not certainty.

The so-called Regal Period of Rome lasted from the city's beginning until the Republic of 510 BCE. The legendary kings of this period include a respected figure from outside the city (Numa), the immigrant son of a Corinthian refugee, Tarquinus Priscus, and also an ex-slave, Servius Tullius. This suggests that Rome had a selective rather than a dynastic monarchy. The formal mechanism of that selection is unknown. To some extent a king could nominate his successor, but the early Roman Senate had a role as the king's *concilium*. The *concilium* was a deeply ingrained Roman institution and several later Roman assemblies were called *concilia* (Botsford 1904). The role of *concilia* was to advise, so it is most likely that it helped to choose a Roman king. It is also most likely that the *concilium* handled administrative affairs during the succession (Livy [25 BCE] 1853: 1.47–9). The office of *interrex* survived as an institution for centuries longer than the office of *rex* itself. Membership of this early *concilium* was by election or nomination by summons as is confirmed by the very ancient name for Roman senators, the *patres conscripti*, conscript fathers.

The earliest known constitution of Rome is the so-called 'Servian Constitution'. In the historical tradition, King Servius faced opposition from the aristocracy. Because the Servian Constitution allowed the army a considerable say in public affairs, a king in Servius' position may well have sought to outflank his opponents by giving the army an investment in his regime. Servius was allegedly overthrown in a palace coup, but once the army had a seat among Rome's power brokers it would have been very risky to take this away, and under Servius' successors the constitution stood. Rome's army was made up of an annual levy of all male citizens, so under the Servian Constitution these had a taste of power. Practice at exercising power, and a constitutional framework for state administration, made it easier for the Romans to eventually dispense with kings altogether and set up their Republic. So it can be argued that some democratic institutions not only pre-dated the Roman Republic, but were a vital precondition for it (Last 1945). Others argue that the Servian Constitution was a construct of the early Roman Republic (D'Arms 1943). Either way, as the Roman Republic was founded in 509 BCE, the Servian constitutional arrangements, with some alterations and adaptations, lasted well into the imperial period 500 years later, which makes the Roman version of 'democracy' one of the most durable on record.

Elements of the Roman Republic

Originally, the patricians were the old Roman aristocracy and the plebeians the common people. The patricians held both state offices and social power, but by the early Republic they faced increasingly vehement objections from the overwhelmingly plebeian majority of the population (Raaflaub 2005). Rome was unhealthy, so averting demographic decline required net immigration and, therefore, a dwindling number of patricians who were forced to selectively share power with the rising plebeian elite (Strachan-Davidson 1886). Removing the king from Rome did not remove his *concilium*, the Senate, which continued as the advisory body to the Republic as a whole. The Senate was a social rather than a constitutional body, and this remained the case – at least in theory – throughout its existence. In the Republic, when the Senate made law, it did so indirectly. A legislative body would refer an issue to the Senate for its opinion – a *senatus consultum* – and then usually rubber-stamp the result of senatorial deliberations into law. The Senate also traditionally provided the pool from which Rome's senior administrators and generals were drawn. Membership of the Senate was restricted by age and property qualifications, and later a somewhat democratic element was added in that senators had to have previously been quaestors, junior administrative officials elected annually. The Senate was always vastly influential in Roman politics, but in the Roman Republic the influence of the Senate as an institution was largely extra-constitutional (Gruen 1992).

The basic Roman legislative body was the *comitium*, the large-scale meeting summoned by a magistrate (or king) (Botsford 1904). The oldest *comitium* was the *comitia curiata*, which was composed of the religious authorities of Rome and presided over by the Pontifex Maximus. As priesthood was a state office rather than a religious calling, the membership was a select group of senators. The *comitia curiata* originally fixed the date of religious celebrations and the calendar, but it also gave (or withheld) the blessing of the gods for state enterprises and so was a powerful political tool. Many of the functions of the *comitia curiata* were subsumed into the newer *comitia centuriata*, which had some legislative powers and could declare war or peace. It was also judicial and voted on the death penalty for condemned Roman citizens who appealed to it. It also elected senior magistrates and gave them their *imperium*, the right to command armies. These functions continued unchanged for almost half a millennium, though the *comitia* itself underwent considerable change (Ammerman 1996). While voting was probably originally by actual military units (centuries), when the *comitia centuriata* enters the historical record, the centuries were arranged by property class. The aristocracy had eighteen centuries, of which six were reserved for patricians, while the main part of the Roman infantry had 170 centuries, 85 for younger men and 85 of older men. The significant factor undermining Rome's early democratic arrangements was that voting was by timocratically weighted blocks. The *comitia centuriata* had fewer and richer people in the senior centuries, so the votes of these individuals counted for much more than the votes of those in the poorer centuries, since it was the vote of the century which counted, not the number of individuals within it. These centuries were later increased in number and further subdivided according to property, with the richer voters in the upper centuries and the poorer in larger centuries further down the voting order. The final century was the *capite censi*, those with little or no property. This last group was effectively disenfranchised, as the centuries voted in order of wealth and prestige and voting was abandoned on reaching a majority.

The *comitia tributa* was an assembly of Rome's tribes. A tribe was an administrative and voting division of the Roman people and unrelated to ethnicity. The Servian division had four urban tribes and seventeen rural tribes, though the number and composition of rural tribes were significantly amended in later years (Sherwin-White 1980). Allocating new citizens into tribes was one of the tasks of the Censors as discussed below. The tribes of the *comitia tributa* elected the minor offices of *quaestor*, *curule aedile* and military tribune. It was also an elective assembly, which passed most of the laws of the later Republic and legitimised legislation proposed by the Senate. Tribes voted as a bloc so a majority of votes within a tribe constituted that tribe's vote. The order in which the tribes voted was by lot and voting stopped once a majority was reached. While the tribe may seem the more equitable arrangement, this too was timocratically biased, because wealthy landowners in the rural tribes could more easily come to Rome to vote than peasants tied to the land. The majority of those who actually voted were in the urban tribes, which were greatly outnumbered by the rural tribes where fewer votes counted for more.

Apart from the potential for intimidation in a society without a police force, the client–patron ties of Roman social networks ensured that the will of powerful individuals usually determined the public choice (Yakobson 1999). Only in the first century BCE were serious efforts made to keep an individual's vote secret. The franchise was also heavily restricted because the vote did not extend to women, slaves, *peregrini* (resident non-citizens) or *infames* (those in unsuitable professions or otherwise officially considered disreputable). Also, anyone not physically present could not vote. As the Roman state expanded, the requirement that voters register their vote in person became, first, onerous and, later, impossible. This effectively disenfranchised many citizens serving in the army, and this disinvestment of the military from the admittedly limited democratic process had disastrous results in the later Republic. Magistrates were central to the checks and balances that provided stability in the early Republic. They were elected offices that exercised executive power, but the term of office was one year and the positions were collegial, that is, held by at least two men simultaneously with each able to veto the other. The early system was more flexible than the later *cursus honorum*, which rigidly dictated the sequence of offices and the age and qualifications of office-holders. While magistrates were elected, there was considerable manoeuvring among the elite to determine which candidates were presented for selection (Stewart 1998).

Consuls were the leading magistrates of the Republic and performed many of the senior administrative functions of the former monarchy. The consulate was collegial, so for the system to work candidates for consul usually presented themselves to the voters as a team, since two serving consuls holding diametrically opposite views resulted in political gridlock. This was less prevalent in the early Republic because the consuls were primarily war leaders who spent much of their terms leading Roman armies. This was one reason why consuls were picked by the *comitia centuriata*: unlike most armies – ancient or modern – it allowed the soldiers a choice of commander. The praetor was another ancient office (Brennan 2001). Early Rome may have experimented with a *praetor maximus* as the leading figure of the state, however, by the time the office enters the historical record, praetors were secondary to consuls. They led armies when consuls were unavailable and had a judicial role after 336 BCE. The praetorian prefect of Rome annually announced the body of law that he was adopting for his year in office. This body was codified in the late imperial period, and still forms the basis of many legal systems today. The office of censor was created in 443 BCE to register Roman voters. The censors also allocated state contracts and maintained public morals. Election was by the *comitia centuriata*. This was Rome's most prestigious magistracy, usually held only once, often by two ex-consuls working together. Originally held by patricians, the office was later opened to plebeians, but was abolished in 22 BCE when Augustus and his successors pre-empted the role (Lintott 1999: 114). Aediles were relatively junior magistrates for whom the city of Rome itself was their primary responsibility. Aediles arranged matters as diverse as the city's annual festivals and games, the licensing of markets, bars and brothels, flood prevention and the removal of refuse from the city streets. Because they worked closely with and for the public, ambitious aediles supplemented their official budgets with their own funds in order to gain popularity, which might carry them to yet higher office. Quaestor was the bottom rung of the *cursus honorum*. In the late Republic quaestors had to be at least thirty years of age. They usually had financial respon- sibilities and might serve as second-in-command to a provincial governor. The office qualified the holder for membership of the Senate. Even before entry to the *cursus honorum*, ambitious young men sought appointment as military tribunes. Though just junior officers in the army, nomination to the office by the *comitia tributa* was an essential start to a political career.

In the early years of the Republic an experimental government by a college of consular tribunes elected annually was tried, but the constitution rapidly reverted to the standard type. While Republican Rome was a long way from a perfect democracy, this mix of public councils and elected offices, and the debate and elections they sponsored, provided not only checks and balances in the political process but also ensured that the people had a voice.

The Effect of Social Conflict

'The struggle of the orders' is the name given to a period of prolonged social stress that began even before the foundation of the Republic and continued until the start of the second century (after which it arguably continued in a different form). The intention here is not to describe this struggle in detail, but to point out the effect on the democratic processes of the Roman Republic (Raaflaub 2005). The last king of Rome, Tarquinius Superbus, is infamous for oppressing the common people. Consequently, the people – as the army – supported the overthrow of the king by his close relatives, who collaborated with other aristocrats in a coup. However, the plebeians had no intention of accepting oligarchic oppression in the place of autocratic oppression. Less than a decade after the foundation of the Republic, the plebeians literally seceded from the city, withdrawing their support for the patrician government, and, crucially, refusing to serve in the Roman army. Faced with extinction by foreign foes, the patrician government was forced into a series of concessions, all of which made Rome more democratic. Two of the most important institutions which developed were the *concilium plebis* and the tribunate. The *concilium plebis* may have been intended as the plebeian answer to the (then) patrician senate. Patricians were excluded, but otherwise the composition and voting procedures were similar to the *comitia tributa*. However, the *concilium plebis* began to pass edicts (*plebiscita*) that were originally binding only on Rome's plebeian population, but from 287 BCE applied to all Roman citizens. Thus, unlike the Senate, which had minimal powers to initiate legislation, the *concilium plebis* evolved to become one of the main law-making bodies of the Republic alongside the *comitia tributa* (Lowenstein 1973).

As seen above, the military tribune was a junior office in the army, but a much more important office was the *tribuni plebis*, the tribunes of the people. Though tribunes had probably begun as spokesmen for the individual tribes, they gained constitutional power after the first secession of the plebs in the early sixth century. The main function of tribunes was to protect the plebeians in Rome from overweening authority. The tribunes had no power outside the boundaries of the city, and other Roman cities of the expanding empire made their own arrangements in this respect. Tribunes were sacrosanct. Plebeians swore an oath to protect tribunes by any and all means in their power, which implicitly included riot, secession or armed insurrection. The pretext for Julius Caesar's march on Rome in the mid-first century was to protect tribunician sacrosanctity. The tribune had the right of *intercessio*, by which he could overrule the decision of any magistrate, and the right of *ius agendi*, by which he could summon the *concilium plebis*.

As representatives of the people, tribunes had none of the pomp of other Roman magistracies and, indeed, it was only in the second century BCE, 300 years after the creation of the office, that tribunes were considered magistrates of the Republic with the right to attend senate meetings. By then the office had largely been captured by the Roman political elite. This was possible because there was not one tribune, but a college of between six to a twelve members. This college often came under the sway of a single powerful individual who set the political agenda. The final stage of the capture of the tribunate by the Roman elite came during the early imperial period when Augustus awarded himself the powers of a tribune. This *tribunica potestas* was thereafter one of the constitutional foundations of the imperial principate. Despite the democratic impulses in the foundation of the Roman Republic, the *concilium plebis* and the tribunate were not brought into being by constitutional processes, but by the plebeian threat of secession, riot and constitutional disruption. In short, extra-constitutional means were necessary to enforce the popular will, which suggests that the institutions of the early Roman state were inadequate for this purpose. Throughout this period, the citizen army remained the main guarantor of the people's rights. The army restored the Republic after it fell into the grip of the tyrannical Decemvirate (a group of legislators who used their power to create laws to make themselves masters of Rome). While the secession of the plebs was often threatened it actually only happened twice. A counter-measure by the aristocracy was the creation of the office of dictator. A dictator was chosen by the Senate for the duration of a particular emergency and a dictator was outside the reach of even a tribunician veto. Unsurprisingly, some dictators, such as the famous Cincinnatus, took the opportunity to crush popular dissent between dealing with the original foreign threat and resigning their office (Nippel 1995).

Assimilation and Alienation

From the outset Rome was geared towards demographic and territorial expansion, and consequently there was an early split between *civitas* (city-state) and citizen. The institutions of the city had to adjust to the fact that not all Romans lived in Rome. Indeed, the policy of adding wholesale to the citizenry meant that some new Romans were former soldiers of recently conquered Italian cities still resentful of Rome. Means had to be found to give these citizens a voice without creating a subversive faction driven by a desire for lost independence. Rome was successful in finding such means, as is evident by the many famous 'Romans' including Cicero, Martial and Virgil who came from peoples conquered and assimilated by the Roman state. One technique for incorporating and assimilating large numbers of disgruntled citizens was to award them citizenship without the vote (*sine suffragio*). This was a common practice until the end of the third century BCE. It was successful as the new citizens enjoyed the right of appeal (*provocatio*) and the right to trade with and marry their fellow Romans. Usually the right to vote was granted after a generation had grown up as Romans (Nicolet 1980). Block enrolments of new citizens were largely abandoned between the Second Punic War that ended in 201 BCE and the Social War of 91 BCE. When large-scale induction of new citizens did resume, these citizens were given the vote immediately. A second means of peacefully incorporating new citizens into the Roman state was by allocating them into voting tribes. This could nullify the effect of a large and hostile constituency in two ways: the disaffected citizens could be distributed through the voting tribes so that their vote would not greatly affect the overall vote of any single tribe, or all the newcomers could be lumped into a single tribe that the other tribes would easily outvote in the assembly. There was considerable controversy as to which tribes the new citizens should be allocated after the Social War of 91 BCE (Gardner 1993).

Another very distinctive characteristic of Roman society was the relative ease of upward mobility, which avoided social conflict by allowing capable (male) individuals to move themselves and their relatives up the social hierarchy. This inclusiveness meant that the people of a captured city could see their own elite rapidly become equestrians or even senators in Rome. The knowledge that they had a voice in the body politic helped with the Romanisation of conquered peoples. Upward mobility was not confined to free men. Slaves, if they were 'civilised' and educated, had a good chance of being manumitted by their masters and a manumitted slave was a Roman citizen. Thus, a man could go from being human property to a voter in good standing overnight. For example, Horace the poet and dinner companion of the Emperor Augustus was the son of a freedman. In the Julio-Claudian empire some ex-slaves became important power brokers, while Rome's conflicts in Greece and Judea gave the capital large Greek and Jewish constituencies – especially as the Jewish community made it a matter of policy to buy the freedom of their countrymen whenever the opportunity presented itself (Donfried 2003).

The Late Republic

The Polybian Republic was the Roman Republic as described by the historian Polybius, who wrote during the mid-second century BCE (Polybius [150 BCE] 1889). In Book VI of his *History*, Polybius presents a somewhat idealised description of the Roman political system. His argument is that government takes three forms: autocracy, oligarchy and democracy. Each of these forms has a developed and a degenerate form. Thus, autocracy begins as monarchy, but degenerates into tyranny (in the modern sense of the word); aristocracy becomes a self-serving clique of oligarchs; and democracy degenerates into mob rule. According to Polybius, the Roman Republic achieved stability by making each of the three elements serve as a check on the other. Thus, consuls (and dictators) exercised monarchical powers, but these were restrained by the aristocratic element in the Senate and the democratic element represented by the tribunes and voting assemblies of the Roman people. Polybius was writing of a time when he considered the Roman system of government fully evolved and operating at its peak. However, the aristocratic element was already having a deleterious effect: it had taken over large tracts of farmland, both by buying or forcing out peasant farmers, and by the *de facto* seizure of land owned by the Roman state, the *ager publicus* (White 1967). Tiberius Gracchus was an aristocratic reformer who attempted to reverse the situation by democratic means while he was tribune of the people. When the Senate used political chicanery to repeatedly thwart his attempts to pass land reform legislation, Tiberius retaliated by using the tribunician veto to bring the state machinery to a standstill. First Tiberius and then his brother Gaius were killed in violence provoked by the conservative element. Though many of the reforms of the Gracchi survived, the Roman oligarchy had increased its grip on power to the point where the Polybian system of balance no longer applied.

In the later years of the Roman Republic some politicians used popular sentiment to further their political aims. Whereas most senators worked within a nexus of connections created by marriage and the exchange of official posts and favours (known as *beneficia* or the client–patron system), those with more radical agendas turned to the people for support. Such politicians were called *populares*, in contrast to the more conservative element who were *optimates* or the *boni* (good men) (Scager 1997). Throughout the history of the Republic, Roman politics was a highly individualised process, and taking an *optimate* or *populares* stance was a means to a particular goal rather than an endorsement of a collective ideology. Nevertheless, by the end of the Republic the divisions between the outlook of the *optimates* and the common people had widened to the point where it is possible to talk of two factions within the Roman state, each with different priorities and aims (Brunt 1986). The popular agenda included land settlement for the dispossessed, the urban poor and discharged soldiers, debt relief, and a stable food supply at reasonable or no cost.

By the employment of extra-constitutional means (bribery, propaganda, the exchange of favours and coercion), the office of consul had been largely captured by the *nobiles*. Whether *optimates* or *populares*, this group of closely linked aristocratic families manipulated the constitution for their own short-sighted, personal ends and often prevented both the free exercise of democratic politics and the rise of capable outsiders; factors which had previously kept the army sympathetic to the Republic. In this environment, the army became alienated from the political process and more attached to individual commanders (Gruen 1995). Politicians, earnest reformers and outright demagogues alike, pushed bills through the legislative process with clauses that supported their own interests. All parties abused the political process with coercion, bribery, riots and religious interdicts, and in so doing destroyed much of the credibility of the democratic system. The corruption and chaos became so bad that the army intervened, not least because the capture of the constitutional process by the aristocracy had sidelined and alienated the military.

In 88 BCE, Cornelius Sulla used the army to take control of Rome by casting his opponents as demagogues who had staged an unconstitutional coup. Significantly, these 'demagogues' had replaced a popular army commander – Sulla himself – with their own candidate. After the Social War (91–88 BCE), Rome had granted citizenship to many Italians who had fought the war against Rome to demand a place in Roman politics. This meant that while internal politics had become dysfunctional, Rome's army contained large numbers of soldiers who had recently been fighting against it. Individual aristocratic commanders found it easy to subvert the army for their own purposes. From that time until the end of the western empire 500 years later, forcible military intervention in politics was always a factor. After a succession of coups and attempted coups, in 49 BCE Julius Caesar's broadly *populares* stance received the backing of his legions, who replaced the machinery of the Republic with a dictatorship which the military felt was more responsive to their wishes (Goldsworthy 2006). The breakdown of democracy, the subversion of the army and the spiral into civil war had caused the failure of the Roman Republic and the emergence of the military dictatorship with constitutional trappings known today as the Augustan principate.

Conclusion

Democracy remained a vibrant force in urban life for the duration of the principate that extended from 27 BCE to CE 284. Though voting assemblies ceased to be significant in Rome itself, the support of the Roman people was essential for the survival of the *princeps*, as any emperor who lost popular support became vulnerable to a Senate-inspired coup. Emperors were well aware of this and sought the people's endorsement of their reigns by entertaining and feeding them, a process condemned by the satirist Juvenal who claimed that the Roman people had abandoned their rights for 'bread and circuses' (Juvenal [CE 100] 1974: 10.77–81). In many urban centres elsewhere in the empire, democracy flourished. The administrative units of the empire were provinces autocratically run by imperial appointees (though some appointments were indirect via the Senate), but the *civitates*, the city-states that collectively made up these provinces often had a lively democratic process. This has been captured for posterity in the city of Pompeii in Campania, where an election in CE 79 was interrupted by the eruption of Mt Vesuvius. Official notices and graffiti tell of campaigning and of interest groups expressing support for one or another candidate for municipal office. We see a strong civic tradition both here and elsewhere in the many inscriptions that describe leading men of a city rewarding voters with public works and other *beneficia* for the city.

References

Ammerman, A. J. (1996), 'The Comitium in Rome from the Beginning', *American Journal of Archaeology*, 100(1), 121–36.
Botsford G. (1904), 'On the Distinction between Comitia and Concilium', *Transactions and Proceedings of the American Philological Association*, 35, 21–32.

Brennan, T. C. (2001), *The Praetorship in the Roman Republic*, 2 vols, Oxford: Oxford University Press.

Brunt, P. (1986), *Social Conflicts in the Roman Republic*, London: Hogarth.

D'Arms, E. F. (1943), 'The Classes of the Servian Constitution', *American Journal of Philology*, 64(4), 424–6.

Donfried, K. (ed.) (2003), *Judaism and Christianity in First-Century Rome*, Eugene, OR: Wipf & Stock.

Gardner, J. (1993), *Being a Roman Citizen*, London: Routledge.

Goldsworthy, A. (2006), *Caesar; Life of a Colossus*, New Haven, CT: Yale University Press.

Gruen, E. (1992), 'The Exercise of Power in the Roman Republic', in A. Molho, K. Raaflaub and J. Emlen (eds), *City-States in Classical Antiquity and Medieval Italy*, Ann Arbor, MI: University of Michigan Press.

Gruen, E. (1995), *The Last Generation of the Roman Republic*, Berkeley, CA: University of California Press.

Juvenal ([CE 100] 1974), *The Sixteen Satires*, trans. P. Green, Harmondsworth: Penguin.

Keppie, L. J. F. (1998), *The Making of the Roman Army*, Norman, OK: University of Oklahoma Press.

Last, H. (1945), 'The Servian Reforms', *Journal of Roman Studies*, 35, 30–48.

Lintott, A. (1999), *The Constitution of the Roman Republic*, Oxford: Oxford University Press.

Livy ([25 BCE] 1853), *History of Rome*, trans. D. Spillan, London: Henry G. Bohn.

Lowenstein, K. (1973), *The Governance of Rome*, The Hague: Springer.

Millar, F. (2002), *The Roman Republic in Political Thought: The Menahem Stern Jerusalem Lectures*, Hanover, NH: University Press of New England.

Nicolet, C. (1980), *The World of the Citizen in Republican Rome*, trans. P. S. Falla, London: Batsford.

Nippel, W. (1995), *Public Order in Ancient Rome*, Cambridge: Cambridge University Press.

Polybius ([150 BCE] 1889), *The Histories of Polybius*, trans. E. Shuckburgh, London: Macmillan.

Raaflaub, K. (ed.) (2005), *Social Struggles in Archaic Rome: New Perspectives on the Conflict of the Orders*, Malden, MA: Wiley-Blackwell.

Sandberg, K. (2001), *Magistrates and Assemblies: A Study of Legislative Practice in Republican Rome*, Rome: Finnish Institute at Rome.

Seager, R. (1997), ' "Populares" in Livy and the Livian Tradition', *Classical Quarterly*, 27(2), 377–90.

Sherwin-White, A. N. (1980), *The Roman Citizenship*, 2nd edn, Oxford: Oxford University Press.

Smith, C. J. (2006), *The Roman Clan: The Gens from Ancient Ideology to Modern Anthropology*, Cambridge: Cambridge University Press.

Southern, P. (2007), *The Roman Army: A Social and Institutional History*, Oxford: Oxford University Press.

Stewart, R. (1998), *Public Office in Early Rome*, Ann Arbor, MI: University of Michigan Press.

Strachan-Davidson, J. L. (1886), 'The Growth of Plebeian Privilege at Rome', *English Historical Review*, 1(2), 209–17.

White, K. (1967), 'Latifundia', *Bulletin of the Institute of Classical Studies*, 14, 62–79.

Wiseman, T. P. (2004), *Clio's Cosmetics*, Bristol: Phoenix Press.

Yakobson, A. (1999), *Elections and Electioneering in Rome: A Study in the Political System of the Late Republic*, Historia Einzelschriften 128, Stuttgart: Steiner.

Part III

Medieval Democracy

Chapter 9

Islam

Larbi Sadiki

Nothing is more perilous than trying to wed Islam and democracy, or engaging in endless discussions on Islam's compatibility with democracy via a framework designed within the Western episteme. This episteme assumes that Islam and democracy are two distinct and autonomous systems and, in its worst iterations, it asserts that they are antithetical to one another. Since the European Enlightenment, the scholarly discussion of Islam and democracy has been one-sided. Western intellectuals condemn religion to the margins and Enlightenment's singular practice of rationality denounces religious foundationalism. Fixity, singularity and determinacy have all been attributed to religion, especially Islam, and cited as evidence of its non-democratic tendencies.

The question should never be whether Islam and democracy are compatible or incompatible, but rather how these two idealised models of a better world have never led to a single, determinate or fixed form. While they may share a millennial journey and encounters necessitating mutual inclusion and exclusion, discovering the Islamic in democracy or the democratic in Islam is not always easy, as Muslim philosophers have discovered since the medieval period of heightened disputation between the thinkers of the Islamic and Hellenic worlds until today. This chapter is an attempt to examine that disputative relationship which led to interpretive renditions of both Islam and democracy as systems and values that are forever delayed, defying reification in the present. But in the course of these many disputations, Islam has had to venture into the pagan world of the Greeks or the secular world of the contemporary West with its Judeo-Christian roots. The reverse is not true: those who have espoused democracy have rarely, if ever, considered entering into dialogue with Islam, much less learning from it. The humility of Muslim philosophy has added value to the enterprise of how to consider Islam and democracy.

The question remains: where and how can democracy be situated in medieval Islamic history? This chapter seeks to address this key question by revisiting the works of the classical Islamic scholar Abu Nasr Al-Farabi (Alpharabius in Latin 870–950). Al-Farabi devoted close to fifty years of his life to the study of Greek philosophy in Baghdad, where he was trained by his Arab mentors – Syrian Christians – from the Alexandrian philosophical school. He also lived through a period of dramatic change in Islamic politics, witnessing the decline of the Abbasids who had ruled the Islamic world since 750. While the Abbasids remained the official figureheads for centuries to come (until 1258), their power and influence waned substantially during the ninth century, leading to the ascension of the Persian Buyids (945–1055). Al-Farabi's philosophy, and particularly his political philosophy, cannot be separated from this context. As Abd Al-Ali remarks, the *islhu al-Khalafah* (reform of the Caliphate) shadows every aspect of Al-Farabi's political thought (Al-'Aali 1986: 62, 73). The central focus of this chapter is Al-Farabi's vision of *al-madinatu al-fadilah* (the virtuous city) as a vista into the Muslim perennial search for virtue sanctioned by Allah through the harmonisation of revelation and reason. His works are an integral insight to the intellect of a medieval Muslim seeker of wisdom, eclectically arguing, disputing and re-designing thought within Islamic foundations and ethics.

The Argumentative Muslim and the Interpretive Ethos

No discussion of democracy within the context of Islam can bypass the medieval period and the great Islamic scholars who straddled multiple cultures, languages and ideologies. Such minds never practiced singular command over the interpretation of divine texts, nor did they belong to the category of learned scholars assigned the unenviable task of underwriting political power. The legacy of these other Islamic scholars has been the production of various fixed 'Islams', one of the great tragedies of Islamic history. Instead, for Al-Farabi and those of his ilk, Islam is marked by dynamic contestation and provisional renewal in theology, legalism and politics. Beyond *tawhid* (the unity of God) and the divine scriptures, namely, the *Qur'an*, nothing else was sanctified. God alone was beyond human contestation, everything else was open to critique. To a large extent, the history of early Islam, up to the time when the proverbial *babu al-ijtihad* (the gate of independent reasoning) was supposed to have been closed in the late ninth and early tenth centuries, was characterised by fluidity and contingency in the realms of legalism and politics. This fluidity permanently introduced a tensely multi-focal competition over the interpretation of religious texts in the bid to reify Islam into a religion as life. Notwithstanding the violence that has punctuated Islamic history, this competition was healthy in that it prevented rigidity and the centralisation of power.

The revered institutions of *ijtihad* (independent reasoning) and *tajdid* (renewal) are two powerfully entrenched Islamic ideals. These, along with the institution of *munazarah* (disputation), were instrumental in setting up the ethical and professional obligation of scholars to engage with all learning, even if un-Godly or pagan. The Muslim scholar was a migratory creature, pursuing learning 'even if it were in China', according to one *Hadith* (the sayings or habits of the Prophet). Literally, to be an Islamic scholar was to be in the vocation of searching for wisdom and this motivated scientific engagement and dialogue. The migratory movement and the ethics of scientific research and wisdom-seeking translated and transmitted ancient knowledge to medieval audiences. They created communities of like-minded scholars who were not afraid to venture into unfamiliar territory. Access to alternative non-Islamic frames of reference became possible and was actively encouraged. Islamic and non-Islamic systems of thought fused and were diffused outwards to the wider Islamic community (*ummah*).

This climate of cross-cultural intellectual dialogue is nowhere more evident than in the medieval Islamic scholarly engagement with the legacy of Greek antiquity. For centuries, Islamic scholars worked tirelessly to translate and transmit a large corpus of Grecian texts. By the time of Al-Farabi, they had thoroughly studied the works of antiquity and made substantial contributions of their own. Aside from Greek scholars such as Porphyry, Plotinus, Euclid, Galen, Ptolemy and Socrates, Islamic scholars had a particular penchant for Plato and especially Aristotle. At the tenth-century school of Aristolian studies in Baghdad, for example, students and scholars had access to Aristotle's complete *oeuvre*. Neo-platonic and Aristotelian thought dominated their investigations into natural philosophy, their reflections on ethics and their rich debates on politics. This access to Greek wisdom included their writings on democracy and, as the case of Al-Farabi demonstrates, Grecian *dēmokratia* was rediscovered by Muslims seekers of wisdom who incorporated and discussed it in the light of their Islamic faith.

These debates on the relevance and usefulness of issues raised by the Greeks were discussed both within Islam itself (Islam–Islam debates) and outwith Islam (Islam–philosophy debates). This led to the jostling of hermeneutic enquiries between two distinct overarching schools of thought: the *Ahlu Al-Ra'y* (the rationalists) and the *Ahlu Al-Hadith* (the traditionalists or literalists). Both the rationalists and the literalists mapped out a discursive framework that has never completely subsided within the *Dar Al-Islam* (house of Islam). The rationalists turned to classical philosophy to defend Islam by fathoming the *batin* (subtextual and inner meaning), as opposed to the *ahir* (literal meaning). They sought to engage the divine texts via speculative cognition; to rationalise revelation. The rationalist theology of the Mu'tazilah (Mu'tazalites), who were initially endorsed for nearly forty years by the Abbasids, especially under Caliph Al-Ma'mun (813–33), applied considerable intellect to the revelation–reason question. As Rosenthal observes the Mu'tazilites

> sought to defend revelation against Aristotle by discarding anthropomorphism and opposing the concept of the God of revelation to the god bound to the eternity of matter of Aristotle. They devised a figurative interpretation of scripture to demonstrate that scripture did not contradict reason. This inner meaning of scripture could be ascertained by reason only; it was additional to the literal, external meaning . . . *Kalam*, or dialectic theology, was the result, and this was Islam's official answer to the challenge of Greek-Hellenistic philosophy. (Rosenthal 1962: 114–15)

The work of the rationalists drew strong criticism from the literalists, especially those of the Hanbali school. As a whole, the literalists attacked the rationalists on the basis that their methods were futile and dangerous. They argued that the human intellect was ill-equipped to capture the essence of divine knowledge. Rationalism's danger, they additionally reasoned, lay in the risk of polluting and abusing the divine revelations. Since Islam is believed to have a divine origin and *Qur'anic* texts are claimed to be the word of God, Muslims are obliged, once they accept them, to abide by the religious sanctions contained within them. This rich culture of debate between the medieval Islamic rationalists and literalists, between reason and revelation, philosophy and theosophy, are illustrative of the dynamism of contestation that was central to the evolution of Islam and its contact with ideas and peoples from outside the original precincts of Mecca and Medina. Together, this hermeneutics-based jostling pluralised and revitalised Islam, producing many Muslims with argumentative minds and a thirst for wisdom.

Al-Farabi's Re-framing of Grecian Democracy within Islam

If the Greeks were among the first to discuss and practice democracy, Arabs and Muslims did more than just preserve and transmit it. Of the Arabophones, those who either received the bulk of their education in Baghdad or Damascus or wrote in the ecumenical Arabic of the time, Al-Farabi is certain to have known Greek democracy and the politics of the Greek *polis*. As far as we know, he read more works by Aristotle and Plato, among other Greek philosophers, than any other Muslim student of the Hellenic curriculum. In the Baghdad of his time, while Aristotle was known as the 'First Teacher' (*Al-Mu'allim Al-Awwal*), Al-Farabi was referred to as the 'Second Teacher' (*Al-Mu'allim Al-Thani*) (Nasr 1985). Despite this, it is curious that throughout his works Al-Farabi does not mention 'democracy' by name. However, Al-Farabi's notion of *al-madinah al-jama'iyyah* (the democratic city) is widely considered to correspond with ancient Grecian *dēmokratia* as it was practiced in the *polis* (Mahdi 1969; Rosenthal 1962).[1]

Greek-Hellenistic philosophy such as that of Aristotle and Plato, as well as the neo-Platonic works form the departure point of Arabo-Islamic *falasifah* (philosophers) (Rosenthal 1962). They drew on the work of the Greeks to contemplate the relationships between the real, the ideal and the transcendental (Strauss 1977; 'Umar 1992). They sought answers to cryptic questions regarding this life and the hereafter through *tawfiq* (harmonisation), including the harmonisation of Greek-Hellenistic and Arabo-Islamic civilisations; of revelation (religion) with reason (philosophy); of 'prophetic revealed law' with 'human law' (such as the Greek *nomos*); and of worldly and heavenly happiness (Qumayr 1986: 42; Rosenthal 1962: 114–16; 'Umarah 1988). But harmonising revelation and reason can be a very difficult task. This difficulty is, for instance, apparent in the position taken by Al-Farabi, Ibn Sina (Avicenna in Latin, 980–1037), Ibn Bajja (Avempace, 1095–1138) and Ibn Rushd (Averroes, 1126–98), on the one hand, and Al-Ghazali (Algazel, 1058–1111), on the other, towards the relationship of revelation and philosophy (Rosenthal 1962: 113–21). Al-Ghazali doubts the capacity of human reasoning to fathom divine revelation. The gist of his well-known work, *Tahafutu Al-Falasifah* (*The Incoherence of Philosophers*), is that there can be no harmony between Islam and philosophy.

This was certainly not the case for Al-Farabi and his intellectual descendants, who found no contradiction between philosophy and revelation. In fact, one distinctive imprint of Hellenic rationality on Al-Farabi is his ranking of philosophy above theology. The first thrives on intellectual perception, the latter on imagination. Influenced by Plato and Aristotle before them, Muslim philosophers hierarchised society and knowledge by making philosophy an elite vocation, the bastion of those who have a superior intellect, and religion a public one, for those lacking in philosophical rationality and wisdom. Noteworthy, however, is that the 'Platonised

Aristotelism' of Muslim philosophers was recast in an unmistakably Muslim frame-work. It accorded divinity a great deal of importance, making no separation between this life and the hereafter, between God and man, or religion and politics.

A very specific example of this comes from Al-Farabi's reading of Plato's *Republic* and *Laws* and Aristotle's *Nicomachean Ethics* (Aristotle [350 BCE] 2004; Plato [360 BCE] 1975, [380 BCE] 1975). In *The Republic*, for example, Plato argues that the ideal society should be presided over by a wise philosopher-king. Al-Farabi finds an analogue for this in his concept of the ruler-philosopher and ruler-prophet, that is, the *ra'is* (ruler-leader). As a philosopher, the *ra'is* is endowed with the faculty and virtue of superior intellect, enabling him to engage in a demonstrative form of reasoning for the purpose of esoteric understanding. As a prophet-ruler, the *ra'is* can deploy dialectical and rhetorical types of reasoning in which emotional appeal is the key to making the masses understand religion and flock to it. This included using allegorical exegesis, or the Mu'tazilites twofold device *al-zahir* (external, superficial) and *al-batin* (as distinct from *zahir* – the literal meanings as imparted by the parables in the *Qur'an*) (Rosenthal 1962: 115). Thus, *falasifah* could pursue both philosophical and religious perfection.

The attainment of happiness for a Muslim *failasuf* (singular of *falasifah*) like Al-Farabi pertains not only to a Greek style philosopher-king led polity, but also to a divinely sanctioned state and society where the ideals of revelation and philosophy become mutually reinforcing and inclusive. The theological attainment of perfection, which in its Platonic sense resides in a philosophical kingdom, would be incomplete for Al-Farabi without a philosopher-Imam or philosopher-prophet as the source of both intellectual power (speculative wisdom) and political/temporal/practical power (practical wisdom). From this perspective, Al-Farabi represents two contradictory phenomena. His philosophy is a meeting point of both Islamic and Western civilisations, it represents an early attempt to synthesise the two cultures and the claims of Hellenic rationalism with the religion of Islam. At the same time, Al-Farabi's work is witness to the early tension between Islamic and Western notions of political theory. Plato's or Aristotle's lawgiver or philosopher-king is free of all religion. In contrast, Al-Farabi's *failsuf* is not:

> He should be pious, yield easily to goodness and justice, and be stubborn in yielding to evil and injustice. And he should be strongly determined in favour of the right thing . . . He should have sound conviction about the opinions of the religion in which he is reared, [and] hold fast to the virtuous acts in his religion. (Al-Farabi [935] 1969: 48)

Nonetheless, it is in political philosophy that a common ground is found between revelation and philosophy with law being the lynchpin between the two. As Rosenthal explains:

> This means that the study of the *Republic*, the *Laws* and the *Nicomachean Ethics* led the Muslim philosophers to grasp more fully the political character implied in the *shari'a* [law] of Islam . . . Hence revelation is for them, not only a transmission of right beliefs and convictions, a dialogue between a personal God of love, of justice

and of mercy and man whom he has created in his image; it is also and above all a valid and binding code for man, who must live in society and be politically organized in a state in order to fulfill his destiny. In short, it is the law of the ideal state . . . Greek and Muslim philosophers are agreed that without law there can be no state and that unlawful behaviour is damaging to the state . . . In the state under *shari'a* such deviations will cause error, heresy and schism, and prove the undoing of the state. (Rosenthal 1962: 116–17)

The above forms part of the backdrop against which Al-Farabi's politics, reflections on Greek democracy and his own response must be understood. His theorising is rooted in a process of dialectic between his Islamic faith and Greek philosophy. Like Aristotle, he conceives of a person as a *zoon politikon* (a political being), and of politics as 'the royal political art' (Rosenthal 1962: 119). Al-Farabi, however, parts company with Aristotle and Plato on certain points. For example, as Mahdi points out, Al-Farabi makes *tahsil al-sa'adah* (the attainment of happiness) the function of political science (Mahdi 1969: xi–xii). Political science inquires, *inter alia*, into the 'right actions' that help perfect a people's way of life. It is quite natural for a believer (and Al-Farabi is one) not only to distinguish between the transient happiness of this world and the hereafter, but also to consider the latter more important. This is concordant with Al-Farabi's position, which sees happiness in the hereafter to be 'supreme' (Al-Farabi [935] 1969: 13).

The key point, however, is Al-Farabi's positive disposition towards the pursuit of happiness as an intrinsically human endeavour. Thus, his investigation into politics, being 'those actions and volitional ways of life', is an investigation into the variegated forms of happiness, and the frameworks within which they are striven for and approximated (Rosenthal 1962: 119). One condition, however, is indispensable for happiness: human association. Al-Farabi, like Aristotle, sees the state as the ideal site of human association which is both *fitriyyah* (natural and intuitive) and necessary for maximising happiness (Al-Huluw 1980: 74). Accordingly, for Al-Farabi, 'individuals living in isolation forfeit their chance of true happiness, which they can attain only as citizens performing their civic duties' (Rosenthal 1962: 138). In the same vein, Al-Farabi holds that decay befalls people upon their 'abandoning political society' (Rosenthal 1962: 165).

If the state is Al-Farabi's ideal site for attaining happiness, what then is his ideal state? Al-Farabi's discussion of the ideal state centres around the Greek *polis*. It is one foundation upon which he builds his treatises on various forms of political society. The *polis* is *al-madinah* (city), the incubational milieu of democracy. Hence, Al-Farabi's concept of *al-madinah al-jama'iyyah* is inexorably tied to the city. He clearly states that:

The democratic city is the one in which each one of the citizens is given free rein and left alone to do whatever he likes. Its citizens are equal and their laws say that no man is in any way at all better than any other man . . . And no one . . . has any claim to authority unless he works to enhance their freedom . . . Those who rule them do so by the will of the ruled, and the rulers follow the wishes of the ruled. (Al-Farabi [940] 1963: 50)

However, Al-Farabi both praises and deprecates *al-madinah al-jama'iyyah* in tune with his open 'Islamicity'. In terms of his praise for the democratic city, Al-Farabi applauds its legal freedom and the equality of its citizens, seeing in them equivalence to the Islamic concepts of *musawat'itq* (emancipation of slaves) and *al-la ikrah* (non-compulsion) which are associated with freedom. However, the best indication of Al-Farabi's approval of the democratic city is his distinction of *al-madinah al-jama'iyyah* as 'the most admirable and happy city' (Al-'Aali 1986: 51). It provides a foundation from which his *al-madinatu al-fadilah* (virtuous city) can develop, governed by virtuous rulers (Al-Farabi [940] 1963: 51–2).

Nonetheless, Al-Farabi does find imperfections in the democratic city, classifying it among the cluster *al-mudunu al-jahilah* (ignorant states), the antithesis of his virtuous city, albeit the least imperfect of the imperfect (Al-'Aali 1986: 61–73; Al-Huluw 1980: 101–5). But Al-Farabi's reservations are not unique; both Plato and Aristotle, among other Hellenes, had reservations about democracy and its tendency to empower the ignorant masses. His disapproval of *al-madinah al-jama'iyyah* can be put down to three main reasons. The first, is its earthly and sensual materialism which contradicts Islam's spiritualism, and Al-Farabi's own life of *zuhd* (asceticism). As in all ignorant cities, the democratic city's leadership 'aims at having its fill of bare necessities', including domination and freedom (Al-Farabi [940] 1963: 51). What can be presumed is Al-Farabi's aversion to the kind of material freedom that is deleterious to supreme happiness. For those who are materially free can buy power:

> Rulerships are actually bought for a price, especially the positions of authority in the democratic city . . . Therefore, when someone finally holds a position of authority, it is either because the citizens have favoured him with it, or else because they have received from him money or something in return. (Al-Farabi [940] 1963: 51)

The second reason for Al-Farabi's suspicion of the democratic city is its alienation of virtuous people of learning, which perhaps offends Al-Farabi's own high esteem of like-minded literati. Thus, he laments:

> As for the truly virtuous man – namely the man, who, if he were to rule them, would determine and direct their actions toward happiness – they do not make him a ruler. If by chance he comes to rule them he will soon find himself either deposed or killed or in an unstable and challenged position. (Al-Farabi [940] 1963: 51)

The third explanation for Al-Farabi's criticism of *al-madinah al-jama'iyyah* is its diversity and 'contesting interests', which for Al-Farabi represents a deviation from the Islamic concept of *tawhid* and the one *ummah*. He appears to deride the democratic city's citizenry in whose 'eyes the virtuous ruler is he who has the ability to judge well and to contrive well what enables them to attain their diverse and variegated desires and wishes' (Al-Farabi [940] 1963: 51). This rather sophisticated view of the democratic city in terms of vying 'desires and wishes' somewhat contradicts his functional approach in the crafting of his virtuous city in which he presents a view of a society bound by a common interest.

Aside from the democratic city, Al-Farabi considered other states antithetical to his virtuous city, such as *madinatu al-karamah* (timocracy), *madinatu al-khissah* (plutocracy) and *madinatu al-taghallub* (tyranny) (Al-Huluw 1980: 65–72; Qumayr 1986: 76–8). Relevant to this analysis is Al-Farabi's opposition to tyranny and despotism. His repetitive highlighting of domination, subjugation and humiliation – the ways of tyrannical despots which he describes as 'the enemies of all men' – divulge Al-Farabi's strong belief in human dignity (Al-Farabi [940] 1963: 47). Tyranny is dualistic: domestic, involving abuses of power and travesties of justice; and external, akin to modern-day colonialism and imperialism (Rosenthal 1962: 136). He seems to be aware that tyranny is most likely to result from military rulers and thus Al-Farabi overlooks those who hold military positions in his virtuous city, and, furthermore, lists no martial qualities in the essential requirements of the virtuous *al-ra'isu al-awwal* (the first ruler) (Al-'Aali 1986: 41). Martial qualities are considered inferior to scholarship, knowledge, insight, truthfulness, justice, magnanimity and eloquence. Al-Farabi lists – last – only one martial requirement out of six qualities for the second ruler. That this is indicative of Al-Farabi's opposition to the increasingly praetorian nature of the declining Abbasid era is a fairly safe assumption.

Al-Farabi's virtuous city constitutes the process of dialectic or, more aptly, the process of its resolution. It is *mithaliyyah* (ideal) and it approximates divinity, for *al-kamal* (perfection), an Islamic quality reserved to Allah, is obtainable in the virtuous city. That Al-Farabi expects perfection from mortals in an earthly virtuous city would seem to verge on *ishrak* (polytheism), for it is an Islamic axiom that *al-kamal Allah* (perfection is only for God). The Farabian notion of human perfection indicates a dialectic between Hellenistic and Islamic tenets. On the one hand, the *Qur'anic* notion of *al-qawmu al-salihum* (the righteous people) is in concordance with Al-Farabi's idea of virtuosity. On the other hand, the notion of human perfection appears to derive from the Platonic influence on Al-Farabi's own philosophy. Overall, Al-Farabi

> realized the importance of politics in the philosopher's search for truth about God, the universe, reality and man. Philosophy aims at the perception of the Creator, and the philosopher must strive 'to become in his actions like God' as far as this is humanly possible. For man, the way to this end is first to improve himself and then to improve others in his house or state. (Rosenthal 1962: 122)

Al-Farabi also realised the ultimate fallibility of one-man rule. He therefore appears to advocate a form of collegial rulership, and 'rule through councils' in *al-ri asatu al-thalithah* (the third rulership) (Al-Huluw 1980: 63). This can be interpreted as a way to harmonise the institutions of both the democratic and virtuous cities. Al-Farabi stresses that supreme happiness derives from the virtues of loving justice and loathing injustice, and the strong sense of community and cooperation for the common good. Al-Farabi's virtuous city is multifaceted. It is differentiated in that 'There will be certain ranks of order', and yet it is integrated as 'The function of the city's governor . . . is to manage the cities in such a way that all the city's parts become linked and fitted together.' It is also civic and participatory because 'the citizens . . . cooperate to eliminate the evils and acquire the goods' and the ruler can 'enjoin the citizens [to be active on] certain matters'. The virtuous city is also universal in that 'There may be a number of virtuous nations and virtuous cities whose religions are different, even though they all pursue the very same kind of happiness. For religion is but the impressions of these things or the impressions of their images, imprinted in the soul' (Al-Farabi [940] 1963: 39–41). In this way, Al-Farabi's discussion of both Islam and democracy, and his attempt to harmonise the democratic city with the virtuous city, are indicative of both the calibre of Islamic scholarship during the medieval period and the extent to which Grecian notions of *dēmokratia* were known and understood.

Conclusion

The interpretive and argumentative Muslim repository left behind by Al-Farabi and other medieval Islamic scholars can, at least partially, illuminate a path, a trajectory and a framework for modern Muslim seekers of knowledge from which to raise questions about democracy and Islam. This work serves as a powerful legacy and provides a plethora of questions with few answers. But this is the essence, if there is one, of both Islam and democracy: openness to interrogation and open-endedness – projects of determinate indeterminacy. It is no easy task to discover correlations between these two open-ended projects, to correlate Islam with democracy, but Al-Farabi was the first to systematically explore and affirm the possibilities for such a correlation. By raising pertinent questions and developing lines of inquiry along them, Al-Farabi, for instance, points to congruence between Islamic societies and the Grecian notions of *dēmokratia*. Today, as in the time of Al-Farabi, the difficulty resides in constructing a polity that is loyal to the Arabo-Islamic heritage, morality and identity and yet bold enough to tap into the Western tradition of political philosophy and practical instrumentality to forge a government that achieves democratic and Islamic cohesion.

Note

1. It should be noted here that one Arab scholar challenges the otherwise accepted notion that Al-Farabi's *al-madinah al-jama'iyyah* translates to mean 'the democratic city' (Al-'Aali, 1986: 73).

References

Al-'Aali, A. A.-S. I. A. (1986), *Al-Falsafatu Al-Siyasiyyah 'inda Al-Farabi [Al-Farabi's Political Philosophy]*, Beirut: Dar Al-Tali'ah.
Al-Farabi, A. N. ([940] 1963), 'The Political Regime', in R. Lerner and M. Mahdi (eds), trans. F. M. Najjar, *Medieval Political Philosophy: A Sourcebook*, New York: Free Press of Glencoe, pp. 31–57.
Al-Farabi, A. N. ([935] 1969), *Al-Farabi's Philosophy of Plato and Aristotle*, trans. M. Mahdi, Ithaca, NY: Cornell University Press.
Al-Huluw, A. (1980), *Al-Farabi: Al-Mu'allimu Al-Thani [Al-Farabi: The Second Master]*, Beirut: Bayt Al-Hikmah.
Aristotle ([350 BCE] 2004), *The Nicomachean Ethics*, trans. J. A. K. Thomson, London: Penguin.

Mahdi, M. (1969), 'Introduction', in M. Mahdi (ed.), *Al-Farabi's Philosophy of Plato and Aristotle*, Ithaca, NY: Cornell University Press.

Nasr, S. H. (1985), Why was Al-Farabi called the Second Teacher? *Islamic Culture*, 59, 357–64.

Plato ([360 BCE] 1975), *The Laws*, trans. T. J. Saunders, 3 edn, London: Penguin.

Plato ([380 BCE] 1975), *The Republic*, trans. D. Lee, 2 edn, London: Penguin.

Qumayr, Y. (1986), *Falasifatu Al-Arab: Al-Farabi* [*The Arab Philosophers: Al-Farabi*], Beirut: Dar Al-Mashriq.

Rosenthal, E. I. J. (1962), *Political Thought in Medieval Islam: An Introductory Outline*, Cambridge: Cambridge University Press.

Strauss, L. (1977), 'Farabi's Plato', in A. Hyman (ed.), *Essays in Medieval Jewish and Islamic Philosophy*, New York: KTAV Publishing, pp. 391–427.

'Umar, Y. K. (1992), 'Farabi and Greek Political Philosophy', in A. J. Parcel and R. C. Keith (eds), *Comparative Political Philosophy*, New Delhi: Sage, pp. 185–216.

'Umarah, M. (1988), *Al-Mu'tazilah wa Mushkilatu Al-Hurriyyatu Al-Insaniiyyah* [*The Mu'tazilite and the Problematic of Human Freedom*], Cairo: Dar Al-Shuruq.

Chapter 10

Venice

Stephen Stockwell

A dense mythology surrounds the origins of Venice and its early development as a democratically inclined republic. This mythology was lovingly crafted by propagandists of the later regime, ably assisted by itinerant intellectuals, then and now, all keen to establish Venice as a republican exemplar for their own political purposes. Venice has a remarkable history. It is a rare example of an autonomous polity that survived for more than a millennium, from the barbarian invasions that presaged the fall of Rome at the start of the fifth century CE to the arrival of Napoleon in 1797, when the city surrendered rather than face bombardment. In that time the city grew from a dozen small settlements around the Venetian lagoon into the most technologically advanced and economically active city in Europe, and then declined into a minor power living off the tourist trade. Venice's political arrangements developed along a similar trajectory from a confederacy of self-governing villages on the fringes of the Byzantine empire to an independent city, with sovereignty resting in a people's council, to an aristocratic republican empire in slow decline, where sovereignty was balanced between the *doge* (a 'duke' elected for life) and the *maggior consiglio* (great council) consisting of the men of leading families. Its location in the lagoon guaranteed Venice escape from barbarian hordes and empires to the east and west, and its freedom gave it the chance to explore and adapt a range of political ideas and transmit them along trading routes into Europe generally. Oliver Logan points to how deeply 'the European consciousness of the sixteenth and seventeenth centuries' was underwritten by 'the myth of "Venice state of liberty" and the allied vision of Venice as a supreme exemplar of "the mixed constitution"' because these concepts, along with Venice's institutional stability, 'provided a framework within which thinkers both in Italy and beyond the Alps could work out their ideas of the best practicable form of state' (Logan 1972: 2). This chapter explores the myth of Venice and the alternative mythologies propounded by the myth's critics to arrive at the scant factual material available to gauge the strength of the early republic's claim to democracy, particularly in the period 800–1200 before Venice's aristocratic tendencies became established. In exploring the mythologisation of Venice, it quickly becomes apparent that its physical location and liminality – between past and present, land and sea, east and west, Christianity and Islam – contributed to its egalitarian, neo-democratic early republic, persisted in the liberality of the later republic and is still evident in the active Venetian community politics of today.

The myth of Venice is neither a single nor a simple narrative, but an accretion of historical propaganda, remaking events, often for short-term political gain. The myth begins even before Venice exists. Livy claims in his *History of Rome* that the Trojan, Antenor, escaped the destruction of Troy and sailed to 'the furthest parts of the Adriatic', defeated the locals and founded the nation of the Veneti near where Venice now stands (Livy [25 BCE] 1853: 1:1). This story conveniently mirrors the mythology of Rome's foundation by the descendants of the Trojan prince, Aeneas, and suggests the unity of Italians required for Rome's imperial ambitions. The myth begins to take form with the most serene republic, or *Serenissima* as Venice styled itself, a city founded in liberty, serenely free from foreign control. This was the position of the early chroniclers of Venice, including John the Deacon whose semi-official account of the city's origins is haphazard and at times fanciful, but is the source of much of the later official history (Angold 2007: 87–8; Diacono [1008] 1890). The myth of Venice continued to grow in the early centuries of the second millennia to include altruistic leadership, responsible citizens and a mixed constitution that was well adapted to manage internal and external challenges. These were themes taken up by Andrea Dandolo, *doge* and scholar, who produced an official chronicle to 1280 using state documents and emphasising the stabilising influence of the office of *doge* and other elite Venetian institutions that justified the republic's shift to aristocracy (Dandolo [1352] 1938). Niccolò Machiavelli provided some support for this position in his *Discourses on Livy*, in which he judged Venice to be an aristocratic republic like ancient Sparta and saw that limiting factions in both had provided stability and longevity until they over-reached in their imperial ambitions (Machiavelli [1517] 1893: 23–33). While Venice lost a large portion of its territory on the Italian mainland in the early sixteenth century, its institutions recovered so that by mid-century Gasparo Contarini could enunciate the full form of the Venetian myth and argue that Venice's peace and serenity were the product, not of military might or sea power, but of its excellent constitution (Contarini [1543] 1599). Contarini's account was influential in the Enlightenment and, even after its fall to Napoleon, the myth of Venice and its 1,400-year reign of relative harmony contributed to the development of liberal constitutionalism. William Carew Hazlitt, grandson of the radical essayist, William Hazlitt, continued a long tradition of British admiration for the myth of a liberal Venice built on social solidarity and tolerance that was not always evident in Venetian politics (Eglin 2001; Hazlitt [1900] 1966).

By the middle of the twentieth century, the myth of Venice as the serene product of a carefully balanced, mixed constitution was under challenge from Marxists, who were sensitive to any hint of class conflict. They soon found that they had support from empirical students of Venetian state and family archives that revealed more problems than the traditional myth admitted. Contrary to the myth of a serene democracy, Venice was unremittingly 'tyrannical, oppressive, unstable, contentious, divided, inconstant, treacherous, covetous, impious' (Grubb 1986: 44). The leadership was hegemonic: self-regarding and self-obsessed, irresponsible and corrupt (Queller and Swietech 1977). The constitution encouraged conflict, faction, fraud and procedural abuses (Finlay 1980; Romano 1988). The Venetian republic was violent, oppressive and exploitative of the very citizens on which it depended (Keane 2009: 205; Ruggiero

1980). But even those intent on deconstructing the myth of Venice rarely point out that this purported liberal utopia condoned the slave trade from the eighth to fifteenth centuries: 'They were incorrigible slave traders, and Pope Zacharias . . . seeing in Rome groups of Christian slaves, men and women, belonging to Venetian merchants . . . paid their price and set them at liberty (Okey 1910: 14–15; Verlinden 1969: 1–2). Late twentieth-century anti-mythologists portrayed Venice as just another autocracy with little proletarian participation (Cracco 1967; Ventura 1964). These scholars provided a service in establishing that Venice was subject to the same class divisions as elsewhere, but their dismissal of Venice's differences and specificities along its long historical trajectory became its own ideological orthodoxy (Blanshei 1976: 10).

The proponents of myth and anti-myth form a symbiotic whole: 'Image and counter-image contend within a single arena' (Grubb 1986: 44). The result is a thriving academic industry where all sides rely on facts useful to them while treating Venice as a single, ahistorical unity rather than as a complex and developing entity and judging it against external criteria from before or after its time. From 1297, when Venice closed the books on new participants in the *maggior consiglio*, it was somewhere between the myth and the anti-myth: at best an 'aristocratic republic' with a relatively free press and where artistic and scientific investigation was encouraged; at worst a paranoid, corrupt and totalitarian oligarchy (Carrithers 1991; McCormick 2001; Rubinstein 1973). But the period before 1297 is of particular interest in this chapter because it was then that Venice's institutions gradually developed in the interplay between a strong leadership and the people's forum, generating checks and balances to evolve from simple popular government into something approaching a mature democracy. While layers of myth eddy and swirl like the mists of the lagoon, through them the early republic sparkles as a city-state taking a pragmatic approach as it pursued imperfect but brave experiments with popular government.

Democracy in the Dark Ages

Sitting in the lagoon between land and sea, Venice avoided the worst of the barbarian invasions, the wars between empires and the serfdom that gripped Europe as the western Roman empire teetered into oblivion. In the so-called 'Dark Ages', from the fall of Rome in CE 410 to the first stirrings of the Renaissance around 1300, European politics were dominated by kings and aristocrats savagely enforcing their inequitable system of feudalism (Castelar 1885: 411; Norwich 2003: 280). Through this same period Venice was arguably 'the exuberant democratic Serenissima' (Munk and Munk 1972: 417). While never an avowed democracy in the Athenian model, evidence suggests that amid the factionalism and violence, early Venice kept democratic tendencies alive and passed them on to the Renaissance from whence they informed modern Western democratic politics (Stockwell 2011).

Venice's location in the tidal waters of the northern Adriatic is a major contributing factor to the development of the city. As Elizabeth Crouzet-Pavan says: 'Perhaps no other city on earth has a more striking relationship with its environment than Venice, a thriving human community improbably built upon water and nestled in the lagoon . . .' (Crouzet-Pavan 2000: 39). Venice's environment contributed to the equality on which the city's claim to democracy is based, but, rather than praising Venice's mythological serenity, recent writers have pointed to 'the violence of location' inherent in the city's geographical position (Geer-Ryan 1999: 143–50). Venice began as a cluster of small towns where Roman citizens sought refuge from the violence of the invading Goths and Huns in the fifth century (Lane 1973: 4; Okey 1910: 2–6). The refugees fleeing to the mudflats of the lagoon were confronted by the violence of the elements and the tides. To escape they built houses of wattle and daub on planks driven into the mud (Hazlitt [1900] 1966: 3–8; Norwich 2003: 5–6). The road to the Venetian state began in CE 466 when the settlements of the lagoon sent tribunes to a coordinating council in Grado (Hazlitt [1900] 1966: 3–8; Norwich 2003: 6).

The survival of these foundational settlements was dependent on 'an endless series of public and private works . . . people had to shore up banks, drain swamps, and build, at first with flimsy materials but later with brick and stone . . .' (Crouzet-Pavan 2000: 45). Economically these early Venetians depended on fishing and drying salt, activities where the collective provision of infrastructure improved the rewards for individual effort. Contemporaneous accounts from this early period emphasise that the equality and independence of the people was based in their common struggle against the elements and their common economic activities: their food was the same, their houses were the same, envy was pointless (Cassiodorus [523] 1886: 515–18). The equality of all in the battle for survival and the importance of neighbourly assistance to overcome the hazards of the environment contributed to Venice's egalitarian world view, an approach that is embedded deeply in the Venetian psyche and that informs its democratic tendencies. In the earliest years of Venetian politics, governmental activities were organised through tribunes, a traditional Roman office that represented the interests of commoners to aristocratic authorities as part of the checks and balances that democratised the Roman republic (Finer 1997: 405). The tribune's re-emergence clearly marks early Venetian politics as emanating from the people.

Around the mid-sixth century, the Byzantine or eastern Roman empire based in Constantinople was once again making its presence felt in the Adriatic. The empire called on the settlements of Venice to help in a blockade of Ravenna in 539 and to ferry mercenaries to join the imperial troops there in 551 (Nicol 1988: 2). As the empire re-established itself in the west, there was one striking innovation: 'provincial governors were not now to be appointed by decree of the emperor. They were to be elected from among the inhabitants by the choice of their bishops and leading citizens' (Nicol 1988: 3). This step away from autocracy, whether or not it is a step towards democracy, was an important harbinger of future developments. There is a tradition that the Venetian leadership struck a favourable treaty with the Byzantine empire at this time and told the emperor's representative that 'we fear no invasion or seizure . . . not even by the emperor himself' (Norwich 2003: 9). This is probably 'patriotic fiction', but relations with the empire became inconsequential as Venice was again inundated with refugees when the Lombards, the final wave of invaders, swept the empire from northern Italy in 568 (Nicol 1988: 4–5).

While tribunes continued as significant players in local politics, their power was balanced by the emergence of 'periodical conventions . . . termed in the Venetian dialect *Arrengi*, composed of the whole adult male population of the islands . . . held in the open air' (Hazlitt [1900] 1966: 9). Sometimes termed the *arengo*, or later the *popolare concio* or people's council, these 'conventions' were held intermittently from 574 to 1297 and for much of that time were the effective sovereign body which was called on to steer the fledgling state when all other options were exhausted (Hazlitt [1900] 1966: 10; Lorenzetti 1961: 272). The word *arengo* has a cognate in the medieval Latin word *harenga*, a speech to a public assembly that is in turn the root for the modern English word harangue, an impassioned monologue usually directed at opponents. Political assemblies were not uncommon in medieval Europe and, like Venice: 'it was mainly at assemblies that early and high medieval polities were able to act' (Reuter 2001: 432). But the Venetian *arengo* was active earlier than any others and while most were called at the behest of the monarch to legitimate tax increases, the assembly of Venice was a power unto itself and of most use when leadership was spent and new directions required. Guided by the *arengo*, the settlements of the lagoon avoided conflict with the final wave of barbarians and maintained their trade with Constantinople and the east. Its political openness allowed Venice to become the conduit between the Byzantine and Holy Roman Empires, then between Islam and Europe, and its place in the ebb and flow of ideas fuelled not only its military and artistic success, but also the political experiments that allowed it to adapt to changing conditions.

Democratic Developments

The Venetian settlements were far from unified in the seventh century as the Lombards' advances pushed more refugees, sometimes whole towns, into the lagoon settlements (Nicol 1988: 4). Heraclea was the formal provincial capital, but it had an uneasy relationship with trading centres such as Torcello and Malamocco. Tensions developed between the Byzantine Orthodox Church in Grado and the Roman Catholic Church based in Aquileia (Nicol 1988: 8). Personal vendetta all too often turned into civil war and 'tribunes conspired against each other, family rose against family, clan against clan [and] sanguinary affairs were of constant occurrence' (Hazlitt [1900] 1966: 16–20). Venice may have disappeared in a bout of clan war, but chroniclers claim that in 697 (John the Deacon puts it a little later in around 714) patriarchs and bishops called all Venetians together in a common council to elect a single leader, Paulicius, to negotiate with the Lombards and unify the lagoon settlements (Nicol 1988: 9–10). Unfortunately, this history, so redolent in democratic possibilities, is supported only by unreliable chronicles from many centuries later. However, the revised history with some factual basis has interesting lessons never-theless. When Constantinople ordered the destruction of all icons in 726, the people rebelled against Byzantine rule and the local garrison at Heraclea declared inde-pendence by electing their own leader, Orso as *dux*, softened in the local Venetian dialect to *doge* (Nicol 1988: 10; Norwich 2003: 13).

As the Lombards continued to encroach on their territory, the Venetians made peace with Constantinople and, by balancing the two major forces against each other, Venice flourished in the space between. The political power of the scattered settlements consolidated in a republican direction when: 'In 742 the people of Malamocco had rebelled against the administration in Heraclea and elected as their own *dux* a son of Orso called Teodata' (Nicol 1988: 11.) The early Venetian constitution provided a system of government where towns elected municipal tribunes annually, while the sovereign *arengo* elected the *doge* as leader for life (Lane 1966: 287–8). At first this approach produced stability, but the question of transition to a new leader soon caused strife. Teodato was blinded before he was deposed, a fate that awaited his successors. Then, in 756, the *arengo* took the power to elect two tribunes annually with responsibility 'to prevent the abuse of ducal power' (Norwich 2003: 17). Thus, the *arengo* reasserted its sovereignty every twelve months and kept the *doge* responsive to the popular will. *Doges* were still elected for life and many ran strong, unifying administrations, undertaking civic works, fighting pirates and managing diplomatic relationships to foster trade. But the management of succession continued to bedevil Venice, particularly when the Doge Maurizio Galbaio, 'co-opted his son Giovanni as his colleague in authority, a practice which he learnt from the emperors in Constantinople' (Nicol 1988: 12). This hereditary approach provided stability for limited periods, but, as dynasties became over-confident and self-satisfied, the social situation deteriorated and the rule of particular families ended with blindings and assassinations that were resolved only when the *arengo* was again convened to exercise its sovereign authority. When the Doge Antenori sought to avoid the *arengo* in 810 by calling for foreign support from the Franks, the people of the lagoon united under the command of Agnello Participazio to see off the interlopers and depose the *doge*.

The first century of unified Venetian governance between 727 and 827 was marked by a very raw form of democracy: citizens were free to elect tribunes and *doges*, but leadership all too often descended into factions, which sought external support and made hereditary claims to forestall the will of the people. This led to a politics of violent catharsis where the power of the *doge* was brutally balanced by the people. Of the eight *doges* in Venice's first one hundred years, all but one was assassinated or exiled after blinding (Muir 1999: 384). Thus, to avoid political excess, checks and balances were instituted to ensure that the *doge* worked within the authority of the assembly. The Venetian *doge* was unlike other leaders in the region: 'All the princes of Italy are tyrants except for the Doge of Venice' (Bernardo Bembo quoted in Munk and Munk 1972: 418).

Democracy Comes of Age

The spirit of unity and the search for greater security after the attempted Frankish invasion led to increased settlement on the neutral and comparatively safe Rialto islands in the centre of the lagoon where Venice stands today (Norwich 2003: 20–3). Agnello Participazio, who became *doge* after the Franks were repulsed, lived on Rialto and so did all *doges* after him. While still technically part of the Byzantine empire, the victory over the Franks reaffirmed Venice's independence and kept it outside the feudal sphere. Venice found the autonomy to manage trade not only between Constantinople and the Franks, but also with emerging Islamic markets in the Middle East (Nicol 1988: 21). As the Islamic caliphates grew: 'Venice began to establish trading contacts with the expanding Moslem world and to exploit its tempting links to

VENICE 137

the spice markets of Central Asia and India' (Howard 2000: 1). As feudalism spread through Europe, Venice watched liberal developments in the Islamic east. The caliphs, like the *doges*, were elected and there were many other 'shared cultural characteristics in Venice and the Levant evolving independently from similar roots, fostered by a common Mediterranean mercantile outlook and urban mentality' (Howard 2000: 1). To trade with, and learn from, the Islamic east, Venice needed to exercise all its diplomatic skills and cultural openness; traits that were also useful in the processes of political reform.

In 864, Venice's failures against Adriatic pirates and the early death of the younger, co-opted *doge* lured the older *doge*, Pietro Tradonico, into a series of political blunders that resulted in his assassination. While the new *doge*, Orso Participazio, was from the same family, he was elected in 864 by an independent and reconfigured *arengo*. He reformed Venetian government by legislating for: 'the institution of judges (*judices*) elected to be magistrates as well as counsellors to the *doge* (Nicol 1988: 35; Norwich 2003: 35). For the next century, the checks and balances on the elite worked well as Venetian democracy matured. Ducal successions were non-violent, and all levels of society participated in decision making. As feudalism engulfed the rest of Europe, Venice provided the liberty to pursue science and commerce, which translated into technological leadership and maritime power (McNeill 1974: 9–11). In 976, the Doge Pietro Candiano IV showed that there were problems still inherent in the government of Venice when he grabbed the wealth of the state for himself, married into a noble Frank family and took on the role of a feudal lord (Norwich 2003: 41–3). Pietro was assassinated, but his rule was followed by nepotism with short-term, weak *doges*. Nepotism finally came to an end in 1032 when the *arengo* elected an opponent of hereditary succession, Domenico Flabanico, as *doge*. He put an end to the co-appointment of family members, or anyone else, to the position of *doge* and he enforced existing 'legislation providing for the proper election of *doges* and giving adequate powers to the popular assembly' (Norwich 2003: 65–6). Flabanico also broadened the base of his advice to a regular council (Finer 1997: 987).

The government of Venice between 800 and 1200 was far from an ideal democracy: elections were often by 'acclamation' and the *doge*, elected for life, could only 'fall by popular riot' (Finer 1997: 987). But the Venetian system gradually developed from rough justice, with regular blindings and assassinations, into a democratic state, with debate in council and assembly and oversight from the *arengo* to restore order and reconcile divergent social views. By the late twelfth century, growing trade saw Italian city-communes emerge from feudalism and Venice's balanced constitution of elected leader, council and assembly 'became the republican ideal' (Jones 1965: 73). Venice's competitors, the maritime republics of Genoa, Pisa and Amalfi, similarly favoured mixed and anti-monarchical constitutions resting on sovereignty from 'the people gathered in assembly' (Herlihy 1973: 54–68; Holmes 2001: 21–33, 218; Shaw 2005: 53–4). As Frankish influence declined in 1167, Venice helped to found the Lombard League where classical ideas such as democracy informed a new civic humanism (Jones 1965: 73; Norwich 2003: 103). These newly independent city-states evolved into broad-based communes with active participation by the *popolo* (Finer 1997: 953–4; Jones 1965: 75). By the fourteenth century there were anti-feudal, self-governing constitutions influenced by Venice in many Italian city-states including Florence (Gilbert 1968; Keane 2009: 251–2).

The End of Democracy

But just as it transmitted democratic methods across Italy, Venice itself moved from a people's government to formal aristocracy. A trade dispute with Byzantium in 1171 prompted Doge Vitale Michiel II to embark on a popular mission to avenge Venice's honour. Returning defeated and with the plague, he was the first *doge* assassinated in 200 years and a review of the catastrophe established that his venture lacked constitutional authority. Reforms in 1172 began a trend 'to *narrow* the popular base and to *expand* the ruling apex' (Finer 1997: 988). The *arengo's* powers were thus limited to approving war and acclaiming the *doge's* selection, while all its other powers went to the *Consiglio Maggiore*, the great council of 480 members who became a self-perpetuating oligarchy (Finer 1997: 987–9). It was this government that redirected the Fourth Crusade against Christian Constantinople and debilitated the West's bulwark against the caliphates (Norwich 2003: 127–42). The aristocracy's power grew in 1229, when a new senate was instituted to instruct ambassadors, regulate navigation and manage debates in the great council, further sidelining the *arengo* and the *doge* (Finer 1997: 989). The *doge* was still elected for life and remained the chair of committees, but the aristocrats around him were growing in power and the *arengo* was without authority to intervene. The closure of the great council (*serrata*) in 1297 to all but recent members and their descendants was the end of Venice as a popular republic (Finer 1997: 990). The *arengo* was redundant, though formally extinguished only in 1421. The aristocratic republic excluded the common citizen, and as the aristocracy grew the great council became a large, unwieldy ritual assembly subject to factionalism, nepotism and personal ambition. The emerging oligarchy was not keen on the responsibilities of high office, which interfered with its commercial pursuits and forced its members to do their duties by a mix of fines and shame (Norwich 2003: 119; Queller 1969: 223–35).

Yet even when Venice effectively became an aristocracy, it still exhibited democratic traits of equality, collectivity and cooperation based in the economics of cross-class solidarity whereby the wealth of trade spread through society and wealthy commoners became a strong middle class (Finer 1997: 992; Norwich 2003: 156). To counter factions, bans were applied to bribery, corruption and the display of coats of arms and other family insignia (Norwich 2003: 165). To diminish political organisation through social activities, banquets and weddings were limited to family members and excessive god-parenting was outlawed (Muir 1999). To minimise the intensity of factional conflict, vendetta was criminalised and electioneering was banned (Bouwsma 1968; Finer 1997: 997; Lane 1973: 109; Ruggiero 1980). Yet debate was prized: the republic avoided Vatican censorship of books and new scientific knowledge; it protected the astronomer Galileo and the free-thinking priest, Paolo Sarpi, who argued for the separation of church and state (Bouwsma 1968: 71–83; Norwich 2003: 511–12). In the fourteenth century Petrarch complained ironically that Venice had 'far too much freedom of speech', and three centuries later Sir Henry Wotton could still report that 'all men speak willingly' (Finer 1997: 1017). Venice also remained a cosmopolitan city: 'it signified nothing if a man be a Turk, a Jew, a gospeller, a papist or a believer in the devil, nor does anyone challenge you whether you are moneyed or not . . .' (Goffman 2002; Munk and Munk 1972: 428).

Commoners retained some democratic capabilities through the *scuola*, neighbourhood-based self-help groups that provided basic social services to members and access to state officials (Finer 1997: 1015; Lane 1973: 105–6). Thus, while the common people, and even the prosperous middle class, were excluded from participation in government, they channelled their civic energies into these fraternal organisations. The *scuola* carefully managed the balance between rich and poor in their membership: members of the aristocratic class could join for their own political purposes, 'but for this honor they were assessed heavy dues, and they did not participate in making policy' (Munk and Munk 1972: 421). The *scuola* were civic institutions, managing welfare, food relief and hospitals, but they also demonstrated their power by organising religious processions, decorating their halls with work from leading artists and displaying their political self-sufficiency (Grubb 1986: 50).

Conclusion

Venice was never a complete democracy. The mythology of the enlightened and benevolent republic was institutional propaganda during the *Serenissima* and, since 1797, a vehicle for various political entrepreneurs. Anti-mythologists are right to point out problems of oligarchy, nepotism and elective despotism which recurred during the period of the republic. Its early history was violent and popular assembly in the *arengo* was often a last resort after extended vendetta among aristocratic families undermined their attempts at government. It is also a history of democratic decline as the aristocratic regime gradually sidelined the *arengo*. By looking beyond the mythology, however, and at the historical specificities instead, particularly in the early republic from 800 to 1200, it can be seen that, while the mythologisers were wrong in portraying a utopia, the anti-mythologists were also wrong to see a picture of unremitting oppression, exploitation and gloom: while the rest of Europe slipped into feudalism, Venice's constitution rested on a sovereign popular assembly and gradually developed the checks and balances and rule of law that are associated with mature democracy. Its liberal perspectives influenced the progressive demeanour of the later, aristocratic republic that embraced the collectivity of the convoy where the fastest ship had to wait for the slowest and produced a politics where the rich had some responsibility to assist the poor to prosper (Lane 1973; Muir 1999). Venetian democracy was an accommodation between people and power, the citizens and the oligarchs. Democracy and the debate it engenders are practical tools by which common people can mould and manage their interactions with power and push the benefits of the state a little their way. The Venetian republic began in equality and still reminds us today of the efficacy of civil conversation, the power of gradual reform and the malleability of the democratic enterprise. Scholars have found Venice an inspiration for ways to manage the power of oligarchies: 'appointment procedures combining lottery and election; offices or assemblies excluding the wealthy from eligibility; and political trials enlisting the entire citizenry in prosecutions and appeals' (McCormick 2006: 147).

The myth of a democratic Venice still has resonance not only in the active community politics of the city today, but also during carnivals, traditionally 'celebrations of civic solidarity' where anonymity hid class, race and social origin and allowed escape from 'the constraints of normal social roles' to produce 'catharsis' and positive social effects (McNeill 1974: 93–4). Some would even argue that the aristocratic spectacle of the opera has been 'reworked . . . based on democratic principles . . . reimagining time and space . . . (particularly) the period prior to the Serrata of 1297' (Feldman 2000; 217). The 'temporary autonomous zones' that carnival and opera create is inescapably egalitarian, symbolising the autonomous zone that early Venice created for itself in myth, and in practice (Bey 1985: 1).

References

Angold, M. (2007), 'The Venetian Chronicles and Archives as Sources for the History of Byzantium and the Crusades (992–1204)', *Proceedings of the British Academy*, 132, 59–94.

Bey, H (1985), *T. A. Z.: The Temporary Autonomous Zone, Ontological Anarchy, Poetic Terrorism*, New York: Autonomedia.

Blanshei, S. R. (1976), 'Perugia, 1260–1340: Conflict and Change in a Medieval Italian Urban Society', *Transactions of the American Philosophical Society*, New Series, 66(2): 1–128.

Bouwsma, W. J. (1968), *Venice and the Defense of Republican Liberty*, Berkeley, CA: University of California Press.

Carrithers, D. W. (1991), 'Not so Virtuous Republics', *Journal of the History of Ideas*, 52(2), 245–68.

Cassiodorus ([523] 1886), *The Letters of Cassiodorus: Variae Epistolae*, trans. T. Hodgkin, London: Henry Frowde.

Castelar, E. (1885), 'The Progress of Democracy in Europe', *North American Review*, 141, 409–20.

Contarini, G. ([1543] 1599), *The Commonwealth and Government of Venice*, trans. L. Lewkenor, London: Windet.

Cracco, G. (1967), *Societa e stato nel medioevo veneziano*, Florence: Olschki.

Crouzet-Pavan, E. (2000), 'Toward and Ecological Understanding of the Myth of Venice', in J. Martin and D. Romano (eds), *Venice Reconsidered*, Baltimore, MD: Johns Hopkins University Press, pp. 39–64.

Dandolo, A. ([1352] 1938), *Chronica per extensum scripta*, ed. E. Pastorello, Bologna: Rerum Italicarum Scriptores.

Diacono, G. ([1008] 1890), 'Cronaca Veneziana', in G. Monticolo (ed.), *Cronache Veneziane antichissme*, Rome: Forzani.

Eglin, J. (2001), *Venice Transfigured: The Myth of Venice in British Culture, 1660–1797*, New York: Palgrave Macmillan.

Feldman, M. (2000), 'Opera, Festivity and Spectacle in "Revolutionary" Venice', in J. Martin and D. Romano (eds), *Venice Reconsidered*, Baltimore, MD: Johns Hopkins University Press.

Finer, S. E. (1997), *The History of Government*, Oxford: Oxford University Press.

Finlay, R. (1980), *Politics in Renaissance Venice*, New Brunswick, NJ: Rutgers University Press.

Geer-Ryan, H. (1999), 'Venice and the Violence of Location', in M. Bal (ed.), *The Practice of Cultural Analysis*, Stanford, CA: Stanford University Press, pp. 143–50.

Gilbert, F. (1968), 'The Venetian Constitution in Florentine Political Thought', in N. Rubenstein (ed.), *Florentine Studies*, London: Faber & Faber, pp. 463–500.

Goffman, D. (2002), *The Ottoman Empire and Early Modern Europe*, Cambridge: Cambridge University Press.

Grubb, J. S. (1986), 'When Myths Lose Power: Four Decades of Venetian Historiography', *Journal of Modern History*, 58(1), 43–94.

Hazlitt, W. C. ([1900] 1966), *The Venetian Republic*, 4th edn, London: Adam & Charles Black.

Herlihy, D. (1973), *Pisa in the Early Renaissance*, Port Washington, NY, Kennikat.

Holmes, G. (2001), *The Oxford History of Medieval Europe*, Oxford: Oxford University Press.

Howard, D. (2000), *Venice & the East*, New Haven, CT: Yale University Press.

Jones, P. J. (1965), 'Communes and Despots: The City State in Late-Medieval Italy', *Transactions of the Royal Historical Society*, 5(15), 71–96.

Keane, J. (2009), *The Life and Death of Democracy*, New York: Simon & Schuster.

Lane, F. C. (1966), *Venice and History*, Baltimore, MD: Johns Hopkins University Press.

Lane, F. C. (1973), *Venice: A Maritime Republic*, Baltimore, MD: Johns Hopkins University Press.

Livy ([25 BCE] 1853), *History of Rome*, trans. D. Spillan, London: Henry G. Bohn.

Logan, O. (1972), *Culture and Society in Venice, 1470–1790*, New York: Charles Scribner.

Lorenzetti, G. (1961), *Venice and its Lagoon*, Trieste: Edizioni Lint.

Machiavelli, N. ([1517] 1893), *Discourses*, trans. N. H. Thomson, London: Kegan Paul, Trench.

McCormick, J. P. (2001), 'Machiavellian Democracy: Controlling Elites with Ferocious Populism', *American Political Science Review*, 95(2), 297–313.

McCormick, J. P. (2006), 'Contain the Wealthy and Patrol the Magistrates', *American Political Science Review*, 100(2), 147–63.

McNeill, W. (1974), *Venice: Hinge of Europe 1081–1797*, Chicago, IL: University of Chicago Press.

Muir, E. (1999), 'The Sources of Civil Society in Italy', *Journal of Interdisciplinary History*, 29(3), 379–406.

Munk, J. and W. Munk (1972), 'Venice Hologram', *Proceedings of the American Philosophical Society*, 116(5), 415–42.

Nicol, D. (1988), *Byzantium and Venice*, Cambridge: Cambridge University Press.

Norwich, J. J. (2003), *A History of Venice*, London: Penguin.

Okey, T. (1910), *The Story of Venice*, London: J. M. Dent.

Queller, D. E (1969), 'The Civic Irresponsibility of the Venetian Nobility', in D. Herlihy, R. S. Lopez and V. Slessarev (eds), *Economy, Society and Government in Medieval Italy*, Kent, OH: Kent State University Press, pp. 223–35

Queller, D. E. and F. R. Swietek (1977), *Two Studies on Venetian Government*, Geneva: Droz

Reuter, T. (2001), 'Assembly Politics in Western Europe from the Eighth Century to the Twelfth', in P. Linehan and J. L. Nelson (eds), *The Medieval World*, London: Routledge, pp. 432–50.

Romano, D. (1988), *Patricians and Popolani: The Social Foundations of the Venetian Renaissance State*, Baltimore, MD: Johns Hopkins University Press.

Rubinstein, N. (1973), 'Italian Reactions to Terraferma Expansion in the Fifteenth Century', in J. R. Hale (ed.), *Renaissance Venice*, London: Faber & Faber, pp. 197–217.

Ruggiero, G. (1980), *Violence in Early Renaissance Venice*, New Brunswick, NJ: Rutgers University Press.

Shaw, C. (2005), 'Principles and Practice in the Civic Government of Fifteenth-Century Genoa', *Renaissance Quarterly*, 58(1), 45–90.

Stockwell, S. (2011), 'Democratic Culture in the Early Venetian Republic', in B. Isakhan and S. Stockwell (eds), *The Secret History of Democracy*, London: Palgrave Macmillan, pp. 105–22.

Ventura, A. (1964), *Nobilta e popolo nella society veneta del '400 e '500*, Bari: Laterza.

Verlinden, C. (1969), 'Medieval "Slavers"', in D. Herlihy, R. S. Lopez and V. Slessarev (eds), *Economy, Society and Government in Medieval Italy*, Kent, OH: Kent State University Press, pp. 1–14.

Chapter 11

The Nordic Countries

Frode Hervik

The Middle Ages should be studied and understood in its own terms and on its own premises, but a historian must also be able to explain progress, development and the great lineages of history. One of these great lineages is the history of democracy, in which the 'Dark Ages' are assumed to be a black hole. The experience of the Nordic countries during this period provides a worthy case study to test the accuracy of this assessment. The word 'democracy' directly translated from the Greek means a form of government where the people rule. In the city state (*polis*) of Athens, the popular assembly that consisted of all free men was the basis of sovereignty and the ultimate arbiter for their whole political system. Thus, democracy in the Greek *polis* can be said to be direct. However, by the end of the twentieth century, it was not direct democracy, but rather representative democracy that was the pre-eminent political system. The main focus in this chapter is to inquire as to whether the Nordic countries in the 'Dark Ages' were black holes in democratic terms, whether they had elements of direct democracy or whether they contained some proto-democratic features that contributed to the development of representative democracy.

There are many ways of defining democracy, but when it comes to the Middle Ages a constitutional approach which concentrates on the laws a regime enacts concerning political activity seems to be the best approach (Tilly 2007: 7–11). This is because, when dealing with the Middle Ages, the aim is not to search for an optimal model of democracy, but rather to look for proto-democratic features in the political system before the age of modern democracy. Following a constitutional approach, proto-democracy is apparent when it contains some core elements, such as representation, citizenship, human rights, rule of law and limitations of power (Touraine 1997: 21–73). The notion of democracy was first introduced to the Middle Ages in the middle of the thirteenth century with the translation of the political works of Aristotle into Latin, then the intellectual language of Western Europe (Hanson 1989: 71). However, the word 'democracy' did not become widely used in the Middle Ages and is not known from Nordic sources. The absence of the word 'democracy' does not necessarily mean that some proto-democratic features did not exist, and constitutional laws enacted in the Nordic countries in the Middle Ages will be analysed below to seek such features. The focus below will be on the state, but it is also possible to find relevant case studies in other levels of medieval society, for instance, the Church, the guilds and the political systems in cities.

The Medieval Icelandic Constitution

The so-called 'Icelandic freestate' in the far north Atlantic was a result of a process of colonisation without a kingly command in the early Middle Ages, and lasted from 930 until CE 1264 when Iceland was brought under the dominion of the Norwegian king. In this period the assembly, the *Althing*, was where all free men could meet and it was the dominant political institution in Iceland. Many historians have pointed out that the formation of the political system in the 'Icelandic freestate' was influenced by the society most of the immigrants had left behind, namely, the western part of Norway (Jóhannesson 1974: 50–1; Taranger 1924: 20–1). German romantics have also considered the social and political arrangements in the 'Icelandic freestate' to be a preservation of ancient Scandinavian practice that was, in turn, a preservation of even more ancient German practice (Miller 1990: 16–17). Connected to this is the claim that the German tribes were ruled by a principle of popular sovereignty in their assemblies, known as *things*, and thus contained a democratic aspect (Gierke [1881] 1958: 37–8; Ullmann 1961: 22). Such claims are, however, considered to be outdated by modern research. First, because it is impossible to talk of one single 'German' practice as the barbarian tribes were far from homogeneous and were under various degrees of Roman influence, so it is difficult to distinguish between the 'German' and 'Roman' origins of their political practice. Secondly, the main populist practice in the German tribes was the election of kings, and these elections implied the singling out of a man already belonging to a royal dynasty. The royal blood-right is often considered to have been sacral, and thus it is claimed that kingship in 'German' tribes had a more sacral than a democratic character (King 1988: 147–53; Oakley 1983: 309–13).

During the 'Freestate' period the lack of a king resulted in a slow state-building process, with the *Althing* and the common law as the only institutions of a rather weak state formation. Beyond that there was no executive power, no bureaucracy, no authority to enforce the law and no organised military power to defend the island (Miller 1990: 20–1). There has been much discussion and debate about the strength of Icelandic constitutional arrangements in this period. Traditionally, it was thought that a common law for all of Iceland was implemented about the same time as the *Althing* was established around 930, and further that the constitutional arrangements could be traced back to the same time. The latter is problematic because tenth-century Iceland lacked a literate culture and the law was not written down until the twelfth century. The two surviving law codes are even more recent, dating from the thirteenth century, and only one of these contains the constitutional arrangements. Against this background, and because these law codes do not correspond to the description of the political system in the sagas, it has been claimed that the constitutional arrangements in the code date from the thirteenth century and, further, that it is not even certain that they were implemented at all (Sigurðsson 1999: 71–83). If they were, they probably lasted for only a short period in the thirteenth century and not for the whole 'Freestate' period.

However, if we take a look at the constitutional arrangements they contain some proto-democratic features. There was a clear distinction between the legislative and the judicial functions of the *Althing*, a separation of power that reflects more recent democratic thinking. The legislative authority was given to a representative assembly within the *Althing* called *lögrétta*, which consisted of thirty-nine chieftains (*goðar*), nine additional regional representatives, the two bishops and the law-speaker: a total of fifty-one men. All these, with the probable exception of the bishops and the law-speaker, could in addition bring two advisers each. By contrast, the judicial functions were taken care of by four quarter courts (*fjórðungsdómar*), and eventually by a fifth court as well. While under these arrangements it appears that the *Althing* was more of a meeting place where legal announcements, new laws and judgements were publicised, rather than a decision-making assembly, it was the *Althing* that elected the law-speaker (Jóhannesson 1974: 35–83; *Laws of Early Iceland – I*: 53–138). Thus, these constitutional arrangements contained elements of both political representation and direct participation. Based on these constitutional arrangements, the 'Freestate' has been described as a medieval society with unusually strong proto-democratic and republican tendencies. This is because the *Althing*, its representative legislative body and its courts are considered to have been the centre of Icelandic political and governmental life without a coercive overlord. Additionally, the many alternatives in handling grievances in the legal system protected the rights of the free men (Byock 2002: 1–14). The principle that all free men could participate in the *Althing* and the fact that there was no coercive overlord were clearly a tendency to the egalitarian.

Nevertheless, a question remains as to how egalitarian the political society in the 'Freestate' was. The legislative assembly – according to the constitutional arrangements in the law code – had a more aristocratic composition. Further, recent research indicates that a gradual process of concentration of power had already started in the tenth century and not in the thirteenth as previously has been claimed (Sigurðsson 1999: 39–83). In this process the dominant political feature was not popular participation in the *Althing*, but the competitive struggle for power between the chieftains and their followers. It is problematic to use the notion of democracy in relation to a more or less stateless society like medieval Iceland, and there is some concern that proto-democratic features have been exaggerated. This concern arises because even though the *Althing* and its legislative assembly made decisions in cases that concerned the community, their power was rather weak when it came to enforcement. The public sphere was small and there were few tasks that demanded a common policy for the community. The assembly seems to have been mainly an arena for conflict-solving and a meeting place that had the maintenance of peace as its main purpose. However, the separation of the judicial and the legislative power seems quite modern, although this arrangement was probably enacted for practical reasons rather than ideological principles. Popular participation and influence in the judicial system was a common feature in all the Nordic countries. A question regarding Iceland is whether the rights of the free men were better protected by chieftains than they would have been by a coercive king. It is interesting to note in this context that every free man, in principle, could chose which chieftain he would support. As there was no public power to maintain law and order or to enforce judgements, all legal cases were private matters where the support of family, friends and chieftains played an important role. On the other hand, the presence of a just king could imply a better protection of the rights of the free men, while a king that ruled arbitrarily implied the opposite. In summary, there is no conclusive evidence that the early Icelandic society was more violent or unjust than the Scandinavian kingdoms, nor is there evidence that the 'Freestate' was particularly more 'democratic', in the sense that it better protected individual rights and gave people access to governmental discussions, than other Scandinavian legal and political systems of the time.

The Mixed Constitution in the Scandinavian Kingdoms

Institutions similar to the *Althing* played an important role in the Scandinavian kingdoms as well as Iceland, but when they were under the king's rule it cannot be said that *things* gathered men into sovereign political entities. The Scandinavian kingdoms in the later Middle Ages were state formations, with the king and his civil servants as the executive power, a small bureaucracy, representative assemblies, taxation and an organised military system. After a period of state-building and strong kings, Denmark and Sweden developed constitutions that limited their monarchies at the end of the thirteenth century and in the first half of the fourteenth century. Thus, the king had to share power with an aristocratic assembly and monarchs were elected by a broader assembly that included popular participation as well aristocratic influence. During the Scandinavian union (1397–1523), a similar constitution was also adopted by Norway. In 1282, the first Danish *Håndfæstning* was issued. This was a constitutional document that was a treaty between the king and the aristocracy on behalf of the whole kingdom, and has been called the 'Danish Magna Carta' (*Diplomatarium Danicum* 1938–: 2(3): 45; Erslev 1902: 116). Almost three decades later, in 1319, the so-called 'Swedish Magna Carta' or 'The Charter of Liberties' was issued (*Diplomatarium Suecanum* 1829–2004: 2199; Drar 1980: 29). The comparison with Magna Carta is pertinent as it is the same type of constitutional document as with some similar arrangements. Such documents were issued in other parts of Europe around this time as well. The main purpose behind these charters was to limit the power of the king and to strengthen the rights and privileges of the aristocracy. In the fourteenth century, another four Danish constitutional documents of the same type as the *Håndfæstning* of 1282 were issued. Similar arrangements were also instituted in Sweden from the 1330s via a written oath that the king had to take and which was incorporated into the national law of Magnus Eriksson around 1350 (*Magnus Erikssons Landslag* 1962: V; *Svenska Landskapslagar* 1933–46: 3:237–8). In the fifteenth century constitutional documents of the Danish *Håndfæstning* type were issued in all three Scandinavian kingdoms. From 1282 onwards, these documents incorporate constitutional principles that include the rule of law, political representation, the separation of powers and individual rights.

   The principle of the rule of law was not a revolutionary change when it was established in the Danish *Håndfæstning* document of 1282, because from around 1100 the Danish kings had already committed themselves to maintain the laws even though the implications of this commitment remains unclear (Christensen 1977: 239–40). The principle became fixed in 1282 when the king had to commit to maintain the 'law unbreakable', which meant that he himself could not be exempt from the law (*Diplomatarium Danicum* 1938–: 2(3): 45). In Sweden, the principle of the rule of law was established in 'The Charter of Liberties' in 1319 but, as in Denmark, there was also an earlier forerunner to this principle (*Diplomatarium Suecanum* 1829–2004: 2199; *Svenska Landskapslagar* 1933–46: 5:109). The Danish *Håndfæstning* document of 1282 not only contained the general principle of the rule of law, but also laid down the principle that no one could be imprisoned unless he was legally convicted according to the law, caught red-handed in a crime or had confessed to a crime. A similar principle had earlier been established in the English Magna Carta and later also appeared in the oath of Swedish kings, which was integrated into the national law for the whole kingdom around 1350. In the Swedish law, the king had to pledge not to punish anyone unless they were subject to a legal conviction. Such arrangements instituted an individual right and sought to secure justice for the people. It can be seen as a predecessor to the similar arrangements in modern declarations of human rights. The enactment of this principle in medieval Denmark and Sweden did not imply a legal revolution because a law-based judicial system had been in place long before. Fundamentally new though was the introduction of an individual right into a constitutional document.

In the Scandinavian kingdoms there were sporadic aristocratic assemblies in the twelfth century that were held with an increasing frequency throughout the thirteenth century (Helle 1972: 302; Hude 1893: 37–9). The term parliament came into use in the Scandinavian kingdoms in the late thirteenth century as a term for these aristocratic assemblies (Helle 1972: 106–7, 296; Schück 2005: 24). At this time these parliaments considered themselves as representative of their respective realms, and in both Denmark and Sweden they sometimes put themselves forward as the king's counterpart. However, the parliaments were only minimally institutionalised. The Danish parliament, *Danehoffet*, became the most developed and met annually on a fixed date and at a fixed place according to the *Håndfæstning* document of 1282 and all subsequent, corresponding documents from the fourteenth century (*Diplomatarium Danicum* 1938–: 2(3):45, 2(8):176, 2(9):273, 3(5):325, 4(1):40). However, this arrangement was probably not fulfilled. In the fifteenth century, the role of the aristocratic assemblies was partly continued by the councils of the realm and they eventually became institutionalised. In the second half of the fifteenth century, assemblies of the estates of the realm were instituted as an addition to councils of the realm (Schuck 2005: 96–121). The crucial aspect of this development was that the powerful magnates involved in politics went from being aristocrats representing no one but themselves to a group also representing the estates of the realm and thus the concept of political representation developed (Reynolds 1984: 250–1, 302–3; Tierney [1983] 1997: 25–9).

The aristocratic assemblies sought to constantly enlarge their authority and competence. In the Danish constitutional document of 1320, it became law that the king could no longer start a war, issue prohibitions against the export of any commodities or implement new laws without the consent of the parliament (*Diplomatarium Danicum* 1938–: 2(8):176). In Sweden, the charter of 1319 gave the parliament authority in questions of extraordinary taxation (*Diplomatarium Suecanum* 1829–2004: 2199). In Norway, constitutional documents like those in the neighbouring kingdoms were not issued before the fifteenth century, but in 1449 it was established that the king could not start a war, start negotiations that concerned Norwegian interests, give away or pawn castles or fiefs or give foreigners fiefs or a place in the council of the realm without counsel from the council of the realm (*Norges Gamle Love* [1388–1604] 1912–: 2(2):3). The term counsel in this sense was probably more binding than just implying a consultative duty (Helle 1972: 38–9). The constitutional documents of 1483, one Danish–Norwegian and another corresponding Swedish one, represented the high point in the limitation of the king's power and the advance of the aristocracy. According to these laws, the management of castles and fiefs, the pledging of properties of the realm, changes in tariff rates, declarations of war, the issue of privileges to foreign towns and the issue of prohibitions could be implemented only after the counsel of the councils of the realms (*Norges Gamle Love* [1388–1604] 1912–: 2(3):1; *Sveriges Traktater med Fræmmande Magter* 1895: 3: 529). The decisions in the councils of the realms were originally based on consensus, but in the fifteenth century majority decisions were also acceptable on some issues (Steenstrup 1932: 457–61). From the preceding discussion it becomes clear that Denmark and Sweden, and eventually Norway, were not pure monarchies in the later Middle Ages, but had became political systems based on power-sharing between king, aristocracy and, eventually, some commoners in a mixed constitution.

This diffusion of power gradually extended further to all commoners who participated in the regional *things*. The introduction of extraordinary taxation measures required the involvement of the regional *things* in Sweden in the fourteenth century, and in Denmark and Norway in the century after. The support of the *things* was also required to enact new laws in Sweden. The regional *things* were composed not only of commoners, but also included regional nobility; they involved participation from a much broader cross-section of the people compared with the aristocratic assemblies on a national level. In the fifteenth century, the rise of assemblies of the estates led to more popular participation at a state level. One issue where it was considered important to involve a broader spectrum of the people was the election of the king. While Norway was a hereditary kingdom from 1260 to 1449, Denmark and Sweden were elective kingdoms throughout the Middle Ages. Originally, the elections were the province of the regional *things*, but in the latter part of the thirteenth or at the beginning of the fourteenth century this was changed so monarchical elections were held on a national level. Unfortunately, the details of the procedure to elect the king have only been passed down in Sweden. With regard to Denmark, it is known that the aristocrats of the realm gathered with commoners to elect the king in the fourteenth century (*Diplomatarium Danicum* 1938–: 2(8):176, 2(9):273, 4(1):40). In Sweden, the election procedure was incorporated into the national law code around 1350. According to the code, each of the presiding judges (*lagmännen*) of the nine regional *things* appointed twelve wise men from their respective judicial districts or regional *things* with the consent of the inhabitants. Then the presiding judges and the appointed delegates would go to Mora on a fixed date to make the election. Each delegation consisted of six commoners and six aristocrats in addition to the presiding judge who belonged to the temporal aristocracy. This means that the election assembly consisted of 117 men including 54 commoners, which was a much broader standard of participation than was found in the aristocratic parliaments. However, the election also contained a hereditary element as it was preferable that a king's son born in the realm was elected (*Magnus Erikssons Landslag* 1962: I–VIII). The Scandinavian union (1397–1521) spread the idea of an elected monarch and laid down the premises for other kingdoms. Eventually, this led to an arrangement where the council of the realm from each kingdom gathered to make the election (*Norges Gamle Love* [1388–1604] 1912–: 2(2):21). Hence, the election became more aristocratic and less based on popular participation. Nevertheless Norway finally moved to elective succession to the throne in 1449/50 (Imsen 1987: 169–79; *Norges Gamle Love* [1388–1604] 1912–: 2(2):3, 5, 21).

Ideological Foundation

From the twelfth century onwards the Nordic countries were an integrated part of Western Christianity both culturally and politically. This meant that political ideas developed in the intellectual centres of Europe, spread throughout Europe and eventually reached the Scandinavian periphery. Particularly important to this flow of knowledge were the Nordic students who studied in universities abroad and brought new ideas back home. Further, while the Icelandic constitution from the thirteenth century onwards was still a version of the old Norse society based on *things*, it incorporated a representative element for the legislative assembly that was most likely a result of external influence. The European context explains much regarding the ideological foundation for the formalised sharing of power between the king, the aristocracy and even the commoners in the Scandinavian kingdoms of the late Middle Ages. The development of parliaments in the European kingdoms of the Middle Ages saw the rise of the concept of political representation. This was closely linked to the introduction of Roman and canon law and was probably inspired by similar arrangements in the organisation of the Church (Tierney [1983] 1997: 25–9). A crucial step in the development of the concept of political representation was the introduction of the notion of *communitas*, meaning community or fellowship, which came into use in Denmark and Sweden at the beginning of the fourteenth century. Eventually, *communitas* was used as a term for the unprivileged third order of society, the commoners, but it was also used as a term for the people as a whole. Grouped together as *communitas regni*, the community of the realm, the meaning connected to the political body of the realm as a whole, including the king and the aristocracy, both temporal and spiritual, who also had the responsibility to represent the people (Black 1992: 14–15 Dunbabin 1988: 482). This form of political representation was realised in the Scandinavian kingdoms without any delegation of authority through elections, but through quiet acceptance that the 'best men of the kingdom' represented the whole realm and all its inhabitants.

Canon law and the practices of the Church organisation not only played a role in the development of representative assemblies, but they were also influential in the development of mixed constitutions. The point of departure was the position of corporations in Roman law, where a crucial principle that applied was 'what concerns all, should be approved by all'. In the later Middle Ages both the Church and temporal political entities could be considered to be corporations, which led to the development of theories on the relationship between the leader or ruler of a corporation and its members or subjects, especially in canon law. Canon lawyers were concerned that the pope could fail and, therefore, they saw the need for another institution to be ready to represent the whole Church. The solution was a general council which was above the pope on questions on faith. As a consequence, the pope was considered to be greater when he acted together with a council than when he acted alone, and canon lawyers followed up by claiming that the ruler was greater than any single individual, but less than the sum of all individuals. Canon lawyers also maintained that bishops had to act with the counsel or even consensus of their local chapter. Thus, a mixed constitution was developed in the Church, which, in addition to canon law, itself influenced political practice across the European realms (Tierney 1966: 1–17; 1982: 13–28, 87–92).

The mixed constitution was also an element of Aristotle's political philosophy that began influencing European political thought after his political works were translated into Latin in the middle of the thirteenth century. Aristotle listed the three positive elements of a constitution as monarchy, aristocracy and the *politia*, the well-ordered democracy (Aristotle 1988: III:7, IV:8). Thomas Aquinas and many of his intellectual successors concluded that a mixed constitution of monarchy, aristocracy and democracy was the best constitution. According to Aquinas, the democratic element was required only for the election of kings, while the aristocracy should rule together with the king (Aquinas 1959: 149–51). Thus, the mixed constitution that Aquinas suggested was quite similar to the mixed constitution that developed in Denmark and Sweden in the first half of the fourteenth century. There the popular participation in politics on a national level was mainly attached to the election of kings, but also to some extent to questions of taxation and legislation, especially in Sweden. In other questions the commoners were represented by the aristocracy in parliaments that had broader authority than the commoners alone, but still within defined fields. However, it is not known for certain whether the framing of the Scandinavian constitutions was influenced by Thomas Aquinas or not. The election of kings by the people had a long tradition, the popular influence was not a new phenomenon. Regarding the formalisation of the authority of aristocratic assemblies, canon law and the Church organisation seem to be the most obvious channels of influence, particularly as knowledge of canon law at the beginning of fourteenth century was common among bishops and other prelates throughout Western Christianity. The reception of Aristotle and Aquinas was, on the other hand, a rather slow process from the middle of the thirteenth century onwards (Füeler 1992: 127–51). It cannot, however, be excluded from consideration that there may have been such an influence present in Scandinavia in the first half of the fourteenth century. Knowledge of the political teachings of Aristotle and Aquinas may have been acquired by Scandinavians at the university in Paris, and the Dominican order may have played a role as well.

Conclusion

The 'Icelandic freestate' in the thirteenth century and the Scandinavian kingdoms in the later Middle Ages were quite different political societies. While the first was a more or less a stateless society, the latter were state-formations. This implies that in Iceland the political culture was dominated by a relatively private competition for power between different chieftains and their followers. In this context the constitutional approach could be criticised for putting too much weight on an essentially weak institutional frame, a point that several studies of the Icelandic judicial system confirm (Byock [1982] 1993: 98–113; Miller 1990: 179–299; Sigurðsson 1999: 151–85). Even though the institutional frame was still weak in the later medieval Scandinavian kingdoms, the rise of the state implied more common tasks and a distinction between the private and the public sphere. The latter distinction was, of course, not as clear as in modern societies and contained many grey zones, but, nevertheless, it existed. The medieval Scandinavian kingdoms also saw the rise of more complex political cultures dealing with a mixture interests. Of course, private interests were still highly important, but they were supplemented by class interests, especially those espoused by the aristocracy, common interests for the whole community and also by emerging national interests, particularly during the Scandinavian union in the later Middle Ages.

In Iceland the *Althing* was a popular assembly where all free men could meet, and hence it contained elements of direct political participation. The legislative assembly within the *Althing* also contained elements of political representation as the chieftains in a way represented their own particular regions and their followers. It is probably fair to call these proto-democratic features. However, it is problematic to extend the notion of democracy much further when applied to medieval Iceland because democracy is a form of government and it is debateable whether a political system in a predominantly stateless society, without an executive power, can actually count as a form of government. The Scandinavian kingdoms in the later Middle Ages were, on the other hand, state-formations that clearly contained a form of government. This form was not democracy, but, in the Aristotelian vocabulary, a mixture of monarchy, aristocracy and democracy, even though the latter played a less important role. Constitutional documents issued in the Scandinavian kingdoms contained some crucial principles, such as the rule of law, individual rights, political representation and power-sharing in a mixed constitution. In sum, these principles, along with many special arrangements intended to limit the power of the king, can be said to have produced some proto-democratic features. In particular, the development and implementation of the concepts of political representation and a mixed constitution can be seen as important medieval contributions to the development of modern democracy. Indeed, the representative democracies of today have some roots that go back to the Middle Ages, and hence it is possible to talk about proto-democratic features in medieval Scandinavian history.

References

Aquinas, T. ([1274] 1959), 'Summa Theologica', in *Selected Political Writings*, Oxford: Blackwell.
Aristotle ([350 BCE] 1988), *The Politics*, Cambridge: Cambridge University Press.
Black, A. (1992), *Political Thought in Europe 1250–1450*, Cambridge: Cambridge University Press.
Byock, J. ([1982] 1993), *Feud in the Icelandic Saga*, Berkeley, CA: University of California Press.

Byock, J. (2002), 'The Icelandic *Althing*: Dawn of Parliamentary Democracy', in J. M.
    Fladmark (ed.), *Heritage and Identity: Shaping of the Nations of the North*, Shaftesbury:
    Donhead, pp. 1–17.
Christensen, A. E. (1977), 'Tiden 1042–1241', in I. Skovgaard-Petersen, A. E. Christensen and
    H. Paludan (eds), *Danmarks historie, vol. 1: Tiden indtil 1340*, Copenhagen: Gyldendal, pp.
    211–399.
Diplomatarium Danicum: Danmarks riges breve (1938–), Copenhagen: Ejnar Munksgaards
    forlag.
Diplomatarium Suecanum: Svensk diplomatarium (1829–2004), Stockholm: Riksarkivet.
Drar, K. (1980), *Konungens herravälde så som rättvisans, fridens och frihetens beskydd*, Stockholm:
    Almqvist & Wiksell International.
Dunbabin, J. (1988), 'Government', in J. H. Burns (ed.), *The Cambridge History of Medieval
    Political Thought*, Cambridge: Cambridge University Press, pp. 477–519.
Erslev, K. (1902), *Danmarks riges historie: Bind II: Den senere middelalderen*, Copenhagen: Det
    nordiske forlag.
Füeler, C. (1992), 'Die Rezeption der *Politica* des Aristoteles an der Pariser Artistenfakultät im
    13. und 14. Jahrhundert', in J. Miethke (ed.), *Das Publikum Politischer Theorie im 14.
    Jahrhundert*, Munich: Oldenbourg Verlag, pp. 127–51.
Gierke, O. von ([1881] 1958), *Political Theories of the Middle Ages*, Cambridge: Cambridge
    University Press.
Hanson, R. L. (1989), 'Democracy', in T. Ball, J. Farr and R. L. Hanson (eds), *Political
    Innovation and Conceptual Change*, Cambridge: Cambridge University Press, pp. 68–89.
Helle, K. (1972), *Konge og gode menn i norsk riksstyring ca. 1150–1319*, Bergen: Universi-
    tetsforlaget.
Hude, A. (1893), *Danehoffet og dets plads i Danmarks statsforfatning*, Copenhagen: G. E. C. Gad.
Imsen, S. (1987), 'Den tronfølgerettslige situasjonen i Norge ved utgangen av middelalderen',
    Historisk tidsskrift, 66, 169–79.
Jóhannesson, J. (1974), *A History of the Old Icelandic Commonwealth*, Winnipeg: University of
    Manitoba Press.
King, P. D. (1988), 'The Barbarian Kingdoms', in J. H. Burns (ed.), *The Cambridge History of
    Medieval Political Thought*, Cambridge: Cambridge University Press, pp. 123–53.
Laws of Early Iceland – I (1980), trans. A. Dennis, P. Foote and R. Perkins, Winnipeg:
    University of Manitoba Press.
Magnus Erikssons Landslag: Rättshistoriskt Bibliotek, vol. 6 (1962), trans. and ed. Å. Holmbäck
    and E. Wessén, Stockholm: Nordiska bokhandeln.
Miller, W. I. (1990), *Bloodtaking and Peacemaking: Feud, Law and Society in Saga Iceland*,
    Chicago, IL: University of Chicago Press.
Norges Gamle Love ([1388–1604] 1912–), Oslo: Grøndahl.
Oakley, F. (1983), 'Legitimation by Consent: The Question of Medieval Roots', *Viator*, 14,
    303–35.
Reynolds, S. (1984), *Kingdoms and Communities in Western Europe 900–1300*, Oxford: Clar-
    endon Press.
Schück, H. (2005), *Rikets råd och män. Herredag och råd i Sverige 1280–1480*, Stockholm:
    Kungl.
Sigurðsson, J. V. (1999), *Chieftains and Power in the Icelandic Commonwealth*, trans. J.
    Lundskær-Nielsen, Odense: Odense University Press.
Steenstrup, J. (1932), 'Flertal og Mindretal', *Historisk Tidsskrift*, 10(2), 449–83.
Svenska Landskapslagar, vols 1–5 (1933–46), Stockholm: Hugo Gebers förlag.

Sveriges Traktater med Fræmmande Magter, vol. III (1895), Stockholm.

Taranger, A. (1924), 'Alting og lagting', *Historisk Tidsskrift*, 5(5), 1–45.

Tierney, B. (1966), 'Medieval Canon Law and Western Constitutionalism', *Catholic Historical Review*, 52(1), 1–17.

Tierney, B. (1982), *Religion, Law and the Growth of Constitutional Thought 1150–1650*, Cambridge: Cambridge University Press.

Tierney, B. ([1983] 1997), 'The Idea of Representation in the Medieval Councils', in B. Tierney (ed.), *Rights, Laws and Infallibility in Medieval Thought*, Aldershot: Variorum.

Tilly, C. (2007), *Democracy*, Cambridge: Cambridge University Press.

Touraine, A. (1997), *What is Democracy?*, Boulder, CO: Westview Press.

Ullmann, W. (1961), *Principles of Government and Politics in the Middle Ages*, London: Methuen.

Chapter 12

The Christian Church

John P. Hittinger

In the classic account of democracy, rule by the majority formally establishes a regime as democratic. Any such organisation is characterised as allowing the rise of those who are neither rich nor distinguished, but who utilise their equality to bring together a numerical majority of supporters (Aristotle [350 BCE] 1980: 3.11; Simon 1951: 76). Democracy emerges as a cluster of concepts and practices sustained by a set of ideas about human equality and popular sovereignty. Participation in actual self-rule is also an aspirational standard of democratic movements. It is commonly acknowledged that many aspects of modern democracy arise from beliefs, practices and theories of the Christian Middle Ages, including the concept of representation, constitutionalism, the self-rule of guilds and communes, the mitigation of slavery and the idea of submitting the power to wage war to political rule (Schall 1999). Debates about whether the medieval ideal is inherently monarchical and theistic often distracts attention from the clear stirrings, seeds and models of the democratic movement in this era.

One must attend to various sources for a true understanding of the era. In his essay 'Medieval Political Thought', Ernest Barker wrote that in addition to political theory one must also look at political thought as an 'immanent philosophy of the whole age, which determines its actions and shapes its life', because while political theory is explicit and self-conscious, political thought is 'implicit, unconscious, and immersed in the stream of vital action' (Barker 1923: 10). He goes on to explain that the Middle Ages were 'ages of formation and fermentation, in which the Christian leaven . . . was steadily permeating society' (Barker 1923: 10). Jacques Maritain would also look to 'the thoughts and aspirations which the Christian message has by degrees awakened in the depths of the consciousness of peoples, and which moved along underground for centuries before becoming manifest,' noting that these ideas are often 'misunderstood and distorted . . . in the course of this hidden journey in the secular consciousness' (Maritain 1944: 34–5; MacIver 1947: 136)

The claim that Christian teaching is a deep source of democratic inspiration does not exclude the possibility of other sources, nor does it mean that Christianity alone is the sole basis upon which to proceed with the democratic movement. Indeed, the notion of pluralistic society is not only one of the great challenges for democratic society today, it is also one of its greatest advantages and the basis of its claim to inclusivity. Nevertheless, it is important to acknowledge historic precedent and sources, and also to be open to and encourage responsible Christian participation in the public political order, as the Christian churches have since the key Lateran Councils discussed later in this chapter. In order to appreciate the various inspirations for democracy arising from the Church in the medieval era, it is useful to consider various factors, including the Church's advocacy of equality, individual conscience and the limits to the powers of Caesar and all governments. Next, this chapter considers the contribution of the new communities and forms of participation that emerged in the religious orders, guilds and dioceses of the medieval period. The new developments in the ecclesiastical offices of cleric, bishop and pope are also significant. Finally, it is useful to understand how the medieval Church contributed to representation and popular sovereignty becoming the basis for political authority and its part in defusing political tension through its advocacy of diarchy and the mixed regime.

Equality, Conscience and the Limits of Caesar

Democracy thrives on the power of ideas. A democracy presupposes an idea of human equality and dignity as the basis for the claims of those who have no special claim to rule, such as property, wisdom or skill. A democracy must allow free exchange of ideas for common deliberation and persuasion; it prefers persuasion to coercion as a means of implementation of policy. And, finally, democracy, as presently understood, entails a form of limited government so as to respect boundaries for freedom of individuals and intermediate groups. These ideas are deeply embedded in the philosophy and practice of the Christian Middle Ages, even if their implications are not fully recognised.

First and foremost, is the idea of equality. Shaking the ancient pagan order of natural hierarchy to its core, Christianity posited the utter equality of all before God and exalted the lowly with the special dignity of being a child of God. Maritain formulates well the series of evangelical ideas that have served as a powerful leaven for democracy over the course of centuries:

> Christianity announced to the peoples the kingdom of God and the life to come; it has taught them the unity of the human race, the natural equality of all men, children of the same God and redeemed by the same Christ, the inalienable dignity of every soul fashioned in the image of God, the dignity of labor and the dignity of the poor, the primacy of inner values and of good will over external values, the inviolability of the consciences, the exact vigilance of God's justice and providence over the great and the small . . . Christianity proclaimed that where love and charity are, there God is; and that it is up to us to make every man our neighbor, by loving him as ourselves and by having compassion for him. (Maritain 1944: 29)

This development of the idea of equality had a powerful impact because it worked the notion from both ends, so to speak: it placed the high and mighty in the same condition as human beings, not a god but a creature and also subject to the same sin and need for redemption as everyone else; it also elevated the lowly through its models of the beloved poor and the dignity of labour of the holy family. The fundamental equality of all calls into question the absolute relevance of the distinctions of birth and class (Hattersley 1930: 76).

As the reception of the faith requires free assent, the respect for personal conscience places clear limits upon the power of coercion and the inculcation of true belief through the agency of the political authority. Thomas Aquinas endorsed Augustine's precept that without free will or choice, there is no faith because 'other things a man can do against his will but to believe he must will' (Aquinas [1259] 1953: 14.1). Aquinas concluded from this that there should be no forced baptisms and that conscience should be followed in a more profound way than the order of a political authority or even a Church prelate. The coercion of heretics he thought another matter, since it involved a prior promise and served as the basis for social unity (Aquinas [1274] 1947). Although the question of practice took some time to reach consistency, the idea of personal freedom as a basis for true faith is a clear principle. The idea that 'the citadel of personality' is free of governmental control is an essential condition for the way of democracy (MacIver 1947: 138).

A powerful new critique of the political order emerges from the words of Jesus Christ when tested by the Pharisees asking: 'Is it lawful to pay taxes to Caesar, or not?' He said, 'Show Me the tax money . . . Whose image and inscription *is* this?', and when they said 'Caesar's', he replied, 'Render therefore to Caesar the things that are Caesar's, and to God the things that are God's' (Luke 22–5; Mark 12: 14–17; Matthew 22:17–21). This charge works to establish clear limits to the power and status of Caesar. The political power is not a unified power with the aura of the divine sanction: at best it is an instrument of the divine, but with its own law and weight; at worst the state seeks to replace the divine and the law of God prevails. The Christian experience of religion and politics resisted a monistic system by which either politics rules and the rational and temporal powers absorb the transcendent and replace or substitute for it, or, alternatively, the dominance of divinely inspired fidelist or theocratic regime in which revealed truth and prophetic or religious authority substitutes for proper temporal and political authority (Schall 1999: 192; Sturzo 1962: 37). Pope Gelasius I in his letter to Emperor Anastasius on spiritual and temporal powers proposed the idea of two swords, which clearly distinguished the powers, but left the precise organisation of temporal and spiritual powers open to various determinations (Gelasius I [494] 1905: 72–3). John Keane argues that democracy requires a freedom from the tyranny of a big ideal, the arrogance of a rule representing the principle of justice (Keane 2009: 852). By stripping the temporal power of its pretension to divinity, the distinction between God and Caesar firmly established the subordination of the political ruler, if not to the people as such, at least to a standard by which they must be judged, and oft times be corrected (O'Donovan and O'Donovan 1999: 202, 408).

New Communities and Participation

Ernest Barker comments that the notion of 'group life' is one of the most important contributions of the Middle Ages (Barker 1923: 25–7). Local groups and townships, communes and guilds, religious orders and dioceses, all exercised their own form of self-governance. The society as a whole was understood to be a *communitas communitatem* or a federal group of groups. Aquinas argued in his defence of the religious orders that men have a right to associate for good works across classes and states of life;

going beyond standing custom and privilege, Aquinas defends the new religious orders with a right for the founding of 'new forms of associational liberty' (Hittinger 2001: 16–17). This is part of the long cultural development that led to the contemporary forms of democracy. The new religious communities emerged out of the evangelical consciousness of a shared life, the hope for renewal and new possibilities for human living. First, the Benedictines built upon the shattered order of the Roman empire to create the basis for a new order. The rule of Benedict made explicit provision for listening to the youngest and providing hospitality to all. The stability of the rule allowed for long-term familiarity and brotherhood as an ideal for relating, under the aegis of charity above all. There was also an autonomy to each monastery that protected the local rule of the abbot and the custom of the community.

There began a notion of participation in the life of the community by every member. As each monk labours and prays as part of a community there is a strong current of human equality that would be reflected throughout society at large. The Benedictines have been hailed as the 'intellectuals with dirt under their fingernails' (Schmitz 2005: 37). Such a motto subverts any Greek or Roman Platonic claim to a natural inequality based upon intelligence or philosophical achievement. The philosopher-king or aristocratic 'wise' are replaced by the humble wisdom of the worker or the child. Such a view does not eliminate all rank or hierarchy, but it certainly modifies its harsh impact. The Dominican order instituted an elaborate arrangement for representation from chapters to general meetings. Democratic practice may be observed in the practices of the major religious orders (Burns 1988: 555). The diocese, the religious orders and the canonists did much to more deeply understand and implement the principle *quod omnes tanget debet ab omnibus approbari*, or 'what touches all should be approved by all' (Monahan 1987: 97–110). The principle extended the notion of consent of the community to the laws affecting the community, and thereby consent was considered to be essential to any community. It was further understood that some matters not only touch the community, but also individuals, and therefore consent should be obtained in some cases from the individuals affected by a communal decision. Nevertheless, Monahan points out that while the majority must make a determination, consent by all is at least a procedural goal and both majority and minority groups must acknowledge the primacy of the common good (Monahan 1987).

The rise of the guilds provided a model for self-rule. As a 'professional group' it could set its own standards and terms of admission to the profession. Not only was this out of the control of the political authority, it also provided a model for common deliberation. As the same idea of common life and deliberation extended to the community at large, the small commune emerged as a political unit similar to the ancient city or republic of old (Troeltsch 1949: 248; Ullmann 1961: 220). The guilds influenced the governing of the town, and in some cases, such as Marseilles, the guilds directly participated in self-governance (Hattersley 1930: 87). At the level of the diocese, the faithful would have a hand in electing their own priests and bishops. St Augustine would explain that as bishop he was the teacher 'for the people,' but as a Christian he was 'with them'. Being with the people is the basic state of being in the world as a Christian; authority is a special mission or call and not some intrinsic claim to rule over others.

The bishop stood forth as a representative of God in the community. On the basis of the two swords and the rendering to Caesar and to God, the bishop had a standing against the power of the prince. The bishop could call the prince to repentance, thus reducing the absolute claim of any ruler. The bishop represented a group that was free of property, special interests and the right to force or violence. The right to Church property was outside the prerogative of the king. The investiture controversy brought into play 'the right of the community concerned to admonish and even depose its ruler if he failed in his obligations to his subjects' (Morrall 1958: 40). The bishop could call the political ruler to special chastisement for the abuse of power, particularly in time of war. War was subjected to some measure of moral standard, thereby lessening the absolute power of the king. The Benedictines and Dominicans prompted a new possibility for the cleric: they opened a new path for any man to rise up to a higher status and obtain education, respect and decision-making authority within the community. Again, because priesthood is a calling and imposed by holy orders, it is not the intrinsic merit of the designated person, but a gift or elevation from within. Hattersley comments: 'ecclesiastical preferment is open to humblest man' and the lowly parish priest is superior to the king, in some respects (Hattersley 1930: 78).

Popular Sovereignty and Representation

Ironically the very idea of the pope as the vicar of Christ, would stimulate a parallel notion that the political ruler was the vicar of the people. Aquinas developed this notion, which was later made an explicit argument for democracy by his Jesuit commentators in the sixteenth century. Authority flows from the people to the ruler. Ullmann contrasts the ascending and descending principles of justification, and he shows that the ascending of authority from people to ruler became a dominant motif in medieval accounts of politics (Ullmann 1966: 20, 190). The law that creates power belongs to the people or the community as a whole because it serves the common good, which is the rationale for any political choice or law. Law derives its authority from the common good; the common good, in turn, is that from which all members of society should benefit. In addition, one could understand the ruler as a representative of the people. In practice, various arrangements were developed such that a representative group of people was assembled to give advice to the king or eventually to decide some matter of importance. This is one origin of parliament as a representative body. There was further development of the idea of popular sovereignty through the reversion of authority to the people when a king or sovereign was absent or deficient.

In addition to the more theoretical discussions about the origin of temporal rule and the doctrine of popular sovereignty, there were profound developments in the practice and theory of representation. Admittedly, the theory and practice of representation did not rise to the full level of democratic political representation as we know it today. That is, the notion did not mean strict political representation by which one must balance the wishes of the represented with the judgement by the delegate about what is best for the group. Instead, we find a twofold understanding of 'spiritual representation' and a 'practical representation' (Faggioli and Melloni 2006: 42). The first brings together members of a whole ecclesiastical body to discern and formulate the permanent wisdom of the tradition. Such a spiritual representation culminated in the general councils of the Church. In addition, the growth in administration of the Church and the expansion of its territory, necessitated a means to coordinate and assure uniformity (Hattersley 1930: 78; Monahan 1987: 112). It culminated in the Conciliar movement, which led to significant reform in the Church in the medieval period, even if it could not stave off the later Reformation.

The Lateran Councils, so-called because they were held in the Basilica of Saint John Lateran in Rome, were of particular significance not only in the coordination they provided, but also in the independence and autonomy they established for the operations of the Church. The first Lateran Council was held in 1123 under Pope Callistus II to confirm the Concordat of Worms (1122) between the pope and Holy Roman Emperor Henry V, which established that all bishops and abbots should be elected freely by the proper ecclesiastical authorities (electors). In Germany, the emperor was to preside over these free elections and then bestow temporal power on the bishop so chosen in return for temporal fealty. Outside Germany, the emperor was to have no part in any elections. Also dealt with at this council was the subject of clerical marriages. It was decided that once ordained, a priest could not marry in either the Latin or Eastern Rites. The second Lateran Council was held in 1139 under Pope Innocent II. This council voided the acts of the deceased anti-pope, Anacletus II, ending the papal schism of the time and showing the authority of the council to overrule even popes. It also condemned the anti-materialist heresies of the neo-Manicheans. The third Lateran Council in 1179 under Pope Alexander III, regulated the election of popes (two-thirds majority vote by the College of Cardinals was required for the pope to be elected) and the emperor (then Frederick Barbarossa) was excluded from voting. The fourth, and final, Lateran Council was held in 1215 under Pope Innocent III and provided for the democratic election of pastors and the education of poor scholars.

Otto von Gierke believes that the spiritual representation has a deeper or dual origin in German tribal custom: the leader represents the tribe and thus a leader represents the community subject to him (Gierke [1881] 1958: 65–7; Hattersley 1930: 96). The right of communities, according to Gierke, became the doctrine of popular sovereignty. The assembly of representatives could also be the agent who exercises the right of the community. In other words, the community is deeper than the ruler and the ruler rules as the vicar or *gerant* of all. The personification of the community is designated by the community to be the instrument for its collective action. The practical assembly of representatives grew out of the need to provide the king or monarch with advice and counsel. The representatives did not really have the full authority to act in such a case. Nevertheless, they did shape and limit the power of the sovereign and gave voice to the people and their various groups. Indeed, Keane celebrates the very practicality of such representation in the case of the Spanish *cortes* of Alfonso IX in 1188 (Keane 2009: 171–6). The English also developed various means of representation to give advice and counsel to the monarch. Robert MacIver asserts that the practice of electing two representatives from the boroughs introduced in 1265 by the earl of Leicester, Simon de Montfort, is the beginning of the House of Commons and the direct ancestor of political democracy (Hattersley 1930: 79; MacIver 1947: 139).

Political Tension: Diarchy and Mixed Regimes

Finally, we must return to the notion of the two societies and two authorities that derives from the distinction between the things of God and the things of Caesar, the spiritual and the temporal. As society vied with society, institution with institution and even ruler with ruler, it became clear that neither side could be reduced to the other and that neither could eliminate or absorb the other. There were many points of conflict. But the social order remained a diarchy in which there are principles of order that must be brought into proper harmony (Sturzo 1962: 46–8). Dante speaks of the grave disorder when the two orders are merged (Dante [1312] 1996). This provides a boost to democracy because it opens up an intrinsic pluralism to social order. The rise of the modern state plants a seed of totalitarian order when the some spiritual powers are absorbed by the state. This serves to highlight all the more the seeds of democracy contained in diarchy and the eventual separation of Church and state as a constitutional principle.

The notion of mixed regime is the final model to be examined as a medieval contribution, albeit one that derives explicitly from the classical heritage, transformed by the biblical basis of belief in the Middle Ages (Kayser 1982: 196). Aristotle, of course, speaks about the mixed regime as a positive type of regime that includes, besides a king and aristocracy, an element of the rule by the many for common good, thus, it is democratic in principle (Aristotle [350 BCE] 1980: IV:9, V:8–9). What we call democracy he would call 'polity' or mixed regime. Polybius also devotes an important passage to the Roman concept of a mixed regime – the various orders of monarch, *aristoi* and the many are each given a place in the constitutional order or political practice (Polybius [150 BCE] 1889). Aquinas also argues that the mixed regime is the best form of government overall. In the *Summa*, Aquinas combines Aristotle and the Bible to make his case, although he does favour monarchy, he acknowledges in this passage the need to balance its claim with that of the few and the many (Aquinas [1274] 1947: I–II:105, a.1; Blythe 1992: 39–59).

At the very least the notion of diarchy of Church and state, and the ideal or model of the mixed regime supported the idea of constitutional limits to the monarch. If the practice of the political regimes of the medieval era favoured monarchy, it was a monarchy limited in scope; limited from above by the sovereignty of God, and the moral order and the authority of the bishops and pope; limited from below, if you will, by its service to the common good, the openness to the participation of the best or *aristoi*, and the input from the many. The great document, the Magna Carta, although strictly speaking a limitation of the royal power by the privilege or right of the barons, nevertheless serves as a great model and inspiration for democracy: the king must respect the rights of his subjects.

When such a notion of right and limitation is combined with popular sovereignty, representation and freedom of conscience, the transition to explicit embrace of democracy is close behind. The exhaustion of the Inquisition as a political force, the destabilising effects and moral repugnance of wars of religion, the deeper under-standing of the relative autonomy of the temporal sphere, and the rise of the new commercial classes eventually galvanised a new understanding of the political order which we call modern. There is no doubt that its various elements are present for centuries, suspended in the solution of *Christiana respublica* requiring Church membership for citizenship and the achievement of the noble, elevated goal of justice through religious strength. That pluralism of beliefs and the dedication to temporal liberty provided a new 'sky' or horizon for understanding the political order (Maritain 1973: 20). Democracy would become a more self-conscious process and the goal of political order.

Conclusion

Writing after the end of the Second World War, various thinkers wondered whether the medieval contribution could continue to strengthen the democratic movement precisely because of its link to a transcendent good. J. W. Allen, for example, praises the medieval political philosophers because they asked the right questions:

> What is the nature of obligation as between man and man, and, in connection with and dependence on that, what is the nature of political obligation? What is the purpose which justifies to reason all that we mean by government? Or, in other words, what is the true function of government? And, finally, what is the character of that state the realisation of which will satisfy man's needs and aspirations? This last is the question Plato had asked in *The Republic*. These questions, though not exactly in the form I have given them, are raised at every point in the writings of the twelfth and thirteenth century. The question of the extent of civil authority and law-making power was wholly bound up with the question as to moral obligation in general. The controversy as to the relations between Pope and Emperor, stripped of its non-essentials, was a controversy as to the end and purpose of life on earth. (Allen 1949: 260–1)

Now there is a tendency to 'reject the idea of a transcendent purpose of end of human existence and to seek a sufficient purpose for life within the walls of matter' (Allen 1949: 267). Allen questions whether we have yet found an end or purpose that will satisfy human beings. Keane argues that the distinction between worldly and otherworldly is ultimately salutary for democracy, and tends towards the view, admittedly stretched, that democracy is a secular ideal (Keane 2009: 854). Yet Alexis de Tocqueville argued strongly that religion is much more needed in a democracy than in a monarchy because it provides a source of hope, discipline and moral inspiration (Tocqueville [1835] 1988: 290–301). Thus, perhaps James Schall is profoundly correct when he says that we still need to study medieval political philosophy and medieval political order, if not to clarify our politics, at least to clarify our minds (Schall 1999: 191).

References

Allen, J. W. (1949), 'Politics', in F. J. C. Hearnshaw (ed.), *Mediæval Contributions to Modern Civilization: A Series of Lectures Delivered at King's College, University of London*, New York: Barnes & Noble, pp. 255–68.

Aquinas, Thomas ([1274] 1947), *Summa Theologica*, New York: Blackwell.

Aquinas, T. ([1259] 1953), *Questiones Disputatae de Veritate Questions 10–20*, trans. R. W. Mulligan, Chicago, IL: Henry Regnery.

Aristotle ([350 BCE] 1980), *The Politics*, trans. E. Barker, Oxford: Oxford University Press.

Barker, E. (1923), 'Introductory: Medieval Political Thought', in F. J. C. Hearnshaw (ed.), *The Social and Political Ideas of Some Great Mediæval Thinkers: A Series of Lectures Delivered at King's College, University of London*, London: G. G. Harrap, pp. 9–33.

Blythe, J. (1992), *Ideal Government and the Mixed Constitution in the Middle Ages*, Princeton, NJ: Princeton University Press.

Burns, J. H. (ed.) (1988), *The Cambridge History of Medieval Political Thought c. 350–c. 1450*, New York: Cambridge University Press.

Dante ([1312] 1996), *Monarchy*, trans. P. Shaw, Cambridge: Cambridge University Press.

Faggioli, M. and A. Melloni (2006), *Repraesentatio: Mapping a Keyword for Churches and Governance*, Berlin: LIT-Verlag.

Gelasius I ([494] 1905), 'Letter to Emperor Anastasius on Spiritual and Temporal Power', in *Readings in European History*, trans. J. H. Robinson, Boston, MA: Ginn, pp. 72–3.

Gierke, O. von ([1881] 1958), *Political Theories of the Middle Ages*, Boston, MA: Beacon Press.

Hattersley, A. F. (1930), *A Short History of Democracy*, Cambridge: Cambridge University Press.

Hittinger, R. (2001), 'Reasons for a Civil Society', in T. Fuller and J. Hittinger (eds), *Reassessing the Liberal State*, Washington, DC: Catholic University of America Press, pp. 11–23.

Hittinger, J. (2003), *Liberty, Wisdom, and Grace: Thomism and Democratic Political Theory*, Lanham, MD: Lexington Books.

Kayser, J. (1982), 'Aquinas' "Regimen Bene Commixum" and Medieval Critique of Classical Republicanism', *Thomist*, 46, 195–220.

Keane, J. (2009), *The Life and Death of Democracy*, New York: Simon & Schuster.

MacIver, R. M. (1947), *The Web of Government*, New York: Macmillan.

Maritain, J. (1944), *Christianity and Democracy*, trans. D. C. Anson, New York: C. Scribner.

Maritain, J. (1973), *Integral Humanism*, Notre Dame, IN: University of Notre Dame Press.

Monahan, A. P. (1987), *Consent, Coercion, and Limit: The Medieval Origins of Parliamentary Democracy*, Kingston: McGill-Queen's University Press.

Morrall, J. (1958), *Political Thought in Medieval Times*, London: Hutchison.

O'Donovan, O. and J. L. O'Donovan (1999), *From Irenaeus to Grotius: A Sourcebook in Christian Political Thought, 100–1625*, Grand Rapids, MI: Eerdmans.

Polybius ([150 BCE] 1889), *The Histories of Polybius*, trans. E. Shuckburgh, London: Macmillan.

Schall, J. (1999), 'On the Point of Medieval Political Philosophy', *Perspectives on Political Science*, 2, 189–93.

Schmitz, K. L. (2005), *The Recovery of Wonder: The New Freedom and the Asceticism of Power*, Montreal: McGill-Queen's University Press.

Simon, Y. R. (1951), *Philosophy of Democratic Government*, Chicago, IL: University of Chicago Press.

Sturzo, L. (1962), *Church and State*, Notre Dame, IN: University of Notre Dame Press.

Tocqueville, A. de ([1835] 1988), *Democracy in America*, trans. G. L. Lawrence, New York: HarperCollins.

Troeltsch, E. (1931), *The Social Teaching of the Christian Churches*, 2 vols, New York: Macmillan.

Ullmann, W. (1966), *Principles of Government and Politics in the Middle Ages*, 2nd edn, London: Methuen.

Part IV

Early Modern Democracy

Chapter 13

The English Parliament

Ann Lyon

The English Parliament is the subject of much mythology, both in its origins and in its development. It is often suggested that prior to the Norman Conquest, rather than having government imposed from above, the English governed themselves through local assemblies often referred to as folk moots (Oman 1919). The best evidence for pre-Conquest folk moots comes from place names such as Thingwall on the Wirral peninsula, Merseyside, and a lost *Tingwala* in the Yorkshire Domesday, cognate with modern Icelandic *Thingvellir* – meeting place of the *thing* or assembly (Mills 1998). The Icelandic Parliament, whose origins can be traced to 930, is the *Althing.* That such place names are Old Norse in origin and situated in areas of Scandinavian settlement in England suggest strongly that the *thing* was a Scandinavian import in the period c. 850–1000, rather than a native Anglo-Saxon development. This hypothesis is supported by the existence of a Dingwall in a strongly Scandinavian area of northern Scotland.

There is a tendency for writers to extrapolate backward from the seventeenth century and assume that parliament in the medieval period took its seventeenth-century form as it was created, rather than developing by a long process of evolution (Sayles 1974: 3–20). Recent work postulates the emergence of 'national assemblies' in the reign of King Athelstan (924–39), though perhaps these assemblies were not the representative bodies that the term implies, but gatherings of the king's leading men – landowners, bishops and senior figures in royal administration, whose identity is evidenced by charter witness lists – coming together at the king's behest to provide counsel (Maddicott 2010: 2–41).

The origins of parliament seem to lie in the custom by which successive kings of the English, whether native or Norman, called together their chief men, ecclesiastical and lay. Kings 'wore their crowns' three times a year, at Christmas, Easter and Whitsun, a practice which seems to have become established by the time of Edward the Confessor (1042–66). John Maddicott suggests that these crown-wearings began under Athelstan, as a response to the vastly increased geographical extent of the territory ruled by his dynasty, and the disparate blend of peoples and traditions (Maddicott 2010: 2–4). Day-to-day government was handled by the king and a small group of regular advisers, termed the *Curia Regis* in the Norman period and later the King's Council, but the crown-wearings, termed *colloquia* in contemporary documents and referred to by modern historians as Great Councils, seem to have been occasions when major policy decisions were made, the king received the counsel of his magnates and prelates, and dispensed justice. For example, it was at his Christmas crown-wearing in 1085 that William I 'had much thought and very deep discussion with his council about this country – how it was occupied and with what sort of people', and made the decision to embark on the Domesday survey to provide a record of landholdings for taxation purposes (Swanton 1996: 1085).

Henry III: The Early Parliament

From the reign of Henry III (1216–72) the term *parliamentum* begins to be used regularly for assemblies, and at the same time the crown-wearings started to evolve into the meetings of a recognisable parliament, as some members were summoned on a representative rather than a purely personal basis (Sayles 1974: 32–4). Further, a Great Council began to be used as a forum for dealing with disputes between the king and his leading men. The confirmation of the charters of February 1225 was agreed at a Great Council called by the *justiciar* (effectively regent), Hubert de Burgh, for the purpose of agreeing a general tax at a time of crisis – the French had occupied Poitou in 1224 and now threatened Gascony, and an invasion of England seemed possible. After a week of negotiation, a tax grant was made by 'the archbishops, bishops, abbots, priors, earls, barons, knights, free tenants and everyone in our kingdom', and the king's confirmation of the charters was made to the same groups except the knights and free tenants. Those named as present at the Great Council were the two archbishops, eleven bishops, twenty abbots, nine earls and twenty-three barons (Maldicott 2010: 107).

   The representative element first appears overtly during Henry III's dispute with a faction among his magnates which climaxed in the Barons' War of 1264–5. At Easter 1258, Henry summoned a Great Council to consider his demands for money to finance an expedition to Sicily, whose crown he had earlier accepted on behalf of his younger son, Edmund, and to deal with rebellion in Wales (Prestwich 1997: 24–53). Shortly before the Great Council assembled, Simon de Montfort, earl of Leicester, and six other earls went in full armour to the king's chamber in the palace of Westminster and would not depart until the king and his heir, the future Edward I, had sworn on the Gospels to accept their counsel at the Great Council and to agree to what they proposed. This dramatic episode demonstrates that the Great Council was now regarded as a proper forum not only for the king to receive the counsel of his great men, but also for the resolution of disputes. Along with similar instances, it is also the origin of the prohibition on attending sittings of Parliament wearing armour. De Montfort and his confederates went to the Great Council of Easter 1258 seeking the removal of the king's favourites and thorough reform of royal administration. Only if their demands were met would they agree to the necessary taxation for the Sicilian expedition. Their terms formed the basis of the Provisions of Oxford, a detailed programme worked out by a council of twenty-four: twelve members appointed by the magnates and twelve by the king.

   Initially the reformers, working through established systems, met with some success in dealing with perennial problems, such as corruption among the sheriffs. However, from 1260 the reform programme fizzled out and the reform party became divided.

There followed a gradual descent into civil war, the capture and imprisonment of Henry III after the battle of Lewes on 14 May 1264, and a period in which the country was ruled by a cabal headed by Simon de Montfort. For the purposes of the evolution of Parliament, a major event was the summoning – nominally by the king – of a parliament to meet on 20 January 1265, which included not only magnates and prelates, but two men as representatives of each shire and two more as representatives of each borough. After 1265, representatives of the shires and boroughs were included intermittently in summonses to parliament, but it was not until well into the four-teenth century that they became a normal element. Parliament remained very much under the control of the monarch, who summoned parliament, usually when he needed consent to extraordinary taxation, and any parliament sat only for as long as the king wished. It is to be noted, however, that parliaments were summoned much more frequently when kings were under pressure – Henry III summoned no fewer than eleven between midsummer 1258 and Easter 1262 (Sayles 1974: 60).

Parliamentary Power Grows

By this time, parliament was producing recognisable legislation. Initially, a statute was the body of legislation produced by a particular parliament, and which might cover a wide range of topic areas, hence, the Statute of Westminster 1275 and the Statute of Gloucester 1278, though some parliaments sat to consider specific issues only. For example, the Caernarvon Parliament of 1284 was summoned to create a framework for English administration in Wales after the conquest of 1282, and the results formed the Statute of Wales 1284. Statutes were also passed to deal with specific areas of concern brought to king's attention by petitions. A good example, from a slightly later period (1351), is the statute *De Natis Ultra Mare* (*Statutes of the Realm* 1810: 310). This law was passed in order to remedy the difficulties that persons born outside England faced in proving their entitlement to inherit land (Kim 2000: 107–24).

Parliament also came to acquire an important symbolic role. Both kings and those deposing kings made use of parliaments to regularise their positions, and it seems to have become accepted from 1225 that taxation could be properly granted only by a parliament (Maddicott 2010: 106–18). This is seen in the crisis of Edward I's reign in the autumn of 1297, stemming from his insistence on mounting a campaign in Flanders against the French at the same time as dealing with rebellion in Scotland headed by William Wallace. The specific concerns were Edward's financial exactions. Unprecedentedly, there was widespread refusal among the magnates and knightly class to do military service abroad (Prestwich 1997: 412–35). The threat of civil war during the king's absence in Flanders was stayed by the defeat of the English by William Wallace at Stirling Bridge on 11 September 1297. This led Edward's opponents to moderate their demands and a settlement was reached by the King's Council, via a confirmation of Magna Carta and the Forest Charter, together with other concessions set out in the document known as the *Confirmatio Cartarum*. The settlement was granted in a parliament summoned and presided over by the king's heir, Edward of Caernarvon, acting as keeper of the realm in his father's absence. A keeper of the realm was appointed by the king to act on his behalf during his absence from England. He was normally an adult male relative of the king – Edward of Caernarvon, then aged thirteen, was unusually young for his position.

In relation to the evolution of parliament, this episode shows, first, that formal recognition had been given to the principle that taxation, as distinct from normal royal revenues such as income from royal *demesne*, feudal wardships and treasure trove, could take place only with the assent of representatives of the realm, though it was not yet clear what the composition of a parliament should be to make it representative. Secondly, a parliament could sit in the absence of the king, although no precedent was established as to whether it could sit in the absence of the king's chosen representative or be summoned other than by the king. Henry III had remained on his throne despite imprisonment by his enemies and Edward I's place as king was never threatened. Henry III was perhaps fortunate during the Barons' War of 1264–1265 that his enemies could not produce an alternative king. Henry's sons, brother and the sons of his brother were all implacably opposed to Simon de Montfort and his faction. Edward II (1307–27) has the melancholy distinction of being the first post-Conquest king to be deposed, and a parliament summoned on behalf of his enemies played a role in the deposition proceedings, a pattern which was followed in subsequent depositions.

Edward II: Deposed by Parliament

As king, Edward II was a largely passive figure, the tool of his favourites and enemies, only occasionally displaying the energy of his ancestors. His reign involved a series of crises, culminating in invasion by his queen, Isabella of France, and her lover, Roger Mortimer, who landed near Ipswich on 24 September 1326. Crucially, they had with them the king's heir, the future Edward III, aged thirteen (McKisack 1959: 84–94). The king was unable to rouse any significant support, and at the end of September he fled from London towards Bristol with his two favourites, Hugh Despenser, earl of Winchester, and his son, also named Hugh. London declared for the queen and the townsfolk of Bristol opened their gates, while the king and the younger Despenser fled into Wales. On 26 October, the magnates assembled at Bristol proclaimed young Edward as keeper of the realm which his father was held to have deserted. In November, the king surrendered at Neath Abbey. Both Despensers were speedily executed, but what was to be done with Edward II? There was then no legal mechanism for deposing a king and doubt as to whether a lawful deposition was even possible. The queen, Mortimer and their cohorts were therefore concerned to give Edward II's deposition on grounds of 'unworthiness to rule' an aura of legality. They did this through parliament.

On 28 October, before the king's capture and presumably on the initiative of his mother and Mortimer, young Edward issued writs in his father's name for a parliament at Westminster. These stated that the king would be absent from the realm and the business would be heard before the queen and young Edward. This parliament, which met in January 1327, was summoned so as to appear fully representative, with representatives of Wales, the Cinque ports and the people of London. In order to maintain the fiction that this was a true parliament, the king was asked to attend, but he refused, or was said in a proclamation of 12 January to have refused. On 12 January, the mayor, aldermen and commonalty of London sent a letter to the magnates now assembled in parliament asking whether they were willing to be in accord with the Londoners, to maintain the cause of the queen and her son, to crown young Edward and to depose Edward II for his frequent offences against his oath and crown.

On 13 January representatives of all estates of the realm – bishops and magnates, representatives of the clergy and the boroughs – took an oath at the Guildhall to maintain the queen's cause, 'to uphold all that has been ordained or shall be ordained for the common profit' and to maintain the liberties of the city of London (Stubbs 1882–3: 323). On 15 January, the archbishop of Canterbury announced at Westminster Hall that, by the unanimous consent of the magnates, the clergy and the people, Edward II was deposed from his royal dignity, never more to reign and govern the people of England, and that the magnates, the clergy and the people unanimously agreed that young Edward should be king. This was an attempt by a small group, most of its leaders motivated by personal grudges against Edward II, to give an aura of legality to acts which were unprecedented and on that basis illegal. Their fiction was that Edward was deposed by the will of the English people. Also on 15 January, a deputation of representatives of all estates went to Kenilworth, where the king was imprisoned, to inform him of his deposition. Two bishops went ahead, charged with persuading him to abdicate, promising that if he did so young Edward would succeed him and that he himself would be maintained in a state of royal dignity for the remainder of his life. If he refused, the people would take a person not of royal blood as the new king. Edward, a broken man, immediately capitulated. Young Edward was then proclaimed king as Edward III. The fiction was maintained that Edward II had abdicated voluntarily, but can the 1327 assembly properly be called a parliament? The 1297 parliament was summoned and presided over by a keeper of the realm appointed by the king, who was kept informed of developments and apparently approved them. Even if the assembly of 1327, summoned first by young Edward as keeper of the realm (but not appointed as such by the king), then postponed and re-summoned under the fiction that Edward II was still the ruler, was a lawfully summoned parliament, it rapidly became a revolutionary body.

Edward III: Parliament Asserts its Authority

Edward III's fifty-year reign was largely peaceful on the domestic scene, but in its penultimate year parliament, particularly the Commons, took new powers upon itself and acted directly against the king's closest confidants: his mistress, Alice Perrers; steward, Lord Neville; chamberlain, William Latimer; and an unscrupulous London merchant, Richard Lyons. The Good Parliament of 1376 is noteworthy for acting of its own volition and largely independently of the ruler, now effectively John of Gaunt, duke of Lancaster, the king's second surviving son, because of the incapacity of both Edward III and his heir apparent, the Black Prince (McKisack 1959: 387–93; Saul 1997: 19–20).

The Good Parliament took upon itself the power to impeach the king's ministers, and, for the first time, the initiative was taken by the Commons. It was summoned because extraordinary revenue-raising powers were required. Throughout its previous history, much of parliament's business had involved dealing with Commons petitions to the king. Unhappiness with the government of the realm in 1376 was manifested in no fewer than 146 petitions, the largest number so far recorded. The Commons concluded that there would have been no need for further taxation had the king been properly advised and decided to deliver that message to the government by the hand of their chosen representative. This was Sir Peter de la Mare, a knight of the shire for Herefordshire and steward of the earl of March, since considered to be the first Speaker of the Commons. De la Mare appeared before Gaunt on 12 May 1376 and informed him of the Commons' concern that the king had 'with him certain councillors and servants who are not loyal or profitable to him or the kingdom', making it clear that he was acting on behalf of the Commons. A process by which a charge could be brought jointly by a group of accusers acting in the name of the king had already developed at common law, and here it was used for the first time by parliament as a means of dealing with the traditional problem of the king's 'evil counsellors'.

The charges against Perrers, Neville, Latimer and Lyons were brought by the Commons and tried by the Lords, presided over by Gaunt. It was alleged that Latimer and Lyons had organised loans to the Crown at extortionate interest rates and sold licences exempting merchants from the Calais Staple. All traffic in wool to and from England was channelled through Calais under the scrutiny of royally appointed officials, who ensured that the proper duties were paid. Exemption from this duty was therefore a valuable privilege. In addition, Latimer was blamed for the loss of two fortresses in Brittany. The charges against Perrers and Neville were less serious. The Lords having found all four guilty, Latimer and Neville were dismissed from their offices and stripped of their emoluments, Lyons was imprisoned for life and Perrers banished from the royal household. However, that the monarch, or his representative, still largely controlled parliament is shown by events over the next few months, in which Gaunt gradually dismantled all the achievements of the Good Parliament. By the time Edward III died on 21 June 1377 all those impeached had resumed their former positions – notoriously, Alice Perrers was able to remove the rings from the king's corpse. Parliament also for the first time claimed a role in relation to the royal succession. Following the Black Prince's death on 8 June 1376, the archbishop of Canterbury, Simon Sudbury, brought the prince's nine-year-old son, the future Richard II, before the Commons. The House loudly demanded that he be created prince of Wales at once to guarantee his succession to the throne (Bennett 1999: 15). The Lords refused to put the matter to the king, but this event may have prompted Edward III to issue a charter that October formally naming Richard as his heir, followed by his three surviving sons and their issue (Bennett 1999: 15).

Richard II: The Merciless Parliament

Richard II's reign also ended in parliament being used as a vehicle for his deposition. Like that of Edward II, the reign was marked by confrontation with factions among the magnates. That parliament had come to be seen as a proper mechanism for the resolution of disputes between king and subjects is shown in the events of 1386–8

(Bennett 1999: 27–33). The 1386 parliament called for the dismissal of Richard's leading ministers, and after a period in which he haughtily declared that he would not dismiss even a scullery boy at parliament's insistence, the king backed down and dismissed his chancellor, Michael de la Pole, earl of Suffolk, on 23 November. The Commons then impeached Suffolk and committed him to prison. Richard's enemies imposed conciliar government on him for twelve months, but this only delayed a further confrontation, which followed in November 1387 as the council's term was about to expire. Richard's leading opponents, his uncle, Thomas, duke of Gloucester, and the earls of Warwick and Arundel, rode to Westminster Hall with 300 armed men. Richard again backed down, agreeing that the accusations would be tried before a parliament to be summoned for 3 February 1388. This 'Merciless Parliament' proceeded to try the 'appeal' of treason brought by Richard's enemies against five of his leading supporters, including the chief justice of the King's Bench, Robert Tresilian, who was dragged out of sanctuary and hanged. The Merciless Parliament went on to condemn six other judges who had ruled in favour of Richard the previous summer in a dispute over the powers of parliament vis-à-vis the king, though their death sentences were commuted to exile in Ireland.

The Merciless Parliament marked the beginning of the practice of obtaining condemnation for treason through parliament and outside the courts, mainly via Bills of Attainder introduced into parliament at the behest of the king and passed by parliament at his direction. These allowed a range of actions which did not properly fall within the relatively narrow purview of the Statute of Treasons, itself passed by the Parliament of 1351/2, to be considered treason in the case of the individual specified. Following the Merciless Parliament, Richard II reached an accommodation with his chief enemies and a period of stability followed. However, another confrontation ensued in 1397, when Richard sought belated revenge against Gloucester, Arundel and Warwick, employing parliament's own weapon of impeachment. The so-called Great Parliament ended in triumph for Richard, whose leading enemies were now dead, imprisoned or converted to his cause. However, within two years his intervention in a private dispute between his first cousin, Gaunt's son, Henry Bolingbroke, and Thomas Mowbray, duke of Norfolk, in 1398 ultimately led to his deposition and murder.

The events of 1399 are strongly reminiscent of those of 1326/7, but the role of parliament in the deposition process was much more prominent, showing that its symbolic importance had grown considerably over the course of seventy years. Bolingbroke landed in the Humber estuary with an army on 4 July, support for Richard melted away, and the king surrendered in mid-August at Flint Castle in North Wales (Bennett 1999: 156–91). Unlike Isabella and Roger Mortimer, Bolingbroke was not seeking to replace a king with his existing heir apparent, but to place himself on the throne. The succession after Richard was unclear. He was childless and had no siblings. Although Bolingbroke was his male heir, he had earlier named as his heir Roger Mortimer, earl of March, grandson through his mother of Richard's deceased uncle, Lionel, duke of Clarence. Mortimer was killed in a skirmish in Ireland in 1398, and it is by no means clear whether Richard regarded his young son, Edmund Mortimer, as the new heir. There is no evidence to support the official statement that Richard agreed to renounce the crown. Around 16 August, he was taken to Chester under guard. Bolingbroke began to rule in his name, issuing writs for a parliament to be held at Westminster on 30 September. As Richard was escorted south, a deputation of Londoners came to Bolingbroke at Lichfield and petitioned him to behead Richard and his companions. Bolingbroke declared that the proper course was to leave matters to the judgement of the parliament which was shortly to meet.

As in 1326/7, the problem was in finding a satisfactory mechanism for the king's dethronement. Edward II's collapse into complete passivity allowed his enemies to present his subjects with the fiction that he had renounced the crown of his own free will and in favour of his son. Richard was a tougher individual altogether. Bolingbroke set up a panel of clergy and canon lawyers to consider precedents for deposition. This found a suitable example of a deposition of a monarch for 'major crimes' in that of the Emperor Frederick II by Pope Innocent IV in 1245. Interestingly, this precedent does not seem to have been noted in 1326/7, though perhaps it was unnecessary, as Edward II's enemies relied on his 'abdication'. The panel ruled that Richard's 'perjuries, sacrileges, sodomitical acts, dispossession of his subjects, the reduction of his people to servitude, lack of reason and incapacity to rule' provided the necessary grounds in canon law (Bennett 1999: 176). However, Frederick II was deposed by a pope and a General Council of the Church, neither of which was available to Bolingbroke. The panel decided that, as in 1327, it was necessary to secure an 'abdication' by the king and then, to prevent any reneging on that abdication, a deposition. The question of whether a parliament summoned in the name of a king could depose that king remained open, for Richard was finally deposed only 'if anything of his dignity shall remain in him'.

The next issue was the way in which Bolingbroke was to prove his right to the crown. He might be the obvious successor to Richard, but was he the lawful heir? Consideration was given to impugning Richard's paternity or legitimacy, and then to utilising an old story that Edmund 'Crouchback', earl of Lancaster, Bolingbroke's direct ancestor through his mother, had been the elder son of Henry III rather than Edward I, but no evidence could be produced to support this. When parliament met on 30 September, Bolingbroke settled for a title with three elements. First, that the throne was vacant through Richard's voluntary abdication and his deposition by parliament; secondly, that Henry was a member of the royal house through both parents; and thirdly, though much less stress was laid on this at the time, he was the lawful king by conquest and by the will of the people. Bolingbroke and his allies sought to break Richard's resistance, confining him in the Tower and subjecting him to interrogation. The official 'Record and Process' against Richard claimed that on being visited by a deputation of notables on 29 September, he renounced his crown voluntarily and placed his coronation ring on Bolingbroke's finger. The following day parliament assembled in Westminster Hall although, as in 1327, it could not be considered a true parliament in the absence of the king or his appointed representative and the throne was left empty. Richard Scrope, archbishop of York, read Richard's statement renouncing the throne and absolving his subjects from their allegiance. Thomas Arundel, archbishop of Canterbury, then asked those present whether they wished, for the good of the realm, to accept this, and Lords and Commons gave their consent. It was then declared that, for the avoidance of doubt, a statement of Richard's crimes and specific instances of misgovernment, meriting his deposition, had been prepared by Bolingbroke's panel of canon lawyers and this was read to the assembly.

The assembly was then asked, both together and singly, whether the accusations contained in the Articles of Deposition and Richard's own 'confession of inadequacy' in the statement of abdication were sufficient grounds for him to be deposed and, according to the 'Record and Process', the assembly assented unanimously. Commissioners representing the three estates were appointed to depose Richard from 'all his royal dignity, majesty and honour, on behalf of, in the name of, and by authority of, all the estates, as has been observed in similar cases by the ancient custom of the realm'. The only similar case in which this 'ancient custom' had been observed was a mere seventy years old. Parliament now turned to the enthronement of his usurper. Bolingbroke spoke first, claiming the throne on the basis of his descent from Henry III twice over and God's grace in sending him to save the kingdom from bad government and bad laws. Again, the Lords and Commons were asked for their assent and, this being given, Bolingbroke was raised to the empty throne by the two archbishops. Archbishop Arundel preached a sermon stressing Bolingbroke's manliness and Richard's shortcomings as a ruler, before Bolingbroke spoke again to re-state his claim to the throne. Once more, he now stated his intention of ruling in accordance with established law and insisted that neither that law nor the rights of his subjects would be compromised by the manner of his succession. On 1 October, the commissioners of the three estates went to Richard II in the Tower, led by the chief justice, informed him of all the stages of the deposition process and then renounced their homage and fealty. A Spanish chronicler alleges that he was subjected to a process of degradation reminiscent of that of John Balliol in Scotland in 1296, being first seated in majesty and then stripped successively of crown, sceptre, orb, sword and finally the throne itself. Edward had dealt with the royal succession by charter. Henry IV did so via parliament in a statute of 1404 entailing the throne on his four sons and their issue. In 1406, he issued a charter confining the entail to his sons and their *male* issue, but this was repealed after only three months. The 1404 statute stands as the first example of what has become a universal practice since.

Conclusion

What was the composition of these medieval parliaments? Peers, bishops and 'mitred abbots' – the heads of the major religious houses – continued to be summoned by name. Indeed, a writ of summons to parliament in the name of an individual and his heirs became the usual means of creating peerages. The means by which members of the Commons were chosen is much less clear. Evidence suggests that many knights of the shire were chosen by the sheriffs of their counties. Richard II's biographer, Michael Bennett, has suggested that sheriffs selecting members for the Great Parliament were specifically told to choose men favourable to the king's cause (Bennett 1999: 99). Certainly, most were men of substance, often considerable landowners in their own right and members of the main aristocratic 'affinities' of their day. The Paston Letters record that John Howard, later the first Howard, duke of Norfolk, was put forward for election as a knight of the shire for Norfolk in 1455 by his kinsman John Mowbray, duke of Norfolk, whose follower he was. There was indignation on the part of some of the Norfolk gentry at having Howard forced upon them, especially as Mowbray had reputedly promised them a free election (Stephen 1891: 42–4). The reference to a free election shows that by this time elections were taking place, and legislation in 1430 gave the franchise in the counties to forty-shilling freeholders, a qualification which was to continue until as late as 1883, though, as much later, the elections were controlled by the great landowners. Borough representatives seem to have been chosen by the borough corporations.

By the mid-fifteenth century, a pattern seems to have been firmly established. The king summoned parliaments, usually when taxation was required, but that was now so often that parliaments were frequent. They were also dissolved by the king, on completion of the king's business – as yet no parliament had sought to remain in session against the king's will. Parliament was also now considered the proper forum for dealing with other matters, in particular in legitimating the accession of a usurper. In 1485, a parliament summoned by Henry VII simply declared that the new king had taken the throne upon himself and title to the crown now vested in him and his issue, though not without some issues for Henry (Chrimes 1972). However, the extent of parliament's power was not clear, nor was its precise relationship with the monarch, as these issues had yet to be tested, as they sorely were in the seventeenth century.

References

Bennett, M. (1999), *Richard II and the Revolution of 1399*, Stroud: Sutton Publishing.
Chrimes, S. B. (1972), *Henry VII*, London: Methuen English Monarchs Series.
Kim, K. (2000), *Aliens in Medieval Law: The Origins of Modern Citizenship*, Cambridge: Cambridge University Press.
Maddicott, J. R. (2010), *The Origins of the English Parliament 924–1327*, Oxford: Oxford University Press.
McKisack, M. (1959), *The Fourteenth Century*, Oxford: Oxford University Press.
Mills, A. D. (1998), *Oxford Dictionary of English Place Names*, Oxford: Oxford University Press.
Oman, C. W. C. (1919), *England before the Norman Conquest*, London: Methuen.
Prestwich, M. (1997), *Edward I*, 2nd edn, New Haven, CT: Yale University Press.
Saul, N. (1997), *Richard II*, New Haven, CT: Yale University Press.
Sayles, G. O. (1974), *The King's Parliament of England*, London: Edward Arnold.
Statutes of the Realm, vol. I (1810), London: Records Commissioners.
Stephen, L. (ed.) (1891), *Dictionary of National Biography*, vol. 28, New York: Macmillan.
Stubbs, W. (ed.) (1882–3), *Chronicles of the Reigns of Edward I and Edward II*, 2 vols, London: Longman.
Swanton, M. (ed.) (1996), *The Anglo-Saxon Chronicle*, New York: Routledge.

Chapter 14

The Levellers and Diggers

Andrew Bradstock

It often takes a national crisis to prompt popular reflection on issues of fundamental social and political importance, and it is no coincidence that the most significant debate in England concerning the nature of democracy occurred in what was arguably its most turbulent decade, the 1640s. As the country endured three civil wars, which culminated in the execution of the king and the abolition of monarchy, and as other great institutions like the Established Church and House of Lords disappeared, so people of all classes began openly to debate the meaning of the crisis and the shape of the new order they hoped would emerge (Bradstock 2011). A key question was how government might better reflect the interests of 'the people', many of whom had invested so much in bringing about change. The most influential and creative popular movements promoting debate on issues of liberty, representation, sovereignty, rights and the law were the Levellers and the Diggers. Neither was in any sense a 'party' or a formal organisation, but through a combination of direct action and dissemination of pamphlets, tracts and petitions, both sought popular support for more radical solutions to the constitutional crisis than the leaders of either the Parliament or army seemed willing to countenance, even though they had spearheaded the campaign against the king. At the heart of the Levellers' programme was a call for a significant extension of the franchise; for the Diggers, change had to be much more fundamental and embrace wholesale economic reform.

Leveller Origins

The Levellers first came to prominence in July 1646 with the publication of a tract entitled *A Remonstrance of Many Thousand Citizens*, setting out their main demands in terms of religious toleration and reform of Parliament (Overton and Walwyn 1646). Its cover depicted one of their leaders, John Lilburne, set behind bars, an allusion to the imprisonment which prevented him from signing the tract. Lilburne, along with other prominent Levellers like Richard Overton, William Walwyn and Thomas Prince, spent much time in prison, testimony to the potential to subvert good order which their ideas were thought to contain. Leveller ideas evolved over time and in response to a rapidly changing situation, but they did share a core of beliefs, including a conviction that all people were created equal and none had a God-given or natural right to govern or rule over another. Rule could be tolerated only where the governed had given their consent, Levellers believed. Thus, governments could act only by the will of the people, in whom resided ultimate sovereignty.

Levellers held that the government under which they lived precisely did *not* reflect the will of the people: the question therefore was how could it be reconstituted so that the 'sovereignty of the people' could be expressed – and who, for that matter, were 'the people' in a political sense? It was in response to such questions that the Levellers produced their manifestoes, calling some 'An Agreement of the People' to indicate their aim of establishing popular consent to a new form of government. For Parliament to be more truly representative of the people's interests, Levellers thought, its undemocratic elements had to be stripped of their power and those which were formally democratic had to be made more so in practice. Included in the first category were the king and the House of Lords. The Levellers made it plain to members of the House of Commons, to whom they addressed their *Remonstrance*, that they looked to them to 'show the intolerable inconveniences of having a kingly government . . . and . . . to publish your resolution . . . to acquit us of so great a charge and trouble forever' (Overton and Walwyn 1646: 1). In the case of the Lords, a body not chosen by the people but 'intruders . . . thrust upon us by kings', the Commons should likewise 'free us from . . . their negative voices, or else tell us that it is reasonable we should be slaves' (Sharp 1998: 36–8). The title of a tract by Overton really said it all: *An Alarum to the House of Lords: Against their Insolent Usurpation of the Common Liberties, and Rights of this Nation* (Overton 1646).

Levellers wanted to make the one institution that did purport to speak for the people, the Commons, *more* representative. One of its failings was that not every region or sector of the country was equally represented: everybody had to pay taxes, but not everybody was represented in Parliament. Levellers therefore called for a redistribution of seats, with the number of Members of Parliament each county chose proportionate to the rate each was assessed to pay. Greater accountability could also be ensured by more frequent elections; removing the corrupt practice of candidates 'buying' votes to get elected; the introduction of salaries for MPs to prevent their dependence on rich patrons; and an extension of the franchise to embrace all men aged twenty-one and above, with the exception of servants, recipients of alms and supporters of the king (who were required to wait ten years). Leveller views on who should be entitled to vote varied over time, and much debate has ensued over what they meant by categories like 'servant' (Macpherson 1962). But in broad terms they wanted the franchise to reflect their belief that no one should be governed against their consent. As Thomas Rainsborough put it in his famous contribution to the debate on democracy at Putney in 1647: 'the poorest he that is in England hath a life to live as the greatest he, and therefore . . . I think it's clear, that every man that is to live under a government ought first by his own consent to put himself under that government' (Firth 1992: I:301; Vallance 2009: 164). The use of the word 'man' here is deliberate. While in many respects Levellers were far-sighted, they appear never to have considered the vote for women despite the high profile of women within the movement and their publication of *A Petition of Women* affirming women's 'equal interest with the men of this nation in those liberties and securities' discussed elsewhere (Bradstock and Rowland 2002: 111–13).

A Democratic Programme

Levellers wanted clear limitations on governmental authority, the better to rein in rulers' potential to misuse their power. Government was necessary, Walwyn affirmed in *A Manifestation* (1649), because 'we know very well the pravity and corruption of man's heart is such that there could be no living without it' (Sharp 1998: 162). But this 'pravity and corruption' was as evident among those in power as in those they ruled, and therefore people should cede only limited powers to their rulers. Even the most truly representative government should not be free to touch *all* rights, including freedom to practise one's religion, to be treated equally under the law and not to be conscripted into the military against one's conscience. Freedom of conscience was a central Leveller concern: everyone should have the right to make up their own mind in matters of religion and not be compelled by another. However, they had to agree that 'freedom to practise religion' could not encompass behaviour that was 'destructive to humane society' or could endanger the state: where a person claimed that their religion entitled them to commit a criminal act, natural law would trump 'religious law'. But Levellers did hold that religious toleration must extend to all, including Jews, Muslims and those accused of atheism and idolatry, a radically consistent position at a time when Catholicism was still illegal.

Unlike many of their contemporaries, Levellers understood that religious liberty was the other side of the coin from political liberty: as Brian Manning has said, 'it may be argued whether the Levellers' ultimate aim was religious liberty, for which political liberty was the means, or whether their overriding objective was political liberty, for which religious liberty was the means', but they certainly understood that the two could not be separated (Manning 1984: 81–2). So Levellers held that no one should be compelled to attend a state church, pay tithes to it or in any way conform to it; although they did agree that governments could 'instruct' the public in matters of religion, provided that this was done without compulsion. Parishioners should be able to choose for themselves their ministers and agree the terms of their employment, rather than have them appointed over their heads and paid through a compulsory tithe. If implemented, this would have amounted to a *de facto* separation of church and state.

Equal treatment for all under the law was another issue that Levellers pressed, and they consistently attacked the privileges enjoyed by members of the Lords and Commons. These had the right to send others to prison without showing cause, but were themselves above the law and free from the general obligation to pay taxes. Levellers were also concerned that the ordinary people (who *were* subject to all the laws) were generally prevented from knowing their rights because those laws were still couched in Latin and Norman French – or in some cases not even written at all, but based on supposed 'precedent'. Levellers wanted the law translated into the vernacular so that all might understand its demands. Levellers called for freedom from arbitrary arrest and imprisonment without trial and the restoration of the right to trial by an independent jury, free of any party interest. They held freedom of the press to be fundamental if political and religious liberty were to be guaranteed and called for an end to the licensing of the press. Suppression of the truth kept people in ignorance and the nation enslaved to tyrants and oppressors, they argued.

Levellers wanted democratic reforms at local as well as national level. Local communities should be allowed to elect their own officials, and justice should be administered through local law courts by locally elected officials. Local militias should also replace the centralised professional army. These policies were consistent with their belief in the sovereignty of the people and that power should be concentrated less in a small number of people in central government and brought nearer to the common people. What we would now call 'decentralisation' or subsidiarity would better ensure the protection of individual rights and freedoms, Levellers believed. Levellers were concerned about the inequitable distribution of wealth in society, but, unlike the Diggers (or 'True Levellers' as they preferred to be known), had no interest in the redistribution of wealth or land. Rather, they upheld the right of the individual to own property, believing that no representative of the people should have the power to level people's estates or make all things common. Their nomenclature had been thrust upon them against their will – they were, as they often said, 'commonly (though unjustly) styled Levellers' – and they did not want anyone to take it literally (Sharp 1998: 158).

Levellers and Religion

Religious beliefs helped to shape the views of the Leveller leaders. John Lilburne, for example, saw the inherent equality of all people rooted in biblical texts as well as natural law and spoke of God engraving upon his heart the golden rule, do unto others as you would have them do unto you. This was not just a rule for Christians, he argued, for God had written it on every heart intending that all should live by it. Overton thought this rule the foundational principle which made civil society possible, and from it Levellers derived their doctrine of equity. They saw no contradiction in arguing for the essential rationality of human beings and the implanting of that rationality in them by God: God made each person 'naturally a rational creature, judging rightly all things and desiring only what was necessary', Walwyn claimed (Lakoff 1964: 63; Manning 1984: 72). The strong individualism in Leveller thinking had its roots in the Calvinistic Puritanism that the movement's leaders encountered in their youth and, in varying degrees, subscribed to in later life. Calvinism stressed the importance of the individual's one-to-one relationship with God, a relationship that gave to that person worth, value and dignity, which Levellers held in tension with Christianity's stress on the importance of community and membership together of the 'body of Christ'. The doctrine that God had 'predestined' some to salvation, which Calvin drew from Augustine and St Paul, also spoke of the inherent equality of all. It affirmed that no one merited God's favour on account of status, wealth or birth (Wootton 1991: 437).

Leveller thinking on equity, and the need for laws based on this principle, was also informed by their experience of meeting and worshipping with gathered churches. In contrast to the established Church, dissenting groups followed an essentially demo-cratic pattern of government, with ministers elected by the congregation and paid by the voluntary contributions of members (not the extraction of tithes). These con-gregations also established themselves on the basis of covenants or contracts freely entered into, which Overton believed reflected the practice of the early Christians. Levellers would have witnessed at Baptist and other separatist meetings people who ordinarily would not have had a public voice accorded the right to speak, including women.

Levellers' Influence

Levellers worked hard to garner support for their ideas among the rank and file of the army, and in the autumn of 1647, Cromwell and the other army leaders agreed to a debate in Putney church with 'agitators' chosen by the army and specially invited Leveller spokespeople. The document on the table was the first 'Agreement of the People', which set out the case for a fairer distribution of parliamentary seats, religious toleration, an end to conscription and equality under the law. Putney afforded the Levellers their best opportunity to persuade Cromwell of the merits of their case, but although they spoke with skill and passion, the argument ultimately went the way of the chief speaker for the grandees, Henry Ireton, who demonstrated the inconsistency of the Levellers' position regarding the franchise and property. Ireton did not oppose extending the franchise, but, with a greater concern for political realities, contended that if the Levellers upheld the principle of private property *and* argued for more men to be given the vote, then 'why may not those men vote against all property?' (Firth 1992: I:314).

The Levellers flourished for at most six years. On one level their impact was small, none of their leaders living to see any of their major proposals established. With hindsight we might conclude that the only way those proposals *could* have come into being was by the inherently contradictory manner of imposition. From the perspective of the political establishment their programme had little to offer and there was no prospect of it being realised by consent. The Levellers themselves failed to gain sufficient support among those whose interests they represented to build a mass movement for change. Yet their key proposals – universal franchise, salaries for MPs, elimination of 'pocket boroughs', frequent parliaments, decentralisation of power – are now largely taken for granted in the West, having been promoted by later movements (notably, in England by the Chartists) and implemented in more recent times. As David Wootton has argued, it is hard today to grasp how revolutionary the Levellers were: in seeking a written constitution based on inalienable natural rights and measures, such as equality of all under the law, freedom of conscience, limitations on government power in accord with the principles of natural justice and voting rights for the poor, they

> were not merely seeking to establish in England freedoms that existed elsewhere . . . but . . . for the first time freedoms which (outside of a mythical historical past, that of Anglo-Saxon England) never had existed, and were not to come into existence for over three centuries. (Wootton 1991: 412–13)

Diggers' Programme

If the Levellers never resolved the tension created by their commitment to both extend the franchise and maintain the right to property, the Diggers faced no such dilemma. They were clear that merely giving more people the vote would not bring about the 'freedom' that Parliament had promised to those who had risked their lives fighting the king, nor would it end the hunger to which so many were subject if the rich were allowed to continue parcelling off areas of land for themselves. What people needed was *economic* and not merely *political* freedom, the restoration of the land to communal ownership and the abolition of the concept of 'thine' and 'mine'. Diggers saw political liberty as inseparable from economic liberty and stood apart from most of their contemporaries in wanting to see the overthrow of monarchy consolidated in the establishment of a truly communitarian order. While many in the 1640s and 1650s called for thorough-going religious and political change, few apart from the Diggers argued that, without a fundamental re-structuring of the pattern of land ownership, no political or social change would benefit the poor and dispossessed. With the king gone, Diggers argued, Parliament must seize the opportunity to dismantle the whole inequitable system of private land ownership over which the monarchy had presided and restore the land to its rightful owners, the people. The Diggers not only *pleaded* for such a restoration, they took up their spades and began to cultivate some waste and common land in the south of England, hoping to set in train the process of making the earth once more a 'common treasury' for all to enjoy.

Our knowledge of Digger ideas can be gleaned from the writings of their main theorist and spokesperson, Gerrard Winstanley, a Wigan-born merchant tailor who moved to Surrey from London in the 1640s. In a tract entitled *The New Law of Righteousnes*, published in January 1649, Winstanley explains his belief that poverty is rooted in the practice of 'buying and selling the earth from one particular hand to another': because some people have the right to say of the land, 'this is mine', others are prevented from seeking nourishment from it and survive only by working for landlords for small wages (Corns *et al.* 2009: I:481). It is as if the earth were made for a few people, not all and such practices will end shortly when Christ begins to 'rise up' in his people and lead them once more to till the land and live together and act righteously toward one another (Bradstock 1997; Corns *et al.* 2009: I:503, 506). Writing during the heady weeks before the execution of Charles Stuart and con- fronting widespread hunger occasioned by the worst run of bad harvests for more than a century, Winstanley begins with the premise that the earth was originally created for all to share: 'In the beginning of time the great creator Reason made the earth to be a common treasury', as their 'manifesto', *The True Levellers Standard Advanced*, put it (Corns *et al.* 2009: II:4). The concept of individual ownership of the land was not written into the creation narrative and originally the earth was common to all, with the more physically able helping the weaker by working harder. However, this simple arrangement became corrupted once the stronger began to argue their right to a larger share of the earth than the weaker – Winstanley's understanding of 'the fall' – and began appropriating land for themselves. For Diggers the earth must be restored to communal ownership and so they went further than most of their contemporaries. The conventional wisdom of the time was that 'fallen' humankind had lost the innocence it once enjoyed in Eden and was now so subject to impulses of greed, fear, envy and lust that for society to exist in any organised form, accommodation had to be made to the need to own and protect private property. Hence, the concern of political philosophers was to construct the most workable social structures permitted by humanity's limitations and weaknesses – in the case of Winstanley's contemporary, Thomas Hobbes, one where anarchy, the inevitable consequence of unbridled competitiveness, was held at bay by a strong authoritative sovereign figure (Hobbes [1651] 1994).

Winstanley, however, not only rejected the position Hobbes was to articulate in *Leviathan*, but in a passage that remarkably anticipated much later thinking, suggested that human nature is largely shaped by the prevailing social conditions:

I am assured that if it be rightly searched into, the inward bondages of the mind, as covetousness, pride, hypocrisy, envy, sorrow, fears, desperation, and madness, are all occasioned by the outward bondage, that one sort of people lay upon another. (Corns *et al.* 2009: II:296)

For Winstanley, there would be no need for laws or punishments once people had put an end to the practice of buying and selling. The prelapsarian community will be attainable once private property is abolished and Reason reigns in the human heart. His understanding of the fall as the introduction of private property led him to envisage a situation in which, as Reason once again held sway, people embraced the idea of communitarian living as the only rational and just way to co-exist. The breakdown of the system of private ownership would then become unstoppable as people in different localities, seeing the benefits of living communally, followed the Diggers' example, thereby bringing about the disintegration of the system of hiring labour, the only way that the rich could manage their own huge estates.

The Diggers' programme was effectively a call for a 'general strike' against landowners and it sought to transform English society in the most radical way. As James Holstun has commented: 'the Diggers threatened the landed ruling class precisely because they inserted local knowledge into a national revolutionary project: preaching and publishing epistles to other disaffected tenants and wage labourers, to the Army, to Parliament, to London, to the universities; forming links among the scattered Digging communes; and developing a programme for revolution based in a transformation of productive relations at the local level' (Holstun 2000: 393). Some commentators have seen the act of digging as largely symbolic, a signal that the new age was dawning where God would transform society in some supernatural way so the Diggers would not have to realise that transformation themselves (Bradstock 2002: 98). There is a sense in which Winstanley must have understood that the fulfilment of his vision of England becoming a common treasury required divine intervention because in purely *economic* terms it was unworkable: it would have required a large section of the population to be fed from land which was not arable. Yet this should not obscure his consideration of how *practically* he might realise his vision, since believing that his programme coincided with the divine purpose did not preclude the necessity of working to bring that purpose about. In fact, quite the reverse, as his reflection in *A*

Watch-word to the City of London that 'action is the life of all, and if thou dost not act, thou dost nothing' makes clear (Corns *et al.* 2009: II:80). Further, while the Diggers' action was inspired by their conviction that this was a propitious time to begin remaking the earth as a common treasury, they were also driven by their hunger and the simple need to feed themselves and their dependants.

The Diggers took other practical steps to pursue their vision, including the employment of new agricultural techniques that were designed to make more land fertile. These included the planting of crops that could survive in dry and sandy soil, the use of those crops to maintain more animals and produce more manure, and the pasturing of animals on land that would also be rotated for crops. The common land on which the Diggers operated was common only because its soil was poor and suitable mainly for grazing, whereas their attempts to work the soil would have gradually rendered poor land into ground suitable for growing corn and other staples. Winstanley worked out that of all the potentially fertile land in England: 'scarce one part [in three] is manured: so that here is land enough to maintain all her children' (Corns *et al.* 2009: I:523). Winstanley believed in the sacred quality of the land and acknowledged it as the source and sustainer of life. The earth is our Mother who brought us forth and her love means she wants to give 'all her children suck . . . that they starve not', but she is hindered from doing this while the landlords enclose off the land (Corns *et al.* 2009: II:18–19).

The Diggers versus Kingly Power

Like the Levellers and many others, Diggers had no time for the established clergy whom they saw, along with landlords and lawyers, as an 'unholy trinity' upholding an iniquitous system. But whereas many were content to attack these groups individually, the Diggers developed an analysis of their interconnectedness, what Marxists might call their shared 'class interest' (Turner 1983: 145–6). The strongest hint of this is to be found in Winstanley's concept of 'kingly power', a collective term he employs for those institutions that maintained the economic system burdening the poor. The word 'kingly' acknowledged, not only that it was the monarch himself who was the 'figurehead' of established order, but the role of William the Conqueror in originally uniting various components of power under himself. Winstanley shared the Levellers' distaste for the Norman character of the English legal system, particularly the way that it continued to reinforce the division of land William effected in the interest of his lieutenants. Winstanley believed that, to enforce his laws, William appointed two 'national officers': the lawyer, whose 'work is conversant about nothing but the disposing of the earth', and the clergy, whose duty was to persuade people to accept the king's claim to call the land his own and not rebel against him (their reward for this being the tithe system) (Corns *et al.* 2009: II:297–8).

The concept of 'kingly power' played a vital role in shaping Winstanley's response to the crisis of the 1640s. While he welcomed the removal of the monarchy and the Lords, he recognised that in themselves these developments would not be sufficient to lift the people's burden: kingly power was not in the hands of the king alone, but in the hands of the landlords, the lawyers and the 'tithing-priests'. With Charles' execution, the 'top-bow is lopped off the tree of tyranny, and kingly power in that one particular is cast out; but alas oppression is a great tree still, and keeps off the sun of freedom from the poor commons still', he wrote (Corns *et al.* 2009: II:112). His solution was straightforward and more radical than the Levellers': in addition to taking away the king and the Lords, the new government should remove the power of landlords, priests and judges, and then people would be free.

Like Levellers, Diggers met with opposition from those most threatened by their actions, including local landowners (Gurney 2000). So ferocious were the attacks on Winstanley's community that it lasted barely twelve months, being wound up after the destruction of their crops and houses. Yet even in defeat Winstanley continued to picture the new society that might emerge from the ashes of the old, and in what proved to be his final work, *The Law of Freedom in a Platform* (1652), he set out his vision of a communitarian order: land communally tilled, and food and commodities available for collection from storehouses without the need for money. Though Winstanley never admitted using any source for his ideas other than Scripture, his new society has some similarities to Thomas More's *Utopia* (More [1516] 2003). Winstanley stressed the importance of the family as the primary unit of society and described the legal system he envisaged being necessary in his society. The need for laws is consistent with his belief that they would only disappear when the practice of buying and selling finally disappears. The offences for which the death penalty will be invoked are significant: buying and selling the land; practising law for money; preaching and praying for hire; homicide; and rape. As John Gurney has written, if this tract was drafted during the period of the digging, as Winstanley claimed, it 'can help us better understand the kinds of social arrangements, and means of production and distribution, that he may have envisaged for Digger communities had they spread as successfully as he had hoped' (Gurney 2007: 212). That these communities did not spread, or even survive, means we can only speculate how far the Diggers' call to the oppressed to join them in remaking the earth might have transformed England and beyond.

Conclusion

The concerns which motivated Levellers and Diggers – democracy, liberty, equality before the law, access to the land – remain central in every age. While many of the Levellers' demands have now been met, other questions they addressed, such as freedom of speech, assembly and conscience, continue to be hotly debated. The question of protecting parliamentary privilege is still as critical in the twenty-first century as it was in the Levellers' day, as is the debate about the necessity or otherwise of written constitutions. Liliburn and his collaborators aspired to provide the framework for England's first constitution and, as Tristram Hunt has pointed out, 'what the Levellers posited nearly 400 years ago was precisely the kind of secular constitution guaranteeing freedom of conscience and speech alongside a sovereign parliament which many regard today as much needed political safeguards' (Hunt 2007: 7).

The Levellers' concern that liberty should be understood in a deeper sense than simply protecting individual rights and take into account the interests of wider society has relevance to contemporary debates. As Melissa Lane has argued, while Levellers used their liberty to argue for the common good, and lived and suffered for the values that they sought to promote, today we are prone to define liberty in terms of a bare, neutral list of rights, isolated from any wider social values (Lane 2009). Whereas contemporary theorists tend to draw no distinction between the values that those seeking rights want to promote, Levellers can help us reconnect liberty with values, to find the grounds to differentiate between *defending* the liberty of all and *valuing* that liberty that is used to help rather than harm others (Lane 2009).

The questions that preoccupied the Diggers also remain relevant, not least in an age of widespread concern about the environment and future well-being of the planet. Even leaving aside the wider question of whether 'the earth' should *in principle* be 'owned' and traded by individuals or corporations or nation-states – which Diggers, of course, were not afraid to ask – issues as diverse as the right to roam, the building of motorways, land tax, land-use planning, the selling-off of school playing-fields and squatting are all manifestations of the core concern of the Diggers, namely, how the earth can once more give sustenance to all her children.

References

Bradstock, A. (1997), *Faith in the Revolution: The Political Theologies of Müntzer and Winstanley*, London: SPCK.

Bradstock, A. (2002), 'Restoring all Things from the Curse: Millenarianism, Alchemy, Science and Politics in the Writings of Gerrard Winstanley', in C. Jowitt and D. Watt (eds), *The Arts of 17th-Century Science*, Aldershot: Ashgate.

Bradstock, A. (2011), *Radical Religion in Cromwell's England: A Concise History from the English Civil War to the End of the Commonwealth*, London: I. B. Tauris.

Bradstock, A. and C. Rowland (eds) (2002), *Radical Christian Writings: A Reader*, Oxford: Blackwell.

Corns, T. N., A. Hughes and D. Loewenstein (eds) (2009), *The Complete Works of Gerrard Winstanley*, 2 vols, Oxford: Oxford University Press.

Firth, C. H. (ed.) (1992), *The Clarke Papers: Selections from the Papers of William Clarke*, 2 vols, London: Royal Historical Society.

Hobbes, T. ([1651] 1994), *Leviathan*, Indianapolis, IN: Hackett.

Gurney, J. (2000), ' "Furious divells?" The Diggers and Their Opponents', in A. Bradstock (ed.), *Winstanley and the Diggers 1649–1999*, London: Frank Cass.

Gurney, J. (2007), *Brave Community: The Digger Movement in the English Revolution*, Manchester: Manchester University Press.

Holstun, J. (2000), *Ehud's Dagger: Class Struggle in the English Revolution*, London: Verso.

Hunt, T. (2007), 'A Jewel of Democracy', *The Guardian*, g2, 26 October.

Lakoff, S. A. (1964), *Equality in Political Philosophy*, Boston, MA: Beacon Press.

Lane, M. (2009), 'Liberty as a Social Value: Lessons from the Levellers', Convention on Modern Liberty, London: openDemocracy.

Macpherson, C. B. (1962), *The Political Theory of Possessive Individualism: Hobbes to Locke*, Oxford: Oxford University Press.

Manning, B. (1984), 'The Levellers and Religion', in J. F. McGregor and B. Reay (eds), *Radical Religion in the English Revolution*, Oxford: Oxford University Press.

More, T. ([1516] 2003), *Utopia*, trans. P. Turner, London: Penguin.

Overton, R. (1646), *An Alarum to the House of Lords: Against their Insolent Usurpation of the Common Liberties, and Rights of this Nation.* London: n.p.

Overton, R. and W. Walwyn (1646), *A Remonstrance of Many Thousand Citizens*, London: n.p.

Sharp, A. (1998), *The English Levellers*, Cambridge: Cambridge University Press.

Turner, D. (1983), *Marxism and Christianity*, Oxford: Blackwell.

Vallance, E. (2009), *A Radical History of Britain*, London: Little, Brown.

Wootton, D. (1991), 'Leveller Democracy and the Puritan Revolution', in J. H. Burns and M. Goldie (eds), *The Cambridge History of Political Thought*, Cambridge: Cambridge University Press.

Chapter 15

The Swiss Cantons

Thomas Lau

Although sixteenth-century humanists regarded Switzerland as an old nation populated by the descendants of the ancient Helvetians, the country, while built on even
earlier charters and treaties, emerged as a confederated alliance in a gradual process
between 1350 and 1450 (Fossedal 2002: 11–42; Sablonier 2008). It consisted of rural
communes in the central Alps and urban communes at Lake Constance, the Upper
Rhine and the eastern part of Burgundy. The main reason these communes stayed
together was their military success. The conquered territories they administered
together could be protected only if the confederates found a way to solve their internal
disputes without the help of foreign allies. In 1481 the Swiss Confederacy consisted of
eight members: Schwyz, Uri, Unterwalden, Glarus, Zug, Lucerne, Berne and Zurich.
In the years to come they were joined by Fribourg (1481), Solothurn (1481), Basel
(1501), Schaffhausen (1501) and Appenzell (1513). The new members were equal in
status. In case of internal warfare, however, they were obliged to remain neutral. The
confederacy of the thirteen cantons was surrounded by associates – allies that were
connected to all or some cantons by treaties. Some of them, like the League of Valais,
were highly complex political systems, others were independent cities like Rottweil,
Mulhouse or Geneva, or princely territories like Neuchatel or the bishopric of Basel.
At least until 1648 the confederacy was part of the Holy Roman Empire, however, its
cantons did not pay taxes nor did they accept an imperial subpoena.

After the Peace of Westphalia dissolved the confederacy's bonds to the empire
step-by-step, Switzerland claimed independence (Fossedal 2002: 11–42). While the
emperor played a rather insignificant role in Swiss politics, other European leaders
were quite influential. Close ties were kept with the king of France, the king of Spain,
the duke of Savoy and the doge of Venice. All of them paid subsidies to the
confederates in return for the services of Swiss mercenaries. While Switzerland
developed amid a range of governmental systems – monarchical, aristocratic, ecclesiastical and oligarchic – there was at the heart of many of the original cantons a system
of governance by assembly of free men that informed a democratic approach
historically and still guides Swiss government today.

The Confederal Diet

At the confederal diet (*Tagsatzung*), matters concerning the administration of the
Swiss condominiums (*Gemeine Herrschaften*) were decided by a majority of participat-

ing cantons. On any other issue unanimity was required among the delegates of the cantons. Those of the urban cantons (Basel, Berne, Fribourg, Lucerne, Solothurn, Schaffhausen, Zurich) were elected by their town councils. In the rural cantons (Schwyz, Uri, Unterwalden, Appenzell) this right was reserved to the cantonal assembly of all eligible citizens, men from the traditionally recognised, free peasant families (*Landgemeinde*). In Zug, one delegate was appointed by town council and one by the rural assemblies. In Glarus, it was the Grand Council's privilege to make this decision. Any canton could ask for a diet. The proposed agenda was sent to Zurich as the presiding canton (*Vorort*) and it invited the other cantons usually to the city of Baden or (after 1712) to the city of Frauenfeld. The representatives of cantons served under a fixed mandate. After the diet any canton had the right to declare any decision at any time to be null and void. The right to nullify, however, was rarely administered in early modern times (Church 2004: 35–48).

Most delegates were given only vague instruction on how to cast their votes. Those who sent them generally lacked the political knowledge to make informed decisions on confederal matters. Those who were elected belonged to the canton's top elite and usually served in confederal meetings for many years – sometimes for decades. In most cases, they were given a free hand to find a compromise with the other delegates. The *Tagsatzung* could decide on any matter all members agreed to decide on. It passed statutes regulating currency problems, it ratified foreign treaties and organised common defence. The delegates expressed their opinion on the matters under discussion one by one. The very formalised procedure (*Umfrage*) followed a fixed order. The first allowed to speak was always the mayor of Zurich. Those who were the first in line (like Zurich, Berne, Schwyz and Lucerne) were the most influential. The others usually agreed with one of these leading opinion makers. The procedure went on until a unanimous vote was reached or the cantons agreed to drop the matter. Some associates also sent delegates to the diet and influenced its decisions.

The most powerful observers visiting the *Tagsatzung* were undoubtedly the ambassadors of foreign powers, especially France, Spain, the Netherlands, England, Savoy, Venice and the Holy Roman Empire. They were allowed to join the assembly after the confederates solemnly greeted each other as brethren and friends. Before the doors were closed they had the chance to give a speech. In the seventeenth and eighteenth centuries these public orations were usually printed and achieved considerable influence in the public debate on political matters. The diplomat's chief business, however, was to observe the proceedings and to keep in contact with the decision makers. They were interested mainly in Swiss mercenaries and they were ready to pay a good price for their services. France and Spain gave high subsidies to cantons in return for the military service of their citizens. The French and Spanish ambassadors also gave political assistance in internal matters. Between 1523 and 1536 four confederates (Basel, Schaffhausen, Zurich and Berne) and four associates (Bienne, and the cities of St Gallen, Mulhouse and Geneva) became Protestant. Appenzell, Glarus, the Grision and most subject territories became religiously mixed areas, while the rest of the confederacy, especially in central Switzerland, remained Catholic. The religious split caused considerable unrest. Four wars were fought over religious matters between 1529 and 1712. They culminated in a fragile balance of power.

The foreign diplomats – particularly the ambassador of France – played an important part in keeping this system working. In the seventeenth century, the Swiss cantons could hardly survive without being on good terms with France. Her ambassador thus was able to ease the way to compromise by turning the delegates' focus to matters of common interest.

How is the constitution of this confederation to be described? Josias Simler (1530–76) proposed a classical answer to this question. Switzerland, he pointed out, had a mixed government, but with only two components – democracy and aristocracy (Simler 1576). It was composed of the aristocratic urban cantons and the democratic rural cantons. Some early modern scholars developed a different approach. The historian Jean Baptiste Plantin tried to show that the Swiss constitution integrated three different elements (Plantin 1666). Zurich, Basel and Schaffhausen, where citizens elected the city councillors, were to be defined as democracies. In Berne and Lucerne, Plantin pointed out, the patricians ruled. These cities were aristocracies. In the rural cantons the principles of popular rule applied. The Catholic scholar Franz Michael Bühler in his *Tractatus von der Freyheit* went one step further (Bühler 1689). Because the equal vote of the cantons' delegates was guaranteed, Switzerland, he explained, was a democracy. No canton claimed legal precedence over another. The idea that Switzerland was a democracy was also put forward in pamphlets warning the cantons not to cooperate with foreign monarchs. The author of the influential *Renovirter Wecker* (1662) tried to convince the readers that princes were always the enemies of democracies and they always would be.

The unique nature of the Swiss diet has been stressed and the confederation hailed as an example of state-building from below (Gierke 1868). Although its insufficiencies in matters of decision making were evident, the diet was successful in keeping the delegates talking to each other. On some matters they agreed to disagree and turned to the matters they could agree on. Other historians emphasise the insufficiencies of this system, drawing attention to the long-term consequences of the religious split (Lau 2008). Matters of crucial importance – such as the definition of Swiss law – were silently banned from the diet's debates. Once one side broke these taboos, the outbreak of a military conflict was likely. Without the economic and political assistance of monarchical powers, the Swiss republic thus was hardly able to survive.

The Rural Cantons

While the rural, Catholic cantons had some claim to democracy in their assemblies, it was avowedly majoritarian and prone to manipulation by leading families. In October 1655, only weeks before a short but bitter war between Protestant and Catholic cantons began, the council of Schwyz issued a declaration explaining why it was ready to take up arms. Zurich, the neighbouring canton, had granted asylum to small group of crypto-Calvinists that had emigrated from their territory. This was – Schwyz made clear – unacceptable. Schwyz, they pointed out, was a democracy. All citizens enjoyed the same rights. Everybody had a share in the supreme power of the state. The majority ruled and citizens were expected to follow. This was – Schwyz's councillors declared – the very reason why their canton still kept her freedom and still preserved the old, Catholic religion. The Protestant refugees had broken this principle and therefore should be handed over to Schwyz officials. Zurich's refusal to comply was criticised fervently. From the Schwyz point of view, the idea that all people living in the confederacy enjoyed an inalienable right to choose their religion did not exist. The cantons were sovereign entities that cooperated only on issues where they decided to do so. No single person could claim any individual rights protected by the confederacy (*Schwyzer Manifest* 1655).

The conflict over the Protestant refugees led to the first war of Villmergen and casts light on the rural cantons' self-perception in early modern times. In Schwyz, Uri, Unterwalden, Appenzell and Glarus, the assemblies of the citizens acted as the supreme powers. In Schwyz, these assemblies were held once a year on the last Sunday in May. When questions of crucial importance were left unresolved at this meeting, a second one was summoned two or three weeks later. The assembly acted as a high court of justice, decided on new laws and charters, ratified treaties and elected the main office-holders of the canton. The head of the administration (*Landamann*), his deputy (*Statthalter*) and the treasurer (*Säckelmeister*) served for two years. Other officers and members of the court were appointed by the assembly for life. The members the council served as custodians of the assembly's rights between sessions and were elected by local meetings held by each of the six quarters. They were responsible for their acts to the assembly and all acknowledged the assembly as the supreme power of the canton. Although office-holders usually proposed the agenda, any member of the assembly had the right to put forward a motion. Freedom of speech was guaranteed. Once a resolution had been passed, every citizen was expected to obey it. The assembly's competence was unlimited. It arranged compromises between conflicting families and administered ecclesiastical rights. In central Switzerland, the parishes and the assemblies were so influential in all matters concerning the Church that there was simply no need for the Reformation. The main office-holders stood for election every two years and that increased the competition among the canton's elite. In Schwyz, about 120 families possessed citizenship in 1700. Only the members of these families were eligible for state offices and only a few of these families were successful in the political competition. The Reding family exerted significant social and political influence because of their perceived ability to keep the ties between Schwyz and the kingdom of France strong. Whenever decisions were made by the Schwyz, a member of the family Reding had to be present. The Redings distributed the French subsidies, organised the salt trade and were successful mercenary leaders (Sowerby 1892: 26–35, 144–5). They lived on French money and shared their wealth with others. The assemblies of the canton were not only a test of the leading families' popularity, they were also places where those families bought electors with money or simply with beer and bratwurst.

At the end of the seventeenth century this system of patronage in the rural cantons became increasingly fragile. The prevalence of Swiss mercenaries in the French infantry came to an end. Their reliability and ferocity still made them valuable to the French king, but the price he was ready to pay decreased. The elite's ability to organise the distribution of economic resources was diminished. The influence of families like the Redings could be saved only if they followed a new political strategy. The ties between the leading families of the Catholic cantons in central Switzerland became stronger during the seventeenth century. The aristocratic habits of the families and their education distinguished them from the ordinary citizens. In a new Europe of sovereign states, a Europe becoming more complex and dangerous, the leaders promised orientation and leadership. Power, they argued, was to be transferred from the canton to regional and confederal institutions because a single canton could not defend itself and was unable to pursue its interests alone. The project to reorganise confederal defence aroused the peasants' suspicion. The cantonal assembly was unwilling to transfer the command of its troops to a confederal body. The citizens of Schwyz not only refused to ratify the defence treaty, they also decided to send envoys to the cantonal assemblies of Zug, Glarus, Unterwalden and Uri. The direct contact between the assemblies' citizens was intended to counter-balance the networks of the elite. In the following decades the antagonism between the elite and the citizens increased. In Schwyz, but also in Zug and Appenzell, considerable unrest was observed. In 1712, the situation went out of control. The second war of Villmergen, the last religious war in Swiss history, ended with a military defeat for the Catholics. Their representatives agreed to an armistice, but the assemblies refused to ratify the treaty. The protests started in Unterwalden, where its assembly sent representatives to other cantons and the unrest spread speedily. Backed by the Catholic clergy, the rural cantons decided to resume the war. When Lucerne hesitated to join the campaign, an uprising of its subject territories made the city councillors change their minds. If the rural canton had won the war, a contemporary Protestant minister in Zurich remarked, they would have turned Zug and Lucerne into democracies (Fries 1724). The renewal of the war, however, was a military and political disaster. The protestant aristocracies won the war that they regarded as a war against democracy. Religion added to the uneasy relationship between the elite and the assemblies in the early modern rural cantons. In two of them at least, religious tensions were on the rise because cantonal assemblies could not decide whether to implement the Reformation or not. In Glarus, Protestants and Catholics lived side by side and they tried to find a compromise in five treaties. In the end, the canton was ruled by two distinct assemblies that cooperated uneasily. In Appenzell, another solution was found: in 1597 the canton was geographically divided between Protestants and Catholics.

The right to participate in the decision-making process was not granted to all inhabitants of the rural cantons. Women and foreigners were excluded from the cantonal assemblies. The supreme power was in the hands of the free peasants. In 1797, long-term resident foreigners claimed what they regarded as their natural rights. Schwyz, however, refused to change its political system. From their point of view the canton was already a democracy and everyone had the rights that were due to him. Recent studies have refuted the idea of an unbroken tradition of Swiss democracy, pointing to the inequality of its inhabitants, the influence of foreign ambassadors and the sophisticated social engineering of the cantons' elites. The democrats of the peasant republics, Randolph Head explains in his path-breaking work on the Grisons, developed a radical language of equality, but the rule of the assemblies was nevertheless not to be confused with modern democracy (Brändle 2005; Head 1995). In the early eighteenth century, however, the manipulation of the cantonal assemblies by old elite became more and more difficult. In political and economic crises, charismatic leaders rose to power using the democratic strength of the assemblies. These leaders depended on foreign money and foreign political support as the old elites had (Lau 2008). But manipulation of the assemblies did not cease as new elites learnt how to manage the citizenry. The rural assemblies' contribution to the development of Swiss direct democracy in the nineteenth century is predominantly a myth (Adler 2006).

The Urban Cantons

While democracy was on the decline in the rural cantons in the eighteenth and nineteenth centuries, the reverse was the case in the urban cantons where the Enlightenment brought more debate and deliberation. In 1713, a new constitution of Zurich was agreed on by its Grand Council. Considerable protest by the civic opposition had prompted only the seventh change to its political system since 1336. Unlike the city of Berne, the nobility in Zurich enjoyed few political privileges. They were allowed to form a noble society, the so-called *Constaffel*, which elected two of the 24 members of the senate and 18 of the 212 Grand Councillors. The true power was in the hands of the twelve guilds. They were political bodies that organised elections and much of the social life in early modern Zurich. In theory Zurich's government had short terms. The mandate of the senators and the mayor only ran for six months after their election, but after another six months the old senators could be re-elected, and they usually were. What was the role of the citizens in this never-ending circle of power? They not only had to elect the senators, but also to pledge allegiance to the new heads of the republic. Although the town's small elite had the means to manipulate these acts, the citizens' approval of the political order remained an indispensable source of legitimation. This very fact eased the way for opposition movements. In Zurich scholars, craftsmen and second-rank senators organised protests against the ruling elite after the war of 1712. Although the Protestants had won the conflict, the city's military and political performance showed remarkable shortcomings. Those who were excluded from power demanded change. The political elite was prompted to adopt a new style of government: in all important matters, the senate should ask the assembly of citizens for consent. The rural cantons were praised for their democratic constitution, and it was pointed out that in Zurich the supreme power was with the people as well. The senate's promise to consult the people on important issues came to nothing, but the impact that public debates had on political decisions began to increase dramatically. Zurich became a stronghold of the Enlightenment movement. The people of Zurich were still not permitted to participate in formal politics, but they were heeded.

In Schaffhausen and Basel, the call for reform led to more efficient constitutional changes. Both cities suffered under the rivalries between the leading merchants, craftsmen and mercenaries, and between pro-imperial and pro-French factions. The old constitution was based on the equal participation of the guilds, but proved to be unfit to deal with these conflicts. New elites came to power, most of whom were merchants and businessmen, but they rapidly adopted aristocratic habits and values. Many of them studied law and proved to be skilled administrators, but the commoners looked on these families with distrust. From their point view, the patrician public servants appeared to be busy filling their pockets with public money. In Basel the protests escalated. The senators and their families were attacked and only the threat of a military intervention by the confederates caused the opposition to stop the violence. The decline of trust in government was evident. In order to reverse this development the senators agreed to changes to the constitution. The Grand Council became – at least in theory – more influential. Matters of importance could be decided only after it had been consulted. Moreover, new elaborated electoral systems were introduced: fair elections were guaranteed by a combination of secret ballot and the drawing of lots. However, no system proved to be sophisticated enough to check the dominance of the elite's networks for long.

In other urban cantons, demands for democracy and the surreptitious consolidation of the power of the leading families was managed in other ways. In Solothurn, the assembly of the citizens still elected the main officeholders, but vacant seats in the senate were filled by cooptation. Further, those who obtained citizenship after 1681 were excluded from political participation, a strategy that was also introduced in Fribourg (1684), Berne (1651) and Lucerne (1773) (Fossedal 2002: 25). Exceptions to this rule were made only infrequently, and those who were admitted to voting rights had to pay a considerable amount of money. The inequalities between citizens were significant. In Berne, most families belonging to the community of citizens hardly ever got the chance to participate in the city's government. The exclusion from honourable and profitable offices caused unrest, and in 1749 a group of citizens lead by Samuel Henzi challenged the senatorial elite. From their point of view the supreme power was in the hands of all citizens and the usurpation of political power by a small elite was not acceptable. Henzi was sent into exile. To ensure that the majority of the citizens remained calm, however, the electoral system was reformed. In Fribourg, revolt brought the city senate to the edge of political disaster. The opposition came from the subject territories that opposed religious reforms. Patricians joined them because noble families were banned from certain offices and they now asked in the name of equality for an end to this kind of discrimination. All citizens were equal and all should have the same rights. It was easy for the subjects in the territories to agree to this principle as they regarded themselves as citizens of the town. This, they argued, was their ancient status of which they were being deprived illegally. These arguments referring to equal rights for the members of a privileged community became increasingly influenced by other arguments stressing the equal rights of men given by nature.

The democratic heritage of Switzerland's early modern cities has divided experts. The important decisions were made by a small elite (Goppold 2007). The towns were places where personal contacts were more important than the rituals of the assemblies, so, whatever the formal position, ordinary citizens hardly had a share in political power. Others emphasise the role of the cities in developing in new culture of public debate (Würgler 2009). From Würgler's point of view, the birthplace of modern democracy is to be found in these debates (Würgler 1995). The conflict over who possessed the supreme power changed the cities (Maissen 2006). A new political language – the language of the modern republic – was adopted; the emerging, modern middle class insisted that the language was honoured; and the deep-rooted distrust of the urban elite against democracy slowly began to vanish.

The Subject Territories

By the end of the seventeenth century it could be claimed that every village in Switzerland was a republic of its own, and that the subject territories enjoyed considerable independence (Rahn 1697). They were governed by reeves (*Landvögte*) who were appointed by the ruling cantons and, depending on the wealth of the territory, it was an office that could make its holders rich. However, compared with other European countries, the tax burden was extremely light and efforts to increase the tax yield by making the rule of the reeves more efficient were blocked by the rural elite. A currency revaluation in 1653 led to uprisings in central and western Switzerland. On 14 May, thousands of farmers opposing the revaluation met at Hutwil and established a federation of free men. They were armed and they wanted a fairer share of political power. Their new federation was intended to become a permanent institution and make Switzerland's rulers accountable to representatives of the peasants. Presumed ancient rights provided the legal basis for this opposition movement and the peasants claimed to be the true heirs of Wilhelm Tell. The troubles of 1653 ended with a compromise. The opposition surrendered to government troops and the ruling elite promised to respect the rights of the peasants. From this time on, Swiss state-building was possible only with cooperation between those who governed and the governed. The increasing influence of the core cantons on the subject territories was based on economic dominance and a new capability to collect information about frictions and interests in villages, but the legal autonomy of the peasants remained untouched. The senators of Berne, Lucerne and Zurich were quite successful in giving their territories common legal standards, but the assemblies of eligible citizens remained indispensable partners with the elites. The rights of the ruling cantons differed. In some villages they appointed local officers after consulting the rural elite, in others, they accepted the results of the elections to the assemblies.

In many of the subject territories the legal situation was complex. Some of the territories belonged to one canton, but others were condominiums where two or more cantons had interests. Early modern Toggenburg, for example, belonged to the territories of the prince abbot of St Gallen – an associate of the confederation. However, since medieval times the protectors of Toggenburg had been the cantons of Glarus and Schwyz, and it was they who guaranteed the privileges Toggenburg had been granted by its late rulers, the counts of Toggenburg (Sowerby 1892: 21, 59). Toggenburg's reeve was appointed by the prince abbot, and an assembly of the territory's citizens pledged him reverence and homage. In return, their privileges were confirmed and approved. Besides these extraordinary occasions, the assembly met only if the reeve decided to call it together. In between these occasions, the council protected the rights of the citizens. Besides the general assembly, regional and local meetings were held. The rights citizens enjoyed differed from village to village. Sometimes, they elected local office holders and councillors, in other cases, they participated in the appointment of judges. Religious questions were discussed on local level as well. The Reformation was quite successful in the 1520s. Toggenburg's elite hoped that an alliance with the Protestant cantons could free them from the abbot's overlordship (Sowerby 1892: 76). However, the defeat of the Protestants in the second war of Kappel in 1531 left Toggenburg at the mercy of the Catholics. A forced reversal of the Reformation was possible, but the abbot confirmed the right of the parishes to stay with their Protestant clergy, although those who wanted to return to the Catholic faith were encouraged to do so. From the middle of the sixteenth century Toggenburg was a religiously mixed area, with some churches being used by both Catholics and Protestants. Although both groups worked together to administer local and regional self-government, religious conflict permanently endangered political stability.

It was their antagonism towards the abbot that finally brought both groups together. In 1707 the conflicts between Toggenburg and the abbot escalated when Toggenburg's council resisted the abbot's orders and formed an independent council to govern the region. From the outset this opposition had to incorporate many different interest groups. Catholics and Protestants, Upper and Lower Toggenburg, rural areas and the town of Lichtensteig fought bitter political battles against each other. Zurich and Berne acted as Toggenburg's protectors and tried to stabilise its government. Ulrich Nabholz, Zurich's representative, criticised his senators sharply for this attitude. In his report he described the rule of the elected councillors as a disaster (Nabholz 1707). The councillors were bribed and too busy struggling against each other. They had, from Nabholz's point of view, no authority concerning the local assemblies so the villages did what they wanted do. Some of the assemblies supported the council and others showed sympathy for the abbot. There were even villages that declared their independence and claimed to be sovereign republics. The process of fragmentation was stopped only by Zurich's military intervention. It was the only way to avoid the failure of the new council. Toggenburg's democratic experiment ended in disaster, and it survived only with outside intervention. The direct rule by the citizens evidently worked only under certain circumstances. Without a strong democratic tradition, working social networks, religious homogeneity and the absence of interfering external powers, democracy appeared to be doomed and the system could hardly survive. But as the subject territories moved beyond religious conflict, Swiss democracy began the long process of maturation.

Conclusion: From Old Democracy to New Democracy

In most parts of Switzerland, the model of direct rule by the citizens proved to be a highly flexible and popular instrument. In spite of the failure in Toggenburg, the call for a stronger role for the assemblies was a key issue for opposition groups. In practice, the citizen assemblies were becoming tremendously successful; religious, social and political antagonisms were discussed, but the struggle to find solutions was difficult, particularly as each year the winners had to fight for the cause again. The elite was in permanent danger of losing its position. Skilful social engineering by the leading families was necessary for them to stay on top. The opposition groups in the urban cantons observed this system carefully. From the start of the eighteenth century especially, Protestant scholars showed sympathy for direct rule by the peasants.

Moreover, the increasing importance of pamphlets and newspapers in public debates eased the exchange of information between town and country. The revolutionary risings of 1798 thus not only took place in the cities, but also in rural areas. The freedom trees were erected in Toggenburg as well as in Basel and Zurich. The step from political enlightenment to revolution was a small one (Weinmann 2002).

The new governments did not meet the high expectations of the intellectual elite. The Helvetic republic, as the new government styled itself, met bitter resistance in the Catholic cantons in central Switzerland. Due to the financial burden incurred by the republic in order to pay the French army to guarantee stability, its unpopularity became more and more evident. In 1803, the centralised republic was replaced by a confederal system. Switzerland changed rapidly in the next decades: after a radical restoration in 1815, the country turned liberal in 1830 and became the modern confederation in 1848. The debate on direct democracy played an important role in the victory of the new system (Adler 2006; Suter 1997). The Helvetic republic was detested as an expensive experiment of centralisation. The direct rule of the people and a power shift to the local assemblies seemed to guarantee an efficient, but relatively weak, state. Even among the liberals this idea found friends and promoters. A strong society and efficient local communities seemed to be the perfect basis for a progressive state. At the same time, the traditions of the old republic also appealed to the conservatives. They pointed to the exclusive character of the people's assemblies in early modern Switzerland. The resistance of these bodies against any central government, their refusal of religious reform and their defence against foreign influence were regarded as a model for a future Switzerland. Thus, Switzerland became the only country in Europe where anti-liberal and progressive movements both favoured democracy and this unanimity saw direct democracy with a weak central state flourish.

References

Adler, B. (2006), *Die Entstehung der direkten Demokratie: Das Beispiel der Landsgemeinde Schwyz 1789–1866*, Zurich: Verlag Neue Zürcher Zeitung.

Brändle, F. (2005), *Demokratie und Charisma: Fünf Landsgemeindekonflikte im 18. Jahrhundert*, Zurich: Chronos.

Bühler, F. M. (1689), *Tractatus von der Freyheit*, Baden: Baldinger.

Church, C. H. (2004), *The Politics and Government of Switzerland*, London: Palgrave Macmillan.

Fossedal, G. A. (2002), *Direct Democracy in Switzerland*, New Brunswick, NJ: Transaction.

Fries, J. H. (1724), *Weltliche Meist Vatterländische Geschichten*, Zurich: Handschriftenabteilung Zentralbibliothek Zurich.

Gierke, O. von (1868–1913), *Das deutsche Genossenschaftsrecht*, 4 vols, Berlin: Weidmann.

Goppold, U. (2007), *Politische Kommunikation in den Städten der Vormoderne*, Zurich: Böhlau.

Head, R. C. (1995), *Early Modern Democracy in the Grisons: Social Order and Political Language in a Swiss Mountain Country, 1470–1620*, Cambridge: Cambridge University Press.

Lau, T. (2008), *Stiefbrüder: Nation und Konfession in der Schweiz und in Europa (1656–1712)*, Cologne: Böhlau.

Maissen, T. (2006), *Die Geburt der Republik: Staasverständnis und Repräsentation in der frühneuzeitlichen Eidgenossenschaft*, Göttingen: Vandenhoeck & Ruprecht.

Nabholz, U. (1707), *Beschreibungen des Toggenburger*, MS. E7, Zurich: Zentralbibliothek.

Plantin, J.-B. (1666), *Abrégé de l'histoire générale de la Suisse*, Geneva: De Tournes.

Rahn, J. H. (1697), *Politisches Gespräch*, UB Basel, Falk, 2916, 31.

Sablonier, R. (2008), *Gründungszeit ohne Eidgenossen: Politik und Gesellschaft in der Innerschweiz um 1300*, Baden: Hier und Jetzt Verlag.

Schwyzer Manifest (1655), Staatsarchiv Schwyz, Schwyz, 13/2314.

Simler, J. (1576), *Regiment Gemeiner loblicher Eydgnoschafft: Beschriben und in zwey Bücher gestellet durch Josiam Simmler von Zürych*, Zurich: Christoph Froschauer.

Sowerby, J. (1892), *The Forest Cantons of Switzerland: Lucerne, Schwyz, Uri, Unterwalden*, London: Percival.

Suter, A. (1997), *Der schweizerische Bauernkrieg von 1653: Politische Sozialgeschichte – Sozialgeschichte eines politischen Ereignisses*, Tübingen: Bibliotheca Academica.

Weinmann, B. (2002), *Eine andere Bürgergesellschaft: Klassischer Republikanismus und Kommunalismus im Kanton Zürich im späten 18. und 19. Jahrhundert*, Göttingen: Vandenhoeck & Ruprech.

Würgler, A. (1995), *Unruhen und Öffentlichkeit: Städtische und ländliche Protestbewegungen im 18. Jahrhundert*, Tübingen: Bibliotheca Academica.

Würgler, A. (2009), 'Reden und Mehren: Politische Funktionen und symbolische Bedeutungen der eidgenössischen Tagsatzung (15.–18. Jahrhundert)', in T. Neu, M. Sikora and T. Weller (eds), *Zelebrieren und Verhandeln. Zur Praxis ständischer Institutionen im frühneuzeitlichen Europa*, Münster: Rhema Verlag, pp. 89–106.

Chapter 16

The American Revolution

Andrew Shankman

To consensus era historians of the 1950s, democracy in late colonial British North America scarcely needed to be explained. Colonists were middle class, jealous of their liberties and determined to assert their rights in powerful colonial legislatures (Brown 1955; Greene 1963). Since the 1970s this story has been dismantled; it is now clear that democracy was not inevitable in the region that became the United States. Between 1720 and 1760, from Massachusetts to Georgia, the colonies became more British in their political practices, social relations and cultural tastes. Each colony produced ruling elites who wielded economic power and monopolised political office (Kornblith and Murrin 1993). By the mid-eighteenth century, colonists had replicated much of English society, economy and politics. Most colonies had, to varying degrees, mixed economies of agriculture, commerce and even manufacturing. They produced class structures based on wage labour, unequal ownership of property, and educational and cultural institutions modelled on British schools, universities and learned societies. Colonists embraced British views about ideal forms of government, which made them cautious, even ambivalent, about democracy. Sophisticated colonists, such as Bostonian, James Otis, believed that absolute monarchies violated natural rights. But the remedy was not government by majority or even allowing the institutional participation of the governed. Democracy was not a system of politics colonists believed, but rather one part of a polity properly comprised of monarch, aristocracy and landowners: the one, the few and the many (Maier 1972: 3–48; Wood 1991: 3–89).

Taxation, Representation and Democracy

Many landowners zealously cared for liberty, and vigilantly observed monarchy and aristocracy to ensure they did not become despotic or oligarchic. Thankfully, the mixed and balanced British constitution gave a meaningful voice to property-owning subjects in Britain – the many whose rights to property would be violated if the one and few misbehaved. Taxation with representation protected the rights of life, liberty and property of Britons, while the mixed and balanced constitution ensured that the people's zeal for liberty would be responsibly tempered by the power and wisdom of the one and few. In 1764, even as he protested Parliament's Sugar Act, James Otis proclaimed that 'the British constitution in theory and in the present administration of it, in general comes nearest the idea of perfection of any that has been reduced to practice' (Otis 1764: 14–15). Yet distance and the Atlantic Ocean added complexity to this constitution. Colonists valued their colonial legislatures and insisted that they were vital to the proper functioning of a constitutional order that governed Britain and its far-flung oceanic empire. The colonists were concerned that governments only protected property when those who raised the taxation were chosen by taxpayers and also had to pay the same taxes they imposed on others. Clearly, then, the House of Commons in London could not tax the American colonists, for the colonists sent no members to Parliament (Greene 1986).

In believing that Parliament could not tax them, the colonists were not advocating democracy. Limiting Parliament's authority did not require actual representation, universal suffrage or even the right to vote for every taxpayer. Colonists like Maryland lawyer Daniel Dulany, who wrote the most influential pamphlet to protest the 1765 Stamp Act, argued that the House of Commons virtually represented non-voting taxpayers whenever those taxpayers owned property similar to property owned by voting taxpayers (Dulany 1765). When the latter voted in ways that protected their own property, they also protected the non-voters' property. This virtual representation was legitimate within Britain, but the House of Commons represented no colonists at all so there would be none who could vote to protect themselves, and who, by doing so, would protect non-voting taxpayers. Only if the colonial legislature of Maryland taxed Maryland would the concept of virtual representation work in that colony as it did in Britain (Dulany 1765). The eighteenth-century colonies, then, had the ingredients of democratic politics. They possessed a language of rights and liberties. They were devoted to legislatures and believed that only their elected representatives could interfere with their property. Yet their acceptance of governors and upper houses appointed by the Crown, and their acquiescence to governance by colonial elites shows how far they were from democracy.

Britain's emphatic victory over France in the Seven Years War (1756–63) encouraged reform of the empire. New laws, particularly unprecedented taxation of the colonies, provoked an acrimonious argument about British liberty and Britain's relations with the American colonists. By 1775, what many in Britain saw as necessary taxation, many in the colonies viewed as encroachment by a tyrannical imperial government (Jensen 1968; Rakove 2010). The decade after 1765 shattered colonists' illusions about their place in the empire. It also placed explosive and slippery words such as liberty, equality, freedom, slavery and tyranny at the centre of American culture. The colonists protested against parliamentary taxation and onerous legislation by forcing a discussion about the nature of government and, eventually, by indicting British forms of governance. Thomas Paine, in his 1776 pamphlet *Common Sense*, summed up what many colonists had already concluded: Britain's mixed and balanced government had not prevented the king and his ministers from acting tyrannically (Paine [1776] 1986). Since the British constitution was the best structure ever conceived for constraining monarchy, the American experience showed that kings could never be constrained. The answer was not simply independence. Independence from Britain, Paine insisted, also required independence from things British, particularly hereditary governance (Paine [1776] 1986). By 1776 the vast majority of colonists understood with Paine that their new nation must be a republic.

But what sort of republic? Americans built theirs in a highly charged atmosphere where devotion to liberty, equality, autonomy and freedom was common currency. Such ideals were slippery and could be applied, defined and redefined based on place and circumstance. Wealthy merchants defined these concepts differently to lowly artisans, women, subsistence farmers or slaves (Countryman 2003). The colonies, with their particular concentrations of wealth and power, had produced inequality, frustration and resentment. Prior to the imperial crisis, colonial elites governed and even overawed those below them. Yet these same elites felt it necessary to provoke a radically disruptive conflict with Britain. To critique the empire, the elites placed concepts and language at the cultural core of America that could be used to challenge their own hierarchical positions. By 1776, it was clear that colonial elites could not start a revolution to overthrow imperial authority without also having their own authority seriously tested.

Towards a Democratic Constitution

The revolution introduced the possibility of democracy to America. The protracted warfare between 1775 and 1783 caused the disintegration of central authority. In New York, for example, most rural communities became self-governing for years and participated in the revolution by enacting laws, policing behaviour, setting wages and prices, defending the local area, printing money and providing supplies for the war. In Pennsylvania, where most of the Quaker colonial elite remained neutral, previously obscure small property-holders seized power and transformed the state's political culture. These men enacted the new nation's most radical experiment with democracy: the Pennsylvania Constitution of 1776 enfranchised all adult, white male taxpayers, and created an annually elected unicameral legislature and a weak plural executive. It allowed the legislature to propose bills, but prevented those bills from becoming law unless they received majority support in the next legislature (seated after the annual election). In the interim, before the next election, prospective legislators had to take a stand on the bills, which were printed and widely distributed. Thus, voters could decide which bills would become law by choosing to vote for candidates who supported that legislation. The Pennsylvania revolution showed that, though conservative elites might favour a mixed and balanced constitution where the many were merely one of three constituent parts, many others held that democracy alone was the only legitimate system of politics (Countryman 1981; Ryerson 1981).

The American Revolution transformed government from a mixed, tripartite polity to a democratic system that could legitimate the processes of republican politics. During the 1780s, the decentralised nature of government under the Articles of Confederation meant that most decision making took place at the state or local levels. The more intimate and immediate nature of politics allowed for less exalted figures to hold political office. In virtually every legislature, many officeholders in 1785 were less educated, less wealthy and closer to the average citizen than they had been in 1765 (Main 1966). These developments reinforced the idea that government of the people could and should be by the people and for the people, and that each voter, being a rights-bearing citizen, was capable of governing. Though largely unexpected in 1776, by the mid-1780s democracy in America was a visible and likely outcome of revolution.

From the 1780s onwards, the general view of democracy switched from outright dismissal to debate about what democracy was and how it would actually work. Discussions explored the limits to a majority's power, the powers and prerogatives of minorities, the existence of fundamental natural rights that the majority was enjoined from violating. These were not solely abstract concerns. Pennsylvanians stripped neutral Quakers of the right to vote. Many state legislatures confiscated and redistributed loyalist property. In addition, they created highly inflationary paper currencies by printing massive amounts of notes. Legislatures then enacted laws requiring creditors to accept the currency of little value as payment for private debts, even though the debts had been borrowed in much more valuable currency prior to passage of the inflationary currency laws. In effect, legislatures forgave large amounts of privately contracted debt in democratised polities where debtor voters outnumbered creditor voters (Holton 2005; Wood 1969).

This taste for majority rule also produced arguments about who precisely constituted a legitimate majority. Some rural communities became so accustomed to self-government that they questioned whether there could be any legitimate government beyond the local community. As many states and communities explored democracy in the 1780s, one possible conclusion was that democracy demanded a politics immediately responsive to the demands of each majority within each small community. With the most radical conceptions of democracy it was unclear how to justify any constraint on local majorities or policy making at state, let alone national, level where government could be viewed as too distant and unaccountable (Bouton 2000). The arguments concerning whether to ratify the United States Constitution and the conflicts of the 1790s between the Federalist Party, led by George Washington, Alexander Hamilton and John Adams, and the Democratic-Republican Party, led by Thomas Jefferson and James Madison, were primarily about the desirability and structure of democracy. Some supporters of the Constitution (also called Federalists) accepted democratic developments, while many others did not. Many anti-Federalists opposed ratification because they associated democracy with localism and feared a much more centralised and strengthened national government. To a great extent, regardless of where one fell on the question of ratification, one's political stance in the 1790s could be predicted by one's views of the democratising trends of the 1780s. Those who could, at least to a degree, accept democracy became Democratic-Republicans. Those who could not do so became Federalists. For example, James Madison, a Federalist in 1787 because he supported ratification, became a Democratic-Republican during the 1790s. Madison believed the Constitution provided a framework for a responsible democracy and feared that the Federalist Party of the 1790s used the new national government to silence and overawe the people (Sheehan 2009). The American Revolution did not turn everyone into a democrat, but it did ensure that conflict about the nature and practicalities of democracy would be the driving force of American politics.

The Federalist Debates

Supporters of a stronger national government in the 1780s and 1790s confronted the central question posed by democracy: could constraints be placed on the majority?

After the revolution, the traditional methods of relying on the intervention of monarchy and aristocracy to balance the democratic process were anathema. The solution of those democratically inclined Federalists of the 1780s, such as Madison, was to take the idea of democracy and popular sovereignty seriously. Madison argued that the sovereign people alone could declare fundamental law, but he also insisted that each citizen be protected from arbitrary treatment (Wood 1969). He reasoned that the sovereign people, once they articulated their authoritative views in written constitutions, had to be obeyed. The governments they created to efficiently enforce their views had to operate within the people's sovereign authority expressed in their sovereign statements: their written constitutions (Wood 1969). Once the people in their constitutions declared the right to the protection of property, the sanctity of contracts and equal protection under the law – even for unpopular minorities – a majority in a legislature was bound to obey the constitution. The constitution was the direct expression of the people, a legislature a mere instrument of the people. The instrument could not countermand the will of its wielder (Wood 1969).

This subtle and complex conceptualisation of popular sovereignty provided a remedy for the tendency of majorities to abuse minorities, but it did so by drawing on the most radical and democratic language to emerge from the revolution. Like so many other revolutionary concepts, popular sovereignty was also slippery. With ratification of the Constitution in 1788, popular sovereignty was universally embraced, at least by constitutional ratifying conventions and in the written constitutions they produced. For some, the concept of popular sovereignty allowed an elegant argument for how the people produced the fundamental laws and documents by which all citizens, individually and in groups, even very large groups, must live. For others, well into the nineteenth century, popular sovereignty meant that even local majorities were sovereign and could define acceptable behaviour within their communities (Fritz 2008; Shalhope 2009). For James Madison, a written constitution emanated from popular sovereignty and confined the people's governments within the boundaries established by the constitution, so for Madison this conception of popular sovereignty was democracy (Wood 1969). Yet for Madison's mercurial ally, then enemy, the Philadelphia newspaper editor William Duane, a constitution that was very difficult to alter, that constrained even the largest popular majorities, was simply an act unable to be repealed. Duane argued that the convention that imposed the constitution was little better than an absolute monarchy (Shankman 2004: 157). Madison's conception of popular sovereignty, Duane concluded in the early nineteenth century, was the gravest threat to true democracy. Yet while Madison and Duane had serious philosophical disagreements, during the 1790s they were allies in the party led by Thomas Jefferson. Both agreed that the Federalist Party posed a terrible threat to democracy, while Alexander Hamilton, Washington's treasurer and the most powerful mind among the Federalists, believed that the revolution and subsequent democracy would make the new republic ungovernable. The Federalists argued that the ancient republics showed that too much liberty led to chaos and then people would accept tyranny in exchange for restored order. Too much democracy, concluded the Federalists, destroyed the conditions for liberty.

Federalists argued that the French Revolution illustrated the process of liberty giving way to anarchy and then despotism, and they concluded that the followers of Jefferson, who supported the French Revolution and criticised the Federalists, were enemies of order and the rule of law. With a series of financial policies and laws regulating speech and immigration, over the course of the 1790s the Federalists sought to restore something of the stable and deferential hierarchical society that had existed before the revolution. Hamilton hoped to strengthen the new national government and attach the wealthiest and most prominent American citizens to it. The core of the Washington administration's policies was Hamilton's proposals for handling the $80 million debt left over from fighting the American Revolution (Shankman 2003). During the economically depressed 1780s, many of the debt's original holders, often soldiers, farmers and artisans, had despaired of ever being repaid. They had sold their debt very cheaply and by 1790 a much smaller number of the wealthiest Americans owned most of the debt. Hamilton hoped to use the debt to reorganise American society and so restore something of the lost social order destroyed by the American Revolution (Roberts 2006).

In 1790 Hamilton proposed that the new government assume full responsibility for the debt and fund it (that is, pay interest on the debt at 4 per cent). His proposals quickly became law and enriched the wealthy speculators who had bought debt cheaply. Now that the debt commanded regular interest payment, it quickly rose to its face value, which was far above what most current holders had paid for it. Hamilton next proposed that the debt should become the primary source of investment capital for a large national bank and a grand manufacturing enterprise (Roberts 2006). Congress and President Washington quickly created the Bank of the United States and Hamilton oversaw the formation of the Society for Establishing Useful Manufactures, which was intended to be the largest industrial enterprise in the nation (Shankman 2003). Hamilton hoped that as the nation's financial system developed and as its manufacturing capacity grew, both would be overseen from the top down by substantial, sober and responsible citizens. Debt-holders were not hereditary aristocrats, but Hamilton was, in a sense, seeking to create a republican version of the few, a small group of the economically and politically powerful and the socially and culturally prominent who would direct the affairs of the nation on behalf of the over-zealous many whose unthinking actions threatened ordered liberty. Hamilton's ally John Jay, a collaborator on the *Federalist Papers* and Supreme Court chief justice during the Washington administration, summed up Federalist philosophy best when he explained that 'those who own the country are the most fit persons to participate in the government of it' (Kornblith and Murrin 1993: 29). The Federalist version of republicanism insisted that the best republics kept the *demos*, the people, firmly in their place (Roberts 2006; Shankman 2003; Wood 2009).

The Democratic Backlash

Federalist concerns intensified after 1792 when the French Revolution entered its radical phase. In the mid-1790s many of the farmers and artisans, who were meant to relearn deference under Hamilton's system, instead formed Democratic-Republican societies. These vocal political groups cheered the French Revolution and denounced

Hamilton's programmes and Federalist foreign policy, which favoured Britain over France. Washington, in turn, denounced the societies as 'self-created', which he considered a damning indictment. But in the democratised atmosphere of the early republic, the President's remarks revealed how ill-prepared the Federalists were to function in a democratic society (Estes 2006; Hale 2009; Schoenbachler 1998). By the mid-1790s the Federalists had provoked a diverse opposition. Southern planters such as Jefferson and Madison associated independence with landowning and agriculture and believed that republican institutions would survive only in a nation predominantly of farmers. Madison's favourite example of the connection between an agrarian society and sound republican institutions was the plight of the London shoe-buckle makers (Madison 1792). During the late eighteenth century, when the style suddenly changed to ribbons and buttons for shoes, a whole class of skilled artisans became destitute. Such men, concluded Madison, could never be truly independent because they depended on the patronage of others. Therefore, they could never be reliable republican citizens. But eating, Madison argued, never went out of style. Farmers working land that they owned would always remain independent republican citizens. 'Those who labor on the earth', said Thomas Jefferson, Madison's close friend and mentor, 'are the chosen people of God' (Jefferson [1784]: 1954 164–5). Agrarians were horrified by Hamilton's programme, which seemed to imitate Britain and move the United States away from an agrarian society and economy (McCoy 1980).

Craftsmen in the nation's cities and smaller towns did not share the southern planters' agrarian sensibilities. But most craftsmen were just as infuriated by the Federalists' elitist methods for promoting manufacturing, methods that were intended to turn craftsmen from independent artisans into employees of much larger manufacturing concerns funded by public debt. Artisans joined an opposition led by southern agrarians, as did many small farmers attracted by the prospect of rapid western settlement. Movement across space, allowing the recreation of the conditions best suited for small, independent farms, was the core commitment of the Democratic-Republican Party (McCoy 1980). After 1793, this opposition to the Federalists grew in size and complexity as English and Irish immigrants poured into the United States. This group became important, especially in states such as New York, Pennsylvania and Maryland, and helped the opposition to gain strength outside the south. Radicals like the Irish-American William Duane became leading spokesmen of the emerging Democratic-Republican Party and led the charge against the Federalists. The conditions of the 1790s consolidated the democratisation of American society and ensured that the future would be much more hospitable to self-created societies than to denunciations of them (Bric 2008; Durey 1997).

Facing conditions they could not control, the Federalists responded with repression, and in 1798 passed the Alien and Sedition Acts. The Alien Act extended the period of naturalisation before citizenship from five to fourteen years and was aimed at the radical émigrés, particularly the Irish (Bric 2008). The Sedition Act sharply limited criticism of the government by treating it as seditious libel. The laws hurt the Federalist cause because the opposition argued that their most sinister depiction of the Federalists was true. In reality, the Federalists' inability to govern by the end of the 1790s showed just how quickly conditions were changing as the nation rapidly became much more a democracy (Kohn 1975). During the 1790s a majority of voters mobilised to defeat the Federalists. Jefferson's election to the presidency in 1800 helped to ensure a democratised political culture, while questions remained about the nature of American democracy and who would define it (Banning 1978; Waldstreicher 1997). Over the three decades after 1800 disagreements about the meaning of popular sovereignty continued to produce political conflict. Yet the Madisonian conception of popular sovereignty prompted the separation of powers and checks and balances within government. Madisonians argued that the people were sovereign and that each branch of government was equally not the people (Fritz 2008). Thus, the people's will, expressed in their written constitutions, was best protected when no branch could overstep its duties and when the other branches could check it if it tried to do so. This theory legitimated judicial review, gave credence to the important role played by the Supreme Court in the early nineteenth century, and provided a way to argue that legislatures made laws, executives enforced laws, and judiciaries interpreted and reviewed them to ensure that they were in accordance with the people's constitutions – the expressions of their sovereignty (Fritz 2008).

   This view of the separation of powers and of checks and balances did not go unchallenged in the early nineteenth century and arguments arose as to how the less accountable, unelected branches of government got to check the most democratic branch. These years also saw rapid economic development, the rise of the cotton south, the expansion of slavery and questions about who could be a voting and full rights-bearing citizen (Morrison 1997; Wilentz 2005). Prior to 1776 the right to vote was dependent on land ownership and high office was usually reserved for the wealthiest voters. But the revolution had begun to dismantle this system and the increasingly democratic language shaping American attitudes made it impossible to justify elites of rich, white men in charge (Wilentz 2005). Next to go was the connection between landowning and the franchise. After about 1810 it became even more imperative to sever this connection because the boom and bust economy produced large numbers of adult, white men who failed to meet the property requirements for voting rights. In a polity increasingly saturated by democratic language and ideals, disenfranchising large numbers of white men was unthinkable (Wilentz 2005). So if one traditional marker could fall perhaps others could too: if hard economic times meant white men need not own property to vote, then perhaps free, black men, with property or without, were entitled to vote too (Egerton 2009; Morrison 1997; Nash 1988).

Conclusion

Democracy, it seemed, raised never-ending questions and prevented stable and consensual definitions of even its most basic and fundamental concepts, such as popular sovereignty, citizenship, majority rule and the right to vote. Demands for democracy had initially proved to be quite subversive by allowing obscure, white men to challenge the claims of traditional colonial elites. In effect, colonial elites had hoped to challenge the authority of Britain while maintaining their own positions at the top of a society of increasingly vertically organised households in their colonies. When, beginning with the revolution, ordinary, white men thrust forward and demanded that they would also govern, they insisted that no citizen was more capable of governing, or more deserving of respect and deference, than any other. In other words, they insisted that relations among households should be much more horizontal, as befitting the egalitarianism and equality among all white, male citizen heads of household in the new republic. This commitment to horizontal social relations among heads of household even had a material dimension, as the land redistribution and paper money laws of the 1780s show. In the nineteenth century, the demand for free western lands would result from the effort to maintain these horizontal social relations among heads of household (Foner 1971; Morrison 1997).

Yet as subversive of an older colonial social order as the demand for equality among heads of household was, it was not the most potentially subversive possibility produced by the advent of democracy. By the early nineteenth century, the radical and slippery language that was the currency of democracy had permeated within the walls of each household. In order for there to be horizontal relations among households, each head of household had to keep a firm grip on the resources that sustained that household, and keep them independent of the resources controlled by other heads of household. He needed, therefore, sole claim to the land of his household and the labour necessary to work it productively. A white, adult male head of household could maintain his independence, and stand eye to eye with his fellow citizens, in part due to laws that prevented married women from owning property and that allowed him sole control over the labour of his wife and children. In more complex households, such as plantations, laws rendering blacks property served the same function. Thus, once the egalitarian language of democracy slid within the household walls, once the dependants living within those walls began to imagine more horizontal social relations, not just among households but also within them, the language of democracy could be turned against even the ordinary. white men who were its earliest speakers (Zagarri 2007).

This development was only further encouraged by the decoupling of land ownership and voting rights: white men formerly considered dependent were now full rights-bearing citizens, the conception of dependence and its relationship to citizenship could be rethought more generally. Certainly, the slippery, egalitarian language of the revolution provided Americans with the vocabulary for doing so. This most unexpected legacy of democracy threatened to tear apart the nation's most intimate private relations. Of course, that mattered only if the structures of those intimate relationships were worth preserving: where there was something important in how parents should relate to children, husbands to wives or masters to slaves. Few would have considered these to be political questions prior to the American Revolution. Then, again, prior to the revolution few would have predicted that democracy would become the only legitimate system of American politics. By 1830, it decidedly was, but precisely what democracy meant, who would benefit and whether some would benefit at the expense of others, were now important questions in what was clearly an explosive, never-ending and thoroughly democratised conversation.

References

Banning, L. (1978), *The Jeffersonian Persuasion: Evolution of a Party Ideology*, Ithaca, NY: Cornell University Press.

Bouton, T. (2000), 'A Road Closed: Rural Insurgency in Post-Independence Pennsylvania', *Journal of American History*, 87(3), 855–87.

Bric, M. J. (2008), *Ireland, Philadelphia and the Re-invention of America, 1760–1800*, Dublin: Four Courts Press.

Brown, R. (1955), *Middle-Class Democracy and the Revolution in Massachusetts, 1691–1780*, Ithaca, NY: Cornell University Press.

Countryman, E. (1981), *A People in Revolution: The American Revolution and Political Society in New York, 1760–1790*, New York: W. W. Norton.

Countryman, E. (2003), *The American Revolution*, New York: Hill & Wang.

Dulany, D. (1765), *Considerations on the Propriety of Imposing Taxes in the British Colonies, for the Purposes of Raising Revenue, by Act of Parliament*, Annapolis, MD: Jonas Green.

Durey, M. (1997), *Transatlantic Radicals and the Early American Republic*, Lawrence, KS: University of Kansas Press.

Egerton, D. (2009), *Death or Liberty: African Americans and Revolutionary America*, Oxford: Oxford University Press.

Estes, T. (2006), *The Jay Treaty Debate, Public Opinion and the Evolution of American Political Culture*, Amherst, MA: University of Massachusetts Press.

Foner, E. (1971), *Free Soil, Free Labour, Free Men: The Ideology of the Republican Party Before the Civil War*, Oxford: Oxford University Press.

Fritz, C. (2008), *American Sovereigns: The People and America's Constitutional Tradition before the Civil War*, Cambridge: Cambridge University Press.

Greene, J. (1963), *Quest for Power: The Lower Houses of Assembly in the Southern Royal Colonies, 1689–1776*, Chapel Hill, NC: University of North Carolina Press.

Greene, J. (1986), *Peripheries and Center: Constitutional Development in the Extended Polities of the British Empire and the United States, 1607–1788*, Athens, GA: University of Georgia Press.

Hale, M. R. (2009), 'On Their Tiptoes: Political Time and Newspapers during the Advent of the Radicalized French Revolution, circa 1792–1793', *Journal of the Early Republic*, 29(1), 191–218.

Holton, W. (2005), 'An Excess of Democracy: or a Shortage?: The Federalists' Earliest Adversaries', *Journal of the Early Republic*, 25(3), 339–82.

Jefferson, T. ([1784] 1954), *Notes on the State of Virginia*, ed. William Peden, Chapel Hill, NC: University of North Carolina Press.

Jensen, M. (1968), *The Founding of a Nation: A History of the American Revolution, 1763–1776*, New York: Oxford University Press.

Kohn, R. (1975), *Eagle and Sword: The Federalists and the Creation of the Military Establishment in America, 1783–1802*, New York: Free Press.

Kornblith, G. and J. Murrin (1993), 'The Making and Unmaking of an American Ruling Class', in A. F. Young (ed.), *Beyond the American Revolution: Explorations in the History of American Radicalism*, DeKalb, IL: Northern Illinois University Press, pp. 27–79.

Madison, J. (1792), 'Fashion', *The National Gazette*, 20 March.

Maier, P. (1972), *From Resistance to Revolution: Colonial Radicals and the Development of American Opposition to Britain, 1765–1776*, New York: Vintage.

Main, J. T. (1966), 'Government by the People: The American Revolution and the Democratization of the Legislatures', *William and Mary Quarterly*, 23(3), 391–407.

McCoy, D. (1980), *The Elusive Republic: Political Economy in Jeffersonian America*, Chapel Hill, NC: University of North Carolina Press.

Morrison, M. (1997), *Slavery and the American West: The Eclipse of Manifest Destiny and the Coming of the Civil War*, Chapel Hill, NC: University of North Carolina Press.

Nash, G. (1988), *Forging Freedom: The Formation of Philadelphia's Black Community, 1740–1840*, Cambridge, MA: Harvard University Press.

Otis, J. (1764), "The Rights of the British Colonies Asserted and Proved", Boston, MA: Edes & Gill, pp. 14–15.

Paine, T. ([1776] 1986), *Common Sense*, New York: Penguin

Rakove, J. (2010), *Revolutionaries: A New History of the Invention of America*, New York: Houghton Mifflin Harcourt.

Roberts, C. (2006), 'Alexander Hamilton and the 1790s Economy: A Reappraisal', in D. Ambrose and R. W. T. Martin (eds), *The Many Faces of Alexander Hamilton: The Life and Legacy of America's Most Elusive Founding Father*, New York: New York University Press, pp. 234–54.

Ryerson, R. A. (1981), 'Republican Theory and Partisan Reality in Revolutionary Pennsylvania', in R. Hoffman and P. J. Albert (eds), *Sovereign States in an Age of Uncertainty*, Charlottesville, VA: University of Virginia Press, pp. 95–133.

Schoenbachler, M. (1998), 'Republicanism in the Age of Democratic Revolution: The Democratic-Republican Societies of the 1790s', *Journal of the Early Republic*, 18(2), 237–61.

Shalhope, R. (2009), *The Baltimore Bank Riot: Political Upheaval in Antebellum Maryland*, Champaign, IL: University of Illinois Press.

Shankman, A. (2003), 'A New Thing on Earth: Alexander Hamilton, Pro-manufacturing Republicans, and the Democratization of American Political Economy', *Journal of the Early Republic*, 23(3), 323–52.

Shankman, A. (2004), *Crucible of American Democracy: The Struggle to Fuse Egalitarianism and Capitalism in Jeffersonian Pennsylvania*, Lawrence, KS: University Press of Kansas.

Sheehan, C. (2009), *James Madison and the Spirit of Republican Self-Government*, Cambridge: Cambridge University Press.

Waldstreicher, D. (1997), *In the Midst of Perpetual Fetes: The Making of American Nationalism, 1776–1820*, Chapel Hill, NC: University of North Carolina Press.

Wilentz, S. (2005), *The Rise of American Democracy: Jefferson to Lincoln*, Oxford: Oxford University Press.

Wood, G. (1969), *Creation of the American Republic, 1776–1787*, New York: W. W. Norton.

Wood, G. (1991), *The Radicalism of the American Revolution*, New York: Vintage.

Wood, G. (2009), *Empire of Liberty: A History of the Early Republic, 1789–1815*, Oxford: Oxford University Press.

Zagarri, R. (2007), *Revolutionary Backlash: Women and Politics in the Early American Republic*, Philadelphia, PA: University of Pennsylvania Press.

Chapter 17

The French Revolution

John Markoff

On 17 June 1789, deputies elected to an old institution with an important but limited purpose announced that they were forming a new body with a much broader purpose. France's Estates-General had been convened after a hiatus of 175 years as part of the royal attempt to manage a severe financial crisis. But many deputies hoped to make this crisis an occasion for significant reform, especially those who represented the Third Estate. After several weeks of fruitless dealing with the deputies of the first two estates – the nobility and the clergy – the Third Estate took a great leap into the unknown by announcing themselves to be the National Assembly, invited the other deputies to join them and soon proclaimed that they would undertake the writing of a constitution. Without command of any armed force of its own and in danger of suppression by military units summoned by the king, the new assembly's existence was saved by a popular uprising in Paris in mid-July, all of which became the stuff of instant legend. The new body began issuing laws and decrees against a background of widespread insurrection in town and country. On 26 August, the 'representatives of the French people constituted as a National Assembly' adopted a *Déclaration des droits de l'homme et du citoyen* (*Declaration of the Rights of Man and Citizen*), setting out some fundamental precepts for a new social and political order. This new order would be one of personal freedom and equality since 'Men are born and remain free and equal in rights'; collective purposes could be realised because 'The law is the expression of the general will' and 'All citizens have the right to participate personally or through their representatives in its formation' (*Déclaration* 1789).

These words and actions have commonly been taken as foundational episodes for modern democracy, not only because France was a large and powerful country, but because the revolutionaries embodied core ideas in abstract terms that were meaningful well beyond France, arousing hope and fear. Immediate expressions of admiration in England, for example, triggered Edmund Burke's condemnation of 1790, *Reflections on the Revolution in France*, which triggered in turn the following year Thomas Paine's *Rights of Man: Being an Answer to Mr. Burke's Attack on the French Revolution* (Burke 1790; Paine [1791] 1985). The varied forms of political organisation and action of the revolutionary decade continued to serve as inspiring or distressing reference points for political debate as nineteenth-century revolutionaries and reactionaries claimed to have learned important lessons from French experience. At the turn of the twenty-first century scholars could still find in aspects of that experience dramatic examples of democracy in multiple forms, and of multiple forms of anti-democracy as well.

Representative Democracy

When the National Assembly declared that it acted as the 'representatives of the French people', that 'No body and no individual may exercise authority which does not emanate expressly from [the Nation]', and that citizens would participate 'by themselves or through their representatives' (*Déclaration* 1789), it left unresolved the ways in which citizens would choose representatives, how government would be organised and in what ways citizens would participate in person. These matters proved to be extremely contentious and were never definitively resolved in the changing legislation of the revolutionary period, nor did any of the revolutionary models settle the future form of French democracy. By one count, France adopted fifteen constitutions between 1791 and 1959 (Woloch 1994: 21). At the onset of revolution, the French already had significant experience with meetings at which local affairs were discussed and decided. Villages and urban guilds commonly had participatory institutions, although seventeenth- and eighteenth-century monarchs had largely dismantled such mechanisms in town government. Such bodies varied enormously from place to place in their authority, organisation and level of participation, as well as the extent of their continuing vitality in the 1780s (Babeau 1893; Babeau [1878] 1978; Jones 2003). In its increasingly desperate search for revenue, the French monarchy began to institute a system of multi-level elective assemblies in 1787 with restrictive suffrage in much of the country to provide representation for landowners in tax allocation. This fledgling consultative structure was soon overtaken by the intensifying crisis that led to the decision to call the Estates-General from which emerged the revolutionary National Assembly.

The elections to the Estates-General were an amalgam of very different social visions (Shapiro and Markoff 1998). Some argued that deputies should have full powers to negotiate with the king; others that they should be bound by imperative mandates to do the bidding of those who elected them. Some argued that deputies represented France's legally distinct statuses and recognised corporate groups so that each of the three estates would have its own elections; others argued that deputies represented the French people as a whole. It was generally accepted that the meetings choosing deputies had the right to draw up statements of grievances, although there was a great deal less agreement over whether those deputies were bound to follow that document. Almost all of France's 40,000 rural communities produced such statements, a remarkable form of national popular consultation. After much debate, the election regulations provided an extremely broad right to participate at these meetings. Not only could almost all heads of rural households (who were sometimes women) attend a primary assembly in the Third Estate's multi-stage process, but ordinary priests as well as bishops elected the clergy's deputies, and most male nobles (and some female nobles too), not just those of illustrious rank or ancient pedigree, could participate. Not only did the entire complex process stimulate a national discussion on the meanings of representation, but the elections and drafting of grievance lists engaged an extraordinary diversity of French people in collectively thinking through their views of a better world at a moment of great crisis. Some of those thus engaged kept on meeting and acting collectively after they had chosen their deputies. France thus lurched into revolution with an intense nationwide experience of both election of deputies and local collective deliberation.

The National Assembly's declaration that all authority was to be exercised either by citizens directly or through their representatives was a radical departure from a political order that included authority that was inherited, purchased or appointed from above. In the early years of revolution, an extremely significant deviation from the new principle of popular sovereignty was the figure of the king, to whom, after considerable debate, the new Constitution of 1791 gave a suspensive veto on legislation and the authority to name ministers. Although broad categories of citizens were denied voting rights, no distinctions by estate were recognised. Eligible voters were to participate in a primary assembly that would name a variety of local officials and would also name 'electors': participants in a higher assembly that would chose both regional officials and deputies to the new national Legislative Assembly. The electoral principle was quite radical. Town councils, judges and prosecutors were to be elected. So were new priests and bishops, and, in separate processes, National Guard officers and, later on, non-commissioned military officers as well (Blaufarb 2002; Woloch 1994: 63). Elections were extremely numerous throughout the entire revolutionary decade. In the view of some, the people's representatives were the supreme authority, with the role in government of other citizens confined to the act of electing them. Governing was commonly understood as the action of a united people finding the only course of action that reasonable people could find, but debate was held to be the particular responsibility of the people's representatives. The primary assemblies that chose the electors, therefore, were not supposed to be places of debate, only of voting, and there was no referendum on the Constitution of 1791 once the people's representatives had adopted it.

The idea of rival parties was anathema at first, a betrayal of the unitary ideal and open campaigning for office was also taboo, so there were no approved party lists. Voting was nominally secret, but, continuing the practice from the Estates-General elections, carried out at the primary assembly, which meant that the vote was observed by others and, for the many illiterates, had to be said aloud to be recorded. Without lists of eligible candidates, citizens had to write or state the names of fellow citizens they hoped to elect. Since such a procedure might not yield the required majority for anyone, let alone for all the many elective offices, there was a rather complicated multi-ballot procedure (Aberdam et al. 2006; Gueniffey 1993; Rosanvallon 1992). Who got to vote remained deeply contested. Despite the claim that all citizens were equal in rights, the National Assembly quickly accepted the notion that there were 'passive' as well as 'active' citizens. Society was to serve all, but only some were to actively shape society. Active citizens were those who had the faculty of independent judgement, something that might be conferred by nature, shaped by education, reinforced by occupation and supported by resources. Those with inappropriate dispositions or inadequate educations, in deferential occupations or deficient in resources were not suitable. On these grounds women, domestic servants and those beneath a certain level of tax payments were excluded. But the precise boundaries of inclusion and exclusion were readily challenged and expanded or contracted at many points. In December 1789, for example, the National Assembly enacted civil equality for 'non-Catholic' citizens, giving Protestants a vote, though Jews had to wait until September 1791 when they were assimilated to the 'active' category if otherwise qualified (McCloy 1957: 78).

There were other, evolving requirements for voting, including willingness to serve on juries and register in the National Guard. Since the actual voting procedure was extremely protracted and the primary assemblies were held not in the local village but at the centres of the newly created 'cantons', participation in electoral life was rather demanding. It is therefore striking that turnout initially was as high as recent historians have demonstrated: an average national turnout of about 40 per cent in 1790 with enormous variation from a high of 73 per cent in rural Aube to 16 per cent in super-urban Paris (Crook 1996: 60; Edelstein 1994; Woloch 1994: 72). A noteworthy generalisation is that turnout was considerably higher in rural France than it was in urban France, which may owe something to continuities in collective decision making in villages. But it may also derive from the greater engagement in other forms of citizen action in urban areas, the rival vision of a more direct democracy (discussed below). In later elections, turnout was notably lower. There is no consensus on the degree to which the fall-off represents disillusionment with revolution, the onerous character of voting in the revolution's many elections, the absence of campaigns between clearly distinguishable candidates and parties on clearly distinguishable issues or, at many moments in many places, the sense that it was safer to keep one's preferences to oneself. Nonetheless, a large number of people engaged in an even larger number of public acts as the result of elections during the decade of revolution.

Every aspect of these electoral procedures occasioned conflict. Some were revised several times. A women's movement produced a *Declaration of the Rights of Woman*, but never won voting rights (Gouges [1791] 1980). Income-based restrictions on the right to vote in primary assemblies and even more stringent requirements for eligibility for elective positions drew fierce criticism. When an uprising in Paris effectively terminated the monarchy on 10 August 1792, elections for a Convention to write a new constitution were called almost instantly, with radically expanded suffrage and no restrictions on who qualified as electable. The voting age was lowered from twenty-five to twenty-one and all men other than domestics, paupers and those without fixed residence could now vote. The primary assemblies, moreover, now gave deputies instructions and often deliberated and formulated policy resolutions. When the Convention produced its new constitution in 1793, it organised a national referendum with an extremely broad suffrage. In a few places, small numbers of women and children participated, possibly a result of local sympathies for a broad understanding of citizens' equality, although the document on which they voted excluded them. But democracy as envisaged in this most radical of the revolution's constitutions, although overwhelmingly approved, never came into force. The Convention, confronting a series of grave crises – foreign invasion, collapse of the currency, insurrections, defiance of Parisian authority by local governments, armed counter-revolutionary mobilisation – empowered its Committee of Public Safety with renewable dictatorial authority, which it used with great and violent effectiveness, curtailing or eliminating many of the rights that only shortly before had been hailed as great human achievements.

With the fall of the Committee, what was left of the Convention drafted yet another constitution, held another plebiscite and produced yet another mode of government. Avoiding the concentration of authority in a single legislative chamber, a bicameral legislature now confronted a five-member executive Directory, tax qualifications were reintroduced for voters and new restrictions on who could be elected were introduced as well. In the first of the annual legislative elections, two-thirds had to be chosen from members of the Convention. What is more, those in power, when faced with election results not to their liking, quashed the results, arrested opponents or called in the military to overturn the voters' choices. Finally, the numerous officials elected locally now shared power with others appointed from above and from Paris, an ongoing transformation that culminated in a national system of centrally appointed administrators established after the seizure of power by General Bonaparte in 1799.

Direct Democracy

The convening of the Estates-General not only launched the revolution's electoral practices, but was a national experience of local meetings and deliberations as well. Many electoral assemblies continued to meet and to correspond with their deputies. In the spring and summer of 1789, not only was there an insurrectionary climate in Paris, but in other cities local movements seized power. Over the next several years, elected national officials had to contend with politically organised clubs, local governments claiming independent authority, self-organised armed groups that went under the label of National Guards, and other bodies as well. These organisations pressured local governments, organised covert campaigns to support favoured candidates for office despite the taboo against parties and sometimes supported insurrection. Political clubs organised around the country, corresponded with one another and formed national networks (Kennedy 1982). In many villages, peasants would gather, often after Sunday Mass, and plan direct action in search of grain, or against an over-bearing lord or an unsympathetic tax official (Markoff 1996). In larger cities, militant citizens ran their neighbourhoods, attacked and intimidated those holding contrary views, and, from time to time, attempted to pressure or even overturn the elected authority of the new revolutionary institutions.

In early revolutionary Paris, to take the best-studied example, delegates were elected to a town council, while the sixty neighbourhood districts into which Paris had been divided for the elections to the Estates-General developed organs of self-government that collectively claimed to be the legitimate local governing authorities rather than their own elected council. The sixty districts were superseded by the forty-eight 'sections', which claimed the right to meet 'permanently', that is to say, when they chose, to arm themselves, debate national as well as local questions, issue documents, negotiate with each other, make demands of the national legislature and even pull down national governments not to their liking (Tønnesson 1988). The overthrow of the monarchy in 1792 was largely organised by the radicalised sections of Paris in collaboration with a large unit of National Guards that came up from

Marseille, where local activists were busy making their own policies. In justifying their continuing activism, such bodies claimed that direct action by the people had greater authority than anything done by elected officials who, without constant monitoring by the watchful citizenry, could easily turn into a new form of aristocracy (Sutherland 2009). Local and central authorities had complex relationships oscillating between intense militancy and authoritarian suppression, resigned acceptance and active facilitation, depending on the crisis of the moment (Soboul 1958; Tønnesson 1959; Woloch 1970).

Tensions in French Revolutionary Democracy

French revolutionary democracy justified actions by appeals to conflicting concepts and resorted to institutions justified by those concepts that were inherently in conflict as well. Sovereignty was lodged not in kings, gods or past practice, but exclusively in human beings who were identical in rights. In abolishing 'privilege', etymologically 'private law', in favour of the universal law for all, no one was to differ in rights due to noble status, occupation, region or locality. The detailed legislation actually accomplishing this was often a source of fierce debate. There was enormous resentment on the part of ex-nobles, for example, over the abolition of their rights to family coats-of-arms (Doyle 2009). But having justified such annihilation of differences on universal grounds, they could hardly deny voting rights to Protestants or Jews, or those in stigmatised occupations such as executioners or actors, or twenty-one year olds, free men of colour or women. The pull and tug of social movements went on, abolishing, maintaining or renewing one or another form of exclusion from full rights. But with equality among abstractly conceived individual citizens given such weight, exclusions would now need some justification, too. While some would claim, for example, that Jews were not really citizens at all since their ancestors came from afar, the debate itself was a sign that exclusions could not just be taken for granted any more. Not that there was anything automatic about the results of any of these conflicts. Women formed political clubs and appropriated revolutionary rhetoric, but only achieved voting rights in a democratic France in 1944 (Hunt 2007: 171). But exclusions could now be challenged. Some challenges met strong resistance, some less and some democratising movements were stronger than others. The night of 4/5 August 1789 became the occasion for the National Assembly to decree the abolition of feudalism in France and to extend that abolition not just to the seigneurial rights but to a multitude of privileges of various kinds. This was not simply the working out of the logical consequences of notions of equality and liberty, but also a practical political response to the enormous explosion of rural insurrection that had peaked in late July (Markoff 1996).

Conspicuously absent from the vast collection of inequalities and deprivations of liberty now slated for history's dustbin was colonial slavery, despite the compelling arguments of the Society of the Friends of Blacks that slavery was obviously incompatible with equality and freedom. However, there was not yet a slave rebellion as there was a peasant rebellion, and the planters, slavers and port-city merchants had their own powerful arguments, especially the threat to shift the fabulously wealthy sugar production of St Domingue to the British Empire. But the boundaries of rights were no easier to fix in the Caribbean than in metropolitan France. First, the white plantocracy demanded its inclusion in the rights-bearing French nation. Then, two challenges arose as less wealthy island whites demanded their own inclusion, as did the very significant group of 'free coloureds' who owned an important portion of St Domingue's land and slaves. Initially, the white planters sought alliance with the free coloureds to resist the demands of less prosperous whites. When the slaves revolted, the National Convention declared the end of colonial slavery, as much in deference to the slaves' movement as to be consistent in the application of the abstract principles of liberty and equality. Napoleon was to rescind the abolition of slavery, but was unable to restore it everywhere, since the Haitians had defeated the French forces, as well as the British and Spanish who attempted to take advantage of the violent chaos (Drescher 2009: 146–80; Dubois 2004).

Embodying the sovereignty of the people in a unicameral elected legislature was inherently problematic as well. As we have seen, all sorts of locally rooted groups claimed that democracy inhered in their own direct action, rather than in locally or nationally elected bodies; local officials and national legislators denounced direct action for defying the legitimate authority of the people's representatives. The relationship of elected legislature and hereditary monarch was also extremely troubled. The Convention's solution was to kill the king, but this did not settle the question of the organisation of the state for long because the revolution soon installed a new monarch in Napoleon Bonaparte who strongly curtailed legislative power. The fundamental notions that there was some meaningful sense in which 'the people' could be said to be a singular actor or that parties and electoral campaigns were illegitimate were challenged by the way actual people organised to defend and advance their particular interests and conceptions of right action. 'Parties' were incessantly condemned, yet the national legislatures and local councils were continually getting petitions and demands from people organised for that purpose and covert support for favoured candidates existed as well. In the period of the Terror in 1793–4, the Committee of Public Safety abolished previously cherished individual rights and carried out incarcerations, property confiscations and executions (but not torture) on a vast scale. Yet even then the government could be said to exemplify the notion of the supremacy of elected legislative authority: when the Convention revoked the Committee's mandate, its rule was over.

After the fall of the Committee of Public Safety, what was left of the Convention treated elections as instruments to acquire rulership, even as they did not rule out other means. Regulations were crafted to keep themselves in place, most dramatically by requiring that two-thirds of newly elected legislators were to be chosen from among those already sitting in the Convention. Over the next few years, if the electorate veered too far left or right, political clubs could be closed, activists imprisoned, schisms in electoral assemblies encouraged and then the favoured fragment of the schism recognised as the rightful assembly. Rather than the citizens choosing their sovereign representatives, the legislators organised the elections to bring themselves back into power: voting results were ignored and the military invited to prevent unwanted outcomes. In 1799, General Bonaparte went beyond the governing establishment's bidding in suppressing threats to its rule, installed himself in power and closed down what was left of the revolution's democracy.

But this does not mean that elections were an insignificant element in political contestation. For a decade, elections were the key element in claiming legitimate authority. At the local level, there is much work for historians still to do, but it appears that beginning with those very first local elections, the local structure of authority changed radically (Jessenne 1987). The conception of the people as a singular collective actor hung over efforts to create such a people where it did not yet exist and was in tension with stirring commitments to the rights of individual persons. The penchant for national standardisation in law, administration, weights and measures, and taxation extended to considerable disdain for the rich fabric of local custom and culture. The relevant committee's report to the Convention on language policy was titled: 'Report on the Necessity and Means to Annihilate Patois and Universalise the Use of the French Language' (Certeau *et al*. 1975: 302). The disdain for parties and the valorisation of the unity of the sovereign people made it difficult to organise disagreement, let alone establish dissent as legitimate. The notion of a 'loyal opposition' was anathema to the French Revolution.

Extending Revolution in the World

The impact of the revolution beyond France was immediate and enormous (Godechot 1956; Palmer 1959–64). It committed an enormously powerful country to one side of an ongoing struggle in many places between what had been described shortly before as 'aristocrats' versus 'democrats'. It provided powerful evidence that the hope of a democratic political order might be viable, not simply along the American coastline far from the aristocratic-monarchical states of the Old World, but in Europe as well. The old claim that democracy was not only extremely undesirable, but impossible on a scale larger than an ancient city-state evaporated when the aristocratic armies of Europe failed to crush the democratic rabble of France. Democracy might still be highly undesirable, but conservatives could no longer take comfort in its impossibility. When the mutable fortunes of battle proved favourable, the French exported their new political models by force, annexing adjoining territory and supporting satellite republics in alliance with local democratic movements. The scale of the extensive French mobilisations of military forces, essential for a country whose armies eventually, if briefly, dominated Europe from Madrid to Moscow, provoked defensive imitation of some French practices even on the part of regimes determined to set the clock back. The writing of constitutions took hold even among some of France's foes, not to mention its satellites, thereby diffusing the foundational democratic notion that human beings can set down the fundamental rules for shaping or reshaping their own states and societies. Those constitutions had other important democratic features. The constitution adopted in Cádiz in 1812, for example, provided for a broad suffrage in the Spanish empire and was an important framework for subsequent democratic developments in Latin America.

At the start of the twenty years of warfare that began in 1792, French legislators proclaimed their intention to democratise the places they occupied, to extend to

Europe their own social and political virtues. As one famous formulation had it, they would go to war against the palaces but make peace with the cottages. A few doubters suggested that they would merely arouse resistance, since 'no one loves armed missionaries' (Robespierre [1791] 1950–67: 8:81). As the long war unfolded, the extraction of resources from occupied places and the consequent multiple forms of resistance against French armies meant the French were more likely to be seen as oppressors than as liberators, as new tyrants rather than as champions of freedom. Wartime exigencies fuelled the closure of France's own sites of democracy, particularly in the brief murderous rule of the Committee of Public Safety and the more durable new monarchy of Bonaparte.

Conclusion

Three days after its establishment by the National Assembly, the Committee on the Constitution announced that it would prepare a 'declaration of the rights of man'. It issued a statement of the seventeen articles on which it could agree in August. These rights were taken to be prior to any particular form of government since 'the purpose of all political association is to preserve the natural and irrevocable rights of man' (*Déclaration* 1789). Although sociologists have generally been of the view that rights are meaningful only to the extent that there is an enforcement mechanism, the *Déclaration des droits de l'homme et du citoyen* had it the other way around. There is almost no specific mention of France, its institutions and mode of government at all. Rather, all governments must take measures to ensure the rights people have simply because they are human beings. It is because 'Men are born free and equal in rights' that the law must see to it that there is equality among citizens (*Déclaration* 1789). According to Article 11: 'The free communication of ideas and opinions is one of the most precious of the rights of man. Every citizen may therefore speak, write and print freely' (*Déclaration* 1789). Perhaps no word is more important in this Article than 'therefore'. Citizens must have certain rights as citizens because all human beings have them.

Ferociously denounced as a threat to established authority everywhere and equally passionately defended for the same reason, the *Déclaration des droits de l'homme et du citoyen* was at the same time a challenge to democracy as it was a powerful defence of it. The defence is in the claim that democracy is a better protector of human rights than imaginable alternatives. The challenge is that actual realisations of democracy are deficient in the achievement of human rights and therefore always a source of social movements for their extension. For twenty-first-century critics of democracy in the era of globalisation, it would no longer be as clear as it seemed in 1789 that the achievement of citizens' rights in the separate nation-states was an adequate vehicle for securing the fundamental rights of humanity.

In the decade that followed the elections to the Estates-General, the drama, complexity and multiplicity of France's revolutionary experience made that upheaval an endless source of models of democracy and of anti-democracy. It developed the practice of democracy through representative institutions and the often contrary practice of democracy through intensive personal participation. At different points it provided deeply eloquent formulations of freedom and equality, eliminated long-standing forms of inequality and many abusive practices, filled enormous numbers of public positions by popular election, inspired large numbers of people in villages and urban neighbourhoods to participate in making their own history, deeply involved its army in political life, crushed political dissent and excoriated cultural difference. It demonstrated that a modern nation-state could be organised without monarchs and aristocrats, and it also demonstrated how deeply contentious the future of democracy would be.

References

Aberdam, S., S. Bianchi, R. Demeude, E. Ducoudray, B. Gainot, M. Genty and C. Wolikow (2006), *Voter, élire pendant la Révolution française, 1789–1799, Guide pour la recherche*, Paris: Éditions du CTHS.

Babeau, A. ([1878] 1978), *Le village sous l'ancien régime*, Geneva: Megariotis.

Babeau, H. (1893), *Les assemblées générales des communautés d'habitants en France du XIIIe siècle à la Révolution*, Paris: Rousseau.

Blaufarb, R. (2002), *The French Army, 1750–1820: Careers, Talent, Merit*, Manchester: Manchester University Press.

Burke, E. (1790), *Reflections on the Revolution in France*, London: Dodsley.

Certeau, M. de, D. Julia and J. Revel (1975), *Une politique de la langue. La Révolution française et les patois: 'l'enquête de Grégoire*, Paris: Gallimard.

Crook, M. (1996), *Elections in the French Revolution: An Apprenticeship in Democracy, 1789–1799*, Cambridge: Cambridge University Press.

Déclaration des droits de l'homme et du citoyen (1789), Paris: National Constituent Assembly.

Doyle, W. (2009), *Aristocracy and its Enemies in the Age of Revolution*, Oxford: Oxford University Press.

Drescher, S. (2009), *Abolition: A History of Slavery and Antislavery*, Cambridge: Cambridge University Press.

Dubois, L. (2004), *Avengers of the New World: The Story of the Haitian Revolution*, Cambridge, MA: Belknap Press.

Edelstein, M. (1994), 'Electoral Behavior During the Constitutional Monarchy (1790–1791): A "Community" Interpretation', in R. Waldinger, P. Dawson and I. Woloch (eds), *The French Revolution and the Meaning of Citizenship*, Westport, CT: Greenwood Press, pp. 106–22.

Godechot, J. (1956), *La Grande Nation: l'expansion reìvolutionnaire de la France dans le monde de 1789 à 1799*, Paris: Aubier.

Gouges, O. de ([1791] 1980), 'Declaration of the Rights of Woman', in D. G. Levy, H. B. Applewhite and M. D. Johnson (eds), *Women in Revolutionary Paris, 1789–1795*, Urbana, IL: University of Illinois Press, pp. 87–96.

Gueniffey, P. (1993), *Le nombre et la raison. La Révolution française et les élections*, Paris: Éditions de l'École des Hautes Études en Sciences Sociales.

Hunt, L. (2007), *Inventing Human Rights: A History*, New York: W. W. Norton.

Jones, P. (2003), *Liberty and Locality in Revolutionary France: Six Villages Compared, 1760–1820*, Cambridge: Cambridge University Press.

Jessenne, J.-P. (1987), *Pouvoir au village et Révolution: Artois, 1760–1848*, Lille: Presses Universitaires de Lille.

Kennedy, M. (1982), *The Jacobin Clubs in the French Revolution: The First Years*, Princeton, NJ: Princeton University Press.

Markoff, J. (1996), *The Abolition of Feudalism: Peasants, Lords, and Legislators in the French Revolution*, University Park, PA: Pennsylvania State University Press.

McCloy, S. (1957), *The Humanitarian Movement in Eighteenth-Century France*, Lexington, KY: University of Kentucky Press.

Paine, T. ([1791] 1985), *The Rights of Man*, Harmondsworth: Penguin.

Palmer, R. R. (1959–64), *The Age of the Democratic Revolution: A Political History of Europe and America, 1760–1800*, 2 vols, Princeton, NJ: Princeton University Press.

Robespierre, M. ([1791] 1950–67), *Œuvres complètes de Maximilien Robespierre*, 10 vols, Paris: Société des études Robespierristes.

Rosanvallon, P. (1992), *Le sacre du citoyen. Histoire du suffrage universal en France*, Paris: Gallimard.

Soboul, A. (1958), *Les Sans-culottes parisiens en l'an II: mouvement populaire et gouvernement révolutionnaire, 2 Juin 1793–Thermidor an II*, Paris: Clavreuil.

Shapiro, G. and J. Markoff (1998), *Revolutionary Demands: A Content Analysis of the Cahiers de Doléances of 1789*, Stanford, CA: Stanford University Press.

Sutherland, D. M. G. (2009), *Murder in Aubagne: Lynching, Law, and Justice During the French Revolution*, Cambridge: Cambridge University Press.

Tønnesson, K. (1959), *La deìfaite des Sans-culottes. Mouvement populaire et reìaction bourgeoise en l'an III*, Oslo: University Press of Oslo.

Tønnesson, K. (1988), 'La démocratie directe sous la Révolution française – le cas des districts et sections de Paris', in C. Lucas (ed.), *The French Revolution and the Creation of Modern Political Culture, vol. 2: The Political Culture of the French Revolution*, Oxford: Pergamon Press, pp. 295–307.

Woloch, I. (1970), *Jacobin Legacy: The Democratic Movement Under the Directory*, Princeton, NJ: Princeton University Press.

Woloch, I. (1994), *The New Regime: Transformations of the French Civic Order, 1789–1820s*, New York: W. W. Norton.

Part V

Colonialism and Democracy

Chapter 18
Africa

Maxwell Owusu

Africa is the cradle of humankind and human culture. It is linguistically and culturally the most complex and diverse continent with hundreds of ethnic divisions, ranging from the Asante in the west to the Zulu in the south. In general, Africa lacked indigenous writing and therefore written records and literature with the exception of Amharic in Ethiopia. Although some examples are known of indigenous attempts, mostly after the mid-nineteenth century, to start elementary writing systems in West Africa, such as the Vai in Liberia, the Bamoun script in the Cameroons (the only one used in writing books) and a few others, there was no technological breakthrough to a fully-fledged writing system for practical purposes and to write books (Goody 1965: 110–11). As a result, it is the last major continent to have a recognised history (Curtin 1986). Faced with deep-seated racial prejudices and negative stereotypes, the world has been slow in accepting or crediting African achievements and original contributions to knowledge, law, ethics, morals, politics and philosophy. Thus, in any account of Africa's contribution to noble human ideals and values such as democracy (universally considered to be of Western European origin and diffusion), one has to overcome 'ethnocentric stereotypes and misguided notions of a civilising mission [that] bedevil relations with the Third World as much today as they ever did' (Mair 1975: 14).

With the discovery of the importance of the use and evaluation of oral traditions of pre-literate peoples as sources of history, and the mastery of indigenous languages as tools of ethnographic analysis in the study of local communities based on direct participant observation over extended periods, it has become possible to understand and describe the different types of indigenous African political systems. Significantly, traditional African history 'is concerned predominantly with political events' (Mair 1975: 7) and 'more typically . . . the organization of power [is] the field in which, it appears, the African genius has really concentrated its efforts' (Fallers 1966: 142).

A most important and lasting contribution to knowledge of British social anthropology is the classification of indigenous African political systems, describing the principles governing political relations and political institutions. These anthropologists were generally concerned to show that African chiefs and kings were not despots activated by arbitrary whims. The anthropologists stressed the importance of the restraints against the arbitrary exercise of power and the dependence of rulers on tribute, taxes and labour to perform what is seen as the welfare functions of government. British social anthropology detailed the reciprocal relations between rulers and subjects, and explained they were based on consensus and legitimate authority rather than simply on force. Antropology provided a defence of indigenous African institutions against the derogatory interpretations put on them by colonial administrators and missionaries who sought to 'improve' them (Mair 1975: 14). What follows is a brief survey of the principles of indigenous African political theory and practice, which can be shown to have been essentially 'democratic'. The question is, what is indigenous African democracy? What are its prospects for survival and its role in consolidating and legitimising democratic governance in post-colonial, twenty-first-century Africa?

Concepts of Democracy

The holistic, comparative, interdisciplinary approach to political systems in British social anthropology is characterised by Jack Goody's call for 'a political sociology that does not limit itself to the party politics of the Western World' (Goody 1969: 11). Also important is Abner Cohen's view of social anthropology as 'essentially a branch of political science', and social change as 'essentially a change in the forms, distribution and exercise of power' (Cohen 1969: 213). This led anthropologists to research and challenge political and legal concepts, such as 'democracy', 'law' and 'government', assumed by political scientists and political sociologists to be generally absent in 'tribal', pre-literate, non-Western cultures before colonialism or Western contact.

In its basic meaning the word 'democracy' refers to a 'system of government in which sovereignty is vested in the people' (Comfort 2005: 198). In the literal sense, democracy is rule by the people. The term itself is of Greek origin and was used to refer to the political systems then found in some Greek city-states, notably Athens in the middle of the fifth century BCE. However, it is possible to identify many early political systems in different parts of the world, including Africa, that had long traditions of some form of 'rule by the people' even if they were not fully 'democratic' by contemporary standards (Kuiper 2010: 204–9). Arend Lijphart argues that modern democracy 'was not fully established anywhere . . . until the beginning of the twentieth century' (Lijphart 1992: 1).

In pre-colonial Africa, the idea of 'democracy' – that is, rule by consent and participation of the people – if not the word, is as old as the social evolution of small, stable village communities that formed the basis of large urban centres and their complex systems of chiefdoms, kingdoms and empires going back thousands of years. These were supported by an equally complex economic system of hunting and gathering, fishing, agriculture, pastoralism, handicrafts, local and long-distance trade and an intricate system of markets (Murdock 1959; Skinner 1973). In pre-literate, pre-colonial Africa, the idea of 'democracy' and its principles and practice were embodied in oral traditions found in myths of origin, animal stories, song and drum texts, proverbs, aphorisms, ceremonies and rituals passed on from generation to generation.

African Political Systems Classified

Meyer Fortes and Edward Evans-Prichard group African political systems into three principal types, namely: (1) societies with centralised authority, administrative machinery and judicial institutions, that is, state societies, such as the Asante (Ghana) and the Zulu (South Africa); (2) societies without centralised authority, formal bureaucratic and judicial institutions, that is, the so-called stateless societies, such as the Igbo (Nigeria) and the Nuer (Sudan); and (3) societies in which the kinship system and the political system are coterminous and indistinguishable, such as the Bergdama (Botswana) and the !Kung (Botswana/Namibia). They provide a representative sample of the first two types, covering all the major principles of African political systems (Fortes and Evans-Pritchard 1940: 1–23). Scholars building on Fortes' and Evans-Pritchard's classification have provided additional subtypes and other variations of the principal types of political systems identified by them (Murdock 1959; Owusu 1979a).

The first group of state societies – chiefdoms, kingdoms, empires – are multi-ethnic, culturally heterogeneous and consist of units bound together territorially by common interests and loyalty to a political superior, usually a paramount chief or the king-in-council. In the second group of decentralised, chiefless societies, power and authority is shared by a number of elders and representatives of kin groups, age-set and age-grade associations and secret societies that maintain law and order, perform public services and defend their communities. In some of the societies, the village head is the highest authority, but in times of war and for trade and ritual purposes, many villages may come together *pro tem* and accept the authority of the most senior elder. Among the Gikuyu of Kenya, for example, age-grade associations perform administrative functions, protect village land and cattle and enforce laws. This is a highly democratic system in which every individual passing through successive age-grade associations has a say in the management of the affairs of the village community. This system of government, resting not on kinship, though still important, but on a structure of formal age-grades and age-sets with specific communal and political functions, has a fairly extensive distribution in East Africa, notably the Galla, Karamojong, Maasai, Nandi and Gikuyu.

In other societies without centralised authority, such as the Igbo of eastern Nigeria, each village enjoys political autonomy. A village consists of a group of lineages and sublineages, each occupying its own compound. There is a village head, an elder who presides over a village assembly where adult members are allowed to speak freely. The assembly may have legislative functions and elders take decisions by consensus. Lineage heads have authority over members of their lineage. Indeed, one of Africa's contributions to political theory and practice is, according to Kwasi Wiredu, the success of consensus democracy practiced in traditional Africa, such as among the Akan (Ghana), which stands in sharp contrast, and arguably, is superior to, 'adversarial' democracy imported from the modern Western world, which has had only limited success in post-colonial Africa. Kwasi Wiredu claims that traditional Africa's 'adherence to the principle of consensus in politics is based on the belief that ultimately the interests of all members of society are the same, although the immediate perceptions of those interests may be different' (Wiredu 1996: 182–90; see also Busia 1967: 17–34; Owusu 1979b: 89–108).

Elias identifies a fourth type of political system not mentioned by Fortes and Evans-Pritchard, namely, pre-colonial African societies subject to Islamic theology and law in parts of northern Nigeria, Northern Territories of Gold Coast (Ghana), Gambia, Sudan, Uganda and Zanzibar. These are traditional theocracies. In general, the emirs or sultans heading these theocracies tend to be autocratic and their power and authority is often feudal (Elias 1956: 13). It is noteworthy, that these traditional northern Nigerian 'autocratic' or 'authoritarian' theocracies provided 'the nursery (in the horticultural sense) of Lord Lugard's theories of Indirect Rule', a controversial and, to educated African nationalist elites, an unpopular political imposition (Low 1964: 238).

A brief and balanced survey of African political systems in all their variation and dynamic complexity is always daunting. As Ronald Wraith notes:

> In one place the people might give their loyalty to a King, powerful in his own right; in another to a paramount or lesser chief, powerful only so long as he held and deserved the respect of his subjects, but removable by their will; in another to the heads of a clan; in another to a group of villages; in another to a 'town'. In others the real seat of authority might be difficult for a stranger to discern even after patient inquiry and research. (Wraith 1953: 13)

The Nature of African Democracy

Concerning the *democratic* nature of indigenous African political systems, there is a large measure of agreement among scholars and African peoples. Fortes and Evans-Pritchard observed correctly that:

> the government of an African state consists in a balance between power and authority, on the one side, and obligations and responsibility, on the other. Everyone who holds public office has responsibilities for the public weal corresponding to his right and privileges. The distribution of political authority provides a machinery by which the various agents of government can be held to their responsibilities. A chief or a king has the right to exact tax, tribute and labour service from his subjects; he has the corresponding obligation to dispense justice to them, to ensure their protection from enemies and to safeguard their general welfare by ritual acts and observances. The structure of an African state implies that kings and chiefs rule by consent. A ruler's subjects are all fully aware of the duties he owes to them as they are of the duties they owe to him and are able to exert pressure to make him discharge these duties. (Fortes and Evans-Pritchard 1940: 12)

This is the indigenous constitutional arrangement. But Africans recognise, as clearly as Europeans, that power corrupts and that men are liable to abuse it, and that it may be, in practice, impossible to prevent abuse entirely (Fortes and Evans-Pritchard 1940). Both rulers and subjects, actuated by their private interests, infringe the rules of the constitution (Owusu 2006). In cases where infringements of constitutional rules become too serious, popular reaction certainly occurs and may result in a movement of secession or revolt by the people and the deposition of the ruler (Owusu 1986). In societies with chiefs and kings, there are constitutional checks and balances, consisting of such mechanisms as the king's council of chiefs; the queen mother's courts; sacerdotal officials with a decisive voice in the king's investiture; powerful secret societies in which the king is only *primus inter pares*; powerful commoners' organisations, such as the *Asafo* among the Akan people of Ghana acting on behalf of the public to exercise a check on arbitrary actions, monarchical absolutism and political tyranny. T. O. Elias stresses that this mechanism of constitutional checks and balances involves the vital principle that all sections of the people and all major interests in the community are able in the final analysis to have an effective say in the ordering of public affairs. Indeed, no king or local chief can disregard the voice of the people and the intangible, but effective, factor of public opinion serving to protect law and custom by controlling the arrogation of executive power (Elias 1956: 13). In this respect, G. P. Murdock is absolutely wrong in characterising African kingdoms as incurably despotic on the model of 'oriental despotism' (Murdock 1959: 37).

In countries without chiefs or kings, the non-centralised political systems include different mechanisms of checks and balances to prevent abuse of power. In these acephalous segmentary societies, power is dispersed among all the component units of lineage segments of local communities. There is no central authority to exploit divergent local loyalties and interests for its own ends or to keep in check any inter-territorial conflicts. Any conflict between two or more local segments is also conflict between two or more component lineage segments, since all are closely interlocked. The mutual interest and desire of the equivalent local and lineage units for political and social balance is the stabilising factor. The societies without rulers are considered the first, simplest and most widespread type of African political system and, perhaps, the most equalitarian and democratic. Murdock refers to this type of political system as *primitive democracy*, without any negative connotation to the word 'primitive' (Murdock 1959). In both the centralised and decentralised political systems, leaders, whether chiefs or village heads or councils of elders, are made and unmade according to their effectiveness and proven concern for the welfare of the community. The people are always the final judges of the indigenous democratic ideal as understood in local communities. Elias points out correctly that 'whether the society is a monarchy or a gerontocracy [both tend to have a strong male bias] one common denominator is the constant aspiration towards the democratic principle in constitutional government' (Elias 1956: 21). In this respect, Ghana's post-colonial coups against one-party authoritarian rule are linked ideologically to the long tradition of the Akan *asafo* populist rebellions against unworthy chiefs (Owusu 1989).

Lord Hailey summarises the overwhelming evidence for indigenous African democracy as follows:

African sentiment attaches special importance to the due observance of the procedure by which all members of the communities concerned are able to have some voice in determining issues which are of major interest to it. It is rare to find in

British Colonial Africa any instance in which the indigenous form of rule previously in force could be described as autocratic and there are not many cases in which it could be described as authoritarian. It was a prevailing characteristic of the indigenous system of rule that whether power was vested in the hands of individual chiefs or of a ruling class, these had (*unlike the absolutist regimes of a certain stage in European history*) no machinery by the use of which they could enforce obedience to their orders. (Hailey 1951: 2, emphasis added)

This is a fair estimate of the vast majority of indigenous African political systems before Islamic or colonial rule. The representative character of indigenous political institutions is well established, and their constant preoccupation with the goal of democracy in popular government is duly emphasised.

Among the few glaring cases in which traditional political leadership could, in a strict sense, be considered authoritarian are the Islamic emirates of northern Nigeria, the military empire of the Dahomean kings and the regime of King Shaka of the Zulu. But such is the indigenous constitutional order that the tyrant or the despot is ultimately overthrown or killed by popular uprising by the subordinate chiefs and people alike. On the Akan constitution, for example, R. S. Rattray observes that 'a "paramount chief" who endeavoured to centralise too much in olden times generally paid with his life for his folly in having allowed his ambitions to override his knowledge of his own Constitution' (Rattray 1969: 406). Reverence for authority is deeply ingrained in the African, as well as a natural propensity for the practical democratic ideal of a fair and orderly life, both of which are passed on from generation to generation.

Colonialism and Change

It is more than a little ironic that the same Western powers who claim to be spreading – as a moral duty – democracy across the non-European world colonised by the West, are the very powers who, in their relentless pursuit of empire, undermine(d) or nearly destroy(ed) the pre-existing indigenous democratic institutions of the non-Western world. In Africa, in the name of the civilising mission of European powers, Africans lost their sovereignty and democratic political traditions. In British colonial Africa, chiefs, whether created and imposed on the people by the colonial authority (such as in eastern Nigeria) or elected by their own people, but required to gain official recognition as chiefs by the colonial power, found themselves in an untenable position as both paid and titled agents of the colonial government and as representatives of their people. Chiefs, whose legitimacy depended ultimately on the colonial authority in the performance of their statutory duties, increasingly grew corrupt and autocratic. In general, what happened to African political institutions after colonisation depended, according to D. A. Low, on the 'initial imperial situation'. In one type, an imperial power superseded a pre-existing political authority, which was very much the basis of French and Belgian imperial power. The French believed in a unified form of government, and the French system both in colonial Africa and in metropolitan France was highly centralised and authoritarian. In a second type, an imperial power established and maintained its dominance over a pre-existing political order that continued to exist, albeit transformed. In a third type, the case of the stateless societies with non-centralised kinship and lineage-based political systems, no distinctly political authorities existed who could be either superseded or subordinated, so the imperial power had to engage in the extremely difficult project of creating a distinctly political authority for the first time by appointing as chiefs and agents of colonial authority individuals who might have been ex-interpreters or ex-policemen and who had no traditional basis of legitimation. The latter two types of imperial situation were particularly typical of British imperial rule (Low 1964: 236; see also Owusu 1997).

Democracy and Post-colonial Africa: The Role of Traditional Political Institutions

The problem of the future of indigenous rulers and political institutions in Africa remained largely unresolved during the colonial period and the nationalist struggle for independence, as well as after independence. What was to be the relationship of traditional chiefs and kings to the new educated and Westernised political leadership, and of indigenous political institutions to parliamentary forms instituted to govern new states whose international boundaries were nearly all the result of the colonial partition of Africa? Thus, with independence, African governments faced three major inter-related problems in organising their post-colonial political systems; problems foreseen before decolonisation, but the decisions now had to be made by African nationalist leaders. The first, was the problem of national integration: how local identifications – the diverse ethnic and other communal loyalties – could be aggregated and harnessed to strengthen national unity. The second, was how to integrate indigenous political institutions, particularly chiefs and kings, into the new structures of local and national government. The third, problem had to do with the kind of political culture that could best function to promote rapid socio-economic transformation and welfare. With respect to the second problem, which is the focus here, the solution has varied from country to country. Ghana, for instance, moved to bring the chiefs under the control of the central government. Their customary role was recognised, but they were made relatively powerless, if still influential. Guinea stripped traditional leaders of all power in favour of the ruling party organisation, headed by Sekou Toure. Other countries like Tanzania and Rwanda abolished chieftaincy and kingship in the name of republican or socialist values (Owusu 1997).

Significantly, a growing number of African countries, notably Botswana and lately Ghana since the Constitution of the Fourth Republic came into force in 1992, have managed to work out realistic and satisfactory solutions to all three problems: promoting national integration; adjusting traditional political institutions and leadership to modern parliamentary representative democratic forms ensuring political stability; and achieving respectable socio-economic development. As Gloriah Somolekae writing on Botswana observes: 'the liberal democratic system . . . is being built on and continues to find its support and continuity in the foundations of the traditional political system' (Somolekae 1989: 75). Briefly, the constitution of the Republic of Botswana is substantially the same constitution adopted at independence from British rule on 30 September 1966. The National Assembly is elected at five-year intervals by universal adult suffrage in single-member constituencies on a multi-party basis. The President, who is both the head of state and head of government, is elected by a simple majority of the declared preferences of the elected members of the National Assembly. A second chamber, the House of Chiefs, comprises the chiefs of the eight principal Botswana traditional ethnic communities, four subchiefs elected by and from their own members, and three members specially elected by the other twelve members. The House may consider draft bills when they affect the constitution or are matters that relate to traditional communities. Botswana's democracy retains the widely shared traditional character of responsible chieftaincy based on representation by lesser chiefs and elected district councils. Local government consists of nine elected district councils in which collective land rights are vested (subject to recent amendments) and four town councils. At the local level, magistrates on the English model preside in district courts, but chiefs and headmen administer traditional law and custom in traditional courts (Kgotla) (Owusu 1992). In democratic constitution making, it is always important to remember, as Sir W. Ivor Jennings points out, that 'every people is unique, and accordingly that every country must have a Constitution to suit itself, a Constitution made to measure, not one bought off the rack' (Jennings 1956: 2).

Conclusion

It is important to end this introductory survey of African democracy by drawing attention to the serious challenges faced by post-colonial democratic constitutional development mainly as a result of the contradictions of the 'mixed' or dual heritage of contemporary African democracy – indigenous as well as colonial, plus the widespread illiteracy and poverty of African populations and the deep-seated political corruption in African states. In nearly every African country efforts have been made to incorporate into their modern democratic constitutions adaptable elements drawn from the country's vibrant indigenous political traditions consistent with the state's cultural identity. It is not uncommon, despite this effort, for post-colonial African democratic constitutions to reflect utopian aspirations rather than the achievements that gave them form. Post-independence African constitutions often reflect borrowed Western institutional models whose working assumptions are neither shared nor understood by the bulk of the populations concerned.

Most of these modern democratic constitutions provide for or sanction elaborate bureaucratic, legislative, executive, judicial and consultative superstructures that assume levels of mass literacy, communication, cultural homogeneity, national integration and identification that simply do not yet exist. Thus, not surprisingly, democracy beyond periodic elections becomes largely the preserve of the educated political elite, and irrelevant and meaningless to the ordinary and mostly illiterate populations in villages and small towns. In this respect, the admonition of the chairman of the Committee of Experts which drafted the proposals for the 1992 Constitution of Ghana, Dr S. K. B. Asante, is particularly revealing:

Ghana's democratic order would only be meaningful if the humblest person in the remotest village has been made aware of his/her constitutional rights, and the prospects for enforcing such rights, have been assured. Only then will the ordinary Ghanaian feel that he or she has a vested interest in the preservation of the constitution. (cited in Owusu 2006: 7)

This comment addresses the common failure of African democratic constitutions, namely, their tendency to remain mere legal declarations of intent having little or no relation to existing socio-economic and political realities. It also highlights one of the biggest challenges facing democracy in Africa today: in a continent riddled with socio-economic and political problems, can democracy be both culturally relevant to the people and responsive to their many complex needs?

References

Busia, K. A. (1967), *Africa in Search of Democracy*, London: Routledge & Kegan Paul.

Cohen, A. (1969), *Custom and Politics in Urban Africa*, London: Routledge & Kegan Paul.

Comfort, N. (2005), *The Politics Book*: *A Lexicon of Political Facts from Abu Ghraib to Zippergate*, London: Methuen.

Curtin, P. D. (1986), 'Africa in World History', in I. T. Mowoe and R. Bjornson (eds), *Africa and the West: The Legacies of Empire*, New York: Greenwood Press, pp. 13–31.

Elias, T. O. (1956), *The Nature of African Customary Law*, Manchester: Manchester University Press.

Fallers, L. (1966), 'Social Stratification and Economic Processes in Africa', in R. Bendix and S. M. Lipset (eds), *Class, Status and Power*, New York: Free Press, pp. 141–9.

Fortes, M. and E. E. Evans-Pritchard (1940), 'Introduction', in M. Fortes and E. E. Evans-Pritchard (eds), *African Political Systems*, Oxford: Oxford University Press, pp. 1–23.

Goody, J. (1965), 'Tribal, Racial, Religious and Language Problems in Africa', in G. Wolstenholme and M. O'Connor (eds), *Man and Africa*, Boston: Little, Brown, pp. 98–120.

Goody, J. (1969), *Comparative Studies in Kinship*, London: Routledge & Kegan Paul.

Hailey, Lord W. M. (1951), *Native Administration in the British African Territories*, Pt IV, London: HMSO.

Jennings, W. I. (1956), *The Approach To Self-Government*, Boston, MA: Beacon Press.

Kuiper, K. (2010), *The Ideas that Changed the World: The Essential Guide to Modern Philosophy, Science, Math, and the Arts*, New York: Fall River Press.

Lijphart, A. (1992), 'Introduction', in A. Lijphart (ed.), *Parliamentary versus Presidential Government*, Oxford: Oxford University Press, pp. 1–27.

Low, D. A. (1964), 'Lion Rampant', *Journal of Commonwealth Political Studies*, 2(3), 235–52.

Mair, L. (1975), 'How Far Have We Got in the Study of Politics?', in M. Fortes and S. Patterson (eds), *Studies in African Social Anthropology*, London: Academic Press, pp. 7–20.

Murdock, G. P. (1959), *Africa: Its Peoples and Their Culture History*, New York: McGraw Hill.

Owusu, M. (ed.) (1979a), *Colonialism and Change: Essays Presented to Lucy Mair*, The Hague: Mouton.

Owusu, M. (1979b), 'Politics Without Parties: Reflections on the Union Government Proposal in Ghana', *African Studies Review*, 22(1), 89–108.

Owusu, M. (1986), 'Custom and Coups: A Juridical Interpretation of Civil Order and Disorder in Ghana', *Journal of Modern African Studies*, 24(1), 69–99.

Owusu, M. (1989), 'Rebellion, Revolution and Tradition: Reinterpreting Coups in Ghana', *Comparative Studies in Society and History*, 31(2), 372–97.

Owusu, M. (1992), 'Democracy and Africa: A View from the Village', *Journal of Modern African Studies*, 30(3), 369–96.

Owusu, M. (1997), 'Domesticating Democracy: Culture, Civil Society and Constitutionalism in Africa', *Comparative Studies in Society and History*, 39(1), 120–52.

Owusu, M. (2006), *Uses and Abuses of Political Power: A Case Study of Continuity and Change in the Politics of Ghana*, 2nd edn, Accra: Ghana University Press.

Rattray, R. S. (1969), *Ashanti Law and Constitution*, New York: Negro University Press.

Skinner, E. P. (1973), 'West African Economic Systems', in E. P. Skinner (ed.), *Peoples and Cultures of Africa*, Garden City: Doubleday/Natural History Press, pp. 205–29.

Somolekae, G. (1989), 'Do Batswana Think and Act as Democrats?', in J. Holm and P. Molutsi (eds), *Democracy in Botswana*, Athens, OH: Ohio University Press, pp. 75–88.

Wiredu, K. (1996), *Cultural Universals and Particulars: An African Perspective*, Bloomington, IN: Indiana University Press.

Wraith, R. E. (1953), *Local Government*, London: Penguin.

Chapter 19

Native Americans

Bruce E. Johansen

Europe did not discover America, but America was quite a discovery for Europe. For roughly three centuries before the American Revolution, the ideas that made the American Revolution possible were being discovered, nurtured and embellished in the growing English and French colonies of North America. America provided a counterpoint for European convention and assumption. It became, for Europeans in America, at once a dream and a reality, a fact and a fantasy, the real and the ideal. To appreciate the way in which European eyes opened on the 'new world', we must take the phrase literally, with the excitement evoked in our own time by travel to the moon and planets. There was one electrifying difference: the voyagers of that time knew that their new world was inhabited (Grinde and Johansen 1991: xvii).

European colonists' lives were pervaded by contact with Native American peoples to a degree that we, today, sometimes find difficult to comprehend. The new Americans looked inland across a continent they already knew to be many times the size of England, France and Holland combined. They did not know with any certainty just how far their new homeland extended. Maps of the time did not comprehend accurately the distances between the Atlantic and Pacific oceans. A few Spanish and French trappers and explorers had left their footprints in this vast expanse of land, but at that time at least 90 per cent of North America was still the homeland of many hundreds of different native peoples. Increasingly, native societies in America came to serve the transplanted Europeans, including some of the United States' most influential founders, as a counterpoint to the European order. They found in the native polities the values that the seminal documents of the time celebrated: life, liberty, happiness, a model of government by consensus, with citizens enjoying rights due to them as human beings (Weatherford 1988, 1991). The fact that native peoples in America were able to govern themselves in this way provided advocates of alternatives to monarchy with practical ammunition for a philosophy of government based on the rights of the individual, which they believed had worked, did work and would work for them in America.

Native American Confederacies

All along the Atlantic seaboard, Native American nations had formed confederacies by the time they encountered European immigrants, from the Creeks, which Hector St

John de Crèvecoeur called a 'federated republic' (Crèvecoeur 1801: 461), to the Cherokees and Choctaws, to the Iroquois and the Wyandots (Hurons) in the Saint Lawrence valley, as well as the Penacook federation of New England, among many others. The Illinois Confederacy, the Three Fires of the Chippewa, Ottawa and Pottawatomi, the Wapenaki Confederacy, the Powhatan Confederacies, and the tripartate Miami also were members of confederations. Each of these native confederacies developed its own variation on a common theme of counsellor democracy. Most were remarkably similar in broad outline. By the late eighteenth century, as resentment against England's taxation flared into open rebellion along the Atlantic seaboard, the colonists displayed widespread knowledge of native governmental systems. Thomas Jefferson, Benjamin Franklin and others the length of the coast observed governmental systems that shared many similarities.

Colonists arriving in eastern North America encountered variations of a confederacy model, usually operating by methods of consensus that were unfamiliar to people who had been living in societies usually governed by queens, princes and kings. The best-known of these consensual governments was the Haudenosaunee (Iroquois Confederacy), which occupied a prominent position in the diplomacy of the early colonies.

The Importance of the Iroquois Confederacy

The Iroquois' system was the best known to the colonists, in large part because of the Haudenosaunee's pivotal position in diplomacy not only between the English and French, but also among other native confederacies. Called the Iroquois by the French and the Five (later Six) Nations by the English, the Haudenosaunee controlled the only relatively level land pass between the English colonies on the seaboard and the French settlements in the Saint Lawrence valley, later the route of the Eire Canal. Without authority to command, Iroquois and other Native American political leaders honed their persuasive abilities, especially their speaking skills. In his *History of the Five Nations*, Colden attributed the Iroquois' skill at oratory to the republican nature of their government. Colden described the intense study that the Iroquois applied to the arts of oral persuasion, to acquisition of grace and manner before councils of their peers (Colden [1727, 1747] 1958). Franklin compared the decorum of Native American councils with the rowdy nature of debate in British public forums, including the House of Commons. This difference in debating customs persists to our day.

Each Iroquois nation has its own council, which sends delegates to a central council, much as each state in the United States has its own legislature, as well as senators and representatives who travel to the central seat of government in Washington, DC. When representatives of the Iroquois nations meet at Onondaga, they form two groups: the Elder Brothers (Mohawks and Senecas) and the Younger Brothers (Cayugas and Oneidas). The Iroquois built certain ways of doing business into their Great Law to prevent anger and frayed tempers. For example, an important measure may not be decided the same day it is introduced to allow time for passions to cool. Important decisions must take at least two days, to allow leaders to 'sleep on it' and not to react too quickly. The Great Law may be amended just as one adds beams to the rafters of an Iroquois longhouse. The Great Tree of Peace is regarded as a living organisation. Its roots and branches are said to grow in order to incorporate other peoples.

A leader is instructed to be a mentor for the people at all times. Political leaders must strive to maintain peace within the League. A chief may be 'de-horned' (impeached) if he engages in violent behaviour of any kind. Even the brandishing of a weapon may bring sanction. The traditional headdress of an Iroquois leader (an emblem of office) includes deer antlers, which are said to have been 'knocked off' if the sachem has been impeached. Chiefs of the Iroquois League are instructed to take criticism honestly, that their skins should be seven spans thick to absorb the criticism of the people they represent in public councils. Political leaders are also instructed to think of the coming generations in all of their actions. Sachems are not allowed to name their own successors, nor may they carry their titles to the grave. The Great Law provides a ceremony to remove the 'antlers' of authority from a dying chief. The Great Law also provides for the removal from office of sachems who can no longer adequately function in office, a measure remarkably similar to a constitutional amendment adopted in the United States during the late twentieth century providing for the removal of an incapacitated president. The Great Law of Peace also includes provisions guaranteeing freedom of religion and the right of redress before the Grand Council. It also forbids unauthorised entry of homes, one of several measures that sounds familiar to US citizens through the Bill of Rights.

In some ways, the Grand Council operates like the US House of Representatives and Senate with their conference committees. As it was designed by Deganawidah the Peacemaker (founder of the Confederacy with his spokesman Hiawatha), debating protocol begins with the elder brothers, the Mohawks and Senecas. After debate by the Keepers of the Eastern Door (Mohawks) and the Keepers of the Western Door (Senecas), the question is then thrown across the fire to the Oneida and Cayuga statesmen (the younger brothers) for discussion in much the same manner. Once consensus is achieved among the Oneidas and the Cayugas, the discussion is then given back to the Senecas and Mohawks for confirmation. Next, the question is laid before the Onondagas for their decision. At this stage, the Onondagas have a power similar to judicial review; they may raise objections to the proposed measure if it is believed inconsistent with the Great Law. Essentially, the legislature can rewrite the proposed law on the spot so that it can be in accord with the constitution of the Iroquois. When the Onondagas reach consensus, Tadadaho asks Honowireton (an Onondaga sachem who presides over debates between the delegations) to confirm the decision. Finally, Honowireton or Tadadaho gives the decision of the Onondagas to the Mohawks and the Senecas so that the policy may be announced to the Grand Council as its will.

Benjamin Franklin and the Lancaster Treaty Council, 1744

If the US government's structure closely resembles that of the Iroquois Confederacy in some respects, how did the founders observe the native model? The historical trail begins in 1744, as Pennsylvania officials met with Iroquois sachems in council at Lancaster, Canassatego, an Onondaga sachem, advised the Pennsylvania officials on Iroquois concepts of unity. Canassatego and other Iroquois sachems were advocating unified British management of trade at the time. While the Iroquois preferred English manufactured products to those produced in France, the fact that each colony maintained its own trading practices and policies created confusion and conflict:

> Our wise forefathers established Union and Amity between the Five Nations. This has made us formidable; this has given us great Weight and Authority with our neighbouring Nations. We are a powerful Confederacy; and by your observing the same methods our wise forefathers have taken, you will acquire such Strength and power. Therefore whatever befalls you, never fall out with one another. (Doren and Boyd 1938: 75)

Benjamin Franklin probably first learned of Canassatego's 1744 advice to the colonies as he set his words in type. Franklin's press issued Indian treaties in small booklets that enjoyed a lively sale throughout the colonies. Beginning in 1736, Franklin published Indian treaty accounts on a regular basis until the early 1760s, when his defence of Indians under assault by frontier settlers cost him his seat in the Pennsylvania Assembly. Franklin subsequently served the colonial government in England. Using Iroquois examples of unity, Franklin sought to shame the reluctant colonists into some form of union in 1751:

> It would be a strange thing . . . if Six Nations of ignorant savages should be capable of forming such an union and be able to execute it in such a manner that it has subsisted for ages and appears indissoluble, and yet that a like union should be impractical for ten or a dozen English colonies, to whom it is more necessary and must be more advantageous, and who cannot be supposed to want an equal understanding of their interest. (Smyth 1905–7: III:42)

As he often did, Franklin put a backward spin on the phrase 'ignorant savages'. He showed that the original peoples of America had much to teach the immigrants. In October 1753, Franklin began a distinguished diplomatic career, which would later make him the United States' premier envoy in Europe, by attending a treaty council at Carlisle, Pennsylvania. During the same year, Franklin also recognised the enormous appeal of American Indian ways to the American people. He wrote that American Indian children reared in Anglo-American society returned to their people when they took but 'one ramble with them'. Furthermore, Franklin asserted that when 'White persons of either sex have been taken prisoners young by Indians, and lived a while among them, tho' ransomed by their friends . . . [they] take the first good opportunity of escaping again into the woods, from whence there is no reclaiming them' (Labaree 1950–1962: IV:481).

Anglo-Iroquois Synthesis in the Albany Plan of Union

James DeLancey, acting governor of New York, sent a special invitation to Tiyanoga (c. 1680–1755), a Mohawk sachem whom the English called Hendrick, to attend the Albany Conference in 1754. Here, Tiyanoga provided insights into the structure of the

League of the Iroquois for the assembled colonial delegates. The Albany Plan of Union, which proposed a federal union of the colonies but retained their autonomy except for matters of mutual concern, such as diplomacy and defence, was therefore a structure very similar to the Iroquois Confederacy that Canassatego had urged the colonists to emulate ten years earlier. Although the Albany Plan was not approved by the colonies or the Crown, it became a model on which the Articles of Confederation were later based.

Tiyanoga was a major figure in colonial affairs to 1755, when he died in battle with the French as an ally of the British. A member of the Wolf Clan, Tiyanoga knew both Iroquois and English cultures well. Tiyanoga died at the battle of Lake George in the late summer of 1755 in the initial stages of the Seven Years War, which was called the French and Indian War (1754–63) in North America. The elderly Mohawk was shot from his horse and bayoneted to death while on a scouting party on 8 September. On the same day, the colonial delegates were in the early stages of debate over the plan for the type of colonial union that Tiyanoga, the Iroquois and Franklin had advocated. Franklin's Albany Plan of Union included a Grand Council, a Speaker and called for a 'general government . . . under which . . . each colony may retain its present constitution' (Labaree 1950–62: V:387–92). The plan also included an English-style chief administrator. While representation on the Iroquois Grand Council was deter- mined by custom, the number of delegates that each colony would have had on Franklin's council was to be determined by each colony's proportional tax revenues. In 1943, after editing Franklin's Indian treaties, Julian P. Boyd stated that in 1754 Benjamin Franklin 'proposed a plan for union of the colonies and he found his materials in the great confederacy of the Iroquois'. Boyd also believed that 'the ability of the Iroquois to unite peoples over a large geographic expanse made their form of government . . . worthy of copying' (Boyd 1942–50: 239, 246).

The Boston Tea Party's 'Mohawks'

Symbols were important in the intellectual battles that accompanied the bullets of the American Revolution. The image of the Indian (particularly the Mohawk) appears at about the same time, in the same context, in revolutionary songs, slogans and engravings, always as a symbol of American freedom vis-à-vis European tyranny. The symbol is often (but not always) female, similar to the statue that was erected atop the US Capitol dome. Paul Revere, whose 'Midnight Rides' became legend in the hands of Longfellow, played a crucial role in forging this sense of identity, contributing to the revolutionary cause a set of remarkable engravings that cast as America's first national symbol an American Indian woman, long before Brother Jonathan or Uncle Sam came along.

The best-known Native American image used by the revolutionaries was the tea- dumping Mohawk. The image of the Indian was figured into tea-dumpers' disguises not only in Boston, but also in cities the length of the Atlantic seaboard. Few events of the revolutionary era have been engraved on America's popular memory like the Boston Tea Party. Nearly everyone, regardless of sophistication in matters American and revolutionary, knows that the patriots who dumped tea in Boston Harbor dressed as American Indians – Mohawks specifically. The Tea Party was a form of symbolic protest – one step beyond random violence, one step short of organised, armed rebellion. The tea dumpers chose their symbols with utmost care. As the imported tea symbolised British tyranny and taxation, so the image of the Indian, and the Mohawk disguise, represented its antithesis: a 'trademark' of an emerging American identity and a voice for liberty in a new land. The tea parties were not spur-of-the-moment pranks, but the culmination of a decade of colonial frustration with British authority. Likewise, the Mohawk symbol was not picked at random. It was used as a revolutionary symbol, counter-poised to the tea tax. While they emptied British tea into Boston Harbor, the 'Mohawks' sang:

> Rally Mohawks, and bring your axes
> And tell King George we'll pay no taxes
> on his foreign tea;
>
> His threats are vain, and vain to think
> To force our girls and wives to drink
>   his vile Bohea!
>
> Then rally, boys, and hasten on
> To meet our chiefs at the Green Dragon!
>
> Our Warren's here, and bold Revere
> With hands to do and words to cheer,
>   for liberty and laws;
>
> Our country's 'braves' and firm defenders
> shall ne'er be left by true North Enders
>   fighting freedom's cause!
>
> Then rally, boys, and hasten on
> To meet our chiefs at the Green Dragon!
>   (Goss 1972: 123–4)

The Iroquois and the Debate over Independence

As symbolic protest turned to armed rebellion against England, delegates of the Continental Congress met with Iroquois leaders at several points along the frontier to procure their alliance in the coming war for independence. At Cartwright's Tavern in German Flats, near Albany, New York on 25 August 1775, treaty commissioners met with the sachems and warriors of the Six Nations. The commissioners (acting on instructions from John Hancock and the Second Continental Congress) told the sachems that they were heeding the advice that Iroquois forefathers had given to the colonial Americans at Lancaster, Pennsylvania in 1744, as they quoted Canassatego's words:

Brethren, We the Six Nations heartily recommend Union and a good agreement between you our Brethren, never disagree but preserve a strict Friendship for one another and thereby you as well as we will become stronger. Our Wise Forefathers established Union and Amity between the Five Nations . . . We are a powerful Confederacy, and if you observe the same methods . . . you will acquire fresh strength and power. (Proceedings 1775)

After quoting Canassatego, the Americans said their forefathers had rejoiced to hear his words and that it had

sunken deep into their Hearts, the Advice was good, it was Kind. They said to one another, the Six Nations are a wise people, let us hearken to their Council and teach our children to follow it. Our old Men have done so. They have frequently taken a single Arrow and said, Children, see how easy it is broken, then they have tied twelve together with strong Cords – And our strongest Men could not break them – See said they – this is what the Six Nations mean. Divided a single Man may destroy you – United, you are a match for the whole World. (Proceedings 1775)

The delegates of the Continental Congress then thanked the 'great God that we are all united, that we have a strong Confederacy composed of twelve Provinces'. The delegates also pointed out that they have 'lighted a Great Council Fire at Philadelphia and have sent Sixty five Counselors to speak and act in the name of the whole'. The treaty commissioners also invited the Iroquois to visit and observe our 'Great Council Fire at Philadelphia' (Proceedings 1775).

Native American Political Systems and the Thoughts of Franklin, Jefferson and Paine

As Americans, and as revolutionaries who believed in the universal moral sense of all peoples, Benjamin Franklin, Thomas Jefferson and Thomas Paine bristled at suggestions that nature had dealt the New World an inferior hand. Under the guise of science, so-called degeneracy theories had gained some currency in Europe during the late eighteenth century. This particular school of pseudo-science was pressed into service as a justification for colonialism in much the same way that craniology (which linked intelligence to the volume of a race's skulls) would be a century later.

Jefferson wrote *Notes on the State of Virginia* partially to refute the assertions of the Comte de Buffon, among others, that the very soil, water and air of the New World caused plants and animals (including human beings) to grow less robustly and enjoy less sexual ardour than their Old World counterparts. The ongoing debate over the innate intelligence of American Indians also was factored into this debate. Franklin and Jefferson took the lead in countering the degeneracy theorists, maintaining that the native peoples of America enjoyed mental abilities equal to Europeans. In *Notes on Virginia*, Jefferson used the eloquent speech of Logan (delivered after whites had massacred his family) as evidence that American Indians were not lacking intelligence and compassion (Jefferson [1784] 1954). While serving as ambassador to France, Jefferson was fond of describing a dinner attended by Franklin, a few other Americans and French degeneracy theory advocates while Franklin was representing the new

United States there. Franklin listened to Abbé Raynal, a well-known proponent of American degeneracy, describe how even Europeans would be stunted by exposure to the New World. Franklin listened quietly, then simply asked the French to test their theory 'by the fact before us. Let both parties rise,' Franklin challenged, 'and we shall see on which side nature has degenerated.' The table became a metaphorical Atlantic Ocean. The Americans, on their feet, towered over the French. 'The Abbé, himself particularly, was a mere shrimp,' Jefferson smirked (Boorstin 1948: 307).

A few months before the Constitutional Convention, Jefferson wrote to James Madison about the virtues of American Indian government. 'Societies . . . as among our Indians . . . [may be] . . . best. But I believe [them] . . . inconsistent with any great degree of population' (Boyd 1942–50: XI:92–3). While Jefferson, Franklin and Paine were too pragmatic to believe that they could copy the 'natural state', ideas based on their observations of native societies were woven into the fabric of the American Revolution early, and prominently. Jefferson wrote: 'The only condition on earth to be compared with ours, in my opinion, is that of the Indian, where they have still less law than we' (Commager 1975: 119). When Paine wrote that 'government, like dress, is the badge of lost innocence' (Paine 1892: 1), and Jefferson said that the best government governs least, they were recapitulating their observations of Native American societies, either directly or through the eyes of European philosophers, such as Locke and Rousseau. Franklin used his image of Indians and their societies to critique European society:

> The Care and Labour of providing for Artificial and fashionable Wants, the sight of so many Rich wallowing in superfluous plenty, while so many are kept poor and distress'd for want; the Insolence of Office . . . [and] restraints of Custom, all contrive to disgust them [Indians] with what we call civil Society. (Labaree 1950–62: XVII:381)

As primary author of the Declaration of Independence and the Bill of Rights, Jefferson often wove his perceptions of Native American polities into his conceptions of life, liberty and happiness. Conversely, Jefferson described the class structure of Europe as hammers pounding anvils, horses mounting riders and wolves gouging sheep. As a student of government, Jefferson found little ground less fertile than the Europe of his day. The political landscape of England was, to Jefferson, full of things to change, not to emulate (Boyd 1981: 239).

Jefferson characterised the Native societies he knew in his *Notes on Virginia*. This wording was inserted into the 1787 edition as the Constitutional Convention was meeting. Native Americans, wrote Jefferson, had never

> submitted themselves to any laws, any coercive power and shadow of government. Their only controls are their manners, and the moral sense of right and wrong . . . An offence against these is punished by contempt, by exclusion from society, or, where the cause is serious, as that of murder, by the individuals whom it concerns. Imperfect as this species of control may seem, crimes are very rare among them. (Jefferson [1784] 1954: 93)

The lesson here seemed clear to Jefferson: 'Insomuch that it were made a question, whether no law, as among the savage Americans, or too much law, as among the civilised Europeans, submits man to the greater evil, one who has seen both conditions of existence would pronounce it to be the last' (Ford 1892–9: III:195). Writing to Edward Carrington during 1787, Jefferson associated freedom of expression with happiness, citing American Indian societies as an example:

> The basis of our government being the opinion of the people, our very first object should be to keep that right; and were it left to me to decide whether we should have a government without newspapers or newspapers without a government, I should not hesitate for a moment to prefer the latter . . . I am convinced that those societies [of the Indians] which live without government enjoy in their general mass an infinitely greater degree of happiness than those who live under European governments. (Boyd 1942–50: XI:49)

To Jefferson, 'Without government' could not have meant without social order. He, Franklin and Paine all knew Native American societies too well to argue that their members functioned without social cohesion, in the classic Noble Savage image, as autonomous wild men of the woods. It was clear that the Iroquois, for example, did not organise a confederacy with alliances spreading over much of northeastern North America without government. They did it, however, with a non-European conception of government, one of which Jefferson, Paine and Franklin were appreciative students who sought to factor natural law and natural rights into their designs for the United States during the revolutionary era (Johansen 1982: 35–9). Franklin's Articles of Confederation (1775) resembled the political structure of the Iroquois and other native nations that bordered the thirteen colonies. This resemblance included the language Franklin used when he called the proposed confederacy 'a firm league of friendship'. The new states retained powers similar to those of the individual tribes and nations within many native confederacies: local problems were to be solved by the local unit of government best suited to their nature, size and scope; while national problems, such as diplomacy and defence, were to be handled by the national government.

Discussion of Native Governance in John Adams' Defence of the Constitutions

Sensing the need for an analysis of American and world governments, John Adams wrote his *Defence of the Constitutions . . . of the United States* in 1786 and published it in 1787 on the eve of the Constitutional Convention (J. Adams 1787). The *Defence* has been called 'the finest fruit of the American Enlightenment' (Wood 1969: 568). Adams saw two conflicting views on the nature of government in America on the eve of the Constitutional Convention. He recognised in Franklin's admonitions of a unicameral legislature (as in the Pennsylvania Constitution of 1776) a sense of serenity of character, since the Pennsylvania Constitution placed a great deal of faith in one house as the best way to express the will of the people. However, Adams believed in balancing the interests of the aristocracy and the common people through two houses.

The *Defence*, which was used extensively at the Constitutional Convention, examined the strengths and weaknesses of ancient and modern forms of government, including an analysis of American Indian traditions. Rather than having faith, as Franklin did, in the voice of the people, Adams was more pessimistic about human nature and all orders of society in his *Defence*. He believed that the separation of powers in government was crucial to maintain a republic. Adams remarked that in Native American governments the 'real sovereignty resided in the body of the people'. Adams also observed that personal liberty was so important to the Mohawks that in their society they have 'complete individual independence' (C. F. Adams 1851: IV:511).

Adams' *Defence* was not an unabashed endorsement of Native American models for government. Instead, Adams was refuting the arguments of Franklin, who advocated a one-house legislature resembling the Iroquois Grand Council that had been used in the Albany Plan and Articles of Confederation. Adams did not trust the consensus model that seemed to work for the Iroquois. He believed that without the checks and balances built into two houses, the system would succumb to special interests and dissolve into anarchy or despotism. When Adams described the Mohawks' independence he exercised criticism, while Franklin wrote about Indian governments in a much more benign way. Adams sought to erect checks on the caprice of the unthinking heart. Thus, he cited the Iroquois Grand Council (the fifty families) as a negative example, ignoring the fact (as Franklin had written to his printing partner James Parker in 1751) that it 'has subsisted for ages' (Smyth 1905–7: III:42). Franklin was more of a utopian: he still sought a government based upon the best in human nature, calling its citizens to rise to it. He did not fear unrestrained freedom as did Adams. These two poles of opinion have been present in US politics ever since.

Conclusion

Having migrated from societies based on hierarchy, early European explorers came to America seeking kings, queens and princes. Quickly, they began to sense a difference: native leaders had few trappings that distinguished them from the people. In most native societies they only rarely sat at the top of a class hierarchy with the pomp of European rulers. More importantly, Indian 'kings' usually did not rule. Rather, they led, by mechanisms of consensus and public opinion that Europeans often found admirable. During the 170 years between the first enduring English settlement in North America and the American Revolution, the colonists' perceptions of their native neighbours evolved from the Puritans' devil-man, through the autonomous Noble Savage, to a belief that the native peoples lived in confederations governed by natural law so subtle, so nearly invisible, that it was widely believed to be an attractive alternative to monarchy's overbearing hand.

The Europeans' perceptions of Indian societies evolved as they became more dissatisfied with the European *status quo*. Increasingly, the native societies came to serve the transplanted Europeans, including some of the United States' most influential founders, as a counter-point to the European order. They found in existing native polities the values that the seminal European documents of the time celebrated in theoretical abstraction: life, liberty, happiness, a model of government by consensus, under natural rights, with relative equality of property. The fact that native peoples in America were able to govern themselves in this way provided advocates of alternatives to monarchy with practical ammunition for a philosophy of government based on the rights of the individual, which they believed had worked, did work and would work for them in America.

This is not so say that the United States' founders sought to replicate native polities among societies descended from Europe. The new Americans were too practical to believe that a society steeped in European cultural traditions could be turned on its head so swiftly and easily. They chose instead to borrow, to shape what they had with what they saw before them, to create a new order that included aspects of both worlds.

References

Adams, C. F. (ed.) (1851), *Works of John Adams*, Boston, MA: Little Brown.

Adams, J. (1787), *Defence of the Constitutions . . . of the United States*, Philadelphia, PA: Hall & Sellers.

Boorstin, D. J. (1948), *The Lost World of Thomas Jefferson*, New York: Henry Holt.

Boyd, J. P. (ed.) (1942–50), *The Papers of Thomas Jefferson*, Princeton, NJ, Princeton: University Press.

Boyd, J. P. (1981), 'Dr. Franklin, Friend of the Indian', in R. Lokken, Jr (ed.), *Meet Dr. Franklin*, Philadelphia, PA: Franklin Institute, pp. 239–45.

Colden, C. ([1727, 1747] 1958), *The History of the Five Nations Depending on the Province of New York in America*, Ithaca, NY: Cornell University Press.

Commager, H. S. (1975), *Jefferson, Nationalism and the Enlightenment*, New York: George Braziller.

Crèvecoeur, H. S. J. de ([1801, in French] 1964), *Journey into Northern Pennsylvania and the State of New York*, Ann Arbor, MI: University of Michigan Press.

Doren, C. van and J. P. Boyd (eds) (1938), *Indian Treaties Printed by Benjamin Franklin 1736– 1762*, Philadelphia, PA: Historical Society of Pennsylvania.

Ford, P. L. (ed.) (1892–9), *The Writings of Thomas Jefferson*, New York: J. P. Putnam.

Goss, E. H. (1972), *The Life of Colonel Paul Revere*, Boston, MA: G. K. Hall/Gregg Press.

Grinde, D. A., Jr and B. E. Johansen (1991), *Exemplar of Liberty: Native America and the Evolution of Democracy*, Los Angeles, CA: UCLA American Indian Studies Center.

Jefferson, T. ([1784] 1954), *Notes on the State of Virginia*, ed. William Peden, Chapel Hill, NC: University of North Carolina Press.

Johansen, B. E. (1982), *Forgotten Founders: Benjamin Franklin, the Iroquois, and the Rationale for the American Revolution*, Ipswich: Gambit.

Labaree, L. W. (ed.) (1950–62), *The Papers of Benjamin Franklin*, New Haven, CT: Yale University Press.

Paine, T. (1892), *The Political Writings of Thomas Paine*, New York: Peter Eckler.

Proceedings of the Commissioners appointed by the Continental Congress to Negotiate a Treaty with the Six Nations (1775), *Papers of the Continental Congress*, 1774–89, National Archives, MS 247, Roll 144, No. 134. See: 'Treaty Council at German Flats, New York, August 15, 1775', u.p.

Smyth, A. H. (ed.) (1905–7), *The Writings of Benjamin Franklin*, 10 vols, New York: Macmillan.

Weatherford, J. (1988), *Indian Givers: How the Indians of the Americas Transformed the World*, New York: Fawcett Columbine.

Weatherford, J. (1991), *Native Roots: How the Indians Enriched America*, New York: Fawcett Columbine.

Wood, G. S. (1969), *The Creation of the American Republic*, Chapel Hill, NC: University of North Carolina Press.

Chapter 20

Australasia

Tim Rowse

'Australasia' refers to Australia and New Zealand, two liberal-democratic nation-states arising from British colonisation – beginning in 1788 – of peoples that we now call Aborigines, Torres Strait Islanders and Maori. With Britain's blessing, by the early twentieth century, the colonists of Australasia had replicated Westminster's democratic model. However, the two dominions approached differently the enfranchising of Indigenous people. After the Second World War, the United Nations (UN) entrusted the Australasian democracies to establish democratic institutions in Pacific colonies. 'Democracy' was among their colonising projects.

Settler-Colonial Democracy

The British began to create civil institutions in the penal colonies of eastern Australia in the 1820s. As of March 1829, the New South Wales Legislative Council consisted of seven official and seven non-official members, nominated by the Crown. Events in Britain and Canada over the next ten years raised the issue of whether such colonial councils should be, at least in part, elected. In composition and purpose New South Wales was then changing from a penal colony to a colony of free settlement. 'Exclusives' (who had never been convicts) mingled with 'emancipists' (former convicts and their descendants) and an increasing flow of free settlers seeking land and fortune. Exclusives, emancipists and free settlers debated, from the early 1830s to the early 1850s, how to apportion colonising authority between the Crown (its servant, the Governor), officials, the propertied elites (whether or not of convict origins) and those (convict-descended or free immigrant) who lived by selling their labour. Their underlying common interest was to combine capital, land and labour prosperously. To this end, all colonists relied on the Crown's continuing conversion of Aboriginal land into either public or private estate. They thus urged Britain to devolve to colonial legislatures the power to make laws regulating the sale and settlement of land. For a labour supply, neither convicts nor Aborigines would suffice. Continuing convict inflow – though still welcome to a conservative faction of landed capital – would compromise the replication of a British social order, and thus delay the grant of responsible government. Aborigines, in number, skills and disposition, would never satisfy the labour demands of the emerging capitalist class. Free immigration was to be financed, in part, by selling land taken from increasingly mendicant Aborigines.

A fractious alliance among colonists over the securing of land framed debate on 'responsible government' in the 1840s. Some hoped for an oligarchy of landowners and senior officials in dialogue with the Crown's appointed governor, while more radical immigrants from Britain drew on the Chartist movement demands: universal manhood suffrage; equal electoral districts; vote by ballot; annually elected Parliaments; and the abolition of property qualifications for MPs. No one then thought of Aborigines as practitioners of democracy; they seemed, frustratingly, to lack any arts of government. Though the British encouraged some cooperative individuals to be 'kings', an Aboriginal polity was barely discernible to early observers (Troy 1993). Subsequent study characterised Aboriginal society as mobile (within a territory) and loosely bounded small groups without legislature or judiciary, high degrees of individual autonomy, leadership according to manipulable combinations of age, birth order, gender and individual initiative (that combined physical and metaphysical forces) – with a tendency to male gerontocracy qualified by substantial female homosociality (Keen 2004: 243–72).

The Australian colonies enfranchised settlers in several steps. Propertied men (restricted male suffrage) got the vote in Tasmania in 1854, New South Wales and Victoria in 1855, South Australia in 1856, Queensland in 1859, and Western Australia in 1890. Universal male suffrage began in South Australia in 1856, Victoria in 1857, New South Wales in 1858, Western Australia in 1893, Tasmania in 1900 and Queensland in 1905. Female suffrage was conceded in 1894 in South Australia, 1899 in Western Australia, 1902 in New South Wales, 1903 in Tasmania, 1905 in Queensland and 1908 in Victoria. The ballot became secret and then, about two to three generations later, compulsory in 1858 and 1928 in New South Wales and Tasmania, 1857 and 1926 in Victoria, 1856 and 1942 in South Australia, 1859 and 1915 in Queensland and 1877 and 1936 in Western Australia.

When the colonial elites began, in the 1880s, to discuss federation, they viewed Aborigines as doomed to extinction either physically (as a distinct race no longer reproducing itself in the purity of its descent) or culturally (the hunter-gatherer way of life rapidly giving way to impoverished fringe-dwelling). However, colonial judges had since 1836 deemed Aborigines to be British subjects, and humanitarians believed that native peoples could be preserved physically and uplifted culturally. Thus, four colonies did not prohibit Aborigines from voting (as they had prohibited women). They had merely neglected – with few exceptions – to enrol them. In two colonies, Aborigines were excluded by law from voting. Queensland – a self-governing colony from 1859 – passed laws in 1872, 1874 and 1885 that allowed 'Aboriginal natives' the vote only if they met very unlikely property qualifications. Western Australia, awarded self-government in 1890, legislated Queensland's 'property' hurdle for Aborigines in 1893. Thus, when the new (1901) Australian government considered the machinery of democracy in 1902, Aborigines could be excluded in two ways from the franchise: legislative proscription and administrative neglect.

However, there were some Aboriginal voters. In the 1896 South Australian election, Point McLeay Mission – where Ngarrindjeri people had converted to Christianity and to agriculture – had a polling station. These exceptional few became voters in the Commonwealth in 1902, because their situation was analogous to that of women.

Section 41 the Australian Constitution stated that a person could not be excluded from the Commonwealth franchise if they had been voting, in any of the six colonies, before Federation. Though devised as a concession to women – enfranchised in South Australia in 1896 and Western Australia in 1899 – section 41 had the incidental effect of enfranchising the few Aborigines who had become voters in colonial elections. As those fortunate individuals died out, the anomalous category – Aboriginal voter – would cease to exist (Goot 2006: 522–5; Stretton and Finnimore 1993). The Commonwealth, after taking over the Northern Territory in 1911, excluded Aboriginal people from the vote from 1922.

In the years from 1893 to 1908, Australasian men conceded women the vote (New Zealanders did so in 1893) in response to arguments that women, like men, were subject to the law and should therefore help to make the law; some laws were especially about women; parliaments elected by men were unrepresentative of 'the people'; female enfranchisement was neutral in respect to party and sect; 'the votes of women would add power and weight to the more settled communities'; women's sense of responsibility would deepen if they could vote; 'public spirited mothers make public spirited sons' (Chesterman and Galligan 1999: 91). That women – as mothers – were a moralising influence on the nation was then a prominent theme (Mein-Smith 2005: 103). These grounds were thought not to apply to Aborigines. In 1902, Senator Matheson contrasted the nobility of the recently enfranchised Australian woman with the 'horrible, degraded, dirty creature' whose right to vote must now be denied (Matheson, cited in Chesterman and Galligan 1999: 95). In a few remote electorates in Western Australia and Queensland, some fearful Commonwealth MPs pointed out, Aborigines still outnumbered whites (Chesterman and Galligan 1999: 95–6). Thus, the Commonwealth Franchise Act of 1902 excluded those described as 'aboriginal native of Australia, Asia, Africa or the islands of the Pacific, except New Zealand'.

Maori Franchise

That Australia allowed 'natives of . . . New Zealand' but not (generally speaking) Aborigines to vote in 1902 requires explanation. Australia and New Zealand were of the British Empire, and Australian legislators were obliged to respect the terms by which New Zealand then enfranchised Maori subjects of the Crown. The colonial doctrine of humanitarian duty to civilise the native had been more influential in New Zealand. Maori showed three promising characteristics: their polity was clearly hierarchical (chiefs, commoners and slaves); many of their rangatira (chiefs) were entrepreneurial (willing to trade goods and labour, and to sell land to the Crown, as envisaged in the 1840 Treaty of Waitangi); and many Maori had been converting to Christianity since the 1810s. It was thus plausible for colonists to hope for the rapid acculturation of Maori – in particular, the recession of customary collective land ownership in favour of individuated proprietary interest. Encouraged by signs of Maori transformation, Governor George Grey advised, and the Colonial Office agreed in 1848, to delay implementing the New Zealand Constitution until 1853, in the hope that more Maori would by then have become men of property and thus have qualified for the restricted male franchise. Grey feared that race relations would degenerate if the electorate consisted of no more than a self-interested non-Maori minority that was likely to use its new legislative power to abridge or terminate colonists' treaty obligations to Maori.

When the New Zealand Constitution came into effect in 1856, the colonists got a House of Representatives elected by males over twenty-one who satisfied modest criteria of 'propertied' and a Crown-appointed Legislative Council. However, Maori were neither selling nor acculturating as rapidly as colonial optimists had hoped. The British government, noting that the racial composition of New Zealand suffrage was almost entirely non-Maori, reserved native policy to the governor, directed by the Colonial Office. A legal opinion in 1859 confirmed that Maori men, as long as they persisted in communal tenure, did not fulfil the 'property' qualification to vote. Meanwhile, the colonists had begun to surpass the Maori in number. Antagonised by pressures to sell, some Maori campaigned against land sales. Thus, rapid immigration, slow Maori land sales and slow Maori acculturation combined to militate against the kind of democracy that would, arguably, have obliged the treaty as then understood: an electorate of propertied men, in which both Maori and non-Maori were numerous. That the governor controlled Maori land sales and legislation specific to Maori frustrated colonists' aspirations. In 1859, the legislature passed an Act to allow direct land dealing between Maori and colonist. The British government disallowed this law, as violating the treaty. Nonetheless, London transferred Maori affairs to New Zealand in 1861. The Native Land Act of 1862 provided that Maori could individualise their title through the Native Land Court, and then sell land direct to settlers.

By then, the British New Zealanders (aided by some Maori tribes) had begun to fight a series of regional wars against those Maori who were alarmed by British ascendancy. Conquering recalcitrant Maori (1860–72) took more effort than the British expected. As a gesture of conciliation towards a people who were all too slowly acquiring 'property' (by individualising their tenures) and thus the vote, in 1867 the New Zealand government set aside four seats in parliament that could be elected only by Maori voters exempted from the property qualification. That is, by 1867, the contest of arms and cultural resistance had combined to extract from the pragmatic New Zealand settlers the inclusion of adult Maori males without 'property' (including 'half-castes') in democracy. The Maori Representation Act of 1867 was promoted as a short-lived healing gesture, until Maori qualified for the common roll by individualising their land titles.

By the time the Commonwealth of Australia defined its electorate in 1902 – enfranchising Maori but excluding Aborigines – New Zealand's expedient inclusive measure was entrenched. For several years there had been an anomaly: the non-Maori franchise (propertied males) had been more restricted than the Maori. However, this disparity of democratic right had been reduced in 1875 when all male rate-payers were enfranchised. In 1876, with the Maori still slow to become 'propertied', the four Maori seats and a Maori electorate had been made permanent, and the 'property' distinction between Maori and non-Maori franchise disappeared altogether in 1879 when all non-Maori males qualified to vote by mere residence. Finally, as we have seen, women in New Zealand got the same voting rights as men in 1893, and this applied in both Maori and non-Maori electorates. By the time (1894–1908) Australian parliaments were getting around to universal (as long as you were not 'aboriginal') suffrage, the 'natives' in New Zealand – both men and women – were already voters and legislators.

The Aboriginal Voter

As Aborigines became literate in English, learned more about the wider British world and claimed membership of it as 'civilised', the political rights of the Maori impressed them. In the 1930s, Yorta Yorta activist William Cooper demanded Aboriginal representation in parliament, 'until the time that there is no aboriginal problem . . . on the same footing as the Maoris' (whose greater 'militancy' he acknowledged) (Attwood and Markus 2004: 35, 60, 67, 81). However, Australian attitudes and policies were slow to change. Making explicit in law what other jurisdictions achieved by neglect, Queensland in 1905 and 1915 forbade 'Aboriginal natives' from voting except under a property qualification that they were very unlikely to meet; in 1930, the law was amended so that Torres Strait Islanders and half-castes also were excluded. In 1965, Queensland allowed Aborigines and Torres Strait Islanders to vote, but exempted them from compulsory enrolment and made it an offence to influence their decision about enrolment.

By that time, in renewal of the duty to 'civilise', Australia had embraced a policy of 'assimilation' designed, among other things, to train Aborigines for citizenship and to phase out legal restrictions on its practice. In 1961, a Select Committee of the Commonwealth Parliament asked whether some or all 'Aboriginal natives' should be allowed to vote in Commonwealth elections. Since 1949, Aborigines had been so entitled if they voted in state elections or if they had served in the defence forces. Aborigines classified as 'half-caste' (legally distinguished from the Constitution's 'aboriginal natives') were beyond laws abridging Aborigines' citizenship. The Committee urged administrative outreach to such Aborigines who were unaware of their right to vote and it recommended legal amendment to extend that right to all other Aborigines. The Commonwealth legislated in 1962 that all adult Aborigines could vote in Commonwealth elections.

However, in 1962, it was realistic to exempt Aborigines from compulsory voting that applied to other citizens. Some Aborigines had only recently begun to abandon their traditional way of life and perhaps 2,000 – an official (over)estimate – were thought still to be living in their traditional way in the remote desert. In 1979, the Commonwealth initiated an Aboriginal voter education programme, and in 1984 made their voting compulsory. From 1973, Australia has also experimented fitfully with a distinct Indigenous voter entitlement to elect advisory bodies (the National Aboriginal Consultative Committee 1973–1976, the National Aboriginal Conference 1977–1985) and a statutory authority with limited executive powers (the Aboriginal and Torres Strait Islander Commission 1989–2005). Though campaigns for an Australian 'treaty' have demanded parliamentary seats elected by Indigenous voters, no Australian parliament has seriously considered legislation.

The Samoan Situation

Australia's inclusion of Aborigines in its democracy coincided with Australasia's export of a Westminster version of democracy to the southwest Pacific between 1960 and 1975. Both New Zealand and Australia had been mandated by the League of Nations in 1920 to administer, in the interests of the natives, Western Samoa and New Guinea, respectively. Their C-class Mandates did not oblige them to prepare the native peoples for self-government. Nonetheless, after instituting a civil administration in 1922, New Zealand had to consider the articulate wishes of Samoans because the previous German colonial authority (1899–1914) had made concessions to Samoan forms of political authority, including an assembly (*fono*) made up of *faipule* (locally nominated district spokespersons) in 1905 and a *fautua* (two high-born advisers) in 1913. The New Zealand Administration legally recognised the *fono* in 1923, seeking its advice on 'Samoan' matters, while an appointed Legislative Council advised on 'European' matters. However, from 1926, a native political movement (called Mau, or 'opinion') with its own newspaper challenged New Zealand authority, including the policy of assuming that the *fono* of *faipule* (then appointed by the administrator) was the only authentic forum of Samoan opinion. The Samoans were beginning to produce leaders who were hybrid in both descent and outlook. Through the Mau they not only voiced, but also enacted models of customary authority, and they expected the New Zealand administrators to learn from and adapt to them. New Zealand suppressed the Mau from 1927, claiming to act for true Samoans.

How Polynesian traditions might adapt to meet the demands of a modern government and economy had been a topic for Maori thought since 1840. The Maori-elected MP, Apirana Ngata, drew in 1929 on his personal experience of 'the best example of success in the government of a Native race not only in the Pacific, but perhaps in the world' (Ngata 1929: 32). Ngata saw in Samoa an opportunity for an alliance between native modernisers – educated in the colonists' schools – and colonists who had studied the 'native mind'. Together, through education and public policy, natives and colonists would undermine only those customs that held native peoples back from health and prosperity. When the New Zealand Administration was in initial recoil from Mau assertiveness, Ngata commented that officials had not yet realised how resilient were Samoan customs of land tenure and chiefly authority (Ngata 1929: 44). In 1938, one observer presented the New Zealand Administration as acting upon a latent Samoan popular mandate to prevent usurpation by 'the existing feudalistic privileges of the chiefs and orator-class on the one hand, and . . . the big trading companies and the mission stations on the other'. What features of Samoan tradition was such a custodian to undermine and what to encourage, this observer wondered (NZIIA 1938: 214). By then, New Zealand had ceased to suppress the Mau, and its reforms of the legislature, judiciary and public service tended to confirm and enable Mau influence (Davidson 1967: 147–8).

In 1946, New Zealand negotiated a trusteeship agreement with Britain, Australia, the Unites States and France and submitted it to the UN. Samoan leaders accepted that they must persist with New Zealand, while demanding self-government. In August 1947, New Zealand designed a new structure intended to concede much to

Samoan political tradition: a Council of State (consisting of the New Zealand High Commissioner and three *fautua*) and a legislature with absolute Samoan majority, with powers over finance, whose decisions the High Commissioner could still veto. European members of the Legislative Council had been elected by secret ballot and universal suffrage since 1938, but in a concession to Samoan respect for customary governance at the local level (Davidson 1967: 262) the *fono* would collaborate with the *fautua* to select the eleven Samoan members. In Prime Minister Peter Fraser's view, 'there was no use in implanting the most democratic constitution in Samoa if the Samoan did not want it, and if their social ideas would make its functioning completely impossible' (quoted in Boyd 1969: 196).

The UN urged further discussion of the institutions of Samoan self-determination; in 1953 a UN delegation called for a constitutional convention, which met in 1954. New Zealand mapped out a sequence of steps to responsible government: a reconstituted Executive Council in 1956, a cabinet and premier by 1960.

In constituting Samoa as a democracy, the most contentious issue was whether to extend universal suffrage to Samoan voters or to continue to restrict the vote to *matai* (titled head of a land-holding family). Both the *fono* of *faipule* and the Legislative Assembly affirmed the *matai* franchise in 1953 (Boyd 1969: 225, 1956). A Working Committee on the constitution, responsible to the Administrator, reinforced this view in 1954: only *matai* could vote and be candidates, voting for *matai* need not be secret and there should not be a common Samoan and European electoral roll (Boyd 1969: 227). The Constitutional Convention in 1954 supported *matai* franchise, though a significant minority of Samoan members of the Convention argued for universal suffrage (Davidson 1967: 328). 'For Samoans [differentiated franchise] was an effective means of restricting the access of Europeans to their land and titles, for local Europeans it was a safeguard of separate political representation based on adult suffrage' (Boyd 1969: 228). The constitutional convention that sat from August to October 1960 was reluctant to re-open the question of universal suffrage, though it was 'uneasy that this attitude might unfavourably impress the United Nations and hinder independence' (Boyd 1969: 265). In the draft Constitution of 1960, the two electoral rolls were no longer racially distinguished, so as not to compromise the ideal of a single Samoan community (Davidson 1967: 375–7), but Samoa nonetheless became independent with *matai* franchise.

The nations on the UN Trusteeship Council sought reassurance that Samoans wanted democracy in this (to them imperfect) form. A plebiscite, in May 1961, would test popular support for a constitution designed by bodies (Legislative Assembly and Constitutional Convention) that had not been elected by universal franchise. Those favouring universal franchise restrained themselves: a vote against the proposed constitution would defer independence (Davidson 1967: 405). Eight out of ten voters endorsed the constitution, and Samoa became an independent nation in 1962. The continuing tension between adherence to the customary authority of the *matai* and the desire to embrace universal franchise was felt in the opening up of *matai* status. After independence, the creation of *matai* titles became 'a feature of every election year . . . mainly . . . by splitting existing ones or creating new ones' (Lafoa'i 1991: 71). The resulting weakening of *matai* status – as some Samoans saw it

– became a ground to re-argue the case for universal franchise. The constitution had left suffrage open to legislative reform. In 1990, a parliament dominated by the Human Rights Protection Party conducted a referendum that showed a slight majority in favour of universal suffrage. As many conservative voters abstained from the referendum, its mandate was debatable. To some, the referendum and consequent legislation of universal suffrage shamefully installed 'the rule of the majority, regardless of rank and status'. Effectively, universal suffrage also enfranchised women, as few women had been *matai*; and it assured the secrecy of an individual's vote (Lafoa'i 1991: 70–3). To one female authority on Samoan culture, critical of universal suffrage, the *matai* franchise had been 'a perfect and logical manifestation of the will of the people' (Tagaloa 1992: 131). The referendum had not been 'decisive', she argued, and universal franchise gave 'the young and uninitiated the august task of steering the ship of state' (Tagaloa 1992: 130–1).

Papua New Guinea

Like Samoa, Papua New Guinea was not a colony of settlement for Australia, and it was central to Australian policy that Papua New Guineans retained control of their land, albeit with strong encouragement to convert customary to formal legal title. In the eyes of the anti-colonial UN, however, Australia's respect for indigenous property rights should be matched by zealous cultivation of Papua New Guinean capacity for self-rule. Warfare between local groups had been characteristic of the native polity. In suppressing conflict (a project still beginning in the 1960s, in remoter regions), Australian rule erected unprecedented forms of unelected local authority. The UN urged the formation of national representative bodies, similarly unprecedented.

In programming Papua New Guinea's transition to Westminster democracy, Australia's steps exemplified the emergent, post-Imperial, applied political science that Schaffer outlined in 1965. His model of British 'preparation' serves as a narrative template for the milestones in Papua New Guinea's transition to democratic self-government:

> The first [stage] consists of a division of legislative and executive councils and a nomination of unofficial members to the legislative council, leading to election of some unofficial members . . . [achieved by 1951, but only European non-officials elected to the Legislative Council]. In the second or 'representative' stage, the unofficial members are a majority . . . [achieved in 1961, Papuans and New Guineans among those elected to the Legislative Council, with further increases in the non-official majority in the House of Assembly (successor to the Council) in 1964, 1968 and 1972]. This creates problems in the relation between the legislative and the executive councils [this tension had emerged by the mid-1950s]. The third semi-responsible stage ensues when the majority of the executive council comes from or is related to the majority of the legislative council . . . [ten Papuan–New Guineas members of the 1964 House of Assembly were appointed 'Under-Secretaries' – effectively Ministers-in-training – who were expected to support Administration policy]. In the fourth stage, nominated officials disappear from the

legislative council . . . [the 1972 House of Assembly was the last to include official members (4 out of 107 members)]. This may be self-government, full self-government, independence; but perhaps a fifth stage should be distinguished to demarcate the actual transfer of power from the preparatory process [Papua New Guinea became self-governing in December 1973 and fully independent of Australia in September 1975]. (Schaffer 1965: 47–8)

In this sequence, the initiative lay with Australia, as it mediated between different views on the pace of transition. While several times in the 1960s the UN queried the slowness of Australia's preparatory work, many Papuan New Guineans – especially those more recently subject to colonial administration – feared that self-government entailed the end of Australia's benefits. A study of the 1968 House of Assembly election found widespread apprehension that:

The continuance of Australian financial and technical support is endangered by any move towards indigenous political autonomy, especially home rule or independence. Papua and New Guinea need Australian support as long as possible. Hence Papuans and New Guineans must reject those who advocate moves towards home rule or independence, or who otherwise radically oppose Australian policies. (Parker and Wolfers 1971: 19)

The Australian Labor Party, aligned with UN criticism of Australia while in opposition (1949–72), hastened political development after gaining power, reaching out to elements in Papua New Guinea's emerging political elite. However, House of Assembly Members on the Constitutional Planning Committee (formed against the advice of the Australian government in June 1972) felt hurried by Australia in the period 1972–4; members warned Australia not to pre-empt the Committee's popular consultations by imposing a constitutional design. Australia's allies in this accelerated progress to political independence narrowly escaped the House of Assembly's censure. The contentious constitutional issues in 1974 were the qualifications for citizenship, the head of state and – tragically – the relationship between provincial and central governments. It took a war (1989–2001) costing perhaps 15,000 lives before the mineral-rich province of Bougainville could re-negotiate its place within the polity bestowed by Australia in 1975.

Universal suffrage, introduced in 1964, was not in dispute in Papua New Guinea's truncated constitutional debate, unlike Samoa in the 1950s. However, a common feature of the two polities' democratic evolution has been that each, after almost twenty years of independence, sought to change by legislation a vital feature of its democratic process. In Samoa, it was the shift from *matai* to universal suffrage in 1991; in Papua New Guinea, it was the 'Integrity Law' of 2001, specifying grounds on which an MP could desert a party. This law sought not only to curb MPs' corruption, but also to shore up a party system – a central feature of the Westminster model as it had evolved in Britain in the 1840s and flowered in Australia and New Zealand in the 1890s. The Australian government had been wary of parties in Papua New Guinea in the 1960s, considering them – against UN advice – to be premature (Parker and

Wolfers 1971: 30). Much training in government in the 1950s had focused on village councils in which party played no role; those welcoming slow, gradual development by Australia had been bemused by the precocity and irrelevance, as they saw it, of the urban, educated elite's facility for party formation. Since 1975, party loyalties have been fragile among the political elite. Electorates expect members to access resources available to MPs who support the government coalition, and little value is attached to being in opposition. Policy debates are not clashes between stable, party-based ideological frameworks. Much of government MPs' effort is devoted not to government, but to retaining – by honest or other means – the support of individual MPs. Since the first post-independence election in 1977, there have been twelve governments and seven elections. Okole refers to 'the overlay of democracy on Melanesian politics', but his explanation of the character of Papua New Guinea democracy is less 'cultural' than this phrase suggests. He points to poverty, high material aspirations, the disincentives of poor governance to private investment and the resulting competition for resources mediated by the state, making 'politics . . . the only game left in town' (Okole 2005: 201).

The 2001 Organic Law on the Integrity of Political Parties and Candidates was intended to defend governing coalitions against opportunistic no-confidence motions. The Somare government in 2004, nonetheless, found it necessary to adjourn parliament for many months. Recent interactions between the two nations has confirmed that Australian aid – in finance and in skilled governmental personnel – remains conditional and largely determines the viability of this independent nation. Also, because of the faltering commitment, skill and honesty of the New Guinea political elite in the last thirty years, 'Australians hold key posts in the economy, the bureaucracy and the uniformed armed forces' (Denoon 2005: 190).

Conclusion

The four indigenous political cultures mentioned here differed enormously in their customs of combining hierarchy with accountability. Each of them has been presented with a model of democracy derived from the North Atlantic (largely from Britain) and spurred by UN advocacy. British settler colonists have been the primary agents of this diffusion. From 1838, Chartists had demanded universal manhood suffrage, equal electoral districts, vote by ballot, annually elected parliaments and the abolition of property qualifications for MPs. While that programme was being fulfilled and (with feminist agitation) extended, humanitarian colonists envisaged that native peoples would eventually be 'civilised' to exercise the rights enjoyed by all Britons. Australasia's settler colonial elites found themselves under two waves of external scrutiny as bringers of 'civilisation'. In the nineteenth century, Britain was quick to devolve to colonial elites responsibility for decisions about the extension of the franchise – to un-propertied male colonists, to women and to native peoples. In the twentieth century, the League of Nations and the United Nations exercised oversight of the Australasian democracies' inculcation of the norms and procedures of 'democracy', as they understood it, into Melanesian and Polynesian peoples. In the period of heroic decolonisation (c. 1945–75), a sense of post-Imperial urgency exacerbated and dramatised the contradiction within the global project of democratic self-determination: prescribing procedures of self-determination and notions of individual and collective 'self' that are novel and (at least at first) alien to those destined to use them.

A 1992 vignette from Papua New Guinea illustrates the cultural challenge of 'democracy'. Tony Deklin reports about 'a wife who received a black eye from her husband after she voted for a candidate she fancied rather than the one for whom her husband wanted her to vote'. Deklin contrasts this couple with another: the 'smart' wife, emerging from the booth, responds to her husband that she had voted for his favourite, 'though she had actually voted for a different candidate of her own choice! In the first case, the wife was politically unsophisticated whereas the opposite was the case with the second. Level of education plays a large part in engendering sophistication' (Deklin 1992: 42). The ballot's secrecy – a radical working-class demand in the nineteenth century, propagated by liberals in the twentieth – enables the 'smart wife' to deceive her husband. In both Samoa and Papua New Guinea, Westminster democracy has been a cultural shock, to which these Pacific peoples are still, more or less peacefully, accustoming themselves.

References

Attwood, B. and A. Markus (2004), *Thinking Black: William Cooper and the Australian Aborigines League*, Canberra: Australian Institute of Aboriginal and Torres Strait Islander Studies.

Boyd, M. (1956), 'Political Development in Western Samoa and Universal Suffrage', *Political Science*, 8(1), 44–69.

Boyd, M. (1969), 'The Record in Western Samoa since 1945', in A. Ross (ed.), *New Zealand's Record in the Pacific Islands in the Twentieth Century*, London: Longman Paul for the New Zealand Institute of International Affairs, pp. 189–271.

Chesterman, J. and B. Galligan (1999), *Defining Australian Citizenship: Selected Documents*, Carlton: Melbourne University Press.

Davidson, J. W. (1967), *Samoa mo Samoa*, Melbourne: Oxford University Press.

Deklin, T. (1992), 'Culture and Democracy in Papua New Guinea: Marit Tru or Giaman Marit?', in R. Crocombe, U. Neemia, A. R. von Busch and W. von Busch (eds), *Culture and Democracy in the South Pacific*, Suva: Institute of Pacific Studies, University of the South Pacific, pp. 35–48.

Denoon, D. (2005), *Trial Separation: Australia and the Decolonisation of Papua New Guinea*, Canberra: Pandanus Books.

Goot, M. (2006), 'The Aboriginal Franchise and its Consequences', *Australian Journal of Politics and History*, 52(4), 517–61.

Keen, I. (2004), *Aboriginal Economy and Society*, Melbourne: Oxford University Press.

Lafoa'i, I. (1991), 'Universal Suffrage in Western Samoa: A Political Review', *Journal of Pacific History*, 26(3), 67–73.

Mein-Smith, P. (2005), *A Concise History of New Zealand*, Port Melbourne: Cambridge University Press.

New Zealand Institute of International Affairs (NZIIA) (1938), *Contemporary New Zealand: A Survey of Domestic and Foreign Policy*, Preparatory Paper for the Second British Commonwealth Relations Conference, Sydney, Wellington.

Ngata, A. T. (1929), 'Anthropology and the Government of Native Races in the Pacific', in Institute of Pacific Relations *New Zealand Affairs*, Christchurch: L. M. Isitt, pp. 22–44.

Okole, H. (2005), 'Papua New Guinea's Brand of Westminster: Democratic Traditions Overlaying Melanesian Cultures', in H. Patapan, J. Wanna and P. Weller (eds), *Westminster Legacies: Democracy and Responsible Government in Asia and the Pacific*, Sydney: University of New South Wales Press, pp. 186–205.

Parker, R. S. and E. P. Wolfers (1971), 'The Context of Political Change', in A. L. Epstein, R. S. Parker and M. Reay (eds), *The Politics of Dependence: Papua New Guinea 1968*, Canberra: ANU Press, pp. 12–47.

Schaffer, B. B. (1965), 'The Concept of Preparation: Some Questions about the Transfer of Systems of Government', *World Politics*, 18(1), 42–67.

Stretton, P. and C. Finnimore (1993), 'Black Fellow Citizens: Aborigines and the Commonwealth Franchise', *Australian Historical Studies*, 101, 521–35.

Tagaloa, F. L. (1992), 'The Samoan Culture and Government', in R. Crocombe, U. Neemia, A. R. von Busch and W. von Busch (eds), *Culture and Democracy in the South Pacific*, Suva: Institute of Pacific Studies, University of the South Pacific, pp. 117–37.

Troy, J. (1993), *King Plates: A History of Aboriginal Gorgets*, Canberra: Aboriginal Studies Press

Chapter 21

Singapore

Christine Doran

In Singapore the period from 1890 to 1914 was one of social transformation, demographic shifts, rapid economic development and intellectual ferment. This chapter explores the contributions to democratic thought made by two Chinese Singaporean intellectuals: Lim Boon Keng and Tan Teck Soon. Both were born in Singapore, of Chinese descent, and both became very influential in the dynamic intellectual scene that emerged at the turn of the twentieth century. Lim and Tan sought and found in Chinese religion, political philosophy and history a powerful democratic tradition. They believed that this could become the foundation upon which could be constructed a more democratic future for both Singapore and China.

The period from 1890 to the outbreak of the First World War was the zenith of British imperialist domination in Asia, and indeed throughout the world. The government they imposed in the colony of Singapore was far from democratic. The system of administration consisted of a Governor, an Executive Council made up of British officials and a Legislative Council also composed mainly of British officials together with a small number of non-official members who were nominated directly by the British rulers. This was also the time when China had just been carved up by Western imperialist powers. The great priority in the minds of Sinophiles all over the world, including the descendants of the great Chinese diaspora resident in Singapore, was the aim of reinvigorating China so that it could reclaim its sovereignty. Discussions about democracy became an integral part of this intense rethinking of the Chinese political tradition. The questions uppermost in their minds then are still relevant today. Were the autocratic tendencies of the Chinese imperial system responsible for China's weakness in the face of international challenges? Was there a Chinese tradition of democracy? If so, could it or should it be revived? How should the political system be reformed to make it more democratic?

The basic question to be addressed in this chapter is: how was it possible for Chinese Singaporean thinkers of the *fin-de-siècle* to imagine democracy, given the inherently undemocratic, apparently unconducive, circumstances in which they found themselves? To what intellectual resources could they turn in order to begin to think about democratic change? In their published seminar papers, scholarly articles, newspaper contributions and pamphlets, both Lim and Tan developed the notion that China and Singapore could move forward politically by looking backwards in a fresh manner. The recovery of a Chinese tradition of democracy became an essential part of their political strategies. Singapore is not usually thought of as a site of intellectual creativity, but it is one of the implications of this study that this assumption is in need of revision.

Lim Boon Keng: Confucian Democracy

Lim Boon Keng (1869–1957) was a second-generation Singaporean-born Chinese. He attended mainly English language schools, including the elite Raffles Institution. Lim was the first Chinese to be awarded the Queen's Scholarship in 1887, which allowed him to study medicine at Edinburgh University. After returning to Singapore, he was nominated to the Legislative Council in 1895, where he served five three-year terms. He was also on the Municipal Commission and the Chinese Advisory Board, and was also a JP and an officer in the Singapore Volunteer Corps. After the Chinese revolution in 1911, Lim was appointed as Sun Yat-sen's confidential secretary and personal physician. He was awarded an Order of the British Empire (OBE) in 1918. In 1921, he became the first president of Amoy University, returning to Singapore in 1937. When the Japanese invaded Singapore in 1941 Lim was imprisoned, but later represented the Chinese community in negotiations with the Japanese. Lim wrote a large number of books and articles and was the editor of an English-language newspaper in Shanghai, as well as being involved in several newspapers in Singapore. He was also a successful entrepreneur in the rubber industry, with other investments in the tin, shipping, insurance and media industries.

In order to develop his thinking on democracy in the seemingly uncongenial ambience of colonial Singapore, Lim Boon Keng turned to the theoretical resources of Confucianism. Lim's conversion to Confucianism was gradual, but by 1899 he identified himself as a convert. He objected strongly to Western commentators' attempts to deny that Confucianism was a religion (Lim 1917: 1). Lim Boon Keng claimed quite explicitly and repeatedly that Confucian principles of government were democratic. Like Tan Teck Soon (see below), he believed that democracy had already been achieved in China's early history, referring proudly to the 'important democratic institutions of the ancient Chinese' (Lim 1915a: 94). He argued that the Confucian conception of the state was based on democratic foundations (Lim 1915a: 97). According to Lim Boon Keng, Confucianism comprises a number of closely inter-related 'departments': (1) philosophy; (2) theology; (3) anthropology; (4) ethics; and (5) politics. This range of concerns made Confucianism, in Lim's view, a complete and rounded study of humanity, chiefly from a pragmatic point of view, as well as an 'all-sufficient religion' (Lim 1913: 142). In order to understand Lim's political thought, it is necessary to outline briefly his interpretation of Confucian principles within each of these departments.

Of particular interest are Lim's thoughts on theology and politics. Lim's theology was based on the claim that behind all the multiple phenomena of the world there is a Supreme Being, or Supreme Ruler. The terms of Lim's argument here slipped easily from theology to theocracy. However, the wishes of this divine ruler were to be interpreted according to the common aspirations and ideals of humanity. As he put it, the '*Vox Populi* is the only recognisable *Vox Dei*' (Lim 1915a: 94). This is, to say the least, a marked democratic move in Lim's argument. By identifying the *vox populi* as the only accessible and intelligible source of information about the desires of the divine authority available to humanity, he gives the people the ultimate word. In this formulation the source of political legitimacy is not the will of the people as such; instead, legitimacy is established on transcendent sacred origins. Nevertheless, the will of the people is recognised as a direct and directly perceptible reflection of the will of the transcendent deity or of Heaven.

Under the heading of politics, Lim Boon Keng puts all the emphasis on democratic principles. Under Confucian conceptions, the state is to be governed for the benefit of the people. The chief authority to whom Lim turned to support this view was Mengzi (Mencius 371–289 BCE). Mengzi is generally acknowledged to be the most creative and influential follower of Kongzi (Confucius 551–479 BCE). Mengzi laid out an order of priority in the political realm: 'the people are the most important; next comes the country, and lastly stands the ruler' (Lim 1915a: 95). Thus, according to Mengzi, it was the ruler's first duty to provide for the welfare and prosperity of the people. In much of his thinking on democracy, Lim Boon Keng revealed a heavy debt to Mengzi. Lim followed Mengzi in the view that human nature is essentially good and for this reason government should interfere with human activities as little as possible (Lim 1915b: 47–8). Mengzi argued that the political legitimacy of a government derives from the acceptance or consent of the people. He stated clearly that the people may always justly overthrow a ruler who harms them. Mengzi's idea of the right to rebel can be compared with John Locke's right to revolution, as expounded in his *Two Treatises of Government* (Locke [1689] 1988).

In his discussion of democratic politics, Lim also appealed to the contributions of a more recent Confucian authority, Kang Youwei (K'ang Yu-wei 1858–1927). Kang had almost lost his life by proposing a programme of reforms to the rulers of the moribund Manchu dynasty during the 1890s. Kang had set out the progressive stages of development of the state as follows: (1) nomadic tribal state; (2) territorial chieftaincy; (3) feudal state; (4) imperial state; (5) republic; and (6) communist state. Lim endorsed this categorisation as representing the progressive changes in the form of the state over the course of Chinese history. He certainly saw no contradiction between Confucianism and republicanism, and also believed that certain socialistic policies, such as nationalisation of land, means of communication and public utilities, could be justified by Confucian arguments (Lim 1915a: 97–8).

From these premises and arguments Lim drew significant conclusions about the proper functioning of a Confucian state:

> The people are the foundation of the State. The country is for the benefit of the people. The ruler and administrators are to serve the people . . . The sole *raison d'être* of the State is for the preservation and maintenance of the people, and for the provision of all human requirements in peace and prosperity. (Lim 1915a: 96)

From the fundamental principles could also be deduced the appropriate rights and duties of the component parts of the state. The ruler is in theory 'the vice regent of God.' He (never she) must 'serve the State in the interests of the governed'. An embodiment of virtue and excellence, the ruler represents the meeting point of the spiritual and the material world and is responsible both to God and to the people (Lim 1915a: 96). The people have the right to life and liberty if they discharge certain definite obligations to the state. In return, they are to receive protection, education and government. The reciprocal rights of the people also encompassed rights to justice, property, freedom of religion and a share in administration or self-government. The right to rebel against tyranny or misgovernment Lim, like Mengzi, considered 'inalienable' (Lim 1915a: 97).

Lim readily admitted that these Confucian ideals had not always been put into practice during the course of Chinese history. He conceded that 'tyrants have oppressed the people from time to time', but pointed out that China was 'not the only land where high ideals have failed to become realised to their fullest extent' (Lim 1915a: 97). Furthermore, even though Confucian principles had never been thoroughly applied in practice, they 'had achieved greater moral results than any other system of religion or morals' (Lim 1913: 136). Despite the existence of oppression in reality, in the end what he wanted to emphasise was that government as conceived by Confucian philosophers was essentially democratic: 'Though in practice rulers and people have often forgotten the real constitutional principles, the fact remains that the institutions are intrinsically democratic' (Lim 1915a: 96). Even in 'degenerate times', when Chinese governments had become oppressive, no central government had dared to deny that the people were paramount. At the end of the last dynasty in 1911, even the Manchus declared when abdicating that the emperor yielded to the will of Heaven and the voice of the people (Lim 1913: 136).

Lim traced the democratic foundations of Chinese civilisation back to the earliest period of ancient Chinese history, or prehistory, associated with the emergence of culture heroes and sage kings. Like most Confucian scholars, he stressed the prime importance of this era, which laid the foundations and established the cultural patterns that would guide Chinese development for nearly five millennia. Lim characterised this formative period as one of social equality. For leadership, the people willingly gave their allegiance to a number of morally outstanding rulers. According to Lim, the principles of the sage founders of Chinese civilisation were 'essentially democratic'. He regarded the kings of this time as moral exemplars and model rulers. In this ancient period, the principle was established that the divine right of kings consisted in the right to 'nurture the people, to educate them, and to raise them to the highest excellence' (Lim 1913: 134). According to Lim, these altruistic sage rulers regarded themselves as the servants of Heaven with the duty to bring to the people 'every conceivable happiness'. About 2,000 years later, Kongzi and his disciple Mengzi talked a great deal about the merits of these legendary kings, endorsing and preserving these ideas about correct political relationships and 'thus imparting upon the politics and administration of China the democratic characteristics which distinguish Chinese institutions from those of the West' (Lim 1913: 135).

Lim Boon Keng most definitely did not look to Western concepts of democracy as the source of his ideas. In fact, the historical trajectory he described was one where the Jesuit missionaries who arrived in China from the sixteenth century were so impressed by Chinese political developments 'and with their profound democratic import' that, when they reported what they had seen in Europe, the Chinese model inspired the works of Voltaire, Montesquieu, Diderot and the Encyclopaedists (Lim 1913: 138). For Lim, it was one of the great ironies of history that these European philosophical works were then being imported into republican China and avidly consumed by Chinese as new insights.

Lim repeatedly drew contrasts between China and the West, always with a sharply critical eye on Western theory and practice. At times these contrasting pictures must have been unsettling for his European audience, threatening to overturn their preconceptions about the general hopelessness of the Chinese and the superiority of all things Western. For instance, Lim pointed to an immense gulf separating social relations in Europe and in China. Whereas in Europe there had existed slavery and serfdom until very recent times, 'the free people of China have been contented with their domestic and village liberties' (Lim 1913: 134). Contrasting the Confucian conception of the state to comparatively recent Western notions, Lim insisted that ' "*L'état s' est* [sic] *moi*" is the very antithesis of the Confucian conception', and that 'it is, from the beginning to the end, the very opposite of the prevalent idea of Machiavelli, that in the interests of the State the ends may justify the means, even if immoral' (Lim 1915a: 95).

Another important source of Lim's democratic thinking was the *Zhouli*, or the *Institutes of Chou* in his terminology, whose authorship he credited to the duke of Zhou (Zhou Gong, Ji Dan) of the eleventh century BCE. This ancient source underscored the principle that 'Government is an organisation carried out entirely in the interests of the masses governed', while 'the State is an ethical organisation for the preservation of the Common Weal' (Lim 1915a: 95). The duke of Zhou is credited with originating the doctrine of the Mandate of Heaven. According to this critically important political doctrine, rulers would receive the support of Heaven only as long as they acted virtuously, but would lose the mandate and be overthrown if they tried to take selfish advantage of their position. In Chinese religious thought, Heaven (*Tian*) was neither a place nor the equivalent of a God as creator of the universe; instead, Heaven referred to moral forces that determine how the universe operates. Rulers were expected to act in harmony with these universal forces; if they did not, it would be their downfall. The Confucians called the emperor the Son of Heaven, underlining his special relationship to the powers of the universe. The *Zhouli* also emphasised that a righteous person has the duty to fight against any wrong committed against the people, thus enjoining resistance against corrupt government. Kongzi and Mengzi and the Confucian tradition in general put great emphasis on the importance of the *Zhouli* and the concept of the Mandate of Heaven. Lim's interpretation of the end of the Manchu dynasty was that the 'masses had resolved that autocracy had lost the mandate of Heaven' (Lim 1913: 140).

Confucians considered the period of high antiquity discussed above as a Golden Age. As well as appealing to the distant past, Lim also drew upon utopian ideas of a future Golden Age. These notions were derived mainly from the *Liji* or *Book of Rites*, one of the five classics of the Confucian canon. As Lim saw it, the *Liji* offered a striking portrait of an ideal republic in which altruism would override all selfish considerations. There would be a federation of all humanity, of all the nations, inaugurating an era of universal peace. Social classes and social hierarchy would become meaningless.

Confucians referred to this ideal future society as *datong* (*ta-t'ung*), or the Great Communism as Lim called it (Lim 1913: 135). This represented the ultimate stage in Kang Youwei's ascending scale of state formations, to which Lim gave his assent.

In making his argument for the consistency of Confucianism and democracy, Lim found the intellectual resources available within Confucianism sufficient to his needs. He was able to appeal to Confucian authorities such as Kongzi, Mengzi and Kang Youwei. The emergence of the doctrine of the Mandate of Heaven was definitely relevant to his case. He called upon idealised portraits of Golden Ages, both of the distant past and the distant future. He also drew unfavourable comparisons between Europe and China, in terms of both theory and practice, explicitly challenging Western claims to own democratic thought.

Tan Teck Soon: The Chinese History of Democracy

Tan Teck Soon (1859–1922) attended the prestigious Raffles Institution, where he was an outstanding student, excelling in Chinese studies. In 1873, he became the first recipient of the Guthrie Scholarship for Chinese boys, which enabled him to go to Amoy to continue his Chinese studies. Unlike other distinguished students of the period, such as Lim Boon Keng, Tan chose to pursue higher studies in China rather than in Britain, and became fluent in Chinese. When he returned to Singapore, he took up employment with the government and later in the private sector (Doran 2006: 50–1). Tan is a more enigmatic historical figure than Lim. Although very active in commercial life and on the intellectual scene in Singapore during this period, he died relatively early (at sixty-three, compared with Lim who died aged eighty-seven); moreover, in the latter years he lived a more reclusive life, increasingly attracted to the beliefs and practices of Buddhism.

Tan's involvement in public life in Singapore was multi-faceted. Together with his friend, Archibald Lamont, a Presbyterian missionary, he purchased a newspaper, the *Daily Advertiser*, as a vehicle for communicating to the public ideas about the need for change within the Chinese community. Tan was editor and proprietor of the paper from 1890 to 1894. Together with Lamont, from 1891 he was involved in running the Singapore Chinese Educational Institute, a type of night school for working adult Chinese. Tan and Lamont also collaborated on a novel entitled *Bright Celestials: The Chinaman at Home and Abroad*, which portrayed the often harrowing experiences of expatriate Chinese in Singapore and was critical of British policies towards Chinese immigrants. In 1893, Tan was invited to become a foundation member of the Straits Philosophical Society (1893–1916), an influential gentleman's debating club whose membership included the administrative elite of the colony (Jose 1998). From 1898 to 1905 he was the general manager of an important Chinese-language daily, the *Thien Nan Shin Pao*, whose aim was to communicate reformist ideas to the large non-Anglophone local audience. For many years Tan contributed actively to the intellectual life of Singapore, delivering lectures, chairing committees, writing articles and editing newspapers. From his contemporaries among the Chinese intelligentsia, Tan received accolades for his outstanding abilities both as a thinker and as a writer. In his book, *One Hundred Years' History of the Chinese in Singapore*, first published in the year of Tan's death, Song Ong Siang paid tribute to Tan's literary prowess as 'a brilliant writer on Chinese subjects' with 'a wonderful command of the English language' (Song [1922] 1985: 598, 94). Tan was at times intensely critical of the arbitrary and undemocratic character of British colonial administration. For example, in the Straits Philosophical Society in 1894, in response to a paper by Hugh Fort on 'Liberal Principles as Applied to the Government of Oriental Dependencies', Tan expressed trenchant criticism of the unrepresentative nature and lack of inclusiveness of the local government (SPS 1894: 237; Jose 2010: 206–7). On another occasion, Tan argued forcefully against the use of special discriminatory regulations by the British to exempt particular groups, notably Chinese immigrants, from the usual application and protection of the law (Tan 1899: 117).

Tan's significant intellectual contribution was to offer a particular interpretation of Chinese history that gave strong emphasis to democratic themes. An outstanding example was his essay, 'The Middle Kingdom', the first substantial paper he presented to the Straits Philosophical Society, delivered in May 1894. In this paper, Tan presented a coherent vision of Chinese history progressing through defined developmental stages towards a consummatory idealistic future characterised by democratic egalitarianism and universal peace. Tan approached his task by first confronting headlong what he took to be the generally prevailing derogatory Western view of China and its history. It is notable that the points he made were consistent with, indeed could be said to have prefigured, many of the ideas developed by Edward Said in his now classic study of Western attitudes towards Eastern cultures, *Orientalism* (Said [1978] 1995). Tan's prescience in this respect and the forceful language in which he expressed himself justify direct quotation:

Notwithstanding its size and population, its ancient civilisation and natural achievements, its vast literature, and the domestic industry and commercial activity of its people, even the most fair-minded of Western historians are unable to regard it as anything else than 'A withered branch on the historical tree of life, an embalmed memory painted with hieroglyphics and swathed in silk.' It is clear enough to these historians that Europe and true civilisation had nothing to gain and have gained nothing in the way of culture from such an eccentric nation. Everything Chinese is therefore simply glanced at for its grotesqueness and valued perhaps as a mere curiosity. The skilful handiwork of Chinese artisans but serves to heighten the effect of the ludicrous on the European mind as the paltry results of a pretentious, antiquated, and inherently unprogressive order of civilisation. Such is the general European testimony of things Chinese. (Tan 1894: 17)

Tan Teck Soon fashioned a conceptual counter to prevailing Western notions that China lacked a history, that its historical development had ceased long ago (Schrecker 2004: 100; Waley-Cohen 1999). The European author whom Tan quoted was Johann Gottfried Herder (1744–1803), a German writer usually considered deeply sympathetic towards cultural diversity, plurality and equality, and who denounced imperial rule for its destructive effects on cultural autonomy (Berlin 2006: 223–36). Yet, as Tan noted, when he turned his attention to China, even Herder could not resist metaphors of withering and embalming. Tan's choice of the term 'Middle Kingdom' for the title of his paper should also be seen as a counter to the reductive Western tendency to marginalise the Chinese. Europeans were often incensed by the Chinese claim to civilisational centrality and thus by the use of this term, so Tan's assertion of it before the colonial elite of Singapore was a bold gesture.

The first, and crucially important, period of Chinese history delineated by Tan in his paper was that of a mythical idealised past before the beginning of history as such. Fabulous Chinese legends recounted the character of this misty ancient epoch. Tan discussed how the earliest available records described the Chinese as a distinct community of people inhabiting a region in central China south of the Huang He or Yellow River. Significantly, it was to this area that the name Middle Kingdom was first applied. The transition from nomadism to settled agriculture and family life was the outstanding achievement of this period. According to Tan, the system of government in this mythical period was republican in nature, while the structure of society showed an absence of social inequalities. In this foundational society no coercion was necessary to secure the spontaneous obedience of the people to a leader elected for the good of the community. Tan rejected the idea that the industriousness of the people was the result of state regulation or control. In the Confucian tradition this prehistoric golden age was usually represented as under the leadership of dominant sage-kings of superior virtue. In Tan Teck Soon's depiction of this mystical era, he put the stress on its egalitarianism and the elective principle as the foundation of government. This was a significant shift of emphasis. Another notable feature of social life in this period, according to Tan, was the adoption of monogamous marriage, which he saw as a transitional phase from an earlier polyandry to a later polygamy.

As Tan was well aware, the characteristics imputed to such mythical ancient epochs deeply influence the course of social development, highlighting 'the unconscious function of imagination in the construction of all great civilisations' (Tan 1894: 20). Showing the influence of Freudian psychology on his thinking, Tan expressed in a later paper his belief that the 'province of subconscious activity in a man's soul is very large, by far larger than the narrow circle that under the stress of attention appears on the surface of consciousness' (Tan 1910: 177–8). Paul Ricoeur has discussed the contradictory significance of the literary figure of utopia, ostensibly merely 'a place that has no place, a ghost city', impossible of realisation and outside of reality; but also perhaps an essential aspect of social imagination:

From this 'no place', an exterior glance is cast on our reality, which suddenly looks strange, nothing more being taken for granted. The field of the possible is now opened beyond that of the actual, a field for alternative ways of living. The question therefore is whether imagination could have any constitutive role without this leap outside. (Ricoeur 1991: 320)

The spectral images of ancient legendary times could thus perform the functions of a *fabula rasa*, in which could be inscribed a vision of social development and reform. Tan sought and found in antiquity the sanction for contemporary social and political change.

The next era of Chinese history featured the development of a feudal system, with detrimental results for social unity and for the interests of the common people. As Tan wrote, 'The Feudal States so multiplied that they became petty kingdoms in themselves, engaged in internecine strife with each other, and all belittling the authority of the ruling sovereign and oppressing the people' (Tan 1894: 23). Importantly, the common people (Tan often referred to them as the 'Chinese democracy') thereby lost their 'inborn privilege of nominating and removing their rulers' (Tan 1894: 23). In addition, they also had to provide for the maintenance of an oligarchy as well as a monarchy. In this period an ethos of militarism came to the fore, which also became an instrument to oppress the people. In Tan's view, the transition to the next great stage of China's history was mainly attributable to the influence of Kongzi (Confucius). Kongzi contributed a powerfully influential social and political model and founded the class of *literati*. Tan emphasised the duties and responsibilities assigned to the emperor, the progressive role of the scholar-officials, and the rights given to the people within the Confucian state:

> To the Imperial power he assigned the first fundamental force of Chinese civilisa-tion, the element of unity, of consolidation; of guardianship over the people. As a counterpoint to the arbitrary display of Imperial power, diminishing the military element in it, and as a regular organ of progress, developing the pacific and industrial qualities of the race, he organised the literary classes, recruited from the people. And, as an instrument for combating the oppression so prevalent in his times, he placed in the hands of the populace that terrible power of retribution, the 'Right of rebellion' against tyrants, even the highest. (Tan 1894: 24–5)

Tan put a marked populist spin on Confucian ideology, emphasising the emperor's role of guardianship over the people, the popular origins of the *literati* and the people's right to rebel when the emperor lost the Mandate of Heaven.

During the succeeding dynasties China made great achievements in many fields, but, as Tan saw it, there were some notable areas of deficiency in Chinese national progress. Significantly, the democratic tendencies of the Chinese nation, evident from the earliest mythological times, had been blocked. Popular rebellions broke out against the Ming dynasty and helped to bring it down and effect its replacement by the Manchu Qing. However, the 'consummation of democratic demands was by this indefinitely delayed, and has remained unfulfilled down to the present day' (Tan 1894: 32). This was a serious defect that Chinese society would need to overcome if it were to progress to the next stage of historical development.

In achieving this, Tan believed that contact with Europeans had much to offer Chinese civilisation. However, European faults were interfering with that promise. International intercourse had been jeopardised by the 'commercial selfishness' and greed of the Western powers, as a result of which 'oppression and the exploitation of the other peoples of the world have in the West been reduced to a system, under the specious pretext of spreading civilisation' (Tan 1894: 35). At the same time 'those who desire the amelioration of China by its contact with the West' – the missionaries – 'unfortunately bring nothing but the narrowest prejudices to the appreciation of a civilisation which they completely misunderstand' (Tan 1894: 35). In Tan's view, it was 'problematical' whether the challenges from the West would encourage an alliance between the populace and the other centres of power, the emperor and the *literati*, but this was the outcome he hoped for and envisaged.

If these problems could be overcome, Tan saw Chinese society progressing to the next stage of history. This would be characterised by the values of egalitarianism and universalism. The originary social equality and democratic polity of the Chinese nation would be reclaimed. Through international contacts the horizons of social relationships would be broadened, from the level of the family in the first stage of historical development, to that of the nation in the second stage, to that of an international community of nations. Thus, the constrictions and limitations symbolised by the Great Wall of China would be surmounted. In Tan's utopian vision of an ideal society of the future the original democratic spirit and potential of the Chinese people would be recaptured and fulfilled. The future would bring a return to the essence of the Chinese nation. As Michel de Certeau has pointed out, the relationship between tradition and modernity is often rather paradoxical, and subject to continual reworking:

> The 'return to origins' always states the contrary of what it believes, at least in the sense that it presupposes a *distancing* in respect to a past (that space which precisely defines history: through it is effected the mutation of lived tradition by which one makes a 'past', the 'ob-ject' of study), and a will to *recover* what, in one fashion or another, seems lost in a received language. In this way the 'return to origins' is always a modernism as well. (Certeau 1988: 136, emphasis in original)

Tan's reconception of the history of China represented an attempt to accommodate traditional thought to modern democratic ideals and objectives.

Conclusion

There was an honourable tradition within Chinese thinking whereby an individual, especially, though not necessarily, one from the scholarly class, could, by exercising his own conscience and creativity, discover new meaning in past traditions, thereby providing a foundation for the reform of existing deficiencies and the renewal of humanity. This concept was often referred to as 'repossession of the way', and had been enshrined in the culture of the *literati* from at least the twelfth century. It emphasised the dynamic potential of Chinese tradition and the scope for reshaping the intellectual resources of the tradition in progressive ways. There is no doubt that both Lim Boon Keng and Tan Teck Soon saw themselves as working in this respected role. Through their creative reworking of the resources available within Chinese religion, philosophy and history, they succeeded in overcoming the unpropitious circumstances of life in an authoritarian British colony, at the zenith of European imperialist domination in Asia, to imagine the possibilities of a democratic future.

References

Berlin, I. (2006), *Political Ideas in the Romantic Age*, Princeton, NJ: Princeton University Press.

Certeau, M. de (1988), *The Writing of History*, New York: Columbia University Press.

Doran, C. (2006), 'Bright Celestial: Progress in the Political Thought of Tan Teck Soon', *SOJOURN: Journal of Social Issues in Southeast Asia*, 21(1), 46–67.

Jose, J. (1998),'Imperial Rule and the Ordering of Intellectual Space: The Formation of the Straits Philosophical Society', *Crossroads: An Interdisciplinary Journal of Southeast Asian Studies*, 12(2), 23–54.

Jose, J. (2010), ' "Like Prussic Acid in a Bottle of Medicine": Liberal Principles and Colonial Rule', *Postcolonial Studies*, 13(2), 199–214.

Lim, B. K. (1913), 'Socialism among the Chinese', *Straits Philosophical Society Proceedings*, 21, 134–42.

Lim, B. K. (1915a), 'The Confucian Conception of the State', *Straits Philosophical Society Proceedings*, 22, 93–8.

Lim, B. K. (1915b), 'The Principles of Education from the Confucian Standpoint', *Straits Philosophical Society Proceedings*, 23, 47–51.

Lim, B. K. (1917), *The Great War from the Confucian Point of View and Kindred Topics*, Singapore: Straits Albion Press.

Locke, J. ([1689] 1988), *Two Treatises on Government*, 3rd edn, Cambridge: Cambridge University Press.

Ricoeur, P. (1991), *From Text to Action: Essays in Hermeneutics*, vol. 2, London: Athlone.

Said, E. ([1978] 1995), *Orientalism*, London: Penguin.

Schrecker, J. (2004), *The Chinese Revolution in Historical Perspective*, Westport, CT: Praeger.

Song, O. S. ([1922] 1985), *One Hundred Years' History of the Chinese in Singapore*, Singapore: Oxford University Press.

Straits Philosophical Society (SPS) (1894), 'Abstract of Discussion on Liberal Principles Applied to Oriental Dependences', *Straits Philosophical Society Proceedings*, 2, 237–43.

Tan, T. S. (1894), 'The Middle Kingdom', *Straits Philosophical Society Proceedings*, 2, 17–36.

Tan, T. S. (1899), 'Criticism on Essay on "The Application of English Law to Asiatic Races" ', *Straits Philosophical Society Proceedings*, 7, 116–26.

Tan, T. S. (1910), 'Buddhism', *Straits Philosophical Society Proceedings*, 17, 168–80.

Waley-Cohen, J. (1999), *The Sextants of Beijing: Global Currents in Chinese History*, New York: W. W. Norton.

Part VI

National Movements

Chapter 22

1808: South American Liberation

John Fisher

Although not used significantly in academic discourse until the early twentieth century, the term 'Latin America' – coined in Paris in the mid-nineteenth century to describe the Francophone Caribbean as well as Spanish and Portuguese America – now defines all the mainland American territories south of the border between the United States and Mexico (including Anglophone Belize and Guyana, as well as Dutch-speaking Suriname). It excludes, however, the former French and Spanish colonies acquired by the United States in the first half of the nineteenth century: Florida (purchased from Spain in 1819); Louisiana (purchased from France in 1803); Texas (declared independence from Mexico in 1836, annexed into the United States in 1845); and Arizona, California, Nevada, Utah and parts of New Mexico, Colorado and Wyoming (ceded at the end of the Mexican–American War in 1848) (Fisher 2008: 181–2). To the south, vast regions remained beyond the frontiers of European settlement because of indigenous resistance or the absence of immediate rewards for potential settlers: parts of the Caribbean and Pacific coasts of New Granada (modern Colombia); the eastern lowlands of Peru and the kingdom of Quito (modern Ecuador); the pampas of the River Plate, Patagonia and southern Chile; and the Amazon and Orinoco.

Nevertheless, the territories that had been settled by Spaniards and Portuguese during the previous three centuries were huge, if thinly populated. They were colonial regimes with few democratic characteristics. The Portuguese vice-royalty of Brazil had an estimated 3.25 million inhabitants by 1800, half of them black slaves, concentrated along the coast and at some interior locations where gold and diamonds had supplanted sugar as Brazil's most profitable export. By 1800, Spanish America had an estimated population of almost 17 million, a third of them in the vice-royalty of New Spain (modern Mexico and Central America, excluding Panama). Panama formed part of the vice-royalty of New Granada along with the kingdom of the same name (modern Colombia) and Quito (modern Ecuador). This entity had been detached from the vice-royalty of Peru in 1739 to improve the defences of the Caribbean coastline against British warships and privateers. Similarly, in 1776, to counter Portuguese intrusion southwards from Brazil, Spain had established the vice-royalty of the River Plate (modern Argentina, Bolivia, Paraguay and Uruguay) with its capital in Buenos Aires. These changes meant that the old vice-royalty of Peru, founded in 1542, had been reduced drastically in size, but it remained important to Spain because of its continued role as a major silver producer. The captaincy-general of Chile enjoyed, like Venezuela and Cuba, practical autonomy from the respective vice-regal authorities, although during the impending wars of independence successive viceroys of Peru assumed the responsibility for sending troops to Chile to bolster the royalist cause.

Prelude to Revolution

Spanish America had experienced significant economic growth in the last quarter of the eighteenth century because of expanding markets in Europe for their sugar, cacao, indigo, cotton, tobacco and hides, and a successful policy of commercial reform which opened their American ports to direct trade with the principal ports of Spain (Fisher 1985: 60–86). The Spanish colonies were enjoying unprecedented levels of prosperity by the early nineteenth century, and remained mostly content with their continued subjection to the Bourbon and Braganza dynasties with little agitation for democracy. In the last quarter of the eighteenth century there were some regional protests in both Brazil and Spanish America against increased fiscal burdens: in the former, the so-called Tiradentes conspiracy in Minas Gerais in 1786; and in the latter the 1780 Rebellion of Túpac Amaru in Peru and the 1781 Rebellion of the Comuneros in New Granada (Fausto 1999: 61–2; Fisher 2003: 31–2; Phelan 1978: 98). These uprisings did not provide any clearly articulated demands for practical independence or functioning democracy, notwithstanding the claims to the contrary of modern nationalist historians. There were, of course, a few isolated champions of the independence cause, notably the veteran Venezuelan revolutionary Francisco de Miranda, who sought in vain prior to 1810 to persuade Spanish Americans to emulate the precedent set by Britain's Thirteen Colonies in taking up arms against colonialism to create democracy in 1776 (Lynch 1986: 29; Racine 2003: 5–6). Similarly, the exiled Peruvian Jesuit Juan Pablo Viscardo y Guzmán – one of 2,600 members of the Society abruptly expelled from Spanish America in 1767 by Carlos III (1759–88) – had articulated in his 1799 *Lettre aux Espagnols-Américains*, the case for full independence to rid Spanish America of the evils of colonialism (Viscardo y Guzmán [1810] 2002). Although his work was subsequently recognised as a key text in disclosing colonial grievances, it had a negligible impact upon the attitudes of his Creole (that is, American-born Spanish) contemporaries (Brading 1991: 535–40).

Within this seemingly harmonious context, the seeds of what would become major crises for Spain and Portugal began to be sown in the mid-1790s. Having gone to war with revolutionary France in 1793, Carlos IV of Spain (1788–1808) made peace in 1795, ceding first Santo Domingo (the modern Dominican Republic) and then Louisiana before joining France in war against Britain, Spain's traditional imperial rival. The outbreak of hostilities in mid-1796 had disastrous strategic and commercial consequences for Spain. The British navy's tight blockade of Cádiz – which handled 80 per cent of Spain's trade with Spanish America – forced the Spanish Crown to grant unprecedented permission in 1797 for neutral ships to enter its American ports (Fisher 1997: 201–2). The principal beneficiaries of this decision – which the Crown tried to rescind in 1799 with only limited success – were US industrialists and merchants and Spanish-American producers, who very quickly worked out a mutually beneficial relationship whereby US vessels brought slaves and manufactures to ports such as

Vera Cruz, Havana and La Guairá in exchange for silver, sugar, tobacco, cacao and indigo, taking the merchandise directly to ports in the United States and northern Europe, notwithstanding the official requirement to sail for peninsular Spain.

The 1802 Peace of Amiens brought Spain some respite, and increased customs revenue, as the merchant houses of Cádiz restored some of their former business. But the renewal of fighting in 1804 brought in its train the battle of Trafalgar in October 1805, which eliminated Spain and France as serious maritime powers. It also led many colonial officials to connive at permitting direct trade with British Caribbean islands, notwithstanding the formal state of warfare (Pearce 2007: 119–219). Even so, Spanish-Americans remained reluctant to embrace the independence cause, as Miranda discovered in 1806 when, with the tacit consent of British officials in the Leeward Islands, he sailed from New York to mount two abortive raids on the coast of Venezuela. One factor in his failure to attract support from the Venezuelan elite was its fear that revolutionary activity might unleash the massacre of landowners by blacks, such as had occurred in nearby Haiti, following its 1804 Declaration of Independence from France (Geggus 1982: 382–91; Racine 2003, 5–6). The British, too, had their fingers badly burned when in 1806 and 1807, they entered the River Plate estuary and seized the ports of Buenos Aires and Montevideo, only later to be forced into an ignominious surrender in the face of the ferocious hostility from local militia regiments (Lynch 1986: 40–2).

The Onset of the Revolutions for Independence, 1807–1810

The impending crisis for the Iberian powers deepened in mid-1807, when Napoleon, antagonised by Portugal's persistent refusal to close its ports to British warships and merchantmen, decided to send thousands of troops across the Pyrenees to undertake a full-scale invasion of Britain's traditional ally (Esdaile 2003: 5–96). The hapless Carlos IV and his Prime Minister Manuel de Godoy, the latter seduced by Napoleon's suggestion that he might make him prince of the Algarve, had little option but to agree to collaborate, despite their apprehension in allowing French troops to pass through northern Spain (in reality the only available route, given Britain's maritime control of the Bay of Biscay). In November, 50,000 French troops invaded Portugal from León, with some Spanish support, and captured Lisbon on 30 November, only to discover that a day earlier a convoy of thirty-six vessels had sailed out of the port, en route for Brazil under the protection of British warships. The fleet carried the Braganza royal family headed by Queen María I (1777–1816) and her dim-witted son Dom João, regent since 1799 because of his mother's insanity. They took with them thousands of courtiers and wealthy inhabitants of Lisbon, along with the contents of the royal archive, library, art collection and treasury. They reached Salvador in January and Rio de Janeiro in March 1808, and immediately inaugurated a period of unprecedented prosperity for Brazil by opening its ports to direct trade with Britain and other friendly countries. Having succeeded his mother as João VI in 1816, the king (and his court) refused to return to Lisbon from their comfortable exile until 1821; when they did so, the king left behind as regent of Brazil his son Pedro, who on 7 September 1822 declared its independence from Portugal, and on 1 December was crowned Emperor

Pedro I. Token resistance from some army units and, more seriously from republicans in the north, was soon overcome, as Brazil made an almost entirely peaceful transition to independence (Fausto 1999: 64–72; Haring 1958: 1–17).

In Spain, Carlos IV, too, contemplated flight to America, but vacillated, confused by riots against Godoy, and on 19 March 1808 abdicated in favour of his son Fernando VII (1808–1833). Both were summoned to Bayonne by Napoleon, where, on 5 May, the new king, too, agreed to abdicate, leaving the way clear for the emperor to make his eldest brother, Joseph, king of Spain and America, an outcome formally proclaimed on 6 June. By then popular risings against the French occupation had occurred in most major Spanish cities, as regional juntas (governing committees) were formed to coordinate resistance and the Spanish army pledged its support for their cause. The juntas also received a powerful boost in June from the success of a delegation sent to London by the junta of Asturias, which persuaded the British to abandon hostilities and instead send arms, money and some 40,000 troops to Spain, including the 13,000 that had been training in Cork under the command of Arthur Wellesley (the future duke of Wellington) for an attack on Venezuela. In the interim, the combined forces of the Spanish army and thousands of hastily mobilised guerrillas had won a stunning victory over the French at the battle of Bailén in mid-July, paving the way for the re-occupation of Madrid at the end of the month and the flight of Joseph Bonaparte a mere ten days after his arrival there (Anna 1983: 29–30). This deceptively easy triumph was followed on 25 September by the agreement of the representatives of the regional juntas, assembled in the royal palace of Aranjuez, to install the *Junta Suprema Central Gubernativa del Reino*, commonly known as the Junta Central. The body, composed of two representatives from each of the regional committees, claimed to govern, in the name of the absent Fernando VII, both Spain and the kingdoms of America, each of which was invited to send two representatives to join it. Thus, for the first time in three centuries the need to provide Spanish-Americans with representation was recognised on the peninsula. In practice, however, the mechanisms for identifying and despatching envoys were left to the absolutist senior administrators in the principal cities of America, whose only minor concessions to democratic processes involved conferring with the oligarchic city councils.

News of the dramatic events in Spain reached the overseas kingdoms slowly, and often in a confused fashion. The most remote vice-regal capital, Lima, did not learn of the formation of the Junta Central until January 1809. Despite his concern that the information received was 'confused, misleading and equivocal', the viceroy, like the overwhelming majority of the royal administrators in the other towns and cities of Spanish America, persuaded his city council to swear allegiance to the Junta Central in March 1809; he also despatched Peruvian troops to suppress local juntas that had been set up in La Paz and Quito (Fisher 1970: 202–3). These expressions of support were of greater symbolic than substantive importance for the Junta Central, which was forced by a new French onslaught to flee southwards from Madrid in December 1808, establishing its headquarters in Seville. While the Junta enjoyed some military success with the support of Portuguese and British troops, when the British withdrew to Portugal, the initiative passed very quickly to the French. Six months later, the Junta Central abandoned Seville, taking refuge in the Isla de León (now better known as San

Fernando), whose fortifications defended the city of Cádiz. There, on 29 January 1810 the Junta Central dissolved itself and handed power to a five-man Council of Regency, which met for the first time three days later. In the event, the defences of León held firm and Cádiz did not fall to the French, in part, because of the constant bombardment of the besiegers by the guns of British warships. Accordingly, the Council of Regency embarked upon a programme of political reform, a key feature of which was its call for all cities in Spain and Spanish America to send deputies to an extraordinary Cortes (parliament). This was a more comprehensive recognition of Americans' rights than the earlier summons of the Junta Central, although few deputies had reached Cádiz when the assembly began to meet. More seriously, by then insurrections refusing to recognise the authority of the Council of Regency had broken out in many parts of Spanish America and while these insurrections were predominantly oligarchic they were not without democratic aspirations.

Bolívar the Liberator

The city of Caracas, capital of the captaincy-general of Venezuela, was the first to react to the news of the collapse of the Junta, which it received on 17 April 1810. What followed there set the pattern for similar events in Buenos Aires in May, Bogotá in July, and Quito and Santiago de Chile in September. Invoking the fear – real or simulated – that the fall of Spain to the French would lead the invaders to attempt to take control of Spanish America, on 19 April 1810 the city council of Caracas – an oligarchic, unelected body representing the upper echelons of Creole society – forced the captain-general to agree to the formation of a national junta, independent of the Council of Regency, to govern Venezuela during the captivity of Fernando VII. Democracy seemed a long way off. Having been shouted down by a hostile crowd, which he tried to address in the main square of Caracas, the captain-general weakly acquiesced, and soon afterwards, along with other prominent peninsular Spaniards, was deported to the United States. In an obvious attempt to emphasise its loyalist character, the Caracas junta – initially composed of twenty-three individuals, presided over by the city's two magistrates – adopted the rather cumbersome title *Junta Conservadora de los Derechos de Fernando VII* when it met for the first time on 25 April. However, it also immediately declared the ports of Venezuela open to free trade, in defiance of long-standing peninsular policy. Other cities and provinces in Venezuela, notably Coro, Guyana, Maracaibo and Valencia, asserting that they had just as much right as the *Caraqueños* to set up their own juntas, soon took up arms not so much to defend the Regency as to preserve their local autonomy. At the other extreme, radical Creoles like Simón Bolívar, already committed to the idea of seeking full independence rather than temporary autonomy for Venezuela, reluctantly accepted the authority of the Caracas junta in the hope of pushing it towards a more revolutionary position (Lynch 2006: 47–9).

During these heady April days the rich, well-travelled, well-connected Bolívar was lying low on one of his rural properties, having been warned informally in 1809 by the captain-general of the dangers of associating with known radical groups in Caracas. Always the pragmatist, however, he promptly made his services available to the junta by offering to pay the costs of a diplomatic mission to London, in the hope of securing from Britain formal recognition and a guarantee of armed support in the event of hostilities with either the French or royalists loyal to the Regency. The offer was accepted and Bolívar promptly sailed for Portsmouth, accompanied by a fellow commissioner, Luís López Méndez, secretary to the delegation, and Andrés Bello. In the event, López would remain in London until recalled to the emerging Gran Colombia in 1821, and Bello until 1829, when he left not for Caracas but for Santiago de Chile, where he pursued a glittering academic and political career until his death in 1865.

Although well aware that the Caracas Junta had resolved not to permit the return to Venezuela of Francisco de Miranda, resident in London since 1796, the delegation made a beeline to his home as soon as it landed (Salcedo Bastardo 1981: 7–12). Miranda opened many doors for the commissioners, introducing them to, among others, important contributors to the emerging British democracy such as Jeremy Bentham, William Wilberforce, the educational reformer Joseph Lancaster (whose system of mutual education made a deep impression on Bolívar) and James Mill, as well as various Latin Americans resident in London. These encounters gave the impressionable Bolívar an indelible admiration for British institutions, except for monarchy. The most important door opened to them was that of Apsley House, the private residence of Foreign Secretary Richard Henry Wellesley (eldest brother of Arthur), where the commissioners had five meetings with the minister between mid-July and early September. Impressive though this venue was, the reason for its choice was the British government's need to make it clear to the Spanish ambassador that the discussions were unofficial and that Britain would maintain its policy of supporting Spain against the French, doing nothing to undermine the authority of Fernando VII in America (Racine 2003: 200). Accordingly, as Miranda had predicted, Wellesley was unwilling to stray from the official line that British recognition of the Caracas Junta would be incompatible with the Anglo-Spanish alliance, thereby forcing Bolívar to resort to the argument that, although the legitimacy of the Regency had been denied by the Caracas Junta, loyalty to Fernando VII was of paramount importance to that junta (Lynch 2006: 51–2; Racine 2003: 201–3). The minister did eventually confirm that Britain would provide protection against any attempted French incursion into Venezuela, and instructed its naval and military commanders in the Caribbean to facilitate trade between British and Venezuelan subjects by ignoring any attempted blockades, while ruling out either providing armed assistance against other Venezuelan provinces that had recognised the Regency or the possibility of negotiating a commercial treaty with the Caracas Junta.

By then a wiser man, Bolívar took his leave of Wellesley in September and reached Venezuela in December, taking with him Miranda's luggage and papers, but leaving the veteran revolutionary to join him a few weeks later, thereby giving himself time to persuade the more conservative members of the Caracas Junta to allow Miranda's return to Caracas after twenty-seven years. In March 1811, a congress, convened by the junta without representatives from many parts of Venezuela, began to meet and declared independence on 5 July. Armed resistance from Coro and Valencia led to significant hostilities in which Miranda distinguished himself. However, the military advantage passed gradually to the royalist forces, particularly as their commanders succeeded in recruiting slaves and poor *pardos* (blacks of mixed ancestry) to take up arms against their hated Creole masters. Following a devastating earthquake in March 1812, which killed an estimated 10,000, Miranda was given dictatorial powers, but failed to prevent either the royalist advance or Bolívar's surrender to them of the fortress of Puerto Cabello. On 25 July 1812, Miranda gave up the struggle, signing the Treaty of San Mateo with the royalists, which supposedly granted him and other patriot leaders immunity from punishment. Believing that Miranda had betrayed the cause to save himself, Bolívar prevented his escape to Curaçao and handed him over to the royalists for eventual shipment to Cádiz, where he died in prison in 1816. Bolívar, however, was allowed to leave Venezuela with a royalist passport – perhaps as a reward for handing over Miranda – and made his way to Cartagena, the major city of the vice-royalty of New Granada on the Caribbean coast.

In Cartagena, Bolívar found a situation similar to but even more complicated than the one in Venezuela. Two rival juntas had been established in New Granada, one in Bogotá, the other in Cartagena, and each was striving to persuade other provinces to recognise its authority. Displaying his military and political prowess, Bolívar secured men and arms in Cartagena for a new expedition into Venezuela. Following a bitter 'war to the death' against the royalists, he was able to return to Caracas in August 1813 and soon gained dictatorial powers as captain-general of the patriot forces. He was driven out of Venezuela again in mid-1814 by a royalist army composed largely of horsemen from the interior plains. The royalist reconquest was completed in April 1815 with the landing on the coast of Venezuela of an expeditionary force of 10,000 Spanish troops, led by General Pablo Morillo, despatched by the vengeful Fernando VII (Stoan 1974). On his return from his long exile in France in 1814, Fernando VII immediately abolished the 1812 constitution, declared all the work of the Cortes null and void and resolved to reconquer America by force of arms. Thus, for Spanish-Americans who had been seduced by the offer of a constitutional monarchy with democratic elements, there was now a stark choice: accept the restoration of absolutism or take up arms for full independence. The latter was easier said than done, for Morillo and other commanders imposed harsh reprisals in a conflict that had become a civil war rather than a simple struggle between Americans and peninsular Spaniards. It is sometimes suggested that Fernando's intransigence destroyed the opportunity of reconciling moderate Creoles to continued Spanish rule on the basis of constitutionally guaranteed autonomy. The evidence from Mexico contradicts this: there the early insurgency led by Miguel Hidalgo and José María Morelos was destroyed by the Creole elite of landowners, churchmen, merchants and mine owners because its popular character threatened their socio-economic power. It was only in 1821, following the restoration in March of the liberal constitution in Spain, that Agustín de Iturbide was able to persuade Mexican conservatives that independence would provide a better guarantee of their privileged status than continued subservience to an increasingly anti-clerical Spain (Anna 1978: 209). There, as in Brazil, the institution of monarchy was preserved after independence, but it soon collapsed, paving the way for Mexico's adoption in 1824 of a federal constitution closely modelled on that of the United States.

Having taken Caracas, Morillo captured the bastion of Cartagena in December 1815, and reached Bogotá where he restored the old vice-regal regime in May 1816. These events led Bolívar, who had taken refuge first in Jamaica and then in Haiti, to rethink his entire strategy. He resolved to bypass Caracas, establish a base in the Orinoco, take the war to New Granada, then return to defeat the royalist strongholds on the coast of Venezuela, and so create a powerful state, Gran Colombia, incorporating both Venezuela and New Granada. In pursuit of this plan Bolívar was able to draw upon the personal credit that he had accumulated in London in 1810, where from 1816, despite protests from Spanish diplomats, the British government took no effective steps to prevent López Méndez from purchasing arms and recruiting British military personnel for the patriot cause. All told, some 7,000 European adventurers, the majority of them British and Irish, served between 1816 and 1825 in Bolívar's armies (Brown 2006: 1, 40). Half of them perished from fever or died on campaign, and 1,000 deserted, but the remainder joined Bolívar in his Orinoco capital of Angostura (now Ciudad Bolívar). He declared the independence of the republic of Colombia on 17 December 1819, insisting that the new state should have not only a people's house, but also a strong executive, a hereditary Senate and a Chamber of Censors intended to moderate the popular will. In the event, its 1821 constitution, approved by the congress of Cúcuta, encouraged by his declaration 'I am a soldier by necessity, and also by choice . . . A Government office is a torture chamber to me', watered down the more authoritarian of Bolívar's demands (Johnson 1968: 92, 172). For his part, Bolívar left the politicians to it, while he, bolstered by his foreign legionaries, took the battle to the royalist stronghold of Ecuador. His 1822 victory at the battle of Pichincha secured the existence of formally democratic Gran Colombia, albeit for only eight years, and barely six months beyond the death of Bolívar, as he waited in Santa Marta to go into self-imposed exile, convinced that his work had been in vain.

The Southern War of Liberation

In South America the other great focus of the Revolutions for Independence was Buenos Aires, where on 25 May 1810 an open meeting of the city council, supported by the officers of the militias that had defeated the British in 1807, deposed the viceroy and established a governing junta, which immediately despatched expeditionary forces to spread the revolution. By the time that the formal independence of the 'United Provinces of South America' was declared in 1816, the province of Paraguay had declared its own independence in 1811, the Banda Oriental (that is, the territory on the eastern bank of the River Plate, now modern Uruguay) had declared itself for the royalist cause in an attempt to preserve its autonomy from Buenos Aires, and three expeditions to Upper Peru (modern Bolivia) had been beaten off by a combination of genuine royalists, provincial separatists and powerful forces motivated by the hope of restoring Upper Peru to the rump of the old vice-royalty (Lynch 1986: 89–127). For successive regimes in Buenos Aires, the defection of Paraguay was an irritant, but that of the Banda Oriental was more serious because it allowed Brazil to spread its influence to the River Plate. The 1831 independence of the 'Oriental Republic of Uruguay', agreed in 1828 after a sterile war lasting three years between Buenos Aires and Brazil, was designed to create a buffer state between the two bigger countries. But the critical problem was Upper Peru: as long as powerful royalist forces survived, willing and able to expand their power into the interior provinces around the River Plate, the revolution was not secure.

The solution, requiring meticulous planning and organisation, was devised by the other great hero of South American independence, José de San Martín. As John Lynch's recent biography explains with superb clarity, San Martín took an army of 5,000 men through the high passes of the formidable southern Andes in January 1817 and won major victories against the surprised royalists (many of them Peruvian) at the battles of Chacabuco and Maipú in February and April, thereby securing the independence of Chile (Lynch 2009). In collaboration with its first president, Bernardo O'Higgins, San Martín then created a liberating expedition of 5,000 men, which was landed on the coast of Peru, south of Lima, in September 1820 by the newly created Chilean navy under the command of Thomas Cochrane. Following the evacuation of Lima by the royalist forces and their retreat to the interior of Peru, San Martín declared independence on 28 July 1821. Peruvians celebrate this as their national day, but the job was far from complete. Realising his inability to persuade the Peruvian elite to take the war to the royalists, San Martín travelled north to Guayaquil in July 1822 for his only meeting with Bolívar. On his return to Lima, he resigned his title of Protector and returned to Chile, leaving the way open for Bolívar, aware of its classical roots, to accept the title of 'Dictator' from the Peruvian congress and bring down his Colombian army to eventually end royalist resistance at the battle of Ayacucho in December 1824. Some mopping-up operations were required in Upper Peru in early 1825, and a few royalist fortresses refused to surrender until 1826, but essentially the Wars of Liberation were over. The once mighty Iberian empires on the mainland of Latin America were no more, although Spain was able to hang on to Cuba and Puerto Rico until 1898, when finally ousted by that emerging imperial power, the United States.

Conclusion

The successful outcome of the Latin American liberation movements brought at least constitutional forms with some democratic promise to new nations that had previously known only absolutism. Their lack of constitutional experience was apparent. Peru, for example, had six constitutions by 1860 (Pike 1967: 116–17). Chile had four constitutions in the first fifteen years after independence, until the country's oligarchy rejected democracy and imposed a new code in 1833 that restricted suffrage to literate, affluent men, thereby achieving the remarkable result that the presidency was held by only four men, each serving two consecutive five-year terms, until the 1870s (Collier 1967: 345–7). In Brazil, Pedro I imposed a constitution in 1824 with some democratic features, but that reserved for the emperor the 'moderating power', enabling him to dismiss a ministry when he saw fit, and then engineer elections to provide a majority for a new one. Mexico's 1824 constitution was democratic but largely ignored by military leaders, who gave the country thirty different presidencies in as many years. The 1819 and 1826 constitutions of the United Provinces of South America proved to be unworkable because of irreconcilable differences between the largest state, Buenos Aires, and the others, with the result that Juan Manuel de Rosas, *de facto* president between 1835 and 1852, simply held the office of governor of Buenos Aires.

Behind the political instability, liberation brought some increased social mobility for ignorant, sometimes illiterate, generals, but very little for the indigenous masses: those on the frontiers of empire were slaughtered to make way for farms and ranches, while those who had paid tribute in the colonial period found that their communal holdings came under increased pressure from liberals keen to turn them into small farmers. Blacks gained little, for slavery continued, and indeed intensified after independence, surviving until 1888 in Brazil. Brazil, like Chile, now has its first woman president, a precedent set by Argentina. When we see a black president in Brazil or one of mestizo origins in Chile or Argentina, it will be safe to conclude that true democracy has finally arrived, two centuries after the conclusion of the Wars of Independence.

References

Anna, T. E. (1978), *The Fall of the Royal Government in Mexico City*, Lincoln, NE: University of Nebraska Press.

Anna, T. E. (1983), *Spain and the Loss of America*, Lincoln, NE: University of Nebraska Press.

Brading, D. A. (1991), *The First America: The Spanish Monarchy, Creole Patriots and the Liberal State, 1492–1867*, Cambridge: Cambridge University Press.

Brown, M. (2006), *Adventuring through Spanish Colonies: Simón Bolívar, Foreign Mercenaries and the Birth of new Nations*, Liverpool: Liverpool University Press.

Collier, S. (1967), *Ideas and Politics of Chilean Independence, 1808–1833*, Cambridge: Cambridge University Press.

Esdaile, C. (2003), *The Peninsular War: A New History*, London: Penguin.

Fausto, B. (1999), *A Concise History of Brazil*, Cambridge: Cambridge University Press.

Fisher, J. R. (1970), *Government and Society in Colonial Peru: The Intendant System 1784–1814*, London: Athlone.

Fisher, J. R. (1985), *Commercial Relations between Spain and Spanish America in the Era of Free Trade, 1778–1785*, Liverpool: Centre for Latin American Studies.

Fisher, J. R. (1997), *The Economic Aspects of Spanish Imperialism in America, 1492–1810*, Liverpool: Liverpool University Press.

Fisher, J. R. (2003), *Bourbon Peru, 1750–1824*, Liverpool: Liverpool University Press.

Fisher, J. R. (2008), 'Imperial Rivalries and Reforms', in T. H. Holloway (ed.), *A Companion to Latin American History*, Malden, MA: Blackwell, pp. 178–94.

Geggus, D. (1982), *Slavery, War and Revolution: The British Occupation of Saint Domingue, 1793–1798*, Oxford: Clarendon Press.

Haring, C. H. (1958), *Empire in Brazil: A New World Experiment with Monarchy*, Cambridge, MA: Harvard University Press.

Johnson, J. J. (1968), *Simón Bolívar and Spanish American Independence, 1783–1830*, Princeton, NJ: Van Nostrand.

Lynch, J. (1986), *The Spanish American Revolutions, 1808–1826*, 2nd edn, New York: W. W. Norton.

Lynch, J. (2006), *Simón Bolívar: A Life*, New Haven, CT: Yale University Press.

Lynch, J. (2009), *San Martín: Argentine Soldier, American Hero*, New Haven, CT: Yale University Press.

Pearce, A. J. (2007), *British Trade with Spanish America, 1763–1898*, Liverpool: Liverpool University Press.

Phelan, J. L. (1978), *The People and the King: The Comunero Rebellion in Colombia, 1781*, Madison, WI: University of Wisconsin Press.

Pike, F. B. (1967), *The Modern History of Peru*, London: Weidenfeld & Nicolson.

Racine, K. (2003), *Francisco Miranda: A Transatlantic Life in the Age of Revolution*, Wilmington, NC: Scholarly Resources.

Salcedo Bastardo, J. L. (1981), *Crucible of Americanism: Miranda's London House*, Caracas: Cuadernos Langoven.

Stoan, S. K. (1974), *Pablo Morillo and Venezuela, 1815–1820*, Columbus, OH: Ohio State University Press.

Viscardo y Guzmán, J. P. ([1810] 2002), *Letter to the Spanish Americans*, Providence, RI: The John Carter Brown Library.

Chapter 23

1848: European Revolutions

Mike Rapport

Between February and April 1848, the conservative order which had dominated Europe since the fall of Napoleon in 1815 was felled by the hammer-blows of revolution across the continent. The revolutions swept liberal governments to power, tasked with forging a new political order based on the principles of civil rights and parliamentary government. By the end of 1849, all the revolutions had collapsed and the short and violent European experiment in liberal (and, in some countries, democratic) politics was over. For the history of democracy, the fascination of 1848 lies in the variety of democratic forms that emerged in such a short space of time and in such a diversity of places. The revolutions witnessed, if only incipiently, the application of the rich and conflicting variety of democratic ideas and practices that have since been identified and closely defined as part of the modern democratic experience. These sharp divisions within democratic thought – over the right level of popular participation, over the relationship between the people and the leadership, and over the role of the state in society – were all present in 1848 (Duncan 1983: 6).

There was, first, an outright conservative rejection of democracy. Secondly, the more moderate liberals of 1848 thought of democracy in terms of universal civil liberties, not political enfranchisement: all citizens would benefit from civil equality, meritocracy and civil rights, but not all would have the right to vote. Thirdly, there were liberals who embraced what is generally taken to be the modern meaning of democracy, that is, representative government based on universal (in 1848, male) suffrage. Yet, fourthly, there were more radical strains of democratic thought in 1848, proponents of a 'pure' or 'direct' democracy who virulently opposed the notion of representative democracy, seeing it as a perversion of the popular will, as 'a mystification . . . the perpetual duping of political democracy', according to French socialist Victor Considérant (cited in Rosanvallon 2000: 172). There were, fifthly, those who rejected democracy altogether: for the French revolutionary socialist Auguste Blanqui, the term itself was a label deployed by those who would 'steal' the revolution and let it fall to the reactionaries. Democracy was 'a vague, banal word, without precision, a word made of rubber' (Rosanvallon 2000: 167). Finally, in France at least, the Revolution of 1848 culminated in a curious offshoot of democracy: Bonapartism, or plebiscitary dictatorship combining authoritarian government with social reform, while appealing to popular sovereignty.

Experiments in National Democracy

Quentin Skinner has argued that to describe a political system as 'democratic' today means, implicitly, to praise it (Skinner 1973: 298). This was not yet universally the case in mid-nineteenth-century Europe. For conservatives who lost power in the spring of 1848, 'democracy' was anathema, conjuring up the long shadows of the guillotine, the bloodthirsty 'mob' and the social 'anarchy' of the French Revolution of 1789. The liberals, who wanted to stabilise the new order as quickly as possible, shared some of these anxieties and in most places sought to restrict the franchise. Yet they accepted that civil liberties would supply the fundamental principles of the new order. The revolutions of 1848 therefore had an important impact in the development of democracy, because they drew hundreds of thousands of Europeans into politics, even when they did not enjoy the suffrage.

As nineteenth-century nationalists, the liberals sought to forge their new order within the framework of the nation-state. For the Germans and the Italians, this necessarily entailed national unification. For the Czechs, Slovaks, Hungarians, Transylvanian Romanians, Serbs, Slovenians and Croats, it meant autonomy within the multi-national Habsburg Empire, or even full independence. For Polish and Romanian liberals, whose countries were split between foreign empires, it meant winning *both* independence and national unity. The liberals were also confronted by the 'social question': the revolutions were born of a desperate economic crisis made worse by dislocation and distress from the relentless press of population growth and industrialisation. The liberals therefore faced forceful demands for social intervention by the state, which thrust forward questions of social and economic rights, as well as political freedom. For socialist critics of the emerging liberal order, including Marx and Engels, political liberty and civil rights were not enough to resolve the social question. For them, 'democracy' came to mean bourgeois and petty-bourgeois radicalism, which sought to overthrow autocracy and establish representative government, but to do so within an emerging capitalist social order excluding the proletariat from power. Marxists would support democracy in the struggle against royal absolutism and noble privilege, but would then oppose it (Levin 1983: 79). These issues of democracy, nationalism and the 'social question' engendered bitter conflicts among the revolutionaries, giving the conservatives their chance to strike back – and they did so everywhere by the end of 1849.

The revolutionaries of 1848 generally agreed that political stability would be attained through constitutions providing representative government and guaranteeing civil rights. One of the achievements of 1848 was the destruction of royal absolutism in many states and the emergence of constitutional, if not democratic, government. The counter-revolution restored absolute monarchy in most places, but in two important states, Piedmont-Sardinia and Prussia, absolutism was permanently abolished – and those states eventually led the push for the unification of Italy and Germany. Moreover, the revolutionaries hurled a further ideological challenge to royal authority: their emphasis on the nation-state threatened the very legitimacy of Europe's dynastic states and multi-national empires.

The Spread of the Franchise

Yet not everyone was to enjoy full political enfranchisement. Nowhere were women given the suffrage. Many liberals were anxious that a broad electorate would bring political chaos and social revolution. Universal male suffrage was therefore introduced only in a few places. Foremost amongst these was France, where the enfranchisement of all adult male citizens had been a central demand of the republican opposition before 1848. The new Second Republic could scarcely deny it now. Even so, there were two conflicting views as to how the new democracy should function: moderates thought in terms of representative government, while radicals pressed for a system of direct democracy in which every citizen had a direct role in making the laws. Following the Parisian *sans-culottes* and their sectional assemblies of 1793, the logic of direct democracy was that it could only operate locally – there would be no central state. 'We want no authority,' declared the tract, *Gouvernement direct du peuple*, 'neither legislature, nor executive, nor judiciary . . . and if we take the words State and government in the sense that they have been used up to now, we could say that we want neither one nor the other' (Considérant 1851; Rosanvallon 2000: 192). This came close to the 'anarchism' of Pierre-Joseph Proudhon, but the friction between the proponents of direct democracy and the adherents of the representative system presages later debates between 'classical' and 'empirical' theorists of democracy. Democratic suffrage in France was in any case curtailed during the conservative backlash, which took the vote away from a third of the electorate in May 1850. This disenfranchisement of 2.8 million men allowed Louis-Napoleon Bonaparte to pose as the defender of universal male suffrage when his coup d'état of 2 December 1851 established his plebiscitary dictatorship (Agulhon 1973: 169).

In Germany, some 75 per cent of adult males were allowed to vote in the elections of spring 1848 to the Frankfurt Parliament, charged with drafting a German constitution. This figure masks considerable local variations: the regulations stated that all 'independent' males could vote, but each of the thirty-nine states of the German Confederation interpreted that provision as they chose. In Prussia, only 5–10 per cent of adult males were excluded, but in Baden, Hanover and Saxony, up to 25 per cent were denied the suffrage (Siemann 1998: 80–1). The disillusion with these limits led thousands of radicals to rise up in a vain bid to provoke republican, democratic revolution in Baden in April 1848.

In Austria, the imperial suffrage law of 11 May excluded servants and those dependent upon a weekly or daily wage. Four days later, the imperial government was cowed by a *Stürmpetition* – mass protests backed by the threat of force on the streets of Vienna – to promise Austrians a much wider electorate. Even so, the new law restricted the number of voters by insisting a subject had to live in the constituency for six continuous months, which excluded the poorest migrant workers and journeymen. Workers also had to be 'independent', a term interpreted in a restrictive way to exclude potential voters (Siemann 1998: 82–5). In the Czech lands, servants, the poorer peasants and the urban workers were excluded from the elections to the Estates of Bohemia and Moravia (Pech 1969: 62). In Hungary, the emperor's constitutional concessions to the Magyars enfranchised some 25 per cent of the population: landless peasants and wage-earners were excluded (Deak 1979: 96–7). Some governments quite deliberately enfranchised only a small elite, in order to satisfy the moderate liberals and split them from the more radical opposition. In Piedmont-Sardinia, voting qualifications included a literacy test and property ownership, which restricted the suffrage to 8 per cent of the adult male population (Beales and Biagini 2002: 105). Some states avoided revolution by timely concessions on the suffrage: Belgium and the Netherlands enfranchised wider sections of the middle class. In Sweden-Norway (in a regal union since 1815) and Britain, the governments managed to weather the storm without making any constitutional concessions, the former by suppressing the opposition, the latter by facing down a strong challenge from the Chartists, a well-organised working-class movement which demanded the democratic reform of Parliament.

The ability of the electorate to influence the legislature's political colour was often hemmed in by systems of indirect election, as happened almost everywhere in Germany (one exception was Württemberg). The Austrian parliament was indirectly elected, allowing landowning farmers, local officials, judges and clergymen to dominate the second round of voting. The voices of the electorate might also be tempered by a bicameral legislature, as in Piedmont, Denmark, Prussia and the short-lived German Imperial Constitution. In Hungary, the April Laws replaced the old two-house Diet by a single-chamber National Assembly, but the suffrage was far from democratic. Electoral systems could also be weighted to benefit the wealthiest parts of the electorate: the Prussian constitution granted universal male suffrage, but in May 1849 voters were broken down into three classes, ensuring that the rich chose a third of the delegates to parliament. Only in the French Second Republic was a unicameral system based on direct elections and the suffrage for all adult males introduced immediately. The short-lived Roman Republic, founded in February 1849 after the flight of Pope Pius IX, proclaimed itself a 'pure democracy' and followed the French example.

In practice, the political impact of such a system was blunted by the way in which voting was carried out: in France, every commune was summoned to vote collectively at the capital of each department. Consequently, villagers marched *en masse* to the polls, often led by their priest or local squire, which gave ample opportunity for these figures to assert their influence and exploit habits of rural deference and village solidarity (Tocqueville [1850–1] 1964: 129–30). At the polls, there were neither ballot papers nor voting booths: a voter wrote out his own preference – or, if he was illiterate, had someone write down his choice for him (Agulhon 1973: 65). In practice, therefore, individual choice could be circumscribed by communal pressures. In East Prussia, peasants were disappointed that their monarch did not appear among the candidates, so they wrote 'Frederick William IV' on their ballots (Orr 1980: 316).

Some incipient forms of party organisation were witnessed in 1848. Hungary's parliamentary system had already witnessed the emergence of political parties. When the Habsburg government prodded the emperor's Hungarian supporters into forming a 'Conservative Party' in 1846, the liberals, led by Lajos Kossuth, coalesced into a 'Party of United Opposition' (Deak 1979: 54–6). The development of a proto-party system was most sophisticated in the Frankfurt parliament, where deputies of particular political tendencies, following the tradition set by the French Revolution in 1789, sat according to their views on the 'right', 'centre-right', 'centre-left' and 'left'. They acted like modern parties, imposing voting discipline, forming coalitions, forging political platforms and disseminating manifestos (Siemann 1998: 122–6). In France, the different tendencies in republican opinion were initially given coherence by the newspapers that had existed prior to 1848: *Le National* for the moderates and *La Réforme* for the radicals. After the elections of April 1848, they faced a strong grouping of royalists and monarchists. It was the far left, the 'democratic socialists', who led the way in developing sophisticated ways to mobilise their supporters and convince voters, particularly in the countryside. Yet across Europe, the eighteenth-century equation of 'party' with 'factionalism' still lingered: a third of the Frankfurt delegates belonged to no group. The full emergence of modern forms of pluralistic politics did not materialise in 1848.

Emancipation

Yet some achievements of 1848 did prepare for the future of democracy. Most important of all was the emancipation of hundreds of thousands of peasants, religious minorities and colonial slaves. Peasants had played an active role in the revolutions in 1848, and landowners were nervous about the emerging momentum for an assault on property, but the revolutions freed the peasants from the last traces of the *seigneur* and the burdens of serfdom. In Hungary, the abolition of serfdom was decreed after Kossuth played on landlord fears of peasant insurrection: labour obligations, tithes and manorial rights were abolished. In western Germany, the *Grundherren*, the last landlord rights over the land and its inhabitants, were abolished, and the compensation payments which remained from the destruction of *seigneurialism* under Napoleon were cancelled. Some monarchs saw emancipation as a way to secure peasant loyalty for a counter-revolutionary strike back. In the Austrian Empire, the imperial court at Vienna issued edicts emancipating Czech peasants from the *robot* (labour obligations towards their landlords) and the Ukrainian peasants of Galicia from serfdom. The Austrian parliament later moved the formal abolition of 'all servile relationships', but Emperor Ferdinand took the credit.

There were limits to peasant emancipation almost everywhere. The landlords were to be paid compensation, which they could invest in their estates, while the peasants were impoverished by the debts incurred. In Hungary, nobles clung onto lucrative rights, such as monopolies on selling wine, keeping doves and pigeons, holding fairs and charging road tolls and ferry dues (Deak 1979: 102–3). The terms of emancipation were therefore crafted to ensure the survival of the social and economic pre-eminence of the great landowners. Yet the emancipations of 1848 served to shape the future of European democracy in important ways. Until 1848, the relationship between the state and the peasant in Central and Eastern Europe had been mediated by the noble landlord, who had responsibilities for policing and taxing 'his' peasants on behalf of the government. The state now assumed these roles and the peasantry theoretically had the same rights as other subjects. In the long run, therefore, the emancipations of 1848 prepared the ground for the integration of the peasants as citizens of the modern nation-state (Blum 1978: 373–4).

Religious minorities were also emancipated, particularly Jews (who won equal rights in France in 1791). The legal status of German Jews had varied from one state to another, but they were granted the same rights as all German citizens under the German Constitution. All German states, except Bavaria, enacted similar legislation (Siemann 1998: 186). In Hungary, the road to Jewish emancipation was rockier: when the Diet proposed to enfranchise everyone with enough wealth, regardless of religion, anti-Semitic riots forced the liberals to delay. Yet when the revolution developed into an all-out war of independence from Austria in 1849, Jews were granted the full rights of citizenship (Deak 1979: 85–6; Deme 1976: 29–30, 48–9). Jews and the Protestant Waldensians in Piedmont-Sardinia were emancipated in 1848 (Beales and Biagini 2002: 93–4). The Jews of the Papal States had to wait until the Roman Republic in 1849. The counter-revolution, currying the favour of the peasantry (many with traditional prejudices against the Jews), rolled back some of these gains. In Austria, Jews had to wait another twenty years before they definitively won equal civil rights. In Prussia, they were excluded from state service after 1848, although they were meant to enjoy civil equality. In Italy, after the restoration of Papal authority, Roman Jews were forced back into the ghetto, but in Piedmont-Sardinia, Protestants and Jews enjoyed civil rights until Mussolini turned back to repression in the next century. Yet the religious emancipations in 1848 had great significance: they posited a pluralistic definition of 'nationality' when it was otherwise equated with ethnicity. It was also a step away from the confessional state (where political loyalty was associated with an established religion) towards the modern, secular state, which defined citizenship on the basis of rights, duties and a shared sense of national identity. The Roman Republic's Constitution made this explicit: 'The exercise of civil and political rights does not depend upon religious belief' (Beales and Biagini 2002: 246).

There were also global ramifications for the events of 1848, since, as a result of the revolutions, slavery was abolished in some overseas empires. In France, anti-slavery had been a plank in the platform of the republican opposition prior to 1848. The revolution swept aside the resistance of the colonial interests and a quarter of a million enslaved people were emancipated. They assumed full civil and political rights, joining the European colonists as political (though not social) equals. In Algeria, European colonists, though not the indigenous population, were given political rights. Denmark and Sweden had avoided the hammer-blows of revolution, but they abolished slavery on their Caribbean island colonies in 1848 (Rapport 2008: 176).

The most serious limit to the emancipations of 1848 was the failure to give women equal political rights. Yet the denial of formal political enfranchisement did not prevent women from engaging in revolutionary politics in other ways. Twelve feminist newspapers were published in Paris, while Italian women wrote for liberal journals such as Cavour's *Risorgimento*. In Prague, the writer Boena Nimcová spoke out against anti-Semitism and German nationalism, and called for social justice and improvements in female education (Pech 1969: 327). Women engaged in the political club movement across Europe, including some French socialist and German democratic societies, or by establishing associations of their own. Kathinka Zitz-Halein's Humania Association, founded in Mainz in May 1849, supported the democratic, republican uprising in defence of the German constitution. Eugénie Niboyet founded a Parisian women's political club that boasted a network of corresponding members from across western Europe. Pauline Roland and Jeanne Déroin organised the 'Fraternal Association of Democratic Socialists of Both Sexes for the Liberation of Women' and established a union of 104 workers' associations aiming for equal pay and conditions. Déroin stood for the National Assembly in May 1849, although her candidacy was declared illegal because she was a woman. In Prague, the Club of Slavic Women sought to improve women's education, protested against the Austrian occupation and secured the release of political prisoners (Rapport 2008: 176–9). In Italy, upper- and middle-class women were involved in the campaigns for Jewish and protestant emancipation (Belgiojoso [1848] 1971: 375–6). In the United States, women – already mobilised by the anti-slavery campaign – met at Seneca Falls, New York, to demand equal rights of property and education, equality within marriage and the vote. Women did not win the right to vote in 1848, but women's rights were thrust onto the political agenda.

The Rise of Democratic Rights

If they were not democrats, the liberals of 1848 were universally committed to civil rights, including freedom of conscience, speech, the press and association. Associations within American civil society were admired by Alexis de Tocqueville because he saw a vibrant civil society as essential for stopping democracy sliding into a tyranny of the majority: 'There is no end which the human will despairs of attaining by the free action of the collective power of individuals' (Tocqueville [1835–40] 1994: 189–90). European liberals agreed and the revolutions opened the wide public space in which civil society, released from the restrictions of the previous regime, could freely act. The secret police evaporated and censorship collapsed. The press flourished: the United States *chargé d'affaires* in Vienna, William Henry Stiles, observed that bookshop windows were suddenly crammed with works, 'which, like condemned criminals, had long been withdrawn from the light of day; boys hawked throughout the city addresses, poems, and engravings, illustrative of the Revolution – the first issues of an unshackled press' (cited in Rapport 2008: 65). There was an explosion in print everywhere. Before the revolution, Austria had seventy-nine newspapers, most of which avoided political discussion, but in 1848, 388 titles rolled off the presses, most of them political. In Paris, 300 new newspapers appeared, totalling a print run of 400,000 copies. Prussian newspapers mushroomed from 118 titles to 184. By 1849, Germany had 1,700 newspapers and, for the first time, the country had an engaged 'partisan' press reflecting opinions from across the political spectrum (Siemann 1998: 112).

People organised themselves into clubs, associations and societies to shape opinions and argue their points. The public engagement with politics was unprecedented in Europe, except in France, which had its traditions dating back to 1789. Yet even there, the effervescence of political clubs was striking: at their height in April 1848, Paris had 203 popular societies, with an estimated membership of 70,000 people (Amman 1975: 33–5). Less widespread, but still vocal and influential, were the radical Italian clubs espousing Mazzini's vision of a unitary Italian republic, putting pressure on the liberals. German democratic associations aimed to push the revolution towards republican democracy. The First Democratic Congress was held in Frankfurt in June, with delegates representing eighty-nine associations from sixty-six different German towns. By October 1848, Prussia alone had an estimated 250 democratic associations. The Central March Association, half-a-million strong and representing 950 democratic associations by the spring of 1849, mobilised democrats to force the German states to ratify the constitution passed by the Frankfurt Parliament (Siemann 1998: 94–9).

The political stirring of the people did not necessarily work in the revolutionaries' favour. Some of the most successful organisations were those that served the counter-revolution. The conservatives quickly learned that they could defeat the revolution with its own weapons. They played on popular fears of disorder and anarchy, but also appealed to religion and monarchy. In southern Germany, Catholics were mobilised in defence of the old order by the 400 'Pius Associations' (named after the then pope), with a 100,000-strong membership. In Prussia, Lutheran pastors drummed up Protestant support for the 'King and Fatherland' associations, which boasted 300 branches by the spring of 1849, with a membership of around 60,000 (Sperber 1994: 161). In Austria, a Constitutional Club attracted conservatives with its emphasis on law and order, swelling its membership to 30,000 (Rath 1969: 304).

For mid-nineteenth-century liberals, one of the essential rights and duties of a citizen was to bear arms: like the vote, it was a mark of citizenship. In 1848, this was no mere ideal, but an absolute necessity: the incipient liberal order owed its existence to the uprising of armed citizens. An organised militia was deemed vital to protect the new regime from counter-revolution. A common feature of the revolutions was therefore the creation (or expansion) of the militia. In Vienna and Prague, where 'civic guards' already existed, the ranks were now swollen by liberal bourgeois, and joined by 'Academic Legions' of militant students. Elsewhere, new militias were created, as in Berlin, Milan and Venice, where the republic's leader, Daniele Manin, took his turn at guard duty (Ginsborg 1979). Hungary formed a National Guard on the French model. Yet the liberals also hoped that the militias could be used to protect private property against social revolution. For this reason they sought to restrict membership to middle-class citizens.

This was a hotly contested issue. In France, the National Guard was democratised and the elite companies abolished. The ranks of the National Guard swelled, more than doubling its size in Paris from 85,000 to 190,000 in a matter of weeks. Moreover, these militiamen elected their own officers (Harsin 2002: 279–81). Consequently, the National Guard could not always be relied upon to defend the existing order. During the bloody June Days, in which a democratic-socialist uprising was crushed by the moderate government, many National Guards failed to muster and some joined the insurgents. It was precisely for this reason that, in other countries, the liberals were deeply reluctant to arm all citizens. Membership of the Hungarian National Guard was dependent upon property ownership, although once the war of independence erupted anyone willing to serve was enlisted. In Berlin, the liberalised regime in March 1848 permitted everyone to bear arms, even if they were not part of the civic guard. Students and workers duly formed themselves into paramilitary 'mobile associations' serving the radical cause rather than the liberal order. In October, when the Prussian parliament decided to disarm these groups, eleven protesters were shot dead in the process. Central to the militia problem in 1848 was the question of who possessed the monopoly of legitimate force in a democratic state. The militia could support the new regime, but it might also back the democratic aspirations of the radicals. Unsurprisingly, civic militias were usually disbanded with the counter-revolution. Moreover, nowhere except in France and Hungary were the revolutionaries able to wrest control of the regular armed forces from the monarchs. This was one of the major causes of their failure: the revolutions did not extend democratic control over the military.

Working-class Initiatives

The liberals also fell because the revolutions stirred fears of social upheaval, driven by the anger and misery of European workers. Sparked as they were by the worst economic crisis of the nineteenth century and coming at a time when artisans were facing the intense pressures of early industrialisation, the 1848 revolutions aroused workers into defending their social and economic interests. Yet this, too, was part of the democratic mobilisation of that year and this was a lesson of 1848 in socialist theories of democracy. If for Marxists the aim was an egalitarian society, not political democracy, social democrats allowed that democracy was integral to socialism, since it gave workers the means for mobilisation and self-expression (Duncan 1983: 6–7). The French labour movement received a fillip from the Provisional Government, with the establishment of the Luxembourg Commission to hear workers' delegates express their views on industrial relations, wages, conditions and the organisation of manufacturing. Working-class organisations flourished in Germany. Master craftsmen and skilled artisans gathered at a congress in Frankfurt in July 1848, seeking to press the German parliament to restore the guilds, while apprentices and journeymen formed the Workers' Fraternity and met in a Worker Congress, demanding a ten-hour working day, pensions, free education, the abolition of taxes on consumption and a progressive income tax, as well as a fair division of government contracts and cheap sources of credit. The Fraternity boasted 15,000 members from no less than 170 German workers' societies (Siemann 1998: 89–94). More radical were Karl Marx and Friedrich Engels, who forged the Communist League in 1847 as an underground socialist organisation. Early in 1848, they published the *Communist Manifesto*, which offered a potentially explosive analysis of society and class conflict and produced a newspaper, the *Neue Rheinische Zeitung*, in Cologne (Marx and Engels [1848] 1973). Yet most German workers wanted to work within the emerging constitutional framework, so that Communist activity in 1848 is best seen as a portent for the future, a symbol of the difficulty of balancing social justice with political freedom.

This was one of the most destructive issues that dogged the liberals: the fundamental disagreement between moderates and radicals over whether the new order should guarantee social and economic rights, or restrict itself to upholding political freedom and civil liberties. In Paris, the tragedy of the 'June Days', in which the government crushed an uprising by despairing, unemployed workers shouting for a 'democratic and social republic' and the 'right to work', had its bloody echoes elsewhere in Europe, including Vienna and Berlin. These insurrections played into the hands of the conservatives, who offered authoritarian solutions to the dangers of social revolution.

The political mobilisation of the national minorities of Eastern and Central Europe also gave the conservatives the opportunity to defeat the revolutions. While the liberals argued for the equality of all peoples, they pressed for the greatest territorial and political advantage for their own nationality. There was a bitter war of words between Czechs and Germans, a military conflict between the German Confederation and Denmark over Schleswig-Holstein, another between Prussia and Polish liberals over the duchy of Poznań and a civil war in Hungary between the Magyars and a coalition of Serbs, Croats and Romanians. The poisonous ethnic divisions were deepened by social conflicts, because frequently landlords and peasants had different ethnic identities. The Romanian–Magyar conflict was a war of Romanian peasants against Hungarian landlords. The Habsburg court in Vienna abolished serfdom in Galicia to secure the loyalty of the predominantly Ukrainian peasantry against their liberal Polish landlords. The court also armed and financed troops for the Croats, Serbs and Romanians. The mobilisation of nationalist feeling and the exploitation of deep-rooted social grievances empowered the conservatives against the liberals.

Conclusion

The great lesson of 1848 was that popular political mobilisation was not necessarily a force for revolution. Democratic freedoms helped the conservatives as much as the liberals and radicals, particularly if the public was 'managed' by appeals to monarchy, patriotism, religion and property against the spectre of 'anarchy', 'communism' and 'terror'. After the counter-revolutionary triumph, Europe experienced a decade of iron-fisted rule that made the pre-revolutionary conservative order seem positively lax. Yet the mounting social pressures unleashed by industrialisation and international competition forced all governments to confront political reform. By 1914, parliamentary government was the norm, but democratisation was faltering. While Germany, France, Austria, Italy and the Russian Empire had universal male suffrage, it was often hemmed in by complex electoral systems. Democratisation usually occurred on conservative terms: democratic reform was a means of integrating the peasantry and the urban working class into the social order. A populist alliance between the conservative elites and the masses was a way of outflanking troublesome opponents like middle-class liberals and socialists.

For all their limitations, the 1848 revolutions mark an important step in the history of democracy. The introduction of elections where they were previously unknown, the emancipation of large numbers of people and the experience of a civil society unshackled from censorship – all politically mobilised wide segments of European society for the first time. The revolutions might even be called Europe's 'apprenticeship in democracy', even if democracy, when it did eventually come, was open to exploitation by less than democratic interests.

References

Agulhon, M. (1973), *1848 ou l'apprentissage de la République 1848–1852*, Paris: Seuil.
Amman, P. H. (1975), *Revolution and Mass Democracy: the Paris Club Movement in 1848*, Princeton, NJ: Princeton University Press.

Beales, D. and E. F. Biagini (2002), *The Risorgimento and the Unification of Italy*, Harlow: Pearson.

Belgiojoso, C. T. de ([1848] 1971), 'Les journées révolutionnaires à Milan', in J. Godechot (ed.), *Les révolutions de 1848*, Paris: Albin Michel, pp. 373–410.

Blum, J. (1978), *The End of the Old Order in Rural Europe*, Princeton, NJ: Princeton University Press.

Considérant, V. (1851), *La solution; ou, Le gouvernement direct du people*, Paris: Librairie Phalanstérienne.

Deak, I. (1979), *The Lawful Revolution: Louis Kossuth and the Hungarians 1848–1849*, New York: Columbia University Press.

Deme, L. (1976), *The Radical Left in the Hungarian Revolution of 1848*, New York: Columbia University Press.

Duncan, G. (ed.) (1983), *Democratic Theory and Practice*, Cambridge: Cambridge University Press.

Ginsborg, P. (1979), *Daniele Manin and the Venetian Revolution of 1848–49*, Cambridge: Cambridge University Press.

Harsin, J. (2002), *Barricades: the War of the Streets in Revolutionary Paris, 1830–1848*, New York: Palgrave.

Levin, M. (1983), 'Marxism and democratic theory', in G. Duncan (ed.), *Democratic Theory and Practice*, Cambridge: Cambridge University Press, pp. 79–95.

Marx, K. and F. Engels ([1848] 1973). 'Manifesto of the Communist Party', in D. Fernbach (ed.), *The Revolutions of 1848: Political Writings*, vol. 1, Middlesex: Penguin, pp. 62-98.

Orr, W. J., Jr (1980), 'East Prussia and the Revolution of 1848', *Central European History* 13, 303–31.

Pech, S. Z. (1969), *The Czech Revolution of 1848*, Chapel Hill, NC: University of North Carolina Press.

Rapport, M. (2008), *1848: Year of Revolution*, London: Little, Brown.

Rath, R. J. (1969), *The Viennese Revolution of 1848*, New York: Greenwood Press.

Rosanvallon, P. (2000), *La démocratie inachevée: histoire de la souveraineté du peuple en France*, Paris: Gallimard.

Siemann, W. (1998), *The German Revolution of 1848–49*, Basingstoke: Macmillan.

Skinner, Q. (1973), 'Empirical Theorists of Democracy and their Critics: A Plague on Both their Houses', *Political Theory*, 1(3), 287–306.

Sperber, J. (1994), *The European Revolutions, 1848–1851*, Cambridge: Cambridge University Press.

Tocqueville, A. de ([1850–1] 1964), *Souvenirs*, Paris: Gallimard.

Tocqueville, A. de ([1835–40] 1994), *Democracy in America*, ed. J. P. Mayer, London: Fontana.

Chapter 24

1919: After Versailles

Conan Fischer

If a name can be attached to the Treaty of Versailles and the wider Paris Peace Settlement, it is that of the United States President, Woodrow Wilson. Of all the Allied leaders, it was Wilson who caught the international popular imagination, and it was Wilson who appeared to offer the defeated Germans and their allies the best prospects for a tolerable peace within a reformed global order. In December 1918, he arrived in France for the peace conference to a hero's welcome and possessing an aura of moral authority to which many British and French delegates initially willingly deferred. Wilson had consistently campaigned for democratic principles during his earlier political career, whether to contain the power of domestic big business or to intervene in the affairs of Latin American countries to advance the cause of 'order and democracy' (Macmillan 2003: 17). The United States had entered the First World War on the Allied side in April 1917 in response to Germany's unrestricted submarine warfare and the sinking of American shipping. In January 1918, Wilson went on to spell out American war aims in a speech to Congress. These 'Fourteen Points' focused on national self-determination, arms control and the promotion of open diplomacy under the supervision of a new international body (the League of Nations). Democracy as such was not mentioned, but given his unreserved attachment to democratic principles, Wilson regarded national self-determination and democracy simply as two sides of the same coin. Thus, he perceived the war itself as 'a struggle between the forces of democracy, however imperfectly represented by Britain and France, and those of reaction and militarism, represented all too well by Germany and Austria-Hungary' (Macmillan 2003: 12).

Emerging National Democracies

American leaders anticipated steering the entire European continent on the road to democratic renewal and reform, using the new-found financial strength of the United States as a means to this end. As for the European Allied powers, the political mood in France was more conservative, for victory was held to have vindicated the political status quo. Nonetheless, France saw itself as the historic wellspring of modern democracy. It had been a parliamentary republic since 1870 and looked back to the republican and libertarian heritage of the 1789 Revolution as well as French involvement in the American War of Independence. Britain's political ethos was similarly attached to democratic and liberal principles, which could trace their roots back over many centuries of English and Scottish history, finding institutional expression within the English, and from 1707 the British, parliamentary system and in the independence of English and Scottish law. Italy was a much newer political creation, united in 1859–60 under the leadership of the liberal constitutional monarchy of Piedmont whose rulers identified with the democratic values of northwestern Europe. Although Italy had been allied to Germany and Austria-Hungary before the war, and many senior politicians and the bulk of public opinion favoured neutrality, the government joined hostilities on the Allied side in May 1915. It certainly had an eye to territorial aggrandisement, but also sought to align Italy with the democratic powers and secure influence over the peace settlement that an Allied victory would bring.

The war was portrayed by Allied politicians and propagandists as a struggle of civilian-controlled parliamentary democracies against authoritarian, and particularly Prussian, militarism. This was something of an over-simplification, not least because the Allied camp included the repressive and autocratic Russian Empire, although revolution swept away the Tsarist order in Russia in February 1917. Parliamentary democracy appeared briefly to be on the agenda until Lenin's revolutionary Bolsheviks seized power during October and founded what became in 1922 the Soviet Union, the world's first communist state. The prospects for democratic government elsewhere in Central and Eastern Europe did, however, appear much more favourable. At the war's end democratic revolutions swept the former enemy states of Germany, Austria and, briefly, Hungary and new national states emerged from the wreckage of the multi-national Austro-Hungarian Empire and the western borderlands of the defunct Russian Empire. These secessionists legitimised their cause through the espousal of cultural and ethnic nationalism, but also embraced democratic parliamentary government that could be juxtaposed neatly against the principle of dynastic legitimacy that had underpinned the region's old empires.

Not all these nationalist leaders identified immediately with the Allied cause. The Polish patriot and military leader, Jośef Piłsudski, initially sided with Germany and Austria-Hungary, for it was Russia that had controlled the Polish heartlands around Warsaw for more than a century. Austria governed Polish-speaking Cracow and the province of Galicia, and Germany possessed a sizeable Polish minority in its eastern borderlands, but these minorities lived under the rule of law and in relative security. The Tsar's Polish subjects, however, like many minorities in the west of the Romanov Empire, had long resented attempts to 'Russify' them and were subjected to a spate of appalling atrocities as the tide of war turned against Russia. The Jews of western Russia, in particular, were made scapegoats as alleged pro-German Fifth Columnists, often with deadly consequences. As Jay Winter observes: 'It is no irony to say that the advancing German army units were seen as liberators of some Jewish communities, reduced by [Russian] fire and slaughter to a miserable state' (Winter 2006: 97–9). More generally, it was Germany and not the Allies who, between 1916 and 1918, sanctioned the creation of embryonic national states along the western rim of the collapsing Russian Empire: Finland, the Baltic states, Poland, Belarus and the Ukraine. The Germans did so grudgingly, primarily to push back the Russian frontier as far as possible to the east, and in the meantime the German and Austro-Hungarian authorities requisitioned foodstuffs and other resources from occupied Imperial Russian and Romanian territory in order to feed their own starving cities and sustain their struggle against the economically superior Allied powers. Piłsudski fell out with Berlin in 1916 and was interned for the remainder of hostilities. Released at the war's end, he thereafter had no difficulty in aligning the emergent Polish parliamentary republic with the Allied cause.

However, the Allied camp served as the obvious destination from the outset for leaders of the minorities within the Austro-Hungarian and German empires. Most of these leaders came from the relatively small urban intellectual elites of their respective societies, and as such had long been attracted by Western, liberal democratic ideals. Once the war began, many sought voluntary exile in the West, including the future foreign minister of Czechoslovakia, Edvard Beneš, Professor of Sociology at Prague University before the war, and the country's future president, the philosopher Tomaš Masaryk. They lobbied for Czechoslovakia's independence particularly hard in Paris, where their cause was bolstered by the Slovak leader, Milan Štefanik, who had moved to France a decade before the war and then served in the French air force during the conflict. Polish intellectuals, too, possessed long-standing cultural ties with France, which could be traced back to the Napoleonic era or before; ties that included a familiarity with the country's republican democratic heritage. East European exiles also lobbied in the Russian, American and British capitals, and while the Allies were slow to endorse an outright break-up of the Habsburg Empire, and the British doubted the viability of a sovereign Polish state, this nationalist pressure and Austrian military weakness left the Western powers increasingly open to the notion of an Eastern Europe consisting of democratic nation-states. For France, in particular, this outcome also had strategic attractions, for a strong and politically stable Poland and Czechoslovakia offered Paris loyal allies to help contain Germany and also to block any future efforts by the Soviet Union to spread revolution across Europe.

Peace Negotiations

Germany's allies sought armistices during the autumn of 1918 and Germany itself signed a ceasefire which came into effect on 11 November. The victor powers moved swiftly to organise peace negotiations, separately with each of the defeated powers: Germany, Austria, Hungary, Bulgaria and the Ottoman Empire. The German treaty was accorded absolute priority, for Germany remained inherently a great power with the potential to reopen hostilities if it so wished or if the Allies failed to enforce a viable peace settlement. Indeed, once the Treaty of Versailles had been signed in June 1919 and ratified by the German parliament, the Allied leaders left the peace conference and entrusted the drafting of the remaining accords to their officials and subordinates. These efforts left much to be desired, for the remaining settlements were flung together hastily and carelessly, which hardly boded well for the continent's future. As the British diplomat Harold Nicolson reminisced: 'we came to Paris confident that the new order was about to be established', but 'left as renegades', having created a world where 'the new order had merely fouled the old' (Nicolson [1933] 1964: 187). Within a decade the entire peace settlement was unravelling and during the 1930s the European continent slid back into war. What, then, had gone wrong and what consequences did this have for democracy on a continent where, the Soviet Union apart, parliamentary liberalism appeared briefly to have swept all before it? Historical debate has focused on the German treaty, but more on its terms and practicality than its impact on the democratic process (Boemeke *et al.* 1998; Sharp 1991). For one thing, the US Congress refused to ratify the settlement, so depriving the post-war order and the newly created League of Nations of American involvement. It fell to the European Allies to watch over the settlement President Wilson had done so much to shape, even though the terms of the treaty were too harsh to be readily acceptable to Germany and yet insufficiently stringent to be enforceable. Even if the treaty was the 'best available at the time', it was eventually undermined by an unrepentant and bellicose Germany (Sharp and Fischer 2008: 1). Similar concerns were as old as the treaty itself. The Allied Commander-in-Chief, Marshal Ferdinand Foch dismissed the treaty in 1919 as militarily weak and little more than a twenty-year ceasefire. Similarly, the French President, Raymond Poincaré, fretted that his prime minister, Georges Clemenceau, had been browbeaten by his British and American allies into agreeing to far too lenient a treaty. Democracy was inextricably linked both to the process of peace making and the post-settlement era. Woodrow Wilson believed that national self-determination and democracy, a world where governments were accountable to free and informed citizens, would remove the fundamental causes of war. His proposed League of Nations would mediate whatever international disputes arose in a golden era of open diplomacy. It followed that a durable peace could be concluded only with a democratic German government that spoke for and answered to its people.

Meanwhile, the German authorities already faced growing internal pressure for far-reaching democratisation that had its roots in the pre-war era. The country's constitution had been framed in 1871 by the Prussian statesman and architect of German unification, Otto von Bismarck. He had conceded a national parliament whose lower house (the Reichstag) was elected by universal male adult suffrage and which controlled national public finances. He had also granted the individual states of the German federation, such as Bavaria, Prussia, Saxony and Baden, considerable domestic autonomy. Those in southwestern Germany developed essentially democratic forms of state government, but the parliament of the largest state, Prussia, was dominated by its conservative rural gentry, kept in power by a complex property-based franchise. Conservative Prussia's political weight was brought to bear in the upper house of the national parliament where it had sufficient delegates to block any efforts further to democratise German political life. Bismarck's constitution also divided the national legislature from the executive. The government answered to the emperor rather than to the elected chamber of parliament, and it was the emperor who appointed the chancellor (prime minister) and the remainder of the cabinet. These ministers were seldom parliamentarians, still less party politicians, in contrast to the situation in Britain, France or the United States. The army chiefs also answered directly to the emperor rather than to parliament, and the emperor alone could declare war or make peace. In 1918, however, as defeat loomed, the authority and credibility of Emperor Wilhelm II became increasingly threadbare. In this situation United States and German domestic pressure combined to make regime change part and parcel of the peace process.

Germany's politically powerful army chiefs conceded the point and engineered the nomination by Wilhelm II of a liberal prince, Max of Baden, as chancellor on 3 October 1918. Max was a genuine reformer, appointing his ministers from the majority group of parties based around the political centre and left. These parties – the Social Democrats, Progressive Liberals and the (Catholic) Centre Party – had already demanded democratisation and the conclusion of a moderate peace in mid-1917, well before Germany was effectively defeated. On 28 October, this new and representative government passed legislation that transformed Germany into a constitutional monarchy. Henceforward, chancellors and the armed forces would answer to the democratically elected Reichstag.

By this time ceasefire talks with the Americans were well advanced and the German negotiators obtained reassurances that the peace settlement would be based on Wilson's Fourteen Points. To all intents and purposes it appeared that a negotiated and essentially moderate peace accord would follow between the newly democratised Germany and the victor powers. Such a peace would not have been painless for Germany. It had violated Belgian neutrality in 1914 and accepted that the devastated country deserved far-reaching compensation. Damage to the private property of other Allied civilians would also be made good. Berlin also anticipated limited territorial losses and the introduction of arms control, but all within the framework of a new global order in which Germany would participate as an equal and where the country's inherent economic strength offered a route to national recovery.

However, things quickly took a different course when the Allies disagreed among themselves over the terms to be imposed on Germany and it proved impossible for them collectively to negotiate with Berlin at all. French leaders doubted whether Germany had really renounced its imperialistic and militaristic past and demanded a settlement that greatly reduced German territory and economic potential. There was even talk of breaking up the country altogether and returning to the pre-1871 situation when central Europe had consisted of a collection of small- and medium-sized Germanic states (Stevenson 1998: 87–101). The French Socialists, who were in opposition, questioned the wisdom of excessively punishing the new Germany for the transgressions of the old, and the British and Americans also had their doubts. They suspected the French of harbouring hegemonic ambitions of their own and insisted on a settlement that bore at least some resemblance to the Fourteen Points. Too harsh a treaty, the British argued, would prove unacceptable to Berlin and so undermine the very peace the Allies sought. The German delegates in Paris stood by as the main Allied powers thrashed out a series of compromises on territory, the payment of reparations, the seizure of German intellectual property, military sanctions and disarmament, and the future ownership of the German overseas empire. The draft treaty was presented to the Germans for written comment, but not negotiation.

Problems with Democracy in Germany

Meanwhile, a second, mass uprising erupted in Germany early in November 1918, which saw the monarchy swept away and eventually replaced by a parliamentary republic – named the Weimar Republic after the city where the new constitution was framed. The burden of expectation placed on this new, democratic order was immense. German society had suffered appallingly during the war and people expected the privations of bereavement, famine, disease and grinding toil to make way for a just and equitable post-war order. The new republic delivered what it could, including votes for women, the democratisation of Prussia, far-reaching workplace and trade union legislation and educational reform, but money was desperately short. Germany had effectively bankrupted itself fighting the war and the peace treaty now demanded far more in reparation payments to the Allies than initially anticipated. The French, in particular, had been panicked into upping their demands on Germany once it transpired that the Americans expected their European allies to repay the huge loans they had incurred fighting the war. French pleas that their massive 'blood sacrifice' should be offset against America's cash sacrifice fell on deaf ears in Washington. Historians have debated whether the reparations were payable at all, but, as Gerald Feldman remarked, at the end of the day 'the only people who really believed that the Germans could pay their reparations obligations . . . are some historians' (Feldman 1998: 445). Patricia Clavin adds to Feldman's observation: 'It is a fast declining number of historians at that' (Clavin 2005: 515). The economist John Maynard Keynes, who resigned in protest from the British peace delegation, denounced the settlement as grossly excessive and ultimately ruinous, and no one in Germany thought otherwise (Keynes 1920: 119). The only disagreement in Berlin was over whether at least to try and fail to pay reparations (so pressuring the Allies to moderate their demands) or simply to repudiate the entire Versailles settlement. In the end, Weimar Germany continued to work within the parameters of Versailles, but constantly sought revision of its more onerous economic and military provisions.

This crisis exacted a heavy price on German democracy. The collapse of the monarchy during the 1918 Revolution had enraged conservatives, who were influential in the higher echelons of German society, including the armed forces, justice and education. However, the measured character of the revolution, which sought as much to refurbish as to overthrow the 1871 Bismarckian settlement, also exasperated those on the far left, who demanded the creation of an explicitly socialist regime. Radical socialists joined with anarcho-syndicalists to form the Communist Party of Germany, which found a significant constituency among people whose lives had been wrecked by the war or by the economic crises that plagued the post-war republic: hyper-inflation during 1923 and a savage slump after 1929. Never strong enough to topple Weimar, the presence of these communists nonetheless nourished fears that the Bolshevik Revolution might repeat itself in Germany. For many frightened citizens the prevention of such an outcome, if needs be by authoritarian means, outweighed any commitment to democracy. For all this, republican democracy, contrary to the claims of some older histories, did initially enjoy overwhelming support (Fischer 2006: 6–32; Sontheimer 1973: 101). However, extremists of the left and right sniped away at the democratic order and found ready support from some military commanders who were anxious to shuffle off responsibility for Germany's defeat. The anti-democratic narrative accused the democrats, whether socialist, liberal or Catholic, of having undermined the war effort with their pro-peace stance and then of cravenly signing away Germany's future at Versailles. This, the extremists raged, was a dictated treaty to which no man of honour could subscribe, a treaty that had effectively condemned the nation to abject poverty. The German Communist Party similarly accused the republic of selling out to international capitalism and so reducing the German people to slavery. German workers would henceforth toil to pay the reparations that flowed into the coffers of bankers in London, Paris and New York – or so the argument ran.

Not all on the radical right were monarchists. New organisations were formed, still authoritarian and decidedly militarist, but dedicated to rallying support for a dictatorship. By the mid-1920s this gaggle of right-wing groupings had coalesced behind Hitler's National Socialist Party, which subsequently attacked the republic with devastating effectiveness during the Great Depression of 1929–32. The radical right consistently blamed 'greedy bankers,' enriched by unearned bonuses, for Germany's plight (Fischer 2011: 216). The Nazis added racialism to this witches' brew when caricaturing the bankers as cosmopolitan Jews sucking the country dry. The new republic, itself allegedly alien and Jewish, was accused of conniving in this disastrous process. The German business community did not buy this nonsense. Employers had struck a deal with the pro-republican labour movement in November 1918 which significantly enhanced employees' rights, but as the economy and public finances deteriorated the businessmen despaired at Weimar's inability to take tough decisions. Unemployment soared after 1928, itself doing nothing for democracy's prospects, and Germany's farmers were engulfed by a global agricultural crisis, which saw prices for their produce slump and their businesses collapse. Weimar had adopted proportional representation as its electoral system, which resulted in a multi-party, rather than a two-party political system. Politicians appeared condemned to endless haggling and horse-trading bereft of any clear, strategic vision, and even before Hitler took power moves were afoot to strengthen the government at the expense of parliament. If the Nazis never succeeded in gaining majority electoral support, their anti-democratic credentials and calls for strong leadership persuaded many key players in German public life that they should be involved in government. Hitler was appointed chancellor in January 1933 at the head of a right-wing national coalition. He exploited his new position ruthlessly, persuading the president to grant him emergency powers, which enabled him to sweep aside the democratic process within a matter of months.

The Italian Experience

Looking further afield in Europe, Allied victory had confirmed and reinforced the existing democratic order in northwestern Europe, Britain and France included, but Italian reactions to the conflict and the ensuing peace settlement were very different. Most felt that the country had suffered too heavily in a controversial war for disappointingly limited gains. In 1915, Britain and France had promised Italy extensive territory in the Balkans and the eastern Mediterranean to lure Rome into the war, but these commitments cut across their own ambitions and across promises to others, including the Yugoslavs and Greeks who were also represented at the peace conference. Even before the peace talks were complete the Italian delegates felt slighted, with the Foreign Minister Sidney Sonnino declaring: 'I have ruined my

country whilst believing that I was doing my duty' (cited in Macmillan 2003: 306). Far
from consolidating democracy in Italy, the peace settlement did much to undermine it.
Italian irregular paramilitaries seized the disputed city of Fiume on the border with
Yugoslavia in defiance of their own government and the Treaty of St Germain
(between the Allies and Austria), before the city was finally handed to Italy.
Disappointment over the meagre pickings of an empty victory melded with domestic
social upheaval as landless peasants returned from the fighting to demand property
rights and urban workers agitated for workplace and wider social reform. The liberals
had dominated the Italian parliament before the war, but the socialists made striking
gains in the 1919 elections as did the radical, peasant-oriented Popular Party. Deprived
of a working majority, the liberals' self-confidence and effectiveness as the guardians of
the democratic order declined. The socialists joined the Moscow-based Communist
International and the trade unions launched major strike campaigns, which the
minority liberal government appeased to the consternation of middle-class society.
Meanwhile, the Popular Party backed an intense grass-roots rural campaign for land
redistribution, which might eventually have created a large, conservative landowning
peasantry, but more immediately terrified the landlords and large tenant farmers.
Further elections in 1921 failed to restore liberal fortunes. A shaky, unsustainable
coalition was patched together consisting of liberals, moderate socialists and a new
party, the National Fascist Party.

   These fascists emerged from the war and its aftermath. A former socialist newspaper
editor, Benito Mussolini, supported the war from the outset, splitting from the anti-
war socialists. Immediately after the war he founded a war veterans' league, the *Fasci di
Combattimento*, in Milan, which became involved in skirmishes on Italy's disputed
northeastern frontier, but also involved itself in domestic political strife. The *Fasci*
claimed to embody a united Italy and fought in the streets against Popular Party and
socialist activists, whom it accused of dividing and further weakening the country. It
stood for property rights, but simultaneously demanded that employees be given a role
in day-to-day management of the workplace, so complicating any effort to place
fascism on the left or the right. In fact, fascism claimed to stand above the potentially
destructive struggle between labour and capital, leading Martin Clark to observe: 'The
Fascists were "bringing the workers into the system" while making sure they did not
dominate it' (Clark 1984: 218). Mussolini understood that street violence alone would
not bring him to power. In October 1921, he founded the National Fascist Party and a
fascist trade union, which provided him with a route to office within the fracturing
liberal state. By 1922, the Fascist Party had 500,000 members and sufficient seats in
parliament to block the formation of any non-socialist coalition that excluded them. In
October, Mussolini successfully demanded of the king the post of prime minister, and
thereafter reformed electoral law to favour the stronger parties over the weak. By 1925,
with the right merged into the National Fascist movement and the left driven from
public life, he had in effect created a one-party state in which he claimed to embody the
popular will. Fascism demanded a monopoly over political power and locked up or
occasionally killed political opponents who challenged Mussolini's right to rule.
Despite vaunted claims to have created a new style of 'totalitarian' government,
however, he had in reality done no such thing. Key institutions of state, including the

monarchy and army, and also the Catholic Church, retained their independence, and much of cultural life, including the cinema and important artistic movements, retained its autonomy. In this regard fascism contrasted with its racialist, Nazi cousin, whose leaders demanded conformity in every reach of life.

Democracy across Europe

Fascism, a distinctively twentieth-century creed and system of authoritarian rule, soon made its impact in Central and Eastern Europe, where the democratic regimes established after the war ran into difficulties (Eatwell 1997: xix–xx; Griffin 1998: x). The crisis was not universal. In the Scandinavian lands, where democracy had been established before the war, the inter-war economic crisis culminated in a settlement of differences between the agrarian and socialist interests in parliament. In contrast to Germany or Italy, the assertion of a common democratic citizenship had triumphed over social and ideological conflict without recourse to a fascist-style revolution (Hilson 2007: 8–32). In the Netherlands and Belgium, the democratic parliamentary system also accommodated deep-seated social and cultural diversity by accepting it as part and parcel of the fabric of national political life (Conway and Romijn 2007: 84–110). The same could be said for Switzerland, and Czechoslovakia managed to engage its mutually antagonistic nationalities – Czech, German, Slovak and smaller minorities – in the parliamentary process until Hitler succeeded in igniting German–Czech and Slovak–Czech tensions to destroy the country and with it, democratic government (Vyšný 2003).

Elsewhere in Eastern and Central Europe, Woodrow Wilson's dream of a community of democratic national states was realised only fleetingly. The problem lay partly in the character of east European nationalism, which had far less to do with a common citizenship and more to do with ethnic and religious distinction than Wilson appreciated. Furthermore, although the Americans were able to organise food aid and other material relief for the impoverished east of Europe, the Allies' military reach was limited and became ever more so as they demobilised. There were perfunctory negotiations with east European delegations at the Paris Conference; sometimes complicated by the arrival of competing representatives from countries that as yet lacked common taxation, currency, tariff, legal or administrative systems. There was little, if anything, in the way of custom or institutional procedure that bound the members of these nascent states to one another. And discussion in Paris ultimately counted for less than events on the ground where the militarily strong trampled on the weak. The Allies confined their active intervention to key flashpoints such as German–Polish frontier demarcation. The emergent states were left harbouring a series of grievances against one another and within their borders resentful ethnic minorities yearned for liberation.

Keynes was witheringly dismissive of the whole peace settlement because the Allies had settled accounts with the defeated powers rather than laying down a blueprint for the wider region (Keynes 1920: 211). Wilson had imagined that the League of Nations would subsequently resolve any outstanding difficulties. However, the Americans' failure to ratify Versailles left the United States outside the League, so it lacked the will or the military teeth to police the post-war world. Keeping Germany compliant and the wider territorial settlement intact was hard enough, however, little was said about the rise of fascism in Italy, which remained within the League under Mussolini, or about the disintegration of democracy across Eastern Europe and around the Mediterranean. In Spain and Portugal, conservatives and republicans struggled for power before army-backed authoritarian regimes eventually prevailed – in Spain's case only after a brutal civil war (1936–9). In southeastern Europe, where nation-states had been created on territory liberated from Ottoman rule during the nineteenth and early twentieth centuries, a partnership between monarchy and parliamentary government was established before the war, but these regimes struggled to accommodate the socio-economic and ethnic tensions of the inter-war period. Monarchists and republicans, communists and agrarians, civilians and soldiers sought to prevail. An impoverished and often illiterate farming population regarded the small islands of urban sophistication that nourished the traditional political elites with hostile incomprehension, further undermining any prospects for free-minded democratic tolerance (Aldcroft 2006). Even in defeated Austria and Hungary, with their more prosperous and educated peasantry, tensions between the Catholic countryside and socialist-inclined cities quickly exploded into revolutionary upheaval. In Hungary's case, a patrician style of government took over in 1919 and in Austria the democratic republic collapsed in March 1933 to be replaced by an authoritarian Catholic-conservative state.

To the north, in former Russian, Austro-Hungarian or German territory, republics rather than monarchies were established. Finland and the Baltic states of Estonia, Latvia and Lithuania possessed reasonably prosperous agricultural sectors that specialised in stock rearing, but neighbouring Poland struggled to restore economic activity to pre-war levels. Finland – more Scandinavian than Baltic in its history and character – maintained a functioning democratic system throughout the inter-war period, whereas the Baltic states adopted more authoritarian forms of government, albeit still with weakened parliaments. In Poland, a succession of short-lived democratic governments was brought to an end in 1926 when the military strongman Jósef Piłsudski seized power and ruled the country until his death in 1935. In common with the authoritarian regimes across much of Eastern Europe, Piłsudski sought a degree of popular legitimation for his government by holding controlled elections to a weak parliament. Fascist leagues sprang up across the east of Europe, but without managing to displace the patrician authoritarian regimes that came to dominate the region (Payne 1995). Fascism, therefore, influenced rather than shaped politics and Robert Evans' observation that the east of the continent slid into 'rising intolerance, disorder, brutality and misrule' seems a little harsh when considering the alternatives (Evans 2007: 234).

Conclusion

The Versailles era saw many European peoples experience democracy for the first time, but often briefly and temporarily. Democracy had emerged erratically in northwestern Europe through generations of revolution and evolution. A similar process arguably began significantly later in Eastern Europe and Iberia, and the post-

1918 peace settlement marked an important step in the democratic story rather than the end game. In the short term, authoritarian forms of rule prevailed, but in the longer term democracy became entrenched in Iberia and Greece during the 1970s, while Eastern Europe had to wait for the collapse of the Soviet Empire in the late 1980s. By the 1990s, Europe had finally come to resemble that imagined by Woodrow Wilson at the end of the First World War.

References

Aldcroft, D. H. (2006), *Europe's Third World: The European Periphery in the Interwar Years*, Aldershot: Ashgate.

Boemeke, M., G. D. Feldman and E. Gläser (eds) (1998), *The Treaty of Versailles: A Reassessment after 75 Years*, Cambridge: Cambridge University Press.

Clark, M. (1984), *Modern Italy 1871–1982*, London: Longman.

Clavin, P. (2005), 'Reparations in the Long Run', *Diplomacy and Statecraft*, 16(3), 515–30.

Conway, M. and P. Romijn (2007), 'Belgium and the Netherlands', in R. Gerwath (ed.), *Twisted Paths: Europe 1914–1945*, Oxford: Oxford University Press, pp. 84–110.

Eatwell, R. (1997), *Fascism: A History*, New York: Allen Lane.

Evans, R. J. W. (2007), 'The Successor States', in R. Gerwath (ed.), *Twisted Paths: Europe 1914–1945*, Oxford: Oxford University Press, pp. 210–36.

Feldman, G. D. (1998), 'Comment', in M. Boemeke *et al.* (eds), *The Treaty of Versailles: A Reassessment after 75 Years*, Cambridge: Cambridge University Press, pp. 441–5.

Fischer, C. (2006), ' "A Very German Revolution"? The Post-1918 Settlement Re-Evaluated', *German Historical Institute London, Bulletin*, 28(2), 6–32.

Fischer, C. (2011), *Europe between Democracy and Dictatorship 1900–1945*, Oxford: Wiley-Blackwell.

Griffin, R (ed.) (1998), *International Fascism: Theories, Causes and the New Consensus*, London: Arnold.

Hilson, M. (2007), 'Scandinavia', in R. Gerwath (ed.), *Twisted Paths: Europe 1914–1945*, Oxford: Oxford University Press, pp. 8–32.

Keynes, J. M. (1920), *The Economic Consequences of the Peace*, London: Macmillan.

Macmillan, M. (2003), *Peacemakers: The Paris Conference of 1919 and its Attempt to End War*, London: John Murray.

Nicolson, H. ([1933] 1964), *Peacemaking 1919*, London: Methuen.

Payne, S. (1995), *A History of Fascism 1914–1945*, London: UCL Press.

Sharp, A. (1991), *The Versailles Settlement: Peacemaking in Paris*, London: Palgrave Macmillan.

Sharp, A. and C. Fischer (2008), 'Introduction', in C. Fischer and A. Sharp (eds), *After the Versailles Treaty. Enforcement, Compliance, Contested Identities*, Abingdon: Routledge, pp. 1–4.

Sontheimer, K. (1973), 'The Weimar Republic – Failure and Prospects of German Democracy,' in E. J. Feuchtwanger (ed.), *Upheaval and Continuity: A Century of German History*, London: Oswald Wolff, pp. 101–15.

Stevenson, D. (1998), 'French War Aims and Strategic Planning', in M. Boemeke *et al.* (eds), *The Treaty of Versailles: A Reassessment after 75 Years*, Cambridge: Cambridge University Press, pp. 87–101.

Vyšný, P. (2003), *The Runciman Mission to Czechoslovakia, 1938: Prelude to Munich*, Basingstoke: Palgrave Macmillan.

Winter, J. (2006), *Remembering War: The Great War between Memory and History in the Twentieth Century*, New Haven, CT: Yale University Press.

Chapter 25

1945: Post-Second World War Japan

Takashi Inoguchi

This chapter examines the undertaking of the United States to bring democracy to Japan between 1941 and 1952 during both the Pacific War and the American occupation of Japan. It explores the extent to which the United States was successful in its effort to democratise Japan. The United States was determined that the wartime government of Japan must be destroyed by repeated military campaigns. Step by step, the United States helped to craft a small, conservative, pro-American force in Japan into a majority political party, and, in doing so, successfully brought democracy to the island nation. Before discussing US democracy promotion, this chapter begins by showing how, in Japan, war itself was used as an instrument for the spread of liberal democracy (Dower 2010; Hasegawa 2011; Iriye 1965, 1967; Iriye and Cohen 1990). The chapter concludes with a brief discussion of the problems that continue to challenge Japanese democracy, with a specific focus on the debt of history and ontological insecurity.

Japan to 1945

The pre-war Imperial Constitution of Japan (1890–1945) declared parliamentary monarchy as the political system of Japan. In order to see clearly the evolution of democratisation prior to 1945, under this rubric of parliamentary monarchy three phases can be discerned (Masumi 1965–80). First, in the early period of the 1890s and 1900s, the parliament was predominantly occupied by professional politicians of political parties that were by definition opposition parties. A small number of parliamentary members were pro-government parliamentarians. This was the result of the first general election of the Imperial Diet in which voting rights were restricted to adult Japanese males who paid a certain amount of tax to the state in 1889. The government called itself 'a government above parties'. Yet the constitution required that in order for a government budget proposal to be passed by a parliament a majority vote was necessary. The government used the tactics of bribing opposition members and manipulating them in exchange for cabinet positions. Second, recognising the need to have government parties in the Imperial Diet, pro-government political parties were steadily constructed and by the early 1910s the two-party system had been born. In 1925, universal male suffrage was legislated and in 1931 the centre-left party called the Social Mass Party sent a large number of parliamentarians to the Imperial Diet.

This period is referred to as Taisho (1912–25) democracy, which continued to the early period of Showa (1926–89) and lasted until an abortive military coup d'état occurred in 1936. It was during the early Showa period that Japan began its intrusions into China and established Manchukuo in 1931, increasing US apprehension and suspicion regarding Japanese ambitions in the region.

However, with the onset of the second Sino-Japanese War in 1937, Japan entered a third period of pre-1945 politics. It was marked by an upsurge in anti-democratic forces, such as the military and ultra-conservative parties, who centralised power and became increasingly authoritarian. This led the United States to side with China, then under the Kuomintang. In 1939, Germany invaded Poland, which triggered the European powers to enter the conflict that was later to be called the Second World War, and the Triple-Axis Pact connected Europe and Asia. The United States along with Britain, the Netherlands and China confronted Japan with embargoes in 1939 unless Japan withdrew from China. The US war strategy was to insist on Japan's withdrawal from China by stepping up sanctions. The consequence of embargoes was that Japan could either give in to the demand to withdraw from China, or fight back.

Being able neither to disengage its army in China, nor withstand a lengthy embargo, Japan launched military attacks against the Allied Powers. Japan decided to fight a war against the United States before the sanctions incapacitated its military ability as a result of a dwindling energy supply. On 7 December 1941, the Japanese Imperial Navy launched a successful surprise attack on the American naval base at Pearl Harbor, setting the stage for the US Congress to give the president a mandate for war. The vote was almost unanimous except for congresswoman Jeannette Rankin, a Republican from Montana, who argued against the war because of the lack of a clear and imminent danger to the nation (Savage 2007: 18). In the Japanese–American war, the tide turned against Japan as early as 1942 with the Midway naval battle. From then on Japan had to withdraw steadily from its overstretched battle fronts that circled from Micronesia and Melanesia through Dutch Indonesia, French Indochina and British Malaya and from India to China. Nonetheless, the tenacious Japanese resistance to the US attack in the Pacific, especially at Iwo Jima and Okinawa, led the United States to develop strategies specifically to provoke Japan's surrender.

In late 1944, the US government changed its strategy. The Japanese army that was stationed in China had driven the entire Kuomintang forces to the southwestern corner of China. The US government could no longer rely on Kuomintang-led China and chose instead to manipulate the peace-seeking domestic forces in Japan in order to accelerate Japan's surrender. Efforts were made in 1944 by pro-American and peace-seeking Japanese close to the Imperial family, including Prince Fumimaro Konoe and former foreign minister, Shigeru Yoshida, to accelerate Japan's surrender. In the US State Department, Stanley Hornbeck, the main proponent of the strategy to use Kuomintang-led China to destroy Japan, was replaced by Joseph Grew, the leader of the new strategy to use Japan in the coming years as a bulwark against Soviet ambitions to control east Asia. There was disastrous suffering for more than 500,000 civilians and military personnel in the Okinawan Islands. In March 1945, the United States firebombed the city of Tokyo killing more than 100,000 civilians overnight. Robert McNamara, one of the engineers of this massive city bombing, recalled that had the

United States lost the war, they would have been prosecuted as war criminals (McNamara *et al.* 1999). Added to this havoc was the use of nuclear weapons which were used twice when bombs were dropped on Hiroshima on 6 August 1945 and on Nagasaki on 9 August. More than 300,000 civilians were killed.

Despite popular mythology suggesting that US aggression prompted Japan's surrender, Tsuyoshi Hasegawa has argued that, in fact, Japan surrendered because the Soviet Union had entered the Pacific War on 9 August 1945 (Hasegawa 2005). Soviet forces advanced into the Japanese-occupied territories – Manchukuo, Sakhalin, the Kuriles and Korea – forcing 1 million civilians to flee. Up to that point, the Japanese army's argument in refusing peace with the United States was that 1 million troops could be transferred from China to the Japanese mainland to fight key last battles against an invading United States. But the shattered morale of the Imperial Army in Manchukuo and China meant that it was impossible to mount a final defence of Japan from the mainland.

Whatever the reason, the Japanese government finally surrendered on 15 August 1945. The utmost priority was placed on how to keep the emperor politically and physically intact. Although the surrender terms were that of unconditional surrender, the Japanese government, formed by those close to the Imperial family, started to negotiate. Before, on and after 15 August, this loyal group surrounded the emperor, fearing for his life or that the emperor's recorded surrender statement would not be aired on radio. On 2 September 1945, the United States and Japan signed the surrender documents aboard the battleship USS *Missouri* in Tokyo Bay. Utmost priority was given to protecting the emperor from being disgraced politically.

The US Strategy to Promote Democracy in Japan, 1945–1952

The broad convergence between the will of the United States to install a pro-American Japanese democracy and the desperate need of Japan to prevent the emperor from being executed for war crimes enabled a conciliation that made the eventual choice of Japan's regime a relatively predictable one: the emperor remained a figurehead, while his government was pro-American. From the outset, the US strategy was clear: keep the emperor and rule Japan indirectly through its bureaucracy, minus the war-tainted army, navy and Interior Ministry; draft a constitution and then translate it into Japanese; keep existing laws intact except for those from the wartime or consisting of generally anti-democratic sentiments; focus on the Cold War and keep US bases and facilities free and usable; and promote democracy within the framework of the US occupation (Dower 1999; Hata 1976; Iokibe 1985; Schaller 1985; Yergin 1977).

Aside from retaining the emperor, the United States was determined to dismantle much of Japan's wartime military bureaucracy in order to pave the way for democracy. In American eyes, the process of democratisation demanded the end of the old order. In the autumn and winter of 1945, a sweeping list of purges from public office included a wide spectrum of Japanese leaders as well as members of the army, navy, internal security police and several war-tainted bureaucrats. War criminals were identified, tried in court and executed.

This meant that an entirely new generation of Japanese elite emerged. These new elites participated vigorously and passionately after the pro-war upper echelon bureaucrats were purged. While many potential bureaucrats were killed on the battlefields or in naval conflicts, the emerging young conservative elite was fast climbing the ladder. They played a key role in recovery and reconstruction in the 1940s and 1950s, and spearheaded the effort to bring democracy to Japan. While the Americans laid the overarching framework, the Japanese elites were fairly free to do what they wanted to run the country. Needless to say, anti-American sentiments and issues of law and order or security matters were carefully monitored and sometimes censored (Yamamoto 1996). Yet the Japanese Communist Party was allowed to participate in political activities throughout this period and the extreme right-wing fringes were drawn in to the political process by the United States as they crafted a conservative, pro-American political system. Although the left and right political parts of the spectrum clashed fiercely, in particular, over the occupation by US armed forces, the discord did not descend into violence. Rather, friendly relations among political foes ensued.

Cleverly, the Supreme Commander of the Allied Powers, General Douglas MacArthur, sought to utilise the efforts of these new Japanese elites by adopting a policy of indirect rule. The occupation forces were composed of two key groups: the Cold War confrontationists, who had led the campaign to destroy Japan since 1941 (G2); and the left-leaning New Dealers, who introduced a progressive constitution with peace, freedom, social welfare and gender equality as the canon of a new nation (GS) (Itoh 2003: 75–6). The G2 was critical to the promotion of democracy in that it focused on fighting the Cold War. Amid the mushrooming of political parties, the G2 made sure that a conservative, pro-American political party was institutionally crafted. Shigeru Yoshida, an aristocratic and peace-seeking diplomat who was kept under house arrest during the war, became prime minister twice in the chaotic post-war years of 1945–55. Democracy promotion by Yoshida and the Liberal Democratic Party worked well in the sense that the US armed forces provided all the security-related facilities and services. The Yoshida Doctrine interpreted the terms of surrender to suit a new political purpose: free of heavy military burdens, Japan recovered swiftly and prospered for a long period (Dower 1999; Inoguchi 2007, 2011).

The GS, on the other hand, was constituted by a set of very young and idealistic Americans who sought to implement American ideology in the form of the draft constitution. Peace, freedom, social welfare and gender equality were at the heart of the American ideology instilled in post-New Deal America. The American official Beate Sirota Gordon, who inserted Article 24 on the rights of women and gender equality, was twenty-two years old at the time. In 1946, Japan extended the franchise to women and, when Japan regained its independence in 1952, the Japanese Constitution drew heavily on that drafted by the GS. Similarly, social welfare Articles became the basis of legislation in the 1950s and 1960s for medical insurance and pension schemes, which helped Japan to become a nation known for its long life expectancy in the 1990s and beyond. The democratic measures taken by the GS assisted the Japanese populace to mitigate the antipathy towards the occupation and not resort to violence.

In American terms, democracy promotion in Japan was a success story. The Freedom House grading of Japan in terms of civil liberties and political freedom has been continuously high. Free and democratic elections have been held since 1946. The first ten years after the war saw a mushrooming of political parties and then the formation of a one-and-a-half political party system where the Liberal Democratic Party was the long-time governing party (1956–2009, with a brief interruption in 1993–4). The United States was able to transform Japan into a pro-US democracy that would pose little security threat. The United States obtained Japan's compliance for the free provision of military bases, facilities and services for its national, regional and global security purposes. The United States also shifted Japan's primary attention from foreign and security issues to economic development and domestic redistributive issues, while enjoying access to a large market for trade and investment. The Americans had confirmed the Japanese commitment to key principles, such as freedom, democracy, market economy, human rights, gender equality and social welfare.

Today, a two-party system of sorts is functioning: the broadly left Democratic Party versus the centre-right Liberal Democratic Party. Unlike classical European political parties, Japanese political parties are not characterised by class cleavages. Thus, ideological diversity is not easily apparent between the two parties. Rather intra-party diversity is significant inside both parties. The Liberal Democratic Party is a centre-right party, but it contains an extreme right-wing fringe as well. The Democratic Party of Japan is a centre-left party, but it contains a sizable union-based left-wing as well as some members close to the extreme right.

However, Japanese democracy is far from perfect. Since 1945, Japan has become increasingly inward looking even when global and regional developments required their attention and investment. Japanese institutions have been plagued intermittently by their fragmented nature and the lack of political leadership that is due in part to security matters not receiving much attention at the highest level of politics. Japan has been passive in putting forth its emotions and ideas directly to the United States, often to the detriment of national interests.

The Debt of History and Ontological Insecurity

In discussing democracy promotion in Japan, other issues require reflection, namely, the debt of history and ontological insecurity (Zarakol 2009, 2010). The debt of history refers to the conscience deficit a nation can suffer as a result of waging an unjust war and executing it without much consideration of wartime international law. Those victimised in war remain negative towards the Japanese government at home and negative to Japan abroad (Hasegawa and Togo 2008; He 2009; Kimura 2010; Lawson and Tannaka 2011; Lind 2008). Korea and China have the most negative perceptions of Japan of all the countries in Asia (Inoguchi 2009). A partial reason for the debt of history continuing to be such a critical issue is related to ontological insecurity. From the very start of Japan's Westernisation process through to today, Japan has aspired to be on a par with the West through rule of law, freedom, equality, democracy and industrialisation. Yet for their earlier failures during the war and before, Japan still considers itself stigmatised.

In Japan, those vanquished in wartime have been customarily enshrined at Yasukuni

Shrine (Hata 2010). However, commemorating Class-A war crime criminals is a difficult issue for the Japanese government to handle. Yasukuni Shrine itself was originally founded after the Meiji Restoration in 1868 to enshrine supporters of the Restoration killed in internal battles against forces opposing the Restoration; those killed opposing the Meiji Restoration are not commemorated at Yasukuni. Over time, however, sentiments changed and those killed in the first Japan–China war of 1894–5 and the Japan–Russia war of 1904–5 were all enshrined at the Yasukuni Shrine, thereby becoming like the United States Arlington Memorial. General Tojo and other Second World War Class-A war criminals were initially shunned. But since then, the Yasukuni Shrine has changed status from a state institution to a private institution and the remains of Class-A war criminals were also enshrined there some three decades after the defeat.

   This has brought with it a great deal of controversy and stigma. The United Nations effectively excludes Japan as an outlier of a sort. Japan has not become central to the United Nations, nor a permanent member of the Security Council despite its economic contributions to the world and its participation in peace-keeping missions. Japan has also been constrained by its own constitution from having armed forces. National security has been more or less shouldered by the United States. Although Japan's Self-Defence Forces have become increasingly well equipped and well trained, in practice they cannot act alone except in the clearest cases of self-defence. Even when Japan's neighbours, China and North Korea, have become a threat, large or small, a stigmatised Japan does not have the constitutional authority to handle such issues. That Japan feels stigmatised and cannot even defend its own interests properly is internalised by the people, who thus feel something less than a sovereign nation and so something less than a sovereign democracy where the people are in charge of their own fate. This is how the debt of history and the associated ontological insecurity combine as an effective drag on Japan becoming a mature democracy.

Conclusion

The pro-American forces in Japan in 1945 and thereafter were fortunate because disruption did not occur. Emperor Hirohito lived and was allowed to reign continuously, even though his position was circumscribed to being a symbol of the nation while his practical, political authority and power became things of the past. Emperor Hirohito was one of the few long-living monarchs of the twentieth century and his continued presence ensured governmental legitimacy in Japan. Building on this sense of legitimacy, the post-1945 Japanese government laid the groundwork for an economic miracle that saw all elements of society striving together. It produced economic well-being that was translated into strong support for democracy. Yet, at the same time, the Japanese sense of historical debt has not been clearly resolved. Ontological insecurity looms large. Some portions of the Japanese citizenry continue to think that their leaders pursued Westernisation as late-comers and outsiders. While Japanese democracy continues to face a host of challenges, the story of post-1945 Japan nonetheless remains an important chapter in the broader history of democracy. On the one hand, it speaks to the ability of democracy to re-build vanquished nations, while, on the other hand, it reveals that historical memory – both domestically and on the global stage – can constrain the maturation of democracy.

References

Dower, J. W. (1999), *Embracing Defeat: Japan in the Wake of World War II*, New York: W. W. Norton.

Dower, J. W. (2010), *Cultures of War: Pearl Harbor, Hiroshima, 9/11, Iraq*, New York: W. W. Norton.

Hasegawa, T. (2005), *Racing the Enemy: Stalin, Truman, and the Surrender of Japan*, Cambridge, MA: Belknap Press.

Hasegawa, T. (2011), 'America to Hiroshima no kyoukun (Lessons of Hiroshima: Past and Present)', *Chuo Koron*, February, 202–13.

Hasegawa, T. and K. Togo (eds) (2008), *East Asia's Haunted Present: Historical Memories and the Resurgence of Nationalism*, Santa Barbara, CA: Praeger Security International.

Hata, I. (1976), *America no Tai Nichi senryo seisaku* (*United States Policy of Occupying Japan*), Tokyo: Ministry of Finance.

Hata, I. (2010), *Yasukuni jinja no saijintachi* (*Yasukuni Shrine*), Tokyo: Shinchosha.

He, Y. (2009), *The Search for Reconciliation: Sino–Japanese and German–Polish Relations since World War I*, Cambridge: Cambridge University Press.

Inoguchi, T. (2007), 'How to Assess World War II in World History: One Japanese Perspective', in David Koh (ed.), *Legacies of World War II in South and East Asia*, Singapore: ISEAS, pp. 138–51.

Inoguchi, T. (ed.) (2009), *Human Beliefs and Values in East and Southeast Asia in Transition: 13 Country Profiles on the Basis of the AsiaBarometer Surveys of 2006 and 2007*, Tokyo: Akashi Shoten.

Inoguchi, T. (2011), 'Prime Ministers', in T. Inoguchi and P. Jain (eds), *Japanese Politics Today*, New York: Palgrave Macmillan.

Iokibe, M. (1985), *Beikoku no Nihon senryo* (*United States Occupation of Japan*). Tokyo: Chuo Koronsha.

Iriye, A. (1965), *After Imperialism: The Search for a New Order in the Far East, 1921–1931*, Cambridge, MA: Harvard University Press.

Iriye, A. (1967), *The Origins of the Second World War in Asia and the Pacific*, London: Longman.

Iriye, A. and W. Cohen (eds) (1990), *American, Chinese, and Japanese Perspectives on Wartime Asia, 1931–1949*, Wilmington, NC: Scholarly Resources.

Itoh, M. (2003), *The Hatoyama Dynasty: Japanese Political Leadership through the Generations*, New York: Palgrave Macmillan.

Kimura, K. (2010), 'Why the History Issue between Japan and South Korea is likely to Persist', in M. Soderberg (ed.), *Changing Power Relations in Northeast Asia*, New York: Routledge.

Lawson, S. and S. Tannaka (2011), 'War Memories and Japan's "Normalization" as an International Actor: A Critical Analysis', *European Journal of International Relations*, 17(3), 405–28.

Lind, J. (2008), *Sorry States: Apologies in International Politics*, Ithaca, NY: Cornell University Press.

Masumi, J. (1965–80), *Nihon Seitoshiron* (*Japanese Political Parties*), 7 vols, Tokyo: University of Tokyo Press.

McNamara, R. S., J. G. Blight and R. K. Brigham (1999), *Argument without End: In Search of Answers to the Vietnam Tragedy*, New York: Public Affairs.

Savage, C. (2007), *Takeover: The Return of the Imperial Presidency and the Subversion of American Democracy*, New York: Hachette.

Schaller, M. (1985), *The American Occupation of Japan: The Origins of the Cold War in Asia*, Oxford: Oxford University Press.

Yergin, D. (1977), *Shattered Peace: The Origins of the Cold War and the National Security State*, Boston, MA: Houghton Mifflin.

Yamamoto, T. (1996), *Senryouki no Media Bunseki* (*Analysis of Media During Occupation*),Tokyo: Hosei Daigaku Shuppan Kyoku.

Zarakol, A. (2009), 'Ontological (In)security and State Denial of Historical Crimes: Turkey and Japan', *International Relations*, 24(1), 3–23.

Zarakol, A. (2010), *After Defeat: How the East Learned to Live with the West*, Cambridge: Cambridge University Press.

Chapter 26

1989: Eastern Europe

Peter M. E. Volten

The transitions to democracy in Eastern and Central Europe from 1989 onwards not only came as a big surprise both inside and outside the region, they were also characterised by incredible speed and by a radical challenge to the prevailing political cultures during the pressing phase of consolidation. The two companion concepts and processes – transition and consolidation of democratic transformation – are clearly culture-bound and dependent on the historical and present context of the country or region involved. This was particularly the case in Central Europe, where cultural and contextual confusion sometimes led to misunderstanding and friction. Westerners who showed their discontent or disappointment about progress regarding the implementation of norms and rules were rebuffed by their interlocutors in these countries: Westerners did not understand the unique background and situation of these countries, which had seen only rare moments of democracy before; what works in Western countries might not work because Eastern and Central Europe are different. There was a collision of different understandings of transition and democracy.

Even though most Westerners insisted that they did not intend to impose their particular view of democracy, partners in the region were often right in responding that the so-called advanced democracies simply claimed the features of their system as the salient, democratic ones. Democratic theory and practice are Western-centric and Western observers were often inclined to compare the experience in the region with their own history, or worse, – showing a demeanour of condescension – with their so-called advanced or modern democracies. As a conceptual tool, the description of four phases of transition and consolidation is useful, namely: the developmental path from authoritarianism to electoral democracy and via liberal democracy to the higher *qualitative* rank of mature or modern democracy (Schedler 1998). This model leads to helpful research questions and comparisons. For example, the question arises as to how to judge that a particular state or society is moving in the 'right' direction, that is, towards greater democracy. Conversely, there are challenges and dangers during these stages of democratic development that must be met to avoid slipping back into the less desirable arrangements. In practice, though, descriptions of these phased developments are vague and subject to many intangibles, but systematic thought is helpful to establish different stages of transition: 'preparatory, decision and habitation' or 'negative and positive consolidation' (Pridham and Lewis 1996: 2–4). Sceptics in Central Europe have a point when looking critically at the range of democratic models available: unique circumstances do matter. Above all, the legacy of communism – or 'the legacy of that legacy'– and the simultaneous processes of political and economic reform require a new approach, fresh theory and special skills (Berliner 1994: 381).

The important question is *to what extent* the experiences in the 1990s were distinct. Whether it concerns disturbing populism, media-manipulated and finance-driven elections or economic inequality, both Western and the new democracies are subject to these problems. Their situations are different to a certain degree, but not in principle. As Keane asserts, democracy as a 'form of government . . . of the humble, by the humble and for the humble' has always been beleaguered (Keane 2009: xii). A major question in this chapter, therefore, is why democracy has taken such firm root in some places and has been less successful in others. These differences are reflected in not only how the constitution is established and the appropriate rules and laws for elections are selected, but also in the quality of decision-making discussions which require a genuinely democratic style and an internalised, democratic political culture.

This chapter focuses on Central Europe (Czechoslovakia, Poland and Hungary) rather than on all the countries involved in transition after the developments of 1989. An attempt to describe the political transitions across the whole region, including the former Soviet Union and southeastern Europe, is impossible at any depth in a single chapter. It should be noted, however, that in spite of significant historical differences, Bulgaria and Romania are included in the discussion below because both countries have, rightly or wrongly, identified themselves as being part of Central Europe *and* are treated that way by the organisations to which they aspire to become member states: NATO and the EU. Many problems that these five countries faced were similar, but the ways in which they responded to those problems and the degree of success in countering them were different. By the same token, other parts of Eastern and Southern Europe also met their 'unique' circumstances head on. However, all had to overcome the obstacles of the Central European states as described below. The general response to specific predicaments are discussed in the Conclusion.

Transition towards Democracy

Roaming the streets of Prague at the very beginning of 1990, one wondered where the country should begin after the sudden fall of the communists. There was a strange feeling in the air: how was it possible that everything simply continued to move as if the country was still under communist rule?[1] The rusty, over-crowded streetcars moved as slowly as before and with the same frequent stops on the street corners while the driver got off and shifted the switch by hand, but they moved; the shops had the same limited choice of goods, but they were open and people apparently still had the money to buy; and thousands of civil servants continued to receive their pay and walked in and out their offices as if there had been no regime change at all. There was a reshuffled cabinet, but it included some 'old hands' and seemingly nothing had happened to the top layers of the huge departments that were not yet dismantled. Then, all of a sudden, everything went so fast, with great, albeit unguided determination. The secret services building was completely deserted. Václav Klaus, then the new minister of finance in Czechoslovakia and now president of the Czech republic, was one who argued that speed was more important than accuracy (Mastrini 1994).

The semi-competitive, yet free and fair, elections in Poland in June 1989 were followed by fully competitive elections in Hungary in December of the same year and Czechoslovakia in June 1990. The communist parties were challenged by numerous competitors, who, given the pejorative meaning of 'party', now labelled their organisations forum, movement, union, alliance or club. A huge number of these formations participated with a range of new candidates, mostly unknown to the public and sometimes even to one another. Yet they claimed to be trustworthy because they were supposed to share the same, new political preferences. Party structures, let alone a defined role for political parties as powerbrokers or elements of civil society, were not in place. Basically, governments of democrats had to be formed, and quickly. Those governments had to be staffed by experts, rather than those with governmental experience. They were called upon to write constitutions and issue laws. Parliaments had to assume their real task of reflection and end their time as 'the reality between a theatre and a museum', as the citizens of Prague jokingly referred to the old parliament. Formal, electoral democracies were enacted very fast. So fast, that many monthly, even weekly, Western publications were often sent to the waste bin, nicknamed OBEs (Overtaken By Events). Who could have foreseen that, shortly after the Prague Velvet Revolution, Bulgarian communists, seemingly with a firm hold on government, also would be toppled and that the untouchable Romanian dictator, Nicolai Ceaucescu, would flee from his own people and be tried by his own soldiers before Christmas 1989?

There are various explanations for these rapid transitions to electoral democracies. The first, is the evident eagerness to shake off the yoke of some forty years of political suppression and personal dehumanisation. Public life not only excluded millions from any kind of participation, but also alienated people from each other and from society. Public life co-existed with personal life only through double standards for human interaction, characterised by mistrust and selfishness, on the one hand, and by trust in a few friends and relatives, on the other. Under communism personal ambitions, interests and beliefs were circumscribed and civil society was broken, or almost. As the newly appointed director of the Institute of Sociology in Prague, Jiøi Musil, said 'We live in the Biafra of the spirit' (personal communication 1990). For decades his profession had been banned and a vibrant civil society suppressed.

The eagerness for change and the humanisation of one's life brought about a remarkable national unity. The national rally around change also occurred in Romania and Bulgaria, but to a lesser extent since submission to the central authority had been a constant in their history and public exposure to Western life and politics had been extremely limited under communist rule, particularly in the poor and under-developed countryside. Nevertheless, people shared both determination and conviction to move forward on the new democratic wave and to refuse to look back to the political past. The mood was one of optimism with scant fear of gliding back into the grip of authoritarianism. Civil society seemed to rise out of its own ashes, even if this would take far more hard work than the mere expression of hope. Arguably, the Poles may be said to have rallied most successfully, and in a more balanced way, around such shared sentiments, unimpeded by minority questions and conscious of the long recovery from the painful loss of their nation and sovereignty in history. There were still people and institutions entrenched in the habits of hierarchical, autocratic rule. Lust for personal, selfish gains was fed by the socio-economic hardship and by the loopholes that inevitably emerged from systemic chaos. Comparatively speaking, though, in Poland, political and societal developments were taking place more smoothly and in greater unison.

For the region generally, it came as no surprise that populists entered the fertile playground to stir up national or ethnic sensitivities. Vladimir Meèiar, the first Slovak premier after the elections in 1989 and later prime minister of the Slovak Republic (1993–8), was just one case in point where ethnic differences were utilised for political purposes. Elsewhere, as oppositional sentiments were exacerbated by ethnic strife against minorities, such as the Hungarians in Romania, Turkish descendants in Bulgaria and the Roma wherever they lived. At the same time, volatile social–economic conditions also threatened stability. The economic downturn and severe austerity programmes were haunting all political parties and coalitions in the region. Consequently, opposition forces were frequently able to win elections because, no matter how well a government in power performed, it was not perceived as 'enough' by the electorates. This was understandable as the people had to endure a 50–70 per cent loss in purchasing power and wait years before there was a change for the better. Around 1994, economic growth became visible, but it took all countries in transition about ten years before real GNP was to reach the 1989 level (European Bank for Reconstruction and Development 2008).

The determination and conviction in society at large to carry on democratic reform survived, however, and the programmes of the political parties reflected this popular sentiment. Even the Bulgarian Socialist Party (BSP), heir of the Communist Party, originally with the support of a majority and showing reluctance to shift from its traditional political positions, changed its mind in the mid-1990s. Until then, the BSP had no scruples about disregarding parliament and considering its own party's assembly the rightful place for national democratic decision making. However, strong opposition and objective reality forced the doubters to turn from Russian kinship towards Western-style democratic rule. At this point, it is necessary to stress the importance of Western 'contagion'. There was an eagerness for democratic change and detachment from Soviet rule. The West represented a pole of attraction about which more and more people had become aware since the Helsinki process started in 1973. That process was later institutionalised as the Conference on Security and Cooperation in Europe (CSCE) and civil rights groups like Charta '77 in Czechoslovakia hoped to use this international community for national purposes, particularly in the field of human rights. In that respect, the role of the CSCE process can hardly be overestimated.

The 1989 events opened up a genuine possibility of joining international institutions of democratic rule and the new regimes found willing players in the West. Yet there were many times when these new partners were demanding and they operated in an unequal relationship. The psychological factors with regard to the real and perceived backwardness of the region were just one set of hurdles to be overcome. The new regimes had visions of being close to the West, but they were so far away, in terms of material wealth as well as mental predisposition (Janos 2000: 413–18). However, a positive approach to 'conditionality' – soon the name of the game in the West – helped to overcome this psychological burden. Conditionality practiced by NATO and the EU was meant to support political and economic change. The two organisations were not so much looking for strict fulfilment of all the criteria for membership, but rather asking, in a rational and calculated way, 'are these emerging democracies really ready to join the West?' The notion of appropriateness prevailed in the process of accession. It was generally agreed that to become members, aspirant countries had to shed their past and should under no circumstances fall back into any kind of authoritarian rule. So, the Czech Republic, Hungary and Poland were probably not ready for membership of NATO in 1999. Nor were they entirely prepared for EU membership in 2004, while Romania and Bulgaria did not even come close to the requirements by 2007 (perhaps not even today). But lack of preparedness is not the point. What counted was that it appeared appropriate to embrace the countries that had suffered for so long. Bulgaria and Romania were simply lucky to play in the same league with the same entitlement as the other players. All the same, conditionality worked both ways. It is unlikely that the many unpopular measures would have been taken in the emerging democracies without the prospect of membership of NATO and the EU.

In summary, a political and societal understanding about the need for change, a determination to overcome tremendous socio-economic setbacks and access to the West are crucial factors in explaining the success of these rapid transitions from autocratic rule to an 'electoral' democracy. But for all the changes, many substantial obstacles to a 'modern' democracy were ahead.

On Acquiring a Democratic Political Culture

The 'first generation reform' of laws achieved significant advances, such as the constitutional separation of powers and regular and fair elections, but to produce democratic change these reforms need to be followed by a process of refinement, above all an internalisation of democratic principles and norms. The answer to the question 'How are decisions formally reached?' must be complemented by a judgement on 'What is decided and for whom?' This subsequent phase of reform moving towards a modern democracy concerns the way persons and institutions deal with each other and their capacity for learning: how to share knowledge and power effectively and achieve optimal rationality among the inevitable compromises. The crucial challenge is to draw a distinction between formal and substantive democracy (Kaldor and Vejvoda 1997). It is about moving beyond the style of democratisation to the substance: 'regulating power relations in such a way as maximizing the opportunities for individuals to influence the conditions in which they live, to participate in and influence debates about the key decisions which affect society' (Kaldor and Vejvoda 1997: 62). Put differently, political culture rests on the belief and orientations nourished in the political process of democratisation. Keith Baker accurately differentiates between politics and political culture:

If politics, broadly conceived, is the activity through which individuals and groups in any society articulate, negotiate, implement and enforce the competing claims they make one upon another, then political culture may be understood as the set of discourses and practices characterizing that activity in any given community. (Baker 1987: xi)

Politics and political culture are inter-related; if the political process is defunct, political culture will be negatively affected and vice versa. We must take both into account in our assessment of the extent to which consolidation of democracy has taken place in Central Europe. In the following, this process of consolidation and development is examined in a number of case studies regarding how politics are done in the emerging democracies under discussion, in particular, the interaction between the executive, parliament, parties and civil society.

One of the most prominent fears about disruption to liberalisation and the democratic order was a resurgence of sentiments of the past, including the pre-communist history. Would discrimination and ethnic strife lead to the reappearance of nationalism and irredentism? It was an ever-present possibility. For example, the remarks by József Antall that he saw himself – legally and spiritually – as prime minister of all 15 million Hungarians, including those living abroad, provoked fierce criticism and even fear that local pressures in favour of greater autonomy or independence, particularly in Romania could lead to a break up of that state. Was this a reflection of the continuing unease over the Trianon Treaty which, in 1920, reduced Hungary to its present size. Hungarian–Romanian relations were tense for some time after Antall's remarks. Elsewhere, populists savouring the prospects of electoral gain were quick to use these themes as well. Meèiar and the leader of Slovak National Party, Ján Slota, for example, undermined the emerging democratic culture by offending Slovak Hungarians and, among other things, demanding one official language: Slovak. The controversy between nationalist xenophobes and democratic forces cut right through a vulnerable society and even hurt friendships and families. In Romania, the extreme nationalist, Vadim Tudor, aspired to a Greater Romania without Hungarians, Jews or any other ethnic group, or intellectuals. However, these tensions about transnational, ethnic problems were never judged to be more important that the shift to democracy in Central Europe and never escalated to the point of endangering national security, something that did happen in the former Yugoslavia. Neither the Slovak nationalists nor the Romanian traditionalists had their way. Over time they were defeated. In Slovakia, the coalition government of Mikulás Dzurinda, eventually including the Hungarian party, came to power, freeing the way for NATO and EU membership. The people had understood the negative impact of undemocratic rule. In Romania, Tudor managed to enter the second round of the presidential elections in 2004, but was overwhelmingly defeated by the incumbent president, Ion Iliescu. In Hungary, however, nationalism once again looms large after the most recent elections in 2010. The ultra-nationalist party under Jobbik won more than 17 per cent of the votes, while the nationalist party, FIDESZ, with its support for 'autonomous' Hungarians living abroad, garnered an astonishing two-thirds majority in parliament (Chmel 2002).

Political stability was threatened in other ways as well. No government in Central Europe has ever survived its first term. In most cases, this has been primarily a consequence of economic hardship. But there is an important qualification: economic performance does not stand on its own and, in fact, needs democratisation. It is dependent on democratic performance in terms of the quality of the decisions and a 'consolidating' political culture. Where democratic culture lags behind, economic development and growth generally suffer. It is of paramount importance that the executive reveals, explains and justifies its policies – economic and otherwise. The government must be *willing* to communicate and, in addition, it must *be able* to present the substance of its policies in a transparent, properly organised way. On both scores the fledgling democracies have shown shortcomings and serious deficiencies in those countries where the holdover parties, now baptising themselves as 'reformed communists', managed to retake office. Thus, Bulgaria and Romania suffered from the fact that there was no opposition movement like Charta '77 in Czechoslovakia or Solidarnoæ in Poland, from which new leaders could be recruited. Nor had they been subject to 'goulash communism' under moderate, reform-minded leaders as in Hungary during the 'first Transitory Parliament' from 1985 to 1989 (Ágh 1995). Nonetheless, even in these countries with histories of contesting or critical voices, the governments were reluctant to show openness and transparency for various reasons.

The governments in Central Europe were simply not hard-pressed by parliaments or by professional, investigative media. The ruling party or parties were tempted to negotiate within inner ranks – a kind of inherited 'democratic centralism', as in the case of the BSP – and did not respect or fully honour the essential role of parliament in national decision making. Furthermore, an inclination towards secrecy was a leftover of the former regimes, particularly in the security area. Finally, the people looked at results and were not happy with their material well-being. Reached democratically or not, the decisions were judged by the public based on the impact on their daily struggle to survive. Even governments willing to show openness and transparency, still had to display their 'capacity-building' capabilities. This, however, represented a major hurdle because of a lack of workforce continuity and institutional memory. One negative experience in all of Central and Eastern Europe is the fairly consistent use of a 'spoils system', where civil servants depend on the patronage of the political authorities. The party leader in the communist style demanded obedience from top to bottom of the organisation. Consequently, the party or parties in power after democratic elections added their own personnel to the bureaucracy, notably the higher echelon of civil servants. This created animosity within the lower ranks, who saw their upwards progress blocked. Policies were reversed by not necessarily competent, often bullying, superiors. Under such circumstances, retention of knowledgeable public servants proved to be difficult. In the case of career personnel, like the military, diplomatic service or judiciary, the professionals from the old regimes were pushed towards recalcitrance, if not overt, collective resistance. The strong corporate sense among these surviving, professional groups, as well as their strategic positioning within their respective organisation, often compromised government reforms. Meanwhile, the defence ministries were struggling to find competent civil servants and often suffered from the lack of professional insight and expertise among their political leadership. For example, the General Staff in Bulgaria – the almighty body in the Soviet-style defence organisation and repository of knowledge and expertise in security affairs – outnumbered the Ministry of Defence staff by a factor of ten during the 1990s, and it took almost ten years before real reforms were introduced by a competent team of political appointees during the Kostov government (1997–2001). Moreover, the General Staff, moulded in the mentality of Soviet-style mass armies, had no expertise in systematically reducing the armed forces, thereby bringing on massive lay-offs across the board, even among its own ranks. Even though it had the benefit of a knowledgeable and effective team, Bulgaria was still pressed to show actual reforms in the face of the NATO summit in 2002 that would decide on Bulgaria's membership of the Alliance. Even then, the reforms were 're-examined' during the reign of the next government. Ministers come and go, but long-term, professional public servants stay and can take their time to reverse course and annul previous policies. This example does not stand alone; strong personalities like Ion Pascu in Romania and Jozef Stank in Slovakia were also crucial for imposing reform on slow-moving bureaucracies before the NATO summit (Centre for European Security Studies 2001).

In general, vested interests, the legacy of 'old thinking' and the intertwining networks of the surviving elites from the old regime in government and society are hard to fight. These survivors have not been slow to move into business circles, capitalising on the opportunities provided by rapid transition. The process of democratic consolidation runs into a great many political opponents as well as profiteers who are not waiting idly. The simultaneous transformations of economics and politics presented attractive opportunities, particularly for the elites, new and old. Privatisation is a case in point. State and party property was suddenly in private hands and people were left wondering how industrial and media privatisation happened, particularly when much of the profit went to so few persons, creating clubs of millionaires and even billionaires. There is no doubt that there have been many undemocratic activities inside and outside official institutions. It is worth recalling Rudolf Tókés' assessment of the Hungarian experience in 1990:

> In sum, the outcome of current policy debates on the modalities of the transfer of the state's massive economic resources into private hands will have a decisive bearing on the future of Hungarian society and politics. It is certain that . . . it will be the elites – new, old, and holdover – who will be the primary beneficiaries of the process of privatization in Hungary. As undisputed owners of property, rather than managers . . . it will be this new bourgeoisie that will determine the shape of Hungary's politics in the years to come. (Tókés 1992: 171)

Transitional politics are reflected in the relationship between state/government and society during the phase of consolidation. The break with past power structures in Hungary, the Czech Republic and Poland was unlike what happened in the Bulgaria and Romania where no alternative movement existed. Hierarchical relations changed more in the former three countries than in the latter two. Power was redistributed more in the first three cases and this offered a choice in the ensuing elections.

Democracy was better served in Hungary, the Czech Republic and Poland than in the countries where power structures continued to enable powerholders to manipulate the public and maintain the lack of democratic choice.

Democratic consolidation in the relationship between the governmental and party elites, on the one hand, and between them and society, on the other, remained complicated. The winner-takes-all mentality and the paternalistic attitude of the elites were part of the political culture everywhere and caused a schism between them and an increasingly apathetic population. The legacy of top-down rule and over-organisation at the top continued in place, in spite of the liberalisation by the masses. The divide between majority and minority in parliament, where the minority was mostly ignored, was accompanied by government-led discipline in an 'aristocratic democracy'. If confidence in a minister was lost by the parliament, his resignation was not necessarily a consequence. The system of powerholders at the top disregarding respect for other participants persevered. The political elites and parties monopolised the agenda and claimed undisputed leadership of the democratisation process. As a result, the masses were alienated and debilitated. Parliamentary democracy was increasingly seen as a system with only limited control over the government, while lacking healthy communication with society. The political legitimacy of parliament and government decreased and, as a consequence, the population soon listed parliament as their least popular institution. Run by immature parties and hampered by underdeveloped internal institutions and weak committee systems with no hope of overcoming party differences in a rational way, parliaments missed the opportunity to become the most important body in civil society and to act as a bridge to society at large. Regular elections could not make up for this democratic deficit. Genuine citizenship does not grow out of mere elections and campaigns; it needs much more (Touraine 1991: 261).

By the same token, civil society actors were kept at arm's length. Trade unions suffered from the legacy of being an instrument of imposed policies, while organisations of employers were fragmented. Other crucial actors in society, such as an articulate middle class, had not yet matured. Social demands were ever more difficult to communicate in fragmented and volatile societies. But the major shortcoming was that parties and parliament did not reach out to civil society and did not act as social partners. As a consequence, the political parties themselves were doomed to remain weak socially. Capacity-building for the nation as a whole was very much the victim of a political style that entrenched in the political culture of the previous regime. Given the cleavages between those in power and those out of power and the cleavages between the elites and the population, the establishment of a kind of consociational democracy was, however desirable, beyond reach (Lijphart 1977). Parties were not achieving the conditions of strong democracy: neither working towards accommodation among themselves, nor securing unfettered popular support for the institutions. Pluralism abounded, but the outcome of elections was often capricious. Sometimes, parties with a comfortable percentage of votes were swept away in the next election. The centrifugal tendencies in these, nonetheless, pluralist societies proved to be a formidable obstacle in the way of a mature, modern democracy.

Conclusion

The foregoing offers a mixed picture of successes and shortcomings. Formal democratic rules and procedures were generally introduced into Central Europe after 1989, but the region's long history of authoritarian and autocratic forms of government has taken its toll in diverse ways. The centuries-long history of building Western democracies could not be emulated in only a few years. Maturity and internalisation of a democratic culture takes generations. But it is fair to conclude that, although the Central European democracies may be lagging behind in some respects, they have become part of the long, historic, democratic experiment. Some countries, such as Poland, the Czech Republic and Hungary, have fared better than others, such as Bulgaria and Romania, in establishing a democratic political culture and style. The latter two still lack comparable institutional arrangements and show serious flaws in their legal practices, while their societies continue to suffer more from the legacy of the communist era. Moreover, polity and society are significantly beset by corruption and political manoeuvrings. Economic and social conditions are painful, notwithstanding Bulgaria's and Romania's EU membership. Transition was a huge shock in these isolated countries, while consolidation of a democracy was seriously hampered by an uninformed, unaware or unwilling political leadership.

Looking to the experiences in other regions of transition, the harsh Bulgarian and Romanian experiences offer insight into the immense problems one encounters there. While the Baltic states, from early on supported by their neighbours, the EU and NATO, are progressing, the former Soviet and Yugoslav republics have disintergrated and continue to struggle with their past. In addition to the problems outlined in this chapter, they face historic hurdles like autocratic leadership, Russian dominance and lack of self-government in the first case and bitter ethnic strife and unbridled nationalism in the second. Corruption is rampant everywhere. Slovenia joined the West and is an exception. Croatia and Serbia are in the midst of negotiations for membership of the EU, while the poorer republics advance slowly. Consolidation of democracy is patchy in this region. The former Soviet republics minus the Baltic states are generally undemocratic, the role of parliament is docile and the judiciary remains manipulated and under threat by the elites, no matter their political stand. Society is often treated as the vulgar playground of the elites making the socio-economic conditions of the people miserable. The road to democratic consolidation appears to be even bumpier than in Central Europe. There are tricky potholes everywhere.

Note

1. The author was at the time director of research at the Institute for East–West Security Studies in New York and was both a witness to and a (foreign) participant in attempts to foster law-governed democratic rule, in particular, in the field of national security. Much of this account is based on that experience.

References

Ágh, A. (1995), 'The Role of the First Parliament in Democratic Transition', in A. Ágh and S. Kurtán (eds), *Democratization and Europeanization in Hungary: The First Parliament 1990–1994*, Budapest: Hungarian Centre for Democratic Studies Foundation, pp. 249–64.

Baker, K. M. (ed.) (1987), *The French Revolution and the Creation of Modern Political Culture: The Political Culture of the Old Regime*, Oxford: Oxford University Press.

Berliner, J. S. (1994), 'Conclusion: Reflections on the Social Legacy', in J. R. Millar and S. L. Wolchik (eds), *The Social Legacy of Communism*, Washington, DC: Woodrow Wilson Center Press, pp. 379–85.

Centre for European Security Studies (2001), *Organising National Defences for NATO Membership: The Unexamined Dimension of Aspirants' Readiness for Entry*, Harmonie Papers No. 15, Groningen: Centre for European Security Studies.

Chmel, R. (2002), 'Syndrome of Trianon in Hungarian Foreign Policy and Act on Hungarians Living in Neighboring Countries, *Slovak Foreign Policy Affairs*, 1, 93–106.

European Bank for Reconstruction and Development (2008), *Transition Report 2008: Growth in Transition*, London: European Bank for Reconstruction and Development.

Janos, A. C. (2000), *East Central Europe in the Modern World: The Politics of the Borderlands from Pre- to Postcommunism*, Stanford, CA: Stanford University Press.

Kaldor, M. and I. Vejvoda (1997), 'Democratization in Central and East European Countries', *International Affairs*, 73(1), 59–82.

Keane, J. (2009), *The Life and Death of Democracy*, London: Simon & Schuster.

Lijphart, A. (1977), *Democracy in Plural Societies: A Comparative Exploration*, New Haven, CT: Yale University Press.

Mastrini, J. (1994), 'Privatization Chief Held on Bribery Charge', *The Moscow Times*, 4 November.

Pridham, G. and P. Lewis (eds) (1996), *Stabilising Fragile Democracies: Comparing New Party Systems in Southern and Eastern Europe*, London: Routledge.

Schedler, A. (1998), 'What is Democratic Consolidation?', *Journal of Democracy*, 9(2), 91–107.

Tőkés, R. L. (1992), 'Democracy in Hungary: The First Hundred Days and a Mid-term Assessment', in P. M. E. Volten (ed.), *Bound to Change: Consolidating Democracy in East Central Europe*, New York: Institute for East–West Security Studies, pp. 151–90.

Touraine, A. (1991), 'What Does Democracy Mean Today?', *International Social Science Journal*, 128, 259–68.

Part VII

Peoples' Movements

Chapter 27

Anti-Slavery

Seymour Drescher

During the last three centuries democratisation has occurred at three levels. For individuals, it was a process of extending access to equality of status and the security of liberty under law. Within civil societies, it was the process of extending access to the means of communication and association in economic, social and religious spheres of life. Within polities, it meant the formation of constitutional processes for law making, law enforcement and broadening the access to elections of legislators and executives at all levels of the state. In this perspective anti-slavery was a movement and an ideology primarily concerned with changing the status of enslaved individuals. There was no single route to the elimination of the institution. The condition of civil society and the polity profoundly affected both the processes of abolition and their impact on democratisation. This chapter assesses the relationship of anti-slavery to democracy in the century of slave emancipation in the Atlantic world. It examines that process primarily in Britain, France and the United States.

Britain

In 1843, just three years after he had published the second volume of his *Democracy in America*, Alexis de Tocqueville published a series of articles calling on France to emancipate the slaves in its overseas colonies. As a legislator and member of the French Society for the Abolition of Slavery, Tocqueville turned the attention of his fellow citizens to a recently completed 'mighty experiment' – British slave emancipation: 'A hazardous and singular task has just been undertaken and completed before our eyes . . . nearly a million men have simultaneously passed from the extremity of servitude to complete independence, or better said, from death to life' (Tocqueville [1843] 1968: 138). Tocqueville emphasised the political process as much as the result:

> The emancipation of the slaves was a parliamentary reform, the act of the nation and not of its rulers. The English government . . . resisted the abolition of the slave trade for fifteen years, and the abolition of slavery for twenty-five years [more]. When it could not prevent its passage . . . [and] gave up all hope of postponement, it sought to dilate the consequences, but always in vain; the popular torrent prevailed and swept it along. (Tocqueville [1843] 1968: 150–1)

More than 150 years later two outstanding scholars of popular mobilisation, Charles Tilly and Sidney Tarrow, opened their global analysis of social movements and democracy by invoking British abolitionism as the world's first successful transnational movement (Tilly and Tarrow 2007: 1). Like Tocqueville, they noted that British abolitionism emerged within an aristocratic polity, providing narrow, unequal citizenship and a limited consultation by the gentry with unenfranchised citizens. Only individual civil liberty under law and relative freedom of association differentiated this polity from most regimes on the mainland of Europe. This tradition of civil liberty and security, however, did place emergent abolitionism in an especially strong institutional and ideological position. At the end of the eighteenth century, a territorial 'freedom principle' was deeply embedded in British self-identification. Jurists and popular writers alike asserted that the very air of their realm was so free that all servile bondage was removed from slaves arriving on the island.

The establishment of large-scale overseas slave colonies, however, created a long-simmering conflict over the extent to which a status sanctioned overseas could be sustained in the metropolis. Long before the emergence of abolitionism the legal and constitutional problems raised about slaves resident in Britain heightened awareness of the contradiction between the hegemonic freedom principle at home and toleration of the horrors of slavery 'beyond the line' of northwest Europe (Drescher 1987; Peabody 1996). The nation in which abolition first emerged as a political movement was at the forefront of other trends that were to occur throughout the world during the next 200 years. By the last quarter of the eighteenth century Britons enjoyed one of the most highly developed civil societies in the world. Legislatively, its citizens enjoyed a polity where the military was more subordinated to civilian control than in any large state in Europe. The principle of representation with respect to the objects and levels of taxation was well established.

The relation between civil society and the legislative process was also deepening. A network of newspapers nationalised the dialogue between citizens and legislators, and advertisements for public gatherings, political pamphlets and news items about ongoing parliamentary debates in London were daily fare for exchanges in the press. Newspapers also linked provincial readers to interested actors across the island. The leeway for legally sanctioned associations and public gatherings was well established. Libraries, debating societies and formal public meetings offered venues for launching petitions to parliament and for creating networks of extra-parliamentary associations. Within this broader civil and political sphere, British abolitionism came to occupy a distinctively innovative position. Between its emergence as a national social movement in 1787 and the accelerated globalisation of anti-slavery during the half-century that followed, abolitionism was significant in three ways. It became a pioneering organisation in the techniques and practices of mass mobilisation and popular claims making. It opened opportunities for the incorporation of hitherto untapped groups as political actors. Its fortunes also became emblematic of the difficulties entailed in converting popular pressure into changes in law and policy (Innes 2005; Tilly 1995).

The great surprise of British abolitionism was its breadth, duration and impact. Its immediate national popularity was unanticipated by both its founders and its enemies. Abolitionist popular agitation came in successive waves from 1788 to 1838. In 1787, the first petition to Parliament was launched from the newly industrialised city of Manchester. It became the model of mass mobilisation for the next half-century. The city's 10,000 petitioners represented two-thirds of its adult male population. Manchester also pioneered in the nationalisation of petitioning, advertising its own petition's contents in all of the country's major provincial newspapers. The 100 petitions gathered in 1788 also constituted more than half of all public petitions reaching London during that year's parliamentary session. The harvest of signatories for abolition in 1788 outmatched those gathered by all major political movements during the previous generation. Within Parliament both Prime Minister Pitt and the opposition leaders cited popular demand as political action against the transatlantic slave trade for the first time in British history.

Abolitionism was equally innovative in expanding the public sphere. From the outset religious dissenters rallied to the cause. Methodists, Baptists, Congregationalists and Unitarians instantly added their support to the original Quaker cadres. Though Members of Parliament still regarded women's signatures as delegitimising public petitions, women could register their opinions in debating clubs, poetry, pamphlets and newspaper correspondence. Public space opened for an African presence. Olaudah Equiano's 1789 autobiography became the Atlantic world's first popular narrative of an Afro-Britain's lifetime journey from slave to freeman to abolitionist writer and lecturer.

Immediately following the defeat of the first bill to abolish the slave trade in 1791, abolitionists launched a second petition campaign. This time more than 400,000 names reached Parliament, the largest number yet registered on behalf of a legislative issue. Those ineligible to sign petitions were called upon to increase pressure on slaveholders themselves by refusing to purchase slave-grown sugar. Long before the term boycott was coined, abolitionists added consumer mobilisation to their tactical arsenal. Women, as managers of the household budget, were asked to register their sentiments by abstaining from purchasing slave-grown sugar. At the height of the campaign 300,000 families were said to have pledged abstention (Drescher 1987: 78–9; Oldfield 1995).The second abolition bill in the House of Commons in 1792 resulted in overwhelming support for a resolution for the gradual abolition of the slave trade.

A long hiatus followed. Rising waves of internal radical ferment at home and revolutionary war abroad postponed further abolitionist mobilisation for more than a decade. The British were successively threatened by the French Revolutionary and Napoleonic wars in Europe and in the Caribbean. Haiti's victory over Napoleon in 1804 and victory at Trafalgar in 1805, however, left the British Empire more secure than it had been in a dozen years. Abolitionist leaders reorganised their local branches for another effort at pressure from within. They still hesitated, however, to invoke mass agitation tactics in wartime. Instead, they turned to the most hallowed opening for exercising public pressure. The general election of 1806 was the first in which abolition became a campaign issue, and Parliament abolished the Atlantic slave trade in 1807.

With victory over Napoleon in 1814, British abolitionism returned to public meetings and mass national petitioning. An Article of the Anglo-French peace treaty of 1814 sanctioned the reopening of the slave trade to France for an additional five years. The British national response was overwhelming. A popular mobilisation was organised to demand the re-negotiation of the Article. At one point, abolitionists estimated that 750,000 or one-fifth of Britain's eligible population had signed up again, the highest in Britain's recorded history. The result was dramatic: 1,370 petitions reached London against the Article, with none in favour (Kielstra 2000: 25–33). For the British government this popular mobilisation was decisive. Slave trade abolition was simultaneously nationalised and internationalised. As the British foreign minister privately informed his ambassador in Madrid: 'the nation is bent upon this object [abolition], I believe there is hardly a village that has not met and petitioned upon it; both Houses of Parliament are pledged to press it; and the Ministers must make it the basis of their policy' (Murray 1980: 52).

For the next half-century most British foreign ministers were, to one degree or another, 'bent upon this object'. The abolitionists honed their master weapon of the mass petition again and again: in 1823, for gradual emancipation; in 1830–1 and 1833 for immediate emancipation; and finally, in 1837–8 for the immediate abolition of the transitional 'apprenticeship' system.

The feminisation of abolitionism proceeded apace. From the mid-1820s women inserted themselves, organisationally and massively, into the abolitionist movement. By 1833, on the day scheduled for the government's introduction of the Slavery Abolition Bill to the House of Commons, the largest single anti-slavery petition in the movement's history dramatically reached the doors of Parliament. It was 'a huge featherbed of a petition,' bearing 187,000 signatures, in 'one vast and universal expression of feeling from *all the females* of the United Kingdom'. Of the 1.3 million Britons who signed that year's appeal, 400,000 were women. In the final mass round-up of signatures against apprenticeship, in 1837–8, the 700,000 women who directly appealed to the young Queen Victoria, amounted to two-thirds of the 1.1 million signatures delivered to the House of Commons. Anti-slavery's reliance upon non-conformist religious mobilisation also increased. Religious dissenters' share of signers rose to their all-time peak (Colley 1992: 279–80; Midgley 1995: 65).

During the last fifteen years of these mobilisations there was a final major addition to the abolitionist cohort: the intervention of the colonial slaves themselves. Before the 1820s, slave uprisings in the Caribbean usually placed metropolitan abolitionists on the defensive. Given its Quaker roots and commitment to peaceful change the abolitionists' first response was usually to exculpate themselves from association with violence (Costa 1997). During the 1790s and in the wake of the St Domingue slave uprising, British abolitionists made no attempt to protest British conquests of French Caribbean islands and the re-enslavement of many recently emancipated French ex-slaves. As noted, the movement's popular agitation was inversely related to violent threats to the nation. Indeed, until the Barbadian slave revolt of 1816, abolitionists proudly invoked the absence of major British slave uprising wars as *prima facie* evidence that the abolition of the slave trade and controlled experiments in the amelioration of slavery could be freely discussed without fear of violent repercussions. In 1816, a massive Barbados revolt was a setback to metropolitan mobilisation.

When the abolitionists decided to revive mass campaigning for gradual emancipation in 1823, their parliamentary leader carefully invoked the hiatus of slave uprisings during the seven years following the Barbados uprising. Within months of the reopened campaign, however, a new large-scale uprising broke out in Demerara. This time it was the Demerara governor's reluctance to publicise a very minimal metropolitan amelioration policy that occasioned the slave revolt; concealment from above fuelled conspiracy from below. The most innovative aspect of the revolt lay, as in the case of metropolitan abolitionism, in the slaves' pattern of action. Plantations were occupied, but masters and their families were only incarcerated. In the final negotiations the rebels presented the British military commander with signed documents from the masters testifying to their good treatment. Extraordinarily, the leader of the slave revolt was reprieved from execution at the request of the governor himself. Moreover, the death of an English missionary incarcerated by the authorities in Demerara produced a counter-mobilisation in Britain against the brutal suppression of fellow Christians. The parliamentary elections of 1826 were the first since 1806 in which slavery again became a campaign issue (Hall 2002: 107–15; Matthews 2006: 36–7).

Six years later, following the suppression of another great rebellion in Jamaica (1831–2), British abolitionists reached a new level of political influence. In the parliamentary election of 1832 they successfully demanded pledges from hundreds of candidates that they would support immediate emancipation if elected. The result was the passage of the British Emancipation Act of 1833. Five years later, in a campaign to end the transition apprenticeship system, colonial freedmen joined metropolitan abolitionists in threatening a massive cessation of labour if complete freedom was not immediately granted.

For half a century, then, abolitionism remained the most innovative, durable and successful social movement of its day. At the peak of its political power in 1840 the British abolitionist movement had achieved a number of significant transformations. It had eliminated the institution in its own colonies. It had successfully launched a global process aimed at eliminating the transoceanic slave trades. It had made the elimination of both slavery and the slave trade a normative international goal, accepted in principle by all the European powers. It had pioneered the strategies and rhetoric that inspired those who organised for other reforms to democratise both British and other societies. Finally, its trajectory seemed to echo the dominant historiography of British democracy as proceeding by orderly stages from reform to reform, from electoral extension to electoral extension, and from a slavery-sanctioning empire to a slave-liberating empire (Oldfield 1995).

Continental Europe

Continental Europe never remotely approached the British model of anti-slavery as a democratising national social movement. There was no popular movement to match the British panoply of tactics; there was no national newspaper network to mobilise local organisations; there was no sequence of mass public meetings; no consumer boycotts; no mass petitions; no durable anti-slavery society; no outpouring of literary polemic. Continental polities left no records of extended legislative hearings; no mountains of data and testimony about the slave trade and slavery; very little public discussion about slavery's impact upon its victims. For the most part, continental European anti-slavery societies were ephemeral and inconsequential.

There were rare exceptions. There was a flurry of popular celebration in France following the Convention's decree of French slave emancipation in 1794. In 1865, a Spanish Anti-slavery Society was founded in Spain. It thrived among those who favoured secular republican government, an expanded civil society and a search for working-class support. However, in Spain, as in most continental states, nineteenth-century associational activity was intermittent. It was disrupted by both metropolitan and imperial events-revolutions, coups d'états, and by popular counter-abolitionist mobilisations and petitions. The opposition to anti-slavery in Iberia was even more intense within its Cuban colony. Beginning in 1868, the Ten Years War accelerated slave emancipation in one part of the island and postponed it in the other. From first to last, the nineteenth-century Spanish Atlantic empire was riven over questions of independence and emancipation.

Mainland European states, with limited anti-slavery activism, shared other characteristics that differentiated them from the British variant. Neither in predominantly Protestant nor Catholic nations did religious organisations play a major role in mobilising anti-slavery. In Catholic countries the Church was additionally constrained by a papacy that hesitated to vigorously condemn slavery until 1888. Only after slave emancipation in Brazil, the last slave-holding country with an overwhelmingly Catholic identity, did Pope Leo XIII's condemnation of slavery open the door to popular Catholic anti-slavery mobilisations in Belgium, France, Germany, Switzerland, Spain, Austria, Italy and Portugal. In nations with mixtures of Protestants, secularists and Catholics, anti-slavery also became an arena for religious *Kulturkampf* (Clarence-Smith 2008: 149–68; Drescher 1999; Oostindie 1995; Schmidt-Nowara 1999: 51–125). In continental anti-slavery movements women were also rarely politically active. For example, in Spain the one women's chapter of the Spanish Anti-slavery Society, founded by the North American spouse of a Puerto Rican abolitionist, appears to have been quite ephemeral.

A final characteristic of continental anti-slavery was that it was nurtured by, and tainted with, association with British imperial hegemony. The first state to be subjected to direct British diplomatic and financial pressure was the Portuguese monarchy. It was deeply dependent upon British arms and money for its very existence. In 1810, Portugal became the first colonial power to agree to limit its slaving activities. British naval supremacy, economic power and victory over Napoleon allowed post-war Britain to force smaller European powers to adopt slave trade abolition as a pre-condition for the return of their New World colonies.

The French case was probably the most important variant of continental anti-slavery. France never developed a mass abolitionist national movement leading to abolition. For most of the period between the first French slave emancipation in 1794 and the second decree in 1848, there was not even an organised abolitionist movement in France. Its intermittent abolitionist societies were composed of a small elite cohort centred in Paris. The primary catalyst of the first French emancipation was, of course, the successful uprising of the slaves in St Domingue. The French Revolutionary decree of emancipation in 1794 was not tied to large-scale prior popular mobilisation in France itself. In all colonies where the first French decree was enforced, the revolutionary leadership, both white or black, ruled by means of military government and forced labour. Haiti, whose constitution made it the first New World nation-state entirely to abolish the institution of slavery, accepted this legacy of militarism, coerced labour and authoritarian government. The emancipation process in the Caribbean, between 1791 and 1804, clearly did not lead to durable political democratisation.

After his seizure of power in France, Napoleon Bonaparte became the only European ruler to resuscitate slavery (1802) and to re-enslave citizens of his own nation. Both slave emancipation in Haiti and the restoration of the institution elsewhere were therefore correlated with the failure of political and civil democratisation on both sides of the French Atlantic. Napoleon's successor, the restored Bourbon monarch, Louis XVIII, restored the slave trade in 1814. It was only the fortuitous sequence of Napoleon's return in 1815, his strategic abolition of the slave trade and his defeat at Waterloo that enabled the British government to obtain the French king's consent not to rescind Napoleon's decree. The circumstances of France after 1815 were such as to forestall the emergence of any French anti-slavery movement on the British scale. During the Restoration any French parliamentarian who even alluded to the evils of slavery was shouted down as an assassin. Precisely because abolitionism was triumphantly nationalised and internationalised in Britain after 1814, French anti-abolitionists could attack anti-slavery as an English plot, designed to subvert what remained of France's once pre-eminent slave empire. French abolitionists correspondingly averted direct reference to the violence of France's first emancipation. Instead, they re-inserted anti-slavery into the Christian, royalist and centuries-old juridical tradition of the 'Freedom Principle' of the Old Regime. Only obliquely did they appeal for the extension to the colonies of metropolitan civil equality.

By themselves such invocations of values and historical traditions could not ensure progress against slavery in early nineteenth century France. The association of abolitionism with rival British global domination, combined with fear of popular agitation, prevented any recourse to mass anti-slavery mobilisation during the period of constitutional monarchy (1814–48). The second French emancipation, like the first, came via revolutionary decree in the wake of the Revolution of 1848. Anti-slavery still had so little popular base in 1848 that the decree's sponsor pre-emptively published it before the convocation of the Second Republic's National Constituent Assembly. The Provisional Government feared that the Assembly, newly elected by universal male suffrage, might refuse to agree to liberation before an adequate indemnity was arranged to compensate the slaveholders. The second emancipation, like the first, demonstrated that there was no synergy of political democracy and abolitionism in France (Jennings 2000).

The United States

During the half-century after the American Declaration of Independence, emancipations were enacted in many of the new states of North and South America. They all occurred in areas where the slave population represented 10 per cent or less of the population. The usual method was gradual emancipation. All slaves born before a certain date remained in bondage. Those born of slaves after that date were legally free, but served an 'apprenticeship' into adulthood in order to compensate their masters for the costs of rearing (Engerman 1995).

Neither in South nor North America was there any parallel to the British nationwide abolitionist mobilisations that preceded anti-slavery legislation. Spanish-American emancipations followed the French mode of revolutionary emancipation. Long indecisive wars of independence created a bidding war for the loyalty of the region's inhabitants. Slave liberations and gradual emancipation were major strategic weapons in the struggle. As in Haiti, the legacy of these internecine conflicts was unstable polities, fragile civil societies and uneven democratisation. All slave emancipations proceeded in the absence of organised abolitionist campaigns. Only in the 1880s was Brazil to develop a mobilisation of civil society that matched that of Britain and the northern United States (Adelman 2006: 232–45, 312–17, 356–65; Andrews 2004; Castilho 2008: 45–8, 93–106; Conrad 1972: 80–105, 176–92). In North America decisions about slavery were at the discretion of the individual states of the new United States. North of the Chesapeake, gradual emancipation laws were enacted through regular legal procedures. As in South America, there was no analogue to British mass abolitionism. In the northern United States abolitionism took a new turn towards mass mobilisation only in the 1830s. The movement was clearly embedded in the efflorescence of political democratisation and associational activity in Jacksonian America. This new radical abolitionism drew direct inspiration from the British anti-slavery movement, then reaching its peak. American abolitionists adopted many of the tactics of their British predecessors: abundant local organisation; mass propaganda; mass petitioning; and inclusive membership extending to women, blacks and juveniles (Davis 2006).

In some respects American abolitionists outpaced the organisational and propaganda performance of their British contemporaries. In one major respect, however, US anti-slavery was far more constrained than its British predecessor. Support for the new abolitionist movement was virtually absent from the slave-holding South. Abolitionist literature was blocked from entry into the slave-holding states. Petitions were refused consideration by the US Congress. Most significantly, democratic elections remained a powerful weapon *against* abolitionism. In the United States, with a far broader suffrage than that of contemporary Great Britain, the ballot, not the petition, was the ultimate arbiter of public opinion. In every national election during the two decades before the crisis following Abraham Lincoln's election, turnout in the South was higher than in the North. Moreover, a majority part of the northern electorate as well as almost the entire South remained strongly anti-abolitionist. Both antebellum national parties were therefore firmly anti-abolitionist. It was only when enough southerners became convinced that the demographic and territorial expansion of the Union was inexorably tilting away from the slave states that they gambled on secession and independence. Slave emancipation in the United States, as in Haiti and most Latin American nations, was decided more on the battlefield than at the ballot box. Nevertheless, final emancipation was legislated without the long-term breakdown of the democratic or constitutional framework of the North American republic (Drescher 2009).

By 1865, Brazil remained the only independent nation in the New World still sanctioning the institution of slavery. Largely in response to its sense of increasing isolation in the Western world, Brazil's legislature enacted an emancipation law in 1871. A significant intrusion of civil society began only a decade later in the 1880s. Even more than in Britain, Brazilian anti-slavery was a highly localised movement, focusing upon the creation of 'free soil' zones. Civil action merged with civil disobedience. They created opportunities for runaways seeking safe haven in other parts of the country. Not since British abolitionism at its height had extra-parliamentary agitation played so decisive a role in a relatively non-violent emancipation process. One of the striking differences between Anglo-American and Brazilian popular anti-slavery mobilisations was the absence of mass petitioning from the Brazilian anti-slavery repertoire. Popular manifestations in favour of emancipation in Brazil's hinterland therefore occurred in the teeth of national legislative silence or resistance. Indeed, the legislature dramatically curtailed electoral eligibility as popular anti-slavery got underway. This was in vain, however, as desertions increased. The army refused to function as a policing force and cross-racial coalitions abounded. Although cultural barriers against female engagement in overtly political activity remained strong, Brazilian abolitionism opened more space for women. By 1888, the erosion of support for the institution was overwhelming. The final emancipation act in the Americas, 'the Golden Law', was enacted by the Brazilian legislature in five days. Its passage was accompanied by civil street celebrations. Thus ended the process of emancipation in the offshoots of Western colonisation in the New World. Within two years an international treaty committed all imperial nations to the abolition of the slave trade and slavery in Africa. By the Brussels Act of 1890 anti-slavery became the gold standard of the civilising process (Miers 1975).

Conclusion

Paths to democratisation were as varied as those aimed at the suppression of the slave trade and slavery. The complexity of ideas historically identified as sources of democracy sometimes converged with those that sustained abolitionists: the Declaration of Independence in the United States (1776); and the Declaration of the Rights of Man and Citizen in France (1789). They proclaimed that all men are created free and equal. Neither proclaimed the ending of slavery, but both were clearly inspirational to those who sought to end the slave trade and slavery. British popular abolitionist mobilisations more directly acted as inspirational models for movements favouring political democratisation. The techniques and achievements of British anti-slavery certainly encouraged their anti-slavery counterparts in America. In Britain, they also encouraged popular mobilisations for universal male suffrage; equal rights for religious groups; and women's suffrage.

By contrast, in most continental European societies both slave emancipation and political democratisation came with far less input from abolitionist mobilisations. The turbulent path to universal adult male suffrage on the European continent had little to do with anti-slavery. In France, during the same week that the Provisional government of 1848 decreed universal electoral male suffrage for a National Constituent Assembly and preparations for the immediate abolition of slavery, it brushed aside feminist demands for the extension of voting rights to women. This dismissal was subsequently ratified by the National Assembly (Offen 1999). Freed males in the French colonies received the right to vote in French national elections almost a century before metropolitan women.

Two decades later, history repeated itself in the United States. Anglo-American abolitionist mass mobilisations inspired the Seneca Falls Convention for women's rights in 1848. Twenty years later, American feminists re-experienced the bitterness of French feminists when the suffrage was extended to American ex-slaves and denied to women. In Britain, too, anti-slavery initially disappointed those agitating for a dramatic extension of the electorate. The British Chartist movement's mobilisation for universal male suffrage in the 1840s faithfully copied the abolitionist model of mass contention. In 1848, like the women of France, the Chartists were denied the suffrage for which they had far more formidably mobilised. As with British anti-slavery, full access to the British ballot box occurred only by piecemeal steps during the century after the passage of British Slave Emancipation Act.

Brazil, too, demonstrated how easily anti-slavery and democracy could be decoupled. As noted, just before emancipation, the Brazilian legislature confronted by popular abolitionist mobilisation, constricted Brazil's suffrage. Emancipation brought no reversal. Neither the newly liberated slaves nor their popular allies were any more successful in gaining access to the ballot. A year after slave emancipation, those who overthrew the Brazilian empire maintained the restricted eligibility principle of the previous regime. The Brazilian case highlights another trend in post-slavery regimes: the political marginalisation of ex-slaves by law or custom. The economic limitations on the right to vote in Brazil were echoed in more explicitly racial terms in the southern United States and in South Africa. The trend was also clearly illustrated in Britain, the nation that took the lead in the assault on slavery. In a metropole with a very restricted suffrage, political rights for ex-slaves had, of course, not been implied by civil enfranchisement in 1833–8. No restriction, however, was placed upon the rights of ex-slaves to participate in elections to colonial assemblies, as long as they possessed the requisite economic qualifications. During the following generations the empire's overseas white settler societies were allowed to transition from Crown Colony status towards self-government. In regard to its ex-slave colonies, the British Empire moved in the opposite direction: they were deprived of their legislative autonomy and transformed into Crown colonies. The line between zones of free and slave labour was thus reconfigured in racial terms. Half a century after British emancipation, colonies inhabited predominantly by free European citizens lived in democratic (male suffrage) polities. Non-settler regions inhabited by non-European colonies remained subjects, under direct imperial control.

Anti-slavery also contributed to the late nineteenth-century expansion of European-dominated subjects in Afro-Asia. As European empires shifted from colonies where ex-masters had been Europeans to those where the masters were non-Europeans, the anti-slavery ideology shifted from projects of liberation to accommodation to projects of economic development. The Brussels Act of 1890 committed its signatories to end the slave trade immediately in imperialised Africa and to begin a process of emancipation wherever their nation's sovereignty prevailed. While acting in the name of a civilisation pledged to eliminate the institution, however, they were authorised to 'civilise' subjects through various systems of coercion. The institutionalisation of imperial control thus came with a commitment to secure peace, civilisation and individual liberty to the aboriginal populations. There was no parallel obligation to move towards colonial self-government and political democratisation (Miers and Roberts 1988). The second quarter of the twentieth century, of course, shattered the illusion that democracy and anti-slavery were the hallmarks of an ever-expanding Western civilisation, one that had banished slavery to an ever-diminishing area of the non-European world. Thus, it is hardly surprising that among the former subjects of imperial domination the language of Western anti-slavery easily became the language of anti-imperialism.

References

Adelman, J. (2006), *Sovereignty and Revolution in the Iberian Atlantic*, Princeton, NJ: Princeton University Press.

Andrews, G. R. (2004), *Afro-Latin America*, New York: Oxford University Press.

Castilho, C. T. (2008), 'Abolitionism Matters: The Politics of Antislavery in Pernambuco, Brazil 1869–1888', Ph.D. dissertation, University of California, Berkeley.

Clarence-Smith, W. G. (2008), 'Église, nation et esclavage: Angola et Mozambique portugais, 1878–1913', in Olivier Pétré-Grenouilleau (ed.), *Abolir l'escavage: un réformisme à l'épreuve France, Portugal, Suisse, XVIIIe–XIXe siècles*, Rennes: Presses universitaires de Rennes, pp. 149–67.

Colley, L. (1992), *Britons: Forging the Nation 1707–1837,* New Haven, CT: Yale University Press.

Conrad, R. (1972), *The Destruction of Brazilian Slavery, 1850–1888*, Berkeley, CA: University of California Press.

Costa, E. V. da (1997), *Crowns of Glory, Tears of Blood: The Demerara Slave Rebellion of 1823*, New York: Oxford University Press.

Davis, D. B. (2006), *Inhuman Bondage: The Rise and Fall of Slavery in the New World*, New York: Oxford University Press.

Drescher, S. (1987), *Capitalism and Antislavery: British Mobilization in Comparative Perspective*, New York: Oxford University Press.

Drescher, S. (1999), *From Slavery to Freedom: Comparative Studies in the Rise and Fall of Atlantic Slavery*, New York: New York University Press.

Drescher, S. (2009), *Abolition: A History of Slavery and Antislavery*, New York: Cambridge University Press.

Engerman, S. L. (1995), 'Emancipations in Comparative Perspective: A Long and Wide View', in Gert Oostindie (ed.), *Fifty Years Later: Antislavery, Capitalism and Modernity*, Leiden: KITLV, pp. 223–41.

Hall, C. (2002), *Civilizing Subjects: Colony and Metropole in the English Imagination, 1830–1867*, Chicago, IL: Chicago University Press.

Innes, J. (2005), 'Legislation and Public Participation, 1780–1830', in David Lemmings (ed.), *The British and their Laws in the Eighteenth Century*, Rochester, NY: Boydell, pp. 102–32.

Jennings, L. C. (2000), *French Antislavery: The Movement for the Abolition of Slavery in France*, New York: Cambridge University Press.

Kielstra, P. M. (2000), *The Politics of Slave Trade Suppression in Britain and France 1814–48: Diplomacy, Morality and Economics*, New York: St Martin's Press.

Matthews, G. (2006), *Caribbean Slave Revolts and the British Abolitionist Movement*, Baton Rouge, LA: Louisiana State University Press.

Miers, S. (1975), *Britain and the Ending of the Slave Trade*, New York: Africana Publishing.

Miers, S. and R. Roberts (eds) (1988), *The End of Slavery in Africa*, Madison, WI: University of Wisconsin Press.

Midgley, C. (1995), *Women Against Slavery: The British Campaigns 1780–1870*, London: Routledge.

Murray, D. R. (1980), *Odious Commerce: Britain, Spain and the Abolition of the Cuban Slave Trade*, Cambridge: Cambridge University Press.

Offen, K. (1990), 'Women and the Question of "Universal Suffrage" in 1848: A Transatlantic Comparison of Suffragist Rhetoric', *NSWA Journal*, 1(1), 150–77.

Oldfield, J. R. (1995), *Popular Politics and British Anti-Slavery: The Mobilization of Public Opinion Against the Slave Trade, 1787–1807*, Manchester: Manchester University Press, p. 57.

Oostindie, G. (ed.) (1995), *Fifty Years Later: Antislavery, Capitalism and Modernity in the Dutch Case*, Leiden: KILTV.

Peabody, S. (1996), *There are No Slaves in France: The Political Culture of Race and Slavery in the Ancien Regime*, New York: Oxford University Press.

Schmidt-Nowara, C. (1999), *Empire and Antislavery: Spain, Cuba and Puerto Rico, 1833–1874*, Pittsburgh, PA: University of Pittsburgh Press.

Tilly, C. (1995), *Popular Contention in Great Britain, 1758–1834*, Cambridge, MA: Harvard University Press.

Tilly, C. and S. Tarrow (2007), *Contentious Politics,* London: Paradigm.

Tocqueville, A. de ([1843] 1968), 'On the Emancipation of Slaves', trans. and ed. S. Drescher, *Tocqueville and Beaumont on Social Reform*, New York: Harper & Row, pp. 137–73.

Chapter 28

Women's Suffrage

Patricia Grimshaw and Charles Sowerwine

Historians have often treated the introduction of women's suffrage as a narrative of linear progress. In this view, women's exclusion from the suffrage resulted from age-old prejudices, which, gradually and inevitably, gave way to modern egalitarian ideas. Recent scholarship, however, has complicated this story by emphasising the intractability of the issue. Enlightenment and republican discourse talked in universal terms, but constructed the citizen as public man in opposition to private woman, creating a feminine 'other' in order to create a 'universal', which was in fact gendered, masculine (Sowerwine 2010: 19). The idea of equal rights and the subordination of women were both part of Enlightenment discourse. Feminists, abolitionists, temperance advocates and many others all played a role in making equality the dominant discourse.

Until the twentieth century, it was unthinkable to view women as active citizens, casting votes, participating in political debates and representing men and women in parliaments. Breaches in the exclusion of women were opened first outside the continental European countries that had constructed republicanism and citizenship, in frontier and marginal areas, beginning in the last decade of the nineteenth century. The upheavals following the First World War opened the door to women's franchise in Europe and the Americas. After the Second World War, universal suffrage for both men and women came to be the norm throughout the world. How women got the vote in each state is complicated: sometimes partial franchise (on the basis of property, race, marital status, education or age); sometimes women of a majority group, while racial or ethnic minorities were excluded; sometimes granted, withdrawn and granted again. This chapter deals exclusively with women's suffrage and the right to stand for political office. It does not deal with the degree to which the government was democratic or dictatorial; the question is how and when women achieved the same rights as men, however extensive or limited these may have been.

Background

The word 'suffrage' pre-dates the concepts of citizenship and representative government, which originated with the three democratic revolutions of the seventeenth and eighteenth centuries: the English Civil War (1642–51), the American Revolution (1775–83) and the French Revolution (1789–99). Representative government, resulting from these events, led to the question of who would be entitled to representation and thus who could vote. In Britain and the United States, the right to vote was neither fixed nor universal until the twentieth century; it varied with local conditions, traditions and governance. In Britain, the Chartist movement struggled for universal male suffrage from 1838, but was defeated in 1848. In the United States, each state determined who could vote and, while white male suffrage became the norm during the first half of the nineteenth century, there was no concept of a universal right to vote, even for men. In France, however, the concept of universal suffrage on a uniform national basis emerged with the Revolution: the First French Republic introduced universal male suffrage for the election of the Convention in 1792; that assembly wrote the Constitution of 1793, which enshrined 'universal' male suffrage (beggars, vaga-bonds and domestic servants were still excluded); it was repealed in the conservative backlash of 1795.

Ironically, universal male suffrage led to the universal exclusion of women from the right to vote. The concept of universal rights necessarily entailed that of universal exclusion. Once all men were entitled to vote, all women had to be excluded and gender became the major qualification. With the advent of universal male suffrage in 1793, French women were formally excluded from the vote, although during the revolutionary period they often joined in when voting was by acclamation (Foley 2004). To get around the contradiction between the discourse of universalism and the reality of exclusion, the revolutionaries distinguished 'active' from 'passive' citizen-ship, which carried civil but not political rights: in 1791, wealthy men were active citizens, poor men passive; in 1792, all men became active citizens, all women passive.

Before 'universal' suffrage, women had not been completely excluded. Rather, being female had been one of many factors tending against inclusion. In the patchwork quilt of estate societies such as France and England in the seventeenth and eighteenth centuries, rights were determined by status, according to local tradition, and quali-fications were multiple, usually involving wealth, property, rank and independence. Gender was not the primary qualification: in eighteenth-century Sweden, Corsica and New Jersey, wealthy or aristocratic women, widows and others voted for local or provincial assemblies. The British Reform Act of 1832 enlarged the suffrage to include more men of property and, for the first time, specifically mentioned 'male', thus excluding women. The Second French Republic introduced truly universal male suffrage in 1848 and, again, women's exclusion became explicit.

Movements for Change before 1914

The British and American suffrage movements provided the foremost impetus for women's movements not only throughout Europe and the United States, but also among English-speaking expatriate communities across the world. The National Society for Women's Suffrage was founded in London in 1867, but women's voting rights did not have a strong voice until several small suffrage groups merged into the National Union of Women's Suffrage Societies in 1897 under the presidency of Mrs Millicent Garrett Fawcett. This body reached 100,000 members by 1914. The working-class labour movement also acknowledged women's political rights, provided they were granted on a universal and not a property basis. Early in the twentieth century, a group of labour women, led by Mrs Emmeline Pankhurst and her daughter Christabel, began organising to invigorate the Independent Labour Party on the issue. Finally frustrated by the party's refusal to make women's suffrage a major focus, they founded the separate Women's Social and Political Union (WSPU) in 1903.

This clearly separated the militant suffrage advocates from organised labour, a separation that facilitated their enlisting middle-class women. While moderates like Fawcett continued peaceful methods of lobbying, using reasoned arguments, the militants of the WSPU – nicknamed 'suffragettes' as a derisory term – adopted increasingly radical tactics to pressure the Liberal government, which allowed private members' bills for women's suffrage, but refused government support; without it all the bills failed. The Union staged a monster demonstration at Hyde Park in 1908, attracting a crowd of, they claimed, 500,000 women. WSPU militants intensified their violence. From disrupting political meetings, breaking windows, cutting telegraph lines and chaining themselves to railings, they moved to arson, setting fire to post-boxes, railway carriages and even a Liberal minister's country house. As a result, many militants were imprisoned. They went on hunger strikes and resisted forced feeding, attracting wide media interest. The Liberal Party, however, was persuaded neither by the militancy of the WSPU (indeed, it alienated them) nor by the moderation of the Fawcett wing. Britain entered the First World War in 1914 with women still awaiting the suffrage (Offen 2000).

The United States saw even earlier development of a sustained and influential women's suffrage movement. It emerged from the abolitionist movement, the fight to end slavery. A small but significant group of evangelical Protestant women joined abolitionist circles; they began to speak and act publicly for this cause and then faced restrictions on their actions from both convention and law. As a result, some abolitionist women resolved to fight for the rights of women as well as for those of slaves. In 1848, some 300 women and a few men held a convention in Seneca Falls in upstate New York. They articulated a raft of feminist aspirations, including women's right to vote. They held National Women's Rights conventions annually until 1861, when they ceased their campaign to assist the Northern cause in the Civil War.

The outcomes of the Civil War catalysed the expansion of the women's suffrage movement well beyond the small ranks of abolitionists. Advocates of women's and blacks' right to vote founded the American Equal Rights Association, which sought the vote for white and black women as well as for freed slave men and women. But the Fifteenth Amendment to the Constitution, proposed at the beginning of 1869, only prohibited any government from denying the right to vote because of 'race, color, or previous condition of servitude [slavery]'; sex remained a ground for denial. In the debate on ratification of the Amendment, many supporters of women's suffrage, led by Elizabeth Cady Stanton and Susan B. Anthony, argued that all women, whose ranks now included many highly educated women, deserved the right to vote as much as uneducated men, whose ranks included uneducated freedmen.

Stanton and Anthony founded the National Women's Suffrage Association in 1869. It pursued all strategies to win a constitutional amendment to enfranchise all women. Julia Ward Howe, Lucy Stone and others founded another organisation, the American Woman Suffrage Association, to pursue votes for women by more measured means.

Some black activists, however, were concerned that suffragists might, to gain the suffrage for women, make deals with white Southern political leaders which would reduce the freedoms or voting rights of newly enfranchised black men. Only in 1890 did the two groups join as the National American Woman Suffrage Association under the presidency of Carrie Chapman Catt to press more systematically for a constitutional amendment.

From the Association's inception, activists from the temperance movement reinforced its suffrage campaign. Among its founders was Frances Willard, President of the Woman's Christian Temperance Union (WCTU), which had 135,000 members by 1895, making it the largest women's organisation in the United States, if not the world. Temperance was a major issue, as widespread access to cheaper alcohol had increased social difficulties following industrialisation. The temperance cause brought many women into political lobbying and predisposed them to seek women's suffrage.

The WCTU was influential both within the United States and globally. In 1885, Willard joined forces with Lady Isabel Somerset, leader of the British Women's Temperance Alliance, to form the World's WCTU. Through the mission outreach of several effective American envoys, the WCTU forged links across the world, including the British settler colonies of Australia, New Zealand, Canada and South Africa, as well as Asian locations including Sri Lanka, Japan, China, Burma and the Philippines. Everywhere, local temperance reformers advocated a women's rights agenda. The WCTU case for women's political citizenship, grounded in an appeal to women's moral authority, joined with the arguments based on inherent equality of rights; it had particular potency in American western rural states and in Britain's settler colonies.

Early Breaches in Frontier Lands

Women's suffrage was not granted first in the heartland of republicanism nor in one of the great cities associated with advanced views on gender equality, but in sites many regarded as frontiers of settlement, far from the mainstream movements. In many US states, the presence of a substantial African–American minority retarded the suffrage, because whites feared that women's suffrage would mean black women's suffrage. In the Rocky Mountain states, the presence of numerous different competing minorities, such as Asians and Native Americans, appeared to reduce that threat (Grimshaw 1994).

Thus, women gained the vote early in the territories of Wyoming (1869) and Utah (1870). The first real breach, however, occurred when the territories became states and women gained the right to vote and stand for office at federal level – Wyoming in 1890, Utah in 1896 – and when two other western states granted the vote: Colorado in 1893 and Idaho in 1896. Other western states followed: Washington (1910), California (1911), Arizona, Kansas and Oregon (1912), Alaska and Illinois (1913), Montana and Nevada (1914). The eastern seaboard, where republicanism was strongest, and the southern states, where virulent racism remained an impediment, still held out against women's suffrage.

Within the British Empire, the Isle of Man, in effect a colony of Britain, passed universal male and female suffrage in 1881, but royal assent was granted only for votes for single women and widows with property. Of greater significance for the accept-ability of women's political citizenship, three self-governing Australasian colonies granted women the vote in the 1890s. The first was New Zealand in 1893, which was to become an independent nation and is thus considered the first nation-state to grant women the vote, though not the right to stand for office (Macdonald 2009). Maori women got the suffrage at the same time. South Australia and Western Australia followed, in 1894 and 1899, respectively; they became states at the creation of the federal Commonwealth of Australia in 1901. These were settler societies that had already extended voting rights to all men, were politically liberal and nurtured organised labour. Racial anxieties also played a part: settlers in New Zealand were keen to incorporate indigenous Maori into the mainstream, white political system; settlers in the Australian colonies felt threatened by the possibility that Asian countries to the north might compete for the land settlers had recently wrested from Aborigines. In both cases, white women could appear to white male politicians as part of the beleaguered white circle. In 1902, Australia granted white women full political citizenship for federal elections, while curtailing Aboriginal political rights (Grimshaw 2009, 2010); the remaining Australian states fell into line, giving women the vote though delaying the right to representation: New South Wales (1902), Tasmania (1903), Queensland (1905) and Victoria (1908). Indigenous women were fully en-franchised, along with indigenous men, only in 1962.

Building on these precedents, women from the United States, Britain, the Nether-lands, Norway, Sweden, Denmark, Australia and Germany founded the International Woman Suffrage Alliance in 1904. Two key members, the Dutch suffragist Aletta Jacobs and the American Carrie Chapman Catt, toured Europe together to speak for women's right to vote. With New Zealand and Australia having granted women the vote, feminists could point to precedent: women voted in civilised nations and the sky had not fallen in. Women's suffrage became a realistic aspiration.

A second breach opened before the First World War, with enfranchisements in Finland and Norway, lands which, if not frontiers, were marginal to the great European centres where republicanism developed. The Russian Revolution of 1905 led immediately to upheaval in Finland (which Russia controlled) and the tsar quickly agreed to greater autonomy for Finland. The Finnish Diet, which was still based on the old estate structures, with four houses (nobles, burghers, peasants and clergy), moved quickly to implement a new governmental structure with a single house of parliament before the tsar could change his mind. To avoid delay, the Diet accepted the demands of a strong feminist movement for women's suffrage and eligibility in 1906 and the new parliament met for the first time in 1907, with nineteen women sitting among the 200 members. There were many grounds for exclusion, however, and women could not vote in local elections. In Norway, too, political upheaval opened the door. In 1905, Norway demanded independence from Sweden, which had dominated it since 1814, and, to demonstrate support for independence, held a referendum, from which women were excluded. Some 250,000 women of a population of 2 million signed petitions ('pronouncements') demanding the right to vote. The parliament (the Storting) acceded and gave the vote to propertied women in 1907 and finally to all women in 1913. With these two breaches in Europe, women's suffrage moved onto the international agenda and was gaining momentum when the First World War broke out in 1914.

The First World War and its Aftermath

The First World War shattered traditional certainties and catalysed the shift to an emerging new model of citizenship, no longer limited by gender, as women had often taken men's roles in domestic and waged work. Some societies came to accept that women should be rewarded for having sacrificed their sons, husbands and brothers to the war; others that women voters would provide a moral, stabilising force against social upheaval. Whether women were viewed as agents of progressive change or bulwarks against radicalism, feminists had a greater chance of success in these contexts. European feminists also benefited from the support of women of the labour and socialist movements that were increasing in size and political significance. Most European socialist parties had already included universal suffrage for both women and men in their programmes: France (1879), Austria (1888–9), Germany (1891), Russia (1907) and the British Labour Party (1912). The International Socialist Paris Congress of 1900 had reaffirmed it as an aim for all member parties. In Germany, the German Social Democratic Party had an amazing 175,000 members before the First World War. They provided mass support for women's rights. In France, mainstream feminist movements came on board during the 1890s, and in 1914 a mock election drew 500,000 women to cast a 'vote' with the words 'I want to vote' (Sowerwine 2009: 76).

These factors were at work when Denmark and Iceland granted women the suffrage in 1915 (Iceland only to women over forty). In Canada, seven states granted women the vote during the war (Alberta, Manitoba and Saskatchewan in 1916, British Columbia in 1917, Ontario, New Brunswick and Nova Scotia in 1918). At the federal level, the vote was given to Euro-American women in the armed forces and close relatives of soldiers in 1917, and then to women of British or French origin in 1918. Indigenous women did not receive the vote until after the Second World War.

The First World War and the Russian Revolution also catalysed widespread political upheaval, especially across the old Austro-Hungarian Empire, which collapsed upon its defeat at the end of the war. Most of the new nations born of this collapse underwent revolution, liberation or national re-generation and assumed the new model of citizenship, immediately granting universal franchise to women and men. What had been unthinkable was suddenly possible. The Russian Revolution of February 1917 was dominated by progressive parties, from the Constitutional Democrats to the Bolsheviks. Women's suffrage supporters persuaded them to honour their commitment to male and female suffrage. In parallel upheaval, Estonia, Latvia and Lithuania also granted women the vote that year. Austria, Czechoslovakia, Germany, Luxembourg and Poland opened the vote to women in 1918, while Hungary granted limited suffrage. Turkey moved to grant women rights after the Turkish War of Independence and the establishment of a republic in 1922. Women were granted full civil rights in 1926 and full voting rights in 1934. The nationalist victory in Ireland led to full suffrage for women from the inception of the Irish Free State in 1922.

Women also obtained the vote in a number of Allied nations which staved off revolution, though with considerable unrest and fear of revolution. Male supporters of the suffrage often referred to women's 'admirable attitude during the war'. Behind this condescension, women's suffrage was seen as 'a means of controlling society in the interests of the "stable" part of the population, the middle classes' (Evans 1987: 217). Women continued to pressure for their rights, though no longer in militant fashion. Instead, they used the war to justify their claims. In this climate, in 1918, Britain granted the vote to all men and to certain categories of women thirty years of age or older: single women whose property was taxed at £5 a year or more; women married to a man whose property was taxed at £5 or more; and women university graduates. It was not until 1928 that Britain extended the suffrage to all women.

The war played a particular role in Belgium. Socialists and liberals, theoretically committed to women's suffrage, hesitated as the Catholic parties began to support women's suffrage; all assumed that women were more religious than men and would vote more conservatively. In a 1919 compromise, suffrage in local government elections was given to the mothers and widows of soldiers killed in the war and to women imprisoned by the Germans during their occupation of Belgium, enfranchising only 0.6 per cent more Belgian voters. Curiously, women were also granted the right to stand for parliament as well as for local government, although they could not vote for parliament until 1948. In 1919, Sweden and the Netherlands gave women the vote. In 1920, Iceland extended suffrage to all women. The Dutch Women's Suffrage Association, founded in 1894, obtained the right for women to stand for election in 1917, before they could vote. As a result, there was female participation in the decision to grant women the vote in the Netherlands in 1919.

The war also provided the catalyst for further state and then federal enfranchisement of women in the United States. Alice Paul, adopting British suffragette tactics, gathered a militant core, which intensified pressure on the government. More American states granted women the suffrage during the war: in 1917, Arkansas, Indiana, Michigan, Nebraska, New York, North Dakota (presidential elections only) and Rhode Island; in 1918, Michigan, Oklahoma, South Dakota and Texas (primaries only). With the end of the war, a groundswell of opinion led to the Nineteenth Amendment, providing that 'the right of citizens of the United States to vote shall not be denied or abridged by the United States or by any state on account of sex'. President Wilson gave it emphatic support; it was passed by Congress in 1918 and ratified by sufficient states in 1920. Non-white Americans, however, did not share these gains. Southern states had used 'literacy tests' and poll taxes to prevent non-whites from voting, despite the Fifteenth Amendment; these restrictions did not change with women's suffrage, so non-white women were not effectively franchised until the 1960s' civil rights acts. Women in two American dependencies received the vote just before America's entry into the Second World War: the Philippines in 1937 and the Dominican Republic in 1942.

Outside the United States, Europe and their settler colonies, however, progress was still limited (Fletcher et al. 2000). Colonial or neo-colonial powers, conscious of the threat posed by local or indigenous political rights, resisted women's suffrage in their colonies, thinking it contrary to their political interests. Where women obtained the vote, it was usually white women, who could be counted on to reinforce the colonial power's hold. In 1919, Zimbabwe, then the British colony of Rhodesia, granted limited suffrage to wives of wealthy men, except to multiple wives married polygamously, which excluded many wives of wealthy African men. The ex-settler colony of South Africa gave white women the vote in 1930, as a direct attack on the rights of non-white men, some of whom had obtained the suffrage through a property provision. Non-white men's votes would be, it was hoped, lost in the enlarged pool of white votes. Full female and male suffrage would await the end of apartheid in 1994. In the colony of India in 1918, the British government rejected women's suffrage while expanding responsible government, but in 1935 gave all women and men with high education and income thresholds, including Indian women and men, limited suffrage, extending the franchise to some 30 million male Indians, but to only 1 million female Indians, since few women had enough income in their own right. Women could vote in the British colony of Ceylon (now Sri Lanka) from 1931.

Political upheaval continued to be a factor. The new Spanish republic granted women the vote in 1931, but Franco revoked women's suffrage as he took power in the Civil War (1936–9) and Spanish women regained the vote only in 1976. Upheaval worked the other way in Portugal. In 1931, the 'new state' dictatorship permitted women with at least secondary education to vote, in the hope that they would vote conservatively. The following year, Antonio Salazar took power in a quasi-fascist regime and promulgated the constitution of 1933, which proclaimed everyone equal before the law 'except for women'. In 1946, women heads of household and married women who paid a set amount of tax got the vote. In 1968, responding to widespread upheaval, Salazar promised 'equality of political rights for men and women', but only following the 1974 Carnation Revolution would women be granted full and equal electoral rights.

The establishment of representative government in Thailand (1932) led to universal suffrage for women and men. The inter-war period saw the beginnings of women's political citizenship in Latin American states that had their origins in Portuguese and Spanish colonisation. Ecuador gave women suffrage in 1929 (only in 1967 were they put on the same footing of compulsory voting as men); Brazil and Uruguay gave women the vote in 1932, Cuba in 1934 and El Salvador in 1939. By the outbreak of the Second World War, the general notion of citizenship was being reconfigured to include women.

The Second World War and Decolonisation

During the Second World War, the Allies stressed a future of self-determination in such documents as the Atlantic Charter and the Brazzaville Declaration. With the inception of the United Nations, notions of universal human rights were formulated and became hegemonic. The tide turned. While before the war women's suffrage had required a strong women's movement and local factors leading men to accept women's suffrage, after the war universal suffrage without distinction of sex became the norm. Many reconstructing European countries extended suffrage to men and to women. In France as far back as 1919, the lower house had approved women's suffrage, but the measure had been buried in the Senate. In 1944, a coalition of Communists and

Gaullists, sitting as the French government in exile in Algiers, finally approved women's suffrage (Sowerwine 2009). In Romania, women over thirty gained the right to vote in 1930; full suffrage came after the war, in 1946. Women in Japan received the suffrage and the right to stand in 1945, as part of American-led post-war reconstruction. In the same year, they also won the suffrage in Bulgaria and Italy and, the following year, in Albania, Malta and Yugoslavia. In 1948, Belgium granted the suffrage to all women. Greek women obtained the vote in the aftermath of a bitter civil war when, in 1952, the victorious authoritarian government gave women the vote in an attempt to restore stability. Women in Switzerland, less affected by war, awaited political citizenship until 1971.

The fallout from the Second World War extended to Latin American nations that had long been independent, at least in theory, though subject to US hegemony in various forms and to strongly contested, historically shaped social and political divisions. Immediately after the war, women were enfranchised in Guatemala, Panama and Venezuela (1946), and in Argentina (1947). Most other nations followed in the next decade: Chile and Costa Rica in 1949; Haiti in 1950; Bolivia in 1952; Mexico in 1953; Colombia in 1954; Honduras and Nicaragua in 1955; and Paraguay in 1961.

In China, the women's movement had been frustrated by the struggle between the Nationalists and the Communists, which began in 1927. China had not been formally colonised, but foreign nations weighed heavily until Japanese occupying forces withdrew at the end of the war, opening the way to all-out civil war. With the victory of Mao Zedong's Communist rebels in 1949, the new regime gave women the franchise on a uniform, national basis, in keeping with a long-standing commitment in their programme (Edwards 2008; Edwards and Roces 2004).

With the decolonisation of most of Africa and Asia after 1945, new countries extended suffrage to men and women upon independence, if it had not been granted before (as in the cases above). Indonesia, then the Dutch East Indies, offers an example of the interplay between metropolitan feminists and colonial power struggles. Following the granting of the suffrage in the Netherlands, metropolitan opinion swung towards women's suffrage in the colonies, generally assumed to mean white women's suffrage. In 1925, the Dutch Parliament removed the provision that Indonesian electors be male, but only in 1941 did the colonial government propose suffrage for European women. The 'People's Council' demanded, and the government accepted, that Indonesian women also be admitted to the vote on the same restrictive property and tax basis as Indonesian men. The nationalist Indonesian government that took power after the war enabled Indonesian women – but not women of mixed racial descent – to participate in the first national elections in 1955.

In broadly similar fashion, women in many developing countries received the vote as the old colonial structures trembled and the new notion of citizenship spread: in 1946, Liberia (partial suffrage), Cameroon, Romania and Vietnam; in 1947, Pakistan; in 1948, Burma (now Myanmar), Israel and South Korea; and, in 1949, India (universal suffrage for women and men). With the second wave of decolonisation, the vote was extended to women in Tunisia (1959), Burundi, Rwanda and Somalia (1961), Algeria, Uganda and Northern Rhodesia (now Zambia) (1962), Kenya (1963), Bermuda (1968) and Mozambique (1975).

In British colonies, administrators now assumed that women's suffrage was the norm and thus granted or accepted it as they prepared colonies for independence: Jamaica (1944), Trinidad and Tobago (1945) and most of the remaining Caribbean colonies in 1951: Antigua, Barbados, Dominica, Grenada, St Christopher (Kitts) and Nevis, St Lucia, St Vincent and the Grenadines. Other British colonies followed: in 1951, Sierra Leone, in 1954 Belize (formerly British Honduras) and Ghana (formerly the Gold Coast Colony); in 1955, Malaya/Malaysia and Nigeria (but North Nigeria only in 1978); in 1957, Singapore; in 1958, Mauritius and Tanganyika (now Tanzania); and, in 1960, Gambia and the Bahamas. Where decolonisation was late, the vote came even later. In 1975, Australia included universal suffrage in the new constitution of Papua New Guinea, and Portugal granted suffrage to Mozambique. Zimbabwe (formerly Rhodesia), troubled by a difficult post-colonial history, gave women full suffrage only in 1978, the same year as Liberia, a nation heavily dependent on the United States.

In the Middle East, the question of women's political citizenship was complicated, on the one hand, by the imposition of Western control and, on the other, by conservative Islamists and/or oppressive regimes, but most nations granted at least theoretical suffrage to women in the thirty years following the Second World War. In 1949, women in Syria received limited suffrage; full suffrage was granted in 1953, withdrawn later that year after a coup and finally granted in 1972. Also in 1953, Lebanon granted women the vote, but, unlike men, women had to show proof of primary schooling and this still remains the case. In 1956, Egypt gave women the right to vote, but made voting compulsory only for men. Women received the suffrage in Iraq (1958), Morocco (1963), Iran (1963) and Jordan (1974).

In the last decades of the twentieth century, women obtained the vote, at least theoretically, in virtually every country where they had not already obtained it, though in some Arab states this awaited the early twenty-first century: Bahrain (2002, its first elections); Oman (2003); Kuwait (2005); United Arab Emirates (2006 very limited, expansion long promised and long delayed; in 2011, one woman was elected to the legislative body). Qatar gave women the suffrage for municipal elections in 1999 and claims to have scheduled women's suffrage for national elections in 2013. In 2011, King Abdullah of Saudi Arabia decreed that women would have the vote in the next elections (scheduled for 2015), but scepticism reigns: women still do not have even the right to driving licences (MacFarquhar 2011).

Conclusion

Women's rights were not inherent in democratic ideals; they had to be fought for case by case, but the idea of equal rights originated with the European Enlightenment. It was carried across the world in the wake of European expansion and colonisation. In each country, local women and men picked up the struggle, redefined the terms and finally gained rights. By the Second World War, the idea of equal rights had become hegemonic and emerging polities built in women's suffrage.

By the late twentieth century, most women across the globe enjoyed the rights entailed in political citizenship, though in some countries the practical force of such rights was complicated. The courage of women in such strife-ridden countries as Iran, Iraq and Afghanistan, who line up to vote alongside men in fraught elections and especially in the Arab Spring revolts of 2011, reminds the world that women themselves regard their political empowerment as a vital underpinning of human rights and social justice. The force of the reaction against women's role in the Arab Spring reminds the world that the struggle must continue.

References

Edwards, L. (2008), *Gender, Politics, and Democracy: Women's Suffrage in China*, Stanford, CA: Stanford University Press.

Edwards, L. and M. Roces (eds) (2004), *Women's Suffrage in Asia: Gender, Nationalism and Democracy*, London: Routledge Curzon.

Evans, R. J. (1987), *The Feminists: Women's Emancipation Movements in Europe, America and Australasia 1840–1920*, rev. edn, London: Croom Helm.

Fletcher, I. C., L. E. Nym Mayhall and P. Levine (2000), *Women's Suffrage in the British Empire: Citizenship, Nation and Race*, New York: Routledge.

Foley, S. K. (2004), *Women in France since 1789: The Meanings of Difference*, New York: Palgrave Macmillan.

Grimshaw, P. (1994), 'Women's Suffrage in New Zealand Revisited: Writing from the Margins', in M. Nolan and C. Daley (eds), *Suffrage and Beyond: International Feminist Perspectives*, Auckland: Auckland University Press, pp. 25–41.

Grimshaw, P. (2009), 'Colonialism, Power and Women's Political Citizenship in Australia, 1894–1898', in I. Sulkunen *et al.* (eds), *Suffrage, Gender and Citizenship: International Perspectives on Parliamentary Reforms*, Cambridge, MA: Cambridge Scholars Press, pp. 34–55.

Grimshaw, P. (2010), 'Settler Anxieties, Indigenous Peoples and Women's Suffrage in the Colonies of Australia, New Zealand and Hawai'i, 1888 to 1902', in K. M. Offen (ed.), *Globalizing Feminisms, 1789–1945*, New York: Routledge, pp. 111–21.

Macdonald, C. (2009), 'Suffrage, Gender and Sovereignty in New Zealand', in I. Sulkunen *et al.* (eds), *Suffrage, Gender and Citizenship: International Perspectives on Parliamentary Reforms*, Cambridge, MA: Cambridge Scholars Press, pp. 14–33.

MacFarquhar, N. (2011), 'Saudi Monarch Grants Women Right to Vote', *New York Times*, 25 September.

Offen, K. M. (2000), *European Feminisms, 1700–1950: A Political History*, Stanford, CA: Stanford University Press.

Sowerwine, C. (2009), *France since 1870: Culture, Society and the Making of the Republic*, 2nd edn, New York: Palgrave Macmillan.

Sowerwine, C. (2010), 'Revising the Sexual Contract: Women's Citizenship and Republicanism in France, 1789–1944', in C. E. Forth and E. Accampo (eds), *Confronting Modernity in Fin-de-siècle France: Bodies, Minds, and Gender*, New York: Palgrave Macmillan, pp. 19–42.

Chapter 29

Socialism, Communism, Anarchism

Barry Hindess

This chapter examines important divisions in the history of socialism, focusing on the period before the schism between communists and others that followed the First World War and the subsequent revolutions in Russia (1917) and Germany (1918–1919). It considers divisions between anarchist and Marxist socialism (or, as the anarchist, Michael Bakunin framed it: between revolutionary socialism and communism (Bakunin 1950)); and, within European social democracy, the divisions over the projects of a peaceful, democratic road to socialism and the 'dictatorship of the proletariat'.

Before the late eighteenth-century American and French revolutions, democracy was generally seen as government by the people as a whole and, partly for this reason, unsuitable for the government of any populous state (Roberts 1994). Yet, by the beginning of the twentieth century, democracy had acquired a second meaning – as government by representatives elected by the people – and was widely regarded as perhaps the best form of government. The nineteenth and early twentieth centuries saw the development of an influential socialist critique of capitalism and the emergence of powerful socialist movements in much of Europe, thus it is not surprising to find that democracy was a matter of intense concern and debate within the socialist movement. Socialism has been unusual among social movements in its levels of both organisation and theoretical reflection. Socialists have played important parts in the organisation of parties, unions, national liberation movements, international federations and factions within each of these. They have debated how far socialists should attempt a leadership role in these organisations, especially in relation to the working class, and what to do when others neglected to follow their lead; and whether they should aim for radical social change (the revolutionary overthrow of capitalism, national liberation), the promotion of socialist values (democracy, equality, internationalism, anti-imperialism) and/or the immediate promotion of workers' interests. Generally, Marxist socialists have approached these debates through a distinctive theory of the role of class struggle and the state in promoting, or preventing, historical change – a theory which they used to judge whether conditions were ripe for a socialist revolution and to claim an important role for intellectuals within the socialist movement. Disagreements about this theory within Marxism and between Marxists and their opponents have often been the source of factional division. In practice, socialist parties, and the socialist movement as a whole, have always been uneasy coalitions of intellectuals (some committed to Marxist theory, others to socialist values) and unions (or other working-class organisations). The latter, concentrating on what the intellectuals saw as short-term issues, saw the intellectuals in turn as focusing on side issues. As a result, significant groups of their supporters have usually had reason to be sorely disappointed by the conduct of these parties. The disputes between these intellectuals are not the only, or even the most important, things worth noting in the histories of socialism, anarchism and communism, but positions taken up by these early figures offer useful insights into later developments (Sassoon 1998).

Communism and Revolutionary Socialism

Nineteenth-century socialists debated questions of authority and especially of the state. Socialism is usually understood as involving production organised either by a free association of workers, and thus through democracy, operating on both a large (national) and a small (workplace) scale, and/or by central planning (often described by twentieth-century communist states as 'people's democracy'). While appeals to the idea of production organised by freely associated workers – and thus to a kind of democracy, if only in the workplace – can be found in eighteenth-century reactions against the apparent evils of capitalism, the first use of the term *socialisme*, in the early nineteenth century, is often attributed to Henri de Saint-Simon who favoured centralised planning as a way of dealing with the social and economic problems resulting from industrialisation (Durkheim [1928] 1959).

The first international socialist movement, the International Workingmen's Association (often called the First International) was founded in London in 1864 with Karl Marx (1818–83) as an influential member of the committee. Like many nineteenth-century socialists, Marx supported democracy in principle, but regarded representative government as an instrument of bourgeois rule. In *The Communist Manifesto*, written with Friedrich Engels in 1848, Marx insists that:

> the first step in the revolution by the working class is to raise the proletariat to the position of ruling class to win the battle of democracy . . . The proletariat will use its political supremacy . . . to centralize all instruments of production in the hands of the state, i.e., of the proletariat organized as the ruling class; and to increase the total productive forces as rapidly as possible . . . This cannot be effected except by means of despotic inroads on the rights of property. (Marx and Engels [1848] 1968: 52)

Critics read this appeal to despotism as evidence of Marx's authoritarian tendencies. The *Manifesto* claims that communists represent the interests of the proletariat and that they 'have no interests separate and apart from those of the proletariat as a whole' (Marx and Engels [1848] 1968: 46), but without explaining why anyone should believe this claim. Nor does it explain what it meant by 'win the battle of democracy'. The authors may have been thinking here of democracy as representative government and of the battle as parties competing for both electoral support and control over the representative assembly. On these lines, Engels' Introduction to the 1895 German edition of Marx's *The Class Struggles in France* explains how the system of representative government in contemporary Germany could benefit the Social Democratic Party. It 'accurately informed us concerning our own strength and that of hostile parties'. Here, Engels assumes that, like the *Manifesto*'s communists, the party represents the interests of the proletariat. He assumes, further, that votes for the Social Democratic Party reflect support for its socialist objectives. However, because representative government also informed 'the bourgeoisie and the government' of the same facts, they 'came to be much more afraid of the legal than of the illegal action of the worker's party, of the results of elections than those of rebellion' (Marx and Engels [1848] 1968: 660). Thus, if we avoid street fighting (and the repression that goes with it) 'there is nothing left for them to do than to break through this fatal legality (Marx and Engels [1848] 1968: 666). At this point, Engels comes close to suggesting that the Party could win power by peaceful means, but that violence, coming from the other side, might be unavoidable. This equivocation about the prospects for a peaceful road to socialism would come to haunt debates within European socialism.

Returning to Marx's views on socialism and democracy, he also argued that there was no prospect of achieving socialism unless the economic organisation of society had reached an appropriate level. It might be possible for a socialist movement to seize power under conditions inauspicious for the socialist organisation of production. If there were, for example, numerous small-scale capitalist or peasant producers, socialists would rely on centralised state control – the 'despotic inroads on the rights of property' noted earlier – to bring about the social and economic conditions required to establish socialist organisation of production. A strong state would also protect the revolution from hostile intervention by capitalist powers. These points bring the ideal of production by groups of freely associating workers perilously close to that of centrally planned production. Marx's commitment to capturing the state and using it to promote socialist objectives was a major source of conflict between Marxist socialism (communism) and anarchists, who promoted a libertarian rejection of authority and denied the need for any kind of state – and sometimes organised violent attacks on the leaders or agencies of states (Woodcock 1975).

The anarchist Pierre-Joseph Proudhon (1809–65) is best known today for the slogan, 'property is theft', and for his powerful polemics against both government and authority. Proudhon's slogan targeted, not the clothing or tools of artisans, peasants and wage-labourers or the homes in which they lived, but rather the property of the wealthy, which Proudhon viewed as stolen from the people. As for government, his *General Idea of the Revolution in the Nineteenth Century* argues that the useful functions of government could be dissolved into the industrial organisation of workers because otherwise 'to be governed is to be watched, inspected, spied upon . . . valued, censured, commanded, by creatures who have neither the right nor the wisdom nor the virtue to do so' (Proudhon [1851] 1923: 293). There are several things worth noting in this passage. First, is its striking individualism. While governments around the world are expected to provide defence, a range of social and infrastructure services (which vary over time and place) and to maintain some degree of law and order, Proudhon's critique focuses on what governments do to the individuals within their reach. Second is its anti-authoritarian character: what he objects to is government's presumption of authority. In addition, Proudhon's critique of anything that watches, inspects, spies upon, etc., applies as much to government by the democratically organised groups of workers that he appears to favour as it does to government by a capitalist state. Unlike Marx and his followers, Proudhon's anti-authoritarianism led him to be profoundly hostile to any state, even one taken over by the socialists. His 'Solution of the Social Problem' claimed that, since the people cannot be represented, they must act for themselves (Proudhon [1849] 1927). An ideal republic would be a matter of liberty freed from all shackles – with citizens free to do what they wish and only what they wish. This is a formula for a popular democracy that imposes no constraints on the conduct of its members.

While Proudhon clearly thought of himself as a socialist and a democrat, Marx and Engels' *Manifesto* calls him one of those conservative or bourgeois socialists who 'desire the existing state of society, minus its revolutionary and disintegrating elements. They wish for a bourgeoisie without a proletariat' (Marx and Engels 1968: 59). Proudhon published few direct criticisms of Marx's ideas, perhaps because they did not seem important. Yet his anti-statism was taken up in later, more substantial anarchist critiques of Marx and Marxism, notably in the work of Michael Bakunin (1814–76). After the First International was established in 1864, Bakunin and his friends set up an alternative international grouping, the Alliance of Socialist Democracy, and applied unsuccessfully to join the International. Sections of the Alliance were later admitted, but only after the Alliance itself had disbanded. The first congress of the International in 1869 supported Bakunin's proposal that inheritance should be abolished. This marked the beginning of the first major dispute in the socialist movement that bears on democracy: that between Marx and Bakunin. It turned on the role of the state in a socialist platform. Both sides thought of socialism as the democratic organisation of production by the workers themselves., but they disagreed from that point onward. Marx and his supporters maintained that the state would be needed in the consolidation of socialism, whereas Bakunin and the anarchists took the view that the state should be abolished and that it would always be an obstacle to socialism. Where Marx saw the state specifically as an instrument of class domination, the anarchists saw it as oppressing anyone within its reach. Thus, if the working class formed a majority of the population, it made no sense to claim that this class could use the state to bring about the democratic organisation of production. Representative government was not a matter of dispute within the socialist movement at this time. Most of those who commented on representative government took the view that it served to keep the people away from the actual work of government.

A Democratic Road to Socialism?

By the end of the nineteenth century, many European states had representative institutions and socialist parties were accustomed to operating within them, often with some degree of success. In 1891, the most successful of European socialist parties, the German Social Democratic Party, published its Erfurt Program: a statement of socialist objectives with explanatory commentary. Within a few years, Karl Kautsky and Eduard Bernstein, who both had a hand in its drafting, produced books on the program. Developing Engels' point that representative government favoured the socialists, they argued, in effect, that socialism should be introduced by democratic means, but developed this argument in different directions.

Kautsky's *The Class Struggle*, published in German in 1892 and other European languages shortly afterwards, maintains that socialism would result from capitalist development (Kautsky [1892] 1971). Capitalism progressively divides the population into a few capitalists, a large majority of workers, a small middle class and peasantry. Workers' experience of struggle over wages and working conditions leads them to form unions and to make political demands – for representative government and freedom of assembly, speech and the press. In the end, they establish a political party to represent their interests and the experience of working for the party takes them beyond pursuit of sectional interests (which Kautsky portrays as reflecting a 'trade union consciousness') to a sense of solidarity and political cohesion. Kautsky outlines a view of the state that was to be taken up by many European communist parties in the 1970s and 1980s and came to be known as Eurocommunism (Carillo 1977): the state, even in its Western 'democratic' form, was an instrument of the ruling class, as *The Communist Manifesto* had argued, and it could be transformed through parliamentary and electoral struggle. Thus, Kautsky insists, the state will remain a capitalist institution until the proletariat becomes the ruling class (Kautsky [1892] 1971: 110). Yet an elected parliament with a widespread franchise was an arena of class struggle, not 'a mere tool in the hands of the bourgeoisie' (Kautsky [1892] 1971: 188). Thinking of Germany in the 1890s, when parliament had no control over appointment of the cabinet, Kautsky argued that the working class should increase its influence in parliament and the power of parliament in the state, the latter depending on the energy and courage of the contending classes (Kautsky [1892] 1971: 187). Thus, the polarisation of the population and the growing maturity of the working class ensured that the socialist transformation of society by parliamentary means would just be a matter of time and that the party had no need to seek support from other classes or non-socialist parties.

Kautsky's view of representative democracy at this time was largely instrumental. While not the democratic organisation of production that socialism requires, it could still be adapted to socialist objectives. His optimistic view of the combination of representative government and capitalist development was soon to be vigorously disputed from two directions. On one side, Kautsky's championing of a parliamentary road to socialism was disputed by the Russian Bolsheviks, arguing from what they saw as a more orthodox Marxist perspective. On the other side, his view that the polarisation of the population would inevitably produce a socialist majority was disputed by Eduard Bernstein's *Evolutionary Socialism* (1899), the second major socialist commentary on the Erfurt Program (Bernstein [1899] 1961). While Kautsky's argument could be read, for example, by Lenin, as a betrayal of Marxism, Bernstein's rejection of Marx's central claims was unambiguous.

Social democratic parties throughout the West have suffered periodic conflicts as some of their leaders have campaigned to throw out outdated ideas (Sassoon 1998: 187–274). In retrospect, the dispute ignited by Bernstein can be seen as a foretaste of what was to come (Schorske 1983). First, Bernstein disputes the tendencies, cited by the Erfurt Program and endorsed by Kautsky, towards polarisation, insisting that, in

Germany, the middle classes, peasantry and small businesses were not disappearing, and the working class was nothing like a majority of the population. For the foreseeable future, he argued, there would always be a substantial minority that was neither bourgeois nor proletarian, but whose politics would crucially affect the prospects of achieving socialist objectives. Secondly, he noted that, even within the working class, membership of and voting for the socialist party did not necessarily indicate support for socialist objectives. Bernstein used the example of Britain to argue that capitalist development need not lead to the growth of socialist consciousness within the working class. Thirdly, citing Webb's discussion of the poor performance of producer cooperatives in *Industrial Democracy* (Webb 1897), he doubted that the working class could control the practical organisation of production: 'it is simply impossible that the manager should be an employee of those he manages . . . dependent for his position on their favour and their bad temper' (Bernstein [1899] 1961: 119).

A parliamentary road to socialism may still be possible, but to get there the party of the working class must be prepared to cut deals with other parties in parliament and it must aim to win support from members of other classes. If the working class is not going to form a clear majority of the population, then a party that appeals exclusively to their interests is never going to win power. Advancing an early version of the late twentieth-century theory of post-materialist values (Inglehart 1977), Bernstein argues that today's level of economic development 'leaves the . . . ethical factors greater space for independent activity than was formerly the case' (Bernstein [1899] 1961: 15). Accordingly, the socialist party must aim to win support from the workers by appealing to their interests and from the more prosperous members of society by appealing to socialist values. Bernstein's argument here shows how easily a focus on social-democratic principles or values at the expense of the party's economic pro-gramme can be represented as a kind of modernisation. Bernstein directs his arguments against the Erfurt Program's optimistic account of how the socialist party might come to power. Yet his objections to the idea that the working class was ready and able to manage production apply equally well, or badly, to the anarchist idea of the direct takeover of production by the working class.

More interesting, is what Bernstein has to say about democracy. His argument here is in two parts, one concerning the nature of democracy and the other the difference between revolutionary and democratic roads to political power. First, he offers a negative definition: democracy means the absence of class rule, if not the absence of classes. People should not be privileged or penalised by the state simply because of their membership or otherwise of any particular class. This, he says, rules out 'the oppression of the individual which is absolutely repugnant to the modern mind' (Bernstein [1899] 1961: 142). Many of Bernstein's readers would have noticed this oblique reference to the liberal notion of the tyranny of the majority, popularised by John Stuart Mill (Mill [1859] 1946). Yet, secondly, Bernstein invokes the idea, that democracy is a defence against oppression. Bernstein's central claim here is that universal suffrage subjects the state to popular control: 'The right to vote in a democracy makes its members virtually partners in the community, and this virtual partnership must in the end lead to real partnership' (Bernstein [1899] 1961: 114). He recognises that, to many workers, the right to vote simply gives them a say in who is to be 'the butcher'. Yet 'with the growing number and knowledge of the workers' it transforms representatives 'from masters into real servants of the people' (Bernstein [1899] 1961: 114).

To illustrate this process, Bernstein refers to the anti-socialist law, introduced by the German Reichstag in 1878 with the aim of curbing the growth of the Social Democratic Party, and finally allowed to lapse in 1890. Following a usage that was common in Europe at the time, Bernstein takes the 'universal' in 'universal suffrage' to mean all adult male citizens and suggests that Bismarck had introduced suffrage to counter growing support for socialism, thereby implying that the socialist movement was indirectly responsible for democratisation. Bismarck saw universal suffrage as a tool, but 'finally it compelled Bismarck to serve it as a tool' (Bernstein [1899] 1961: 114). In fact, this example offers little support for Bernstein's point, since the anti-socialist law remained in force until after Bismarck had resigned.

The view that representative government brings the government under popular control underlies Bernstein's hostility to the phrase 'dictatorship of the proletariat'. In an era of parliamentary democracy, he insists, talk of dictatorship is anachronistic, something that belongs to 'a lower civilization' (Bernstein [1899] 1961: 146). In fact, far from dictatorship, socialism is: 'an elaborately organized self-government with a corresponding economic, personal responsibility of all the units of administration as well as of the adult citizens' (Bernstein [1899] 1961: 155).

Along with his clear preference for democracy over dictatorship, Bernstein favours a democratic over a revolutionary road to socialism: revolutions are good at destruction, but parliamentary struggle and constitutional legislation are 'best adapted to positive social-political work'. Under democratic conditions the appeal to revolution 'becomes a meaningless phrase' (Bernstein [1899] 1961: 218). In fact, democracy is 'indispensable . . . to the realization of socialism' (Bernstein [1899] 1961: 163). Bernstein also cites Marx's well-known observation about the Paris Commune showing 'that the working class cannot simply take possession of the state machinery and set it in motion for their own ends' (Bernstein [1899] 1961: 156). Bernstein interprets this observation as saying that French state machinery at the time was not attuned to democratic rule. Yet, by the end of the nineteenth century, the political situation of German social democracy was vastly different from that of the Communards, because limited democratic forms of political organisation already existed: they should not 'be destroyed but . . . further developed' (Bernstein [1899] 1961: 163).

Bernstein's suggestion that the oppression of the individual 'is absolutely repugnant to the modern mind' (Bernstein [1899] 1961: 142) invites the response that many states of his time, and since, have engaged in the practice, suggesting that 'the modern mind' may be more open to oppression than Bernstein would prefer. As for his view that 'democracy' is the absence of class domination, many leaders of 'democratic' states in the nineteenth and twentieth centuries have attempted to suppress strikes and make life difficult for unions and other working-class organisations. The anti-socialist laws of Bismarck's Germany, which Bernstein had characterised as democratic, are an interesting early example. The conduct of states showed, Kautsky insisted, that the presence of representative institutions did not render working-class power unnecessary. These points aside, there is little to choose between Bernstein's and Kautsky's views on parliamentary democracy. Their shared view of the power it offers a popular majority is a central issue in the dispute between Lenin and Kautsky outlined below.

The Dictatorship of the Proletariat

The First World War (1914–18), followed by the Russian Revolutions (1917) and the short-lived revolution in Germany (1918–19), resulted in permanent divisions in the international socialist movement (Schorske 1983) between communism and a non-Marxist social democracy; and between communism and Marxist groups critical of the Soviet regime. The dispute between Lenin and Kautsky about the Russian Revolution reflects the character of the first of these divisions. Kautsky's *The Dictatorship of the Proletariat* criticises the Bolshevik seizure of power in the second Russian Revolution of 1917, and identifies 'fundamentally distinct methods [of] . . . democracy and . . . dictatorship' (Kautsky [1918] 1964: 1). Modern socialism involves the social organisation of production and the democratic organisation of society as well. Kautsky aims, first, to show that socialism should be achieved through democratic means and, second, to demonstrate the destructive effects of dictatorship. Following his argument in *The Class Struggle*, he insists that a majority in parliament, backed by a popular majority outside, could force a socialist transformation of society. Since such a popular majority would result from capitalist development and could be expected to elect a parliamentary majority, there was no need for revolution. The only cause of violence might be a right-wing coup, but a working-class majority would block any capitalist attempt 'to suppress democracy' (Kautsky [1892] 1971: 9).

Dictatorship goes beyond the argument of *The Class Struggle*, not in proposing a democratic route to socialism, but in its view of democratic politics. Where *The Class Struggle* supports democracy on instrumental grounds, *Dictatorship* makes a positive case for civil liberties, arguing for parliamentary control over the state apparatus: 'the executive can only be supervised by another central body, not by an unorganised and formless mass of people' (Kautsky [1918] 1964: 26). Kautsky presents civil liberties and protection for minority views as enabling political organisations to form alliances and negotiate over differences, thereby allowing for changes in the policies, or the parties, of government. At this point Kautsky abandons the idea that a single party should represent the working class, suggesting that a plurality of parties might do so: classes rule but parties actually govern. Where he had once seen politics as conflict between classes, Kautsky now sees conflict between parties: 'the abstract simplification of theory [classes] . . . is true only in the last resort, and between it and actualities [parties] there are many intervening factors' (Kautsky [1918] 1964: 31).

In spite of this distinction, Kautsky still follows Engels' view, noted earlier, that votes for parties in a democracy signify the relative strengths of the contending classes. Yet, under absolute rule, the classes are 'fighting in the dark' (Kautsky [1918] 1964: 35–6). Parties still represent classes, but 'the same class interest can be represented in very different ways . . . the deciding factor is the position in relation to other classes and parties' (Kautsky [1918] 1964: 31). To illustrate this point, Kautsky refers to the Liberal and Conservative parties in England. Both represent the bourgeoisie, one in alliance with the working class and the other, with landed interests. Yet, if parties and classes belong to different levels of analysis, it makes little sense to suggest that parties may form an alliance with classes. Leaving this difficulty aside, however, Kautsky's distinction between party and class enables him to separate dictatorship of the proletariat from the dictatorship by a party that he sees emerging in Russia under Bolshevik rule. In 'a real democracy', the former follows from 'the overwhelming numbers of the proletariat' (Kautsky [1918] 1964: 45). Yet, where there are competing proletarian parties, the dictatorship of one party is simply dictatorship of 'part of the proletariat over the other' (Kautsky [1918] 1964: 46).

Lenin responds to these arguments by disputing Kautsky's account of events in Russia, which we have not considered here. Lenin also distinguishes parliamentary democracy from the proletarian democracy he saw developing in Russia, supporting this distinction with the argument that parliamentary democracy is an instrument of bourgeois rule (Lenin [1918] 1964a). Lenin sees a clear contrast between parliamentary and proletarian democracy: where one requires a division of labour between legislature, executive and the people, the other is a 'self-governing, mass workers' organization' and where one selects representatives every few years, the other recalls them on demand (Lenin [1919] 1964b: 459). The Soviet organisation of the state ensures 'the immediate break-up and total destruction of the . . . bureaucratic and judicial machinery . . . which is the greatest obstacle to the practical implementation of democracy for the workers and working people generally (Lenin [1919] 1964b: 466).

Lenin supplements this contrast between two kinds of democracy with the claim that a democratic state is always a machine for class rule: 'Never forget that the state, even in the most democratic republic . . . is simply a machine for the suppression of one class by another (Lenin [1918] 1964a: 269). A parliamentary state is simply a capitalist dictatorship: 'the more democratic it is, the cruder and more cynical is the rule of capitalism' (Lenin [1919] 1964c: 485). Lenin argues that the extent of the franchise makes no real difference, that what really matters are the institutional forms: the separation between legislature and executive; the time between elections; limited state control over economic activity; a standing army; an independent central bank, etc. He also notes, as Kautsky had argued against Bernstein, that the democratic rights of freedom of speech, association, etc. benefit the bourgeoisie more than the workers, and that when it comes to the crunch, the workers get martial law rather than the right of assembly and protection of minorities.

Conclusion

This chapter has examined some of the most consequential debates in the socialist movement in the period up to and including the Russian Revolution. This focus is not intended to suggest that the views of a few intellectuals are more important than other aspects of the movement, but rather to bring out significant issues useful in understanding later developments. With the benefit of hindsight, it is tempting to suggest that Lenin and Kautsky were each right in their critique of the other's preference for proletarian or parliamentary democracy and wrong about their own. While Lenin's view of the prospects for proletarian democracy in Russia may have been optimistic at best, he was right to insist that parliamentary government does not bring democracy into the workplace. Again, while Kautsky's belief that representative institutions are the best available means for keeping governments under limited control seems to be reasonable, now that we have seen established democratic states join an illegal war against Iraq, despite substantial popular opposition, it is hard not to feel that these means are far from perfect.

While Lenin's approach to the pursuit of socialism in Russia was hardly realistic, the same might be said of his critics' pursuit of socialism in Western capitalist democracies. While they have not achieved socialism, they have, at least, given the West its welfare states and helped to promote a brief 'egalitarian moment' in the post-colonial states of Africa and Asia (Low 1996).

The socialist dispute, mainly between anarchism and communism, over authority, the role of the state and the party reached a peak in a destructive internal war on the republican side (which included a substantial 'international' brigade of mostly socialist foreign volunteers) during the Spanish Civil War (Orwell 1938; Thomas 1961) and has continued, rather more peacefully, ever since. Non-anarchist socialism split into many camps after the First World War and the revolutions that followed it in Russia and Germany. The most substantial organisations were Marxist communist parties, many of them with financial and organisational support from the Soviet state, and non-Marxist social democratic parties, which abandoned whatever association they had with Marxism after losing members to the communists.

The differences between Bernstein, Kautsky and other leaders of German social democracy provide a foretaste of what was to become a long-standing division among intellectuals within social democratic and labour parties: one side stressing the need to broaden the base of party support by appealing to socialist values and modernising its platform; and the other, resisting 'modernisation', often in broadly Marxist terms. However, neither of these views found much favour among the unionists and full-time party officials who dominated the party's leadership. Both left the German party at the beginning of the First World War (thereby confirming the party leadership in their distrust of intellectuals) after its parliamentary wing, fearful of losing popular support, ignored its internationalist principles and voted in favour of mobilisation for war. Despite all their debates and differences, however, the key scholars concerned with socialism, communism and anarchism produced an important intellectual and pragmatic legacy that constitutes an important chapter in the history of democracy, leaving behind questions and challenges that remain as pertinent today as when they were first raised.

References

Bakunin, M. (1950), *Marxism, Freedom and the State*, London: Freedom Press.
Bernstein, E. ([1899] 1961), *Evolutionary Socialism*, New York: Schocken Books.
Carillo, S. (1977), *Eurocommunism and the State*, London: Lawrence & Wishart.
Durkheim, E. ([1928] 1959), *Socialism and Saint-Simon*, ed. A. W. Gouldner, London: Routledge.
Inglehart, R. (1977), *The Silent Revolution: Changing Values and Political Styles Among Western Publics*, Princeton, NJ: Princeton University Press.

Kautsky, K. ([1918] 1964), *The Dictatorship of the Proletariat*, Ann Arbor, MI, University of Michigan Press.

Kautsky, K. ([1892] 1971), *The Class Struggle*, New York: W. W. Norton.

Lenin, V. I. ([1918] 1964a), 'The Proletarian Revolution and the Renegade Kautsky', in *Collected Works*, vol. 28, London: Lawrence & Wishart, pp. 227–325.

Lenin, V. I. ([1919] 1964b), 'Theses and Report on Bourgeois Democracy and the Dictatorship of the Proletariat', in *Collected Works*, vol. 28, London: Lawrence & Wishart, pp. 455–77.

Lenin, V. I. ([1919] 1964c), 'The State', in *Collected Works*, vol. 29, London: Lawrence & Wishart, pp. 470–88.

Low, D. A. (1996), *The Egalitarian Moment: Asia and Africa, 1950–1980*, Cambridge: Cambridge University Press.

Marx, K. and F. Engels ([1848] 1968), *Selected Works in One Volume*, London: Lawrence & Wishart.

Mill, J. S. ([1859] 1946), 'On Liberty', *On Liberty and Considerations on Representative Government*, ed. R. B. McCallum, Oxford: Blackwell.

Orwell, G. (1938), *Homage to Catalonia*, Harmondsworth: Penguin.

Proudhon, P.-J. ([1851] 1923), *General Idea of the Revolution in the Nineteenth Century*, London: Freedom Press.

Proudhon, P.-J. ([1849] 1927), *Solution of the Social Problem*, ed. H. Cohen, New York: Vanguard Press.

Roberts, J. T. (1994), *Athens on Trial: The Antidemocratic Tradition in Western Thought*, Princeton, NJ: Princeton University Press.

Sassoon, D. (1998), *One Hundred Years of Socialism*, New York: Free Press.

Schorske, C. E. (1983), *German Social Democracy, 1905–1917: The Development of the Great Schism*, Cambridge, MA: Harvard University Press.

Thomas, H. (1961), *The Spanish Civil War*, Harmondsworth: Penguin.

Webb, S. (1897), *Industrial Democracy*, London: Longmans, Green.

Woodcock, G. (1975), *Anarchism. A History of Libertarian Ideas and Movements*, Harmondsworth: Penguin.

Chapter 30

Civil Rights

Michael L. Ondaatje

The civil rights movement is widely acknowledged as the greatest social movement in US history. Typically associated with the stirring oratory and leadership of Martin Luther King, its philosophies and legacies continue to reverberate throughout America and the world. Demanding freedom and democracy for all, record numbers of black people rose up to challenge the institutional foundations of US white supremacy. They stood nobly and non-violently in the face of police dogs, water cannons and violent mobs, adamant that only love and moral suasion could change America. In overturning segregation and securing black voting rights, the civil rights movement transformed the social landscape that underpinned US racial inequality and opened up new opportunities for millions of African-Americans across the nation. But it also touched the lives and struggles of other historically marginalised peoples. In the United States and overseas, women's liberation activists drew inspiration from the democratic activities of black Americans, as did Native Americans, Indigenous Australians and anti-colonial activists in the Third World. In different ways, and for different reasons, these groups lauded the post-war black struggle, often emulating its methods in their own struggles for democracy and equality.

Yet most of the scholarship on the civil rights movement has understandably focused on its implications for black people in America. The literature is voluminous. Over the past three decades, civil rights history has been intensely scrutinised by scholars, becoming one of the hottest fields in American historiography. Early studies focused on national leaders, national organisations and national battles, culminating in the passage of national legislation. In the 1980s, this 'top-down' approach was supplanted by 'bottom-up' studies, suggesting the movement was actually propelled by community groups at the local level. More recently, scholars have adopted an 'interactive model', highlighting how local struggles and national factors intersected. By synthesising the two dominant schools of interpretation in civil rights history, the interactive model has revealed the dichotomy between 'local' and 'national' to be a false one, and ultimately provided a more complex portrait of the black movement.

There have been other debates, too, most notably over the origins and scope of civil rights activism. Today, many scholars subscribe to the idea of a 'long civil rights movement' stretching back to the 1930s and extending beyond 1968, when Martin Luther King was assassinated (Dowd Hall 2005). In contrast, most popular histories have continued to bracket the movement with King's leadership, focusing on the period 1954–68. Typically, these histories document two distinct phases of struggle: the classical phase (1954–65), centred on the South, in which black organisations fought for citizenship, the right to vote and desegregation, securing important civil rights legislation; and the period 1965–8, centred on the North, when the agenda shifted to a more radical demand for economic equality and self-determination, and few significant victories were achieved. While 'freedom' may have been the goal of black activists both in the South before 1965 and in the North after 1965, the meaning of 'freedom' differed significantly in each context. Rather than simply an extension of the civil rights movement, post-1965 activism is perhaps best viewed as part of a longer 'black freedom struggle' in America (Carson 1986). This chapter is not concerned with that longer struggle. Its focus is the unbroken chain of insurgency that defined the 'civil rights movement' between 1954 and 1965, when freedom for black activists was principally about winning 'civil rights' in the South, not economically restructuring the nation.

Background

In explaining the emergence of the civil rights movement, as defined here, historical context is crucial. In the first half of the twentieth century, the prospect of a frontal assault on white supremacy led by African-Americans seemed remote. The Supreme Court's 1896 decision in *Plessy* v. *Ferguson* provided legal justification for American-style apartheid, with the hollow qualification that separate facilities for blacks were to be equal to those for whites. In reality, they never were. African-Americans who sought to challenge the system faced the daily threat of violent reprisal: lynchings, public executions and the like. This is not to suggest that black people simply bowed down to white supremacy; often against great odds, many fought back as best they could, building schools, churches and homes and initiating small-scale challenges to racism in local communities. Others migrated to the freer North or joined the National Association for the Advancement of Colored People (NAACP), lending support to national campaigns against disfranchisement and lynching. However, the vast majority of African-Americans still lived in the South with few rights and less power. Disfranchised and segregated, most scraped by in agricultural or menial jobs in an economic system that facilitated the super exploitation of black labour. This system of racial exploitation, known as Jim Crow, appeared firmly intact in the late 1940s. Indeed, millions of Americans simply assumed the system would endure *ad infinitum*.

   This assumption proved to be short-sighted because it overlooked a number of pre-conditions for racial change – rooted in the 1930s and 1940s – that eventually made a civil rights revolution possible. Although African-Americans were largely excluded from the 1930s New Deal, the expansion of federal power that took place in Roosevelt's America at least allowed black leaders to imagine how government might also work to protect black rights (Sitkoff 1978). These leaders were also buoyed by the 'Double V' campaign during the Second World War, as millions of blacks committed to securing both a victory over Nazism abroad and a victory over racism at home. Concurrently, the membership of the NAACP soared, reaching half a million in 1945. President Roosevelt was forced by black labour pressure to prohibit discriminatory employment practices in wartime defence industries. And as more than 700,000 blacks left the South to take up jobs in the North and West, many voted for the first time, prompting politicians of both parties to pay more attention to the issue of civil rights (Kryder 2000).

But there were other reasons why concern with the status of African-Americans enjoyed greater prominence during and immediately after the Second World War. At the most basic level, an intellectual redefinition of the 'race problem' took place in American life. In the context of the worldwide struggle against Nazism, the discrediting of the concept of biological racism and rising black demands for equality at home, liberal Americans began to view race as a problem of white attitudes rather than black capacities. Echoing Gunnar Myrdal's thesis in *An American Dilemma*, they called on government to provide black citizens with the same opportunities as whites in line with American principles (Myrdal 1944). In this new environment, Harry Truman became the first US president to address the NAACP and to identify black equality as a moral issue for the nation. Truman also established a Civil Rights Commission that urged the federal government to end segregation and guarantee blacks equal access to employment, education and the ballot box. In 1948 the armed forces were desegregated. In all these decisions, international realities weighed heavily: America's race system was undermining the nation's struggle for hegemony with the Soviet Union over the Third World. Truman noted that if the United States were to offer the 'peoples of the world' a 'choice between freedom and enslavement', then it would have to 'correct the remaining imperfections in our practice of democracy' (Gardner *et al.* 2002: 85).

However, rather than advance the cause of civil rights, as Truman had hoped, the early Cold War years proved to be an inauspicious time to call attention to the flaws within American society. As anti-communism escalated, the widespread sentiment that equated any criticism of the United States with disloyalty seriously hampered efforts to achieve racial progress through mainstream politics. Consequently, fine gestures were rarely matched with substantive action and Truman's initiatives gradually faded, forcing black protest organisations increasingly to place their faith in the courts to confront white supremacy.

The Civil Rights Movement

No one could know completely, however, the new phase of American history that would open up on 17 May 1954 when the Supreme Court declared in *Brown* v. *Board of Education of Topeka* that separate schooling of black and white children was inherently unequal, and thus unconstitutional. Throughout the almost year and a half of hearings, the court heard dramatic evidence of how racial separateness had created and perpetuated glaring inequalities in black education throughout the South, permanently damaging the psyches of black children. The *Brown* decision, which overturned the pernicious 'separate-but-equal' doctrine established in *Plessy* v. *Ferguson*, was nothing less than a dagger in the heart of Jim Crow.

In essence, *Brown* created 'the legal framework for a democratic, color-blind society within the structures of liberal capitalism' (Marable 1995: 18), setting the stage for the civil rights movement of the 1950s and 1960s. All over the country African-Americans were jubilant, believing the dream of a promised land of justice and equality lay within reach. The black press and black leaders anticipated that the decision would break down segregation not only in the schools, but in all public facilities, heralding a speedy end to all the inequities of Jim Crow. The *Chicago Defender* proclaimed *Brown* 'more important to our democracy than the atom bomb or the hydrogen bomb' (Bennett 1979: 36). But it was the NAACP that issued perhaps the boldest statement of all: black people, it predicted, would be 'free by '63' (Garrow 2004: 45).

Unsurprisingly, Southern opposition to *Brown* mushroomed at every level of society, paralysing the drive toward civil rights in the late 1950s. In some states, like Alabama, the NAACP was outlawed, while in others schools that had been ordered to desegregate were simply shut down. During this period, African-Americans also confronted a resurgent Ku Klux Klan, proliferating White Citizens Councils and increasingly rabid segregationist politicians. Throughout the South, civil rights supporters were routinely denounced as communist agents. Believing it was not for government to intervene or legislate on controversial social issues, President Eisenhower rejected the opportunity to provide moral leadership to the nation, remaining silent amid the rising tide of anti-black violence. And yet it was in this region, in Montgomery, Alabama, the so-called 'Cradle of the Confederacy', that the struggle for desegregation would enter its next phase. In December 1955, Rosa Parks, a veteran black activist, was arrested in Montgomery for refusing to relinquish her seat on a city bus to a white passenger, as required by municipal law. What followed – a 381-day boycott of the buses by Montgomery's black citizens – would signal the beginning of the mass action phase of the civil rights movement.

In 1955, the black population of Montgomery remained imprisoned in apartheid-style social relations despite the *Brown* decision the previous year. The frustration this engendered was nowhere more evident than in the anger African-Americans felt towards the city's segregated bus system, which profited primarily from black customers but demanded that they accept second-class treatment for the comfort of whites. For some time, local black leaders, such as E. D. Nixon and Jo Ann Robinson, had been looking for a person around whom Montgomery's black citizens could rally to protest discrimination on the buses, and in Rosa Parks they found that person. A church-going secretary of the NAACP who had participated in numerous voter registration campaigns, Parks' case would fire the community to challenge their subordination in this controversial Jim Crow theatre. Throughout 1956 approximately 95 per cent of Montgomery's black community – including maids, janitors, teachers and students – refused to ride the city's buses, preferring either to walk, car pool or ride an informal network of black taxis. Despite violence and harassment from police and the white public, African-Americans responded with the weapon of non-violence, harnessing the spirit of black religion to boost their morale. In November 1956, the black citizens of Montgomery were vindicated by a Supreme Court ruling ordering that the city's buses be desegregated. The boycott had ended in triumph.

By bringing together an entire African-American community to challenge segregation in the Deep South for the first time, the Montgomery Bus Boycott demonstrated the power of oppressed people to shape a new world through non-violent collective action. It won the support of prominent liberals in the North and the sympathy of international observers. It also heralded the emergence of a charismatic young leader, Martin Luther King, as the movement's national symbol. Dramatising black people's aspirations and their readiness to sacrifice and suffer to achieve them, King's genius lay in his ability to communicate the movement's central messages to appeal to the collective conscience of moderate whites. Drawing on the teachings of Gandhi, King outlined a philosophy of struggle in which evil must be met with good, hate with love, and violence with non-violent demands for change. As David Garrow has pointed out, like no other leader, he came to articulate the struggle for integration as a divinely inspired mission to fulfil one of the central principles of American democracy: 'We hold these truths to be self-evident, that all men are created equal' (Garrow 1990).

Encouraged by the success of the boycott, in 1956 King founded the Southern Christian Leadership Conference (SCLC) to press harder for desegregation and voting rights throughout the South. Yet for most African-Americans the drive towards equality still seemed painfully slow. Few schools had desegregated, while hotels, lunch counters, theatres, churches and government buildings remained as rigidly segregated as ever. It was clear by now that the boycott strategy, employed so effectively in Montgomery, could not secure the ballot or civil rights legislation or economic justice for African-Americans. Boycotting public venues from which one was excluded, for example, made little sense when the objective, ultimately, was to integrate these venues. As hopes for a nationally backed crusade against Southern racial injustice faded in the late 1950s, it became apparent that if America was to change, blacks would have to take matters into their own hands and compel the federal government to protect their rights.

On 1 February 1960, four black freshmen from North Carolina Agricultural and Technical College in Greensboro sat down at the lunch counter of the local Wool-worths and asked for service. When told the counter was reserved for whites, the students politely but firmly refused to move, remaining in their seats until the close of business. The next day they returned, and then the next, until by the end of the week approximately 1,000 students had joined them to protest segregation in downtown Greensboro. Within two months, a cohesive region-wide movement had been born, with over 50,000 people – black and white – participating in demonstrations throughout the South. Local activists were soon employing non-violent direct action to transform other sites of bigotry, staging 'stand-ins' at segregated theatres, 'pray-ins' at Jim Crow churches, as well as 'wade-ins' at white-only beaches and swimming pools. Confused and incensed by these actions, racists assaulted the protestors in a frenzy of brutality. Moreover, thousands of African-Americans were arrested and caged like animals in some of the South's most notorious jails.

By putting their bodies on the line and being prepared to suffer for their principles, young blacks, many barely into their twenties, elevated the struggle for racial justice to a higher level. Despite King's support, it was the students themselves who formed the vanguard of the civil rights movement. On 16–18 April 1960, SCLC Executive Director Ella Baker sponsored the first meeting of the Student Nonviolent Coordinat-ing Committee (SNCC), which in time would stand alone in its determination to confront the segregationist power structure in the South. Viewing the legal strategies of the NAACP as increasingly redundant, and highly critical of SCLC's 'top-down' structure, the organisers and activists of SNCC sought to win their freedom from the 'bottom-up', mobilising hundreds of thousands of working-class blacks to confront segregation and second-class citizenship on a daily basis. In doing so, the organisation made 'direct and often militant action the key criterion for race leadership' (Sitkoff 2008: 70). Stepping onto the nation's racial stage as the leading force for social change, the students' sit-ins were essentially a 'judgement upon middle-class conventional, half-way efforts to deal with radical social evil', which historically had favoured 'fundraising and court action' (Levy 1998: 166).

Though the mass direct action protests still enjoyed the backing of most major civil rights organisations, every so often one of these organisations, inspired by the students' example, would take the lead and force the pace of history themselves. The Freedom Rides were a case in point. On 4 May 1961, six white and seven black 'Freedom Riders' set out from Washington DC on two buses destined for New Orleans, to test a recent Supreme Court decision outlawing segregation on inter-state buses and trains, and in transportation terminals. The plan was hatched by the Congress of Racial Equality (CORE), eager to establish itself as a major voice within the freedom movement, and determined to elevate the struggle to the national level by forcing the Kennedy Administration to intervene in support of desegregation. The philosophy was 'simple', according to CORE leader James Farmer: 'We put on pressure and create a crisis so that they [the federal government] react' (Sitkoff 2008: 73).

When the Freedom Riders entered Alabama, angry white mobs attacked and burned one bus, before savagely assaulting the fleeing passengers. Only days later, the group and its growing band of supporters – mostly members of SNCC – were viciously set upon once more, this time by Klansmen wielding baseball bats and chains. Immediately, newspapers around the world published photographs of the terror, exposing American racism in its rawest brutality and forcing the federal government to intervene. Attorney-General Robert Kennedy, a strong critic of the Freedom Rides, reluctantly dispatched 400 federal marshals to protect the protestors, before calling for a 'cooling off period', in which he hoped the campaign might be abandoned. But the Freedom Riders emphatically rejected Kennedy's suggestion. 'We have been cooling off for a hundred years,' James Farmer quipped. 'If we got any cooler, we'd be in a deep freeze. The Freedom Ride will go on' (Schlesinger 1978: 299). Their travails forced the Kennedy Administration to intervene to uphold a Supreme Court ruling (their original purpose), and their actions also pushed the Interstate Commerce Commission to order that buses and terminals be desegregated.

The lesson of the sit-ins and the Freedom Rides was clear: only white violence, leading to a breakdown in public order, would force a federal government response favourable to the movement. Looking to create a sense of momentum, King and his associates at SCLC planned a protest campaign in Birmingham, Alabama, 'the most thoroughly segregated city in America' (King [1963] 1999: 160), and a citadel of white supremacy. Placing greater emphasis on local civil rights activists than he had previously, King led a series of marches in the city demanding equal access to public accommodations and petitioning business to hire blacks on a non-discriminatory basis. Almost immediately, Birmingham's white power structure responded in a manner befitting the city's reputation as 'America's Johannesburg'. Before national television cameras, police unleashed massive repression using fire hoses, dogs and clubs to assault women, children and the elderly. On one day alone, nearly 1,000 children aged between six and sixteen were arrested and jailed. Confronted by these images in newspapers and on the evening news, millions of white Americans expressed revulsion. Under mounting pressure to restore civil peace, the Kennedy Administration exerted unprecedented pressure on Birmingham's business leaders and elected officials, insisting that they end discrimination in city employment and accept a timetable for the desegregation of stores and restaurants in the downtown area.

That summer, nearly 1,000 protests broke out in more than 100 towns and cities throughout the South, with over 15,000 arrests in one week alone. Filtering these developments through a Cold War lens, and growing increasingly alarmed about the damage to America's international reputation, Kennedy belatedly endorsed the movement's goals, going before the nation to declare his intention to deliver to Congress a comprehensive Civil Rights Bill. America, he said, faced a moral crisis: 'We preach freedom around the world . . . but are we to say to the world, and much more importantly, to each other, that this is the land of the free except for Negroes?' (Barnes 2005: 92) With images of bloodied and battered black bodies in Birmingham 'recorded in the permanent photoelectric file of every human brain' (Gower 2007: 55), and seriously denting American credibility in two crucial Cold War theatres – Asia and Africa – Kennedy responded pragmatically, as he saw it, in the national interest. It was simply no longer possible for the United States to declare itself the champion of freedom and democracy throughout the world while maintaining a system of racial inequality that denied these virtues to millions of its own citizens at home.

Hot on Birmingham's heels, the March on Washington, staged at the Lincoln Memorial on 28 August 1963, marked the climax of a turbulent year. Televised before a national audience, this 250,000-strong inter-racial event exceeded all expectations and turned out to be one of the civil rights movement's greatest triumphs. Eschewing political militancy in favour of political moderation, participants envisioned a democratic society free of racial hierarchy, in which the federal government would take the lead role in promoting justice and equality for all. To a rapturous audience, Joan Baez belted out the movement's anthem, 'We Shall Overcome', but it was King who stole the show with a speech that many in the audience later described as a 'rhetorical miracle'. Suffused with Christian themes and identifying the black struggle with the nation's most celebrated principles and people, 'I Have a Dream' awakened millions of previously indifferent whites to the reality of black suffering and convinced them that the time had finally come to press forward with an agenda for racial equality.

But the March on Washington failed to please everyone, black militants in particular. Bitterly disappointed that King and others had failed to speak out against the recent wave of violence in the South, and convinced that a golden opportunity to exert further pressure on the Kennedy Administration over civil rights had been squandered, these militants condemned the event as the 'Farce on Washington'. Event organisers had tried to strike a balance between idealism and pragmatism, between protest and accommodation. Although this tactic drew criticism in some quarters, it was common to hear movement leaders speak of the March as the highpoint of the desegregation struggle. In fact, the real highpoint of the struggle would come the following year, in 1964, when Lyndon Johnson – who had succeeded the assassinated Kennedy as president – made the passage of his predecessor's Civil Rights Bill his first order of business. The Bill may have enjoyed bipartisan backing in Congress, but far from being the 'product of the charity of white America for a supine black America', it was, as King said, 'first written in the streets' (Sitkoff 2008: 136).

The Civil Rights Act did not, however, address the right of African-Americans to vote in the South. With the support of the NAACP, CORE and SCLC, and thousands of white Northern college students who streamed into the South in 1964, SNCC now sought to dramatise blacks' exclusion from the political process. Critical of King's apparent willingness to work more as a consensus politician than protest leader, SNCC launched a massive voter registration and education drive in Mississippi dubbed 'Freedom Summer'. This grassroots push in the Magnolia state, where less than 5 per cent of the black population was enrolled to vote, was an audaciously creative challenge to white supremacy. An outpouring of vigilante violence greeted the campaign, with black civil rights workers beaten, crippled and, in at least twenty-five instances, murdered by segregationists. However, it was the murder of two white students – along with a black colleague – that focused unprecedented national attention on Mississippi and the seeming inability (or unwillingness?) of the federal government to protect citizens seeking to exercise their basic constitutional rights.

The campaign provoked one of the most dramatic clashes of the civil rights era when, at the 1964 Democratic National Convention in Atlantic City, New Jersey, the newly formed Mississippi Freedom Democratic Party (MFDP) attempted to unseat the state's regular all-white party. Because the latter refused to allow blacks to participate in their conventions, and since blacks throughout the state were barred from voting, civil rights activists established the MFDP, opened it up to all Mississippians, and conducted a 'freedom vote' in which 80,000 blacks cast ballots for MFDP candidates. Even as the convention was meeting, civil rights workers in the South were being brutalised and MFDP headquarters were burned to the ground. When anxious liberal figures within the Democratic Party put forward a compromise plan, promising to seat two black delegates, the MFDP rejected the proposal. African-Americans had suffered too much, and for too long, it seemed, to compromise any more. As one black Mississippi woman railed: 'the compromise would let Jim Crow be . . . Ain't no Democratic Party worth that' (Chafe 1999: 314).

More than any other event of the 1960s, the meagre concession offered to the MFDP in Atlantic City undermined black activists' faith in white liberals and severely dented their confidence in the nation's political system. But the experience also exposed simmering tensions within the black movement. After gruelling years of seemingly endless struggle, in which they had borne the brunt of racist violence, SNCC members had become bitter and resentful of Dr King – and a number of other black leaders – for continuing to evince a profound optimism in the American 'system'. Even as they were inspired by the willingness of their fellow blacks to sacrifice for the cause of civil rights, SNCC activists had come to believe that voting rights and legal equality were not enough, and that only a radical agenda involving a massive redistribution of wealth and power could deliver genuine freedom to African-Americans. Indeed, by the time King launched a voting rights campaign in Selma, Alabama in January 1965, relations between SNCC militants and movement moderates had deteriorated to such an extent that the tensions now seemed irreversible. Yet SNCC and SCLC supporters still marched together in Selma. The fact that they disagreed on almost every tactical issue did not prevent the campaign becoming the greatest victory of the civil rights era.

In 1965, Selma was a city in which only 355 of a possible 15,000 black residents had been allowed to register to vote (Foner 2006: 857). With a strong local movement dedicated to changing that situation, the city seemed like the obvious place for King to focus his attention as the movement pursued its next major objective: formal political equality for African-Americans. President Johnson had already signalled his unwillingness to support a voting rights law so soon after the Civil Right Act, but King, sensing that victory in Selma was possible, made plans for a non-violent campaign to attract publicity to the cause and force the president's hand. Black leaders attempted to lead a march from Selma to the state capital, Montgomery, ignoring a ban imposed by Alabama Governor George Wallace. The event turned out to be jarringly familiar. When the marchers reached the bridge leading out of the city, state troopers on horseback attacked them with cattle prods, nightsticks and tear gas in front of hundreds of cheering white spectators. As one marcher remembered: 'They literally whipped folk all the way back to the church . . . Ladies, men, babies, children – they didn't give a damn who they were' (Kasher 1996: 167).

Once again, graphic scenes of violence against non-violent demonstrators flashed across television screens throughout the nation. As Americans recoiled in horror once more, demands for the federal government to take action inundated the White House and compelled Johnson to speak out before a 70-million-strong television audience and a joint session of Congress. The president now expressed his absolute determination to secure a law that would guarantee Southern blacks the right to vote, heaping praise on the 'American Negro' in the process:

His actions and protests, his courage to risk safety, and even to risk his life, have awakened the conscience of this nation. His demonstrations have been designed to call attention to injustice, designed to provoke change, designed to stir reform. He has called upon us to make good the promise of America. And who among us can say that we would have made the same progress were it not for his persistent bravery and his faith in American democracy? (Kotz 2005: 311)

Wrapping up arguably the finest speech of his political career, Johnson then looked beyond voting rights and into the future, closely identifying both himself and the nation with the civil rights struggle. According to the president, overcoming the 'crippling legacy of bigotry and injustice' was fundamental to the fulfilment of the American creed. Never before had civil rights received such powerful endorsement from the federal government. Passing with overwhelming support in the Senate, the Voting Rights Bill was signed into law by Johnson in August 1965. Its impact was almost immediate. As federal officials arrived in the South to facilitate black suffrage, the number of African-Americans registered to vote exploded. In Selma, for example, the percentage soared from under 10 per cent to over 60 per cent in less than two months, but the city was hardly alone: other areas of the South experienced comparable spikes in African-American registration. By 1968, the number of black voters in the South had tripled and over 400 African-Americans held elective office in the Southern states. It was difficult to see how US politics could ever be the same again.

Yet even at the apex of its success, the foundations of the civil rights movement were crumbling. As violent outbreaks in black ghettos outside the South drew attention to the myriad of problems faced by Northern blacks, the focus of black leaders shifted from South to North, and from legal and political equality to the issue of economic justice. African-Americans in cities like Harlem and Watts appeared not to have benefited from the gains won by the movement in the South – inequalities in jobs, housing and education remained firmly entrenched. To address these problems, King believed that a new struggle would have to be waged for 'basic structural changes in the architecture of American society', to end the economic legacy of slavery and Jim Crow (Jackson 2007: 207). But marches, sit-ins and mass arrests – the major tactics of the civil rights movement – would prove to be largely ineffective in addressing the economic problems of the most disadvantaged African-Americans, North and South.

Conclusion

Today it is common for historians to focus on what the civil rights movement (1954–65) did not achieve. This is hardly surprising when we consider that poverty, crime, drugs and family breakdown are problems that disproportionately afflict black people in contemporary America. School desegregation did not deliver social and educational equality, or 'freedom', for the more than 30 per cent of African-Americans who comprise the twenty-first-century black underclass. Nor has the integration of public accommodations had a significant impact on these people's lives: without marketable skills or resources, the great majority of them continue to languish in a (*de facto*) segregated world. Yet for most African-Americans the civil rights movement was a profoundly positive force. On the whole, desegregation and voting rights did increase opportunities for blacks in American society – in business, government and politics. Along with affirmative action policies, it also helped to fuel the growth of a sizeable black middle class for the first time in American history. Employing non-violent direct action protest in the 1950s and 1960s, civil rights activists had attacked the institutional foundations of white supremacy, leaving the system, as it had existed up to then, in ruins. As Harvard Sitkoff has written: 'Blacks were not at the end of the road, but they were farther along, and the prospects for additional strides were greater than they had ever been' (Sitkoff 2008: 167). The civil rights movement changed American politics and society forever.

References

Barnes, J. A. (2005), *John F. Kennedy on Leadership: The Lessons and Legacy of a President*, New York: Amacom.
Bennett, Jr, L. (1979), 'Have We Overcome?', *Ebony*, 35(1), 33–42.

Carson, C. (1986), 'Civil Rights Reform and the Black Freedom Struggle', in C. W. Eagles (ed.), *The Civil Rights Movement in America*, Jackson, MS: University Press of Mississippi, pp. 19–37.

Chafe, W. H. (1999), *The Unfinished Journey: America Since World War II*, 4th edn, New York: Oxford University Press.

Dowd Hall, J. (2005), 'The Long Civil Rights Movement and the Political Uses of the Past', *Journal of American History*, 91(4), 1233–64.

Foner, E. (2006), *Give Me Liberty! An American History*, New York: W. W. Norton.

Gardner, M. R., G. M. Elsey and K. Mfume (2002), *Harry Truman and Civil Rights: Moral Courage and Political Risks*, Carbondale, IL: Southern Illinois University Press.

Garrow, D (1990), 'Martin Luther King, Jr., and the Spirit of Leadership', in P. Albert and R. Hoffmann (eds), *We Shall Overcome: Martin Luther King, Jr., and the Black Freedom Struggle*, New York: Pantheon.

Garrow, D. (2004), 'Why Brown Still Matters', *Nation*, 278(17), 45–50.

Gower, K. (2007), *Public Relations and the Press: The Troubled Embrace*, Evanston, IL: Northwestern University Press.

Jackson, T. F. (2007), *From Civil Rights to Human Rights: Martin Luther King, Jr., and the Struggle for Economic Justice*, Philadelphia, PA: University of Pennsylvania Press.

Kasher, S. (1996), *The Civil Rights Movement: A Photographic History*, New York: Abbeville Press.

King, M. L. ([1963] 1999), 'Letter from a Birmingham Jail', in W. H. Chafe and H. Sitkoff (eds), *A History of Our Time: Readings on Postwar America*, New York: Oxford University Press, pp. 159–72.

Kotz, N. (2005), *Judgment Days: Lyndon Baines Johnson, Martin Luther King, Jr., and the Laws that Changed America*, Boston, MA: Houghton Mifflin.

Kryder, D. (2000), *Divided Arsenal: Race and the American State during World War II*, Cambridge, MA: Harvard University Press.

Levy, P. (1998), *The Civil Rights Movement*, London: Greenwood Press.

Marable, M. (1995), *Beyond Black and White: Transforming African American Politics*, New York: Verso.

Myrdal, G. (1944), *An American Dilemma: The Negro Problem and Modern Democracy*, New York: Harper & Row.

Schlesinger, A. M. (1978), *Robert Kennedy and His Times*, Boston, MA: Houghton Mifflin.

Sitkoff, H. (1978), *A New Deal for Blacks: The Emergence of Civil Rights as a National Issue*, New York: Oxford University Press.

Sitkoff, H. (2008), *King: Pilgrimage to the Mountaintop*, New York: Hill & Wang.

Part VIII

Democracy Today

Chapter 31

South Africa

Roger Southall

The democratisation of South Africa has become widely celebrated. Apartheid, a legalised system of white domination over a majority black population imposed by post-1948 National Party (NP) governments, was peculiarly vilified in a post-Nazi, post-colonial world. By the 1980s, the polarisation between pro-democratic forces and the regime was threatening conflagration of the most advanced industrial economy in Africa. Yet in 1994 South Africa held a first democratic election following a four-year transition process whereby previously warring parties negotiated a highly praised constitution founded upon human equality, liberal democracy, a separation of powers, minority representation and socio-economic as well as individual rights.

South Africa's democratisation is of particular interest because of the depth, width and intensity of the struggle against white minority domination. Unlike surrounding territories where colonial or settler regimes similarly confronted 'wars of liberation', South Africa was politically sovereign, and was recognised as such internationally. The anti-apartheid movement (broadly conceived) has been depicted as the direct descendant of the anti-slavery movement, itself characterised as the first 'social movement' of modern times. By this is meant that democracy in South Africa was achieved upon the basis of a struggle for equality waged via intimate linkages between internal forces of democracy, an exiled liberation movement and extensive international support. No significant actor besides the South African government formally supported apartheid, this severely detracting from the legitimacy of the *de facto* backing provided to the regime by the major Western powers. Thus, the anti-apartheid struggle was able, simultaneously, to draw its support from liberal democratic, social democratic and communist governments and groupings, as well as from the international trades union movement, human rights organisations, churches and solidarity organisations, many of which took their lead from the African National Congress (ANC) in exile (Southall 1995). Meanwhile, the struggle at its height was given momentum by a powerful, internally based trades union movement and a wide diversity of community groupings, which not only forged close political connections with the ANC but also came to recognise the political hegemony of the organisation.

The Anti-colonial Origins of the Democratic Movement

The struggle against apartheid is inseparable from the wider freedom struggles waged by peoples subjected to colonialism. That its triumph took longer to achieve than

political independence for the overwhelming majority of colonies reflects the particular dynamics of settler colonialism: the imposition of British rule upon the
independent Boer republics of the Transvaal and Orange Free State and their enforced
union with the British colonies of the Cape and Natal, this following a war (1899–1902)
waged by the metropolitan power to bring newly discovered reserves of gold under
British economic hegemony; a subsequent high level of metropolitan investment; the
rapid concession of *de facto* political sovereignty via the Act of Union of 1909 to a
minority of whites at the expense of black political rights; and the rapid evolution
among the militarily defeated Dutch minority of a vigorous Afrikaner nationalism
centred around anti-imperialist sentiment and a sense of manifest destiny. All these
worked to give racial domination in South Africa a degree of political rigidity that
exceeded that to be found in other settler colonies. The formation of the Union of
South Africa in 1910, swiftly followed by passage of highly discriminative legislation
(notably the Native Lands Act of 1913 which reserved only 7 per cent of the country's
land area for 'Native reserves'), threatened the promise of liberalism embodied in the
franchise provisions to which small numbers of Africans, Coloureds and Indians
qualified upon the basis of property and education within the Cape and Natal. Union
also confirmed the outcome of white minority domination following a long history of
wars of dispossession fought throughout the nineteenth century between settlers and
Africans. It thus precipitated the formation of the South African Native National
Congress (later to become the ANC) by a largely mission-educated, progressive
African elite, which from the beginning took pains to construct an alliance with the
established traditional leadership of kings and chiefs as a movement for realisation of
African rights (Welsh 2009: 29–51).
    The early history of the struggle for democracy was constructed around three major,
inter-related themes. The first, was embodied in the attempts of racially subordinated
elites to resist further erosion of black rights. Often lacking organisational coherence
and conducted within separate racial spheres, whilst focusing heavily upon elite
interests, these efforts were to prove largely unavailing. Notable in this regard was the
failure of the All-African Convention (which temporarily replaced a disorganised
ANC as the premier vehicle of African political aspirations) to prevent the passage of
the 'Hertzog bills' – named after the Prime Minister of the day – in 1936. These not
only consolidated African land dispossession, but substituted the right of (a small
number of) qualified Africans to vote in common-roll elections for parliament in the
Cape and Natal with the restriction of their right to vote to four 'Native representatives', all of whom would be white (Lodge 1983: 1–32).
    The second theme was the evolution of a working-class movement which estab-
lished intermittent links to the countryside. This was based upon the advance of
mining-led industrialisation which summoned into being a significant working class.
Historically, this class was to remain divided between white workers, who utilised their
access to the vote to entrench their racial privilege, and a majority of black (largely
African) workers, who lacked political rights, worked upon short-term migrant
contracts and constituted a supply of 'cheap' labour for white industry. Nonetheless,
the working-class movement was to be significantly shaped by socialist influences,
notably the formation in 1918 of the Communist Party of South Africa (CPSA). In

1927, the CPSA adopted the thesis of the 'Native Republic' in line with the decision of Comintern (the Soviet-led communist international), which dictated that the working-class movement should work in alliance with bourgeois nationalist movements to fight for freedom from colonial domination. This was controversial, as South Africa was effectively independent of Britain, and it implied that racial domination predominated over class exploitation. Nonetheless, although the CPSA was subsequently to be divided throughout the 1930s by sectarian disputes, the Native Republic thesis was to provide the ideological basis for an alliance with the ANC which came to fruition in a later era (Simons and Simons 1983: 201–20).

The third theme was the shift of the ANC from elite to mass-based politics. The ANC drew inspiration from pan-Africanism, the grant of independence to India in 1947 and the post-1945 wave of decolonisation that was sweeping through Africa. African upward movement during wartime into semi-skilled and skilled jobs previously held by whites had provided confidence to the black working class, increasing the links between secondary industrialisation and accompanying black urbanisation. Crucially, however, the radicalisation of the ANC was a response to the arrival in power of the NP in 1948. Repudiating the limited gradualism (notably, acceptance of the inevitability of African urbanisation) of the predecessor Smuts government, the NP embarked upon a programme of social engineering premised upon an aggressive affirmation of white domination, which was justified by theological reference to the inherent inferiority of blacks. Thus, the 1950s saw a massive extension of repressive legislation that extended racial separation, confirmed black subordination in the labour market, extinguished the remaining black political rights and sought to reverse African urbanisation (O'Meara 1996: 59–82).

'Grand apartheid', as elaborated by Hendrik Verwoerd (who became prime minister in 1958), confronted political claims by black South Africans to citizenship by insisting that Africans were inherently divided along lines of ethnicity and owed primary allegiance to their chiefs, whose rule was strengthened from 1951 by implementation of a system of 'Bantu Authorities'. By the early 1960s, the government was pressing ahead with plans to base African governance upon eight (later ten) ethnicised political structures located in the different African 'homelands', artificial constructions drawing together territorial fragments of the various 'Native reserves' established in 1913 and extended in 1936. Beginning in 1963 with the grant of 'self-government' to the Transkei, power was to be devolved to conservative, rural, black elites rooted in the chieftaincy. African citizenship, even among urban populations, could, according to apartheid theory, be exercised only through these homelands. From 1976, with the grant of 'independence' to Transkei, the government sought to create a ring of dependent states whose 'sovereignty' would constitute a final block to African participation in the politics of 'white' South Africa (Southall 1985).

The Era of Defiance

The reaction against apartheid was spearheaded by a new generation of African leaders, grouped within the ANC Youth League. Inclusive of individuals such as Oliver Tambo, Walter Sisulu and Nelson Mandela, mission-educated and schooled in the law, the Youth League overthrew a preceding conservative 'old guard' and in 1949 unveiled its Programme of Action. This declared the objective of the ANC to be 'freedom from white domination and the attainment of political independence' and committed the ANC to a radical campaign of boycotts, strikes and civil disobedience.

The Programme of Action set the ANC and allied organisations on a course of direct confrontation with a government that identified black opposition with terrorism and communism. Although strongly influenced by Africanism, the post-1949 Youth League leadership adopted a pragmatic willingness to collaborate with all those opposed to apartheid and prepared to back radical action. This allowed it to work with both left-wing and Africanist elements within the ANC, as well as with a revived Natal Indian Congress, a Communist Party whose revival had been stimulated by Soviet participation in the alliance against Nazi Germany and, importantly, a workers' movement whose militancy had been honed by industrial and political struggles during and after the war. Although never free from tensions (notably Africanist suspicion of communist, white and Indian influence), coordinated action provided the basis for mass actions such as work stay-aways, anti-pass law campaigns and boycotts. These were by no means uniformly successful, for their support was sporadic and regionally uneven. Nonetheless, they were notable on two particular grounds.

First, mass actions (notably the Defiance Campaign against the pass laws in 1952) were premised upon 'passive resistance' and civil disobedience. These drew simultaneously upon Christian and Gandhian precepts of non-violence: Christianity having taken deep root among the African population and the Mahatma having begun to evolve his principles when confronted by white racism in South Africa in the early years of the century. Although pragmatically as much as ideologically based, non-violent resistance imparted to ANC-led struggles a moral legitimacy that the NP government was never able to overcome. Secondly, cooperation between the ANC, a newly radicalised South African Indian Congress (SAIC), the (Coloured) African People's Organisation, the CPSA and the Council of Non-European Trade Unions (CNETU) provided for a convergence of political energies within the 'Congress Alliance'.

The Congress Alliance, subsequently to draw in the South African Congress of Trade Unions (SACTU, the successor to CNETU) and the Congress of Democrats (COD, which provided a home for, among others, white communists following the decision of the CPSA to dissolve before passage of the Suppression of Communism Act of 1953), confirmed the evolving social movement character of opposition. This found particular expression in the Congress of the People in 1955, when 3,000 delegates adopted the Freedom Charter. This affirmed the right of the people to govern, to human rights, to freedom of movement, to equality before the law, and to equal access to education, housing and medical care. Further, it declared that 'South Africa belongs to all who live in it, black and white' and committed itself to transfer into common ownership the country's mineral wealth, banks and monopoly industries. The latter provision led to major debate about whether the ANC and Alliance were steered by the South African Communist Party (SACP, the successor to the CPSA, which established itself as an underground organisation after 1953). The former commitment gave rise to major tensions within the ANC, as Africanist elements came to contest 'non-racialism' as a cover for undue influence exercised by white liberals and communists. More immediately, the government's response to the Charter was a crackdown on the Congress organisations and the arrest of 156 leading activists. The resulting long-drawn out treason trial ended in a triumphant victory for the accused in 1961. However, by removing established leaders, it severely disrupted mass mobilisation and created a dangerous power vacuum within the ANC.

Tension between Africanists and the ANC's pro-Alliance leadership culminated in 1958 to the formation in Johannesburg of the Pan-Africanist Congress (PAC). The PAC made a radical appeal to the Programme of Action, from which it maintained the Alliance had deviated, and adopted a highly confrontational stance to the state that plunged it into bitter rivalry with the ANC. On 21 March 1960, the PAC pre-empted the ANC's own planned anti-pass campaign by organising a demonstration outside the police station at Sharpeville, a suburb of Soweto, the major township outside Johannesburg. When police opened fire in panic, killing sixty-nine, they set off a chain reaction of demonstrations around the country, and prompted the ANC into declaring a day's stay-away in mourning. Significantly, too, Sharpeville earned the government strong condemnation from the UN. Although the state was never fundamentally threatened, international investment confidence was profoundly shaken. The outcome was government's decision to impose a state of emergency, arrest hundreds of activists and to ban both the PAC and ANC.

Both movements moved swiftly to proclaim an armed struggle. The ANC established Umkhonto we Sizwe (MK), which for the moment focused upon a campaign of sabotage of strategic installations designed to persuade the white population to turn away from repression. The PAC established Poqo, which targeted whites and sought to provoke mass uprising. In Pondoland in Transkei, there was a popularly based uprising against Bantu Authorities. However, the early guerrilla efforts of both the ANC and PAC were distinctly amateurish. Poqo was swiftly broken up, the Pondo revolt repressed, and virtually the entire leadership of MK was arrested at Rivonia outside Johannesburg in July 1963. The ANC leadership was subsequently found guilty of planning to overthrow the government and condemned to life imprisonment in 1964. By 1965, mass protest had dissolved, the popular leadership was jailed and the capacity of the internal security forces to contain popular revolt significantly strengthened. Investor confidence was restored and foreign investment poured in to promote an economic boom which extended to the early 1970s. Defeated at home, the ANC and PAC now looked to continue their struggle from abroad.

Exile and International Support

The ANC had dispatched Oliver Tambo abroad to establish an External Mission in April 1960. One of his most urgent tasks was to mobilise support from the UN, African governments and nationalist movements. This required that the ANC should join with the PAC in forming a United Front (UF) so that the 'liberation movements' could speak with one voice. This was particularly important for the ANC for, as Nelson Mandela was to report following a covert trip outside South Africa in 1962, support for the PAC was extensive throughout Africa, with the ANC depicted as communist-dominated and less militant than its rival. Over time, however, the threat of the PAC was to diminish, as it was to become riddled with factionalism, while its espousal of Maoism and half-hearted backing by China was to dramatically reduce its international appeal.

The ANC in exile faced enormous challenges. These extended from issues posed by race and ethnicity through to the difficulties of being cut off from its mass base, the location of its exiled members in different countries, and for individuals, the perils of loneliness and demoralisation. That the ANC overcame these trials owed much to its tradition of non-racialism and the willingness of its Congressional allies to acknowledge its pre-eminence. But significant, too, was the dual membership allowed in the SACP. Although the SACP and ANC in London remained clearly distinct, partly because of the pre-eminence within the former of whites, in Africa the two organisations were to become largely indistinguishable, bonded by their collaboration in MK (Dubow 2000).

With the destruction of the internal leadership of the ANC and SACP, MK was to come under the direction of the ANC's External Mission. In 1963, Tambo relocated the Mission's headquarters from London to Dar es Salaam (and subsequently to Morogoro). Another major office was established in Lusaka, Zambia in 1965. Establishing forward bases was clearly crucial if MK was to pursue the 'armed struggle', yet it also had the effect of asserting the authority of the ANC over the SACP. In part, this was because African host governments remained suspicious of communism. But it was also because the party accepted the primacy of national liberation over class struggle. This was embodied in the theorisation of the 'national democratic revolution', whereby achievement of democracy was regarded as the first stage of the struggle for socialism. However, whereas mass mobilisation had been appropriate during the 1950s, the suppression of the internal movement now meant, according to this theory, that armed struggle came to the fore. The revolutionary experiences of such countries as China, Algeria and Vietnam suggested that military insurgency could inspire popular uprisings within South Africa itself. Yet the reality was that the armed struggle enjoyed little success. Early attempts to infiltrate guerrillas back into South Africa through Botswana were to prove disastrous. Subsequently, the ANC forged an alliance with the Zimbabwe African People's Union, and conducted joint operations against the Smith regime in Rhodesia during 1967–8. These were likewise to prove militarily unsuccessful, and were to result in major deployment of South African military support for Rhodesia. Their major value was therefore to boost ANC morale (Dubow 2000).

Early training for MK guerrillas was provided by countries as diverse as Morocco, Egypt, China and Ethiopia. However, over time military support from the Soviet Union and its Eastern European satellites was to become pre-eminent. Tambo had first visited Moscow in March 1963, his visit facilitated by the SACP. Subsequently, the Soviet Union was to provide the ANC with vital material and military resources. The Soviet connection, mediated through the SACP, also provided a model of organisational discipline, so that over the years the ANC absorbed the tenets of 'democratic centralism' while conducting much of its discourse in terms of Marxism–Leninism. However, its communist links meant also that the ANC came to be regarded by right-wing organisations and governments in the West as a tool of Moscow.

Despite its relationship with the Soviet Union, the ANC proved to be adept at mobilising widespread support across political fault lines internationally. Key to its success was the formation of the Anti-Apartheid Movement (AAM) in Britain in April 1960, born out of a response to Sharpeville by an anti-colonial network. Over the years, the AAM was to enjoy remarkable success, combining traditional pressure group activity with an activism that drew extensive backing from political parties, trade unions, churches and human rights organisations, as well as numerous other local associations dedicated to its cause. Its success was founded upon three pillars. First, as a single issue campaign that stressed the struggle against apartheid as a just cause, it appealed to a broad spectrum of liberal and religious opinion, as well as to those who regarded anti-apartheid as part of a wider anti-capitalist struggle. Secondly, it had to choose between legal action and pressure politics or resorting to illegal and direct action. Overwhelmingly, it opted for the former, although combining this with a capacity to mobilise mass marches and campaigns. Third, AAM – drawing upon both extensive middle-class support as well as the emphasis laid on organisation by its communist allies – developed a sound institutional base that proved to be important for influencing governments and international organisations. AAM was to become the model for similar bodies in many European countries, as well as for a vigorous divestment campaign across university campuses and municipalities in the United States (Fieldhouse 2005).

By the mid-1970s, the ANC had established a solid network of influence throughout Africa, Europe and America. By contrast, its presence within South Africa was minimal. The armed struggle had as yet failed to place a single MK foot on domestic soil, and popular consciousness of the ANC was fading. Under the weight of repression imposed by the regime, the democratic movement had reached its lowest ebb. It was to take a major conflagration, which surprised the ANC as much as it did the South African government, to revive it.

Soweto Erupts: Popular Struggles, Unions and the ANC

On 16 June 1976, schoolchildren in Soweto staged a demonstration against the regime's ideological determination to impose Afrikaans in African schools as a language of instruction. A brutal response by the police sparked demonstrations around the country and provoked outrage internationally. As the depth of student protest intensified over several months and drew in support from parents, churches and unions, the Soweto uprising forced a major reassessment of government strategy, while internationally it brought the longevity of white minority rule into question. Soweto also provided the crucible for a re-connection between the ANC and the internal democracy movement as increasing numbers of student activists escaped a police crackdown by fleeing across the country's borders to be met by the ANC.

Soweto built upon prior foundations for the revival of black protest. A wave of strikes among black workers, which started spontaneously in Durban in 1973, was taken up around the country, and gave major impetus to the emergence of a black trade union movement whose strength was to build throughout the rest of the decade (Friedman 1987). Regionally, too, the collapse of Portuguese colonialism, Frelimo's coming to power in Mozambique in 1974, and the increasing guerrilla challenge to white power in Rhodesia provided major inspiration to a younger generation of blacks that had become increasingly impatient of its parents' political quiescence since the early 1960s.

Younger blacks' political confidence was also boosted by Black Consciousness (BC). This was initially articulated by students studying in universities established in homeland rural areas which became hotbeds of black radical consciousness. In many ways recycling the Africanist tendencies of the early Youth League, BC was suspicious of the ANC, which it initially saw as irrelevant to the current generation. Yet, over time, although BC was to remain a distinct current within the democratic movement, it was also to become simultaneously absorbed within the ANC as it increasingly provided a home for student activists as they found their way out of the country, many determined to join the armed struggle.

Able at last to infiltrate activists back into the country following Mozambican, and in 1980, Zimbabwean independence, the ANC's influence rose accordingly. MK enjoyed particular successes in bombing the state's coal to oil installations in 1980 and launching a rocket assault on the army base in Pretoria in 1981. Indeed, during 1981–2, MK was responsible for over sixty attacks, mostly against police stations, rail tracks and electricity installations. Yet none of these changed the balance of military force, and MK's effectiveness was to decline following Mozambique's accession to the Nkomati Accord in 1984, whereby under South African pressure it agreed to the expulsion of ANC bases. Nonetheless, MK's 'armed propaganda' served as a stimulus to popular mobilisation, as was confirmed by a revival of ANC songs, flags and the demands of the Freedom Charter at mass gatherings. This was to have a marked impact upon both the democratic trades union movement and the countrywide growth of civic organisations (Dubow 2000).

The rapid advance of the democratic union movement reflected the expansion of manufacturing, the increase in strength, size and skill of the urban black workforce, resistance to low wages, and a determination to challenge the established system of industrial relations that denied African workers' rights. Following the Durban strike wave, workers' struggles – carried out in the teeth of employer hostility, police violence and state terror – revolved around demands for 'recognition', whereby firms would agree to negotiate directly with unions at the workplace. By 1977, seeking to de-politicise industrial relations, the state appointed the Wiehahn Commission to consider labour reform. In 1979, the commission recommended that Africans should be able to join established 'registered' unions, unions with African members should be able to 'register' in order to participate in the established industrial relations system, and the state should no longer prohibit the registration of non-racial unions. Although the state initially demurred, Wiehahn inaugurated a major transformation of industrial rela-tions. By November 1985, the culmination of a long-running trade union unity process had resulted in the formation of the Congress of South African Trade Unions (COSATU) by unions that were broadly favourable to the Congress Alliance, even though a 'workerist' stream remained wary of 'Charterism' and subordination to the ANC. This was followed in 1986 by the creation of the smaller National African Council of Trade Unions, which united unions inclined to Black Consciousness and Africanism (Bhulungu 2010).

Widespread employer reluctance to concede to worker demands, countered by worker militancy and unions' astute use of the reformed industrial relations framework, ensured that the 1980s were an era of extensive industrial conflict. Meanwhile, outside the workplace, the unions' growth was matched by the launch of a multiplicity of 'civics' around the country. The union movement, especially the majority tendency, had embodied a deep commitment to worker democracy and leadership accountability. Likewise, the civics – which developed around local struggles for better education, housing, rents and so on – stressed commitment to participatory democracy. In 1983, some eighty civics formed the United Democratic Front (UDF), whose immediate stimulus lay in popular rejection of the government's proposals for a new 'tricameral' constitution, whereby Indians and Coloureds would now be represented alongside whites in racially separate houses in parliament, while Africans would continue to be represented in their 'homelands'. Although the ANC played no part in the UDF's creation, its formation was in line with ANC's concept of 'people's war', whereby a broad unity of all racial groups, classes and organisations would combine illegal with semi-legal activity to ensure mass mobilisation. From its inception, the UDF nominated Mandela and other ANC stalwarts as its patrons and, although it did not formally adopt the Freedom Charter until 1987, it was widely regarded as the ANC's surrogate. That it was not immediately banned was probably because the state did not want to diminish the legitimacy of elections held for the Coloured and Indian houses in the tricameral parliament in August 1984. But over the next few years, the UDF was subject to perpetual harassment (Seekings 2000).

Following Soweto, the state had embarked upon a strategy of structural reform. The tricameral constitution, implemented in 1983, sought to politically co-opt Indians and Coloureds. Increased spending on education, housing and amenities in black townships, changes in local government administration and a relaxation of restrictions on racial mixing were intended to improve conditions for urban Africans. Simultaneously, the state under President P. W. Botha presented itself as beset by a 'total onslaught' by a communist-allied ANC, which could be repelled only by a 'total strategy'. Top-down reform was to be accompanied by military containment of ANC-supportive Marxist regimes in Angola and Mozambique and facilitated by a determined crackdown on radical protest internally. However, the state's reform agenda failed completely to secure black buy-in and political legitimacy.

The UDF's achievement was to provide a national focus for local and regional protests to be woven into sustained popular revolt. The spark was provided by the announcement of rent increases in industrial areas of the Transvaal in August 1984. A widely supported stay-away from work and school ensued. Popular confrontations led to the occupation of the townships and a heavy-handed response by the army and police. But instead of restoring order, state action spread the revolt to the Eastern Cape, Free State and Natal and thereafter to the Bantustans. In July 1985, the government announced a state of emergency. Security forces cracked down on the UDF, arresting most of its national and regional executives. Overall some 19,000 persons were arrested during 1985. Thereafter, a televised speech by President Botha, in which he dashed hopes for significant political reform, dramatically worsened the crisis. The United States declined to roll over loans, and – often spurred by popularly backed divestment campaigns – international investors withdrew, collapsing the value of the South African currency and forcing the government to default on debt repayment. When confronted by further protest, the government imposed a more severe state of emergency in June 1986, before, in February 1988, effectively banning the UDF. However, in alliance with COSATU in early 1989, the UDF was resurrected with the creation of the 'Mass Democratic Movement' (Welsh 2009: 269–343).

Both COSATU and the UDF struck up covert contact with the ANC from the mid-1980s. Likewise, both absorbed numerous former ANC activists, some of whom were by this time being released from long terms of imprisonment. In 1985, Oliver Tambo had called for South Africa to be rendered 'ungovernable', yet the ANC itself could claim little responsibility for the unprecedented surge of popular resistance. By the time of its banning, the UDF itself had nearly 800 affiliates, and was the by far the biggest organisation among blacks, far eclipsing rival organisations, such as the BC-aligned Azanian People's Organisation. Yet in two ways its political hegemony was incomplete. First, the UDF was little more able than the security forces to contain the violence that the continuous waves of protest unleashed, this expressed in reprisals directed at those – vigilantes, councillors, local warlords and armed militias – who were deemed to be 'collaborators'. Secondly, in Natal, supporters of the UDF and COSATU were thrust into violent confrontation with Inkatha and its allied United Workers' Union of South Africa (UWUSA). The former was led by Mangosutho Buthelezi, Chief Minister of the KwaZulu-Bantustan. It had been founded in 1975 with the support of Tambo in the hope that it could utilise legal space to open opportunities for the ANC's underground activities. But a breach between the two organisations in 1979 had left a legacy of bitter rivalry. Although Buthelezi consistently resisted pressures for KwaZulu to become 'independent', the political apparatus of the Bantustan provided him with authority and patronage to which COSATU and the UDF constituted a major threat. The result was a vicious war that divided local communities throughout Natal between 1985 and 1994.

By the late 1980s, South Africa had reached a violent stalemate. While the popular opposition had failed to overthrow the government, white power was being visibly eroded by the state's loss of control over blacks and a rapidly deteriorating economy. It was to break this logjam that on 2 February 1990, F. W. De Klerk (who had replaced an ailing P. W. Botha as president in 1989) announced the release of Nelson Mandela and the unbanning of the ANC, SACP and other organisations. The era of political negotiation had begun.

Conclusion: The Transition to Democracy

Western support for the apartheid regime had been based on the fear that a Soviet-aligned ANC victory would threaten South African capitalism. Yet from the mid-1980s, the Soviet Union began to show decreasing enthusiasm for involvement in southern Africa. In 1988, the ANC's regional ally, SWAPO, had acceded to power in Namibia following agreement between the Unites States and the Soviet Union to bring to an end a proxy war in Angola. In 1989, the collapse of the Berlin Wall effectively buried communism as a global force. Even conservative politicians were now prone to view white power as dispensable, and to join with business interests that, from the early 1980s, had already begun to seek an accommodation with the ANC. Indeed, for all the government's intransigence, Afrikaner and liberal elites had themselves begun to debate the need for fundamental political reform and had held informal meetings with the ANC outside South Africa. By 1990, white power-holders were prepared to negotiate a transition to democracy that would protect the rights of the white minority and property.

The transition was to be fraught with difficulties. Fundamentally, it was a process of negotiation between political elites that were buffeted from the right by extremist whites resistant to a concession of power and from the left by radicals who feared that the ANC was 'selling out'. Likewise, Inkatha's involvement was constantly problematic, protesting its perceived marginalisation by walk-outs, instigating political violence and a destabilising brinkmanship that continued to fuel bitter civil strife in Natal. With the government in uncertain control of the security forces while trying to drag out the negotiation process in the hope of dividing the ANC, the ANC itself was beset by the pressures of finding agreement with the NP while retaining the backing of its mass constituency. The negotiation process therefore took place amid continuing violence. Yet, ultimately, the principal political actors recognised that the negotiations were too important to fail.

The Convention for a Democratic South Africa (CODESA), which first met in late 1991, was composed of delegations from political parties and independent homeland governments, although Inkatha was to walk out within six months. Negotiations collapsed in June 1992 following the deaths of some forty-five protestors in Boipatong for which Inkatha and state agents were widely blamed. Following a campaign of rolling mass action initiated by the ANC, Mandela and De Klerk rescued the situation by signing a Record of Understanding in September 1992. Negotiations were resumed in March 1993 within a Multi-Party Negotiating Forum, where progress was facilitated by the practice of 'sufficient consensus' between the ANC and NP. An interim constitution was finally agreed in November 1993. Amid remarkable scenes of joy, voting took place on 28 April 1994 in the country's first democratic election, with the ANC securing some 67 per cent of the popular vote under an inclusive proportional representation electoral system. The ANC then formed a first democratic government in which it shared power with the NP and Inkatha under an 'interim' constitution that provided substantial protection for minority rights. The fundamental principles agreed during the negotiation process, which established the formal supremacy of the constitution over the executive and legislature, were then confirmed by parliament's passage of a final constitution in 1996 (Welsh 2009: 481–534). While South African politics since 1996 has been besieged by a host of intractable problems – not least of which is the vast economic polarisation between rich and poor – the Anti-Apartheid Movement nonetheless remains a substantial chapter in the history of democracy and has much contemporary relevance, both for the freedoms it achieved and the ongoing struggle (within South Africa and across the globe) towards equality.

References

Buhlungu, S. (2010), *A Paradox of Victory: COSATU and the Democratic Transformation in South Africa*, Scottsville: University of Kwazulu-Natal Press.

Dubow, S. (2000), *The African National Congress*, Johannesburg: Jonathan Ball.

Fieldhouse, R. (2005), *Anti-Apartheid: A History of the Movement in Britain*, London: Merlin.

Friedman, S. (1987), *Building Tomorrow Today: African Workers in Trade Unions 1970–1984*, Johannesburg: Ravan Press.

Lodge, T. (1983), *Black Politics in South Africa since 1945*, Johannesburg: Ravan Press.

O'Meara, D. (1996), *Forty Lost Years: The Apartheid State and the Politics of the National Party, 1948–1994*, Johannesburg: Ravan Press.

Seekings, J. (2000), *The UDF: A History of the United Democratic Front in South Africa 1983–1991*, Cape Town: David Philip.

Simons J. and R. Simons (1983), *Class and Colour in South Africa 1850–1950*, London: International Defence and Aid Fund.

Southall, R. (1985), *South Africa's Transkei: The Political Economy of an 'Independent' Bantustan*, New York: Monthly Review Press.

Southall, R. (1995), *Imperialism or Solidarity? International Labour and South African Trade Unions*, Cape Town: University of Cape Town Press.

Welsh, D. (2009), *The Rise and Fall of Apartheid*, Johannesburg: Jonathan Ball.

Chapter 32

Bolivia

Juan Manuel Arbona and Carmen Medeiros

On December 2005, Evo Morales won Bolivia's presidential election by one of the widest margins in the country's democratic history, while his party, Movement Towards Socialism (MAS), gained control of congress. The margin of victory (54 per cent of the votes and 25 percentage points ahead of his closest opponent) was, perhaps, overshadowed by Morales self-identification as an indigenous person and as a staunch critic of the neo-liberal project as neo-colonial and undemocratic. This victory raised many doubts from critics and opponents, who saw Morales as unprepared to assume the responsibilities of governing a country. However, under his leadership Bolivia is attempting to build a pluralistic democratic process that aims to overcome the long history of exclusion and discrimination experienced by the majority of its indigenous (and impoverished) population. With a new constitution approved by referendum on 25 January 2009, the prospects of building a democratic 'pluri-national state' that represents the hopes and aspirations of the majority of this multi-cultural nation seems to be within reach, though not without tensions and contradictions.

This short, descriptive chapter builds from the premise that the fundamental challenge in building a democratic 'pluri-national state' derives from unresolved colonial tensions and contradictions that have continuously shaped the history of Bolivia since its foundation as an independent republic in 1825. As Bolivian scholar Silvia Rivera has convincingly argued throughout her work, the 'central paradox' in Bolivia's history is how 'successive attempts at economic and political reform and modernisation have reproduced and strengthened the colonial pattern of *mestizo/* Creole domination over the country's indigenous majority' (Rivera 1990: 98). In this context, the different models of political democratisation that ruling elites sought to implement in the process of building a modern nation-state have consistently ignored (and undermined) indigenous forms of social organisation, participation in community processes of decision making and communal democratic practice. The institutional infrastructure of the state and everyday practices of ruling elites conditioned the integration of the indigenous majority as citizens of the state and members of the nation to a previous process of transformation often called 'civilisation' (Larson 2004).

While most nation-building projects have cast their objectives in terms of the establishment of legal mechanisms to extend formal equal citizenship to all, the persistence of the colonial race/ethnic hierarchy as the foundation of all forms of inter-subjective relations of power – that is, what Aníbal Quijano calls the 'coloniality of power' (Quijano 2000) – turned these objectives into unfulfilled promises. Thus, in Bolivia, as in other parts of Latin America, the coloniality of power has constantly shaped the realities of democratic ideals and promises. It is in this sense that, in Bolivia, historical struggles over the meanings of democracy cannot be separated from those over the meanings of citizenship and the process of nation making. It is at the intersection of these three political concepts that the historical realities of colonial forms of domination continue to have a resonating effect: shaping (or erasing) subjects; constructing (or silencing) voices; and naturalising (or dismissing) political projects. This historically complex construction of citizenship and how it corresponds to the construction of a democratic pluri-national state is at the heart of the challenge of the Morales administration.

This chapter presents a general contour of Bolivia's history with the purpose of providing insights into the trials and tribulations of building democratic processes and institutions in present-day Bolivia. The discussion focuses on three particular moments that represent different approaches to addressing the question of how to build a nation with a majority indigenous population: the 1952 national revolution; the neo-liberal project and its democratic promises based on market principles' and the current prospects to shape a democratic 'pluri-national state'.

Context: Shaping a Nation, Building a State

The thirty-six indigenous groups of Bolivia represent 55 per cent of the total population, while 45 per cent of the population identifies as mestizo or white (INE 2001). The largest indigenous groups, Aymaras and Quechuas, have historical roots in the highlands and Andean valleys, while the Guarani and the thirty-three other indigenous groups trace their ancestry to the lowlands. Today, economic activities in the highlands and valleys – the most densely populated regions – consist mainly of mining extraction for export, smallholding agricultural production of Andean crops and informal commerce. The vast lowlands are where the majority of natural gas and oil production occurs, and are also characterised by larger agro-industrial production, cattle raising and timber production.

Significant historical differences highlight the sharp geographical and ecological contrast between the highlands and the lowlands. Prior to the arrival of Spaniards in the early part of the sixteenth century, the territories of the highlands and valleys were an integral part of the Inca Empire and were subjected to elaborate forms of direct and indirect state rule (Larson 1988). The territories of the lowlands, by contrast, were the domain of a variety of non-state forms of organisation that established different relations with – but were never part of – the Inca Empire (Saignes 1985). In spite of the radical changes brought about by Spanish colonisation, this contrast between highlands and lowlands did not change during the 300 years of colonial rule. Indeed, while the highlands were deeply penetrated and greatly altered by colonial institutions and the market forces set in motion by silver production in the mines of Potosí, the tropical jungles proved to be impenetrable and thus the lowlands were left at the margins of the colonial state (with the exception of the establishment of a few isolated religious missions). In fact, the lowlands remained isolated and economically untapped until the rubber boom at the turn of the twentieth century (Soruco 2008). This is why the very brief and general historical background offered here mainly concerns the highlands region.

Without chronicling the three centuries of colonial rule, it is important to bear in mind three general points. First, in the Andean highlands Spaniards encountered the social and political structure of a state capable of mobilising labour for massive public works, extracting (and redistributing) the surplus of agricultural production (Larson 1988). Secondly, through a massive programme of forced resettlement (*reducciones*) the Spaniards reconstituted Indian communities with which the Crown established a particular form of indirect rule, facilitated tribute collection on the corporate ownership of the land and accepted a certain autonomy of internal organisation (Ovando Sanz 1985). Thirdly, the indigenous communities displayed constant resistance to the colonial project through cycles of rebellion, everyday forms of resistance and creative engagement with colonial institutions (Stern 1987).

With independence wars (1809–25) and the formation of the Republic of Bolivia in 1825, the winds of nineteenth-century liberalism came to the Andes (Larson 2004). One of the first decrees signed by Simón Bolívar mandated: (a) the establishment of a private property regime; (b) the institution of a salary for everyone who works; (c) the abolition of Indian tribute; and (d) the elimination of servitude (Barragán 1990). Bolívar sought to eliminate colonial institutions such as Indian corporate landholdings and tribute in the name of 'more advanced' liberal principles. However, the need for indigenous tribute to sustain national finances was more important than the liberal ideals of private property and respect for individual liberties. This dilemma of integrating indigenous peoples as Bolivian citizens equal before the law, but keeping them as a separate population with different rights and particular obligations has been a permanent tension since the formation of the republic.

It was only during the second half of the nineteenth century, with the slow recovery of silver mining and the possibilities of export-led capitalism, that the Bolivian government found alternative sources of revenue allowing for the abolition of Indian tribute and thus a new round of liberal legislation. Late-nineteenth-century land reforms sought to finally eliminate Indian corporate landholdings by privatising indigenous lands (Condarco Morales [1966] 1982). These reforms aimed at incorporating indigenous peasants (as free and equal citizens) and land as a commodity into the market. One of the main outcomes was a considerable expansion of the *hacienda* system, which included turning communal Indians into enserfed indigenous peasantries. However, the sale of indigenous land was regionally uneven and prompted fierce resistance in parts of the highlands, where entire *ayllus* (traditional communities) refused to receive individual land titles and continued to pay tribute which, according to Tristan Platt could be understood as a way of calling for the 'reciprocity pact' to be respected (Platt 1982). This peculiar form of resistance and a new cycle of indigenous rebellions triggered by hacienda expansion revealed that Indians had an ambivalent relation to the promises of modern citizenship. Platt suggests that what they were seeking was the status of 'tributary citizenship', that is to say, that as citizens they could demand individual rights to education and protection from the state, and as tributaries they expected the state to recognise their ethnic territories (Platt 1993).

As Andeanist scholarship has amply demonstrated, indigenous peasantries had all the reasons to mistrust nineteenth-century liberalism and its promises of restricted democracy and citizenship. Indeed, while all citizens were recognised as equal before the law, the colonial hierarchy structure of ethnic/racial difference continued to shape the practices of state institutions. The status of citizen was the privilege of property-owning, literate males: the members of the Creole elite, the only ones allowed to vote and the only ones allowed to occupy state offices. Thus, the illiterate indigenous population was relegated to a subordinate position: Indians needed to undergo a process of 'civilisation' in order to attain equality and citizenship. As Brooke Larson argues:

> policy makers began to tailor a 'civilizing' mission to keep Indians back. Indians were instructed in agricultural skills, temperance, hygiene and crafts, but not literacy. They were to cultivate their crops, but not on their own communal lands. And they were to render their usual labour services and pay property taxes, but they were to remain disenfranchised. (Larson 2004: 244)

Furthermore, Rossana Barragán's analysis of Bolivian nineteenth-century liberal legislation suggests that the construction of citizenship by invoking the need for 'civilising' processes constantly reconstituted what Partha Chatterjee has called the 'rule of colonial difference' (Barragán 1990; Chatterjee 1993). In other words, at the core of this historical construction of citizenship is a constant conflict between the persistent discrimination on the basis of racial and ethnic criteria, and a legally defined equality whereby citizenship is implied as conceiving of others as being of the same nature as oneself, even though he or she might occupy a different (unequal) socio-economic position. This original tension, this complex construction of citizenship, so closely related to the reconstitution of the rule of colonial difference, is constitutive of the coloniality of power knowledge. Since the nineteenth century, citizenship has been an open wound, its construction a battleground.

The model of state and restricted democracy that emerged in the context of this cycle of contradictory nineteenth-century liberal reforms is often referred to as the 'oligarchic state', because of its rigid stratification between the impenetrable ruling elite and the indigenous rural population (Zavaleta 1978). There was little room in this model for the upward social mobility reflecting the economic changes the country underwent during the first half of the twentieth century: an expanding urban middle class and an increasingly politicised working class (for example, in the mines and in the city of La Paz). The social tensions that expanded during this period exposed the limits of the oligarch state that began to unravel during the 1930s and 1940s and culminated in the national revolution of 1952 (Malloy 1970; Rivera 1983).

The 1952 Revolution: The End of a Liberal Cycle, the Beginning of a Populist Cycle

Proclaiming the liberation of the nation from oligarchic elites and colonial forms of domination, the 1952 National Revolution marked the end of the liberal cycle and the beginning of the nationalist-populist cycle (Rivera 1990; Zavaleta 1986). What the nationalist intellectuals of those times and the ideologues of the revolution envisioned was the transformation of the country into a progressive, modern and democratic state with a socially integrated and culturally homogeneous mestizo nation (Sanjinés 2004; Stephenson 1999). Led by the Nationalist Revolutionary Movement Party (the Movimiento Nacionalista Revolucionario, MNR), the new government quickly implemented three major reforms: the nationalisation of mines; agrarian reform; and the establishment of universal vote. Thus, the expanding political rights of the large masses of illiterate indigenous peasantries and working classes set the grounds for a less restrictive and more representative form of democracy. As part of these reforms, *Indios* became *campesinos* (peasants) as a way of abolishing the deep-seated discrimination against indigenous people and integrating them to the emerging mestizo nation. In the context of the mestizo nationalist ideology, however, 'modernizing traditional peasants' became a euphemism for 'civilizing backward Indians' (Medeiros 2001). Despite the significant changes, once again the promise of democracy and inclusive citizenship required Indians to undergo a process of transformation.

In the Andean highlands, the 1953 agrarian reform sought to eliminate the 'feudal' regime of the hacienda and promote the development of a market-oriented smallholding peasantry. Although the Andean peasantry represented an important force for the nationalist revolution, highland agricultural production was not (and still is not) an economic priority for policy makers. Mining, oil industries or agribusiness in the lowlands were considered to be more likely to contain the seeds of an 'economic miracle' of modern industrialisation. The implementation of agrarian reform was not only incomplete, but it gave rise to increasing land fragmentation and new forms of economic exploitation. Land redistribution was very uneven and came together with greater market integration, socio-economic differentiation, new forms of economic exploitation and deterioration of the terms of exchange between the rural and the urban sectors. The organisation of agrarian unions (*sindicatos agrarios*) – promoted by the MNR in the context of hacienda land redistribution – was a way of establishing local political structures and dissolving the remaining vestiges of the localised indigenous political structures (Dandler 1983).

The nationalisation of the mines allowed the MNR government to control the most important source of national income, dismantle the main bastions of the oligarch state (the mining elites), and – to some degree – absorb the most powerful trade union in Bolivia into the institutional infrastructure of the state (Nash 1979). The incorporation of the miner's trade union and the peasant unions into the government gave the MNR a particular form of legitimacy and representation not seen in previous governments. However, it also brought about political tensions between two conflicting political projects and visions of economic development: socialist workers' control, a project defended by the miner's union; and state-led capitalist modernisation, which was defended by the pragmatic leaders of the MNR and actively supported by US aid. Needless to say, the latter vision prevailed and was later embraced by the military regimes that followed the twelve years of MNR governments. The coup d'état led by General Barrientos in 1964 initiated a cycle of coups d'état and military governments which lasted almost without interruption until 1982.

While the achievements of the revolution have been the source of great controversy, most scholars agree that the revolution changed the forms of state–society relations and gave rise to the establishment of a different state model based on state ownership of natural resources and a strongly centralised state administration (Malloy 1970). In this new model, the state was to become the primary agent for economic development and the main interlocutor to address the demands of the new social actors: middle classes; the miner's union (leading the Bolivian Confederation of Workers: COB); and the state-promoted peasant unions. Legitimised within the discursive field of 'revolutionary nationalism' (Antezana 1983), the vision of the state as the guarantor of the nation against the 'anti-nation' dominated the Bolivian political spectrum from the 1950s to the early 1980s in spite of significant political conflicts, regime changes and the repressive military dictatorships of the 1970s. In this context, the indigenous question dissolved into or was silenced by the ideology of *mestizaje*, an ideology that, as Richard Stutzman has already convincingly argued, is an 'all inclusive ideology of exclusion': while all citizens could be entitled to define themselves as *mestizos*, only the lighter-skinned, Spanish-speaking, better educated urban dwellers are respected members of the ideal mestizo nation (Stutzman 1981). Once again, the coloniality of power loomed large on the horizon of failed promises of democratic participation and mestizo inclusion. The end of the military dictatorships of the 1970s exposed the crisis of the state model. The transition to democracy was also the transition out of the populist cycle.

The Neo-liberal Turn and the 'Democratic Pact'

As in many Latin American countries, the 1980s in Bolivia was a decade of transition to democracy after a long period of military regimes and the implementation of structural adjustment programmes. While in most cases the adoption of democratic institutions coincided with the implementation of neo-liberal economic policies, in the Bolivian case there was a gap between the two that re-opened political spaces for the manifestation of different alternative political projects (Medeiros 2001). The early 1980s can also be viewed as that critical moment between and betwixt two states of populist and neo-liberal order. In this tumultuous moment of liminality, as it were, any utopia could be imagined, all repressed voices could emerge, including those that had been explicitly forbidden under dictatorships and those that had been implicitly, but more fundamentally, silenced within the discursive field of the 'revolutionary nationalism' (Antezana 1983: 84).

The democratically elected government that acceded to power in 1982 was a coalition of leftist parties forming the Union Democrática y Popular (UDP) and representing a diverse group that united against the military regime. Once this had been achieved, the unity of the movement fractured into a multiplicity of competing groups with different visions of democracy, both political and economic. The political coalition of the UDP found its limits in an economic crisis of epic proportions and deep intra-party conflicts. Consequently, the democratic potential during this period of transition came to a quick end with the advent of a new political economic model that established the conditions for the construction of an official democratic ideal based on the neo-liberal notion of efficient and effective market performance. The economic crisis in Bolivia was due primarily to the collapse of the international prices for minerals and resulted in one of the most devastating hyper-inflation events in history. With an inflation rate of over 20,000 per cent, the country experienced dramatic mobilisations, particularly from sectors affiliated to the COB, a supporting member of the UDP coalition. As prices rose, the people demanded salary increases that the government accepted and covered by printing more money. This, in turn, deepened the inflationary pressures that generated a new wave of salary increase demands. The pressure exerted by the COB unravelled the governing coalition and elections had to be called one year ahead of schedule.

The winner of this election was the MNR and Victor Paz-Estenssoro – the leader of the 1952 revolution. Paradoxically, Paz-Estenssoro opened the doors for a new model of state that was in opposition to the nationalist state model:

Within three weeks of taking office, in a dramatic reversal of many of the principles he had championed in 1952, Paz-Estenssoro initiated South America's second most radical neoliberal restructuring programme (after Chile) called the New Economic Policy (NEP). Although it incorporated a structural adjustment programme similar to the stabilization plan underwent in 1956, and reflected continuity with centuries of international intervention, the NEP none the less represented a profound change in direction. (Kohl and Farthing 2006: 60)

The signing of Presidential Decree 21060 was successful in curtailing inflation overnight, but in the process it set the country on a path that transformed the institutional infrastructure of the state. The aim of the measure was to restructure the role of the state in economic matters in a way that would make it conform to international standards. The state was to limit its regulatory role in order to enable free-market dynamics: create the conditions for the efficient flow of capital; ensure debt repayments; rationalise spending; and discipline labour. To accomplish this, state enterprises were shut down and (already limited) public programmes were further curtailed. The argument given by the Paz-Estenssoro administration was that the state could no longer be the central economic agent as market mechanisms were believed to be more effective in generating economic growth and promoting a better democracy (Cariaga 1997). In other words, this new state model would create the conditions for better democratic institutions as individuals would be free from the 'artificial pressures' of the state or corporate forms of organisations (that is, unions). From then on, the only model of democracy that was considered to be viable was the one that was tied to free markets, silencing the memory of the many competing models of democracy that have been manifested a few years prior.

The election of Gonzalo Sanchez de Lozada (1993–7) opened a new phase of neo-liberal reforms. His administration recognised that an exclusive emphasis on economic measures – at the expense of 'appropriate governance' – generated political instability that was detrimental to the formation of an efficient market economy and the promotion of democracy. With this in mind, the 1993–7 legal reforms sought to bring back the state and promote democratic governance through the decentralisation of state administration, augmenting the power and autonomy of municipal govern-ments. One of the pillars of these legal reforms was the 'law of popular participation' (*ley de participación popular*) that provided the conditions for decentralised forms of governance, without touching the macro-economic framework. Furthermore, this particular set of reforms sought to quell growing indigenous demands for greater political participation and economic equity by embracing the language of multi-culturalism. In this framework, indigenous forms of social organisation and collective identity gained legal recognition (Postero 2007). However, the parameters of this new citizenship were limited to the municipal level as long as they took place within the precepts of liberal institutions; the politics of identity were emphasised at the expense of the politics of redistribution.

In summary, during this period a handful of political parties established a 'demo-cratic pact' that defined the electoral parameters and political alternatives 'viable' to Bolivians (Mayorga 2007). These multi-party coalitions were effective in establishing a political monopoly that generated a relative democratic stability and framed political expectations. However, the promises and ideals of 'neo-liberal democracy' did not translate into better living conditions for most of the population. In fact, those who were left at the economic margins of the neo-liberal project and on the political sidelines of the 'democratic pact' were the same people who had been left out since colonial times. Social inequalities and economic frustrations grew during this period (Kohl and Farthing 2006). This generated social tensions that began to be expressed in outright social fractures. The 'water wars' of 2000 launched a period of social mobilisations that on the surface challenged the neo-liberal project, but were in fact underpinned by an aspiration for a new type of democracy.

The Prospect for a Pluri-national Democracy

The events of October 2003 marked a key turning point for a new era in the democratic history of Bolivia. During the second term of the Sanchez de Lozada administration (2001–3) thousands of Bolivians – particularly in the 'new' city of El Alto – took to the streets demanding radical changes. The response of the government was brutal, sending the military onto the streets of El Alto in an attempt to quell the growing anger. With the number of dead and wounded climbing, Sanchez de Lozada was forced to flee (Mamani 2006). This was the opening stage for two tumultuous years of political tensions that witnessed two presidents and continuous waves of social mobilisations. While on the surface this could be seen as a moment of political chaos, close scrutiny and broad historical reflection suggest that this was a deep democratic moment. After five centuries in which a small segment of the population spoke and governed on behalf of the country, a new era began in which those who had been historically marginalised were able to shape what would become a new pluri-national state. The elections of 2005 brought the first (self-identified) indigenous president in the 180 years of Bolivian history and a new democratic promise. The Evo Morales administration, fuelled by a strong support from indigenous communities, trade unions and urban middle-class mestizos sought to promote a new set of principles as the highest democratic aspirations for a country with a history like Bolivia's.

One of the new government's principles was the recuperation of natural resources that have been used for the benefit of external interests since colonial times. On 1 May 2006, Morales announced the signing of Presidential Decree 28701, which 'nationalised' natural resources, particularly oil and natural gas. The aim was to return to the state control (and royalties) one of the country's main assets. Morales announced that 'the pillage of our natural resources by foreign companies is over', clearly alluding to the continuing expression of colonialism. The political symbolism of an indigenous president leading the re-appropriation of natural resources was a clear sign that a new approach to nation-building was taking place. In his speech, with a petro-chemical plant and a Bolivian flag as background, he also made clear that his administration was not about to reproduce the abuses of previous governments. The revenues generated were to be redistributed to the impoverished through massive welfare programmes.

A few months later (6 August 2006) a spectacular ceremony took place which inaugurated the constituent assembly in charge of drafting a new constitution for Bolivia. Special delegations and the 255 members of the constituent assembly, elected through popular vote for the first time, watched the parade that included about 2,000 indigenous people. The national anthem was sung in Spanish, Aymara, Quechua and Guaraní, and in his speech President Evo Morales spoke of the mission of re-founding the nation, ending 500 years of colonial forms of discrimination and exclusion, and writing a new history of unity and equality. During a sixteen-month process the Constituent Assembly took place with many tensions, as representatives of traditional parties, outnumbered by indigenous and members of the MAS, tried to derail the drafting of the document. The final document – signed by the president on 7 February 2009 – takes as its political core the pillars of decolonisation and 'living well' (*vivir bien*). Both of these principles represent an effort to capture the long history of the marginalised, to give them a voice and a democracy on their own terms. For the first time in Bolivian history, the indigenous population was present in the constitution not as a minority with limited rights, but as full citizens of the pluri-national state.

It is in this constitutional context that 'living well' was presented as a political principle that attempts to establish a new societal model that breaks away from a 'developmental model' principled on individual welfare and accumulation, or living better than others. The principle of living well appears throughout the constitution on issues relating to education, the organisation of the economy and the use of natural resources:

The state is sustained on the values of unity, equality, inclusion, dignity, liberty, solidarity, reciprocity, respect, complementarity, harmony, transparency, equilibrium, equal opportunities, gender and social equality in participation, common well-being, responsibility, social justice, distribution and redistribution of social products and goods, to live well. (Bolivian Constitution 2009: VIII:2)

While the principle of living well represents an effort to establish a new societal model, its translation into actual policies revealed two crucial dilemmas. One of the dilemmas facing the current government is how to negotiate the new 'democratic revolution' based on a principle of decolonisation and 'living well' with the requirement of generating revenues to pay for the welfare programmes through the exploitation of natural resources. Such forms of exploitation have historically run counter to the principles being espoused. The other dilemma is related to the effort to open up the institutional infrastructure of the state – and thus the definition of democracy – to the majority of the indigenous population by relying on the same liberal institutions that have reproduced their exclusion and discrimination. Thus, the way the Morales administration manages these dilemmas will have an effect on how Bolivians experience this 'democratic revolution' and are able to overcome their colonial legacy.

Conclusion

As this chapter has highlighted, the central issue at stake in the democratic history of Bolivia is how to address the contradiction between the ideals and promises of democracy and the historical continuity of coloniality. Thus, the challenge facing the Morales administration is how to build a democratic future on its own terms, taking into account a very troubled history in which large segments of the population (working poor and indigenous) were placed at the social margins of society. While in the recent past they had the formal rights of a representative democracy, they remained unable to be an active part of it. These marked divisions created the conditions in which these disenfranchised sectors of society found that social mobilisation and protest was their only way of being taken into account. These active demands for inclusion opened the door of history for what could be a new democratic framework under the umbrella of a pluri-national state.

The current political process can be easily criticised and dismissed by 'right' or 'left' lines of argument. There is no doubt that it has many problems and contradictions: the cultural legacy of the colonial and neo-liberal projects cannot be erased with decrees and laws, and continue to be alive and well. However, if we view democracy, not by a series of established requirements, but as ideals in which citizens actively participate in the construction of a nation and notions of citizenship, then the actual political process could be considered as a pivotal moment in the democratic future of Bolivia. It is still premature to pass judgement on the Morales administration's advances to promote a more democratic Bolivia. During its first years this administration has masterfully deployed cultural symbols that clearly signalled the break from the patterns of coloniality. History will judge whether the 'democratic revolution' will yield the types of results that produce a de-colonised citizenship and the conditions for 'living well'. What cannot be denied is that the political process launched in 2005 cannot be undone.

References

Antezana, L. (1993), 'Sistema y proceso ideológicos en Bolivia (1935–1979)', in R. Zavaleta (ed.), *Bolivia Hoy*, México: Siglo XXI, pp. 60–84.
Barragán, R. (1990), *Espacio Urbano y Dinámica Étnica: La Paz en el Siglo XIX*, La Paz: Hisbol.

Bolivian Constitution (2009), The Fundamental Law of Bolivia enacted by President Evo Morales Ayma on 4 February 2009, trans. L. F. V. Valle.

Cariaga, J. (1997), *Estabilización y Desarrollo: Importantes Lecciones del Programa Económico de Bolivia*, México: Fondo de Cultura Económica.

Chaterjee, P. (1993), *The Nation and its Fragments*, Princeton, NJ: Princeton University Press.

Condarco Morales, R. ([1966] 1982), *Zárate: el 'Temible' Willka*, La Paz: Renovación.

Dandler, J. (1983), *Sindicalismo Campesino en Bolivia: Cambios Estructurales en Ucureña (1935–1952)*, Cochabamba: CERES.

Instituto Nacional de Estadísticas (INE) (2001), *Bolivia: Características de la Población*, La Paz: INE.

Kohl, B. and L. Farthing (2006), *Impasse in Bolivia: Neoliberal Hegemony and Popular Resistance*, London: Zed Books.

Larson, B. (1988), *Colonialism and Agrarian Transformation in Bolivia: Cochabamba, 1550–1900*, Princeton, NJ: Princeton University Press.

Larson, B. (2004), *Trials of Nation Making: Liberalism, Race, and Ethnicity in the Andes, 1810–1910*, Cambridge: Cambridge University Press.

Malloy, J. (1970), *Bolivia: The Uncompleted Revolution*, Pittsburgh, PA: University of Pittsburgh Press.

Mamani, J. (2006), *Octubre: Memorias de Dignidad y Masacre*, El Alto: Centro de Estudios y Apoyo al Desarrollo Local-Agencia de Prensa Alteña.

Mayorga, F. (2007), 'Estado y democracia en Bolivia', *Informe Nacional sobre Desarrollo Humano 2007: 'El estado del Estado en Bolivia'*, La Paz: PNUD.

Medeiros, C. (2001), 'Civilizing the Popular? The Law of Popular Participation and the Design of a New Civil Society in 1990s Bolivia', *Critique of Anthropology*, 21(2), 401–25.

Nash, J. (1979), *We Eat the Mines, and The Mines Eat Us: Dependency and Exploitation in Bolivian Tin Mines*, New York: Columbia University Press.

Ovando Sanz, J. (1985), *El Tributo Indígena en las Finanzas Bolivianas del Siglo XIX*, La Paz: CEUB.

Platt, T. (1982), *Estado Boliviano y Ayllu Andino: Tierra y Tributo en el Norte de Potosí*, Lima: Instituto de Estudios Peruanos.

Platt, T. (1993), 'Simon Bolivar, the Sun of Justice and the Amerindian Virgin: Andean Conceptions of the Patria in Nineteenth-Century Potosi', *Journal of Latin American Studies*, 25(1), 159–85.

Postero, N. (2007), *Now We are Citizens: Indigenous Politics in Postmulticultural Bolivia*, Stanford, CA: Stanford University Press.

Quijano, A. (2000), 'Coloniality of Power, Eurocentrism, and Latin America', *Nepantla*, 1(3), 533–80.

Rivera, S. (1983), *Oprimidos pero no Vencidos: Luchas del Campesinado Aymara y Quechwa 1900–1980*, La Paz: HISBOL.

Rivera, S. (1990), 'Liberal Democracy and Ayllu Democracy: The Case of Northern Potosí, Bolivia', in J. Fox (ed.), *The Challenge of Rural Democratization: Perspectives from Latin America and the Philippines*, London: Frank Cass, pp. 97–121

Saignes, T. (1985), *Los Andes Orientales: Historia de un Olvido*, Cochabamba: CERES.

Sanjinés, J. (2004), *El Espejismo del Mestizaje*, La Paz: PIEB.

Stephenson, M. (1999), *Gender and Modernity in Andean Bolivia*, Austin, TX: University of Texas Press.

Soruco, X. (ed.) (2008), *Los Barones del Oriente: El Poder en Santa Cruz Ayer y Hoy*, Santa Cruz: Fundación Tierra.

Stern, S. (ed.) (1987), *Resistance, Rebellion, and Consciousness in the Andean Peasant World: 18th to 20th Centuries*, Madison, WI: University of Wisconsin Press.

Stutzman, R. (1981), 'El mestizaje: An All-inclusive Ideology of Exclusión', in N. Whitten (ed.), *Cultural Transformation and Ethnicity in Modern Ecuador*, Urbana, IL: University of Illinois Press, pp. 45–94.

Zavaleta, R. (1978), 'El proletariado minero en Bolivia', *Revista Mexicana de Sociología*, 40(2), 517–59.

Zavaleta, R. (1986), *Lo Nacional-Popular en Bolivia*, Mexico: Siglo Veintiuno Editores.

Chapter 33

Georgia

Lincoln A. Mitchell

The 'Rose Revolution' in Georgia is a significant part of the narrative of democracy in the twenty-first century, despite not having played an important role in the expansion of democracy or contributed to new understandings of the concept. Instead, the Rose Revolution is important because it has become one of the most extreme cases of a non-democratic country vesting much of its strategic and political capital in being perceived as democratic. The Rose Revolution, therefore, is less a critical moment in the evolution of democracy as a critical event in the evolution of geo-political spin. Nonetheless, the narrative of the Rose Revolution, and much of the debate about the impact and success of the Rose Revolution, is framed by a story of democracy. The Rose Revolution is largely thought of as either the first or second, depending on how the Bulldozer Revolution in Serbia is perceived, of the Colour Revolutions that swept through Eastern Europe and parts of the former Soviet Union in the middle of the first decade of the twenty-first century. The Rose Revolution, like the Orange Revolution in Ukraine, and to a lesser extent the Tulip Revolution in Kyrgyzstan had a storyline, images and characters that lent it the feel of a true democratic breakthrough.

Following a fraudulent election in November 2003 when an ageing Communist era kleptocrat, former Soviet Foreign Minister Eduard Shevardnadze, sought to steal one final election, a group of young, Western-educated, English-speaking reformers led peaceful protests, ultimately forcing the president to resign. These events were followed very quickly by new elections in January 2004, when the charismatic leader, Mikheil Saakashvili, was elected president freely and fairly. The story up to that point, while somewhat simplified, is clearly one of democratic advance (Fairbanks 2004; King 2004; Mitchell 2008). The story, however, did not end there. The development of Georgian democracy since that heady and exciting time has been far less dramatic or unequivocal. In the first few years following the Rose Revolution, democratic development in Georgia was decidedly mixed. Low-level corruption, which had reached endemic proportions by the end of the Shevardnadze period, was substantially reduced. The three elections in 2004, for president, parliament and the Ajaran legislature were far more free and fair than anything the country had seen during the Shevardnadze years. The warlord Aslan Abashidze was peacefully deposed in Ajara, bringing that region of Georgia a level of freedom and democracy which it had never previously enjoyed. This was good news for democracy.

There was, not surprisingly, another side to the story. Within a few years of

Saakashvili becoming president, power had again been consolidated by one political force, media was beginning to be less free, the parliament had become weaker and judicial independence had failed to evolve. These conditions only worsened following the crackdown on demonstrators in November 2007 and the more or less continued state of low-level political crisis since that time (Lanskoy and Areshidze 2007). By 2010, classifying Georgia was something of a challenge. While considerably freer than its neighbours and most of the other countries in the region, Georgia, to a great extent, differs only in degree with regard to the ability to contest for power or civic and media freedom. Georgia exhibits characteristics of being a semi-authoritarian regime. These regimes are described by Marina Ottaway as

> political hybrids. They allow little competition for power, thus reducing govern-
> ment accountability. However, they leave enough political space for political parties
> and organizations of civil society to form, for an independent press to function to
> some extent, and for some political debate to take place. (Ottaway 2003: 3)

Georgia also exhibited some of the characteristics of an electoral authoritarian regime described by Andreas Schedler as 'Political regimes [that] have established the institutional facades of democracy, including regular multiparty elections for the chief executive, in order to conceal (and reproduce) harsh realities of authoritarian governance' (Schedler 2006: 1). Steven Levitsky and Lucan Way use a similar term: 'competitive authoritarianism', which could also apply to Georgia. They describe these regimes as countries where:

> Although elections are regularly held and are generally free of massive fraud,
> incumbents routinely abuse state resources, deny the opposition adequate media
> coverage, harass opposition candidates and their supporters, and in some cases
> manipulate electoral results. Journalists, opposition politicians, and other govern-
> ment critics may be spied on, threatened, harassed, or arrested . . . Yet if
> competitive authoritarian regimes fall short of democracy, they also fall short of
> full-scale authoritarianism. Although incumbents in competitive authoritarian
> regimes may routinely manipulate formal democratic rules, they are unable to
> eliminate them or reduce them to a mere façade. Rather than openly violating
> democratic rules (for example, by banning or repressing the opposition and the
> media), incumbents are more likely to use bribery, co-optation, and more subtle
> forms of persecution, such as the use of tax authorities, compliant judiciaries, and
> other state agencies to 'legally' harass, persecute, or extort cooperative behavior
> from critics. (Levitsky and Way 2002: 53)

Democracy in Georgia, 2004–2010

While the narrative of democracy and democratisation is deeply tied to the Rose Revolution, this storyline was, to a substantial degree, developed outside the country. The Rose Revolution was briefly part of a broader global narrative of democratisation, which was supported from Washington and reached beyond the states of the former

Soviet Union to countries such as Afghanistan and Iraq where US military efforts were increasingly described as efforts to build democracy. Georgia became a success story to which Washington could point, at a time when success stories were badly needed. Georgia continued to play this role throughout the Bush Administration even after it could no longer plausibly be described as a successful example of the spreading of democracy. The new Georgian government, at least initially, pursued a policy of state-building, seeking to modernise the Georgian state. This state had been left in shambles by the corrupt Shevardnadze regime, which followed on the heels of civil conflict and the dismemberment of Georgia during the early 1990s. Saakashvili's government improved tax collection, reduced petty corruption and made government bureaucracies more streamlined and efficient. They also strengthened the reach of the state and reduced the power of non-state actors (Mitchell 2009).

During this period democracy was largely understood by the leadership as something that was required for Georgia to become Western so it could integrate into NATO and the EU, as well as something about which there was occasional pressure from the United States and Europe, but it was not a priority of the new government. More accurately, democracy was viewed as something of a nuisance which could slow down needed reforms, change the legislative outcomes preferred by the leadership and even weaken the power of the new government. The government's emphasis on state-building over democracy was clear almost immediately upon taking office. The constitutional reforms of January–February 2004 sought to concentrate power in the presidency and reduce the checks and balances that could potentially slow down the executive. Sabine Frezier commented on the new constitution:

> Domestic analysts and legal experts tend to consider that the amendments strengthen the presidential system and maintain a centralized state . . . The Prime Minister will be answerable first and foremost to the President. On the flip side, however, it is unlikely that citizens and political parties will be guaranteed maximum public participation and the necessary tools to engage in decision-making. (Frezier 2004)

By rushing the passage of the amendments, President Saakashvili did not promote a democratic atmosphere. He urged parliament to vote almost immediately after he came to office so that he could quickly appoint the new government, thus reducing the time available for public discussion. According to the law, amendments to the constitution were to be made public for discussion one month before being voted upon. The president nevertheless denied the public an opportunity for full participation or discussion. These reforms substantially changed the Georgian government, shifting power away from the parliament and towards the president. The constitution created a prime minister to be appointed by the president, allowing the president to disband parliament and call for new elections if it failed to approve the president's budget and gave the president the right to appoint a substantial range of local and national officeholders. Additionally, it did not call for direct elections of mayors, which had been a central demand of the people who had opposed Shevardnadze during the last years of his regime. In 2009, the law was changed so that there would be elections for the mayor of Tbilisi, but not, as the government had previously promised, for any of Georgia's other major cities.

The constitutional change was significant because it came within the first two months of Saakashvili's presidency, sending an early message about how government structures would look in post-Rose Revolution Georgia. It also brought Georgia more in line with other semi-authoritarian countries in the former Soviet Union that are characterised by presidents who enjoy a great deal of both formal and informal power. Since the Rose Revolution, due to the new constitutional arrangements that created a *de jure* super presidency, and due also to the political skills and influence of Saakashvili himself, the Georgian president has secured a large degree of power. Buoyed by a constitution that gave him a great deal of formal power, strong public support (at least initially) and well-honed political skills, Saakashvili quickly became the locus of political power in post-Rose Revolution Georgia. He achieved this through several means. First, he constantly moved people, including his biggest supporters, around in his government and at times to important non-governmental positions as well, assuring that these people would remain loyal to him and be unable to develop an independent power base. For example, between 2004 and 2009 Alexander 'Kakha' Lomaia served as Minister of Education, National Security Adviser and ambassador to the UN; Zurab Tchiabishvili served as chair of the Central Election Committee, mayor of Tbilisi and ambassador to the Council of Europe; and Giorgi Arveladze served as an MP, general secretary of the ruling party, chief of staff to the president, Minister of Economics and general manager of the pro-government television station, Imedi.

The major exception to this policy has been Vano Merabishvili, who has served as Minister of the Interior since late 2004. Merabishvili has, not coincidentally, been the only individual other than President Saakashvili to build his own power base. Merabishvili's Interior Ministry has become extremely powerful, playing a major role in the erosion of civil liberties and occasional state-sponsored violence that has come to be part of political life in Georgia. Saakashvili has also strengthened his informal power by making certain that other than his United National Movement (UNM), there are no strong political parties in Georgia. While the UNM has remained genuinely popular through most of the period since the Rose Revolution, they have often used undemocratic means to increase their power. Limiting media access for opposition parties, pressuring business people not to contribute funds to opposition parties and frequently accusing various opposition parties of being under Moscow's control are some of the ways that the Georgian government has helped to keep opposition parties weak. Freedom House, for example, rated the Georgian media as 'partly free' in 2009 and 2010 (*Freedom of the Press: Georgia* 2009; *Country Report: Georgia* 2010).

The concentration of formal and informal power in the office of the president contributed to the overall stagnation of democratic development in Georgia after the Rose Revolution. The new regime quickly hardened into a one-party system as the UNM dominated political life, holding constitutional majorities in parliament throughout these years, while also controlling every sub-national legislature in the country. Efforts to weaken opposition parties and, more significantly, the frequent attempts by the government to define opposition parties as treasonous, suggests that the Georgian government saw all other parties as destructive and was unable to conceive of the country being controlled by anybody but the UNM. The power of the presidency has contributed to the failure of an independent judiciary or even an independent legislature to emerge. International monitoring organisations have consistently faulted the judiciary for being too frequently susceptible to pressure from the executive (Dolidze 2007; *Human Rights Report: Georgia* 2010; Nodia 2007). Similarly, the legislature has never achieved independence from the president. In addition to being weakened by the 2004 constitutional reforms, the ruling party remained dominated by the president who had tremendous influence in determining who would be put on the UNM's party list in both 2004 and 2008. Thus, individual MPs owed their loyalty and their place in parliament to the president.

Georgia and the Democracy Story

While the Rose Revolution was not a meaningful step forward for democracy in Georgia and did not lead to a wave of democratisation in the former Soviet Union, it is still important for the broader history of democracy for several reasons, particularly with regard to politics and democracy globally. Democracy in Georgia cannot be separated from the strong rhetorical emphasis placed on freedom and democracy during the middle part of the Bush Administration. Georgia, perhaps more than any other country, provides fodder for those who argue that the United States was never interested in building democracy, but simply interested in bringing to power those who would support it. Thomas Carothers summarised this critique and the changing views of authoritarian regimes to US democracy promotion following the Rose Revolution:

> Some autocratic governments have won substantial public sympathy by arguing that opposition to Western democracy promotion is resistance not to democracy itself, but to American interventionism. Moreover, the damage that the Bush administration has done to the global image of the United States as a symbol of democracy and human rights by repeatedly violating the rule of law at home and abroad has further weakened the legitimacy of the democracy-promotion cause. (Carothers 2006: 56)

More broadly, democracy in Georgia is not just a domestic story. It can be fully understood only by looking at the role of the West both in the lead up to the Rose Revolution and in the years following those events. The Georgia case demonstrates the challenges associated with consolidating democratic regimes after initial democratic breakthroughs. Most of the democratic gains in Georgia, including less petty corruption and fairer elections, occurred early in President Saakashvili's term. The more difficult work of, for example, creating clear lines between state and party, having strong institutional checks on executive power and a genuinely free and empowered civil society and media have required more time and have proven to be more difficult.

Related to this is the need to understand the nature and intentions of regimes that are viewed to be democratising. The rise of semi-authoritarian regimes in the post-Soviet region and elsewhere indicates that many non-democratic regimes are led by people who do not want to move their country towards democracy. Georgia is a particularly useful case in this regard because the government has, more than any other in the region, sought to create an image of itself as democratising while acting in a way that must bring these assumptions into question. The mechanisms used by the Georgian government to restrict democratic development are far more sophisticated than those used in many other countries. Thus, media is not simply censored. Instead, independent and opposition oriented stations are allowed to broadcast, but only in the capital, Tbilisi. Similarly, the government took great pride in their restraint in allowing mass demonstrations in spring and summer 2009. Having learned from their mistake in November 2007, there were no widespread or daytime attacks on demonstrators. Nonetheless, there were numerous reports of abuses by plain-clothes, interior ministry troops in the evenings and other incidents relating to these demonstrations (*Human Rights Report: Georgia* 2010; *Georgia: Events of 2009* 2009).

Elections in Saakashvili's Georgia are not characterised by violence and chaos on election day, which was common during much of Shevarnadze's time in office. Instead, administrative pressure on resources and limiting media access for non-government candidates are the government's preferred tactics to ensure electoral victory. Obviously, when compared with the Baltic states, or other post-communist countries such as Hungary and the Czech Republic, Georgia's democratic credentials fall far short. When looked at in the context of much of the former Soviet Union, however, Georgia looks much better. Saakashvilli's Georgia is more democratic than Russia or any other country in central Asia or the southern Caucasus, but these are increasingly differences of degree, not kind. While it is important to recognise the relative freedom that still exists in Georgia, this should not be viewed as an accomplishment of the Rose Revolution because during the late Shevardnadze years, Georgia was also more free and democratic than any of the countries from the former Soviet Union.

The problems of democratic development in post-Rose Revolution Georgia can also be attributed to the danger of reading too much into elections. The presidential and parliamentary elections of 2004 were considerably more democratic than any that had occurred in Georgia in the previous decade. Even the presidential and parliamentary elections of 2008 were more democratic than those of the late Shevardnadze years. However, neither of these elections led to democratic outcomes, primarily because of the concentration of both formal and informal power in the office and person of the presidency, but also because of the Georgian government's belief that a strong state was more important than anything else. Additionally, the 2008 elections occurred with the media under constraints that could not be considered democratic. Thus, in Saakashvili's Georgia, elections are more democratic than other institutions that ensure democracy day to day, such as a pluralistic media, civil society and checks and balances on institutional power (OSCE 2008, 2010).

Democratisation in an International Context

To fully understand the Rose Revolution and the period following it, one has to look not only at the domestic politics of Georgia, but at the role of Western governments, multilateral organisations, ratings organisations, NGOs and even the international media. The Rose Revolution almost immediately assumed a greater import than was probably appropriate because it dovetailed with the Bush Administration's freedom agenda. Therefore, both supporters and opponents of the Rose Revolution from Moscow to Washington viewed the West, in general, and the United States in particular, as having played a greater role in the Rose Revolution than had probably been the case.

While it is not accurate to describe the Rose Revolution as a Western creation, it is useful to take a closer look at the role of American democracy promotion in the years leading up to November 2003. Georgia received a great deal of resource support for democracy-related activities during this period, but this alone is not meaningful evidence that regime change in Georgia was the goal of the United States. During this period democracy promotion resources allocated to Georgia were dwarfed by direct assistance to the Georgian government. Moreover, although Shevardnadze presided over a corrupt, incompetent and weak government during these years, he maintained strongly positive relations with the United States. Given the problems the United States faced all over the world in 2002–3, it is hard to imagine that even the Bush Administration would seek to oust a leader who had not only agreed to support the war effort in Iraq, but had personally played such a key role in the peaceful resolution of the Cold War and enjoyed enduring political relationships across the political spectrum in the United States.

Assertions that the United States masterminded the Rose Revolution are inaccurate, but that does not mean that it had no role in these events. The battery of democracy projects in Georgia ranged from civil society development to election monitoring to political party support to initiatives improving media freedom. They all contributed to the political environment that led to the Rose Revolution. Thus, while Western democracy assistance was not solely the cause of regime change in Georgia, it did contribute to the Rose Revolution in some ways. In some respects, the democracy assistance programmes that were supported in Georgia by the United States and Europe were similar to programmes that were supported throughout the region. In the first years of the twenty-first century, there was no real plan in Washington to treat Georgia differently from most other countries in the region with regard to democracy promotion. Significantly, the relative freedom of the Shevardnadze period, as well as that government's desire to retain friendly relations with the West, meant that Georgia hosted more democracy promotion programmes than many other countries in the region. Accordingly, there was, at times, more money going into democracy promotion programmes, and these programmes, rather than a desire for regime change in Georgia, were the main reason that democracy assistance played a different role to that in neighbouring countries.

The Rose Revolution changed the political environment for democracy assistance. Although the role of the United States has been overstated, the perceptions remain important. Since the Rose Revolution, particularly because it was followed a year later by the Orange Revolution in the Ukraine, many non-democratic governments, particularly, but not exclusively in the former Soviet Union, have become wary of democracy assistance. There are few countries today where the breadth of democracy assistance programmes found in Georgia in 2002–3 would be allowed by their governments. Since the Rose Revolution, Georgia's democratic development has continued to occur in an international context. From its earliest days, the Rose Revolution government was touted as a success story for both democratic development and democracy assistance. This meant that the West, specifically the United States, was not just vested in the success of Georgia's democracy, but changed from being a force for greater democracy in Georgia to a promoter of the perception of Georgia as a democracy. During the years that Saakashvili and George W. Bush were, respectively, presidents of Georgia and the United States, US policy shifted from seeking to support democratic development in Georgia to offering unconditional support for the Georgian government, and energetically endorsing Georgia's tenuous democratic credentials.

As the United States had become Georgia's primary patron during this period, as long as it felt that Georgia was democratic, there was little incentive for the Georgian government to work more seriously for meaningful democratic gains. The result of this political reality was that Georgia failed to move forward on any democratic continuum during the key initial years of the post-Rose Revolution period; and the United States squandered a unique opportunity to push the Georgian government to make good on their democratic promises. The Georgian government has nonetheless engaged in a form of democratic shadow boxing where democratic institutions, such as legislatures, elections and civil society exist and appear somewhat democratic, but the political reality is always more complex. For example, there is ample space for political parties to campaign and have their voices heard, but the democratic freedom stops short of creating an environment where these parties might win enough votes to control even one city council in the entire country. In the spring 2010 local elections, for example, the UNM retained control of every single local legislature in Georgia. The government's explanation of this is that this outcome reflects their popularity, but there is ample evidence to suggest that it is in fact their liberal use of government resources to influence the outcome of elections that brings about this result. Saakashvili's response to a question about the election demonstrates how cleverly the government can speak the language of democracy:

> A limitation on abuse of administrative resources although I have to say, there will always be a bunch of experts from abroad, [who] would say, oh, you should stop all this road-making and school-building and bridge-building and health care changes and new hospitals and all kinds of stuff because it's helping the government; it's like spending budget for electoral needs. (Saakashvili 2010a)

The abuse of administrative resources was threatening opposition activists, intimidating supporters of opposition parties and the like, not simply delivering services, but Saakashvili very effectively presented it differently. Similarly, there are Georgian television stations that are not controlled by the government and that regularly voice anti-government views, but these stations cannot be viewed outside the capital, Tbilisi. This makes it possible for officials of the Georgian government to easily dismiss foreign concerns about media freedom as 'total bullshit' without having to tell the full story (Saakashvili 2010b).

Conclusion: The Rose Revolution and the Post-Soviet Region

Now that several years have passed since the heady days of late 2003 and early 2004 in Georgia, it is reasonably clear that the Rose Revolution has not catalysed substantial democratic advance in that country. It is less clear, however, what role the Rose Revolution has played in post-Soviet Georgian politics, and whether those events represented a major transition for Georgia or just another stage in its post-Soviet semi-democracy. There is evidence to support at least two different answers to this question. The failure of the Rose Revolution to make Georgia more democratic, alleviate its widespread poverty, integrate Georgia into European or Euro-Atlantic institutions or restore Georgia's territorial integrity suggests that the true story of the Rose Revolution is one of continuity. However, the degree to which the Rose Revolution swept away the Shevardnadze regime and with it all aspects of the Soviet era elite that had ruled Georgia for most of the 1990s, the broad attacks on corruption and the significantly stronger Georgian state that Saakashvili's government helped to create, indicates that the Rose Revolution was something more than just another iteration of post-Soviet semi-democracy.

The Rose Revolution and the story of Georgian democracy in recent years should also be viewed in a regional context, specifically that of the Colour Revolutions in Kyrgyzstan and Ukraine. At the time they occurred, the Colour Revolutions were frequently described as critical democratic breakthroughs which would have an impact throughout the region. The failure not only of the Colour Revolutions to spread beyond these three countries, but also of democracy to move forward in any of these countries following their revolutions belied these initial hopes. In Kyrgyzstan, the post-Tulip Revolution government of Kurmanbek Bakiyev was even more corrupt than the government it ousted in 2005. Bakiyev's government lasted less than five years before being overthrown in 2010 by disgruntled Tulip Revolutionaries. In Ukraine, reasonably fair presidential elections in 2009–10 led to the election of Viktor Yanukovych, the man against whom the Orange Revolutionaries had demonstrated in 2004. Yanukovych's victory can certainly be interpreted as reflecting the strength of Ukrainian democracy, but it also suggests that the Orange Revolution was not a transitional event for Ukraine. The Georgian story of the Rose Revolution leading to little concrete democratic change does not stand out from the rest of the region, as Colour Revolutions in Ukraine and Kyrgyzstan had even more ambiguous effects on democracy in those countries.

The fate of democracy in all three of these countries suggests that the Colour Revolutions in general, and perhaps the Rose Revolution more specifically, played a role in the global story of democracy, albeit different from the one that many in the West had first thought or hoped. The Rose Revolution did not usher in an age of democratic transition in Georgia or elsewhere in the region. Instead, it served as a reminder of the difficulties involved in democratic transitions in the former Soviet Union and helped a semi-authoritarian regime emerge in Georgia which, presentation notwithstanding, is more similar to regimes in the rest of the region than Shevardnadze's freewheeling kleptocracy had been. The Rose Revolution, and the Colour Revolutions more broadly, turned out to be significant, not because they were the harbingers of a new wave of democracy in the region, but because they were the events that led to the end of Western hopes for democratic advance in the former Soviet Union. Since 2003–5, democracy assistance in the region has been downplayed by European and American powers, who seem resigned to their limited ability to meaningfully influence political outcomes in that part of the world. The failure of the Western-trained Georgian leadership who came to office through a peaceful revolution pledging its belief in liberal democracy to actually bring strong democracy to a small, ethnically homogeneous, strongly pro-Western, Christian country made it clear that democracy had stalled in the former Soviet Union. This is the most lasting legacy of the Rose Revolution with regard to democracy.

References

Carothers, T. (2006), 'The Backlash against Democracy Promotion', *Foreign Affairs*, 85(2), 55–68.
Country Report: Georgia (2010), New York: Freedom House.
Dolidze, A. (2007), 'Georgia's Path to Authoritarianism', *National Interest*, 24 August.
Fairbanks, C. (2004), 'Georgia's Rose Revolution', *Journal of Democracy*, 15(2), 110–24.
Freedom of the Press: Georgia (2009), New York: Freedom House.
Frezier, S. (2004), 'Georgia's Constitutional Amendments: A Setback for Democratization?', *Central Asia Caucasus – Institute Analyst*, 11 February.
Human Rights Report: Georgia 2009 (2010), Washington, DC: US Department of State.
Georgia: Events of 2009 (2009), New York: Human Rights Watch.
King, C. (2004), *The Black Sea: A History*, New York: Oxford University Press.
Lanskoy, M. and G. Areshidze (2008), 'Georgia's Year of Turmoil', *Journal of Democracy*, 19(4), 154–68.
Levitsky, S and L. Way (2002), 'The Rise of Competitive Authoritarianism', *Journal of Democracy*, 13(4), 51–65.
Mitchell, L. (2008), *Uncertain Democracy: US Foreign Policy and Georgia's Rose Revolution*, Philadelphia, PA: University of Pennsylvania Press.
Mitchell, L (2009), 'Compromising Democracy: State Building in Saakashvili's Georgia', *Central Asian Survey*, 28(2), 171–83
Nodia, G. (2007), 'Wanted: A Robust System of Checks and Balances', *The Financial Times*, 31 October.
Organisation for Security and Co-operation in Europe (OSCE) (2008), 'Final Report on the 21 May 2008 Parliamentary Elections in Georgia', Vienna: Organisation for Security and Co-operation in Europe.
Organisation for Security and Co-operation in Europe (OSCE) (2010), 'Georgian Local Elections Mark Evident Progress, but Significant Shortcomings Remain to be Addressed', Vienna: Organisation for Security and Co-operation in Europe.
Ottaway, M. (2003), *Democracy Challenged: The Rise of Semi-Authoritarianism*, Washington, DC: Carnegie Endowment for International Peace.
Saakashvili, M. (2010a), 'Transforming Georgia: Transcript Interview', *Atlantic Council*, 15 April.
Saakashvili, M. (2010b), 'Claims on Media Freedom Problems "Bullshit"', *Civil Georgia*.
Schedler, A. (2006), *Electoral Authoritarianism: The Dynamics of Unfree Competition*, Boulder, CO: Lynne Rienner.

Chapter 34

Iraq

Benjamin Isakhan

In March 2003, the world's last remaining superpower launched a pre-emptive strike on a sovereign nation without UN approval or popular domestic or global support. The justification given to the world for such an attack was twofold: Iraq was accused of harbouring weapons of mass destruction (WMD) and of having links to Al-Qaeda, both of which could not be permitted in a post-9/11 world. However, when evidence for either Iraq's WMDs or links to terrorism failed to emerge in the wake of the war and the nine subsequent years of military occupation, the Bush Administration was forced to re-frame the war and redefine the parameters of success. To do this, the United States began speaking about bringing democracy to Iraq as if it had always been one of the goals of the war itself. The notion that the United States could use its superior military might to invade a sovereign state, topple an existing regime and implant democracy set a new and unfortunate precedent that has come to be termed the 'Bush doctrine' (Jervis 2003). In addition, the Bush Administration also held the overly simplistic view that by installing democracy in Iraq they would set off a 'domino effect' across the region where autocratic regimes would have no choice but to convert to robust democracies.

Despite such lofty ideals, the Bush Administration demonstrated a startling gap between rhetoric and action on the issue of democracy in Iraq. On the one hand, they argued that the success of Iraq's democracy was central to their broader geo-political agenda, and, on the other, they repeatedly tried to silence dissent, to limit democratic freedoms and to interfere in due process. In fact, the original plan of the Coalition Provisional Authority (CPA), which managed Iraq after the fall of Baghdad, was to install a puppet Iraqi government that would write the constitution under American auspices and be pliable to their interests in the region. In addition, the United States was quick to nullify the results of a whole series of spontaneous elections that sprang up across Iraq. Unfamiliar with such lively, grassroots democracy, the United States outlawed these elections and the officials who had been elected by their own constituents were promptly replaced. It also went to great lengths to ban several political parties (of which the Baath were only one) and forcibly shut down several of Iraq's independent newspapers that proved to be too critical of the occupying forces and their military operations (Isakhan 2009, 2012).

Despite such interference, the Iraqi people have proven themselves to be remarkably willing to embrace democracy and remarkably adept at utilising its mechanisms and institutions to their advantage. This chapter seeks to document some of the more significant democratic developments that have occurred in Iraq, including the complex array of political parties that (re)emerged in the wake of the former regime; the series of nationwide elections that have occurred since 2005; and the role of various Iraqi media outlets and protest movements in agitating towards greater inclusion, diversity and debate. However, this chapter also documents some of the alarming counter-democratic developments that have occurred, particularly the rise of ethno-religious sectarian politics and violence and the increasingly authoritarian nature of certain elements of Iraq's political elite. The chapter concludes by noting that Iraqi democracy is increasingly precarious and it faces its greatest challenge in renewed violence, rising authoritarianisms and the end to the US occupation.

Embracing Democracy, 2003–2005

When the United States began talking about bringing democracy to Iraq they did not expect the Iraqi people to hold them to their word. However, when news of the CPA's plan to install a puppet government in Baghdad reached the people of Iraq they took to the streets in a series of massive nationwide protests throughout 2003–4. They demanded democracy and called on the United States to make good on its promise to see Iraq transform from an oppressive dictatorship into a modern representative democracy governed by the principles of justice and equality. These early protests were but a forerunner to a movement – particularly among the majority Shia Arab population of Iraq – that gathered enormous momentum over the ensuing months. Indeed, senior religious figures such as Grand Ayatollah Ali Al-Sistani took the unprecedented step of issuing a politically motivated *fatwa* in June 2003 that argued that the United States lacked the appropriate authority to install a government in Iraq and demanded that they instead hold national elections so that the Iraqi people could nominate their own representatives. Although the CPA at first underestimated the importance of such a *fatwa*, it went on to have a profound effect on the US plans for post-Saddam Iraq, as they were soon forced to appease Al-Sistani's demands. Although an interim government was put in place by the United States and not by elections, this body had limited powers and was designed to prepare the way for national elections in January 2005, which would in turn see an elected body responsible for drafting the Iraqi constitution. Although this was a significant compromise for the world's last remaining superpower to make to a religious figure in Najaf, it was not enough for Al-Sistani, who demanded that the United States seek UN approval for their plan. Amazingly, even though the entire world – including pleas from their closest ally, the United Kingdom – had been unable to bring the United States before the UN, Al-Sistani succeeded (Feldman 2005: 6–8).

Once the US plan for democracy in Iraq had UN approval, the political floodgates opened. In the lead up to the January 2005 elections an entire collection of political parties and civil society movements began writing policy agendas, engaging in complex political alliances, and debating and deliberating over the key issues facing the state. Some of these political parties had been formed decades ago, were very sophisticated and had endured the Baathist efforts to flatten Iraq's political opposition, while others were entirely new and spoke for a variety of opinions. Perhaps foremost among these groups is the avowedly ethnic-based politics of the Kurdish people of northern Iraq. Aside from several smaller factions, the Kurds have two key political parties: the Kurdistan Democratic Party (KDP), currently led by Massoud Barzani who is also the President of the Kurdish Regional Government (KRG); and the Patriotic Union of Kurdistan (PUK) under the leadership of Jalal Talabani, who currently serves as State President of Iraq. More religious in tone are the two key political parties that represent the Shia of Iraq. The first of these is *Hizb Al-Da'wa Islamiyya* ('The Islamic Calling', or more commonly referred to as *Da'wa*, the 'Calling'), whose Secretary-General, Nuri Al-Maliki, is also the current Prime Minister of Iraq. The second major Shia Arab party is the Supreme Islamic Iraqi Council (SIIC), currently led by Sayyid Ammar Al-Hakim. Also of real significance is the network of political organisations, militias, media outlets and social services that are more or less controlled by the firebrand Shia cleric, Moqtada Al-Sadr.

However, the immediate upsurge of political parties in post-Saddam Iraq was not limited to those premised on Kurdish ethnicity or Shia religiosity. There are also a number of parties that claim to be both secular and inclusive, including the US and UK backed *Al-Wifaq Al-Watani Al-Iraqi* ('The Iraqi National Accord' or INA), headed by Dr Iyad Allawi, the former Interim Prime Minister of Iraq and the current head of the powerful *Al-Iraqiyya* list (Stansfield 2007: 136–8). There is also the Iraqi National Congress (INC), headed by Dr Ahmed Abdel Hadi Chalabi, Iraq's Deputy Prime Minister throughout much of 2005. Beyond these are the myriad of political parties that seek to represent the interests of Iraq's smaller ethno–religious minorities, such as the Turkomans and Assyrians. Finally, it is also worth mentioning that during this period the Sunni Arab minority of Iraq – who had ruled the nation since its inception in the 1920s – resisted the Coalition effort to 'democratise' Iraq. They did not want to see power transferred to the Shia Arabs or the Kurds and therefore chose initially to abstain from the political process.

Then, in January 2005, around 8.5 million Iraqis (constituting approximately 58 per cent of those eligible to vote) lined up for their chance to partake in the nation's first free and fair election for many decades. Each was acting in defiance of the blood-curdling threats issued by figures such as the head of Al-Qaeda in Iraq (AQI), Abu Musab Al-Zarqawi, who proclaimed an all-out war on the evil principle of democracy. These threats were not entirely empty. There were several attacks across Iraq resulting in a number of deaths and injuries, but given the chaos of the post-Saddam era these attacks fell well short of the promised bloodbath. What was perhaps a much bigger problem was that the Sunni boycott had left them significantly under-represented in the 275-member national assembly. Indeed, when the results were announced on 14 February the Shia coalition, the United Iraqi Alliance (made up of Dawa, SIIC and the Al-Sadr trend), had won 48 per cent of the vote, the Kurdish Alliance (constituted by the KDP and PUK) had garnered around 26 per cent, Allawi's secular Iraqi National List had achieved a paltry 14 per cent, while the Sunni-backed party, The Iraqis, achieved just under 2 per cent (Diamond 2005: 324–7).

Regardless, the elected assembly was charged with the rather prestigious, if laborious, task of drafting a permanent Iraqi constitution by the middle of August

2005. This, along with the need to position the candidates within the new government, brought with it the kind of political in-fighting, jostling and rhetoric that is typical of a fledgling democracy. While the incumbent Shia and Kurdish groups went to great lengths to incorporate the disenfranchised Sunni parties, there remained much friction between the groups and lengthy debates ensued over key issues such as the official role of Islam in the new constitution, as well as extended deliberations over the merits of regional autonomy versus a federated state (Dawisha 2005). With the stakes high and the issues thorny in nature, it is not at all surprising that the draft constitution was delayed from its initial deadline of 15 August until 28 August 2005. This new Iraqi constitution, drafted by a body of representatives elected by the Iraqi people in free and fair elections, was then circulated to all via the nation's diverse media sector. Some six weeks later (15 October 2005), the Iraqi people were once again asked to visit the polls, only this time their ballot paper posed a simple question printed in both Arabic and Kurdish: 'Do you support the draft constitution?' Approximately 10 million Iraqis answered this question and, despite continued Sunni opposition to the constitution (which was strongly reflected in the polls), the overall majority replied in the affirmative (Stansfield 2007: 183–7).

With the constitution officially accepted, the Iraqi people were invited to visit the polls for the third time on 15 December 2005, this time to elect a permanent 275-seat government. This was arguably the most successful of Iraq's recent forays into democratic practice, with strong Sunni participation, very low levels of violence and an estimated 67 per cent of those eligible to vote participating in the election (approximately 11 million people). When the final results of the election were released in early 2006, they revealed that while the Shia and Kurdish parties had retained a significant proportion of the votes, the Sunni minority had garnered considerable political momentum after learning the hard lessons associated with their electoral abstinence in January. Indeed, the Sunni-backed Iraqi Accord Front (led by the Iraqi Islamic Party) managed to secure third place with 15 per cent of the vote, falling behind the Shi'ite United Iraqi Alliance (41 per cent) and the Kurdish Alliance (22 per cent) (Dawisha and Diamond 2006: 99). This political diversity brought with it a more legitimate (if somewhat sluggish) Iraqi political landscape, as the various factions began lengthy negotiations and deliberations over the exact composition of the Iraqi government.

This series of elections and the referendum held in 2005 are remarkable accomplishments in and of themselves. The fact that millions of Iraqis – men and women, young and old, Sunni and Shia, Kurd and Arab, Christian and Muslim – literally risked their lives to vote is a strong testament to the political determination of the people and the degree to which they rapidly embraced democracy. Another strong testament is the often overlooked role that Iraq's many partisan and non-partisan media outlets played during this period. Indeed, the fall of the former regime had seen a rapid transformation of the Iraqi media landscape from a handful of tightly controlled state propaganda outlets to more than twenty radio stations, around fifteen Iraqi-owned television stations and approximately 200 Iraqi-run newspapers across the entire country. Most of these new outlets were started by the seemingly countless political factions of post-Saddam Iraq, but many others claimed to be free of any specific political, religious or sectarian allegiance and desired to report the news in a professional and objective manner (Al-Marashi 2007). Together, this complex array of media outlets fostered the emergence of a renewed public sphere in Iraq and provided Iraqi citizens with a rich array of information on key policies, politicians and parties, as well as encouraging them to defy the threats and take part in the elections (Isakhan 2008).

Violence and New Authoritarianisms, 2006–2010

However, one of the unfortunate consequences of the US effort to bring democracy to Iraq was that many key ethno-religious political factions viewed it as an opportunity to pedal their own relatively narrow and very divisive political rhetoric (Davis 2007). Overwhelmingly, Iraq's key political parties failed to unfold a vision for a united and prosperous Iraq. Similarly, when Iraqis took to the polls, most of them voted along ethno-religious sectarian lines. This meant that the 275-member government they elected was constituted not so much by a body who wanted to draw Iraq together behind a common ideology and to work towards a collective and egalitarian future, as it was by representatives who had been given a mandate by their constituents to fight in the interests of their ethnicity or religion. This meant that – following the December 2005 elections – a six-month political stalemate ensued, with little known Nuri Al-Maliki eventually being nominated as prime minister and his government finally taking office in May 2006 (Stansfield 2007: 187–9). Although the many disagreements on the path to forming a government were resolved peacefully, this short period of divisiveness set the tone for political in-fighting and was a forerunner to the sharp upsurge in ethno-religious motivated sectarianism and violence that was to follow.

Over the next couple of years Iraq descended into a particularly dark and unprecedented period with grim and complex battles fought between the occupying forces, the Iraqi armed services, various insurgent groups and terrorist organisations, as well as between competing ethno-religious sectarian militias (Dawisha 2009: 258–71). In the so-called 'Sunni triangle' a web of insurgent groups (made up of former Baathists, Iraqi nationalists and AQI) stepped up their attacks on the US occupation forces and on various Shia militias. The tide turned somewhat when Al-Zarqawi was assassinated by the United States in June 2006, but also with the rise of the Awakening Council ('Sons of Iraq'), a Sunni alliance of tribal sheikhs mostly from the Anbar province who fought the insurgency throughout 2006 on US salaries. In the Shia-dominated south, powerful militias – such as Al-Sadr's Mahdi Army and SIIC's Badr Brigade – waged a series of deadly attacks against US troops, the Iraqi government, Sunni insurgents and each other. The violence peaked after the February 2006 attack on the *Al-Askari* mosque in Samarra, an iconic edifice highly revered by the Shia population and deliberately targeted by Sunni insurgents. The Sunni–Shia bloodbath that followed led many commentators to argue that Iraq had in fact slipped into a civil war (Fearon 2007).

Although things were much more peaceful in the Kurdish north, members of the Kurdistan Alliance were using their influence over Baghdad not only to press for increasing degrees of autonomy, but also to attempt to bring the oil-rich but ethnically diverse province of Kirkuk under their jurisdiction. However, their obstinacy over such issues was less disconcerting than some of the unfortunate trends that have emerged among those who administer the KRG. Despite the region's reputation as a bastion of relative freedom since 1991 (Stansfield 2003), the KRG became increasingly insular and autocratic from around 2006. They cracked down on intellectuals, dissenters and journalists who experienced waves of harassment, detention and beatings. For example, during both March and August 2006, a series of largely peaceful demonstrations broke into angry protest against the KRG and its denial of basic public services to the region. Kurdish security forces reacted by detaining scores of protestors, including the arrest of twenty-eight journalists. Furthermore, both the KDP and the PUK have become increasingly sensitive to criticism or allegations of corruption or incompetence, even to the point where they have sacked several senior officials who were found to have made remarks considered unfavourable to the party and its leadership (Isakhan 2009: 18–19).

However, such actions pale in comparison with what can only be described as the increasingly authoritarian nature of the Shia-dominated government in Baghdad, especially of the prime minister himself. To consolidate his grip on power, from 2006 Al-Maliki instigated a three-pronged approach. First, he cracked down hard on Iraqi civil society, even going as far as to close down media outlets and political parties that dared to criticise his government, his parliament or his security apparatus (Isakhan 2009: 17–18). Secondly, he successfully harnessed the increasing strength of the Iraqi Security Forces (ISF) to target and undermine much of his opposition. Arguably, this began in 2008 when Al-Maliki orchestrated a series of military manoeuvres, most notably the 'Charge of the Knights' which saw the ISF and the Badr Brigade pitted against the Mahdi Army. Although it was a protracted and bloody fight, Al-Maliki emerged on top, winning a significant victory and severely weakening Al-Sadr in his strongholds as well us building up loyalty towards himself among the rank and file of the ISF. His third approach was to broaden his political support base via a series of tribe-based 'support councils', especially in key Shia and Kurdish provinces. Not surprisingly, the creation of these very un-democratic 'support councils' has been controversial across Iraq, especially among key Shia and Kurdish political organisa-tions who see it as a move to commandeer their political support base (Duss and Juul 2009). All of this has meant that, throughout 2006–8, Al-Maliki was able to silence opposing views, develop his credentials as a nationalist leader and flag the strength of his central government and the ISF (Katzman 2010: 3).

Capitalising on this, Al-Maliki split those loyal to him in the Dawa Party from the UIA to form the State of Law Coalition (SLC) in the lead up to the 2009 provincial elections in Iraq. This effectively left the UIA in ruins and without adequate leadership. Officially secular and multi-ethnic, the SLC sought to advocate a strong, united nationalism. To do this, it cobbled together an odd array of smaller Shia, Kurdish, Turkomen and Christian parties as well as Sunni independents. However, Al-Maliki's list did not attract high profile leaders and it lacked the genuine diversity needed to be truly representative. Nonetheless, the SLC emerged the clear winner of the 2009 provincial elections, winning 126 seats and delivering another strong blow to Al-Maliki's political rivals.

Despite this, it has to be said that the election itself was remarkably successful. The vastly improved security situation – in part, because of the US troop surge in 2007 and the increasing strength of the ISF under Al-Maliki – meant that the election was not only free and fair, but also safe. In total, some 400 parties and 14,500 Iraqi candidates (including a large number of women) registered to compete for the 444 seats. Some 51 per cent of eligible Iraqis (Just over 7 million people) turned out at the polls to cast their vote. As with the lead up to the 2005 national elections, the Iraqi press went to great lengths to provide details on the various parties and candidates who had registered to compete, and to encourage the Iraqi people to vote. Colourful campaign posters were glued to walls all over Iraq, while party volunteers handed out leaflets at security checkpoints. Others used more traditional tactics, such as going door to door, doing radio interviews or calling public assemblies where ordinary citizens were invited to grill leading candidates on their policies.

However, with the break-up of the UIA and the successes of the SLC at the 2009 elections, the various Shia political entities re-ignited negotiations in 2009 and formed a new coalition ahead of the 2010 national elections, the National Iraqi Alliance (NIA) headed by former Iraqi Prime Minister, Ibrahim Al-Jaafari, and made up of ISCI, the Sadrists and other smaller political entities. At around the same time, Allawi banded together a number of largely secular Sunni and Shia parties to form *Al-Iraqiya* (Iraqi National Movement, INM). Allawi represented a credible alternative to Al-Maliki and had far greater credentials as a unifying figure who was determined to root out Shia Islamism and ethno-religious sectarian politics.

On 7 March 2010, around 11.5 million Iraqis (61 per cent of registered voters) again took to the polls, this time in a national parliamentary election. Although there were some violent attacks in the lead up to and during the elections, the Iraqi people demonstrated their will towards a democratic future by once again risking their lives to vote. As with the 2005 and 2009 elections, the Iraqi press did an excellent job of covering the lead up to these polls, demonstrating their ability to serve as the Fourth Estate of this fledgling democracy. However, when the results were announced a few weeks later, it soon became clear that no one list had managed to secure the 163 seats needed to form a government in the 325-member parliament. The INM had received the greatest number of seats at the election (91); the SLC came a close second (89); the NIA followed (70); and then came the Kurdistan list (43).

This meant that the various blocks and their constituent political parties would have to cobble together a coalition government. This was never going to be an easy task, but it was made cripplingly difficult by the obstinacy and incompetence of much of Iraq's political elite, who routinely failed to encourage the mutually beneficial dialogue and debate critical to democracy. Foremost among these was Al-Maliki himself, who was determined to cling to power and undertook an aggressive and multi-faceted campaign towards such an end (Ottaway and Kaysi 2010a). Such misconduct saw the nation plummet into nine months of political stalemate: several long and complex political negotiations ensued; new alliances were forged and then broken; old enemies shook hands and discussed new pathways to peace only to fall back to pre-existing disagreements; various models and options were tabled before being scrapped at the last moment; and the urgency of a prompt political solution was emphasised by figures such as Al-Sistani and President Obama, all to no avail.

The deadlock continued until early November when an agreement was signed that would pave the way for the formation of a government. Finally, a government was announced in December 2010 and – to the grave disappointment of many Iraqis – much remained the same: Al-Maliki would retain the position of prime minister (and actually extend his portfolio to include the powerful defence and interior ministries); Talabani would stay on as president; and many other key positions would rotate between a handful of familiar faces (Ottaway and Kaysi 2010b). For his troubles, Allawi was to enter a power-sharing arrangement with the government as the head of a new National Security Council, but it was not long before Allawi was complaining that there was no real 'power-sharing' in Iraq and he withdrew from the post.

The Arab Revolutions and Beyond, 2010–2011

In the middle of 2010, as the government deadlock continued and Iraqis sweltered in the heat of summer with only sporadic electricity to fuel their air conditioners and poor access to drinking water, frustrations literally reached boiling point. Although Iraq had witnessed a series of strong protest movements emerge since 2003 (Isakhan 2009), 2010 saw religious figures, political parties, women's groups and civil rights movements band together in a series of protests and sit-ins across Iraq, the largest and longest of which were held at Nasiriyah and Basra. Aside from electricity and water, under-pinning these protests was a sense of wide dissatisfaction with the on-going political stalemate.

However, no one could have predicted the dramatic sequence of events that swept across the Middle East and North Africa in late 2010 and early 2011. As long lasting and deeply entrenched regimes fell in Tunisia, Egypt and – with more than a little help from NATO – in Libya, Iraqis were confronted with the failures of their own democracy to deliver on the many promises made to them since 2003. This led to weeks of scattered protests across the nation, culminating in the 'Day of Rage' on 25 February 2011, in which thousands of protestors took to the streets in at least seventeen separate demonstrations across the country following Friday prayers. In the north, tens of thousands of Kurds mimicked protestors in Cairo and elsewhere by setting up camp for days on end in central squares, including Al-Saray Square in Sulaimaniya. In Baghdad's own Tahrir Square protestors gathered carrying Iraqi flags and various political banners, many calling for an end to Al-Maliki's leadership, and even in smaller provincial centres like southern Thi-Qar, more than 10,000 demon-strators gathered to voice their concerns and air their frustrations (*Al-Jazeera* 2011; Al-Khateeb 2011; *Aswat-Al-Iraq* 2011).

On the surface, these protests shared much in common with others across the region, including the use of Facebook and other social media to promote the rallies, and the focus on corruption, unemployment and poor public infrastructure. However, upon closer inspection the Iraqi protests are very different to others across the Middle East and are therefore among the most significant for the future of democracy in Iraq and across the region. The Iraqi people were not protesting against an autocratic regime or an entrenched monarchy that had held power for decades, but a relatively new political elite that had been brought to power in the wake of the US invasion and had manipulated the very institutions and discourses of democracy to retain, rather than diffuse, power. Indeed, while protestors across the region called for more democracy in the form of a written constitution, free and fair elections, a robust media sphere and the rule of law, Iraqis were questioning the efficacy of such democratic institutions (all of which they more or less have) and wondering if they had simply enabled new forms of authoritarianism.

Unfortunately, key Iraqi political figures, such as Al-Maliki and Barzani, reacted to these events in ways that would confirm such anxieties, and in ways very similar to dictators and autocrats across the region. They met Iraqi protests with a mixture of brutal suppression and modest political and economic concessions. Al-Maliki offered token concessions, such as promising to cut his pay in half and to amend the Iraqi constitution so that no leader could serve more than two terms. In terms of suppression, Al-Maliki ordered the closure of the offices and newspapers of the Iraqi Nation Party and the Iraqi Communist Party, both of which had been critical in organising the protests (Schmidt and Healy 2011). Al-Maliki also ordered a brutal crackdown on the Iraqi protestors, journalists and civil society or political actors who had been involved in the events. The ISF and the protestors clashed frequently, leading to many arrests, beatings and deaths. In the Kurdish north, Barzani employed a similar strategy, sending in thousand of his Peshmerga militia to quell demonstrations that demanded his departure, leading to further clashes (Al-Laithi 2011)

While such developments do not bode well for Iraq, these protests nonetheless indicate the continuing struggle of the Iraqi people towards democracy and shed light on the complexities of Iraqi politics post-Saddam. Commenting on these events an anonymous opinion editorial printed in the independent Iraqi newspaper *Azzaman* at the time of the 'Day of Rage' protests captures the complexity:

Iraqis are supposed to have been 'liberated' by their US occupiers. They are supposed to be enjoying the fruits of their occupation by the world's most powerful nation. They are supposed to have democracy, unlike other Arab countries whose nations are rising against their dictators. The US, childishly, thought it could bring democracy to Iraq . . . It thought it could bring its own lackeys and install them as satraps to rule the country democratically. And today, the lackeys it brought with its invasion, who are ruling the country, including its semi-independent Kurdish north, find that their own people are rising against them the way the people of Libya and other Arab countries are revolting against their dictators . . . Iraqis, who think of themselves as the real revolutionaries of the Arab world, are embarrassed and ashamed. They wanted to have the change on their own, the way the Egyptians toppled Mubarak's presidency . . . How glad we the Iraqis would have been if we today, like other Arabs, rose against our dictator and had him toppled. We need to remove this stigma of shame by overthrowing the lackeys the US brought with it and installed over us, whether in the Kurdish north or the Arab centre and south. (*Azzaman* 2011)

Conclusion

This is a critical time for Iraqi democracy. On the one hand, there can be no doubting the Iraqi people's will towards democracy and their willingness to vote, to engage with a robust media sphere and to take to the streets to protest key decisions. On the other hand, the protracted political impasse of 2010, recent escalations in violence and the final withdrawal of all US troops on 18 December 2011, has left an Iraqi populace that is increasingly disillusioned about the efficacy of democracy and its ability to meet their many urgent needs. While the 'Arab Revolutions' and the protests they have inspired in Iraq give some cause for optimism, the Iraqi people face a political elite who have mastered the manipulation of democracy for authoritarian ends like no other Arab regime. If the largely undemocratic trends that have occurred over the last few years continue, especially those espoused by Al-Maliki but also Barzani and Al-Sadr, there remain serious doubts about the prospects of a democratic future beyond occupation. For all its successes and its failures, Iraqi democracy reveals a number of interesting things about democracy in our times: about the perils of imposing a top-down model by a foreign power; about the will of people everywhere towards a fairer political order; and about the myriad ways in which authoritarians can and do utilise the very mechanisms of democracy to dig their talons deeper into the flesh of power.

References

Al-Jazeera (2011), 'Tensions Flare in Iraq Rallies', 25 February.

Al-Khateeb, B. (2011), 'Iraqi Kurdish Protestors to Press Demands for Freedom and Transparency', *Azzaman*, 11 March.

Al-Laithi, N. (2011), 'Tensions Rise in Iraq's Kirkuk as Kurdish Leader Sends in Militias', *Azzaman*, 2 March.

Al-Marashi, I. (2007), 'The Dynamics of Iraq's Media: Ethno-Sectarian Violence, Political Islam, Public Advocacy, and Globalisation', *Cardozo Arts and Entertainment Law Journal*, 25(95), 96–140.

Aswat-Al-Iraq (2011), 'Calls in Thi-Qar for Friday Protests', 3 March.

Azzaman (2011), 'Iraqis Revolt Against their "Liberation" by the US', 25 February.

Davis, E. (2007), 'The Formation of Political Identities in Ethnically Divided Societies: Implications for a Democratic Transition in Iraq', *American Academic Research Institute in Iraq Newsletter*, 2(1), 3–4.

Dawisha, A. (2005), 'The New Iraq: Democratic Institutions and Performance', *Journal of Democracy*, 16(3), 35–49.

Dawisha, A. (2009), *Iraq: A Political History from Independence to Occupation*, Princeton, NJ: Princeton University Press.

Dawisha, A. and L. Diamond (2006), 'Electoral Systems Today: Iraq's Year of Voting Dangerously', *Journal of Democracy*, 17(2), 89–103.

Diamond, L. (2005), *Squandered Victory: The American Occupation and the Bungled Effort to Bring Democracy to Iraq*, New York: Times Books.

Duss, M. and P. Juul (2009), *The Fractured Shia of Iraq: Understanding the Tensions within Iraq's Majority*, Washington, DC: Center for American Progress.

Fearon, J. D. (2007), 'Iraq's Civil War', *Foreign Affairs*, 86(2), 2–15.

Feldman, N. (2005), 'The Democratic Fatwa: Democracy in the Realm of Constitutional Politics', *Oklahoma Law Review*, 58(1), 1–9.

Isakhan, B. (2008), 'The Post-Saddam Iraqi Media: Reporting the Democratic Developments of 2005', *Global Media Journal*, 7(13).

Isakhan, B. (2009), 'Manufacturing Consent in Iraq: Interference in the Post-Saddam Media Sector', *International Journal of Contemporary Iraqi Studies*, 3(1), 7–26.

Isakhan, B. (2012), *Democracy in Iraq: History, Politics and Discourse*, London: Ashgate.

Jervis, R. (2003), 'Understanding the Bush Doctrine', *Political Science Quarterly*, 118(3), 365–88.

Katzman, K. (2010), *Iraq: Politics, Elections, and Benchmarks*, Washington, DC: Congressional Research Services Report for Congress.

Ottaway, M. and D. Kaysi (2010a), 'Post-Election Maneuvering: Rule of Law is the Casualty', Carnegie Endowment for International Peace, 30 April.

Ottaway, M. and D. Kaysi (2010b), 'Can Iraq's Political Agreement be Implemented?' Carnegie Endowment for International Peace, 15 November.

Schmidt, M. S. and J. Healy (2011), 'Iraq Shuts Office of Protest Organizers', *New York Times*, 4 March.

Stansfield, G. (2003), *Iraqi Kurdistan: Political Development and Emergent Democracy*, London: Routledge Curzon.

Stansfield, G. (2007), *Iraq: People, History, Politics*, Cambridge: Polity.

Chapter 35

Burma

Donald M. Seekins

Burma is one of the poorest countries in southeast Asia and its people are among the least free. Since 1962, it has been ruled by a series of military regimes distinguished by their corruption, incompetence and authoritarianism: the 1962–88 Burma Socialist Programme Party (BSPP) regime of General Ne Win; the State Law and Order Restoration Council (SLORC), which staged a bloody seizure of power in September 1988 (its name was changed in 1997 to the softer-sounding State Peace and Development Council, or SPDC); and a new military-dominated regime with a constitutional façade, the Republic of the Union of Myanmar, whose legislators, mostly from the army or pro-SPDC groups, were chosen in a carefully staged general election in November 2010.

As the twenty-first century enters its second decade, Burma continues to face a grim predicament. Not only is it badly-governed and poor, but its politics is in a perpetual state of crisis because of the vicious cycle created by the top-down and distant nature of military rule. Since 1962, the state has repeatedly failed to gain popular support and allegiance, due largely to its economic failures and mis-steps, and has had to resort repeatedly to brute force to remain in power. At the same time, anti-government forces situated in society do not have the resources or organisation to push the military from power and establish a new, democratic political system. For one thing, there has been almost no cooperation between oppositionists in central Burma and ethnic minority insurgents in border areas such as the Karen National Union and the Kachin Independence Army.

Thus, contemporary Burma's history is one of the state threatening and squeezing resources out of society, while society resists – usually covertly and evasively, but sometimes, overtly and explosively. For protesters, the stakes are high, since the army-state has shown it will not negotiate or compromise: troops killed as many as 10,000 protesters nationwide in the wake of the 18 September 1988 SLORC power seizure (Boudreau 2004: 210). Yet protests persist, as the 'Saffron Revolution' reveals, with the emergence of historically-rooted narratives that connect the military-ruled present with past struggles against the injustices of illegitimate states.

Since the SLORC's violent inception in 1988, there has been a growing body of literature on military rule and the struggle for democracy in Burma (Boudreau 2004; Fink 2009; Lintner 1989; Wakeman and San San Tin 2009). Collectively, these works give vivid accounts of people's struggles for both integrity and physical survival, and concern the relatively un-institutionalised and underground nature of Burmese opposition. Foremost among such writing is Daw Aung San Suu Kyi's *Freedom from Fear and Other Writings*, which provides historical background as well as vivid descriptions of the 1988 popular uprising and her role in those events (Aung San Suu Kyi 1995a). Others have focused on the history of political activism by Buddhist monks and lay people in colonial and post-colonial Burma, showing that the popular image of Buddhism as an ethereal, otherworldly religion must be replaced by a more nuanced understanding of the complex relationship between 'world-renouncing' monks, worldly power-holders and the society in which they live (D. Smith 1965). More recent work discusses how Burma's former capital city was the stage for repeated anti-state movements by city residents beginning in the British colonial period. From at least the 1920s until now, there has emerged and re-emerged a powerful and coherent narrative of resistance against the state that has mobilised the city's people (Seekins 2010).

Democracy's Summer, 1988; The Saffron Revolution, 2007

On 15 August 2007, the State Peace and Development Council suddenly decreed the removal of subsidies for fuel, causing a rise of 500 per cent in the price of compressed natural gas, a 100 per cent increase in the price of diesel and a 67 per cent increase in the cost of petrol (AAN on Burma 2007). Largely because of uncontrolled inflation, the great majority of Burmese are economically insecure, even people such as civil servants, teachers and small traders who have middle-class occupations and average incomes higher than the rural or informal sector majority. The SPDC's decree had a shattering impact on the daily lives of practically everyone in central Burma, save the richest and best connected. In cities like Rangoon and Mandalay, public transportation became unaffordable for tens of thousands of commuters, who were obliged to walk to work, and even wealthier city dwellers who had cars often could not afford to fill their petrol tanks.

Food prices, especially for rice, increased due to the higher cost of bringing it in from rural areas, endangering the very survival of many ordinary Burmese who spend as much as 70–80 per cent of their total income on food each month. Observers believe that the jump in fuel prices pushed a large percentage of the population, perhaps more than half, below the poverty line (AAN on Burma 2007). Due to the poor quality of the electric power grid and the frequency of blackouts, most shops and factories in Burma rely on petrol-powered generators, which, became prohibitively expensive to operate after the abolition of fuel subsidies. Teashops and small restaurants not only could not afford to serve their customers, but the latter, hit hard by price increases in virtually every sector of the consumer economy, also cut back on all but the most essential purchases (AAN on Burma 2007; Human Rights Watch 2007: 23–4).

The SPDC never gave an explanation for the price rises. Older Burmese could not help but recall an earlier government economic initiative, the Ne Win regime's sudden demonetisation order on 5 September 1987 that made 70–80 per cent of all *kyat* (Burmese currency) banknotes in circulation worthless, without compensation. The measure's purpose was to deal a blow to 'economic insurgency', the socialist-era black market. However, it did little to undermine the economic power of its targets (wealthy border area warlords and *hmaung-kho*, black market entrepreneurs), while it impoverished ordinary people from all walks of life, including legitimate, small-scale business people and traders, members of the middle class, university students, day labourers and 'sidecar' (trishaw) drivers. In Ne Win's Burma, most people kept their *kyat* savings in cash rather than in the unreliable state-controlled banking system and demonetisation caused their hard-earned savings to evaporate.

Soon after the 1987 demonetisation decree was announced, there were protests by university students and the government closed the universities and sent the students home. But the economic and social impact of the measure – the sudden impoverishment of millions of people – was a major factor in stoking the popular rage that led to the massive protests of 1988. In turn, this led to the collapse of Ne Win-style socialism and the emergence of the pro-democracy movement led by Daw Aung San Suu Kyi, though not an end to military rule. According to Kyaw Yin Hlaing, the Ne Win regime's demonetisation was eventually self-destructive. As well as causing general economic havoc, it sundered patron–client ties between the *hmaung-kho* and high-ranking state and army officials: 'the old social equilibrium that had produced political and social stability in Myanmar [Burma] collapsed and the whole country was overrun by political chaos and violence' (Kyaw Yin Hlaing 2002: 88).

By 2007, Ne Win-era *hmaung-kho* had been replaced by a new generation of monopoly capitalists who had access both to the top generals and to foreign investment capital. However, there was an essential continuity in economic policies between the Ne Win and SLORC/SPDC state: both the 1962 army-state and its 1988 successor have viewed economic resources rather narrowly as something that the state has to 'capture' and control in order to make itself stronger (at the same time depriving potential opponents of economic power, by keeping them chronically insecure and poor). To ensure the regime's survival, much government spending (estimated at around 40 per cent of the total) has been diverted to expanding and modernising the armed forces since 1988. This has included purchasing expensive weapons from abroad (especially China), while public education and healthcare have been starved of funds, creating what observers consider to be a humanitarian crisis in the country, including a large AIDS epidemic and widespread malnutrition among children (M. Smith 1996: 2).

The 1987 demonetisation and the 2007 abolition of fuel subsidies also reveal a still more fundamental problem: the *isolation* of the army-state from the population it claims to have the right to govern in the name of national unity and 'disciplined democracy'. For the junta 'disciplined democracy' means authoritarian rule with a democratic façade (a constitution and multi-party system). The observant visitor to Burma soon learns that the geography of power is not much different from that of the British colonial era, when white *Thakins* ('masters') lived in a privileged world of their own, both spatially and psychologically distant from the Asian masses they controlled with a large and intimidating colonial army (Seekins 2010: 32–4).

Like the colonial elite, the top brass, such as Senior General Than Shwe, General Maung Aye and their fellow military officers, live in comfortable, well-guarded spaces (known in Burmese as *bogyoke ywa* or 'generals' villages) segregated from the humbler dwellings of ordinary citizens. They enjoy access to special shops, hospitals, schools and, after 1988, even a system of military-run universities, much better funded than those available to civilians. The most significant expression of the growing isolation of the state from society was top leader and SPDC Chairman Than Shwe's unexpected decision in late 2005 to relocate Burma's capital away from the crowded, tumultuous city of Rangoon to the entirely new city of Naypyidaw ('Abode of the King'), located in central Burma. This move was not only costly for the junta at a time when it could scarcely afford such monumental projects, but it also caused great hardship for civil servants, who were obliged to leave their families behind in Rangoon, and local people, who were forcibly relocated from their homes to make way for the construction of government ministries, residential areas and a huge Military Zone (Seekins 2009a: 63–70).

Following the 15 August 2007 announcement of the fuel price hikes, there were muted public protests whose participants attempted to draw attention to livelihood issues while steering clear of politics, hoping to avoid the regime's ire. One such demonstration was held on 19 August in Tamwe Township, north of downtown Rangoon. Attended by 400–500 people, it included leaders of the 1988 Student Generation, a group of veterans from the earlier struggle who at the time had been university students. The most prominent of the 1988 Student Generation people was Min Ko Naing, the famed 'conqueror of kings' (Min Ko Naing, is a *nom de guerre*; his original name was Paw Oo Tun). He announced the 8 August 1988 general strike against the Ne Win regime during the high tide of Democracy Summer and established the All Burma Federation of Student Unions. Working underground in Rangoon after the SLORC came to power, he was arrested in March 1989 and served two prison terms (1989–2004 and 2006–7) before being released in January 2007. Although the demonstration was peaceful, it was followed by a wave of arrests of most of the 1988 Student Generation leaders, including Min Ko Naing. The total number of detainees reaching 100 by 25 August (Human Rights Watch 2007: 23–5).

Subsequently, demonstrators in Rangoon were attacked and detained by regular security forces and toughs belonging to two pro-regime groups: the Union Solidarity and Development Association (USDA), a 'grassroots' organisation established in 1993 by Than Shwe; and the *Swan Arr Shin* ('Masters of Force'), a newer paramilitary group that has served as an auxiliary to the police and employs many local thugs, who are paid several thousand kyat a day for their services (Human Rights Watch 2007: 105–11). By the end of August, protests had spread to towns outside the old capital. Had the participants remained confined to members of the 1988 Student Generation, the opposition National League for Democracy and other opposition or civil society groups that struggle to survive in military-ruled Burma, the protests would have probably spluttered out as the SPDC stepped up its arrests and attacks by pro-regime bullies. But on 5 September 2007, a new element emerged during a demonstration by several hundred members of the *Sangha*, the community of Buddhist monks, in the town of Pakkoku, a major religious centre located not far from the old royal capital of Mandalay in Upper Burma. Like previous lay demonstrators, they demanded revocation of the 15 August price hikes. However, army, USDA and *Swan Arr Shin* personnel beat and humiliated several of the monks and there were rumours that one monk had been killed.

The following day, Pakkoku monks briefly took government officials and military officers hostage. A few days later, a new organisation called the 'All-Burma Monks Alliance' (ABMA) demanded an apology from the government for its abuse of the monks. It also demanded a lowering of commodity prices, the release of all political prisoners, including Daw Aung San Suu Kyi, and the beginning of genuine dialogue between the democratic opposition and the regime, setting a deadline of 17 September for an SPDC acceptance of these conditions. If their demands were not met, the monks vowed to impose a boycott on offerings to the *Sangha* given by members of the armed forces and other people connected to the regime. Known in Pali, the sacred language of Theravada Buddhism, as *patam nikkujjana kamma* and colloquially as 'overturning the offering bowl', the monks' refusal to accept offerings or participate in ceremonies connected with army-state personnel would deprive the latter of the major means of earning merit (*kutho* in Burmese). Such merit in the Theravada Buddhism of southeast Asia is essential to winning a happy rebirth in the cycle of *samsara* (death and rebirth) (Yeni 2007). The date of the deadline was historically resonant, since it was one day before the 18 September SLORC power seizure nineteen years before.

The SPDC sought to gain the support of senior monks through generous offerings. However, when it refused to respond to the ABMA's four demands, the alliance began its boycott on the deadline date with, it seems, the support, or at least the acquiescence, of a majority of Burma's 400,000 members of the *Sangha*. On 21 September, the ABMA issued a statement denouncing the 'evil military dictatorship', describing it as 'the common enemy of all our citizens' and committing its members to 'banish the common enemy evil regime from Burmese soil forever' (Human Rights Watch 2007: 30–2). This was not the first time that the *Sangha* had used the sanction of 'overturning the offering bowl' against the post-1988 military regime. In August 1990, after security forces shot monks during a demonstration in Mandalay, abbots at monasteries in the former royal city declared a similar boycott, which quickly spread to other cities, including Rangoon. Given the deeply conservative Buddhism of the army rank-and-file, this protest was possibly more threatening to the new SLORC's hold on power than the 27 May 1990 general election victory of Aung San Suu Kyi's National League for Democracy, which the junta refused to recognise. The regime moved quickly to halt the protest by raiding monasteries and arresting, defrocking and jailing hundreds of monks, including senior monks who had lent their moral authority to the protest (Human Rights Watch 2007: 32).

When the anti-SPDC boycott began on 17 September, the monk leaders organised demonstrations of members of the *Sangha* in the streets of Burma's major towns and cities, including Rangoon, Mandalay, Sittwe and Pakkoku. This movement became known as the 'Saffron Revolution', although the robes of Burmese monks are usually maroon or brown rather than yellow. According to one press report, however, some of the protesting monks wore saffron-coloured sashes (Booth 2007). On 22 September, police surprisingly allowed a procession of several hundred monks to walk to the house of Aung San Suu Kyi on University Avenue in northern Rangoon and she came to the gate to pay her respects. People got their first glimpse of the pro-democracy leader in over four years. She had been arrested and then placed under a renewed term of house arrest in 2003, following an attack on her and her supporters by USDA toughs in

Upper Burma on 30 May of that year. The impact on the public cannot be over-estimated, since she remains highly respected despite SPDC attempts to marginalise her (Kyaw Zwa Moe 2007). However, the police halted further attempts by monks to visit her.

By 24/25 September, as many as 100,000 monks and lay supporters joined together in protests in Rangoon, congregating at the Shwedagon Pagoda, the holiest site in Burmese Buddhism, and at the Sule Pagoda just across from the Rangoon City Hall located in the centre of the old colonial downtown. Both places have deep historical associations with the dynastic and colonial periods, and had been the locations of major demonstrations – and military shootings – during 1988. It was at the Shwedagon that Aung San Suu Kyi, speaking before a crowd of hundreds of thousands of people on 26 August 1988, declared that opposition to the Ne Win regime that year constituted 'the second struggle for national independence' (Aung San Suu Kyi 1995b: 193). Origin-ally, the monks discouraged lay people from joining in the demonstrations. By 25 September, however, when protesters seemed to be taking over Rangoon's streets and the security forces still maintained a low profile, they had stepped up their call for a nationwide movement to overthrow the military regime. Monk and lay street marchers carried pictures of Gotama Buddha, Buddhist flags and the red 'fighting peacock' banner of the old, politically active student unions and renewed calls for Aung San Suu Kyi's release from house arrest.

Predictably, the junta cracked down. Beginning on 26 September, troops and riot police were stationed in strategic parts of Rangoon, especially around the Shwedagon, and fired tear gas, rubber bullets and live ammunition at the protesters. One observer reported that soldiers in red bandanas had the authority to shoot people in the street, while those wearing green or yellow ones could beat and arrest them (Guilford 2007). Monasteries were (as in 1990) raided, monks beaten, de-frocked and arrested, and thousands were detained at special holding centres in various parts of the city where they were subjected to inhuman conditions. The worst day for repression appears to have been 27 September, when the killing of peaceful demonstrators occurred at a high school in Tamwe Township in Rangoon, and around the Sule Pagoda (Saw Yan Naing 2007).

As photos and videos of the crackdown streamed out of Burma on the Internet, international indignation grew and the special envoy of the UN Secretary General to Burma, Ibrahim Gambari, made a special visit to the country to meet with Aung San Suu Kyi and Senior General Than Shwe. But by the end of the month, the streets of Rangoon and other towns had been largely cleared of protesters, and the authorities were ruthlessly hunting down monk and lay dissidents who had gone underground (Wai Moe 2007). On 4 November, the regime arrested the prominent monk U Gambira, leader of the ABMA, and later sentenced him to sixty-eight years in prison (AAN on Burma 2007; Than Htike Oo 2008).

Secular and Sacred Protest: Students, Buddhist Monks and Politics

There are major differences between the popular uprising of 1988 and the 2007 'Saffron Revolution'. The former was far larger in scale and longer in duration, involving millions of mostly urban protesters nationwide throughout a period of over six months. The 2007 movement involved as many as 100,000 in the former capital city and some demonstrations in other towns, but lasted, at most, about six weeks before the SPDC effectively suppressed resistance. The 1988 movement succeeded in toppling the Ne Win socialist regime, though it did not (as mentioned above) end military rule. The 'Saffron Revolution' had few concrete results, save from adding to the intense alienation between state and society that has been evident in some form from the early 1960s. However, the 'Saffron Revolution' was less costly in human lives, due to the security forces' greater use of non-lethal weapons, such as rubber bullets, tear gas and clubs. As mentioned above, thousands died in the streets of Burma's towns and cities in 1988 at the hands of the security forces; credible estimates of the number of victims of the 2007 crackdown range from at least thirty-one during the crackdown and sixteen in detention (including nine monks) to over a hundred (AAN on Burma, 2007).

The two movements also represent different facets of popular resistance, alternative though not mutually exclusive sacred and secular forms of protest that together constitute a *tradition of resistance* to the state with roots going back to at least the British colonial period. The chief agents and organisers of resistance in 1988 were university student activists such as Min Ko Naing. The genesis of such student protest reaches back to the establishment of the University of Rangoon in 1920; student demonstrations against British educational and other policies (which often took place in or near the precincts of the Shwedagon Pagoda) in the 1930s; and the public prominence of the Rangoon University Students Union before the Second World War. The most important student leaders were major figures of the independence movement, such as Aung San and U Nu. Students remained politically active during the Ne Win era, but following the SLORC power seizure, the army-state has kept universities closed, relocated the campuses to remote areas outside Rangoon to discourage contact between students and ordinary citizens, and promoted distance education, usually with very low standards, to keep students isolated from each other. Although there were renewed student demonstrations around the Rangoon University main campus in late 1996, by the opening years of this century, it was apparent that regime attempts to undermine their unity and activism had met with success. It was veterans of the 1988 Student Generation and not young students who were the main secular force behind the September 2007 demonstrations.

Monks, with their own tradition and narrative of resistance, have tremendous moral authority, which is closely connected to Burma's very national identity as the 'land of the Buddha'. In that sense, pagoda-building generals and militant monks not only struggle over specific political and economic issues, but also over the kind of Buddhist country Burma must be: in other words, will the religion be promoted from the top down by the army-state elite, or will it be nurtured within society, among ordinary monks and lay people, largely independent of state control? In other Buddhist countries such as Thailand, these two forms of the religion have been able to co-exist, but the SPDC regards any independent social force as a threat to its very existence. Despite the severe battering that the *Sangha* received at the hands of the SPDC in 2007, the active role that monks played in getting relief to victims of Cyclone

Nargis, which caused as many as 140,000 deaths in the Irrawaddy Delta southwest of Rangoon in May 2008, shows that their moral authority as 'sons of the Buddha' and their status as initiators of defiance, if not resistance, in the face of the army-state remains intact (Seekins 2009b: 717–37).

Since 1988, the SLORC/SPDC junta have tried to place themselves in the traditional Burmese ruler's role as patron and protector of the Buddhist religion, sponsoring ambitious merit-building projects, such as the construction or renovation of pagodas and generous offerings to compliant members of the *Sangha* or community of Buddhist monks. Indeed, the post-1988 period has witnessed what one observer has called a 'Buddhist building boom' (Fraser-Lu 1997: 4–5). In a major development in state–*Sangha* relations, the Ne Win regime in May 1980 gained the senior monks' acceptance of a new organisational framework for the monkhood under tight state control. This enabled his army successors to keep its upper ranks generally coopera-tive, even if lower ranking and younger monks tended to be more critical of the regime. However, as mentioned above, it seems that a majority of the monkhood on all levels backed, or at least did not oppose, the September 2007 boycott.

According to Buddhist doctrine, monks, a distinct category of men separate from and spiritually superior to lay men and women, must stay completely clear of worldly matters. It is their status as ascetics or mendicants striving for spiritual liberation (*nibbana* in Pali [Sanskrit: *nirvana*]) that makes them the most respected group in Burmese Buddhist society. To achieve this highest spiritual state, they live a simple life, meditate and study the Buddhist scriptures. Monks preach the Buddha's teachings (Pali: *dhamma* [Sanskrit: *dharma*]) to lay people, recite sacred texts (which many people believe have magical or protective powers) and advise influential lay people on religious matters. Some errant monks dabble in the occult. But their chief significance in the eyes of lay people is their role as 'fields of merit', recipients of *dana* (offerings) from ordinary people seeking to enhance their sum of accumulated merit. One of the most common scenes in daily life in Theravada Buddhist countries such as Burma, Thailand and Cambodia is groups of monks carrying offering bowls and walking through villages or city neighbourhoods receiving food from householders in the early morning.

As ascetics, monks' involvement in politics in any way would seem to be anathema, though senior monks in the dynastic period occasionally criticised the king for moral lapses or heresy. During the early twentieth century, however, when Burma was a province of British India, groups of monks known as 'political *pongyis*' (*pongyi* is a Burmese title for monks) demonstrated, sometimes in a very disorderly fashion, against colonial rule. The most prominent activist monk, U Ottama (1897–1939), claimed that British rule had not only increased the influence of non-Buddhist religions, especially Christianity, but had also, through profit-oriented economic exploitation, made Burmese Buddhist people so poor that they could not afford to do acts of merit. Because the Burmese had been 'enslaved' by the British colonialists, they could not strive to achieve *nibbana*. U Ottama concluded that under such dire conditions, the first duty of monks was not to meditate or preach the *dhamma*, but to actively fight colonialism (D. Smith 1965: 96–7, 103). Thus, U Ottama justified direct monk participation in opposition politics, and young members of the *Sangha* proved to be ideal political activists, because large numbers of them were concentrated in major monasteries, especially in Mandalay and Rangoon, which became centres of anti-colonial resistance. Their religious pursuits left them much free time and also freed them from family ties that might otherwise have inhibited activism, and the British (unlike the post-colonial indigenous army-state) were reluctant to respond in too heavy-handed a manner towards men who were revered by local society as 'sons of the Buddha' (D. Smith 1965: 96–7).

During the 1930s, the focus of nationalist, anti-colonial resistance shifted away from the monks to secular activists, including members of the Burmese urban professional class such as lawyers and journalists, but especially to university students such as Aung San Suu Kyi's father, independence leader Aung San, and independent Burma's first prime minister, U Nu. But throughout the colonial, parliamentary (1948–62) and army-state periods, younger and to a lesser extent senior members of the *Sangha* lent their support to anti-state resistance. They joined students on the campus of Rangoon University in a massive movement to protest the Ne Win regime's disrespectful attitude towards the late UN Secretary General U Thant by refusing to grant him a state funeral in December 1974. They also marched in the streets alongside student activists and other lay people in the 'Democracy Summer' of 1988 (Seekins 2010: 127–31). It is significant that when U Ottama was arrested and sentenced by the British for stirring up unrest in the early 1920s, a meeting of 1,500 monks at the Shwedagon Pagoda vowed to carry out a similar movement to 'overturn the offering bowl', whose targets were Burmese magistrates and witnesses for the prosecution who cooperated with the colonial authorities during his trial (D. Smith 1965: 103).

Given the high status of Buddhist monks in Burmese society and the resources that the army-state and its supporters have spent on Buddhist pagoda-building and other religious projects as a way of gaining legitimacy, the violent way in which it has treated dissident members of the *Sangha* seems paradoxical. Many monks were killed in 1988 and 2007. Despite the venerable tradition that the *Sangha* must be self-governing and self-disciplining, since 1962 the army-state has taken on for itself the role of defining who is a 'real' (that is, cooperative and compliant) monk, and who is a 'counterfeit' one (that is, a monk who is politically active, engaged in anti-state activities), who can be dealt with using the same lethal violence that is used against rebellious lay people.

Conclusion: Democracy and Traditions of Secular and Sacred Resistance

In conclusion, democratic practices have been very weakly institutionalised in military-run Burma since Ne Win's coup d'état in March 1962. The National League for Democracy, for example, has not been allowed to function as a real political party despite its May 1990 election victory, and it was abolished by the SPDC when those of its leaders not in jail or under house arrest refused to register for the junta-engineered general election held on 7 November 2010. Local promoters of civil society activism have most frequently found themselves in jail or harassed by the regime's growing ranks of paramilitary bully-boys. In one sense, Burma is among the least democratic states in Asia. Freedoms are minimal and the state is ever on the watch to crush dissent, however moderate or non-violent. However, the popular tradition of resistance to the state, which forms an integral part of the nation's history and identity, means that as long as the army-state does not reform itself from within (which is highly improbable, at least in the near future) the (covert and overt) conflict between the aloof state and the people it claims the right to rule will continue. And popular memories of sacred and secular resistance to the state in the past will inspire people to continue to believe that things can change, that the military-run status quo can finally be replaced with a government more responsive to the needs and hopes of ordinary citizens.

References

Alternative Asean Network (AAN) on Burma (2007), *Saffron Revolution: Recap*.

Aung San Suu Kyi (1995a), *Freedom from Fear and Other Writings*, ed. M. Aris, rev. edn, London: Penguin.

Aung San Suu Kyi (1995b), 'Speech to a Mass Rally at the Shwedagon Pagoda', in *Freedom from Fear and Other Writings*, ed. M. Aris, rev. edn, London: Penguin, pp. 192–8.

Booth, J. (2007), 'Military Junta Threatens Monks in Burma', *The Times*, on-line, 24 September.

Boudreau, V. (2004), *Resisting Dictatorship: Repression and Protest in Southeast Asia*, Cambridge: Cambridge University Press.

Fink, C. (2009), *Living Silence in Burma: Surviving under Military Rule*, 2nd edn, London: Zed Books.

Fraser-Lu, S. (1997), '"A Buddhist Building Boom"': Works of Merit Sponsored by the State Law and Order Restoration Council', *Bulletin of the Burma Studies Group*, 59, 4–5.

Guilford, G. (2007), 'Burma after the Crackdown: Waiting for the Military to Turn on their Generals', *Slate*, on-line magazine, 15 October.

Human Rights Watch (2007), *Crackdown: Repression of the 2007 Popular Protests in Burma*, 19(18(c)), December.

Kyaw Yin Hlaing (2002), 'The Politics of Government–Business Relationships in Myanmar', *Asian Journal of Political Science*, 10(1), 77–104.

Kyaw Zwa Moe (2007), 'Suu Kyi Greets Monks at her Home; 10,000 Monks Demonstrate in Mandalay'. *The Irrawaddy*, 22 September.

Lintner, B. (1989), *Outrage: The Struggle for Democracy in Burma*, Hong Kong: Review Publishing.

Saw Yan Naing (2007), 'Witnesses say September 27 was the Worst', *The Irrawaddy*, on-line, 8 October.

Seekins, D. (2009a), '"Runaway Chickens" and Myanmar Identity: Relocating Burma's Capital', *City*, 13(1), 63–70.

Seekins, D. (2009b), 'State, Society and Natural Disaster: Cyclone Nargis in Myanmar (Burma)', *Asian Journal of Social Science*, 37, 717–37.

Seekins, D. (2010), *State and Society in Modern Rangoon*, Abingdon: Routledge.

Smith, D. (1965), *Religion and Politics in Burma*, Princeton, NJ: Princeton University Press.

Smith, M. (1996), *Fatal Silence? Freedom of Expression and the Right to Health in Burma*, London: Article 19.

Than Htike Oo (2008), 'U Gambira to Serve Total of 68 Years in Prison', *Mizzima*, 21
    November.
Wai Moe (2007), 'Prominent Student Leader Arrested', *The Irrawaddy*, 13 October.
Wakeman, C. and S. S. Tin (2009), *No Time for Dreams: Living in Burma under Military Rule*,
    Lanham, MD: Rowman & Littlefield.
Yeni (2007), 'Burmese Monks Demand Government Apology', *The Irrawaddy*, 10 September.

Chapter 36

China since Tiananmen Square

Baogang He

In the wake of the 1989 Tiananmen Square event, the Chinese government has both tightened its authoritarian rule and introduced a wide variety of local mini-democratisation practices, including village elections, township elections, intra-party democracy, participatory and deliberative forums, and participatory budgeting. While these do not jeopardise the monopoly of the Chinese Communist Party (CCP) on political decision making, they illustrate major trends and characteristics of Chinese democratisation and highlight the Chinese hybrid model of democratisation. This chapter focuses on official democratic mechanisms and institutions initiated at the local level, rather than on more general aspects of democratisation, such as rights movements, the media, freedom of speech and the legal protection of rights, which seem to be where most of the retreats from democracy have occurred in recent years.

The meaning of democracy in the Chinese context has had a particular trajectory, and it is important to understand Chinese democratic progress in Chinese terms, rather than just in the more Western terms of multi-party competition through periodic elections. Chinese local democratisation has been led by reformers to improve governance practices that allow for greater public participation while maintaining one-party dictatorship. Chinese local democratisation exhibits elements of Confucian influence in the emphasis on the concept of *minben*, or people-centred governance (He 2010a). In this way the push for democracy in places like Hangzhou, for example, has been facilitated by efforts to improve the people's welfare. The government calls it 'improving the people's livelihood through democracy'. As will be discussed, Chinese local democratisation possesses several identifiable characteristics and has developed along several distinctive pathways.

Village Elections

A quiet process of democratisation started in rural China when village elections were introduced in 1987 through the promulgation of the Provisional Organic Law of Village Committees. In the wake of the collapse of the People's Commune System, rural China encountered challenging issues regarding local stability and order. In order to fill the organisational vacuum and re-establish local order, villagers in Guangxi created autonomous village organisations and introduced village elections in 1979 (He 2007).

Through various forms of protest, villagers have resisted official manipulation and demanded free and fair elections. They have resisted election procedures they consider to be unfair, irregular or corrupt by refusing to pay tax. Such resistance has forced the state to adopt and promote open and transparent procedures; in particular, the state has endorsed *haixuan* (naming from the floor or direct nomination for candidates) to resolve practical problems. For example, in Zhejiang, party secretaries appointed candidates in village elections. Such a practice was justified by one official in the Ministry of Civil Affairs in Beijing as normal since party leaders decide candidates in all elections in China (Personal communication October 29, 1994). The appointment of candidates by party secretaries, however, faced resistance from villagers who did not vote for the officially nominated candidates. Sometimes, official candidates lost elections and sometimes elections failed to produce any village leader, thus leading to a vacuum in village governance. To overcome this practical problem, some villages experimented with direct nomination by villagers, and township leaders had to make a compromise by allowing villagers to nominate candidates.

In the process of resisting manipulated elections, villagers invented and practised *haixuan*, which originated in Lishu County, Jilin Province (China Association 1994; Jing 1999). In one village, 571 out of 693 eligible voters took part in *haixuan* (Chan 1998). *Haixuan* was quickly adopted in the Xiangtan and Suining counties of Hunan Province, as well as five counties and two districts in Gansu Province. *Haixuan* was ultimately endorsed in the 1998 Organic Law. Article 14 stipulates: 'In village elections, candidates should be nominated directly by the eligible voters of the village, with the number of candidates exceeding the number of positions available' (*Zhejiang Daily* 2003). *Haixuan* has dramatically increased the competitiveness of the village elections in many localities. Between April and July 1999, 786 villages in the Yuyao municipality held elections under the Organic Law of Village Committees. The ratio of candidates to positions was 48:1, which was unprecedented in the history of village elections (Yuyao Committee of CCP 1999). In Laofangqiao, a township selected by the Yuyao municipality for test elections, the villagers nominated 959 candidates for the fifty-seven open seats. The candidate–seat ratio was 17:1, promising intense competition.

Competition was also intensified as elections shifted from 'one-candidate' elections, which dominated in 1994, to 'multiple-candidates' elections, which dominated in 1998–9. The Tongxiang municipality of Zhejiang is a good example. In late 1992, what was then Tongxiang County held its second round of village elections. Of its 306 villages, 244 (86.9 per cent) took the non-competitive approach: the same number of candidates for the same number of positions. Only forty villages (13.1 per cent) held semi-competitive elections. By 1998, however, as Zhang Biao has found in his case study of the elections in the ten administrative villages of Taoyuan township in July of that year, competitive elections were common. Quite a large number of villagers nominated themselves as candidates for village committee positions. As the township government made no effort to limit the number of candidates, elections became very competitive (B. Zhang 1998).

The idea of village democracy included an assembly in which all adult villagers participated and made major decisions over village affairs. It was, however, difficult for this to be realised in practice due to many constraints. The first reason has to do with the size of the village, which generally is between 1,000 and 3,000 individuals, but some villages can have as many as 8,000–10,000 people. The second reason has to do with location. In some mountainous parts, a village committee may cover several natural villages, scattered over a large area. The third reason is due to the fact that with the production mode of household responsibility, with no commonly set work schedule, it is difficult to find a time that suits everybody. Finally, in some villages the majority of the labour force may have left to work in cities and/or do business in other areas (Working Committee 1998). Consequently, villages have instituted village representative assemblies (VRAs), which involve representatives who are either elected by villagers or households, or selected by village party secretaries or village committees. By 1997, 50 per cent of the villages in China had instituted VRAs. The rate was even higher in the provinces of Liaoning, Jilin, Fujian, Shangdong, Hubei and Sichuan (Tang and Na 1999).

The timing and the number of the meetings vary in different areas. In Beiwang village, 'the VRA is particularly active, meeting on the third day of every month' (Lawrence 1994). Diyiqiao village holds at least two meetings each year in July and November, respectively. Xiacun village also has two meetings in March and September. Laiwang village has four meetings each year, presided over by the village committee. These figures are consistent with Oi's and Rozelle's 1995 survey finding that the average number of meetings of VRAs is 2.76 meetings a year (Oi and Rozelle 2000). According to a survey by Yang Min, 57.8 per cent of respondents in 1990 and 73.3 per cent in 1996 confirmed that they participated in VRAs only one or two times a year, while 32.7 per cent and 20.7 per cent participated several times a year (Yang 2000). In Kent Jennings' survey, 47 per cent of the respondents reported that they went to all-village meetings, and David Zweig's fieldwork revealed that 16.4 per cent of the 3,078 respondents turn to their village assembly for help if village cadres carry out unfair policies (Jennings 1997; Zweig 2002). The VRA served as the body that decided the final candidate for village elections, with one survey demonstrating that 40.5 per cent of the final candidates for village elections were decided through VRAs in 1998 in Zhejiang (He 2007: 94).

In recent years, village leaders, recognising the importance of the VRAs, are using these meetings more frequently in their decision-making process. One such example is Shuangqiao village in Chengjiao township of Wenzhou. Believing it would pay off in the long run, the village leaders bought a four-storey office building from a business company for 8 million RMB. However, since the deal was made without any consultation in advance with the village representative meeting, some villagers grew angry and suspicious. They challenged village leaders and demanded a say in the decision-making process, and they went to the leadership above to voice their anger and suspicion, which did not die down until six months later. Drawing from its experience of this incident, the village committee began to pay more attention to the views of the representative meeting. Consequently, in the latter half of the year 2000 alone, there were as many as ten meetings held.

Intra-Party Democracy

The CCP is one of the oldest and certainly the largest political party in the world. It is also the wealthiest, with the politburo and central organisation claiming control of forty-two gigantic corporations. As the most powerful organisation in the nation, it has full command over all government and military services. The power of the CCP has been increasing, but this growth in power is accompanied by widespread ideas and experiments in intra-party democracy. There has been a progressive push to promote internal party democracy and generate innovative solutions (He 2010b).

Intra-party democracy is 'inspired by CCP assessment of the causes of collapse of the Soviet Communist Party in the Soviet Union' (Shambaugh 2008). The demise of the Communist Party of the Soviet Union (CPSU) in 1991 was particularly alarming for CCP officials in Beijing. The mechanisms of self-destruction, or the processes of disintegration, are threefold. The bottom-up process is the collapse of local organisations. The centrifugal process is the use of party organisations by ethnic groups for their independence or the dismantling of party branches in the peripheral republican states. The top-down process is the split of the core organisation at the centre. For the CCP, the lesson is in how to prevent the three processes from occurring (Central Institute 2007). In 2002, at the Sixteenth National Congress of the Communist Party of China, intra-party democracy was confirmed as fundamental to the future survival of the CCP. Reform of the party's leadership and rules of governance was considered a foremost priority.

The purpose of intra-party democracy is to guide, protect and promote initiatives. In the experiment of Ya'an in 2003, party representatives were granted five basic rights: the right to elections; the right to discuss major policies; the right to evaluate party leaders; the right to monitor; and the right to propose a motion. Ten or twenty permanent party representatives are able to put forward a motion in the Party Congress. The relevant party or government organisation must answer an inquiry made by any permanent party representative within three to six months. Moreover, in exercising these rights, party representatives are protected by state laws and the party disciplinary committee. The party secretaries have no right to arbitrarily remove party representatives. In July 2008, the central party organisation introduced a new regulation, which provides full protection to the rights of party representatives. In particular, it provided party members with sufficient funding to exercise the right to contribute to the formulation of major policies, such as carrying out an investigation. It also provided party representatives with the right to attend committee meetings and to evaluate the performance of committee members.

A rejuvenation of the party means empowering party representatives. Party democracy needs its own parliament, just as national democracy is dependent on a national parliament. The Permanent System of Party Representatives (PSPR) is the parliament of the party where party representatives engage in deliberation and debate on major policies. In the past, party representatives were restricted from engaging in policy formation after their attendance at meetings. In the PSPR, however, there are *permanent* positions for the period of the Party Congress, 'permanent' in the sense that party representatives exercise daily rights and powers. The PSPR was originally suggested by Mao Zedong and proposed by Deng Xiaoping in 1956. At the Thirteenth Party Congress, Zhao Ziyang's team proposed that a PSPR be established. In 1988, the central party organisation approved twelve experimental sites for this, among them Jiaojiang and Shaoxing. Before the Sixteenth Party Congress, seven out of twelve sites stopped their experiments. The system was improved in Ya'an, however, in August 2002.

In the past, party election was only a formality. However, in Ya'an, Yinjin County, party representatives were competitively elected in August 2003. Among the 5,800 party members, 736 (that is 12.7 per cent of party membership) ran for election, 241 were decided as final candidates and 166 were elected as party representatives. During the election process, seventeen party leaders at township level lost their positions. Several initiatives were taken so that a Party Representative Congress could be held more frequently and more efficiently. The size of the constituency of party representatives was reduced so that one representative could make close contact with, and represent, about a hundred party members. The standing committee and the alternate member system were also abolished to make the Party Representative Congress a decision-making body. Ya'an also set up a new institution for party representatives called the Party Representative Liaison Office. In 2003, in an annual Party Congress in Ya'an, all major leaders were evaluated by party representatives, 40 per cent of whom had to be ordinary members. Crucially, if any leader did not gain a confidence vote of over 70 per cent, a dismissal process would begin automatically against him or her. In practice, a first no-confidence vote will result in such a leader being given a warning and a year to improve his or her work. Dismissal only occurs after a second no-confidence vote.

Ordinary citizens are involved in democratic evaluation. In July 2008, the central party organisation entrusted the State Bureau of Statistics to carry out an independent survey of 80,000 citizens. The survey examined satisfaction levels regarding the performance of cadres and the process of appointing cadres. The result of the social survey influenced future political appointments and promotions (*Nanfang Ribao* 2008).

Political parties around the world are experiencing a loss of connection with the community. While the CCP is not an exception to this rule, it has worked hard to address the issue of representation. In an attempt to safeguard its legitimacy, the CCP has developed non-electoral forms of representation. The introduction of the 'Three Represents' concept has been particularly significant in maximising inclusiveness and representation. In February 2000, in Guangdong, Jiang Zemin proposed the concept of the 'Three Represents' (*san ge dai biao*), that is, the CCP represents the 'most advanced mode of production, the most advanced culture, and the interests of the majority of the population'. Jiang Zemin seemed to realise that the CCP had to reposition itself to be representative of the whole nation instead of just being the vanguard of the working class. Given that the private entrepreneur class forms a large part of 'the most advanced mode of production', Jiang Zemin proposed that the party should recruit more members from this new class. The proposal was adopted in the Sixteenth Party Congress, marking a significant change in the nature of the CCP, and radically transforming it from being representative of the working class and peasants to being representative of all social classes, including the new entrepreneur class. Now in Ya'an, the party branch in each village is required to recruit between two and five private entrepreneurs into the party each year.

Development of Participatory and Deliberative Institutions

China has a long-standing tradition of discussion and deliberation on community-related issues at the local level. Centuries ago Confucian scholars established public forums in which they debated and deliberated national affairs. During Mao's time, the 'mass line' emphasised the need for public consultation to give value to the voice of the people in the political process. In contemporary China, however, some of these institutions are characterised by a number of institutional innovations involving detailed procedures of how deliberative meetings should be conducted; they respond to the needs of people through the articulation and aggregation of individual preferences and interests, mixed with voting, giving a far more 'democratic' design than previously encountered within China.

Since the middle and late 1990s, some villages have developed village representative meetings wherein major decisions on village affairs are discussed, debated and deliberated upon by village representatives. Local urban communities have also developed a number of new participatory and deliberative institutions. The Chinese consultative meeting or public hearing is designed to get people's support for local projects and to be a forum for people's opinions. The popular conciliation or mediation meeting is designed to solve various local problems and conflicts. In the Shangcheng district of Hangzhou, a consensus conference or consultation meeting is held once a month. Citizen evaluation, first introduced in Shangdong and Shengyang, and then in Shanghai and Hangzhou, is designed to give the ordinary people an opportunity to rate and evaluate the performance of local cadres. The rating seriously affects the political career or the level of performance bonus of local cadres (He 2006).

The practice of holding public hearings has also developed at the national level. In 1996, the first national law on administrative punishment introduced an Article stipulating that a public hearing must be held before any punishment is given. Another, the famous Article 23 of the Law on Price passed by China's National Congress in December 1997, specified that the price of public goods must be decided through public hearing. This was followed by the Law on Legislature, passed in 2000, which requires public hearings to be an integral part of the decision-making process for all legal regulations and laws. More than fifty cities have now held legislative public hearings. On 29 September 2005, a public hearing was held by the National People's Congress Standing Committee to decide whether the central government should raise the personal income-tax threshold.

Wenling City's progress is a good example of successful integration of deliberative institutions. It is a county-level city with a vibrant private economy. In 2004, it was awarded the national prize for Innovations and Excellence in Local Chinese Governance. From 1996 to 2000, more than 1,190 deliberative and consultative meetings were held at the village level, 190 at the township level and 150 in governmental organisations, schools and business sectors. Such meetings are called *kentan*, meaning 'sincere heart-to-heart discussion'. Some meetings were 'one shot' discussions, that is, sessions dealing with only one topic and that meet only once. Others were continuing discussions about more complex matters or a series of matters. For example, five deliberative meetings were held to deal with the relocation of the fishery industry. Some meetings were just consultative without connecting with decision-making directly, while others were well connected to policy decision making through the local People's Congresses.

The development of participatory and deliberative institutions in Wenling has involved four stages (Mo and Yiming 2005). In the first stage, local leaders found that traditional ideological mobilisation did not work as a mode of persuasion. In 1996, a democratic 'heart-to-heart' forum was therefore invented to give villagers a genuine opportunity to express their grievances and complaints. However, the villagers who experienced this democratic forum soon discovered that it was a forum for discussion only, not for decision making. Their political enthusiasm decreased, the turn-out rate dropped and disillusion followed. In the second stage, in order to continue to attract people, the local officials turned this discussion forum into a decision-making mechanism. By 2000, local leaders responded to participants' questions and made decisions on the spot.

The third development, in 2004, was a democratic discussion forum attended by the deputies of the local People's Congress. Local leaders had discovered that if the issue being considered was controversial, decisions made in deliberative meetings gained support from some, but faced opposition from others. In order to defuse its responsibility and gain legitimacy for the policy on any controversial issue, the local party organisation decided that deputies of the local People's Congress should vote on certain difficult issues in a deliberative meeting – and the result of voting constituted a final decision that overrode the authority of the local party secretary. Leaders held the view that the only reliable and indisputable source of legitimacy is democratic voting, which generates a basis for public will on certain disputable issues. This is an institutional innovation that combines deliberative institutions with the empowerment so sorely lacking in much experimental deliberative democracy in the West.

In the fourth stage, in 2005, Wenling introduced China's first experiment in deliberative polling on a budget issue, adopting methods of social science to deliver a scientific basis for public policy. Wenling officials realised the deficiencies of their deliberative meetings, such as unscientific representation and insufficient time for a full discussion. Accordingly, they accepted advice from James Fishkin and Baogang He to use a random sampling method to select the participants to avoid selection bias and to provide well-balanced information to all the participants, who would spend an entire day deliberating over the town's budget issue. Officials in Zeguo altered the device by elevating the poll's outcomes from their common exemplary or advisory status to an empowered status by committing in advance of the process to abide by the outcomes (Fishkin *et al.* 2010). In 2006, ten out of twelve projects chosen through deliberative polling were implemented. The device further evolved when the government opened every detail of the city's budget to participants.

Nevertheless, in other places like Chengdu, some so-called randomly selected citizens have been exposed as 'fake citizens' who seem to have been chosen by government officials (Bandurski 2011). The overall pattern is one of 'authoritarian deliberation': that is, a high density of talk-based politics within the context of government-defined agendas and formal government control of outcomes (He and Warren 2011). Most power remains in the hands of unelected elites, operating within the structures of one-party domination, and without the kind of empowerments and protections necessary for democratic inclusion (Nathan 2003). Party officials still decide whether or not to introduce deliberative meetings, determine the agenda, as well as the extent to which the people's opinion will be taken into account. They seek to avoid spillover into non-approved topics, keeping deliberations to specific topics. Although there are divisions of power among layers of government and between agencies, there are no effective separations of powers within government and no independent oversight bodies – though in some areas the judicial system operates with increasing autonomy (Peerenboom 2002).

Participatory Budgeting

While the Brazilian idea and practice of participatory budgeting (PB) was officially introduced to China in the late 1990s (Chen 2007), Chinese villages have been practising a form of PB since the early 1990s. Villagers or village representatives have been participating in citizen processes that have involved the monitoring of budgeting items, ensuring that village leaders collect money for public goods, distribute village income in a fair way and invest village money effectively (Cai and Yuan 2005; Feng 2007). It was not called 'PB' as such, but rather 'the openness of the village account' or 'democratic management of the village account'.

In 1991, the local People's Congress in Shenzhen set up a budget committee in which deputies had an opportunity to examine the budget. In 1998, Hebei province introduced sector budgeting; partial budgets were disclosed to the examination and deliberation of the People's Deputies of the People's Congress. In 2004, the Huinan township in Shanghai undertook an experiment in public budgeting. This was followed by a similar experiment in Xinhe and Zeguo townships in 2005. 'Street-level' PB was introduced between 2006 and 2008 in Wuxi and Helongjiang. Here, a dozen or so street-level administrations organised PB projects that were impressive in scale and mobilisation.

The deputies' examination of the budget in Xinhe is a useful example (Chen and Chen 2007). In 2008, in Xinhe town, Wenling city, Zhejiang Province, citizens first participated in the early stages of the budget process by expressing their preferences and concerns. Then deputies were divided into three groups each examining the budget, followed by heated debates held in the local congress over each budget item. As an outcome of these debates, local deputies proposed a revised version of the overall budget. A final budget proposal was then voted on by the local deputies. During one two-hour session in Xinhe on 23 February 2008, the majority of deputies demanded an increase in a certain section of the budget and voted down government expenses on cars.

The PB experiment has also moved up to city level. In Wenling, Zhejiang Province, more than eighty participants from sixteen towns discussed the public transportation sector budget on 13 January 2008. Four small group discussions were held in the morning and one plenary session in the afternoon. Many suggestions were made. For example, it was proposed that the maintenance cost of village-to-village roads should be included in the city budget, with the limited funds available being used as effectively as possible. It was recommended that the subsidy for senior citizens should not be included in the transportation budget, as this would be seen as corruption (X. Zhang 2008).

The above experiments can be seen as a Chinese form of monitory democracy (Keane 2009). Apart from participatory budgeting, China has also developed a variety of mechanisms and institutions to monitor the government and promote official accountability at the local level. They may not involve electoral democracy, but they are an important part of public oversight. Social media as well as media outlets that operate within the official system have increased public scrutiny of officials, and the government has acknowledged the desirability of 'supervision by public opinion' (*yulun jiandu*). Media has played a significant role in promoting and spreading the idea of participatory budgeting.

In summary, some of the PB projects are showcases, some are substantive and others are a mix of both. The number of PB projects is still very small compared with the number of villages and townships. PB has only really just begun and there are a lot of problems associated with PB experiments. Nevertheless, the direction of PB is clear: more and more PB experiments are being introduced. For example, in the coastal province of Zhejiang, participatory budgeting was introduced in Xinhe and Zeguo townships in 2005, extended to eight neighbouring townships in 2009, to seventy-nine more in 2010, and to the city level in Wenling in 2010–11 (He 2011).

Conclusion

Democratisation in China has a particularly local character. This chapter has discussed in detail a variety of local reform initiatives and experiments in particular locations, but it remains difficult to draw broader conclusions about China as a whole because so many of these practices have their own local characteristics and some seem still to be fairly experimental. While it is clear that there is a great deal of dynamism and variety in the local democratisation process, the overall scale and level of institutionalisation of this process is difficult to perceive. In China, local governments and societies have been at the forefront of the democratisation process, but this highly localised character sometimes makes it harder to get a sense of overall progress or to generalise about democracy in China on a national scale.

The development of these reform practices is uneven across China. Regional differences have been a key feature of the process of Chinese local democratisation. In Sunan, in Jiangsu Province, for example, where the village economies are dominated by the government, past village elections have been more controlled by local officials than has been the case in Zhejiang, where the private sector dominates the economy and village elections have been more competitive (J. Zhang 2008).

There have been different levels and forms of consultative and deliberative institutions in the process of democratisation in different regions. In Zhejiang, more of a deliberative heart-to-heart dialogue has taken place during democratic consultations, whereas in Guangdong there has been a higher level of contestation, with workers striking or even committing suicide and grassroots trade unions being formed. Policies to encourage mass participation in politics have taken yet another form in Chongqing, where there has been a nostalgic campaign to get the public to sing the old revolutionary songs. In regions such as Tibet and Xinjiang, however, there have been few meaningful village elections. The case of Hong Kong is another example of regional variation that is often overlooked. The authoritarian state is able to live alongside and tolerate the freedom and vibrant civil society that exists there.

The Chinese state still maintains a Leninist political structure. Democracy, Premier Wen Jiabao said, is 'one hundred years away' – possible only when China becomes a 'mature socialist system' (MacDonald 2007). This will be a long and difficult process and it seems that gradual shifts are necessary to reduce the resistance from establishment forces. The best chance of success in making democratic progress lies in incremental change rather than revolutionary upheaval.

References

Bandurski, D. (2011), 'Online Scandal Alleges Public Hearings are Rigged', *China Media Project*, 15 July.

Cai, B. and S. Yuan (2005), 'Tuijin cunwu gongkai he minzhu guanli de xin qidian: dui mishan shi guanche luoshi zhongban shiqi hao wenjian de diaocha yu sikao' ('Promoting the Openness of Village Affairs and a New Starting Point of Democratic Management: Investigation and Reflection on Mishan City's Implementation of Document No.17'), *Zhongguo minzheng* (*China Civil Affairs*), 1, 35–7.

Central Institute for Party-building at the Central Organisation Department of CPC Central Committee (Zhonggong Zhongyang Zuzhi Bu Dangjian Yanjiusuo Ketizu) (2007), *Guowai Zhengdang Zhuanti Yanjiu Baogao* (*Foreign Political Party Research*). Dangjian Duwu Chuban She (Party Building Books Publishing House).

Chan, S. (1998), 'Research Notes on Villagers' Committee Election: Chinese-Style Democracy', *Journal of Contemporary China*, 7(19), 511.

Chen, J. (2007), 'Canyu shi yusuan de lilun yu shijian' ('Theory and Practice of Participatory Budgeting'), *Jingji shehui tizhi bijiao* (*Comparative Economic and Social Systems*), 130(2), 52–7.

Chen, J. and Y. Chen (2007), 'Difang zhili zhongde Canyu shi yusuan: guanyu zhejiang wenling shi xinhe zhen gaige de anli yanjiu' ('Participatory Budgeting in Local Governance: A Case Study of Reform from Xinhe Town, Zhejiang Province'), *Gonggong guanli xuebao* (*Journal of Public Management*), 4(3), 76–83.

China Association of Study of Grass-root Institutions & Research Team for Project of Chinese Village Autonomy (1994), *The Chinese Electoral System of Village Committee*, vol. 1993, Beijing: China Social Press, pp. 40–8.

Feng, Y. (2007), 'Guanyu cunwu gongkai he minzhu guanli zhidu jianshe de sikao' ('Reflection on the Openness of Village Accounts and the Construction of Democratic Management System'), *Dangzheng ganbu luntan* (*Cadres Tribune*), 10, 238–9.

Fishkin, J., B. He, R. C. Luskin and A. Siu (2010), 'Deliberative Democracy in an Unlikely Place: Deliberative Polling in China', *British Journal of Political Science*, 40(2), 435–48.

He, B. (2006), 'Participatory and Deliberative Institutions in China', in E. Leib and B. He (eds), *The Search for Deliberative Democracy in China*, New York: Palgrave, pp. 176–96.

He, B. (2007), *Rural Democracy in China*, New York: Palgrave Macmillan.

He, B. (2010a), 'Four Models of the Relationship between Confucianism and Democracy', *Journal of Chinese Philosophy*, 37(1), 18–33.

He, B. (2010b), 'China's Step toward Democratisation: Intraparty Democracy', in K. Lawson (ed.), *Political Parties and Democracy: vol.3: Post-Soviet and Asian Political Parties*, Santa Barbara, CA: Praeger, pp. 127–47.

He, B. (2011), 'Civic Engagement through Participatory Budgeting in China: Three Different Logics at Work', *Public Administration and Development*, 31(2), 122–33.

He, B. and M. Warren (2011), 'Authoritarian Deliberation: The Deliberative Turn in Chinese Political Development', *Perspectives on Politics*, 9(2), 269–89.

Jennings, K. (1997), 'Political Participation in Chinese Countryside', *American Political Science Review*, 91(2), 363.

Jing, Y. (1999), 'Haixuan shi zenyang cansheng de' ('The Origin of Haixuan'), *Kaifang shida* (*The Era of Opening up*), No. 3.

Keane, J. (2009), *The Life and Death of Democracy*, London: Simon & Schuster.

Lawrence, S. V. (1994), 'Democracy, Chinese Style', *Australian Journal of Chinese Affairs*, 32, 61–8.

McDonald, S. (2007), 'Wen: China Democracy 100 Years Off', *Time Magazine*, 1 March.

Mo, Y. and C. Yiming (2005), *Democratic Deliberation: The Innovation from Wenling*, Beijing: Central Compliance and Translation Press.

Nanfang Ribao (*South China Daily*), 14 July 2008, p. A02.

Nathan, A. (2003), 'Authoritarian Resilience', *Journal of Democracy*, 14, 6–17.

Oi, J. C. and S. Rozelle (2000), 'Elections and Power: The Locus of Decision-Making in Chinese Villages', *China Quarterly*, 162, 513–39.

Peerenboom, R. (2002), *China's Long March toward Rule of Law*, Cambridge: Cambridge University Press.

Shambaugh, D. (2008), *China's Communist Party: Atrophy and Adaptation*, Washington, DC: Woodrow Wilson Center Press.

Tang, X. and J. Na (1999), 'Zhongguo Nongcun zhengzhi minzhu fazhan de qianjing ji kunlan: zhidu jiaodu de fengxi' ('Prospects and Difficulties in the Development of Chinese Rural Democracy: an Institutional Point of View'), *Zhengzhixue yanjiu* (*Research in Political Science*), No. 1.

Working Committee of Legality of the NPC Standing Committee (1998), *Cunmin weiyuanhui zuzhifa duben* (*Organic Law of the Village Committee: A Reader*), Zhongguo minzhu fazhi chubanshe (China Democracy and Legality Press), pp. 53–4.

Yang, M. (2000), 'Participatory Consciousness and Behavior of Chinese Peasants', *Studies of Sociology*, 2, 67–75.

Yuyao Committee of CCP (1999), 'Yuyaoshi nongcun jichen zuzhi qingkuang zongji' ('Summary on the Conditions of Grass-root Units in Rural Yuyao').

Zhang, B. (1998), *Guanyu taoyuan cunminweiyuanhui xuanju de diaocha baogao* (*Report on Village Elections in Taoyuan*), Summer Investigation Report, Department of Political Science of Zhejiang University.

Zhang, J. (2008), *Marketization and Democracy in China*, London: Routledge.

Zhang, X. (2008), 'Shenhua gonggong yusuan gaige, zengqiang yusuan jiandu xiaoguo: guanyu Zhejiang Wenlin shi canyu shi yusuan de shijian yusikao' ('Deepening the Reform of the Public Budget and Enhancing the Effect of Budget Monitoring: The Practice and Thinking of Participatory Budgeting in Wenlin City, Zhejiang Province'), *Renda yanjiu* (*People's Congress Study*), 11, 19–22.

Zhejiang Daily, 5 November 2003, p. 5.

Zweig, D. (2002), *Democratic Values, Political Structures, and Alternative Politics in Greater China*, United States Institute of Peace, Peaceworks No. 44, July, p. 44.

Chapter 37

Islam since 9/11

Nader Hashemi

In international affairs, 11 September 2001 was a watershed day. This day will forever be associated with the terrorist attacks in New York and Washington, DC that resulted in the deaths of 3,000 people. Over the course of the next decade more than 7,500 American, British and other allied troops would lose their lives in the wars and occupations of Afghanistan and Iraq. Civilians, too, have been killed and, while exact figures are unknown and often ignored, the widely accepted conservative estimate is that more than 130,000 Iraqi and Afghan citizens have lost their lives during this same time period (Tirman 2011).

As a result, 9/11 has become *the* defining event of this generation. It has the same emotional resonance as the Vietnam War had for a previous generation in terms of shaping our economic, political and moral context. One of the key issues that surfaced in the aftermath of 9/11 was the relationship between Islam[1] and democracy. Knowledge that the attacks originated from within the Muslim world and were justified in the name of Islam led to a major rupture in Islam–West relations. It also led to a new global scrutiny and suspicion of Muslim societies that placed the topic of Islam and democracy at the top of the international agenda. An intense intellectual debate emerged that was sometimes accompanied by reductionist arguments and simplistic generalisations. Long-standing stereotypes about Islam, Arabs and the Middle East were often bandied about, mostly in right-wing political circles. Notwithstanding the ferment aroused by this topic, an interest in the relationship between Islam, Muslims and democracy, after such a cataclysmic event as 9/11, was entirely natural and understandable. The wars in Iraq and Afghanistan and the attempt by leading Western powers to create new democratic polities in these societies have given this topic a pressing new relevance.

Having examined the key schools of thought, points of contention and intellectual arguments on the relationship between Islam and democracy in previous work (Hashemi 2012), this chapter will examine many of the key interpretive themes that repeatedly hinder an objective assessment of this topic. While many of these themes have a long history in the Western interpretation of Muslim societies, they have resurfaced and been given greater global prominence since 9/11. Rejecting the claim of 'Muslim exceptionalism' that is rooted in the assertion that Islamic political thought is essentially anti-democratic, this chapter asserts an alternative analysis and set of arguments that is far more optimistic about the future of Muslim democracy. Recent scholarship and empirical developments on the ground will be utilised, but primarily this chapter is devoted to establishing a critical analytical framework where the reader can understand the subject of Islam and democracy historically and dispassionately.

While the 2011 'Arab Spring' has been widely celebrated in the West, the popularity of Islamist parties, the frequent references to *shariah* by key political actors and the ongoing violence in parts of the Arab world have cast a shadow of doubt over the prospect of democracy. These concerns are clearly warranted, yet a serious engagement with the topic demands that we go beyond emotionally charged references and engage the topic at a deeper historical and comparative level.

Interpretative Caveats on the Study of Non-Western Societies

There was more to the post-9/11 debate on Islam and democracy than a simple concern about the scarcity of democratic political systems in the Middle East. The scholarly literature on the pre-conditions for democracy is remarkably advanced (Lipset [1959] 1981; Linz and Stepan 1996; Moore 1967). Although predicting when a country might undergo a democratic transition is not an exact science, social scientists have identified a key set of variables that make the possibility of a transition more likely. These are usually related to levels of socio-economic modernisation (industrialisation, literacy, mass communications), class structure (the existence of a sizeable middle class), and political culture (cultural norms, habits, values that are democracy-enhancing). The more these variables are in play the greater the prospects for democracy. In the context of the post-9/11 debate on Islam and democracy, however, these issues have rarely been explored.

Instead, the mass media and intellectual arguments have come to represent a different set of concerns rooted in cultural and civilisational differences. The question 'Is Islam compatible with democracy?' by itself has become an all-encompassing catchphrase that expresses a widespread frustration with and condemnation of the general state of under-development in the Muslim world. Specifically, commentators have asked: 'Why is there so much anger, instability and social conservatism in these societies?' 'Why the prevalence of religious fundamentalism, the unrelenting calls to violence and the deplorable state of human rights, particularly women's rights?'

Now that the violence emanating from the Islamic world has come into the heart of Western cities and is perceived to be directly affecting the quality of life of millions of Americans and Europeans, the level of anxiety about these questions has risen to new heights. In short, the 9/11 media and intellectual debate in the West about Islam and democracy has often boiled down to this: 'Why is the Islamic world seemingly so different from societies in North American and Europe?' 'Why are they not more like us?' (Fish 2011). This basic point of departure, of assuming and expecting cultural and civilisational similarity, has formed the backdrop to an inquiry about the relationship between Islam, Muslims and democracy. From the outset, this debate has been framed in ways prone to analytical distortion.

The essential problem with the question, 'Why are they (Muslims) not like us (Westerners)?' is twofold. First, the question mistakenly assumes that the West has always been democratic, peaceful and liberal, and that one can draw a straight line from ancient Athens to twenty-first-century Europe without detours along the way. No serious historian would entertain such an argument. As Mark Mazower has observed in his *Dark Continent: Europe's Twentieth Century*, it is incorrect to think of Europe as the natural home of human rights and democracy. The last 100 years of European history clearly suggest that the continent was often a terrifying laboratory for social and political engineering, inventing and reinventing itself through war, revolution and ideological competition. Fascism and communism, Mazower argues, should be regarded not as exceptions to the general rule of democracy, but as alternative forms of government that attracted millions of Europeans by offering different solutions to the challenges of the modern world. By 1940, the prospects for democracy looked bleak and Europe's future appeared to lie in Hitler's hands. These are sobering reminders that should inform any serious inquiry related to international affairs today, particularly in relation to the study of non-Western societies, their histories and their problems of political development (Mazower 2000).

Secondly, to expect Muslim societies to mirror the West in terms of social norms is to ignore the fact that the historical experience of these societies has been qualitatively different from the Western experience both in the pre-modern and modern eras. To assume that Muslim societies have undergone the same political, economic, social and intellectual transformations as the West is to project and impose Western history onto the Islamic world. This problem is deeply embedded in the broader question of the nature and causes of under-development. What explains the chasm between the northern tier countries and those of the global south? How does one account for the huge differences not only in terms of wealth and economic growth, but also in terms of good governance and constitutional rule? Why did modern representative democracy first emerge in the West, in Protestant-majority societies, and then spread to the rest of the world? There are no simple answers to these questions, nor is there space here to properly explore them. Various theories and explanations have been offered over the years and little consensus exists as to precisely which factors are most salient in explaining divergent developmental outcomes (Dunn 2006; Fukuyama 2011; Handelman 2011; Isbister 2006). The broader interpretative point here is that when one begins to investigate a topic, the assumptions that are brought into the initial inquiry can often pre-determine the outcome.

Historical Notes on Religion and Democracy

This chapter takes the approach that unless one recalls the long and torturous history of democracy in the West, understanding this topic in other cultural or regional settings can lead to misrepresentation. Comparison is indispensable in avoiding the trap of cultural essentialism and religious exceptionalism. Islam is not the first religious tradition to struggle with the relationship between religion and politics, nor will it be the last. It should be remembered that the origins of political philosophy in the West are rooted in the tension between religion and democracy. Socrates was brought to trial and sentenced to death for corrupting the minds of the young *and* for the crime of religious impiety (Colaiaco 2001). Furthermore, prior to the development of political secularism in the West, Church and state were often deeply intertwined. At

the societal level, religion played an influential role in the political life of Europe well
into the twentieth century where Christian Democracy parties were frequently elected
(Kalyvas 1996). Today in the United States, religion continues to play an important
role in American democracy, and as the debate on Barack Obama's Muslim heritage
verses his Christian faith reminds us, one cannot get elected as president today unless
the candidate is openly and explicitly Christian.

Furthermore, in a seminal work on 'World Religious Systems and Democracy',
Alfred Stepan reminded us that all emerging democracies face political conflict and
struggle over the normative role of religion in politics. No democracy is immune from
this dispute and any objective reading of history will reveal that, for many long-
standing Western democracies, a major source of conflict for a protracted period of
time was the tension between religion and politics. In his essay, Stepan explores
various 'maps of misreading' in the history of religion–state relations in Europe. He is
critical of an ahistorical approach to this topic, which often suggests that the
consolidation of democracy requires a hostile and rigid separation between religion
and state. A closer reading of the topic, he suggests, will reveal that virtually 'no
Western European democracy now has a rigid or hostile separation of church and
state'. Instead, most Western countries 'have arrived at a democratically negotiated
freedom of religion from state interference and all of them allow religious groups
freedom, not only of private worship, but to organize groups in civil society'. It is in
the 'constant political construction and reconstruction' of what he terms 'the twin
tolerations' – whereby the institutions of the state and religious authorities learn to
respect certain minimum boundaries of freedom of action – that an understanding
of the relationship between religion and democracy must be rooted (Stepan 2001:
213–53).

In thinking about the tension between Islam and democracy, the case of Catholicism
and democracy is instructive. Just as it is with Islam today, until the 1960s Catholicism
was widely viewed as deeply anti-democratic and illiberal. The Enlightenment critique
of religion was based on the tenets and behaviour of the Catholic Church. For
centuries the Vatican opposed modernisation and secularisation, to wit: liberalism,
democracy, socialism, capitalism, feminism and the sexual revolution (Casanova 2001:
1054). This view was so pervasive that the distinguished American political sociologist
Seymour Martin Lipset, in a widely cited and influential article in 1959, could observe
without controversy that the 'linkage between democratic instability and Catholicism
may also be accounted for by elements inherent in Catholicism' (Lipset 1959: 92, n40).

The relationship between Catholicism and modernity gradually changed. The major
catalyst for this was the reforms of the Second Vatican Council (1962–5), which
addressed and updated Catholic doctrine in the modern world. Soon afterwards, there
was a major expansion of democracy known as the 'third wave of democratization'.
According to Samuel Huntington this spread of democracy was 'overwhelmingly a
Catholic wave' in that 'roughly three-quarters of the countries that transited to
democracy between 1974 and 1989 were predominately Catholic countries' (Huntington 1991: 76). José Casanova specifically credits the *aggiornamento* (reforms) at
Vatican II for allowing Catholicism, for the first time in its history, to openly support
democracy and human rights struggles which contributed significantly to the third

wave of democratisation (Casanova 2001). In thinking about the relationship between Islam and democracy, the long conflict between Catholicism and modernity is a sobering reminder that Muslims are not *sui generis* when it comes to this topic. An examination of other world religions and democracy, such as Orthodox Christianity, Judaism, Hinduism and Confucianism would be very instructive in this context (Diamond *et al.* 2005).

The Crisis of Secularism: Rethinking Religion–State Relations

In 2007, the research firm Gallup published the most comprehensive survey of global Muslim opinion. Based on six years of polling in thirty-five countries that represented more than 90 per cent of the world's Muslim population, it found widespread compatibility of values between Western and Muslim societies in terms of support for human rights, basic freedoms, democracy and gender equality. Where the West and Islamic worlds differed, however, was in their attitudes to the relationship between religion and politics. Muslims do not believe that greater democracy and self-determination require a Western-like separation of Church and state. 'Poll data show that large majorities of respondents in the countries surveyed cite the equal importance of Islam and democracy as essential to the quality of their lives and the future progress of the Muslim world' (Esposito and Mogahed 2007: 35). How can this difference be explained? Again we turn to history.

The history of religion–state relations and the role of religion in public life have been qualitatively different in Muslim societies compared with the West both in pre-modern and modern periods. Different political lessons have been learned on both sides of the Islam–West divide as a result. Part of the problem here is one of historical perception. Any comparative treatment of the role of religion in politics often suffers from the problem of transference. This is the natural and erroneous tendency to assume that the historical experience of the West is a universal experience. Specifically, it is the assumption that because in the West, after centuries of conflict, bloodshed and experimentation from the Renaissance to the Enlightenment, a broad democratic and secular consensus on the normative role of religion in government has been demo-cratically negotiated, then the rest of world should do so as well. This has distorted our understanding of the politics of the Arab–Islamic world primarily because the history and legacy of religion–state relations in this part of the world has been qualitatively different.

There have been no major wars of religion, nor have there been battles over religious toleration that have forcibly generated new moral, political and intellectual arguments on the relationship between religion and political authority in the Muslim world. Most historians are in agreement that in the classical and pre-modern era Muslim societies were more tolerant of religious pluralism than societies in the West, not in an ideal sense nor by twenty-first century liberal democratic standards, but in comparison with Christendom during, for example, the 'Dark Ages'. Secondly, the classic constitution of the historic Islamic state was one where religion served to limit political tyranny, rather than acting as a source of conflict and deep division. As Noah Feldman observes in *The Fall and Rise of the Islamic State*, through 'their near monopoly on legal affairs in a state where God's law was accepted as paramount, the [religious] scholars . . . built themselves into a powerful and effective check on the ruler' (Feldman 2008: 6). These scholars were sometimes able to restrain the autocratic ambitions of the sultans and caliphs by forcing them to recognise certain limits demarcated by Islamic law in exchange for conferring political legitimacy. For example, on 29 May 1807, the Ottoman sultan, Selim III, was deposed after the Chief Mufti issued a ruling that his pro-French modernisation polices had violated Islamic principles.

Religion–state relations in the Muslim world have thus bequeathed different historical lessons and memories to the faithful. Today, religion in the Muslim world is viewed by significant segments of the population not as a natural ally of despotism and a cause of social conflict, but as a possible agent of stability, predictability and as a constraint on political power. This partly explains why demands for a greater role for religion in politics have had a sympathetic hearing in parts of the Arab–Islamic world today, though notably not where Islamists are already in power.

Furthermore, many Arab societies have also been deeply shaped by the negative experiences of post-colonial authoritarianism. The forms of secularism associated with these regimes have had a critical impact on perceptions of the relationship between religion and government. The various modernisation projects and political systems that emerged from this experience were often justified in the name of secular Arab nationalism, and by the late twentieth century most of these regimes were as politically repressive as they were economically corrupt. Ben Ali's Tunisia, Mubarak's Egypt, Saleh's Yemen and Gaddafi's Libya embodied this state of affairs. In Syria, for example, the ruling regime justifies its rule, in part, in the name of secularism (al-Assad 2010). It has responded to pro-democracy protests during the Arab Spring, which have been overwhelming non-violent, with such extreme brutality that Amnesty International, Human Rights Watch and the UN Human Rights Council have characterised the regime's behaviour as 'crimes against humanity'. Thus, for a generation of Arabs, dictatorship, repression and nepotism embodied a strikingly negative 'secular' reality. As a result, the turn to Islam as an alternative source for political inspiration and hope was both logical and natural. At the moment, reliable polling suggests the most Arabs oppose the idea that democracy demands a Western-style form of secularism and large majorities support the idea that Islamic law should be 'a' source (not 'the' source) of legislation.

The 2011 Arab Spring: Reflections on Fundamentalism and Democracy

The 2011 Arab revolutions are best described as uprisings for democracy and dignity. They are democratic in the sense that they are driven by a deep-rooted hunger for political empowerment on a mass level, specifically the replacement of elite rule with popular sovereignty. They are also about dignity in that the protesters are rejecting the humiliation and degradation that has accompanied decades of authoritarian rule, namely, the indignity brought on by massive corruption, nepotism, the absence of the rule of law and political transparency, and the rampant abuse of power. These are the factors that have produced these revolts. The increasingly educated, globalised and young segments of society – the driving force behind these uprisings – are particularly motivated by the ignominy of their political and economic context coupled with a demand to be respected by political leadership; a respect that can be generated only by democratic rule (Hudson 2011; Khalidi 2011; Khouri 2011a, 2011b).

While these uprisings have been widely celebrated around the world, in the West they have also been received with considerable anxiety and foreboding. It is reasonable to wonder what will emerge from this transformative moment when the dust settles. Do the uprisings represent another 1989 Berlin Wall moment in human history? Are they a prelude to a broader democratic transition across an entire region or are these Arab revolts a replay of the 1979 Islamic Revolution in Iran, a landmark event in the modern history of the Middle East that similarly had democratic potential, yet resulted in the triumph of an authoritarian Islamist regime in the heart of the Muslim world?

Much of the concern about the future trajectory of the Arab revolutions has focused on the role of the Muslim Brotherhood in Egypt and to a lesser extent on *Ennahda*, a sister Islamist movement in Tunisia. In *Civilization: The West and the Rest*, Niall Ferguson argues that the 'core values of Western civilization are directly threatened by the brand of Islam espoused by . . . the Muslim Brotherhood leaders', whom he believes are Islamo-fascists that seek 'the restoration of the Caliphate' (Ferguson 2011a: 289, 2011b). But questions remain: 'What role have these groups played in the uprisings?' 'How much popular support do they genuinely enjoy and what are the political consequences for regional stability, international security and democracy if they should emerge triumphant in the aftermath of these revolutions?' While these questions are all legitimate, the mainstream intellectual and policy debate in the West has ignored some basic sociological, historical and ethical questions on political development in the Arab world that deserve critical scrutiny. Two issues are of primary importance: the role of political Islam and the conflict over religion–state relations.

Political Islam and the West

A central trope of the criticism against the Muslim Brotherhood in Egypt runs as follows: it is a deeply illiberal organisation whose commitment to pluralist democracy is as shaky as its commitment to women's rights and minority rights. The centrality of *shariah* to its political platform is often cited as evidence of the same. More recently, one can point to the 2007 draft political platform of the Muslim Brotherhood that called for an Iranian-style religious advisory council to review legislation for its conformity with Islamic law. In the same vein, the platform (which has since been revised) called for the banning of Copts and women from holding the office of president and prime minister.

While there is much to be concerned about with respect to the future role of Islamist parties in the Arab world, it can be argued that for many in the West it is not the commitment to liberal values that is of chief concern, but rather it is the commitment of these religious parties to Western foreign policy goals that really matters. In other words, mainstream Islamist parties are viewed with deep suspicion *not* because of their distance from liberal values, but because of the challenge they pose to long-standing

Western geo-political interests in the Middle East, primarily to Israel and pro-Western regimes in the Arabian Peninsula. It is plausible that, if the Muslim Brotherhood were to announce its full recognition of the state of Israel, accept the legitimacy of the ruling regimes in the Persian Gulf and devote itself to *da'wah* (missionary proselytising) and social welfare work instead of parliamentary politics, the fear and foreboding surrounding this organisation would likely drop precipitously in Western policy and in some intellectual circles.

In an insightful essay on 'Palace Fundamentalism and Liberal Democracy,' written more than fifteen years ago, the Moroccan sociologist Fatima Mernissi provided an intriguing analytical framework for considering this topic. Mernissi noted that there is a long and sordid history of Western liberal democracies supporting and promoting backward and fanatical forms of Islamic fundamentalism. This takes place because it advances Western geo-strategic and business interests related to oil production and arms sales in the Middle East (Mernissi 2003). While Mernissi's analysis focused on Saudi Arabia and Wahhabi Islam, her argument can also be extended to many of the pro-Western Persian Gulf regimes whose record on democratic and liberal values is arguably far worse than the Egyptian Muslim Brotherhood and Tunisia's *Ennahda*. The Western response, or lack thereof, to the crackdown on pro-democracy protests in Bahrain in 2011 is an illustration of her thesis. Support for long-standing dictators and the ordinances of the *shariah* are perfectly acceptable in this context. The point here is that from the West's perspective there are good and bad forms of Islamic fundamentalism. Those fundamentalist groups and illiberal regimes that line up with and enhance Western geo-strategic goals are to be tolerated, supported and sustained (the Afghan Mujahideen and Pakistan's Zia-ul-Haq also fit this profile); those that are politically independent and that operate outside a US foreign policy framework are to be opposed and demonised. In this moral and political calculus, liberal democratic values are of little relevance.

The second point concerns the nexus between authoritarian regimes in the Arab world, the Western support that bolsters them and the political ramifications of this support for the future of democracy. Stated simply, Western support for authoritarian regimes in the Arab–Islamic world has had tremendous negative political consequences for the region's prospects for democracy. Decades of political repression, particularly of secular civil society, has forced political opposition in the Middle East in the direction of more traditional sectors of society such as the mosque. The forces of religion have indirectly and inadvertently benefited from the authoritarian policies of the post-colonial Arab state, in part because all rival secular political organisations have been suffocated or crushed. The 2011 electoral results from Egypt, where Islamist parties emerged victorious confirm this point.

Similarly, it is also instructive to briefly examine the case of Iran. The rise of political Islam in Iran in the wake of the 1979 Revolution made perfect sociological and political sense. The social conditions in the decades before the revolution, a specific by-product of the authoritarian modernisation policies of the Western-backed Pahlavi regime, created fertile ground for the rise of Islamic fundamentalism. These policies undermined the forces of democratic secularism and liberalism, and inadvertently strengthened the forces of political Islam (Keddie 2006: 188–213;

Mirsepassi 2000: 65–95). In short, in the same way that the forces of political Islam emerged from decades of authoritarianism as the only credible and organised opposition in Iran, a similar (though not identical) situation prevails in much of the Arab world today. To decry this state of affairs is to ignore the political consequences of supporting repressive authoritarian regimes. Ultimately, one cannot support the social conditions that give rise to Islamic fundamentalism and then expect secular liberal democrats to emerge after the revolution. Given this enveloping political context, the strength and popularity of religious movements makes perfect sociological sense, *in part* due to long-standing Western support for Middle Eastern dictatorships (Ayoob 2008: 152–69).

Conclusion

To understand the tensions between Islam and democracy, an understanding of history is essential given that the development of democracy and human rights is a historical process that is evolutionary and gradual in nature. One of the key points of tension that most emerging democracies have to grapple with is the place of religion in government. There are no blueprints to follow; democratic bargaining and negotiation over the normative role of religion in politics is an inevitable part of the history and consolidation of democracy in all societies. No religion is born with an inherent predisposition toward democracy, liberalism or secularism. Like other religious traditions that originate in the pre-modern era and are scripturally based, Islam is neither more nor less compatible with modernity than Christianity or Judaism. Not too long ago it was widely assumed that Catholicism was an obstacle to democracy and that only Protestant-majority countries could respect popular sovereignty. Very few people would entertain this argument today.

The key interpretive point that merits consideration is that all religious traditions are a highly complex body of ideas, beliefs and doctrines that, when interpreted in a modern context, contain sufficient ambiguity and elasticity to be read in a variety of ways. This is not to suggest that religious doctrine should be completely ignored when discussing democracy in the Middle East, but rather that the interpretation of religion is always contextual and evolving; at best, it is only one factor among many that affect the prospects for democratisation and liberalisation (Brynen *et al.* 1995). In the context of the contemporary Islamic world, the struggle for democracy has been negatively affected by on-going intervention from outside powers. Long-standing policies, particularly by the United States, of supporting authoritarian dictators such as the Shah of Iran, Hosni Mubarak or the House of Saud have impeded the political development of the Middle East. Coupled with the destabilising effects of the Israel–Palestine conflict, an environment that is more conducive to the growth of radical religious politics than secular democratic politics has flourished. In this sense, the experience of the Middle East has been qualitatively different to that of Europe. External intervention by foreign powers in support of authoritarian regimes was not a factor in the development of democracy in the West.

A final word from historian Richard Bulliet who has written extensively about the relationship between Islam and democracy aptly sums up this comparative analysis:

Notions like human rights, equality and civil liberties did not come from documents. They came from struggles. Anyone who is aware of the feminist movement in this country can see such a struggle taking place; a struggle that has yet to succeed but that probably will in time. Struggles cannot be fought from the outside; they must occur internally. What struggles will take place within the community of Muslims I would not hazard to say. Nor would I venture an opinion as to whether the Muslims of the twenty-first century will follow the direction of the West in their controversies over political and social norms, or whether they will find unique solutions to unavoidable contradictions. Either way, conflict, diversity, and evolutionary change seem inevitable despite the powerful appeal of a traditional core of norms and values. (Bulliet 1994: 10–11)

Note

1. For the purposes of brevity this chapter uses terms such as 'Islam' and the 'West' as if they are monolithic, static and all-encompassing. This is, of course, problematic and the author is sensitive to the nuanced debates and differences within such categories and their dynamic nature.

References

Al-Assad, B. (2010), Interview with Charlie Rose, 27 May.
Ayoob, M. (2008), *The Many Faces of Political Islam: Religion and Politics in the Muslim World*, Ann Arbor, MI: University of Michigan Press.
Brynen, R., B. Korany and P. Noble (eds) (1995), *Political Liberalization and Democratization in the Arab World*, vol. 1. Boulder, CO: Lynne Rienner.
Bulliet, R. (ed.) (1994), *Under Siege: Islam and Democracy*, New York: Middle East Institute, Columbia University.
Casanova, J. (2001), 'Civil Society and Religion: Retrospective Reflections on Catholicism and Prospective Reflections on Islam', *Social Research*, 68, 1041–80.
Colaiaco, J. (2001), *Socrates Against Athens: Philosophy on Trial*, New York: Routledge.
Diamond, L., M. Plattner and P. Costopoulus (eds) (2005), *World Religions and Democracy*, Baltimore, MD: Johns Hopkins University Press.
Dunn, J. (2006), *Democracy: A History*, New York: Atlantic Monthly Press.
Esposito, J. and D. Mogahed (2007), *Who Speaks for Islam?: What a Billion Muslims Really Think*, New York: Gallup Press.
Feldman, N. (2008), *The Fall and Rise of the Islamic State*, Princeton, NJ: Princeton University Press.
Ferguson, N. (2011a), *Civilization: The West and the Rest*, New York: Penguin.
Ferguson, N. (2011b), 'Wanted: A Grand Strategy for America', *Newsweek*, 21 February.
Fish, M. S. (2011), *Are Muslims Distinctive?: A Look at the Evidence*, New York: Oxford University Press.
Fukuyama, F. (2011), *The Origins of Political Order: From Prehuman Times to the French Revolution*, New York: Farrar, Straus & Giroux.
Handelman, H. (2011), *The Challenge of Third World Development*, 6th edn, Boston, MA: Longman.

Hashemi, N. (2012), 'Islam and Democracy', in J. Esposito and E. Shahin (eds), *The Oxford Handbook on Islam and Democracy*, Oxford: Oxford University Press.

Hudson, M. (2011), 'Awakening, Cataclysm, or Just a Series of Events?: Reflections on the Current Wave of Protest in the Arab World', *Jadalliya*, 16 May.

Huntington, S. (1991), *The Third Wave: Democratization in the Late Twentieth Century*, Norman, OK: University of Oklahoma Press.

Khalidi, R. (2011), 'Preliminary Historical Observations on the Arab Revolutions of 2011', *Critical Inquiry*, special online issue available at: http://criticalinquiry.uchicago.edu/preliminary_historical_observations_on_the_arab_revolutions_of_2011, accessed 12 May 2012.

Kalyvas, S. (1996), *The Rise of Christian Democracy in Europe*, Ithaca, NY: Cornell University Press.

Keddie, N. (2003), *Modern Iran: Roots and Results of Revolution*, New Haven, CT: Yale University Press.

Khouri, R. (2011a), 'The Long Revolt', *The Wilson Quarterly*, 35(3), 43–6.

Khouri, R. (2011b), 'The Arab Awakening', *The Nation*, 293(11), 13–15.

Isbister, J. (2006), *Promises Not Kept: Poverty and the Betrayal of Third World Development*, 7th edn, Sterling, VA: Kumarian Press.

Linz, J. and A. Stepan (1996), *Problems of Democratic Transition and Consolidation: Southern Europe, South America, and Post-Communist Europe*, Baltimore, MD: Johns Hopkins University Press.

Lipset, S. M. (1959), 'Some Social Requisites of Democracy: Economic Development and Political Legitimacy', *American Political Science Review*, 53, 69–105.

Lipset, S. M. ([1959] 1981), *Political Man: The Social Bases of Politics*, Baltimore, MD: Johns Hopkins University Press.

Mazower, M. (2000), *Dark Continent: Europe's Twentieth Century*, New York: Vintage.

Mirsepassi, A. (2000), *Intellectual Discourse and the Politics of Modernization: Negotiating Modernity in Iran*, Cambridge: Cambridge University Press.

Mernissi, F. (2003), 'Palace Fundamentalism and Liberal Democracy: Oil, Arms and Irrationality', in M. Sells and E. Qureshi (eds), *The New Crusades: Constructing the Muslim Enemy* , New York: Columbia University Press, pp. 51–67.

Moore, B. (1967), *Social Origins of Dictatorship and Democracy: Lord and Peasant in the Making of the Modern World*, Boston, MA: Beacon Press.

Stepan, A. (2001), *Arguing Comparative Politics*, New York: Oxford University Press.

Tirman, J. (2011), *The Deaths of Others: The Fate of Civilians in America's Wars*, New York: Oxford University Press.

Part IX

Futures and Possibilities

Chapter 38

Democracy Promotion

Christopher Hobson

One of the most notable features of the post-Cold War era has been the ideational dominance of liberal democracy. The majority of the twentieth century was shaped by a conflict between different ruling ideologies but, with the collapse of the Soviet empire, democracy outlasted its rivals. In this context, Amartya Sen proposed that: 'democratic governance has now achieved the status of being taken to be generally right', while one of the leading scholars of democratisation, Larry Diamond, has suggested that 'democracy is really the only broadly legitimate form of government in the world' (Diamond 2008: 13; Sen 1999: 5). Certainly, such claims overstate matters, but not greatly: a distinctive characteristic of the contemporary international order has been the remarkable level of consensus on the legitimacy and desirability of (liberal) democracy. In this sense, it is hardly a coincidence that the spread of democratisation, and the embedding of democracy-promotion practices internationally, has occurred in a world in which democracy is materially and ideationally ascendant. How much longer such a situation will hold for is an open question, but this has been the broad context within which the global push towards democracy must be understood.

The post-Cold War world has been unipolar in both material and ideational terms, with little in the way of systemic challengers to democracy. In such an environment, the value of promoting democracy has been taken as almost self-evident. If one looks more closely, however, one can identify two basic rationales for supporting and promoting democracy abroad. The first is based on the claim that democracy is a universal value. Indeed, it is notable that this position was adopted in the 2005 World Summit Outcome Document, which announced in unambiguous terms that 'democracy is a universal value' (UNGA 2005: 31). From this perspective, the logic of promoting democracy is essentially an extension of protecting and promoting other proclaimed universal values, such as human rights. If democracy is something universally valued and desired, then supporting its advancement seems common sense. Whether democracy can be considered as something universal remains contested as the 'Asian Values' debate in the 1990s made clear (Sen 1997). This is where the second justification becomes relevant: regardless of the normative arguments in favour of democracy, there are strong practical reasons emerging for the instrumental value of democracy. Democracy is seen to be uniquely capable of providing good outcomes; it performs better than other regime types. Democracy provides government that is more accountable and less corrupt; there is considerably less likelihood of genocide, extreme violence, famine and economic disaster; while human rights and individual freedom are better protected (McFaul 2010: 34–7). In this line of thought, democracy is of instrumental value both to the people in the target state, as well as the international community more generally. An influential set of arguments about the 'distinctiveness' of democracies suggests they are more peaceful and cooperative in their international behaviour. To simplify, it is proposed that a growth in democracies will, in time, lead to greater amounts of peace and prosperity. When these two rationales are combined, democracy promotion is justified in both moral and instrumental terms, and any qualms about the impact of such practices on state sovereignty are largely discounted.

The post-Cold War world has been unusually favourable to democracy, and its present positioning is in sharp contrast to the historical record (Hobson 2009a). Democracy's popularity has shaped the way democracy promotion has developed as a practice within international politics, as this chapter will show. The purpose here is to provide an overview of the emergence of democracy promotion as an important factor in determining the shape and nature of democracy in the world today. In doing so, this chapter seeks to consider some of the major ways democratisation is influenced by external forces, as well as identifying how the democracy-promotion agenda has emerged and developed in international politics. The latter part of the chapter focuses on the present and future of democracy promotion. In concluding, it is suggested that even if democracy's appeal may now be under challenge or on the wane, it is likely that democracy-promotion practices will continue to be an important dimension of international politics and contribute to democracy's future development.

Democratisation and the Structure of International Politics

To understand the 'newness' of democracy promotion, it is important to place these practices in a longer historical perspective. Doing so indicates that international politics have often played a role, in one form or another, in shaping processes of democratisation. There are a number of different ways that international relations have shaped democracy. First, on a basic level, the international system has provided the context for democracy itself, insofar as it has historically developed within the bounds of the state. In a seminal article, Dankwart Rustow identified what he termed 'national unity' as the sole 'background condition' for democratisation, explaining that: 'democracy is a system of rule by temporary majorities. In order that rulers and policies may freely change, the boundaries must endure, the composition of the citizenry be continuous' (Rustow 1970: 351). In this sense, the international system plays an important role in creating and structuring the possibility for domestic level democracy to occur. Secondly, staples of international politics over the centuries – primarily war and empire – have played conditioning roles in shaping where and when democratisation has occurred (Hobson 2009b). This is hardly a modern phenomenon. As John Keane observes: 'from its sixth-century beginnings, the whole experiment with democracy took place in a geopolitical laboratory' (Keane 2009: 64). Thirdly, and closely related, there have been numerous cases of direct intervention by an international actor to install democracy, or in contemporary parlance, bring about 'regime change'. The democratisation of Germany and Japan after the Second World War are normally identified as two particularly clear – and unusually successful – examples of this (Smith 1994). Finally, democratic ideas have been liable to be transferred, spread and diffused across borders. This dimension is obviously amplified by the rapid advance of communication and transportation technologies, but again is not new: one needs only to turn to the American and French revolutions for examples of democratic ideas being 'contagious'.

The way in which the external structure of the international system can shape or influence the internal process of democratisation is best illustrated through briefly listing some significant historical examples. A central component of the establishment of the United States as a federation of democratic republics was the context of it breaking free from its former imperial master and joining international society. The violent, chaotic and incomplete attempt to institute democracy during the French Revolution cannot be understood separate from the international environment it took place within: a Europe made up of aristocratic great powers that saw the democratic principles of the French as a fundamental threat to their existence. Not only did the revolutionary wars fundamentally reshape international politics, they also conditioned the possibilities for democracy in France and beyond into the nineteenth and twentieth centuries. The democratisation of Great Britain in the nineteenth century, often taken as a paradigmatic case, was underwritten by the simultaneous expansion of its empire (Zakaria 2003: 48–51). The material benefits accrued through colonisation acted as a safety valve in controlling the pace and nature of democratisation at home (Jahn 2011). Likewise, the remarkably successful democratisation of settler societies, such as America, Australia, Canada and New Zealand, was premised on displacing indigenous communities and dispossessing them of their land (Mann 2005).

In the twentieth century, the conclusion of both world wars helped trigger subsequent democratic waves, and it is impossible to understand the consolidation of democracy in Western Europe in the second half of the twentieth century separate from the consequences of the Second World War (Huntington 1991: 17–18). As Berman notes, 'the silver lining to Europe's final collapse into barbarism . . . is that leaders and publics emerged from the experience with a great appreciation for the virtues of democracy and an understanding that social peace and stability were necessary if it was to work' (Berman 2011: 78–9). Likewise, the third wave of democratisation must be located with reference to the end of the Cold War and the emergence of a unipolar order dominated by a superpower that is also a liberal democracy. In much the same way that the considerable expansion of democracy-promotion practices in the 1990s was partly predicated on a material and ideational balance of power in favour of liberal democracy, it is unsurprising that this agenda has been increasingly challenged as part of the contemporary global power realignment. 'The backlash against democracy promotion', as Thomas Carothers observes, is 'one symptom of a more daunting context . . . for democracy promotion in the decades ahead' (Carothers 2010: 72). There are many examples of how domestic processes of democratisation have been influenced by the larger international framework within which states exist. Collectively it illustrates the fundamental point that international relations have long played an important role in shaping democratisation; democracy promotion represents the latest and most explicit aspect of this dynamic. This is an important coda to the argument that democratisation is first and foremost a domestic phenomenon, in which the international realm serves as little more than a backdrop to internal proceedings (O'Donnell and Schmitter 1986).

The Development of Democracy Promotion

Having acknowledged how international politics contributes, in a general, systemic fashion, to democratisation – helping to shape conditions within which domestic processes take place – it becomes easier to examine democracy promotion as an aspect of foreign policy and acknowledge fostering democratisation as an explicit form of external intervention. In the literature there is sometimes an attempt to distinguish democracy 'promotion' from 'assistance', 'support' or other similar terms (Burnell 2000). The result tends to be synonyms and euphemisms, rather than useful analytical categories. As such, democracy promotion is used here as an overarching, somewhat generic term to cover all of these processes, whereby external agents – most commonly other states, but also international actors, such as international organisations and NGOs – make an active, concerted effort to influence the nature and pace of democratisation in a target state. In understanding democracy promotion, it is necessary to consider closely the United States, historically the most prominent actor supporting democracy abroad. Scholars such as Daniel Deudney, Michael McFaul and Tony Smith do not greatly exaggerate in suggesting that no country has played a more significant part in the defence and spread of democracy (Deudney 2007: 184–5; McFaul 2004–5: 158; Smith 1994: 9). While appreciating the central role the United States has played historically, it also necessary to recognise that these practices are now engaged in by a wide variety of actors: other states, regional bodies such as the European Union, international organisations like the United Nations, NGOs, and even transnational corporations (Carothers 2007a; McFaul 2004–5; Youngs 2004).

The United States has the longest tradition of being actively and explicitly involved in promoting democracy. As Smith observes: 'since 1898 . . . no theme has figured more prominently in the annals of American foreign policy than the repeated presidential calls to promote the creation of democratic government abroad' (Smith 1994: xiii). While the hesitant attempts at bringing democracy to the Philippines (and Cuba to a lesser extent) following the Spanish-American War represent America's first forays into democracy promotion, this tradition is most closely associated with the presidency of Woodrow Wilson. For Wilson, the form of government determined whether states could be trusted to pursue war or peace, with democracies following the latter path and autocracies the former. From this perspective, the extension of democracy was necessary for the safety of America. In Wilson's mind, as long as the autocratic German government remained, 'there can be no assured security for the democratic Governments of the world' (Wilson [1917] 1965: 308). Wilson's efforts at promoting democracy were mixed, but his greatest influence was his legacy: the vision of democracy he announced and its importance in international politics (Ikenberry *et al.* 2009; Smith 1994). The victory of the Entente powers in the First World War helped to pave the way for a democratic wave, but most of the gains were quickly reversed in the inter-war years. Following the Second World War, America played a crucial role in helping to establish liberal democracies in West Germany and Japan. Undoubtedly, there were structural conditions that aided democratisation in these two cases, but the role played by the United States, and in the case of Germany, other European actors, proved to be vital in these being remarkably successful attempts at installing democracy.

The Cold War standoff between liberal democracy and communism, was not conducive to external actors intervening to promote democracy. For much of the twentieth century democracy promotion was neither a prominent nor common component of foreign policy. This would slowly begin to change, however, as the Carter Administration raised the profile of human rights diplomacy, and the third wave of democratisation commenced in Portugal, Spain and Greece. Carter's important forays into human rights diplomacy laid the groundwork for Ronald Reagan's decision to place much greater stress on supporting democracy abroad. In 1982, in a landmark speech at Westminster, Reagan announced that: 'we must be staunch in our conviction that freedom is not the sole prerogative of a lucky few, but the inalienable and universal right of all human beings . . . the objective I propose is quite simple to state: to foster the infrastructure of democracy' (Reagan 1982). It was a pivotal moment in cementing democracy's place in America's foreign policy objectives, and in laying the foundation for the rapid expansion of democracy promotion in recent decades. Meanwhile, the European Community, and notably German *Stiftungen*, played important roles in supporting the democratic transitions that occurred in southern Europe in the mid-1970s (Whitehead 1996).

These successful democratic transitions in Portugal, Spain and Greece – considered as the start of the third wave of democratisation – were fundamental in shaping the emergence of the contemporary democracy-promotion agenda. During the initial stages of the Portuguese transition, it was viewed through a Cold War lens, and there was a serious concern that these events would be destabilising and counter-productive. Once these transitions did not have adverse consequences, the United States and other Western actors became more supportive of the democratisation agenda. In this regard, the transition of Spain came to be an influential example, which would serve as a template for future attempts (Whitehead 2009). This model emphasised political agency – as opposed to structure – and encouraged a voluntarist approach to democratisation. When the tenets of modernisation theory held strong, there seemed to be limited use in pursuing direct policies of democracy promotion: if democratisation was determined by the level of economic development and other social factors, the best route to encouraging democracy was through development projects that assisted in processes of modernisation. If, however, democratisation was primarily driven by political factors, then democracy promotion could potentially play an important role in shifting the balance towards reformers. As Diamond proposed: 'the precarious balance of political and social forces in many newly democratic and transitional countries' provides 'international actors . . . real scope to influence the course of political development' (Diamond 1995: 47). The highly contingent nature of transitional moments, when the potential for agency to be determinative is at its greatest, suggested outsiders could potentially play a crucial role in facilitating democratisation.

Post-Cold War Democracy Promotion

The end of the Cold War provided the material and ideational conditions for democracy promotion to be considerably expanded as a practice in international politics. The bipolar balance of power that previously held was a significant impediment to the West widely engaging in democracy promotion had it wanted to (and until the 1980s it showed little inclination that it did). The emergence of a unipolar order presided over by a great power that was a democracy was a fundamental facilitating factor in the expansion of democracy promotion. This unipolarity was not just material, it was also ideational: liberal democracy had ascended to a position without peer or precedent. The end of the Cold War and the collapse of the Soviet empire was taken by many to represent the 'victory' of liberal democracy, even if this was achieved more by default (Burgess 2001; Fukuyama 1989). The ideational strength of liberalism and democracy strongly shaped the rapidly expanding field of democracy promotion. Indeed, the underlying premise of democracy promotion is a belief in the superiority and greater legitimacy of democracy compared with other regime types, and that target states desire this form of government. Authoritarianism and military rule were thoroughly rejected following decades of human rights abuses, and after almost half a century, the East's experiment with 'really existing socialism' had reached an inglorious end.

Thus, when democracy promotion became embedded in international politics it was imbued with a sense of confidence in the legitimacy of such practices: the incipient universality of liberal democracy and a belief that it was something that target populations desired. As democratic openings appeared across the globe in the 1980s and 1990s, it appeared that a sea-change really was occurring. An emerging sub-field of political science identified a clear model of democratisation, whereby states first went through a short-term period of transition to democracy, which was followed by a longer period of consolidation, in which liberal democracy became embedded within that society as the only option (Linz and Stepan 1996). For the international community, elections were taken as the signifier of this movement towards democracy, with the ballot box becoming the new symbol of legitimacy. The tendency to regard elections as the '*sine qua non*' of democracy (Huntington 1991: 9) quickly gave rise to practices of international election monitoring, whereby the international community seeks to support and advance democratisation by validating election results. One consequence, however, is that there was a tendency to reduce democracy to elections, what has been dubbed an electoral fallacy. While recognising the central role of elections, a more sober assessment has since emerged that that these are a necessary, but not sufficient, condition for democracy, and need to be supplemented by other institutions, notably the protection of basic civil and political rights, and the rule of law.

In tracing the development of democracy promotion and democratisation, the picture throughout the 1990s is rather uneven. In Eastern Europe, the lure of membership in the European Union played a fundamental role in locking in democratic changes and advancing democratisation. Elsewhere, the picture was much more mixed. In Latin America, there were clear elements of democracy, but few examples of transitions where fully consolidated democracies had appeared. Guillermo O'Donnell identified an emergent form he termed 'delegative democracy', where there were elections, but only horizontal accountability was institutionalised, allowing those in power to rule largely unchecked (O'Donnell 1994). An important factor that shaped the direction of democratisation in Latin America was that the form of democracy promoted and instituted there did not address underlying socio-economic inequalities. The liberal democratic model that has prevailed has been limited to the political sphere, with the economic realm remaining largely outside democratic control (Robinson 1996). This was reinforced by the consequences of the neo-liberal Washington Consensus, as structural adjustment programmes operated in a manner that proved to be remarkably corrosive on incipient democratic institutions. In Africa and the former Soviet Union, many states that initially appeared to be moving towards democracy did not progress much beyond an initial breakthrough and the adoption of certain signifiers of democracy. These so-called 'façade democracies' have instituted some superficial trappings of democracy – most notably elections – to placate external donors and the international community, but the ruling party maintains a strong grip on power (Haynes 2001: 6–7).

By the second half of the 1990s it was clear that many states had adopted elections, and certain other democratic attributes, but few had consolidated into liberal democracies and could best be identified as a sub-type of democracy or a 'hybrid' regime (Collier and Levitsky 1997). The promise of the third wave materialised only in a partial and incomplete manner, with a large number of attempted democratisations stalling, reversing or failing to consolidate. The euphoria that prevailed after the fall of the Berlin Wall soon disappeared, and was replaced with a much more sober assessment. It was becoming more apparent that previous assumptions about democratisation and the possibilities of democracy promotion had been overly optimistic. In this context, Fareed Zakaria challenged contemporary wisdom by arguing that what was needed was 'not more democracy but less' (Zakaria 2003: 248). His concern was that an unchecked faith in democracy was fostering an unchecked form of democracy, which was producing perverse results: the rise in democracy was not being matched by a rise in liberty. Instead of continuing to promote democracy unconditionally, Zakaria argued that there is a need to first focus on promoting the rule of law and other features of liberal constitutionalism; elements that work to restrain and channel the dangers of democracy. Emerging from these claims has been an important debate over whether it is possible to sequence the process of democratisation by first building up liberal institutions (Carothers 2007b).

Despite the conservative scepticism, there have been many successful cases of democracy promotion in recent decades. With external assistance, democracy has managed to survive even in particularly hostile environments where most of the usual preconditions for this form of government are lacking. To take one example, against the odds Mongolia has established and consolidated a young democracy. A key factor in this has been the considerable support of external assistance. Countries such as the Czech Republic, Poland and Slovenia represent remarkably speedy and successful examples of democratic consolidation, spurred on by the carrot of EU membership. Nonetheless, today, when democracy promotion is thought about, it is the American attempts at coercive democratisation in Afghanistan and Iraq that dominate. This is unfortunate, as these are exceptions that have been mistakenly presented as the rule. Democracy at the point of a bayonet is not only unlikely to succeed, it is also unlikely to be attempted again.

The Iraq War soon became part of President George W. Bush's so-called 'freedom agenda'. The result, however, was that the United States effectively managed to chart the worst possible course between inflated rhetoric and limited changes in actual democracy-promotion policy. While there may be a wide range of international actors involved in democracy promotion, the United States remains the most prominent and influential, especially in terms of shaping the larger agenda. As such, the flawed democracy promotion policies of the Bush Administration have proven to be particularly damaging for the reputation of democracy promotion in general, to the extent that it has been suggested that the larger democratisation agenda must now be 'decontaminated' (Carothers 2010). This reflects, in part, the unique nature of democracy promotion. When states engage in foreign policy it is natural for them to prioritise their national interests, but given that democracy is not only a set of institutions but an ideal, it creates particularly high expectations. Put differently, the price of hypocrisy is much higher when it comes to engaging in democracy promotion. If there is too great a gap between rhetoric and reality, the legitimacy of democracy promotion as a set of practices comes into question. This is arguably what has been happening in recent years.

The Present and Future of Democracy Promotion

There is now an extensive democracy-promotion global network established, made up of government agencies, quasi-governmental bodies, NGOs and private actors. This community of international actors engaged in supporting democracy now faces a number of significant adverse developments. These include the backlash against their activities by semi-authoritarian states; a changing balance of power and the potential rise of a Chinese model mixing a closed political sphere with a free market economy; the related possibility that their activities are being countered by 'autocracy promotion' (Burnell 2010). Many states nominally engaged in democracy promotion are simultaneously working closely with non-democratic regimes as a result of mutual economic interests and concerns over terrorism.

The liberal international order, developed following the end of the Second World War, and further entrenched and extended in the post-Cold War era, has made for a favourable context for the advancement of democracy abroad. And it is hardly a coincidence that democracy promotion has peaked in a world where the one great power is democratic. There are, however, strong indicators that this situation is fast coming to an end. America's power may be on the wane, in both relative and absolute terms. Meanwhile, China is continuing its rapid emergence as a global player. The growing importance of China helps to reduce pressure for other developing states to democratise, and, in time, it could even provide an umbrella for a group of non-democratic states. Closely related to a changing balance of power is the growing 'backlash' against democracy promotion, led by a resurgent Russia. This reflects a more general shift away from the conditional notions of sovereignty that gained ground in the 1990s, as rising states China, Russia and India all support a return to a more traditional conception of sovereignty based on independence and non-interference. This does not bode well for democracy-promotion practices, given that they are inherently interventionist in nature.

The rise of China, in unison with the strengthening position of other non-liberal democratic powers like Russia, works to further dilute the ideational environment that held in the immediate post-Cold War period. Attending China's rise has been the growth in interest and support for the alternate model of government it embodies, a kind of authoritarian capitalist regime that mixes a highly liberalised economy with a largely closed political system. There are obvious demonstration effects, other states can be expected to mimic China as its position continues to rise and its sphere of influence expands. Notably, it has achieved consistently spectacular growth rates, far more impressive than most democratic states. Those sceptical of the alternative China represents have argued that a mix of an open economy and a closed political realm is an unstable cocktail, and political liberalisation is difficult – if not impossible – to postpone indefinitely (Deudney and Ikenberry 2009). While acknowledging that this combination may contain contradictions, and there are definitely tensions in the Chinese regime, it is not clear that these are *necessarily* sufficient to cause liberalisation. This emergent authoritarian capitalist form could be more stable than some presume, and it would be a mistake for democracy promoters to underestimate the strength of this model as a competitor to democracy.

Greater consideration of authoritarian capitalism is matched by the lessening attraction of liberal democracy itself. In many places where democracy has been attempted, it has failed to meet the expectations of citizens. When the Cold War came to an end, liberal democracy was associated with prosperity, stability and normality. At this time, 'the politics of "normalization" replaced deliberation with imitation' (Krastev 2010: 117). Two decades later the report card is decidedly mixed on the kind of liberal democracy advanced by the United States and other international actors. There may be continuing support for democracy as an *ideal*, but this is offset by diminishing faith in democracy as a *reality*. This situation is hardly limited to transitional states: it is also evident in many established democracies. It can no longer be taken for granted that local populations will necessarily desire democracy, or if they do, that they understand it in the same way as the United States or Europe does. Furthermore, even if there is abstract support for democracy, in real-life situations economic growth and stability may be accorded higher priority (Chu *et al.* 2009). Such a context is far less favourable to democracy-promotion practices, as target populations may become more open to alternatives, and simultaneously more sceptical of external actors seeking to foster democracy.

Conclusion

Processes of democratisation have always been shaped and structured, to a certain extent, by larger international forces. In the latter part of the twentieth century external forces have played an increasingly noticeable role in the nature and speed of moves towards democracy within states. Having only begun to emerge in the mid-1970s, by the start of the new millennium democracy promotion had become embedded in international politics, with a wide range of actors – states, international organisations and NGOs – involved in these practices. Following the rapid expansion of this international agenda, there is now greater contestation over the virtue and validity of engaging in democracy promotion. Furthermore, the triumphalism that shaped an earlier phase of democracy promotion has been replaced by greater uncertainty, if not pessimism. Nonetheless, even if the ideational strength of democracy is not as great as it was at the end of the Cold War, it remains the most politically legitimate and normatively desirable form of rule. Furthermore, few states – if any – are willing to openly repudiate the idea of democracy. And on a more practical level, the democracy-promotion community that has developed now has a vested interest in these practices being maintained. There are strong reasons to expect that Western countries, notably the United States, will continue to place considerable emphasis on supporting democracy abroad as part of their foreign policy. Likewise, the United Nations and other major institutional organisations are committed to supporting good governance in post-conflict and transitional states, and the successful establishment of democracy is a central component of this aim. As such, it is highly unlikely that the global advancement of democracy will disappear from the agenda of the international community, even if the context is much more challenging. The open question is how democracy promotion will operate in an international environment that is far less favourable to such practices.

References

Berman, S. (2011), 'The Past and Future of Social Democracy and the Consequences for Democracy Promotion', in C. Hobson and M. Kurki (eds), *The Conceptual Politics of Democracy Promotion*, London: Routledge, pp. 68–84.

Burgess, A. (2001), 'Universal Democracy, Diminished Expectation', *Democratization*, 8(3), 51–74.

Burnell, P. (2000), 'Democracy Assistance: The State of the Discourse', in P. Burnell (ed.), *Democracy Assistance: International Co-operation for Democratization*, London: Frank Cass, pp. 3–33.

Burnell, P. (2010), 'Is There a New Autocracy Promotion?', Working Paper No. 96, Madrid: FRIDE.

Carothers, T. (2007a), 'A Quarter-Century of Promoting Democracy', *Journal of Democracy*, 18(4), 112–15.

Carothers, T. (2007b), 'The "Sequencing" Fallacy', *Journal of Democracy*, 18(1), 12–27.

Carothers, T. (2010), 'The Continuing Backlash against Democracy Promotion', in P. Burnell and R. Youngs (eds), *New Challenges to Democratization*, London: Routledge, pp. 59–72.

Chu, Y. *et al.* (2009), 'Asia's Challenged Democracies', *The Washington Quarterly*, 32(1), 143–57.

Collier, D. and S. Levitsky (1997), 'Research Note: Democracy with Adjectives: Conceptual Innovation in Comparative Research', *World Politics*, 49(3), 430–51.

Deudney, D. (2007), *Bounding Power: Republican Security Theory from the Polis to the Global Village*, Princeton, NJ: Princeton University Press.

Deudney, D. and G. J. Ikenberry (2009), 'The Myth of the Autocratic Revival: Why Liberal Democracy Will Prevail', *Foreign Affairs*, 88(1), 77–94.

Diamond, L. (1995), *Promoting Democracy in the 1990s: Actors and Instruments, Issues and Imperatives*, Washington, DC: Carnegie Endowment for International Peace.

Diamond, L. (2008), *The Spirit of Democracy*, New York: Times Books.

Fukuyama, F. (1989), 'The End of History?', *The National Interest*, 16, 3–18.

Haynes, J. (2001), *Democracy and Political Change in the 'Third World'*, London: Routledge

Hobson, C. (2009a), 'Beyond the End of History: The Need for a "Radical Historicisation" of Democracy in International Relations', *Millennium*, 37(3), 627–53.

Hobson, C. (2009b), 'Democracy and International Politics: A Conceptual History, 1776–1919', unpublished Ph.D. dissertation, Australian National University, Canberra.

Huntington, S. (1991), *The Third Wave: Democratization in the Late Twentieth Century*, Norman, OK: University of Oklahoma Press.

Ikenberry, G. J., T. J. Knock, A.-M. Slaughter and T. Smith (2009), *The Crisis of American Foreign Policy: Wilsonianism in the Twenty-first Century*, Princeton, NJ: Princeton University Press.

Jahn, B. (2011), 'Liberalism and Democracy Promotion', in C. Hobson and M. Kurki (eds), *The Conceptual Politics of Democracy Promotion*, London: Routledge, pp. 53–67.

Keane, J. (2009), *The Life and Death of Democracy*, London: Simon & Schuster.

Krastev, I. (2010), 'Deepening Dissatisfaction', *Journal of Democracy*, 21(1), 113–19.

Linz, J. and A. Stepan (1996), *Problems of Democratic Transition and Consolidation: Southern Europe, South America, and Post-Communist Europe*, Baltimore, MD: Johns Hopkins University Press.

Mann, M. (2005), *The Dark Side of Democracy: Explaining Ethnic Cleansing*, Cambridge: Cambridge University Press.

McFaul, M. (2004–5), 'Democracy Promotion as a World Value', *The Washington Quarterly*, 28(1), 147–63.

McFaul, M. (2010), *Advancing Democracy Abroad: Why We Should and How We Can*, Lanham, MD: Rowman & Littlefield.

O'Donnell, G. (1994), 'Delegative Democracy', *Journal of Democracy*, 5(1), 55–69.

O'Donnell, G. and P. Schmitter (1986), *Transitions from Authoritarian Rule: Tentative Conclusions about Uncertain Democracies*, Baltimore, MD: Johns Hopkins University Press.

Reagan, R. (1982), 'Address to Members of the British Parliament 8 June', *Public Papers of Ronald Reagan*, Simi Valley, CA: Ronald Reagan Presidential Library.

Robinson, W. (1996), *Promoting Polyarchy*, Cambridge: Cambridge University Press.

Rustow, D. (1970), 'Transitions to Democracy: Toward a Dynamic Model', *Comparative Politics*, 2(3), 337–63.

Sen, A. (1997), 'Human Rights and Asian Values: What Kee Kuan Yew and Le Peng Don't Understand About Asia', *The New Republic*, 217(2–3), 1–9.

Sen, A. (1999), 'Democracy as a Universal Value', *Journal of Democracy*, 10(3), 3–17.

Smith, T. (1994), *America's Mission*, Princeton, NJ: Princeton University Press.

United Nations General Assembly (UNGA) (2005), *World Summit Outcome Document*, New York: United Nations.

Whitehead, L. (1996), 'Democracy by Convergence: Southern Europe', in L. Whitehead (ed.), *The International Dimensions of Democratization*, Oxford: Oxford University Press, pp. 261–84.

Whitehead, L. (2009), 'Losing "the Force"? The "Dark Side" of Democratization after Iraq', *Democratization*, 16(2), 215–42.

Wilson, W. ([1917] 1965), 'The World Must Be Made Safe for Democracy', in A. Fried (ed.), *A Day of Dedication: The Essential Writings and Speeches of Woodrow Wilson*, New York: Macmillan, pp. 301–8.

Youngs, R. (2004), *International Democracy and the West: The Role of Governments, NGOs and Multinationals*, Oxford: Oxford University Press.

Zakaria, F. (2003), *The Future of Freedom: Liberal Democracy at Home and Abroad*, New York: W. W. Norton.

Chapter 39

Transnational Democracy

James Anderson

Transnational democracy is an idea whose time has come, but it does not, as yet, have much substance. It is a thing of the future more than the present, but its future is far from assured. Such democracy as we presently enjoy it is mostly national, rather than transnational, and representative, rather than participatory. It is largely monopolised by elected 'representatives', rather than politically active citizens and almost entirely circumscribed by the territoriality of national state borders. The social communities, relations and processes beyond and across state borders that would constitute transnational democracy largely elude democracy's remit. 'Globalisation' and the burgeoning world of transnational communities of all kinds – cultural, political and economic – may cry out for transnational democracy, for democracy to 'trespass' borders, but it seems as if the different kinds of globalisation have all raced ahead of democracy. Transnational processes generally remain non-, if not anti-, democratic. The globalisation of democracy has generally meant exporting liberal representative democracy to national territories, rather than globalisation itself, or more localised cross-border relations being democratised. E. H. Carr's 1951 conclusion about mass national democracy – which four decades later Anthony Arblaster found he could not improve on – applies with even greater force to transnational democracy: 'a difficult and hitherto largely uncharted territory; and we should be nearer the mark, and should have a far more convincing slogan, if we spoke of the need, not to defend democracy, but to create it' (Carr 1951: 76; Arblaster 1994: 103).

This chapter argues that the creation of transnational democracy needs to be seen in tandem with the development of national democracy, as both are presently inadequate but their futures are interdependent. It sketches out how 'globalisation' has put transnational democracy on the agenda by disrupting and undermining traditional 'inside/outside' dichotomies between the national territory and the world beyond. It then outlines how a structural tendency for 'politics' and 'economics' to be separated in capitalism facilitates the two major and related exclusions of democracy: from the transnational sphere generally and also from economic production both within the national territory as well as transnationally. We shall see that territoriality has distinct benefits for democracy, including helping to 'forget' the paradox of its *un*democratic origins, but territoriality also points to serious limitations for democracy that may be off-set by the advantages of *non*-territorial communities and participatory democracy. Territorially-based representation can sometimes be extended across borders, but the future of transnational democracy (TND) will probably depend more on non-territorial participatory democracy, which is more flexible and amenable to border-crossing.

Disrupting 'Inside/Outside' Dichotomies

The dichotomy between 'inside' and 'outside' state borders, between 'domestic' and 'foreign' affairs, has underpinned – and to a significant degree continues to underpin – the negation of democracy in the transnational sphere beyond the state territory. It is reflected in a debilitating disciplinary division between Political Science, focusing on the internal study of 'the state', typically in the singular and including democracy, and a separate field of International Relations (IR), the study of relations between many states (Walker 1993). IR theorists, with some exceptions, have tended to ignore democracy, while theorists of democracy have tended to ignore supposedly 'anarchical' international society, some arguing that the shared history and culture necessary for a 'democratic community' is largely absent at transnational levels (McGrew 2002). To some, democracy above the state level is utopian or impossible, a sceptical Robert Dahl advising that 'we should openly recognise that international decision making will not be democratic' (Dahl 1999: 23). Friedrich Hayek, concerned to insulate the 'liberty' of capitalists from popular democratic demands and state 'interference', located his ultra-minimal, neo-liberal dream state at the inter-nation state level of governance, above and separated from national democracy – a 'dream' the neo-liberal European Union (EU) with its so-called 'democratic deficit' is in danger of approximating with potentially disastrous consequences for its own legitimacy (Anderson 2006). Liberal democratic theory (with the significant exception of cosmopolitanism discussed below) has mostly focused on the singular, territorially delimited state 'community', effectively ignoring other states, other communities and international relations. And in IR – particularly its dominant 'realist' school – there was a widespread assumption that states were *the* – indeed sometimes *the only* – important 'international' actors.

But 'globalisation' has seriously disrupted the traditional dichotomy between national and international affairs and its reflections in political and geo-political theory. For instance, where multinational corporations and foreign direct investment (FDI) dominate economic production, the familiar 'domestic/foreign' distinction breaks down. Nor is the 'international sphere' simply 'anarchy' as so-called 'realists' claim, rather it is 'already quite dense with networks of communication and associations' (Bohman 2007: 171). These networks range from the transnationalisation of cultural interest groups, such as those around 'World Music', to burgeoning world city networks of global governance (Taylor 2005). So the problem is not a transnational absence of social communities and processes, but rather the relative absence of democracy from many of the communities that are there. Many processes and their effects do cross borders, but democracy generally does not, and the result is *un*democratic trespass (environmental pollution, for instance, seeps through or wafts across the border). Hence, there is an absence of democracy's standard benefits, such as the ruled having some control over their rulers, giving the latter information about the wishes of the former, reducing arbitrary and self-interested decisions, and generally fostering individual rights, more equality and the common good. Increasing overlaps and ambiguities between 'inside' and 'outside' erode what was always to some extent a misleading separation. But conventional thinking still has difficulty coping with a world at least partly turned 'inside out and outside in' (if not yet upside down). David Held notes that territorial borders generally determine which individuals are included or excluded from participating in decisions affecting their lives, but 'the outcomes of these decisions . . . often stretch beyond national frontiers' (Held 2006: 292). As he says:

> The implications of this are troubling, not only for the categories of consent and legitimacy but for all the key ideas of democracy: the nature of a constituency, the meaning of representation, the proper form and scope of political participation, the extent of deliberation, and the relevance of the democratic nation-state as the guarantor of the rights, duties and welfare of subjects. (Held 2006: 292)

It is true that the 'sovereignty of the nation-state has generally not been questioned' (Held 2006: 290), but it must indeed be questioned when causes and effects cross borders (for a general history of sovereignty, see Hinsley 1986). The increased border crossings of 'globalisation' challenge 'taken-for-granted' assumptions about 'political community' being co-terminus with state territory or its standard electoral sub-divisions.

TND is on the agenda because 'globalisation' is eroding our already limited forms of national representation, while at the same time increasing transnational governance and border crossings that need democratising. The spectacular growth of transnational processes has unfortunately been matched by spectacular 'democratic deficits'. New, or newly powerful, non-state actors include supra-state trading blocs like the EU; sub-state regions and their transnational associations; multilateral institutions of global regulation such as the World Bank, the IMF and the WTO; multinational corporations; trades union federations; international non-government organisations (INGOs) such as Oxfam, *Médicins sans Frontières*, Amnesty International and Greenpeace; transnational social movements and meetings, such as the 'anti-capitalist' World Social Forum. Some are inherently undemocratic, but democratisation is central to the agenda of many of them.

So far the effects of transnationalisation are mostly negative for democracy: weakening popular sovereignty and (most) elected representatives within state arenas (though not necessarily weakening states *per se*). State power has tended to act as 'a transmission belt from the global to the national', rather than 'a bulwark defending domestic welfare'; hence, power has tended to become 'concentrated in those agencies in closest touch with the global economy – the offices of presidents and prime ministers, treasuries, central banks', while agencies 'more closely identified with domestic clients . . . become subordinated' (Cox 1992: 30–1). Key decisions about transnational processes are monopolised by a small elite of representatives and unelected officials: by, for example, a minority of those in cabinet government, rather than by the whole government, never mind all the representatives debating together, much less the electorate. Clearly, there are new needs and new opportunities for TND, but the structural rootedness of the 'inside/outside' dichotomy suggests that transnational democratisation will not be easy.

The Separation of 'Politics' and 'Economics'

In his moving account of how in Britain 'the vote was won and then undermined', Paul Foot provides a graphic example of the two-sided historical trajectory of democracy – as electoral representation was widened to become more socially inclusive (with working-class males and all women), the content of the democracy on offer was diluted and reduced in the recurring conflict between:

> parliamentary or political democracy and economic democracy . . . Without some form of democratic control of industry, finance and services . . . political democracy will always be at the mercy of a greedy and predatory economic hierarchy . . . the electoral process, whenever it favours labour and the poor, has been consistently thwarted by undemocratic forces it does not control. (Foot 2006: x, 429)

This is not a new condition. From at least the time of Plato, the rich and powerful openly opposed democracy as so-called 'rule by the mob' and some still do, if not so openly (Arblaster 1994). But the modern British story of 'political power' trumped by 'economic power' has a deeper and wider significance. The twin exclusions of liberal democracy from economic production and from the transnational sphere mean that large swathes of modern capitalist society elude democratic control, for non-territorial as well as territorial reasons. These twin exclusions are perhaps best understood in terms of their structural basis in capitalism's separation of 'politics' and 'economics'. Both exclusions – democracy generally stops at the gates of the workplace as well as at the borders of the state – have the same structural roots in this 'politics/economics' separation which is unique to capitalism (Wood 1995).

In pre-capitalist modes of production economic surpluses were typically extracted from the producers (slaves or serfs, for example) by *extra*-economic means. The direct use of physical force and/or political, ideological and religious 'persuasion' were the central means of surplus extraction in slave-owning and feudal societies and those ruled by priestly castes. In sharp contrast, surpluses in capitalism are generally extracted from the 'free' labour of the producers (workers) through the economic operations of the 'free market'. Here the 'politics' of physical enforcement are apparently absent from the 'economics' of the production process and market exchange. However this formulation has to be qualified. First, the 'politics/economics' separation is only partial. In reality, or despite appearances, 'politics' and physical force are still used, but indirectly rather than directly. They have not been removed or rendered unnecessary, but are only displaced to the realm of the national state which acts as the enforcer of property rights and the 'rule of law' without which 'economic' production and the so-called 'free' market could not operate. There is no such thing as capitalist production or a market that is 'free' of state support, even if that is just the force needed to protect property. This 'politics' of force is less transparent (than in classic feudalism, for example) because it is displaced from the immediate 'economic' sphere of production to the 'political' sphere of the state. Secondly, the separation of economics and politics is politically contested and, hence, can vary significantly, from the extreme of 'economic' separation in *laissez-faire* to the 'political' dominance in state-operated production. Socialists (like Foot), for instance, want more democratic, that is, political, control of the economy and more state ownership, while liberals want privatisation and minimal political regulation of markets – and the latter achieved a high-point of 'politics/economics' separation in the 1980s with the 'Washington Consensus', a set of neo-liberal prescriptions to which countries seeking support from the IMF, World Bank and so on must subscribe.

Although partial and contested, this structural separation of 'politics/economics' has a strong institutional reality and profound implications for democracy, sovereignty and the transnational. It finds expression in separate 'economic' and 'political' institutions and the 'division of labour' between 'business people' and 'politicians' (and in an academic gulf between Economics and Politics which is even more debilitating than the disciplinary division between Political Science and IR). At its simplest, the separation involves a 'public realm' of 'politics' and the state, which is territorially delimited, and a 'private sphere' of economic production, distribution and exchange, which is beyond democratic control and – partly for that reason – more easily straddles state borders. Indeed, the separation can be re-formulated perhaps more accurately as a 'presence/absence' *of* democracy (Anderson 2001). Democratic politics is the key differentiator rather than politics *per se*. It is not politics that is excluded from production – the politics of class characterise the workplace – but more precisely liberal democracy that is excluded (or excludes itself), whether the workplace is within the owner's national arena or outside it. Decisions about what should be produced (or not), about how and where to invest, who to employ and so forth, are almost invariably separated off to the 'non-political' (that is, non-democratic) sphere of 'economics'. Here decisions are predominantly driven by 'market forces', and profitability and technocratic criteria rather than by democratic choices, ethical concerns or human needs (and in practice, although sometimes successfully contested, that can apply to state-owned as much as to privately-owned production). Likewise, it is not politics that is excluded from the transnational sphere – dominated as it is by the politics of imperialism – but rather *democratic* politics (Harvey 2003).

These structural exclusions of democracy are bolstered by the ways in which the partial separation continues to support the 'inside/outside' dichotomy. The separation is a pre-condition both of the claim to national sovereign independence, on the one hand, and the reality of global inter-dependencies, on the other, and it helps to explain their relatively harmonious co-existence when they seem to be in contradiction. It also helps to explain why, despite 'globalisation', the sovereignty of the national state or 'national self-determination' is generally unquestioned, and why, indeed, it can often be fetishised as an 'absolute' fact when in reality it is only a partial and questionable claim. The claim to territorial sovereignty within state borders is unquestioned precisely because the 'politics/economics' separation effectively (if not always explicitly) limits the sovereignty claim to the sphere of 'politics' and leaves most of the 'economic' sphere, including foreign direct investment (FDI), out of consideration.

Conversely, the separation facilitates the globalisation of economic production across national state borders without implying that sovereignty has been breached.

So, for example, far from rejecting FDI as 'foreign interference', the 'sovereign' states and their constituent regions and cities can fall over themselves trying to attract it. For sovereignty is 'political', while investment in economic production is merely 'economic'. Irrespective of ownership, foreign or domestic (or for that matter even state-owned), production is generally beyond the reach of national democracy. And this makes FDI – including the foreign direct *dis*investment of branch plant closures and mass redundancies – *the un*democratic trespass *par excellence*, embodying the 'double exclusion' of democracy from production and from the transnational sphere. In the face of major foreign disinvestments it is sometimes contested on nationalistic grounds, but this is questionable given that 'domestic' disinvestments are also beyond democratic control, which is the main issue. Usually, of course, the undemocratic trespass is not recognised as such because of the plausibility of the 'political' claim to sovereignty. The separation buttresses national territorial democracy by lending it an aura of 'absolute' sovereignty through confining it to 'politics' minus 'economics'. It enables 'economics' to transcend territorial borders unencumbered by 'politics', but at the cost of excluding transnational democracy.

Territoriality, Representation and Participation

Democracy literally means 'rule by the people', the *demos*. But originally *demos* had connotations of 'place', and then referred to 'the people' as the inhabitants of a particular place, already a territorial community. It seems democracy was based on territoriality from the start, and today it shares fully in its strengths and weaknesses. Territoriality is a spatial mode of social organisation where bordered geographical spaces are used for purposes of social classification and control (Sack 1986: 21–34). It operates by delimiting geographical 'territories' to include or exclude things and people, and control cross-border movements in, out and between different areas or places. Its strengths include simplifying issues of control and administration, and giving power relationships material or symbolic tangibility. For liberal democracy territoriality crucially provides the standard hierarchical framework of ready-made and usually accepted electoral 'communities', the bordered territorial units for representation at different spatial scales: electoral wards and the constituencies of local, regional and national government, up to, but usually not beyond, the level of national states (the weak European Parliament being an interesting exception). This all-purpose territorial framework – where elected representatives decide on matters deemed to affect the respective territorial communities – gives legitimacy to decisions in that the framework pre-dates, is independent of, and is clearly not 'biased' by, the particular issues and interests of the moment. Decisions are further distanced from implications of 'bias' by the framework's more abstract *spatial* basis in territory, rather than in the *social* attributes of voters. Furthermore, it prevents the paradox of democracy's *un*democratic origins becoming a recurring problem (except, of course, where the territorial framework is persistently contested as in ethno-national conflicts).

As William Connolly indicates, representative democracy requires an institutional, including a territorial, framework and cannot operate without one, but paradoxically it follows that the creation of the framework itself cannot be accomplished democratically in the first place (Connolly 1991). Any democracy's territorial origins precede the democracy and so are necessarily undemocratic and they have to be 'forgotten' for democratic systems to be accepted as legitimate. Having a standard electoral framework of territorial units helps to 'forget'; and it also avoids having to decide the relevant community of voters each time according to the people actually affected, issue by issue; something which could be difficult, if not impossible, by purely democratic means. In some circumstances, however, territoriality's strengths become weaknesses. There may, for instance, be strong, positive reasons to define the relevant community in terms of the people actually affected, particularly where effects cross territorial borders or borders arbitrarily split actual, functioning communities. Borders can unintentionally or indiscriminately disrupt social processes and democracy is arbitrarily truncated, 'kept inside' like a prisoner and like a trespasser told to 'keep out'.

Territoriality's simplifications easily become *over*-simplifications. *Physical* space can be crudely equated with *social* space, an often unwarranted conflating of the social and the spatial. Not only are particular communities split by borders, but territoriality is in general becoming less efficient in delimiting genuine communities. The territorial 'community' assumes that people who share contiguous physical space also interact socially and share interests and problems in common. However, because of 'globalisation', increased cross-border movements and the general, but socially uneven, access to huge advances in technologies for moving people and information, that assumption is increasingly questionable or only part of the story. Now people's actual social communities are often spatially *dis*continuous and defined by function and interest instead of territory. Some people may have more in common with people living elsewhere in the country, or indeed across national borders, than with their next-door neighbours. They have community without propinquity. Conversely, a territorial community may comprise strangers with little in common except their geographical location of residence. Yet, despite these growing weaknesses of territoriality (and partly because of the inertia stemming from its strengths), communities defined by territory still dominate politically over non-territorial ones based directly on actual social interests, associations or functions. The non-territorial communities continue to be marginalised or crowded out, and with them non-territorial types of democracy – *direct*, *participatory* or *deliberative* (Held 2006: 209–15, 224–52). However, their potential strengths highlight the impoverishment of a democracy largely confined to territorial representation.

Deliberative democracy, for instance, can involve the general public in developing and setting political agendas, rather than simply voting for alternatives on agendas already decided by territorial representatives or even less representative elites. Deliberation is geared to improving the quality of democracy through informed public debate, a public sharing of knowledge and a striving for reasoned decisions (using mechanisms such as opinion polls, referenda and citizens' juries). In the case of *direct* democracy, associated more with socialism than liberalism, and trade union and workplace collectives rather than territorial communities, major decisions can be taken collectively by the people themselves rather than by 'representatives'. Elected delegates are mandated by collective democratic decisions on how to vote on particular issues in higher level assemblies and are subject to 'report back', recall and, if necessary, replacement. In contrast, liberal representative democracy allows people to vote only as individuals, typically at lengthy intervals and with little means of ensuring representatives actually represent their views or keep electoral promises; and even less chance of replacing them – until the next election comes round by which time it may be too late. Participatory forms, by contrast, can draw on a wide range of civil society organisations and active collectives, many of which constitute functioning communities, their members already in regular social contact with one another, their representatives subject to continuous or frequent democratic pressures from the members. In many respects this is superior to representation based on the formal electoral 'community' of individual voters: they often comprise an *ad hoc* collection of diverse interests which not surprisingly lacks its own coherent voice. The more flexible and robust forms of participatory democracy can more readily cross state borders instead of stopping or being stopped at them. Yet, despite its limitations, representative democracy can sometimes be extended internationally across borders with the 'bonus' of fostering the cross-border communities and participation on which the future of TND will probably depend.

International Representation and Transnational Participation

One common model for extending national to international representation is the federal structure of the United States, as in the notion of a federal 'United States of Europe' where the EU's national states become like the 'states' in the US federal structure. But this misleadingly assumes that the EU would become just another state, that it would in fact leave the transnational sphere under discussion (Anderson 2006). John Agnew demolishes the notion that the United States' essentially eighteenth-century form of liberal, limited and rather sclerotic national government is an appropriate transnational guide for the twenty-first century; and in any case, TND is 'not best formulated as a single territorial model' (Agnew 2002: 70). Much more promising, ambitious and specifically cosmopolitan plans are provided by David Held, who persuasively argues for a complex set of new transnational institutional structures for cross-border democracy at various different levels (Held 1995). Drawing mainly on liberalism, he emphasises the extension of 'cosmopolitan democratic law', not as the law of states, or between one state and another, but for all in the 'universal community', in 'an expanding institutional framework for the democratic regulation of states and societies' (Held 1995: 232–4). He includes various supra-state forums, such as continental-scale parliaments and a stronger, more representative UN assembly, with participatory democracy at local levels to complement the representative assemblies of the wider global order (Held 1995: 272–8).

This would substantially increase TND and the architectural plans are impressive. It is, however, quite unclear what agents or agencies might build these cosmopolitan structures. The scenario seems disappointingly 'top-down' with participatory democracy confined to 'local levels'. As Richard Falk rather acidly observed: 'The only elites . . . likely to contemplate world government favourably in the foreseeable future are those that currently seem responsible for the most acute forms of human suffering'; and he concludes that while the cosmopolitan approach encompasses:

> participation, accountability, lawmaking, and agenda-setting by the peoples of the world, through their representatives . . . it doesn't carry us very far. It doesn't tell us whether and in what circumstances governments are representatives of peoples, thereby satisfying democratic requirements, and when they are not. (Falk 1995: 7, 119–20)

Instead, Falk, like others, puts his faith in the participatory democracy of transnational movements from below; plausible considering the historical anti-democratic credentials of the rich and powerful equating democracy with the mob.

However, evidence from the EU and, in particular, the innovative cross-border institutions linking Northern Ireland and the Irish Republic show that in some circumstances representative democracy can be substantially extended internationally. Northern Ireland's Good Friday Agreement (*Agreement* 1998) became possible only when Britain gave up its inconsistent and contradictory search for the chimera of an 'internal solution' to the conflict over the disputed partition border (Anderson 2008). The border remained in place, but its meaning was substantially transformed. A significant 'all-Ireland' dimension was added to internal consociational power-sharing through a partial joining-up of the island's two separate territorial frameworks and some joint decision making. Regular meetings of a 'North–South Ministerial Council' are loosely based on the model of 'sovereignty-sharing' in the EU's Council of Ministers, with government departmental ministers and civil servants from Belfast and Dublin taking joint decisions and coordinating policy in particular sectors, including agriculture, health, education, tourism, the environment, trade and language policy (*Agreement* 1998). There is, moreover, a significant element of cross-border participatory democracy in joint North–South 'implementation bodies'. Subject to approval by the Ministerial Council, they formulate policy on a variety of cultural, social and economic matters that straddle the border; and each is composed of people from a diverse range of civil society organisations, relevant specialist associations, pressure groups and other community organisations, nominated by the two governments and political parties from both sides of the border.

Of course, these democratic developments could have gone further. For instance, a cross-border forum of civil society representatives to give marginalised groups a say in cross-border policy formulation had been proposed, but it was mentioned only as a possibility in the *Agreement* (Anderson and Goodman 1998: 249). Instead, a civic forum for the North alone was established, but, subsequently, it was then marginalised partly because conventional representative politicians disliked it as 'competition' to themselves. This highlights the danger that politicians may play 'zero-sum games' with the different forms of democracy, and leads to some other general points. Ireland's breaching of orthodox notions of state sovereignty happened only because of the pressure 'from below' of a violent ethno-national conflict. On the other hand, the generality of cross-border situations have the advantage of not being soured by such conflict, though they too will need their own 'pressure from below' for cross-border relations to be democratised.

Cross-border representative frameworks are important not just in themselves, but for setting a frame of reference for the growth of active cross-border communities as a basis for participatory democracy; and here they constitute a direct counter to the tendency for national representative frameworks to corral participatory efforts within purely national arenas. TND probably depends most immediately on political struggles using participatory forms within existing transnational institutions and communities. Participatory forms are more suited to transnational arenas, as John Dryzek argues for deliberative democracy (Dryzek 2000). Whereas extending new state-like government structures across borders is inherently difficult, extending looser forms of participatory democratic *governance* through already existing structures is easier by comparison. While democracy is mainly theorised 'in terms of the ideal of a self-governing community within precise territorial boundaries', extending it trans-nationally is easier if we think of it not in terms of voting and representatives, but as participating in deliberations that can be within fixed territories but can also readily cope with fluid borders and with crossing them (Dryzek 2000: 5, 115–22). Further-more, 'democracy without boundaries means that the intimate link between democracy and the state can be severed'; and shorn of state-dependence cross-border participation opens up a variety of additional dimensions for democracy (Dryzek 2000: 128–9). States themselves, as Bohman argues, can become more democratic only if they begin to practice democracy across their borders: we need to think not of the territorial *demos* in the singular, as in the national arena, but of *demoi* in the plural, or a transnational 'democracy of democracies' (Bohman 2007: 188–90).

Conclusion

The different forms of democracy – representative and participatory, territorial and non-territorial, national and transnational – can all be more effective when mutually supporting rather than being played off against each other. Democracy needs to fire on all cylinders, and TND needs all the help it can get considering the urgency and difficulties it faces. Non- and anti-democratic cross-border processes have expanded greatly with 'globalisation'. There are also contradictory and chauvinist pressures to strengthen borders, not to mention the looming transnational dangers of sudden, massive population movements in response to the emerging ecological crisis. 'Inside/outside' dichotomies and traditional assumptions about territorially defined commu-nity have been disrupted, but democracy has not kept pace. The advantages of territoriality for democracy's development are now meeting increasing limitations. Capitalism's structural tendency to separate 'politics/economics' continues to under-pin both state territoriality – not about to wither away any time soon – and the two main absences of democracy from economic production and more generally from the transnational sphere. The separation enables the 'economics' of globalisation to transcend territorial borders, but at the cost of excluding transnational democracy. TND is clearly 'difficult and hitherto largely uncharted' (Carr 1951: 76). Further work is clearly needed, and perhaps especially on the potential for mutual support between national and transnational democracy, representation and participation, and territorial and non-territorial communities. There also needs to be more debate comparing 'bottom-up' and 'top-down' approaches with democratisation and the question of agency and not just with respect to cosmopolitan democracy, but also to TND in general.

But it is possible to provisionally conclude that the future of TND most immediately depends on 'bottom-up' democratisation within existing transnational structures, employing the more flexible and robust forms of participatory democracy that readily cross borders instead of stopping at them. The 'politics/economics' separation and both its associated democratic absences, the economic as well as the transnational, have to be contested. Simply extending liberal representative democracy or the networks of established power beyond state borders cannot create TND. Here a decade-and-a-half later – it is difficult to improve on Richard Falk's conclusion:

> The necessary enlargements of democratization will occur, if at all, only through pressure and struggle. Economic and political elites will not protect the general human interest on the basis of their own values or even through . . . enlightened self-interest . . . Only a transnational social movement animated by a vision of humane governance can offer any hope of extending the domain of democracy. (Falk 1995: 119–20)

References

Agnew, J. (2002), 'The Limits of Federalism in Transnational Democracy: Beyond the Hegemony of the US Model', in J. Anderson (ed.), *Transnational Democracy: Political Spaces and Border Crossings*, London: Routledge, pp. 56–72.

Agreement (1998), The *'Belfast Agreement'*, Belfast: HMSO, April.

Anderson, J. (2001), *Theorizing State Borders: 'Politics/Economics' and Democracy in Capitalism*, Electronic Working Paper Series, Belfast: Centre for International Borders Research.

Anderson, J. (2006), 'Transnational Democracy for European Diversity', in K. Robins (ed.), *The Challenge of Transcultural Diversities*, Strasbourg: Council of Europe Publishing, pp. 81–97.

Anderson, J. (2008), 'Partition, Consociation, Border-crossing: Some Lessons from the National Conflict in Ireland/Northern Ireland', *Nations and Nationalism*, 14(1), 1–20.

Anderson, J. and J. Goodman (1998), 'North–South Agendas for Dis/agreeing Ireland', in J. Anderson and J. Goodman (eds), *Dis/Agreeing Ireland: Contexts, Obstacles, Hopes*, London: Pluto Press, pp. 232–56.

Arblaster, A. (1994), *Democracy*, Buckingham: Open University Press.

Bohman, J. (2007), *Democracy Across Borders: From* Demos *to* Demoi, Cambridge, MA: MIT Press.

Carr, E. H. (1951), *The New Society*, London: Macmillan.

Connolly, W. (1991), 'Democracy and Territoriality', *Millennium*, 20(3), 463–84.

Cox, R. W. (1992), 'Global Perestroika', in R. Miliband and L. Panitch (eds), *Socialist Register*, London: Merlin Press, pp. 26–44.

Dahl, R. (1999), 'Can International Organizations be Democratic? A Skeptic's View', in C. Hacker-Cordon and I. Shapiro (eds), *Democracy's Edges*, Cambridge: Cambridge University Press, pp. 19–37.

Dryzek, J. S. (2000), *Deliberative Democracy and Beyond: Liberals, Critics, Contestations*, Oxford: Oxford University Press.

Falk, R. (1995), *On Humane Governance: Towards a New Global Politics: A Report of the World Order Models Project*, Cambridge: Polity.

Foot, P. (2006), *The Vote: How it was Won and How it was Undermined*, London: Penguin.

Harvey, D. (2003), *The New Imperialism*, Oxford: Oxford University Press.

Held, D. (1995), *Democracy and the Global Order: From the Modern State to Cosmopolitan Governance*, Cambridge: Polity.

Held, D. (2006), *Models of Democracy*, 3rd edn, Cambridge: Polity.

Hinsley, F. H. (1986), *Sovereignty*, 2nd edn, Cambridge: Cambridge University Press.

McGrew, A. (2002), 'Democratising Global Institutions: Possibilities, Limits and Normative Foundations', in J. Anderson (ed.), *Transnational Democracy: Political Spaces and Border Crossings*, London: Routledge, pp. 149–70.

Sack, R. (1986), *Human Territoriality: Its Theory and History*, Cambridge: Cambridge University Press.

Taylor, P. J. (2005), 'New Political Geographies: Global Civil Society and Global Governance through World City Networks', *Political Geography*, 24(6), 703–30.

Walker, R. B. J. (1993), *Inside/Outside: International Relations as Political Theory*, Cambridge: Cambridge University Press.

Wood, E. M. (1995), 'The Separation of the "Economic" and the "Political" in Capitalism', in E. M. Wood (ed.), *Democracy Against Capitalism: Renewing Historical Materialism*, Cambridge: Cambridge University Press, pp. 19–48.

Chapter 40

Digital Democracy

Brian Loader

Political communication and the means of its production and diffusion have always been a significant factor shaping the nature of democratic politics. From the oral tradition of the *Agora*, through the pamphlets and newspapers of early modern Europe, to the prevalence of the mass broadcast media in the twentieth century, the communicative power of citizens has been influenced by their access to and use of the prevailing media technologies. It was no surprise, therefore, that the emergence of new information and communication technologies (ICTs), in the form of digital networks such as the Internet, once again raised the prospect of new directions for democratic governance (Loader 1997). For some commentators the open and collaborative nature, particularly of the latest variants of *social media*, make it almost inherently democratic (Benkler 2006; Hippel 2005; Jenkins 2006). Yet, as in previous incarnations, these optimistic speculations for digital democracy need to be tempered by an understanding that sees communications technologies as socio-cultural artefacts that are shaped by political conflict and open to variable interpretations of use. Consequently, they may just as likely be considered as threats to democratic governance by facilitating apathy, surveillance or social control (Habermas [1962] 1989; Lyon 2003; Postman 1987).

As in the past, new media technologies are positioned to significantly influence democratic politics, but in ways that are likely to be contingent upon contestations between groups and agents who are themselves subject to wider socio-cultural and ecological trends. This indeterminate characteristic, produced by contestation around *communicative technologies of governance* (CTG),[1] and how those technologies articulate contemporary debates about the future possibilities for citizenship and democracy are the principal concerns of this chapter. At its core is the argument that digital democracy is inexorably linked to current anxieties about the closure of the public sphere and the concomitant challenge of multiple alternative political identities in contemporary democratic cultures. Emerging CTG are configured by these trends, but also shape the possibilities and limitations of their development. Crudely this contest can be recognised in at least two quite distinct versions of digital democracy. One version is associated with the early formulations of digital democracy that championed these CTG as a means to construct *virtual public spheres* providing greater access for citizens and enabling deliberative democratic decision making (Blumer and Gurevitch 2001; Tsagarousianou *et al.* 1998). A more recent version of digital democracy draws inspiration from democratic and social theory to see the democratic potential of these CTG being shaped through the autonomous networking of citizens engaged in lifestyle and identity politics (Bennett 2003; Dahlgren 2009; Papacharissi 2010).

The Early Promise of Digital Democracy

Pessimistic accounts of the disengagement of citizens, particularly young ones, from democratic politics in many countries provided a fertile atmosphere for the birth of digital democracy (Loader 2007). Anxiety about poor voter turnout, declining membership of political parties and negative opinion polls about politicians and politics were trotted out with monotonous regularity as indicators of the poor health of democracy. Imbued with a view that democratic politics is sleazy, corrupt and self-serving, attention became directed to a reappraisal of the effectiveness of the media as a conduit between political elites and citizens. Instead of facilitating deliberative democracy, the media was accused of producing apathy and eroding the social capital necessary for civic participation (Putnam 2000). Understandably, the emergence of new CTG offered the prospect of ameliorating this situation to become the potential salvation of democratic politics.

At its simplest, the term digital democracy (or electronic democracy[2]) was used to describe the adoption of computer networked communications technologies, most notably the Internet, for enhancing democratic politics at local, regional, national and international levels. Typically, these manifested themselves through experimental initiatives worldwide. They originated from governments, community groups, social movements and protest activities or the commercial and business sector (Hague and Loader 1998; Tsagarousianou et al. 1998). They were further categorised through media applications used for different democratic processes, such as on-line campaigning and electioneering, deliberative citizen forums, social movements, community politics and political parties (Chadwick 2006). What underpinned the enormous optimism for the potential of digital democracy was the contention that these new CTG could enable more direct, participatory forms of democracy. Anyone with a computer and Internet connection, it was suggested, could access this virtual public sphere at any time and engage in discussion or share information across national boundaries. Citizens could thereby more effectively hold leaders, tyrants and regimes to account. Political activists could protest, challenge and propose. The electorate could get closer to their elected representatives.

A small number of cyber-utopians and cyber-libertarians championed the replacement of representative governments with direct or anarchistic forms (Barlow 1996). However, most interest in the Internet was directed to its potential for creating a public sphere on the model outlined by Jürgen Habermas ([1962] 1989). For Habermas, the crucial democratic aspect of the public sphere is the reasoned manner in which public opinion is formulated through critical deliberative norms in pursuit of the public will. Many of the earliest variants of digital democracy appealed directly to a Habermasian mode of consensual and deliberative democracy (Tsagarousianou et al. 1998). The electronic discussion forum that enabled ordinary citizens to 'have their say' on issues of direct interest to them came to epitomise this new democratic CTG. One of its earliest manifestations was the Public Electronic Network (PEN), which was an email and computer conferencing system owned and run by the Santa Monica city council in California, USA (Doctor and Dutton 1998; Tassel 1994). Going live in February 1989, PEN was designed to give local residents access to information and stimulate participation in local decision making. Computer networked communication presented a cheaper alternative to previous tele-democracy experiments using interactive cable TV to increase the participation of citizens and improve the responsiveness of local government (Becker 1981). Early enthusiasm for the initiative led to the participation of local opinion leaders in online conferences, together with increasing numbers of observant 'lurkers'. The Santa Monica network also fostered the development of citizen groups on particular interests such as homelessness. Indeed, it stimulated the kind of citizen discussions which might approximate to a public sphere. The increasing prevalence of the internet in the last decade of the twentieth century witnessed an explosion in similar digital democracy initiatives, particularly in North America and Europe. Many of these were city or community informatics projects, including Digital Amsterdam City, Manchester Electronic Village Halls, Blackburg Community Network, Minnesota Net and many more (Keeble and Loader 2001; Schuler 1994).

However, evaluation of these early digital democracy experiments and other online political communities such as Usenet, uncovered a number of limitations that questioned their potential to facilitate deliberative forms of online democracy. Contrary to the idealised dream of a Habamasian public sphere widely accessible to a reasoning, deliberative public, the picture that emerged instead was a digital divide, which reflected the Internet's relationship to the offline world of socio-economic inequality (Loader 1998a). Anthony Wilhelm in his analysis of the virtual public sphere concluded that it offered little hope of overcoming the entrenched offline socio-economic problems that undermined access to existing participation in democratic politics (Wilhelm 2000). Instead of the Internet transforming democracy it was more likely that society and politics would change the Internet (Hill and Hughes 1998: 182). By the turn of the millennium our understanding of CTG was becoming embedded in 'everyday life' (Wellman and Haythornthwaite 2002). These more grounded approaches revealed that the quality of online deliberation shared the factionalism, bias, personalisation and abuse of conventional politics (Doctor and Dutton 1998; Dutton and Guthrie 1991).

The early optimism for the Internet as a panacea for democratic ills was replaced by the contention that it would just reinforce the existing crisis in democratic politics. At best, these CTG were a cost-effective means of re-inventing government and providing better public services (Fountain 2001). In these contexts the public either picks up the costs of 'government direct' or are simply ignored by political elites (Loader 1998b). Little evidence had been found that the Internet was a means to stimulating participatory democracy and public sphere deliberation. The remedy of a Habermasian model for democracy's ills was itself critiqued by post-modern and feminist theorists, who found that public spheres were gendered, racist and privileging the communicative power of white, middle-class males (Fraser 1990; Pateman 1989). Instead, more inclusion in the public sphere (online or offline) required displacement of rational forms of deliberation with *discursive* models applicable to the cultural diversity of contemporary societies (Dryzek 2000; Young 2000). Regardless, virtual public spheres continue to garner support despite the paucity of evidence in their favour. One re-statement of the case for an online deliberative commons was made by two veteran scholars, Stephen Coleman and Jay Blumler. They offer the BBC as an example of a publicly supported domain. However, while it may be superior to many public spheres, the BBC is still limited as a forum for the opinions of all citizens because it provides only rare opportunities for alternative lifestyles or politics to be considered seriously. Most discussion fails to move far from the middle ground of mainstream public opinion. Moreover, it is still dependent for its revenue upon the government of the day who set the licence fees (Coleman and Blumler 2009).

Digital Democracy in the Age of Social Media

Despite the limitations of early experiments in digital democracy, a new-found enthusiasm for the transforming qualities of these CTG once again emerged with the recent generation of digital communications applications. Originally described as Web 2.0 to denote the proclaimed disjuncture with previous Internet technologies, it is now more commonly known as *social media*. Throughout the first decade of the twenty-first century, the diffusion of social media platforms has been rapid. Increasingly ubiquitous social media include websites such as *Facebook*, *MySpace* or *Bebo*, which allow participants to personalise their interface and construct friendship channels; blogs that make it possible for anyone to disseminate their opinions; microblogs such as *Twitter*, which enable people to share their brief observations with their followers; wikis, like *Wikipedia*, that let contributors collectively create, share and edit content; content communities such as *YouTube*, *Flickr* and *del.icio.us* that give users the chance to organise and distribute digital content; and podcasting, which allows audio and video content from such sources as *Apple iTunes* or *BBC iPlayer* to be downloaded. What is seen as distinctive about social media is its proclaimed people-centred orientation, which may empower both customers in the marketplace and also citizens in democracy. The 'social affordances' that are facilitated by social media platforms have the potential to reconfigure power relations between users and participants through different modes of communication, transaction, creativity and/or collective action. This shift is predicated upon social media's capacity to enable customers and citizens, rather than being passive recipients of standardised manufactured goods, public services and policy edicts, instead to become capable of participating in the design, construction and consumption of their desires via 'user-centred innovation' (Hippel 2005). Axel Bruns refers to the idea of the breakdown of functional barriers between producers and consumers in the creation of collaborative outcomes as 'produsage' (Bruns 2007).

Furthermore, user-centred innovation is perhaps most effectively undertaken through 'mass-collaboration' (Leadbeater 2008). The open source software movement and *Wikipedia* are examples of the realisation of this potential. Mass collaboration is also said to be responsible for developing 'innovation user communities' or movements that are important for industry, but also for the empowerment of citizens in the political domain: 'democracy is a prime example of our capacity for collective innovation: our ability to make binding decisions together to produce social innovations, from the abolition of slavery and child labour to the collective provision of education and welfare' (Leadbeater 2008: 170). Perhaps as a consequence of the marketing agencies from which they originate, many prophecies about social media are characterised by hyperbole rather than critical conceptual clarification favoured by scholars. Nonetheless, the argument is made that these CTG have distinctive, inherent democratic capacities (Benkler 2006; Jenkins 2006; Leadbeater 2009). Their argument centres upon social media's contrast to traditional mass media and a shift in communicative power. Unlike the centralised control and dissemination of industrial mass media or the top-down initiatives of early digital democracy projects, social media is seen to facilitate grassroots interaction that enables citizens to challenge mainstream political institutions and practices. Social media is financially, technologically and (usually) legally accessible to millions of ordinary people living in advanced societies. The ease with which almost anyone can gain access to social media and publish content without professional knowledge or competence creates new opportunities for the production and communication of ideas, social meaning and culture. Moreover, social media enables an immediacy of publication and response which old-style broadcast media cannot match without incorporating social media into their operations. If the publication of books, TV programmes and films are fixed in their formats, social media are often emergent forms in transition, subject to continual editing, revision and interactive feedback.

Increasingly, citizens can use social media to communicate and exchange information among themselves, rather than primarily with political institutions. Social media may provide opportunities to reconfigure social relations of production, community and power. How it does so and the potential consequences for democracy are far from certain. If these forms of CTG are significantly different from those involved in earlier claims for digital democracy, it is useful to explore these differences and their potential impact on democratic processes. To address these issues it is necessary to recognise the contingent nature of the development of such technologies.

The Shape of Digital Democracy to Come

Scholars working in the field of science and technology studies (STS) have done much to replace simplistic technological determinism and aid our understanding of the contested and problematic nature of the development and diffusion of technologies. As Sismondo observes: 'Knowledge and artefacts are human products, and marked by the circumstances of their production' (Sismondo 2004: 10). Histories of familiar items such as bicycles, Bakelite, electric light bulbs and telephones show many different paths to innovation and the frequently haphazard manner in which these objects were developed. At each stage of the process, the outcome may well have been different from the eventual one. Many socio-cultural factors come into play that favour some options over others. Consequently, despite commonly held assumptions, the development of technologies does not proceed along a linear progression, but is marked by complex processes of 'flexible interpretation' (Bijker *et al.* 1987). Even before the current interest in innovation-communities, these scholars recognised the importance of 'social groups' for shaping the design of technologies, with each group capable of constructing radically different meanings of a technology, often in competition with other groups.

These early insights have been further complemented by feminist, semiotic, actor/ network and 'domestication' approaches, all of which have contributed to our under-standing of the fluid and contingent nature of the shaping of technological artefacts (Oudshoorn and Pinch 2005). Of particular interest is the significance these studies place on the 'user' as an influential agent. In their respective explorations they all foreground the important role of the user in the 'co-construction' of technological innovation, which, as we have seen above, is manifested through social media as user-centred innovation, mass collaboration and 'prosumerism'. While space limitations preclude any kind of extensive discussion of these ideas, what is important to acknowledge is how user-centred innovations undermine the idea that social media technologies can in themselves produce strong democratic polities. Citizens neither withdraw from politics because of a lack of Internet connectivity nor become activists simply because somebody gave them an *iPhone*. What influences the use of social media for democratic politics is a complex and dynamic range of socio-cultural factors. The earlier experiments in digital democracy discussed above failed to produce virtual public spheres not because of the limitations of the technology, but rather because the Habermasian model of the public sphere was itself incompatible with contemporary social culture and political attitudes. An appropriate evaluation of the emancipatory rhetoric of social media requires us to ask what factors are shaping the current generation of communication media and what, if any, are their implications for democratic governance.

Many have suggested that recent social trends represent a profound cultural 'turn' in advanced democratic societies (Bauman 2000, 2005; Beck 1992; Giddens 1991). Without an agreed theoretical model, these theorists nonetheless identify several phenomena that can be seen to have an elective affinity with social media. In particular, there is recognition of a shift towards an individualism which is seen as fragmenting former collective notions of citizenship. The prescription of stable political identities through the traditional structures of social class, family and community declined in late modern societies and have been replaced instead by more fluid processes of individual identity construction (Bauman 2000, 2005). This is characterised by what Giddens, for example, calls 'the project of the self' in contemporary society whereby the individual is required to reflexively narrate their own biography (Giddens 1991: 54). Drawing upon the growing amounts of information and advice available, people are able to tell stories that relate their self-identity to wider social factors and personal experiences. According to Giddens, they are aided in this venture by the choice of 'lifestyles' available to them (Giddens 1991: 81). Such opportunities for the self-actualisation of diverse lifestyles may be severely limited for many people depending on where they live and the resources at their disposal (Bourdieu 1984). Nevertheless, with the assistance of the media, it may now be possible in post-traditional societies to conceive of a much wider choice of lifestyle identities to enfold into one's narrative. Moreover, the reflexive processes involved in the construction of a more personalised political identity lead to two further important developments. They stimulate a self-actualising model of citizenship that emphasises a personalised and experiential orientation to political understanding (Bennett *et al.* 2009). A consequence of this is a decline in deference to traditional authority and a challenge to expertise and dominant discourses.

Democratic politics in this frame are characterised by competing discourses around the construction of lifestyle politics and the self-actualisation of identity. These constructs offer a rich diversity of contrasting lifestyles incorporating race, gender, sexuality, geography and class. Each of these constructs may be capable of providing the individual citizen with greater opportunities for autonomy, control and self-expression. Such interpretations form the focus of much contentious debate among scholars (McKee 2005). For the purposes of our discussion, however, these constructs are important for reinforcing the contention that political identities are contingent upon the nature of a variety of relations that may be increasingly realised through a range of offline and online networked spaces, many of which are facilitated by social media. For evidence of such relational indices of political identity and engagement it is useful to consider the actual use of social media and its manifestation in networked spaces.

User-generated Democracy

A focus upon the co-construction of social media networks reveals initial indications that prompt caution about its positive potential for influencing democratic politics. First examination of the structure of social networks supports the view that it does not present a uniform virtual space enabling the equal representation of interests. Networks are composed of nodes (individual citizens or organisations) connected by social ties (hyperlinks), but these relationships are not constructed in a random fashion. People choose their associations and vary significantly in the number of social ties (friends) they make: the vast majority having very few, and a small minority of nodes having many links (Barabasi 2011). Through individual user preferences the social web is characterised by a few giant nodes, such as *Google*, *Yahoo*, *Facebook* and *YouTube*, which attract the majority of users. These intense associations, formed by millions of hyperlinks, produce important political spaces. Such a connective dominance arguably gives these authoritative nodes a disproportionate influence over the information made available to users. The possibilities for competing or alternative lifestyle discourses to attract or mobilise users becomes increasingly difficult. Ranking algorithms used in search engines appear to privilege some information sources over others (Halavias 2009). Analysis of social networks using *Issue Crawler* mapping software reveals information politics at work through the formation of networks and contests over hyperlinking between competing interests (Rogers 2004). The outcome of such contests provides an indication of the respective communicative power of participants and also the extent to which such networks facilitate or restrict citizen access, representation and equality. Thus, we may see the strength of social network ties and the density of their clusters as visualisations of social relations of power and their sources.

Consideration of the use of, and communication through, social media as manifestations of contemporary culture gives a mixed picture about their democratic affordances. A number of cursory observations may nonetheless be usefully made to contribute to current debate. In the case of social network sites, many of the most active political users are those already politically engaged. Increasingly, politicians, party workers, social movement activists and self-appointed citizen journalists adopt social media as a means to push their messages to new recruits through the infinite scalability of the social web. The political bloggersphere, for example, is increasingly dominated by a few vociferous bloggers (Rettberg 2008). Social network use is often restricted to people connecting to friends they already know rather than seeking out new connections. Even if a user comes across an unfamiliar political message or group, it does not necessarily result in the user actually engaging with them. More typically users are networking to share gossip, embarrassing video or online gaming, rather than debating the respective merits of political arguments. The mistake of political enthusiasts is to assume that the value they place on the growing online opportunities to access and discuss political information is shared by the rest of humanity. They follow past misconceptions of digital democracy as a common virtual space existing independently of real places.

Instead, if we regard social media as reflecting the contested diversity of contemporary culture(s) through its millions of nodes and clusters of identity and lifestyle networks, it may be possible to see a more fluid conception of democratic spaces. One which perhaps foregrounds the actual practice of citizens who no longer identify with the dutiful loyalties of the past, but rather construct personalised political affiliations through their flexible links to numerous alternative spaces. Such a plurality of political spaces clearly resonates with agonistic democratic models predicated upon conflict between different identity positions (Mouffe 1993, 2005). Furthermore, these social networked relations blur the old public sphere distinctions between public and private spaces to enable citizens to engage in public politics from the 'privacy' of their own home (Papacharissi 2010). They can participate in an online campaign through mobile devices while watching television and/or sharing a conversation with family and friends. Indeed, through wi-fi, citizens can interact from a wide choice of locations. By enabling these private spaces to break into the public sphere such practices may also be seen as a manifestation of the feminist assertion that the 'personal is political' (Squires 1998). Equally important is that the variety of visual, text, audio and graphic communication that social media enables may move further from traditional rule-bound deliberative models of consensual, rational exchanges. A wide range of communication, including testimony, story telling, greetings and rhetoric, may all act to stimulate more discursive forms of democratic engagement (Young 2000). Autonomy and self-actualisation may be more widely experienced and performed through less discriminating codes for inclusion in social networks. While not specifically designed for engagement in mainstream politics, *YouTube* videos, for example, may still express alternative identity positions and critiques that have widespread appeal through their playfulness and unexpected nature. Critics of such trends are likely to reject claims for the democratic power of social media and instead regard it as a further threat to serious liberal politics. They will point to its use for negative campaigning and undermining the credibility of representative democracy. Concern is also expressed over the dangers posed to deliberative public spheres by competing personalised viewpoints incapable of rational verification and populist rhetoric that may even incite extremism. Further examples include trivialisation of the public sphere and its debasement by celebrity politics. Moreover, the kind of 'networked individualism' that arises from social networking is seen as additional evidence of the corrosive influence of social fragmentation upon liberal democratic practices (Wellman *et al.* 2003).

Perhaps the most immediate impact of social media upon democratic politics is as a means of challenging dominant mainstream political interests, rather than fostering a significant increase in direct participation. Most controversial are the interventions of hackers who spearhead the use of computers for direct citizen action (McKenzie 2004). Some would argue that 'creative hacking' as opposed to 'black-hat hacking' provides opportunities for liberating information that disrupts the dominant control of governments (Stockwell 2008). The disclosure of US government foreign affairs cables by Wikileaks represents another example of the disruptive power of collaborative sharing to stimulate critical political interest (Leigh and Harding 2011). Thus, much citizen engagement worldwide could be described as 'monitorial', rather than old-style, civic action. The 'monitorial' citizen can reflexively consider competing frames that inform political lifestyle choices, make recommendations to friends and, where appropriate, connect with conventional political institutions and practices through political action and/or protest. In autocratic societies it may even facilitate direct opposition to rulers, as in the Middle East during the spring of 2011 (*The Guardian* 2011a). In the United Kingdom, social media was used by young activists mobilising support for student campaigns against tuition fee increases, while the *UK Uncut* movement led *Twitter* protests using 'smart' flexible tactics to demonstrate against alleged corporate tax avoidance (Guardian 2011b).

Conclusion

The early models of digital democracy as a virtual public sphere assumed that the random connections of millions of people into a global network would provide an open online *agora* for the free and equal deliberation of citizens capable of informing and enriching democratic governance. Perhaps naive in hindsight, such utopian perspectives were quickly replaced by accounts that outlined the limitations of cyberspace as a means of combating the perceived crisis in mainstream democratic engagement. Surfing the new wave of social media and technological optimism, another generation is enthusiastic for digital democracy. While guilty of repeating the utopian rhetoric of the original experiments in digital democracy, these explorations are a departure from the earlier managed public sphere models with their requirement for rational, dutiful citizens. Instead, with its focus upon the citizen-user acting through multiple social networks, it opens the possibility of seeing these CTG as important spaces where the construction, maintenance and defence of political identities are played out. These networked relations thereby become an important source of power through their inclusion and exclusion of lifestyle choices, their access or denial to nodes of authoritative meaning and their capacity to facilitate the competitive advantage of some individuals and groups over others. Mapping and analysis of these networks could reveal significant social distinctions and cultural fissures that inform the nature of contemporary democratic politics. The potential of social media to enhance democracy, however, may lie less in any inherent capacity to stimulate activism than in the opportunity it gives to citizens and social movements to challenge and intrude upon public spheres shaped and controlled by existing political and cultural elites.

Notes

1. The term *communicative technologies of governance* (CTG) refers to the contestability of information and communication within democratic politics and the interpretive flexibility of the artefacts through which such contestations are manifested, resisted or codified.
2. As has been asserted elsewhere (Hague and Loader 1999) it is also useful distinguish between e-government and e-democracy.

References

Barabasi, A. (2011), 'Introduction and Keynote to a Networked Self', in Z. Papacharissi (ed.), *A Networked Self: Indentity, Community, and Culture on Social Network Sites*, London: Routledge, pp. 1–14.

Barlow, J. P. (1996), *Declaration of the Independence of Cyberspace*, San Francisco, CA: Electronic Frontier Foundation.

Bauman, Z. (2000), *Liquid Modernity*, Cambridge: Polity.

Bauman, Z. (2005), *Liquid Life*, Cambridge: Polity.

Beck, U. (1992), *Risk Society: Towards a New Modernity*, London: Sage.

Becker, T. (1981), 'Teledemocracy: Bringing Power Back to the People', *Futurist*, 15(6), 6–9.

Benkler, Y. (2006), *The Wealth of Networks: How Social Production Transforms Markets and Freedom*, New Haven, CT: Yale University Press.

Bennett, W. L. (2003), 'Lifestyle Politics and Citizen-Consumers', in J. Corner and D. Pels (eds), *Media and the Restyling of Politics: Consumerism, Celebrity and Cynicism*, London: Sage, pp. 137–50.

Bennett, W. L., C. Wells and A. Rank (2009), 'Young Citizens and Civic Learning: Two Paradigms of Citizenship in the Digital Age', *Citizenship Studies*, 13(2), 105–20.

Bijker, W. E., T. P. Hughes and T. J. Pinch (eds) (1987), *The Social Construction of Technology Systems*, Cambridge, MA: MIT Press.

Blumler, J. and M. Gurevitch (2001), 'The New Media and our Political Communication Discontents: Democratizing Cyberspace', *Information, Communication & Society*, 4(1), 1–13.

Bourdieu, P. (1984), *Distinction*, London: Routledge.

Bruns, A. (2007), 'Produsage, Generation C, and their Effects on the Democratic Process', *Media in Transition 5th Proceedings*, Cambridge, MA: MIT Press.

Chadwick, A. (2006), *Internet Politics: States, Citizens and New Communications Technologies*, Oxford: Oxford University Press.

Coleman, S. and J. Blumler (2009), *The Internet and Democratic Citizenship: Theory, Practice and Policy*, Cambridge: Cambridge University Press.

Dahlgren, P. (2009), *Media and Political Engagement: Citizens, Communication and Democracy*, Cambridge: Cambridge University Press.

Doctor, S. and W. H. Dutton (1998), 'The First Amendment Online: Santa Monica's Public Electronic Network', in R. Tsagarousianou *et al.* (eds), *Cyberdemocracy: Technology, Cities and Civic Networks*, London: Routledge, pp. 125–51.

Dryzek, J. S. (2000), *Deliberative Democracy and Beyond: Liberals, Critics, Contestations*, Oxford: Oxford University Press.

Dutton, W. H. and K. K. Guthrie (1991), 'An Ecology of Games: The Political Construction of Santa Monica's Public Electronic Network', *Informatization and the Public Sector*, 1(4), 1–24.

Fountain, J. E. (2001), *Building the Virtual State: Information technology and Institutional Change*, Washington, DC: Brookings Institution Press.

Fraser, N. (1990), 'Rethinking the Public Sphere: A Contribution to the Critique of Actually Existing Democracy', *Social Text*, 25/26, 56–80.

Giddens, A. (1991), *Modernity and Self-Identity: Self and Society in the Late Modern Age*, Cambridge: Polity.

Guardian, The (2011a), 'Google and Twitter Launch Service Enabling Egyptians to Tweet by Phone', 1 February.

Guardian, The (2011b), 'Taking Inspiration: New Wave of Activists Follow in Uncut's Footsteps', 11 February.

Habermas, J. ([1962] 1989), *The Structural Transformation of the Public Sphere*, Cambridge: Polity.

Hague, B. and B. D. Loader (1999), *Digital Democracy: Discourse and Decision-Making in the Information Age*, London: Routledge.

Halavias, A. (2009), *Search Engine Society*, Cambridge: Polity.

Hill, K. A. and J. E. Hughes (1998), *Cyberpolitics: Citizen Activism in the Age of the Internet*, Oxford: Rowman & Littlefield.

Hippel, Eric von (2005), *Democratizing Innovation*, Cambridge, MA: MIT Press.

Jenkins, H. (2006), *Convergence Culture: Where Old and New Media Collide*, New York: New York University Press.

Keeble, L. and B. D. Loader (2001), *Community Informatics: Shaping Computer-Mediated Social Relations*, London: Routledge.

Leadbeater, C. (2008), *We-Think*, London: Profile Books.

Leigh, D. and L. Harding (2011), *Wikileaks: Inside Julian Assange's War on Secrecy*, London: Guardian Books.

Loader, B. D. (ed.) (1997), *The Governance of Cyberspace: Politics, Technology and Global Restructuring*, London: Routledge.

Loader, B. D. (ed.) (1998a), *The Cyberspace Divide: Equality, Agency and Policy in the Information Society*, London: Routledge.

Loader, B. D. (1998b), 'Welfare Direct: Informatics and the Emergence of Self-service Welfare?', in J. Carter (ed.), *Postmodernity and the Fragmentation of Welfare*, London: Routledge, pp. 220–33.

Loader, B. D. (ed.) (2007), *Young Citizens in the Digital Age: Political Engagement, Young People and New Media*, London: Routledge.

Lyon, D. (2003), *Surveillance as Social Sorting: Privacy, Risk and Digital Discrimination*, London: Routledge.

McKee, A. (2005), *The Public Sphere: An Introduction*, Cambridge: Cambridge University Press.

McKenzie, W. (2004), *A Hacker Manifesto*, Cambridge, MA: Harvard University Press.

Mouffe, C. (1993), *The Return of the Political*, London: Verso.

Mouffe, C. (2005), *On the Political*, London: Routledge.

Oudshoorn, N. and T. Pinch (2005), *How Users Matter: The Co-construction of Users and Technology*, London: MIT Press.

Papacharissi, Z. (2010), *A Private Sphere: Democracy in a Digital Age*, Cambridge: Polity.

Pateman, C. (1989), *The Disorder of Women: Democracy, Feminism and Political Theory*, Cambridge: Polity.

Postman, N. (1987), *Amusing Ourselves to Death*, London: Methuen.

Putnam, R. (2000), *Bowling Alone: The Collapse and Revival of American Community*, New York: Simon & Schuster.

Rettberg, J. W. (2008), *Blogging*, Cambridge: Polity.

Rogers, R. (2004), *Information Politics on the Web*, Cambridge, MA: MIT Press.

Schuler, D. (1994), *New Community Networks: Wired for Change*, Reading: Addison-Wesley.

Sismondo, S. (2004), *Introduction to Science and Technology Studies*, Maldon, MA: Blackwell.

Squires, J. (1998), 'In Different Voices: Deliberative Democracy and Aestheticist Politics', in James Goog and Irving Velody (eds), *The Politics of Postmodernity*, Cambridge; Cambridge University Press.

Stockwell, S. (2008), 'We're All Hackers Now: Doing Global Democracy', *Createworld Proceedings*, Brisbane: Apple University Consortium.

Tassel, Joan van (1994), 'Yakety-Yak, Do Talk Back', *Wired* 2(1), 78–80.

Tsagarousianou, R., D. Tambini and C. Bryon (1998), *Cyberdemocracy: Technology, Cities and Civic Networks*, London: Routledge.

Wellman, B., A. Quan-Haase, J. Boase, W. Chen, K. Hampton, I. Diaz and K. Miyata (2003), 'The Social Affordances of the Internet for Networked Individualism', *Journal of Computer Mediated Communication*, 8(3).

Wellman, B. and C. Haythornthwaite (eds) (2002), *The Internet in Everyday Life*, Oxford: Blackwell.

Wilhelm, A. (2000), *Democracy in the Digital Age: Challenges to Political Life in Cyberspace*, London: Routledge.

Young, I. M. (2000), *Inclusion and Democracy*, Oxford: Oxford University Press.

Chapter 41

Radical Democracy

Lincoln Dahlberg

What is radical democracy? Karl Marx's definition of 'radical', from his 1844 'Introduction' to *A Contribution to the Critique of Hegel's Philosophy of Right*, states that to be radical is 'to grasp the root of the matter' (Marx [1844] 1970: 137). Thus, 'radical democracy' means to grasp or draw out the root meaning or conditions of democracy that have been obscured in its various historical appropriations. Radical democrats argue that there are two central, intertwined and historically constituted root meanings or conditions of democracy: first, the free and equal participation of 'the people' (the *demos*) in power (*kratos*); and, secondly, that democracy – including any of its criteria, institutions and decisions – has no grounds, justifications or guarantees outside the people, that is, outside itself. This second condition of democracy – its self-grounding, self-legitimation and, indeed, its self-constitution – leads to, when taken seriously, constant anxiety and self-reflexive questioning: democracy is the only regime with a self-revolutionising logic. Thus, at its root, democracy cannot be specified in any detailed, substantive way. Nor does going to the root of democracy mean finding and returning to an 'origin' such as classical Athens. While the root conditions are historically constituted, and excavated, any historical moment in the practice of democracy will involve fixing and limiting democracy in particular, contingently circumscribed ways. The dangers of nostalgia for Athens, for example, would include forgetting the many exclusions upon which Greek democracy was based. Given this lack of external grounds to justify democracy, pinning down a 'true' meaning of liberty and equality is seen as impossible. At the same time, democracy's self-grounding is also the condition of *possibility* for liberty and equality: the absence of external principles is the basis for participants' positive freedom and equality – each is autonomous from external gods and equally qualified and responsible for governance (Rancière 2006: 41).[1]

Radical democratic theorists have added 'radical' as a supplementary term to 'democracy' so as to draw out these root conditions. This supplement would be unnecessary if democracy was understood and practised according to these root conditions: 'radical democracy' would be a tautology. As a supplement, 'radical' does not just add to, but, as intended by the second meaning, problematises current understandings and practices of democracy. A range of radical democrats have drawn out these root conditions. This has resulted in an array of interpretations and conceptualisations of what goes under the name of 'radical democracy'. While some of these conceptualisations stem from the work of Jürgen Habermas and other deliberative democrats, many now draw upon post-structuralist influenced political theory, post-modern anarchism, contemporary Marxist philosophy, autonomist Marxism, Deleuzian theories of abundance and post-Marxism (Critchley 2004; Habermas 1996; Laclau and Mouffe [1985] 2001; Rancière 2006). These post-structuralist currents share with other radical democrats an interest in radicalising democracy through drawing out – although in different ways – the two conditions introduced above. It is post-structuralist radical democrats, however, who take most seriously the implications of the second condition, democracy's self-grounding. This chapter focuses upon post-structuralist interpretations, beginning with some of the background influences on contemporary radical democracy, then introducing post-structuralist conceptualisations in general, touching momentarily on Habermas as a point of contrast and then drawing on Ernesto Laclau and Chantal Mouffe to flesh out the post-structuralist conception, choosing their work for its widespread influence amongst those identifying with radical democracy.

From Participatory to Radical Democracy

The forebears of contemporary radical democracy are largely Western Enlightenment social and political theorists, most prominently Jean-Jacques Rousseau. These Enlightenment democrats argued for an extension of popular sovereignty beyond the limits placed on political participation by other forms of government (monarchy, aristocracy and liberal-capitalist democracy), forms of government that Enlightenment democrats saw as being sustained by extensive social, political, cultural and economic inequality. Here the work of Marx and other critics of liberal capitalism has been very influential upon radical democratic thinking. Contemporary radical democratic thought has been influenced more recently by the 1960's theory and practice of participatory democracy, as well as the New Left and 'new social movements' generally. Participatory democrats, drawing strongly upon Rousseau and Marx, demanded more direct participation in all spheres of society, against the increasing domination of life by state and capital (Macpherson 1977; Pateman 1970). The New Left drew on participatory principles to push for the extension of popular sovereignty, but its particular concern was to emphasise pluralism of identity as against the class essentialist and authoritarian tendencies that could be identified within 'older' Left traditions (Aronowitz 1993). This pluralist recognition of difference is a corollary of the second condition of democracy above: the self-grounding of democracy that allows it to accommodate multiple ways of being. Participatory democratic and New Left theories found practical expression in what came to be referred to as the 'new social movements': the civil rights movement followed by the women's, peace, sexual rights, indigenous peoples and ecology movements. These movements were understood to be 'new' and 'social' as they did not prioritise economic restructuring as did the 'older' workers' movements, nor aim to seize state power as revolutionary Marxist theories would expect of class movements; rather, they struggled for the empowerment of marginalised groups through the transformation of 'everyday life' (particularly through 'cultural politics') as well as the democratic *reform* of state and economic institutions (Melucci 1980). This 'new' democratic politics expressed both conditions of democracy identified above: it involved working for greater liberty and equality without claiming the certainty of absolute moral right or scientific truth. As Mouffe says, the recognition that 'the impossibility of any ultimate foundation or final legitimation is constitutive of the very advent of the democratic form of society' can be seen in the new social movements' claims for particular knowledge and democratic (self-grounded) rights, rather than universal knowledge and the 'rights of man' (Mouffe 1989: 34–6).

Such participatory and pluralist democratic theory and practice continue to be developed today, particularly with respect to periphery and emerging nations (Santos 2005). However, they have now largely been subsumed within 'radical democracy'. The emphasis upon the extension of inclusive and plural participation without external grounds has been drawn upon in various ways by all currents of radical democratic theory. For example, deliberative democracy, particularly through the work of Habermas, is understood by adherents as radically democratic in that it sees legitimate political rule as being based upon the equal opportunity for all those affected by a particular issue to participate in a pluralist public sphere (Habermas 1996). This sphere is constituted by inclusive, reciprocal, respectful and reasoned communication aimed towards the formation of rational public opinion that can scrutinise and guide decision making and so hold power accountable to 'the people'. In this model, free and equal participation in public opinion formation, and hence in public sovereignty, is secured through the institution of universal criteria of democratic communication. These criteria are drawn from the presuppositions of democratically oriented communicative action and so deliberative democracy is self-grounded.

Post-structuralist influenced radical democrats have also drawn inspiration from participatory politics, the New Left and new social movement theory. However, they have brought post-structuralist readings to the root conditions of democracy. In relation to the first condition, they have been particularly interested in how liberty and equality are limited by the politics of inclusion and exclusion that are often seen as hidden within formally liberal democratic norms, practices and institutions. In relation to the second condition, post-structuralist radical democrats have, more than any other democratic tradition, taken seriously the implications of democracy's lack of external legitimating grounds. Given their attention to this self-grounding, it is important to explore how they conceptualise it. Against any ideal of a fully reconciled or democratic society, such as envisioned by Rousseau and Marx, and also against the idea that universal normative criteria can be reconstructed out of social practice (as in the Habermasian model), post-structuralist radical democrats conceptualise democracy as being conditioned by undecidability and, indeed, by the self-consciousness of its own radical contingency (Critchley 2004: 115; Derrida 2005: 86–7; Mouffe 1989: 34). In other words, contingency is not just seen as an empirical fact, but as constitutive. Politics, and thus democracy, is made possible by the absence of extra-political grounds or foundations (apart from contingency itself, which is necessary, and as such there is a necessary/contingent dialectical tension running through post-structuralist radical democracy). Ultimate foundations would make politics, and thus democracy, unnecessary. For post-structuralists, radical democracy is not only post-foundational, but must be, as just noted, self-consciously or explicitly so: democracy is that particular type of politics that seeks to come to terms with – that is, institutionalise – radical contingency. The post-structuralist radical democrat believes that:

> democracy is to be defined as a regime that seeks, precisely, to *come to terms* with the ultimate failure of grounding rather than simply repressing or foreclosing it. While all conceivable political regimes, all forms of political order and ordering, are necessarily grounded in the abyss of an absent ground, most of them tend to [ideologically] disavow their abyssal nature . . . every democracy, if it is worth that name, *will have to be deliberately post-foundational* – a criterion which is not precisely met by everything that goes under the name of 'democracy' today . . . democracy has to accept contingency, that is, the absence of an ultimate foundation for society, as a *necessary* precondition. Otherwise it cannot legitimately be called democracy in a strong sense. (Marchart 2007: 157–8, emphasis original)

We see this institutionalisation of radical contingency spoken of in different ways in post-structuralist conceptualisations of democracy. For Jacques Derrida, democracy is always 'to come', not in the sense that it will be achieved at some future time and not even in the asymptotic sense that we can get ever closer to it without ever finally arriving at it, but in the sense that there is in fact no 'it' to arrive at – 'it' is impossible (Derrida 2005: 86–94). Thus, in accord with the idea of democracy as self-revolutionising, being impossible means that 'democracy is the only system, the only constitutional paradigm, in which, in principle, one has or assumes the right to criticize everything publicly, including the idea of democracy, its concept, its history, and its name' (Derrida 2005: 87). For Claude Lefort, the 'democratic revolution' involves the 'beheading of the king' and thus the 'dissolution of the landmarks of certainty', followed by the institutionalisation of the 'empty place of power' (Lefort 1986: 305–6). In democracy proper, 'the place of power' (sovereignty) can never be fully occupied or pre-determined, neither by a metaphysical principle or Being nor by any human beings with essential qualities endowing them with the right to rule (such as a monarch, an aristocracy or the proletariat).

The institutionalisation of radical contingency means recognising that 'politics goes all the way down', which means the institutionalisation of (political) struggle, ensuring that no social arrangement comes to be seen as final and uncontestable (Tønder and Thomassen 2005: 4). This contrasts with the Rousseauian and Marxist radical democratic understandings that conflict may be eliminated through the realisation of the general will or the communist revolution. It also differs from liberal democratic theory in that it does not try to limit or contain conflict within certain (formal political) spheres. In contrast to liberalism, radical democracy

> emphasizes conflict and dissension as themselves constitutive of democracy, as necessary to maintain its openness. On this view, the main danger to democracy would be freezing or institutionalizing a particular arrangement of power. Politics-

as-conflict is always necessary to renew politics-as-regime by challenging its limits. (Ingram 2006: 38)

Thus, post-structuralist radical democracy involves not only the extension of liberty and equality, but the institutionalisation of contingency, which means the institutionalisation of contestation. This post-structuralist understanding of radical democracy is found in the work of Laclau and Mouffe discussed below. Their extensive engagement with the question of radical democracy has caused the term to become associated with them more than with any other theorist.[2]

Laclau and Mouffe

Radical democracy first became associated with Laclau and Mouffe through their highly influential work *Hegemony and Socialist Strategy*, which has done so much to set the terms for discussion and debate of radical democracy (Epstein 1996). *Hegemony and Socialist Strategy* locates radical democracy as part of a post-Marxist project, a project aimed at the renewal of the left imaginary after the various theoretical and political defeats of the 1970s and early 1980s (Laclau and Mouffe [1985] 2001). Their project offers a post-structuralist deconstruction and reconceptualisation of the emancipatory programme of Marxism and socialism, attempting to resituate left politics in terms of radical contingency. They further develop, particularly through the concept of hegemony, the two conditions of radical democracy introduced above: first, the extension of liberty and equality and, secondly, democracy as self-grounded, or in post-structuralist terms, as self-consciousness of its own radical contingency.

Following on from the first condition of democracy noted above, Laclau and Mouffe see radical democracy as involving a continuing commitment to the expansion of 'liberty' and 'equality' into ever wider areas of social life so as to give 'political voice to the underdog' (Laclau 2004: 295; Laclau and Mouffe [1985] 2001; Mouffe 2000). This means the extension of liberty and equality without formal limits, unlike those placed on democracy by liberalism (Mouffe 1996: 22). However, Laclau and Mouffe see an 'unresolvable tension' between liberty (linked to the extension of differences and recognition of distinction) and equality (linked to the extension of equivalences and the elimination of distinctions), which means there is an ontological limit to radical democracy: neither liberty nor equality can be fully achieved without the elimination of the other (Laclau 2001: 4). Moreover, defining what 'liberty' and 'equality' are is finally impossible. While 'liberty' and 'equality' carry embedded or sedimented significations, any specific claim to their full meaning, given their radical contingency, is always contingent, the result of a political logic (form and practice) that Laclau and Mouffe refer to as hegemony, where a particular understanding comes to be invested with, or comes to represent, a universal meaning. In the process, 'liberty' and 'equality' become 'tendentially empty signifiers': they are partially (or their tendency is towards being) emptied of fixed signification, which allows particular meanings to occupy them (Laclau 2001: 11). These particular meanings become accepted as universal through liberty or equality representing the positive commonality of a set of otherwise differentiated elements, as well as the common negative relation to a named 'enemy'

– what they are 'not'. As a result, the representation articulates the set of elements into a seemingly coherent and total 'discourse' of liberty or equality, ostensibly encompassing all relevant elements while necessarily excluding a potentially infinite – given radical contingency – array of possibilities that remain in 'excess' but also hidden – given the naming of an explicit outside (the 'enemy') that seemingly represents all exclusion.

Liberty, for example, takes on a liberal (as against, say, social democratic or deliberative) meaning when it becomes the representative of a particular articulation of elements – 'free markets', 'individual rights', 'private property', 'privacy', 'religious tolerance', 'citizenship rights' and so on – each of which shares, or comes to share, a common relation to a liberal understanding of 'liberty'. As this 'liberal' articulation comes to stand for the universal meaning of liberty it occludes other possibilities, for instance a deliberative understanding based on the articulation of (some of) the liberal elements with 'inter-subjectivity', 'reciprocity', 'reflexivity' and so on. Liberty is partially emptied in order to represent liberal democracy's or deliberative democracy's specific meanings. This emptying is only partial because 'liberty' carries sedimented meanings from previous articulations, as do all elements in the discourse, which make some articulations more likely than others. For example, one might expect liberty, with its embedded association with human autonomy, as more likely to represent the articulation of, in a liberal discourse, 'private property' and 'individual rights', as against 'surveillance'. However, one can imagine a particular liberal discourse where liberty might represent the articulation of, and thus modification of, all three, for example, the 'right' to freely carry out surveillance within one's own 'property' even if the latter is used for politically-oriented communication (here we can think of the case of digital properties like Facebook). Similarly, 'equality' may be understood in a range of ways through the articulation of a variety of elements, but will resist articulation with any form of explicitly exclusionary or exploitative order. In fact, 'exclusion' and 'exploitation' are likely candidates to represent 'enemies' of equality, as 'totalitarianism' would be for liberty. Hence, different articulations of elements provide for different meanings, and thus practices, of liberty and equality.

As empty signifiers, liberty and equality are historically and politically articulated rather than rationally founded or metaphysically given. The meanings of the terms liberty and equality, like democracy, derive from, and are passed down and developed by, hegemonic struggles over democracy. Democracy – liberty and equality – must not, to be consistent with itself, be limited to any particular conceptualisation: ignoring the particularity of any understanding or practice of liberty and equality, no matter how liberating and equalising such may seem, would mean limiting possibilities for their extension. This, in turn, means that radical democracy must not only promote the expansion of liberty and equality, but encourage the ongoing contestation of their specific conceptualisations. In other words, a radical democracy must make explicit the hegemonic relation underlying its own understanding and practices of liberty and equality (Laclau 2001: 5, 10). This call for hegemony to be made explicit is another way of expressing the second understanding of *radical* democracy introduced above: the type of politics that institutionalises its own radical contingency and thus makes explicit its own ultimate failure and its exclusionary politics, which means the institutionalisation of self-critique and contestation. This is in contrast to failure being ideologically covered over, where ideology for Laclau and Mouffe involves the non-recognition of radical contingency, which takes place when one particular social arrangement comes to be naturalised, comes to be taken to be coterminous with the whole (Laclau 1990: 92). Ideology is thus the name Laclau and Mouffe give to the opposite of radical democracy in its pure – impossible – form.

The logic of hegemony, for Laclau and Mouffe, does not just apply to liberty and equality, but can be found to operate in all politics. Moreover, given that the social is understood as finally contingent and hence political, hegemony is understood to be a principle structuring all aspects of social life. This means that any (seemingly) stable, fully consensual social system or identity involves the occlusion of exclusions (excess) and associated antagonisms. For maximising liberty and equality, such exclusions and antagonisms, and hence radical contingency, must be brought to light, which once again involves making explicit the hegemonic logic at work. To make hegemony explicit requires the contestation of the particular articulations of all seemingly fully explanatory discourses, contestation that can develop out of counter-hegemonic discourses formed from the articulation of excessive particularities. It has already been seen that post-structuralists generally understand radical democracy to involve the institutionalisation of radical contingency: the institutionalisation of perennial contestation of any fixations of meanings and practices. Laclau's and Mouffe's specific contribution is their conceptualisation of hegemony, which offers a means by which to theorise the politics associated with radical contingency. Thus, it becomes possible to understand the institutionalisation of radical contingency in terms of the institutionalisation of hegemonic contestation: keeping contestation going between different hegemonising forces so that no one articulation comes to be finally accepted as total, to be (ideologically) seen as fully incarnating universality (Laclau 2001). Thus, the logic of hegemony helps extend Lefort's understanding of democracy as the institutionalising of 'the empty place' of power.

Four important aspects of this institutionalisation of hegemonic contestation need to be highlighted here. First, democracy is understood as involving the management of power, rather than its (impossible) elimination, bringing power into the open and mediating subsequent conflict. Secondly, the radical democratic motivation in keeping the hegemonic game in play, rather than ideologically masking it, is to allow for the possibility of excluded voices being heard through new discursive articulations. Thirdly, representation is central to radical democracy: 'relations of representation are constitutive of democracy . . . that is why *representative* democracy is not a second best, as Rousseau thought, but is *the only possible democracy*' (Laclau 2001: 13, emphasis original). Representation here is not direct or transparent, but rather mediated and transformative: in the hegemonic process all articulated identities are transformed to a degree. Fourthly, hegemony, as Laclau and Mouffe have strongly emphasised throughout their work, involves passion: there is a subjective identification with, and investment in, the representative identity and against the 'enemy' (Laclau 2005; Mouffe 2005b).

But what is needed practically for realising the institutionalisation of hegemonic contestations? It is at this point that Mouffe's and Laclau's focus diverges somewhat, although remaining complementary. Mouffe argues that the institutionalisation of hegemonic contestation requires the institutionalisation of 'agonistic' spaces that enable the transformation of 'enemies' bent on destroying each other into 'adversaries' that 'recognize the legitimacy of their opponents' to engage in political struggle (Mouffe 2005b: 20).[3] Agonistic conflict is understood to be guided by a minimum agreement among adversaries upon the need for the 'ethico-political principles' of liberty and equality, as well as for some form of 'democratic procedures' to regulate conflict, although the interpretation and content of these principles and procedures always remains open to contestation and decided upon through agonistic struggle (Mouffe 2005a, 2005b: 14–21). Mouffe refers to parliament as one example of such an agonistic institution (Mouffe 2005b: 22–3). In various places she has also suggested the importance of the mass media, as well as critical media and 'artistico-activist' practices for fostering agonistic spaces, although her thinking here remains undeveloped (Mouffe 2007, Mouffe et al. 2006). To institutionalise such spaces of democratic contestation in the first place, however, requires a political (i.e., hegemonic) project: the articulation of the greatest possible number of diverse democratic struggles, with otherwise differentiated demands, into a 'contingent combination of radical democrats' that can then effectively challenge existing liberal and other discourses (Mouffe 1989: 41–2, 1993: 77). Here Mouffe, as well as Laclau, develops earlier thinking on the democratic politics of the 'new social movements', seeing such as enabling the articulation of a range of groups around calls for justice and democratisation (Fenton 2011). And it is also here that Laclau's recent work on populism is useful, helping to extend his and Mouffe's understanding of what is involved in radical democracy, as well as in any attempt to win hegemony (Laclau 2005).

An example of such a hegemonic project aimed at democratisation can be seen in 'anti-globalisation' politics where a wide range of groups – farmers and other local producers, radical environmentalists, indigenous peoples, socialists, anarchists and so on – with a wide variety of (sometimes conflicting) demands become articulated through their common negative relation to capitalist globalisation and positive association with calls for 'democracy' and 'justice'. More recently, the 'Arab Spring' has involved a range of previously unarticulated, and sometime hostile, groups (Muslim, Christian, secular, women and youth) coming together, and modifying themselves in the process, around the demand for 'democracy'. While it remains uncertain as to how radically democratic these movements' ambitions may be with respect to the post-structuralist understanding described in this chapter, they provide a practical illustration of the hegemonic battle that Mouffe and Laclau would see as necessary for a political system to move towards radical democracy.

This discussion suggests that radical democracy must negotiate, as indicated earlier in this chapter, an inherent dialectical tension between necessity and contingency.[4] This can be seen in a couple of inter-related ways. First, hegemonic politics must be deployed in order to fight for the institutionalisation of radical democracy and as such there must be, ironically, a moment of ideological closure and exclusion. Secondly, 'contingency' must be fought for as 'radical', and thus as the only thing *not* operating upon hegemonic logics. This dialectical tension – 'undecidable game' – between contingency and necessity, is presupposed by hegemony and expressed within it, by the tension between universality and particularity (Laclau 2001). The institutionalising of hegemonic contestation makes explicit this tension, which in turn subverts any final institutionalisation. Radical democracy is an ongoing, impossible project.

Finally, it needs to be said that, in promoting this conception of radical democracy, Laclau and Mouffe bring a normative element to their ontology of radical contingency. Along with many other post-structuralist radical democrats, they are committed to not only the 'ethico-political principles' of liberty and equality (even if tendentially empty), but to the institutionalisation of radical contingency and 'the empty place of power', which in their terms means to extend agonistic spaces and institutions so as to ensure the opportunity for contestation and re-articulation of all hegemonic discourses.

Conclusion

Laclau and Mouffe understand radical democracy in terms of the institutionalisation of hegemonic contestation, and thus of the tension between contingency and necessity (and particularity–universality). This institutionalisation is achieved by keeping contestation going as against (the impossible task of) overcoming it. However, this call for the institutionalisation of contestation should not be read as an unrestrained embrace of power and conflict, but rather a shaping of it in accordance with the (always negotiable) principles of liberty and equality, that is, in accordance with 'the people'. This conceptualisation has been thoroughly interrogated and refined through political philosophy. However, there are still significant questions that need attention, relating to political organisation, economy and sociology, areas to which post-structuralist radical democrats have yet to pay adequate consideration. Three questions in particular demand consideration. First, a question of political organisation: how can the practical requirements for instituting radical contingency, or more specifically hegemonic struggle, be further clarified given the limits that a commitment to radical contingency places on prescriptions? In particular, greater consideration is needed of the role of communications media in supporting the institutionalisation of agonistic engagement. Secondly, is the matter of political economy and in particular the relation of radical democracy to globalisation, and specifically global capital. In other words, can the institutionalisation of agonistic struggle between hegemonic forces effectively challenge neo-liberal discourse or, particularly given radical democracy's de-centring of class, will it simply sit on top of, and ideologically legitimate, the already seemingly dislocating rhythms (contingency) of global capital? And thirdly, a question of political sociology: can hegemony be considered the universal form of politics and democracy given that some (e.g. Deleuzian and autonomist Marxist) theorists' claim to recognise in human relations non-hegemonic, non-representative political and democratic logics and practices, including the democratic politics of decentralised (digital) networking, while others argue that alongside hegemonic conflict there are modes of politics based on a disposition to 'receptive generosity, hospitality, or acknowledgement' that must be considered central to radical democracy (Barnett 2004: 505)?

The answers to these questions are complex and have been introduced here simply to indicate that there is still much work to be done in developing a convincing and workable post-structuralist theory of radical democracy. This might be expected given that it is a very recent development in the history of democracy. Yet, to be true to their understanding of the root meaning of radical democracy, post-structuralists cannot be expected to give detailed substantive prescriptions. Such prescriptions can be decided only through political struggle, that is, as the result of the temporary, hegemonically instituted decision of the 'free' and 'equal' body of 'the people', which justifies itself, its rules and decisions, to none other than itself: democracy is founded upon the rule of the people, and the people alone.

Notes

1. Rancière draws on Plato's third book of the *Laws* to see democracy based on the law of chance and decided by lottery, highlighting the contingency of democratic order and equal entitlement to govern (Rancière 2006: 40–1).
2. Others have developed useful strands of poststructuralist radical democracy (Marchart 2007; Tønder and Thomassen 2005).
3. Mouffe uses institution 'in a very wide sense' to refer to 'an ensemble of practices, language-games, discourses, but also traditional institutions such as parties and other political institutions as well as different forms of participations among a diversity of people at local and other levels' (Mouffe 2007: 3).
4. The dialectic here is, as Laclau and Mouffe observe, a 'specific dialectic' (Laclau and Mouffe [1985] 2001: xii). They explicitly reject the singular and total philosophical system that can be found in dialectical materialism or particular readings of Hegel, where there is a single self-unfolding teleological movement towards a resolution – the ultimate return of difference into the one (Laclau, 1990: 26; Laclau and Mouffe [1985] 2001: xi, xiii).

References

Aronowitz, S. (1993), 'The Situation of the Left in the United States', *Socialist Review*, 23(3), 5–79.
Barnett, C. (2004), 'Deconstructing Radical Democracy: Articulation, Representation, and Being-with-others', *Political Geography*, 23(5), 503–28.
Critchley, S. (2004), 'Is There a Normative Deficit in the Theory of Hegemony?', in S. Critchley and O. Marchart (eds), *Laclau: A Critical Reader*, London: Routledge, pp. 113–22.
Derrida, J. (2005), *Rogues: Two Essays on Reason*, Stanford, CA: Stanford University Press.
Epstein, B. (1996), 'Radical Democracy and Cultural Politics: What about Class? What about Political Power?', in D. Trend (ed.), *Radical Democracy: Identity, Citizenship, and the State*, London: Routledge, pp. 127–39.
Fenton, N. (2011), 'Multiplicity, Autonomy, New Media, and the Networked Politics of New Social Movements', in L. Dahlberg and S. Phelan (eds), *Discourse Theory and Critical Media Politics*, London: Palgrave, pp. 178–200.
Habermas, J. (1996), *Between Facts and Norms: Contributions to a Discourse Theory of Law and Democracy*, trans. W. Rehg, Cambridge: Polity.
Ingram, J. D. (2006), 'The Politics of Claude Lefort's Political: Between Liberalism and Radical Democracy', *Thesis Eleven*, 87, 33–50.

Laclau, E. (1990), *New Reflections on the Revolution of our Time*, New York: Verso.

Laclau, E. (2001), 'Democracy and the Question of Power', *Constellations*, 8(1), 3–14.

Laclau, E. (2004), 'Glimpsing the Future', in S. Critchley and O. Marchart (eds), *Laclau: A Critical Reader*, London: Routledge, pp. 279–328.

Laclau, E. (2005), *On Populist Reason*, London: Verso.

Laclau, E. and C. Mouffe ([1985] 2001), *Hegemony and Socialist Strategy: Towards a Radical Democratic Politics*, 2nd edn, London: Verso.

Lefort, C. (1986), *The Political Forms of Modern Society: Bureaucracy, Democracy, Totalitarianism*, ed. J. B. Thompson, Cambridge: Polity.

Marx, K. ([1844] 1970), *A Contribution to the Critique of Hegel's Philosophy of Right*, ed. J. O'Malley, Cambridge: Cambridge, University Press.

Macpherson, C. B. (1977), *The Life and Times of Liberal Democracy*, Oxford: Oxford University Press.

Marchart, O. (2007), *Post-Foundational Political Thought: Political Difference in Nancy, Lefort, Badiou, and Laclau*, Edinburgh: Edinburgh University Press.

Melucci, A. (1980), 'The New Social Movements: A Theoretical Approach', *Social Science Information*, 19(2), 199–226.

Mouffe, C. (1989), 'Radical Democracy: Modern or Postmodern?', trans. P. Holdengräber, *Social Text*, 21, 31–45.

Mouffe, C. (1993), *The Return of the Political*, London: Verso.

Mouffe, C. (1996), 'Radical Democracy or Liberal Democracy?', in D. Trend (ed.), *Radical Democracy: Identity, Citizenship, and the State*, New York: Routledge, pp. 19–26.

Mouffe, C. (2000), *The Democratic Paradox*, London: Verso.

Mouffe, C. (2005a), 'For an Agonistic Public Sphere', in L. Tønder and L. Thomassen (eds), *Radical Democracy: Politics between Abundance and Lack*, Manchester: Manchester University Press, pp. 123–32

Mouffe, C. (2005b), *On the Political*, London: Routledge.

Mouffe, C. (2007), 'Artistic Activism and Agonistic Spaces', *Art & Research: A Journal of Ideas, Contexts and Methods*, 1(2), 1–5.

Mouffe, C., N. Carpentier and B. Cammaerts (2006), 'Hegemony, Democracy, Agonism and Journalism: An Interview with Chantal Mouffe', *Journalism Studies*, 7(6), 964–75.

Pateman, C. (1970), *Participation and Democracy*, Cambridge: Cambridge University Press.

Rancière, J. (2006), *Hatred of Democracy*, trans. S. Corcoran, London: Verso.

Santos, B. (2005), *Democratizing Democracy: Beyond the Liberal Democratic Canon*, London: Verso.

Tønder, L. and L. Thomassen (eds) (2005), *Radical Democracy: Politics between Abundance and Lack*, Manchester: Manchester University Press.

Chapter 42

Deliberative Democracy

Kasper M. Hansen and Christian F. Rostbøll

Over the last twenty years deliberative democracy has become the most discussed theory of democracy. The term was coined by Joseph Bessette in 1980, but academic writing on deliberative democracy really picked up in the early 1990s (Bessette 1980; Hansen 2004). While the idea of giving deliberation a core role in democracy has roots throughout the history of democracy, the most important contemporary theoretical sources for deliberative democrats are the works of Jürgen Habermas and John Rawls (Habermas 1984, 1989, 1996; Rawls 1971, 1996). The theory of deliberative democracy is often directed at two related deficiencies of actual existing democracy, that is, democracy as we know it in the contemporary world. On the one hand, it is directed at the low quantity and quality of political participation: the widespread political apathy and political ignorance (Ackerman and Fishkin 2004: 5). Research within this field has fostered many empirical studies of actual deliberation (Fung 2003; Grönlund *et al.* 2010; Hansen 2004). On the other hand, deliberative theory is directed at the distortion exercised on the political process by money and power (Habermas 1996; Rostbøll 2008). Participation in deliberation is seen as a promising way to gain greater knowledge of politics. But the political process must be insulated from the distortions caused by diverse forms of power and inequality in order for it to be a process of exchange of reasons rather than of threats and rewards.

Simply put, deliberative democracy can be characterised as 'talk-centric' democratic theory (Chambers 2003: 308). Rather than merely adding their votes to one side or the other, the idea is that citizens ought to exchange views and arguments – before they vote (Goodin 2008: 2). Deliberative democrats do not reject the need for voting, but the focus is the process of opinion and will formation that precedes voting. Deliberation is not merely talk, but a specific form of communication, where the participants carefully consider the available information and weigh the different arguments against each other. Deliberative democracy represents a way of thinking about democracy where the decision-making process is infused with deliberation. Thus, it is the quality of the deliberation – not the number of speakers or their degree of representativeness – that is the basis of democratic legitimacy (Dryzek 2000; Dryzek and Niemeyer 2008; Parkinson 2003). Political decisions must be justified in a process of exchanging arguments with mutual respect and a willingness to come to a collective determination. Accountability is achieved through continual deliberation between politicians and citizens, and political equality is achieved by equal uptake of everyone's arguments

(Andersen and Hansen 2007; Bohman 1996, 1997; Hansen 2004; Hansen and Andersen 2004). As an ideal, deliberation requires that citizens exchange arguments as *free and equal* participants. The outcome of deliberation should be determined not by the status or economic resources of the participants, but by 'the peculiarly constraint-free force of the better argument' (Habermas 1984: 24). In the process of deliberation, opinions are not merely stated and recorded (aggregation of preferences); opinions may be changed as a result of new insights gained from the exchange of reasons (transformation of preferences). Thus, deliberation can be defined as 'an unconstrained exchange of arguments that involves practical reasoning and . . . potentially leads to a transformation of preferences' (Cooke 2000: 948).

Deliberative Democracy's Historical Roots

While deliberative democracy is deeply rooted in the republican democratic tradition, researchers often forget these democratic roots in their hurry to 'jump on the deliberative bandwagon'. In order to illustrate how the significance of deliberation has developed historically, the focus turns to three political thinkers who have considered the role of debate and discussion in different parts of their respective bodies of work: Jean-Jacques Rousseau, Alexis de Tocqueville and John Stuart Mill. These three thinkers discussed deliberation with regard to various different aspects of public life, but nevertheless all within the context of democracy. The chapter aims to cast light on how these three key political theorists discussed related aspects of democracy, though fully recognising that their theories are of a much more complex and sophisticated nature. The aim is simply to show that deliberation is not a new phenomenon, that it was not first considered by contemporary political theorists and thinkers in recent decades, but has in fact been part of a lengthy democratic republican tradition (Hansen 2004, 2012).

Jean-Jacques Rousseau (1712–78) was one of the first political thinkers with a plebeian background. In fact, he remained relatively poor throughout his entire life. This might explain why he was so concerned about political equality in a time dominated by the rational outlook of the Enlightenment. Rousseau was one of the first political thinkers since the ancient Greeks to explicitly emphasise deliberation in the political process. The strong belief in the sovereignty of the people and their right to self-government led Rousseau to argue for direct or city-state democracy, whereby citizens would be able to take direct part in the decision-making process. As such, legislation by representatives should not be tolerated, as it enslaves the people and violates their right to self-legislation. As Rousseau emphasised in his famous statement about the people of England: 'The people of England regards itself as free; but it is grossly mistaken; it is free only during the election of the members of parliament. As soon as they are elected, slavery overtakes it, and it is nothing' (Rousseau 1762: 470). Deliberation is essential for Rousseau in the process of self-legislation, as it transforms individual opinion into a public opinion or, in Rousseau's own words:

> particular wills are substituted for general will in public deliberation . . . [and] there are two general rules that may serve to regulate this relation [the relation between

the particular wills and the general will]: First, the more grave and important the questions discussed, the nearer should the opinion that is to prevail approach unanimity. Secondly, the more the matter in hand calls for speed the smaller the prescribed difference in the number of votes may be allowed to become: where an instant decision has to be reached, a majority of one vote should be enough. (Rousseau 1762: 472)

While the first part of the quote emphasises deliberation as a means to transform self-interest to common interest, the latter part of the quote establishes that if important questions are at stake, then deliberation should take the time to lead the participants to unanimity, while the faster a decision is needed, the closer to a bare majority the meeting can go – so there needs to be only a brief deliberation on opinions when speed is of the essence. This view on deliberation as a means to transform opinions towards a unanimous common interest also prevails in contemporary approaches to deliberation (Habermas 1996). Others have provided a critical discussion of consensus arising from deliberation (Hansen 2010). Even though the above reading of Rousseau betokens his partiality for deliberation, he also warns that 'long debates, dissensions and tumult proclaim the ascendancy of particular interests and the decline of the State' (Rousseau 1762: 471). For this reason, some interpret Rousseau as being against deliberation (Freeman 2000: 377). Nevertheless, it could also be argued that Rousseau warns against distorted deliberation; that is, if the deliberation is excessive and marked by factions or tumult (Cohen 2010: 75; Hansen 2004: 83). Regardless of the various interpretations of Rousseau, the examples above illustrate how the concept of deliberation has been relevant to democratic theory for centuries.

Another important political observer who isolated deliberation as important to democracy is Alexis de Tocqueville (1805–59), an enthusiastic student of American society during the 1830s. Tocqueville's analysis of the participation in local institutions, voluntary associations and civil society in general is often highlighted in his writings (Barber 1984: 234–5; Mansbridge 1983: 41). Thus, Tocqueville is interpreted as an advocate of that which has since come to be known as communitarianism. Deliberation and discussion are also part of Alexis de Tocqueville's fascination with American society as described in *Democracy in America*. This aspect emerges in his description of the American debate culture, where he claims that Americans find such amusement in deliberation that some take their entertainment in debate clubs rather than the theatre (Tocqueville [1835] 2000: 289). Tocqueville also describes how discussions carry on as long as the majority is undecided, 'but as soon as its decision is irrevocably pronounced, everyone is silent, and the friends as well as the opponents of the measure unite in assenting to its propriety' (Tocqueville [1835] 2000: 304). This description shows how discussion was very important in the decision-making procedures, but that everyone put aside their particular positions and supported the decision as soon as it was taken. Deliberation in American juries in the 1830s is the institution Tocqueville describes as the 'most efficacious means for the education of the people which society can employ' (Tocqueville [1835] 2000: 330). But the juries are not only important due to their educational effect, but also because they promote attention to the common good among the citizenry: 'By obliging men to turn their attention to other affairs than their own, it rubs off that private selfishness which is the rust of society' (Tocqueville [1835] 2000: 329). Similar to Rousseau, Tocqueville emphasises how discussion can alleviate a narrow focus on self-interest and promote broader interest in public affairs.

John Stuart Mill (1806–73) also emphasised the educational effect of participation and discussion. Deliberation is, in his own words:

> the practical part of the political education of a free people, taking them out of the narrow circle of personal and family selfishness, and accustoming them to the comprehension of joint interests, the management of joint concerns – habituating them to act from public or semi-public motives, and guide their conduct by aims which unite instead of isolating them from one another. (Mill [1859] 1962: 243–4)

Mill's strong advocacy of free speech also has relevance for why he promoted deliberation as an important element of the political process. Mill summarises the arguments for free speech on four grounds. First, if an opinion is not allowed to be expressed, then how would we know whether or not it is true? By denying the expression of an opinion we assume our own infallibility: that is, we assume that the current truth is unquestionable. Secondly, even if the silenced opinions are untrue, they may be part of a new perception of the truth; it is only by the collision of different opinions that the entire truth will prevail. Thirdly, even in the case where the current perception of the truth is entirely correct, liberty of speech is necessary. The truth would otherwise turn into prejudice, and people would forget the rational grounds upon which the truth was based. Finally, the meaning of the truth will be endangered if freedom of expression is violated, as the truth then becomes nothing more than a formula that does not encourage belief to become action based on rational arguments (Mill [1859] 1962: 180–1). These four arguments make clear that Mill believed free speech offers a means by which to arrive at a 'truth'; however, these four grounds for liberty of speech also form a strong argument for deliberation to be part of the political process in order to secure a decision based on 'rational grounds'. Thus, deliberation is not merely a contemporary phenomenon developed in the twentieth century, but rather it has deep roots in the republican tradition of democratic theory.

Key Elements of Deliberative Democracy

Most theorists of deliberative democracy do not see deliberative democracy as an alternative to, but rather as an improvement on and expansion of, representative democracy. There are weaknesses in the way contemporary representative democracy works, and making it more deliberative has the potential to overcome some of these. Making democracy more deliberative is not merely a matter of telling people to deliberate more, but requires institutional and economic reforms; indeed, some proponents think that the social and political conditions of deliberative democracy requires a revolution (Fung 2003). Deliberation has educational effects on the participants. Democratic theory presupposes that all citizens are qualified to take part in ruling, at least indirectly through electing representatives. Deliberative democrats share this view, but hold that citizens can become more qualified (for example, more knowledgeable, better articulated) and that their opinions might become more transitive, coherent and consistent if they take part in a deliberative process. The belief of deliberative democrats is that under other and better institutional and social conditions citizens would be able to form their opinions in a more rational and consistent manner. A deliberative process is thus seen as a learning process. By engaging in the public exchange of reasons, citizens, as free and equal, would be able to learn from each other and attain a more informed and reflective understanding of what their and others' political preferences are. The idea is that there often will be a difference between citizens' pre-deliberative and post-deliberative opinions. It is not just opinions that are confronted in the deliberative process; information is also shared and validated in the dialogue between the participants. Deliberation will thus have an educational effect on the participants.

In deliberation the aim is to articulate and justify personal views as well as listen to the arguments of others. By listening to others, participants learn how the world looks from the perspective of people situated differently to ourselves (with other social and educational backgrounds, for example), and consequently learn how former policy preferences would potentially affect others. Ideally, this should assist participants in changing their preferences in ways that make them more accepting of others. Deliberation tempers self-interest and promotes mutual justification. Deliberation has not only educational effects in the sense that one may learn more about politics, policy and other citizens' viewpoints, it also has the effect of tempering self-interest (Freeman 2000). Deliberation is usually seen as a *public* process of reasoning, and when one is required to defend one's opinions publicly it is difficult to refer to one's self-interest as the only ground for supporting a certain policy (Benhabib 1996; Young 2000). The ideal of deliberative democracy is that participants give reasons that are equally acceptable to all involved. This does not mean that interests should be ignored in deliberation or that one is not allowed to complain that a certain policy ignores one's interests. Often finding the most just solution concerns finding out what is in the equal interest of everyone (Knight and Johnson 1997). The point is that politics ought to be something different from the egoistic pursuit of individual self-interest or a power struggle between self-interested parties; rather, it should be a process that aims at policies that can be equitable to everyone. This shift from self-interest to equity is sometimes presented as the difference between bargaining and deliberation (Elster 1998; Habermas 1996). In bargaining, the participants aim to further their own interests and they do so by means of sanctions and rewards. In deliberation, by contrast, the participants aim to find a solution that is in the equal interest of everyone, and they do so by means of reasoning. Thus, in bargaining the result is determined by the balance of power, while in deliberation the result is determined by the best arguments. Needless to say, this difference is analytical and only under ideal conditions will the result be determined by the best arguments and the merits of the case rather than by the status and power of the participants: 'Deliberation . . . is an ideal whose realisation has preconditions. In the absence of those preconditions, we cannot expect the force of the better argument to prevail' (Cohen and Rogers 2003: 249). The point of deliberative democracy is to reform society to conditions that approximate the situation in which political decisions are the results of good arguments rather than bargaining power.

Deliberative democracy promotes deliberative accountability. The process of exchanging arguments has another important purpose in deliberative democracy, as the process encourages a deliberative sense of accountability in the political system. The participants in deliberation must give 'reasons that can be accepted by all those who are bound by the laws and policies they justify', and not rely only on the mandate given to them at election time (Gutmann and Thompson 1996: 129). Thus, participants should be considered deliberatively accountable in relation to the argument they put forward during deliberation. This form of deliberative accountability is different from accountability as defined in representative democracy, where the focus is on how elected officials can be held accountable for their decisions through formal electoral procedures (Pitkin 1967). In deliberative democracy accountability is understood in terms of 'giving an account' of one's policy preferences, which means one must be able to justify them to everyone bound or affected by them (Chambers 2003: 308). It is not merely elected representatives who must be able to give an account of their views; all citizens must justify their political choices to each other. This is done through deliberation where participants are mutually accountable to the objections made towards their arguments and are, thus, strongly encouraged to look beyond self-interest and consider the interests of others (Gutmann and Thompson 1996: 228, 2004). The epistemic dimension of deliberative democracy is also important here. Most proponents of deliberative democracy see it as an epistemic conception of democracy that not only values the technical benefits of the procedures of deliberative democracy, but also believes the knowledge generated in those procedures to have a tendency to lead to good and rational outcomes (Bohman 1996: 26; Estlund 2008). In other words, democracy is not only the best form of government because it treats everyone equally and fairly, but under conditions that promote public deliberation it also has the capacity to produce wiser and morally better outcomes than other forms of government. A basic assumption underlying deliberative democracy is that no one has privileged access to truth. The only way to arrive at judgements that have the presumption of having right on their side is through public processes of deliberation where everyone is free and able to participate. What makes deliberative democracy produce better outcomes are the educative effects on individual citizens mentioned above and that political decisions must be mutually justifiable. Thus, the wisest and morally best decisions are not those devised by experts, but those decisions that would be equally acceptable to everyone in processes of public deliberation among free and equal citizens (Rostbøll 2008: 176–96).

Deliberative democracy proposes a new account of legitimacy. In many traditional models of democracy, legitimacy is based on consent or on the acceptance of political authority expressed through one's vote. Deliberative democrats object that:

> the source of legitimacy is not the predetermined will of individuals, but rather the process of its formation, that is, deliberation itself . . . a legitimate decision does not represent the *will* of all, but is one that results from *the deliberation of all*. (Manin 1987: 351, emphasis original)

Deliberative democrats do not disagree that legitimate government should embody 'the will of the people', but they insist that it is not insignificant how this will has been formed. If the will of the people is identified with people's pre-deliberative preferences, there is a risk that it is a will that is unreflectively formed, or worse, that it has been manipulated by powerful actors. The idea that the will of the people is not identical to people's expressed preferences might raise the suspicion that deliberative democracy is elitist or paternalistic. However, a basic premise of deliberative democracy is that no one has privileged access to, and uncriticisable beliefs about, what the true interests of anyone are. In deliberation, it is true, there is a substitution of one judgement for another, but it is not of one person's for another's, but rather of what results from deliberation for both (Rostbøll 2005, 2008: 95–102). It should also be noted that even if deliberative democrats insist that 'legitimate lawmaking issues from the public deliberation of citizens', deliberation cannot entirely substitute for aggregation because at some point the talking must stop and, short of consensus, a vote must be made (Bohman and Rehg 1997: ix). Thus, the deliberative account of legitimacy does not mean that legitimate law making can exist without voting and majority decision making. But deliberative democracy differs from other models of democracy in two respects. First, the counting of votes does not confer legitimacy as the aggregation of pre-given preferences, but rather as the pooling of deliberatively formed and reflective judgements. Secondly, majority decisions are seen only as an unfortunate device necessitated by the pressure to decide and never as the final expression of the will of the people. Thus, 'the decision reached by the majority only represents a caesura in an ongoing discussion; the decision records, so to speak, the interim result of a discursive opinion-forming process' (Habermas 1996: 179). This also means that no decision can be perfectly legitimate; the minority is always free to dissent and continue the deliberation.

The Empirical Turn in Deliberative Democracy

Soon after it was formulated by political theorists, deliberative democracy was taken up by researchers for empirical testing. The empirical research in deliberative democracy was not only driven by theoretical models, but also by the claimed increasing democratic gap between the elite and the public, which is commonly interpreted as a democratic deficit. This gap is often related to a lack of trust in politicians, low turnout at elections, a lack of party loyalty and more general tendencies, such as increasing individualisation, globalisation, Europeanisation and pluralisation of norms and values in society (Beck 1992). The empirical research in deliberative democracy has launched new methods designed to integrate the public in decision-making procedures. These methods are wide-ranging and some of them have been used for substantial periods of time, while others are newer, more specialised or narrowly defined. The large variations between the different methods are partly due to the fact that the methods have been designed to explore different democratic governance goals (Fung 2003). Among the methods that are relatively narrowly defined are Consensus Conferences, Planning Cells and Citizens' Juries (Andersen and Jæger 1999; Barnes 1994; Crosby 1995; Renn *et al.* 1995). Also narrowly defined are different forms of citizen panels or 'Minipopulus', focus group studies, town meetings, conferences, workshops, citizens summit and participatory budget procedures and deliberative polls (Avritzer 2002; Baiocchi 2001; Hansen 2004; Nylen 2002). These methods have several common characteristics: they are *ad hoc*; non-institutionalised; have a limited agenda of issues with which to deal; have deliberation as a central element; are independent of the electoral procedure; and are primarily organised by decision makers or external consultants and not by the citizens themselves. The methods vary on many factors, such as number of participants, timeframe and different restrictions on the procedures and the participants.

The various experiments have confirmed many of the theorists' normative expectations of deliberative democracy. Deliberation makes the participants more knowledgeable, opinions change and citizens' post-deliberative opinions are more transitive, consistent and coherent than pre-deliberative opinions. These findings are quite consistent over many studies (Dryzek and Niemeyer 2008; Grönlund *et al.* 2010; Hansen 2004: Luskin *et al.* 2002). Nevertheless, the empirical research has also suggested some challenges to the theory. One challenge concerns the dilemma between free exchange of opinions and that proposals must be backed by reasons. The point being that the exchange is not as free as hoped because deliberation requires a certain kind of communication that gives priority to the most educated, with the best argumentation skills (Hansen 2010). Furthermore, Elster has also pointed out that there exists a dilemma between publicity and deliberation (Elster 1998). Encouraging public deliberation may also discourage opinion change as participants tend to stick to their publicly voiced views, while in closed deliberation more deliberators are encouraged to change views and find it easier because they have not committed publicly to a certain view (Hansen 2004).

Conclusion

The development of theories of deliberation has not merely resulted in deliberative democracy as an alternative model of democracy, but in a 'deliberative turn' in democratic theory. Consequently, anyone writing on democracy today must consider the place of deliberation. While there is still disagreement regarding some of the fundamental aspects of deliberative democracy, it has established itself as a theory that can be applied to specific institutional as well as policy issues, and much current work is in that direction. Moreover, while deliberation for some time has attracted the attention of both political theorists and empirical researchers, there is increasing awareness of the need for interplay between the two research fields (Bächtiger *et al.* 2010). Finally, deliberative democracy is not merely a field of academic research, but a model of democracy that has caught the imagination of many practitioners who work for deepening democracy and has been successful in engaging citizens.

References

Ackerman, B. and J. S. Fishkin (2004), *Deliberation Day*, New Haven, CT: Yale University Press.

Andersen, V. N. and K. M. Hansen (2007), 'How Deliberation Makes Better Citizens: The Danish Deliberative Poll on the Euro', *European Journal of Political Research*, 46(4), 531–56.

Andersen, I. and B. Jæger (1999), 'Danish Participatory Models. Scenario Workshops and Consensus Conferences: Towards More Democratic Decision-making', *Science and Public Policy*, 26(5), 331–40.

Avritzer, L. (2002), *Democracy and the Public Space in Latin America*, Princeton, NJ: Princeton University Press.

Bächtiger, A., S. Niemeyer, M. Neblo, M. R. Steenbergen and J. Steiner (2010), 'Disentangling Diversity in Deliberative Democracy: Competing Theories, Their Blind Spots and Complementarities', *Journal of Political Philosophy*, 18(1), 32–63.

Baiocchi, G. (2001), 'Participation, Activism, and Politics: The Porto Alegre Experiment and Deliberative Democratic Theory', *Politics & Society*, 29(1), 43–72.

Barber, B. R. (1984), *Strong Democracy: Participatory Politics for a New Age*, Berkeley, CA: University of California Press.

Barnes, M. (1994), *Building a Deliberative Democracy: An Evaluation of Two Citizens' Juries*, London: Institute for Public Policy Research.

Beck, U. (1992), *Risk Society: Towards a New Modernity*, London: Sage.

Benhabib, S. (1996), 'Toward a Deliberative Model of Democratic Legitimacy', in S. Benhabib (ed.), *Democracy and Difference: Contesting the Boundaries of the Political*, Princeton, NJ: Princeton University Press, pp. 67–95.

Bessette, J. M. (1980), 'Deliberative Democracy: The Majority Principle in Republican Government', in R. A. Goldwin and W. A. Schambra (eds), *How Democratic is the Constitution?*, Washington, DC: American Enterprise Institute, pp. 102–16.

Bohman, J. (1996), *Public Deliberation: Pluralism, Complexity, and Democracy*, Cambridge, MA: MIT Press.

Bohman. J. (1997), 'Deliberative Democracy and Effective Social Freedom: Capabilities, Resources, and Opportunities', in J. Bohman and W. Rehg (eds), *Deliberatie Democracy: Essays on Reason and Politics*, Cambridge, MA: MIT Press, pp. 321–48.

Bohman. J. and W. Rehg (eds), *Deliberative Democracy: Essays on Reason and Politics*, Cambridge, MA: MIT Press.

Chambers, S. (2003), 'Deliberative Democratic Theory', *Annual Review of Political Science*, 6, 307–26.

Cohen, J. (2010), *Rousseau: A Free Community of Equals*, New York: Oxford University Press.

Cohen, J. and J. Rogers (2003), 'Power and Reason', in A. Fung and E. O. Wright (eds), *Deepening Democracy: Institutional Innovations in Empowered Participatory Governance*, London: Verso, pp. 237–55.

Cooke, M. (2000), 'Five Arguments for Deliberative Democracy', *Political Studies*, 48(2), 947–69.

Crosby, N. (1995), 'Citizens Juries: One Solution for Difficult Environmental Questions', in O. Renn, T. Webler and P. Wiedemann (eds), *Fairness and Competence in Citizen Participation: Evaluating Models for Environmental Discourse*, Dordrecht: Kluwer, pp. 157–74.

Dryzek, J. S. (2000), *Deliberative Democracy and Beyond: Liberals, Critics, Contestations*, Oxford: Oxford University Press.

Dryzek, J. S. and S. J. Niemeyer (2008), 'Discursive Representation', *American Political Science Review*, 102(4), 481–93.

Elster, J. (1998), 'Deliberation and Constitution Making', in J. Elster (ed.), *Deliberative Democracy*, Cambridge: Cambridge University Press, pp. 97–123.

Estlund, D. (2008), *Democratic Authority: A Philosophical Framework*, Princeton, NJ: Princeton University Press.

Freeman, S. (2000), 'Deliberative Democracy: A Sympathetic Comment', *Philosophy & Public Affairs*, 29(4), 371–418.

Fung, A. (2003), 'Recipes for Public Spheres: Eight Institutional Design Choices and their Consequences', *Journal of Political Philosophy*, 11(3), 338–67.

Goodin, R. E. (2008), *Innovating Democracy: Democratic Theory and Practice After the Deliberative Turn*, New York: Oxford University Press.

Grönlund, K., M. Setälä and K. Herne (2010), 'Deliberation and Civic Virtue: Lessons from a Citizen Deliberation Experiment', *European Political Science Review*, 2(1), 95–117.

Gutmann, A. and D. Thompson (1996), *Democracy and Disagreement*, Cambridge, MA: Belknap Press.

Gutmann, A. and D. Thompson (2004), *Why Deliberative Democracy?* Princeton, NJ: Princeton University Press.

Habermas, J. (1984), *The Theory of Communicative Action*, 2 vols, trans. T. McCarthy, Cambridge: Polity.

Habermas, J. (1989), *The Structural Transformation of the Public Sphere*, trans. T. Burger with F. Lawrence, Cambridge, MA: MIT Press.

Habermas, J. (1996), *Between Facts and Norms*, Cambridge, MA: MIT Press.

Hansen, K. M. (2004), *Deliberative Democracy and Opinion Formation*, Odense: University Press of Southern Denmark.

Hansen, K. M. (2010), 'The Equality Paradox of Deliberative Democracy: Evidence from a National Deliberative Poll', in K. Ikeda, L. Morales and M. Wolf (eds), *Political Discussion in Modern Democracies*, London: Routledge, pp: 26–43.

Hansen, K. M. (2012), 'Deliberative Democracy: Mapping out the Deliberative Turn in Democratic Theory', in Christian Kock and Lisa Villadsen (eds), *Rhetorical Citizenship and Public Deliberation*, University Park, PA: Pennsylvania State University Press.

Hansen, K. M. and V. N. Andersen (2004), 'Deliberative Democracy and the Deliberative Poll on the Euro', *Scandinavian Political Studies*, 27(3), 261–86.

Knight, J. and J. Johnson (1997), 'What Sort of Equality Does Deliberative Democracy Require?', in J. Bohman and W. Rehg (eds), *Deliberatie Democracy: Essays on Reason and Politics*, Cambridge, MA: MIT Press, pp. 279–319.

Luskin, R. C., J. S. Fishkin and R. Jowell (2002), 'Considered Opinions: Deliberative Polling in Britain', *British Journal of Political Science*, 32(3), 455–87.

Manin, B. (1987), 'On Legitimacy and Political Deliberation', *Political Theory*, 15(3), 338–68.

Mansbridge, J. (1983), *Beyond Adversary Democracy*, 2nd edn, Chicago, IL: University of Chicago Press.

Mill, J. S. ([1859] 1962), *On Liberty*, New York: Meridian.

Nylen, W. R. (2002), 'Testing the Empowerment Thesis: The Participatory Budget in Belo Horizonte and Betim, Brazil', *Comparative Politics*, 34(2), 127–45.

Parkinson, J. (2003), 'Legitimacy Problem in Deliberative Democracy', *Political Studies*, 51(1), 180–96.

Pitkin, H. F. (1967), *The Concept of Representation*, Berkeley, CA: University of California Press.

Rawls, J. (1971), *A Theory of Justice*, London: Oxford University Press.

Rawls, J. (1996), *Political Liberalism*, New York: Columbia University Press.

Renn, O., T. Webler and P. Wiedemann (1995), *Fairness and Competence in Citizen Participation: Evaluating Models for Environmental Discourse*, Dordrecht: Kluwer.

Rostbøll, C. F. (2005), 'Preferences and Paternalism: On Freedom and Deliberative Democracy', *Political Theory*, 33(3), 370–96.

Rostbøll, C. F. (2008), *Deliberative Freedom: Deliberative Democracy as Critical Theory*, Albany, NY: SUNY Press.

Rousseau, J.-J. (1762), 'The Social Contract', in W. Ebenstein and A. Ebenstein (eds), *Great Political Thinkers: Plato to the Present*, 6th edn, Fort Worth, TX: Harcourt College Publishers, pp. 452–72.

Tocqueville, A. de ([1835] 2000), *Democracy in America*, New York: Bantam Classic.

Young, I. M. (2000), *Inclusion and Democracy*, Oxford: Oxford University Press.

Chapter 43

New Thinking

John Keane

In 1945, following several decades that saw most experiments in democratisation fail, there were only a dozen democracies left on the face of the earth. Since then, despite many ups and downs, democracy has bounced back from near oblivion to become a planetary phenomenon for the first time in its history (Diamond 2008; Dunn 2005; Keane 2009b). Fresh research perspectives are required because democracy has taken root in so many different geographic contexts that several fundamental presuppositions of democratic theory have been invalidated. This metamorphosis remains largely unregistered in the literature on democracy, which still has a distinctively Eurocentric bent, hence precluding references to many anomalous cases, past and present (Dunn 2005; Held 2006). Many analysts of democracy still suppose that the prerequisites of democracy include a 'sovereign' territorial state, competition among political parties, periodic elections, parliamentary government, a 'national identity' with a common language, common customs and a common sense of shared history and a market economy that guarantees citizens a standard of living sufficient to allow an interest in public affairs. These criteria are seen as essential to 'liberal democracy', 'Western democracy' and 'parliamentary democracy', but these terms arguably now function as living-dead 'zombie' categories that suppress the novel dynamics unfolding within actually existing democracies.

Alternative Approaches

India, Taiwan, South Africa, Botswana, Nepal and the Tibetan Government in Exile are just some of the anomalous cases that throw into disarray many presumptions about democracy in such disciplinary fields as political science, sociology, economics and international relations. In each case, the meaning of democracy and the ways in which it took root in local soils prompt new questions about what future research might call the *indigenisation of democracy*. This phrase refers to the complex ways in which the language, institutions and normative ideals of democracy morph when they are carried into environments where they exercised little previous influence.

Indigenisation is always a complex and contested set of processes. What is arguably needed is a twenty-first-century *political anthropology of democracy*: new approaches with fresh perspectives, metaphors, theories and methods to understand democracy as it takes root in unfamiliar soils. In contrast to simple approaches guided by 'end of history' teleology (Fukuyama 1992) or by 'third wave' maritime metaphors (Hun-tington 1991), alternative approaches examine changes in the language and institutions of democracy with more complex analogies. Translation and other literary similes from linguistic philosophy have been utilised, most notably in Frederic Schaffer's study of the Wolof and French speakers in Senegal and how they transformed the European donor language of *démocratie* to make new sense of multi-party electoral practices within a culturally divergent society that calls itself a *demokaraasi* (Schaffer 1998). Some scholars have adapted Michel de Certeau's work to examine how the tactical appropriation of a technical procedure like the secret ballot creates a 'theatrical' performance that results in long-lasting changes in its functioning (Bertrand *et al.* 2007). Other literature (to take a third example) has relied on the language of mutagens and evolutionary biology to suggest that just as mutations sometimes transcend unfitness to produce organisms better adapted to their environment, democracy too can evolve and adapt to changing environments (Keane 2009b: 673–86).

Analogies drawn from linguistics, theatre and evolutionary biology must be handled with great care. But in pursuit of new ways of analysing the global processes by which democratic languages and institutions become 'embedded' in particular contexts (Merkel 2004), one thing seems abundantly clear: the field is wide open for novel metaphors, fresh interpretations and original case studies that add to the thesis of indigenisation and force refinement of our understanding of democratisation. Much can be learned from the reinterpretation of historical efforts to nurture democracy on 'foreign soils', including Athenian efforts at 'democracy promotion'; the invention of the norms and institutions of representative democracy and their diffusion to the British colonies and Spanish America (Hirst 2002; Keyssar 2000; Rosanvallon 2004); and the colonial roots of democratisation in Taiwan, China and Japan during the last great globalisation spurt from 1870 to 1930 (Chang 1971; Dower 2000; Ike 1950; Wu 2003). There is scope for the reinterpretation of the spread of democracy in the present round of globalisation, including much neglected cases such as India, Papua New Guinea, Tanzania and the Muslim world (Guha 2007; Keane 2009b; Reilly 2001; Sadiki 2009; Scheps 2000). The rise of Australian federalism also seems ripe for reinterpretation along these lines. The standard narrative is of piecemeal colonisation propelling various colonies into a new, historically inevitable federation. Instead, the nineteenth-century push towards federation was the contested result of many forces, including post-1776 British reassessment of empire, the resistance of local colonists, visions inspired by the American republic and decentralist initiatives guided by the mental maps and patterns of movement of aboriginal peoples (Brown 2004).

Another significant change that has been taking place in the real world of democracy since 1945 is the growth of power scrutinising mechanisms – human rights organisa-tions, summits, forums, integrity commissions, participatory budgeting and citizens' assemblies – that have gradually altered the political geometry and everyday dynamics of democracy to produce post-electoral or *monitory democracy* (Keane 2009b, 2011). Democracy is coming to mean much more than the periodic election of representatives to a parliament. In the new age of monitory democracy elections still count, but parties and parliaments now have to compete with thousands of monitory organisations and networks that try to keep those who exercise power on their toes. The old meaning of democracy based on the rule of one person, one vote, is replaced by democracy guided by a different and more complex rule: one person, many interests, many votes, many representatives, both at home and abroad. The trend towards monitory democracy prompts many questions. What are the principal drivers of the growth in extra-parliamentary scrutiny? How are the different types of monitory mechanisms best catalogued (for example, auditors-general and public enquiries are adjuncts to parliament, while human rights campaigns and environmental watchdogs operate at a distance from elected representatives and governments)? Do these mechanisms compound the weaknesses of contemporary political parties and parliaments, forcing them further into decline? Can parliaments recover their powers or will they share power with *unelected* representatives whose legitimacy stems from subscription membership, ethical probity, media exposure and resilience in suffering?

Communication Media

The advent of monitory democracy is inextricably linked with the growth of new communication media. With few exceptions, the historical affinities between democracy and communication media are still poorly analysed in contemporary social science literature. Major research initiatives may profitably think of the affinities: ancient forms of assembly democracy belonged to the era of the *spoken word*, supplemented with laws written on stone or papyrus, and messages by foot or horse. Representative democracy in territorial states sprang up in the age of *print culture* – printing presses, books, pamphlets, newspapers, novels and mailed messages – and fell into crisis during the advent of early mass broadcasting media. By contrast, contemporary forms of democracy are tied to the growth of *multi-media-saturated societies*, whose structures of power are overseen by institutions operating within a new galaxy of 'communicative abundance' (Keane 2009c, 2012).

Regardless of how the changing historical relationship between communication media and democracy is understood, many new questions are prompted by the contemporary trends. What are the distinctive qualities of new communication media? Are they best described in terms of overlapping and interlinked media devices that integrate texts, sounds and images, and communicate through multiple user points, in chosen time, either real or delayed, within modularised global networks that are affordable to hundreds of millions of people across the globe? Does this new age of communicative abundance produce disappointments, instability and harmful self-contradictions, for instance, in the concentration of media capital, the commercialisation and erosion of private life or in the gaps between communication-rich and communication-poor? Are the strongly generative qualities of the Internet so vulnerable to degenerative trends (such as spyware, adware, spam, phishing, viruses and cyber-attacks) that new hierarchies of restricted 'gated communities' are likely to develop, weakening the democratic effects of communicative abundance? Is disaffection with political parties, politicians and 'politics' a necessary effect of the new communication media, at least when compared with the era of representative democracy, when print and audiovisual media were closely aligned with political parties and governments? How plausible is the suggestion that such disaffection is dangerous for democracy, because it can be tapped by political leaders who use state-of-the-art rhetorical methods to convince people that their own interests are identical with the leader's (Eco 2008; Ginsborg 2005; Keane 2012; Sartori 2009).

Research on communicative abundance might also profitably concentrate on the past, present and future of journalism. Do democracies require an 'unlovable press' (Schudson 2009)? Is democracy compatible with adversarial journalism that produces 'gotcha' moments driven by ratings, sales and hits? Is there substance to new-style 'churnalists' who hunt in packs, feed upon unconfirmed sources, spin titillating sensations and concentrate too much on personalities and events? Does the new journalism – and the challenges posed to its authority by 'citizen journalists' – add substance to democracy by giving a voice to 'ordinary people' and encouraging citizens' suspicions of power? What about those moments when the public exposure of wrongdoing and poor decisions does not happen? Is it meaningful to speak of 'media decadence' or 'media failures', those junctures when powerful organisations are not subject to scrutiny, or when journalists circulate disinformation around the globe before inaccuracies are corrected (Keane 2009a, 2009c)? Granted that the new communication media are marked by structural defects, are there ways to enhance the quality of democracy by fostering new business models and patterns of media ownership, or by reshaping the contours of journalism through new codes of conduct and public expectations? What is the long-term impact of citizen journalists on social networking sites? Are they profoundly transforming the meaning of journalism or will they have the effect of disorientating, commercialising and ruining public life?

Markets and Democracy

The tensions between journalism and democracy are mired in a larger magnetic field: the potentially contradictory relationship between markets and democracy. New research initiatives in this field are vital. From the early years of the nineteenth century, and especially during periods of capital disinvestment and mass unemployment, this relationship has often been a source of public disturbance. The recent global recession is no exception: it has had the effect of breathing new life into an old subject waiting for fresh research to happen. Enquiries into markets and democracy might profitably reinterpret key historical cases. Investigations are likely to show that the standard formula, 'no bourgeois, no democracy', is implausible (Moore 1967: 418); and that viable democratic political forms, such as citizens' assemblies, public juries, political parties and periodic elections, are contingently related to a wide repertoire of property forms. The early Greek assemblies enjoyed a functional but tense relationship with commodity production and exchange: the life of (male) citizens was seen as standing in opposition to the production of the necessities of life in the *oikos*. Modern forms of representative democracy sprang up in the Low Countries at the end of the sixteenth century and were intimately bound up with profit-driven production and exchange. Since that time, capitalist markets have been a mixed blessing for democracy. The dynamism, technical innovation and enhanced productivity of (unconstrained) markets have been impressive. So, too, has been their rapaciousness, unequal (class-structured) outcomes, reckless exploitation of the environment and the vulnerability to bubbles, whose bursting generates wild downturns and misery in people's lives, in the process destabilising democratic institutions, as happened the 1920s and 1930s (Kindleberger and Aliber 2005).

Future research might be guided by a handy formula: democracies can neither live with markets nor live without markets. The formula helps to explain the divergent political recommendations concerning markets and democracy. According to pro-market observers, democracy distorts the rational calculations markets require; majority rule is at odds with free competition, individual liberty and the rule of law. Required are 'democratic pessimism', the restriction of majority democracy in favour of 'demarchy' and limited government that nurtures 'free markets' (Caplan 2007; Hayek 1979). Other observers stake out the contrary view: market failures require correction by political interventions based on popular consent, equality and solidarity. The democratisation of markets means various things: for Giuseppe Mazzini it means the Principle of Humanity replaces the profit motive; for Karl Marx it provides the opportunity for the development of 'social individuality' and for C. B. Macpherson it raises the possibility of post-market individualism (Macpherson 1973; Marx [1857] 1973). Other analysts have championed social democratic proposals to 'socialise' the unjust effects of competition by 're-embedding' markets within civil society institutions guaranteed by welfare states that protect and extend social citizenship rights (Hall and Soskice 2001; Marshall 1950; Polanyi 1945).

It seems important to revisit the subject of markets so as to develop comparisons among contemporary Anglo-Saxon, Rhineland, Japanese, Indian, Chinese and other 'varieties of capitalism'; and to craft new lines of research concerning the ill-understood phenomenon of *democracy failure* (Keane 2009a). There is evidence, under certain conditions, that democracy failure can breed market failure. For example, in the Atlantic heartlands of global banking, the recent willingness of unelected regulatory bodies, elected governments and self-regulation agencies to encourage the dispersal of credit risk to third-party investors has produced destabilising boom–bust sequence on the whole global economy. Assuming the need for new early warning systems, can more democratic ways be found for producing probity and transparency in markets? Can democracies now build regional and global oversight structures in banking, insurance and securities – credible forums that would crack down on fraud, discourage excessive risk-taking, foster best practice through open-minded counsel and provide redress to those hurt by this crisis?

Global Problems

The struggle to extend the vote to all categories of people largely came to an end during the course of the twentieth century – the question of the universal franchise is now settled. From this perspective, the matter of *who votes* has been replaced by questions concerning *where* people can or should vote (Bobbio 1989). Among the remarkable features of our age is the spread of power-scrutinising mechanisms across borders. Some downplay the significance of these innovations on the definitional ground that democracy in representative form requires a territorial state and a common sense of national identity (Dahl 1998). Future research needs to interrogate this claim, whose empirical, strategic and normative weaknesses seem obvious. Exactly how democracy can be re-imagined across borders is another matter. Analysts of 'global chains' (Sassen 2005) and 'cosmocracy' (Keane 2003), as well as advocates of 'cosmopolitan democracy' (Archibugi 2008; Held 1995, 2006) are agreed that there are forces afoot weakening the conventional mechanisms of electoral democracy within states: the power of global firms; parliamentary hesitation in the face of globalising markets; the disproportionate power of a few states within global bodies such as the G20; and the growth of supranational institutions that are wholly unaccountable to citizens and their elected representatives. Much less agreement follows from the empirical diagnosis of such trends. Some champions of 'global civil society' think of it as the best hope for protecting struggles for justice, freedom and solidarity across borders. Others give priority to the reform of the United Nations by a global constitutional convention and widening the basis of representation in the General Assembly. Still other democrats work for the general proliferation of power-chastening monitory mechanisms.

Each of these approaches has advantages and disadvantages that must be explored. Consider the 'two-tier' thinking of cosmopolitan democracy calls for 'the creation of new political institutions which would coexist with the system of states but which would override states in clearly defined spheres of activity where those activities have demonstrable transnational and international consequences' (Held 2006: 305, 308–9). Cosmopolitan democracy is a brave effort to find a language through which democracy after representation is discussed. But its two-tier thinking and vision of 'an intensive, participatory and deliberative democracy' begs questions about the fiction of a global people participating in global decision making (Held 2006: 308–9). Others seek to re-imagine the architecture or 'political geography' of democracy in new ways. Empirical studies of cross-border mechanisms of integration are likely to yield important insights. East Asia is a case in point: during the past three decades, bilateral and multilateral cooperation among governments, economic networks, development corridors and *ad hoc* problem-solving bodies have brought a greater sense of 'top-down' and 'bottom-up' interdependence and heightened the need for new monitory mechanisms, including peer review panels, cross-border parliaments and summits (Gyngell and Wesley 2003; Pempel 2005; White 2006).

The biosphere is emerging as the major issue facing twenty-first-century democracies (Alonso *et al.* 2010: 74–95, 236–57). How democracies reverse, modify or adapt to environmental changes has prompted some to suggest that 'intergenerational justice' requires the world of nature to have political rights (Hiskes 2009: 2). The earliest and most challenging effort to think along these lines was Heidegger's rejection of the will to universal measurement and domination; he was appealing to the possibility of cultivating an abiding sense of life on earth as poetic dwelling (Heidegger 1973, 1995). Technological hubris, homelessness and their devastating, darkening effects are not necessarily the destiny of the world, he argued. Through meditative reflection, a new preparedness to embrace mystery and release our hold on other beings (*Gelassenheit*), humans can come to terms with the biosphere by becoming shepherds who refuse to lord over other beings, but preserve them in their nearness to the truth of being. His vision involved a short-sighted rejection of politics, the flipside of his earlier infatuation with Nazism. But the fundamental problem outlined by Heidegger must be confronted with new questions from a democratic perspective. To what extent is democracy implicated in the trends that Heidegger spotted? Is political thinking guided by the supremacy of 'the people': incorrigibly arrogant, at odds with the biosphere and its (supposedly) lesser creatures? How can the current 'greening' of democracies be explained? Is democracy equipped to handle the complex, intractable, open-ended and often 'wicked' problems caused by our long-standing quest to dominate nature? Given that democratic mechanisms in territorial state frameworks are often dysfunctional when it comes to environmental problems, can regional and global institutions subject to democratic control do any better? Can new democratic forms of representation be extended to nature, despite the fact that it has no personality, voice or 'subjectivity'? Can democracies stimulate institutional inventions – green parties, green courts, bioregional assemblies and other early warning systems – that change the meaning of democracy itself?

Another topic ripe for investigation in the global sphere is *war, peace and the promotion of democracy*. If democracies intervene in tyrannical and authoritarian states using military means then they are accused of violating the 'sovereignty' of peoples entitled to govern themselves; whereas if they do not intervene then democracies are accused of avoiding their responsibility to protect human rights and other democratic standards. The dilemma is compounded when military intervention is done in the name of 'democracy promotion'. Democratisation requires more than firepower. Can occupying powers build a successful democracy? Historical perspectives are needed: democratic empires have a mixed record in democracy promotion. During the fifth century BCE, there was a strongly symbiotic relationship between Athenian democracy and its war-making prowess (Pritchard 2010). Revolutionary France witnessed new forms of democratic violence at home and abroad; while America's stated global commitment to 'make the world safe for democracy' has been dogged by accusations of double standards and ulterior motives (T. Smith 1994; Wilson [1917] 1965: 308). Are democracies 'peaceful'? Can they enforce democracy? Nearly 85 per cent of the ninety American military interventions from 1898 to 1992 proved democratically infertile, while another study, covering more than 200 US military operations, including peacekeeping and military training, showed that democratic effects were observable in only 28 per cent of cases (Keane 2010; Peceny 1999; Tures 2005).

From a twenty-first-century perspective, the patchy record of success of democracy promotion by military means is complicated by the rise of what might be called *anti-democracy promotion*: new types of criticism and resistance to democracy – para-doxically, often in the name of democracy. Despite recent democratic breakthroughs in the Arab world, contemporary 'democracy pushback' may be the prelude to a repeat of the democratic failures of the 1920s and 1930s (Carothers 2006: 55). Critics of democracy are encouraged by endogenous weaknesses within contemporary democ-racies: the decline of the conventional mechanisms of electoral democracy; deep disaffection with parties, parliaments and politicians; regulatory failures in market economies; and the spread of violence, nuclear weapons, uncivil wars and terrorism using asymmetric warfare. Worthy of fresh research is the growing power of China, which is said by some to be a paragon of authoritarian state capitalism, overtaking the

United States and presenting an alternative to democratic representation (Jacques 2009; Mahbubani 2008). Further research is also required into defective democratic regimes such as Russia, Ukraine, Georgia, Thailand and Venezuela (Keane 2009b; Merkel 2004; Zakaria 2003). These 'phantom democracies' tolerate pluralism and elections, but are corrupted by grave deficiencies in the rule of law, lack of press freedom and populist authoritarianism where strong figures (Vladimir Putin, Hugo Chávez) claim to represent the nation's will. The form of politics unleashed by these regimes is redolent of the popular sovereignty proposed by Carl Schmitt in his critique of parliamentary democracies in the early twentieth century (Schmitt [1923] 1991). Within such regimes, plebiscitary or populist politics is pseudo-representation.

Why Democracy?

Seen from a twenty-first-century perspective, does the term democracy have a precise meaning? Some sceptics doubt whether it does. They like to quote T. S. Eliot, who famously complained that 'when a term has become so universally sanctified as "democracy" now is, I begin to wonder whether it means anything, in meaning too many things' (Eliot 1940: 11–12). The commonplace reply is that democracy rests upon 'the people' as the foundation of political authority. Those who speak of democracy in this way fail to acknowledge the changing historical meaning of the sovereign people principle: while Athenian-style assembly democracy took its authority from 'the people' assembled face-to-face in a public place to decide matters concerning the common good, the invention of representative democracy in the late eighteenth century cast doubt on the presumed homogeneity of 'the people', kept them at arm's length from government and transformed them into part-time judges of how representatives performed. This reasoning is rejected by contemporary scholars who express nostalgia for the age of assembly democracy by agitating for 'real' or 'deep' or 'participatory' democracy to bring back the energies and wisdom of an imaginary 'people' (Barber 1984; Wolin 2004, 2008). This claim avoids the reality that the world is made up of many *demoi* with flesh-and-blood people who may not see eye to eye. German constitutional lawyers say that 'the people' are a '*Zurechnungssubjekt*', a fictional legal subject to whom collective powers are attributed, but a subject not capable of acting in a unified and purposeful way. This raises challenging 'anthropological' questions about how 'peoplehood' is constructed (R. M. Smith 2003). There are also strategic and normative questions about democracies tolerating divergent forms of 'peoplehood', that is, conflicting understandings of who is or are 'the people'. Perhaps it is time to downgrade the 'sovereign people' principle and restrict it to moments when sharp contests of power require for their resolution the fiction of an undivided people as the source of authority.

   The current challenges to democracy make it imperative that research tackles the toughest sets of questions in the field: is democracy worth defending? Given that the twenty-first century has plenty of other ways of handling power, isn't democracy to be seen as just one – dispensable – ideal among many others? Is it really a universal norm, as many observers have claimed? Or, when all is said and done, is democracy actually just a fake universal norm, just a tool useful in the struggle by some for mastery over others? These questions are not easy to answer. New research on the ethics of democracy might note how the history of democracy has been marked by warnings and accusations of its weakness: mass ignorance; mob rule, followed by tyranny; centralisation of state power; new forms of servitude; and bureaucratic organisation that renders equality and freedom impossible.

Urgently needed as well is new research on the long history of positive justifications of democracy. Who today believes that democracy is sanctioned either by the deities or by its military superiority (as many ancient Greeks thought)? Who still thinks of democracy as a Christian gift to humanity or an historical necessity? Democracy has been defended as a universal norm (Sen 1999). But is it wilting under the suspicion that it is stamped with the birthmark of local time–space contexts so it is not for everybody (Keane 2009b; Rorty 1991). There is another possibility: those defending a specific form of life called democracy might conclude that it is worth fighting for, especially in a world riddled with the demons of power, politics and violence. Faced with difficult ethical questions, some scholars have proposed that democracy should part company with philosophical justification and instead follow the path of pragmatic calculation (Rorty 1991). Other scholars seek to justify democracy as an ethical universal because they claim it has positive consequences: promotes peace, is a precondition of market-generated wealth, or the guarantor of human wellness.

Conclusion

New research is likely to show the implausibility of most of these arguments, which raises a fundamental normative question: are there fresh – twenty-first-century – ways of thinking positively about democracy? Is democracy a set of ideals and institutions that can be applied all over the world? Answers to these questions may come from research into older normative defences of democracy and insistence that democracy guarantees freedom from the pseudo-universal claims of norms such as 'the Nation', 'the Market' and 'the State'. Other candidates for consideration include the claim that 'democracy is the worst form of government except all those other forms that have been tried from time to time' (Churchill, 1947: 207). Then there is the bolder conjecture that democracy is not just the best weapon for dealing with human arrogance, folly and hubris, but that it also has a deep sensitivity to uncertainty, complexity and diversity, so that it is indispensable for resolving so-called 'wicked problems' (Fukuyama 2007; Head 2008). This line of reasoning would be new in the history of democracy and the strongest case for democracy's superiority in preventing and addressing mistakes, anticipating and handling unexpected events and consequences, and reversing wrong-headed decisions and their unjust effects.

References

Alonso, S., J. Keane and W. Merkel (eds) (2010), *The Future of Representative Democracy*, Cambridge: Cambridge University Press.

Archibugi, D. (2008), *The Global Commonwealth of Citizens: Toward Cosmopolitan Democracy*, Princeton, NJ: Princeton University Press.

Barber, B. (1984), *Strong Democracy: Participatory Politics for a New Age*, Berkeley, CA: University of California Press.

Bertrand, R., J.-L. Briquet and P. Pels (eds) (2007), *Cultures of Voting: The Hidden History of the Secret Ballot*, London: Hurst.

Bobbio, N. (1989), *Democracy and Dictatorship: The Nature and Limits of State Power*, Cambridge: Polity.

Brown, A. J. (2004), 'Constitutional Schizophrenia Then and Now', *Papers on Parliament*, 42, 33–58.

Caplan, B. (2007), *The Myth of the Rational Voter: Why Democracies Choose Bad Policies*, Princeton, NJ: Princeton University Press.

Carothers, T. (2006), 'The Backlash Against Democracy Promotion', *Foreign Affairs*, 85(2), 55–68.

Chang, H. (1971), *Liang Ch'i-Chao and Intellectual Transition in China 1890–1907*, Cambridge, MA: Harvard University Press.

Churchill, W. (1947), 'British Parliament Bill', *Hansard*, 444, 206–7.

Dahl, R. (1998), *On Democracy*, New Haven, CT: Yale University Press.

Diamond, L. (2008), *The Spirit of Democracy: The Struggle to Build Free Societies Throughout the World*, New York: Henry Holt.

Dower, J. (2000), *Embracing Defeat: Japan in the Aftermath of World War II*, Harmondsworth: Penguin.

Dunn, J. (2005), *Setting the People Free: The Story of Democracy*, London: Atlantic Books.

Eco, U. (2008), 'On Mass Media Populism', in *Turning Back the Clock: Hot Wars and Media Populism*, London: Vintage.

Eliot, T. S. (1940), *The Idea of a Christian Society*, New York: Harcourt Brace.

Fukuyama, F. (1992), *The End of History and the Last Man*, New York: Free Press.

Fukuyama, F. (ed.) (2007), *Blindside: How to Anticipate Forcing Events and Wildcards in Global Politics*, Washington, DC: Brookings Institution Press.

Ginsborg, P. (2005), *Silvio Berlusconi: Television, Power and Patrimony*, London: Verso.

Guha, R. (2007), *India after Gandhi: The History of the World's Largest Democracy*, London: Pan.

Gyngell, A. and M. Wesley (2003), *Making Australian Foreign Policy*, Cambridge: Cambridge University Press.

Hall, P. and D. Soskice (2001), *Varieties of Capitalism: The Institutional Foundations of Comparative Advantage*, Oxford: Oxford University Press.

Hayek, F. von (1979), *Law, Legislation and Liberty: The Political Order of a Free People*, London: Routledge.

Head, B. W. (2008), 'Wicked Problems in Public Policy', *Public Policy*, 3(2), 101–18.

Heidegger, M. (1973), *Holzwege*, Frankfurt: Klosterman.

Heidegger, M. (1995), *Feldweg-Gesprache: 1944–1945*, in *Gesamtausgabe*, vol. 17. Frankfurt: Klosterman, pp. 6–17.

Held, D. (1995), *Democracy and the Global Order: From the Modern State to Cosmopolitan Governance*, Cambridge: Polity.

Held, D. (2006), *Models of Democracy*, 3rd edn, Cambridge: Blackwell.

Hirst, J. (2002), *Australia's Democracy: A Short History*, Sydney: Allen & Unwin.

Hiskes, R. P. (2009), *The Human Right to a Green Future: Environmental Rights and Intergenerational Justice*, Cambridge: Cambridge University Press.

Huntington, S. P. (1991), *The Third Wave: Democratization in the Late Twentieth Century*, Norman, OK: University of Oklahoma Press.

Ike, N. (1950), *The Beginnings of Political Democracy in Japan*, Baltimore, MD: Johns Hopkins University Press.

Jacques, M. (2009), *When China Rules the World: The Rise of the Middle Kingdom and the End of the Western World*, London: Allen Lane.

Keane, J. (2003), *Global Civil Society?* Cambridge: Cambridge University Press.

Keane, J. (2009a), 'Democracy Failure', *WZB-Mitteilungen*, 124, 6–8.

Keane, J. (2009b), *The Life and Death of Democracy*, London: Simon & Schuster.

Keane, J. (2009c), 'Media Decadence and Democracy', Senate Occasional Lecture, Canberra: Australian National University.

Keane, J. (2010), 'Epilogue: Does Democracy Have A Violent Heart?', in D. Pritchard (ed.), *War, Democracy and Culture in Classical Athens*, Cambridge: Cambridge University Press.

Keane, J. (2011), 'Monitory Democracy? The Secret History of Democracy since 1945', in B. Isakhan and S. Stockwell (eds), *The Secret History of Democracy*, London: Palgrave Macmillan, pp. 204–18.

Keane, J. (2012), *Media and Democracy in a Decadent Age*, Cambridge: Cambridge University Press.

Keyssar, A. (2000), *The Right to Vote: The Contested History of Democracy in the United States*, New York: Basic Books.

Kindleberger, C. P. and R. Aliber (2005), *Manias, Panics, and Crashes: A History of Financial Crises*, 5th edn, Hoboken: Wiley.

Mahbubani, K. (2008), *The New Asian Hemisphere: The Irresistible Shift of Global Power to the East*, New York: Public Affairs.

Marshall, T. H. (1950), *Citizenship and Social Class and other Essays*, Cambridge: Cambridge University Press.

Macpherson, C. B. (1973), 'Problems of a Non-Market Theory of Democracy', in *Democratic Theory Essays in Retrieval*, Oxford: Clarendon Press, pp. 39–76.

Marx, K. ([1857] 1973), *Grundrisse*, trans. M. Nicolaus, Harmondsworth: Penguin.

Merkel, W. (2004), 'Embedded and Defective Democracies', *Democratization*, 11(5), 33–58.

Moore, B., Jr (1967), *Social Origins of Dictatorship and Democracy*, London: Penguin.

Peceny, M. (1999), *Democracy at the Point of Bayonets*, University Park, PA: Pennsylvania State University Press.

Pempel, T. J. (ed.) (2005), *Remapping East Asia: The Construction of a Region*, Ithaca, NY: Cornell University Press.

Polanyi, K. (1945), *The Great Transformation*, London: Gollancz.

Pritchard, D. (2010), 'The Symbiosis between Democracy and War: The Case of Ancient Athens', in D. Pritchard (ed.), *War, Democracy and Culture in Classical Athens*, Cambridge: Cambridge University Press.

Reilly, B. (2001), *Democracy in Divided Societies: Electoral Engineering for Conflict Management*, Cambridge: Cambridge University Press.

Rorty, R. (1991), 'The Priority of Democracy to Philosophy', in *Objectivity, Relativism, and Truth: Philosophical Papers*, vol. 1, Cambridge: Cambridge University Press, pp. 583–9.

Rosanvallon, P. (2004), *Le modèle politique français: la société civile contre le jacobinisme de 1789 à nos jours*, Paris: Seuil.

Sadiki, L. (2009), *Rethinking Arab Democratization: Elections without Democracy*, Oxford: Oxford University Press.

Sartori, G. (2009), *Il sultanato*, Rome: Laterza.

Sassen, S. (2005), *Digital Formations: IT and New Architectures in the Global Realm*, Princeton, NJ: Princeton University Press.

Schaffer, F. (1998), *Democracy in Translation: Understanding Politics in an Unfamiliar Culture*, Ithaca, NY: Cornell University Press.

Scheps, L. (2000), 'The Native Roots of Papua New Guinea's Democracy', *Quadrant*, May, 52–9.

Schudson, M. (2009), *Why Democracies Need an Unlovable Press*, Cambridge: Cambridge University Press.

Schmitt, C. ([1923] 1991), *Die geistesgeschichtliche Lage des heutigen Parlamentarismus*, 7th edn, Berlin: Duncker & Humblot.

Sen, A. (1999), 'Democracy as a Universal Value', *Journal of Democracy*, 10(3), 3–17.

Smith, R. M. (2003), *Stories of Peoplehood: The Politics and Morals of Political Membership*, Cambridge: Cambridge University Press.

Smith, T. (1994), *America's Mission: The United States and the Worldwide Struggle for Democracy in the Twentieth Century*, Princeton, NJ: Princeton University Press.

Tures, J. A. (2005), 'Operation Exporting Freedom: The Quest for Democratization via United States Military Operations', *Whitehead Journal of Diplomacy and International Relations*, 6(1), 97–111.

White, H. (2006), *Beyond the Defence of Australia: Finding a New Balance in Australian Strategic Policy*, Sydney: Lowy Institute.

Wilson, W. ([1917] 1965), 'The World Must be Made Safe for Democracy', in A. Fried (ed.), *A Day of Dedication: The Essential Writings and Speeches of Woodrow Wilson*, New York: Macmillan, pp. 301–8.

Wolin, S. S. (2004), *Politics and Vision: Continuity and Innovation in Western Political Thought*, expanded edn, Princeton, NJ: Princeton University Press.

Wolin, S. S. (2008), *Democracy Incorporated: Managed Democracy and the Specter of Inverted Totalitarianism*, Princeton, NJ: Princeton University Press.

Wu, R. R. (2003), 'The Formosan Ideology: Oriental Colonialism and the Rise of Taiwanese Nationalism, 1895–1945', unpublished doctoral dissertation, University of Chicago.

Zakaria, F. (2003), *The Future of Freedom: Illiberal Democracy at Home and Abroad*, rev. edn, New York: W. W. Norton.

Conclusion:
The Future History of Democracy

Stephen Stockwell

In the preceding chapters, the contributors have brought their expertise to bear on many democratic moments, both expected and unexpected, down through history. Together, these chapters tell quite a story of common people taking their chances to create ideas, opportunities and institutions of government where their collective voices have a role to play and often carry the day. But as more people identify themselves as democrats, as more countries embrace democracy, as there is more opportunity for participation at local, national and international levels, there is also evidence of a lapse of faith, a moment of uncertainty, a loss of focus in the democratic project. There is an irony in the present condition of democracy: the more it has been adopted around the world since the end of the Cold War, the less enthusiasm there is for democracy in the heartland of its greatest proponents. What hope is there for people risking their lives to bring about democracy in Iran, Burma or China, when people in established democracies like the United States, the United Kingdom and Australia are just not inspired by it anymore? For too many citizens in 'advanced' democracies, it seems a game played by elites to protect their interests with only adverse consequences for the daily life of the ordinary individual.

These tensions have been played out in daily events during the editing of this book. As discussed in the Introduction, Freedom House's 2011 annual report marked the sixth consecutive year in which countries with declines outnumbered those with improvements. In 2011 the number of electoral democracies declined to 117 from the 2005 peak of 123 and equivalent to the 1995 figure (*Freedom in the World* 2012). The 2011 Arab Revolutions of anti-authoritarian uprisings commenced in Tunisia and spread to Egypt and Libya, but similar uprisings in Bahrain, Yemen and Syria were put down with force. Meanwhile, in the West, inequities resulting from the global financial crisis prompted popular grassroots movements, such as the protests against austerity measures in Greece and other European Union countries and the Occupy Wall Street movement.

Then there was the interesting case of the UK riots, where a police shooting of a family man doing his domestic chores prompted young people to riot and plunder shops. Many critics blame this behaviour on poor parenting, slack education and personal ethical failures and all of these issues are relevant, but society also contributed when the government alienated young people by giving police the powers for repeated, close surveillance of them and when the advertising industry and mass media provided them with world views hedged by brands, celebrity and obscene but easy rewards for a modicum of sporting, theatrical or financial talent. When the police were initially slow to respond to the rioting, young people saw an opportunity for excitement while obtaining the brands they have been taught to desire. Wayne Halliburton, a reformed criminal whose son avoided joining the riots, brings the gap between East and West into focus: "The way how I look at it is in Libya and Syria in the Middle East they're fighting for peace and democracy and in London the kids are fighting for plasmas and free jewellery" (Halliburton cited in Fowler 2011).

This is a refreshingly frank insight into the problems that democracies presently face in the West. There is no doubt that individuals bear the responsibility for their actions, but at the same time it is incumbent upon democratic society to ask why these well-fed, materially well-off and politically free individuals feel so disaffected and are so distant from their society. Democracy has been successful in addressing the urgent questions of material scarcity in the West: people do not starve; they mostly have accommodation; their basic health and education needs can be met. But Western liberal democracy has failed to address the ethical, personal and even spiritual needs of the citizenry to find meaning and purpose in their lives through their political and civic participation. It was David Marquand who first coined the term 'democratic deficit' to refer to the lack of political oversight for the institutions of the European Economic Community, oversight to which they would have been subject if they were initiatives of individual nation-states (Marquand 1979). Since then, the term has come to encapsulate many of the flaws in modern representative democracy that prevent popular control of political decisions and public policy: elite domination of politics, privileging business, finance and capital; powerful people, politicians and bureaucrats pursuing their own or sectional interests; citizens with little knowledge of, and little interest in, politics; minimal opportunity for social movements or the public interest to influence governments; political parties bereft of ideas; elections dominated by wealthy interests, spin, negative advertising and legal manoeuvring which citizens find irrelevant; alienated minorities; and incivility (Dryzek and Dunleavy 2009: 207–8).

There are some commentators who see the promises of meaningful participation in democracy as an impossibility and appeal for scholars and political actors to move on, to accept democracy as an affectation bogged down in a pre-modern mythology and to take a scientific approach to the electoral and administrative practices that constitute the actual society regardless of ideology and ideals (Rubin 2001). But the current representative regimes should not be the final word in governance systems, just as the ancient assemblies practising direct democracy were not the end of democracy's development. As has been observed in the body of this book, democracy is an open system, in its best iterations it is constantly seeking improvement and always goaded on by the possibility that the people collectively attempting to better their lives, their situation and their world is the highest aspiration available to humans, and if not that, is at least an entirely rewarding project to grab whatever meaning may be available among the vagaries of existence.

Having considered the hard-won heritage of democracy in disparate times and places in preceding chapters, this companion to the history of popular rule is now at the point where it provides an excellent vantage point from which to study the utility, pitfalls and future of this most controversial and contested form of governance. This Conclusion seeks to draw out the ramifications of this book and, in particular, to raise questions about how we think about democracy, its history, its current form and its future. On the positive side of the ledger, the breadth of examples in this book prompt reflection on the claim that democracy arises from universal human values and its strength lies in its adaptability to different circumstances, from small hunting bands to large technological societies. On the negative side of the ledger, the preceding chapters remind us of democracy's limitations: its propensity to backslide, most spectacularly into autocracy, but more pervasively to let itself be used by oligarchy. Further, despite the hope that democracy is an antidote to war, oligarchs all too often use the promise of empire to justify violence. Finally, the forty-three chapters of this book remind us of the challenge that is always before democracy – to improve itself, to adapt to new conditions, to overcome oligarchy, to democratise democracy.

Democracy is Universal

In considering the chapters of this book as a whole, one striking observation emerges: democracy has the potential to thrive, and very frequently has thrived, among all of the peoples of the earth. This contradicts the conventional wisdom on democracy and its history, which tends to emphasises only some key moments of Western civilisation (Isakhan and Stockwell 2011). The argument here is that democracy is re-emerging in new and interesting ways from within a variety of human civilisations that have – in one time or another, in one form or another – practised it before. Democracy is not the exclusive invention of any one civilisation, culture or context. It has a deep and universal history that must be acknowledged if we are to continue to strive towards it, and make it better suited to the many peoples who want it.

This claim to universality is a recurring theme of this book. In Chris Boehm's chapter on prehistory, it was seen that a rudimentary democracy emerged in the interstices of evolving human behaviour as an antidote to authoritarianism among our earliest ancestors. Tracing the behavioural phylogenetics of the early Great Apes, the natural history of democracy is seen to have some antiquity. Our ancestors' egalitarian processes of coalition-building and providing checks and balances on leadership suggest that deliberative and democratic tendencies may have supplied the human race with certain evolutionary advantages that go some way to establishing why the will to democracy is so deeply ingrained in human society. Other evidence for the universal and deep roots of democracy is provided in chapters by Maxwell Owusu on Africa, Bruce Johansen on Native America and Tim Rowse on Australasia. In discussion of the experience of traditional societies before and after colonial contact, indigenous people are seen to have had their own distinctive, democratic tendencies resting predominantly on processes of extensive and egalitarian consultation, deliberation and debate. Of course, these examples are far from perfect democracies from the modern, Western point of view, but they all throw up models of discussion, decision making and organisation that have developed over millennia, stood the test of time and may provide models for the future.

These deep roots suggest that democracy may in fact have originated before many of the cultures and religions that are so often thought to prevent or inhibit it. If democracy was practised by our pre-human antecedents and among tribal societies generally, then it most certainly predates civilisation itself as well as modern, particularly monotheistic, religion. To put it another way – democracy probably predates the very earliest civilisations, and therefore the notion of civilisation itself; it also probably predates organised religion and therefore religion itself. If this is true, no particular civilisation or religion could be antithetical to democracy by necessity. Rather, those who hold that the Islamic religion or Chinese culture are incapable of democracy are duped either by Eurocentrism or by authoritarian leaders manufacturing ideology in order to cling to power.

This is the territory to which Amartya Sen points when seeking the universal value in democracy: when the particular regional characteristics or cultural claims are put aside, what remains are *intrinsic* values of political participation and freedom in human life, the *instrumental* value of keeping political decision making accountable and the *constructive* part democracy plays in establishing values in the context of the needs, rights and duties of all humans (Sen 1999). John Keane is just one commentator who is sympathetic to democracy and its goals, but wary of any claim it would make to universality. He points out that not everyone agrees that democracy is a good thing and quotes Afghan warlords and Russian oligarchs to support his case before concluding: 'Democracy is a geographic, not a global morality, and that's that' (Keane 2009: 842). Keane goes on to report his conversation with philosopher Richard Rorty where they conclude that 'modern representative democracy was a "peculiarity" of "North Atlantic culture". It had no ultimate justification, it was neither True nor Right nor Universal' (Keane 2009: 843). Nevertheless, it emerges that Rorty does not think democracy needs philosophical justification because democrats should:

> whistle their way through the world, with an air of 'philosophical superficiality and light-mindedness . . . democracy was 'morally superior' because it was part of 'a culture of hope – hope of a better world as attainable in the here and now by social and political effort . . . So even though democracy is only one norm among others, it is self-evidently superior when put into practice. (Keane 2009: 843)

However, Keane does produce a broader argument that where democracy avoids hubris and embraces humility, then its commitment to equality and problem solving means it becomes 'a universal ideal because it is a basic precondition of people being able to live together on earth freed from arrogant power' (Keane 2009: 852).

Sen and Keane both point to the pragmatic rationale for the universality of democracy: it has universal applicability because it can work everywhere (Keane 2009; Sen 1999). The histories presented in this book reinforce the point that elements of democracy have been practised successfully by people from all over the world. All inhabited continents and most of the world's significant cultures are represented in the book at least once: China, India, Mesopotamia, Greece, Rome, Modern Europe, Africa, Indigenous Australasia. This volume also presents convincing evidence for the applicability of democracy across religious borders and that, while democracy can find itself in conflict with theocracy, religions of all stripes can accommodate and even make use of democracy. The early Jewish Israelites practised it in electing their leaders, and their contribution in insisting that their leaders were subject to the same laws as those they led made a major contribution to the development of democracy. Chapters by Steven Muhlberger and Victoria Tin-bur Hui show how the Hindu and Buddhist traditions, as well as Confucian philosophy, developed a remarkable archive of democratic prescriptions that contested autocratic rule and were often put into practice. Chapters by Larbi Sadiki and Nader Hashemi establish how democratic tendencies in Islam have long histories that are informing contemporary democratic initiatives. John Hittinger's chapter establishes how the medieval Christian Church persisted with a democratic ethos as a counter to feudal monarchy, in the defence of the common people and their customary law and in the councils of the Church itself. And, of course, democracy had its humble beginnings in the polytheistic and pagan societies of the Assyrians, Phoenicians, Greeks and Romans.

While this book does much to establish the universal applicability of democracy, it does not mean that democracy will always succeed or that its triumph is inevitable. Indeed, the book does not give the impression that the history of democracy is a litany of success stories that will ultimately end with its global triumph. Democracy is a fragile system of governance and is all too easily quashed, averted and destroyed as is borne out in many chapters, including those by Mike Rapport on the revolutions of 1848 that by the end of 1849 had been suppressed, by Conan Fischer on the democratic flourishing after the Treaty of Versailles at the end of the First World War that provided no competition to the rise of fascism, and by Lincoln A. Mitchell on the less than democratic outcomes of the 2003 Rose Revolution in Georgia. This book has not ignored those who have agitated for democracy, but remained frustrated and disappointed: Christine Doran explains how nineteenth-century, ethnic Chinese, Singaporean intellectuals used ancient Asian experience to develop their own distinctive, democratic ideology that never matured into a robust democratic reality; Donald M. Seekins tells of the Burmese people and their inspirational leaders, such as Aung Sun Suu Kyi, who have fought for democracy but never fully realised their dreams. But these failings – just as much as the well-known successes – indicate the universal appeal of democracy. The willingness of people to persevere in the pursuit of democracy, even against insurmountable odds and without the promise of glory, wealth or easy access to heaven, indicates the power of this idea and its broad appeal. Then, again, all too often democracy is expected to be a complete success or otherwise it is judged a complete failure – and that does not necessarily tell the whole story. For example, Barry Hindess' chapter on socialism, communism and anarchism reveals how the initial democratic energy underpinning these movements produced, in the case of communism, abuse and tyranny, but that while socialism has faltered, its contribution has nevertheless pushed parliamentary politics into introducing social welfare, expanding education availability, providing health support and supporting other egalitarian policies. That the pursuit of democracy, even when it fails by the aspirants' standards, produces unexpected, unpredicted democratic outcomes further substantiates democracy's pragmatic claim to universality: even in defeat, democracy cannot stop producing results.

Democracy is Adaptable

Democracy's claim to universality rests in part on its high level of adaptability. One reason democracy can take root, and has often flourished, in so many different geographical, religious and cultural environments is that it defines itself with a set of principles that are sufficiently dynamic and flexible to find resonance in an array of different contexts. Democracy has not been given due credit for its adaptability. In addition to the Eurocentric expectations of democracy outlined earlier, much of the literature on democracy has sought to set preconditions and constraints that limit democratic possibilities. These high standards became especially pronounced during the middle of the twentieth century as the Western liberal model of democracy began to spread across much of the world and the quality of its uptake was judged against criteria that had only recently been instituted in London and Washington after hundreds of years that had seen civil war, political trials and executions, as well as summary disenfranchisements and factional struggles. The expectation that former colonies would suddenly emerge as mature democracies was mostly doomed to failure.

Many commentators had the expectation that a successful democracy required cultural unity and religious homogeneity, but a review of academic literature shows that there were three further preconditions suggested as necessary for the spread and stability of democracy. The first of these was *economic development*, the hope being that greater degrees of wealth would free up labour and enable citizens to further their education, improve their literacy and move to urbanised environments where citizens could participate in political life and the creation of better and more democratic institutions (Downs 1957; Lipset [1959] 1971). Wealth was then expected to generate a second key precondition of democracy, *a civil society* (or communal pluralism) represented by a healthy and peaceful mix of competition and cooperation among various stakeholders, who would work together towards the common good (Dahl 1966, 1971; Lijphart [1968] 1975, 1977). A final key precondition for democracy evident in much of the literature is the need for *a pre-existing functioning state* with strong political institutions and the rule of law prior to democratisation (Dahl 1971; Huntington 1968). There was also the ancillary expectation that such a state would be governed by elites with an interest in promoting democracy, but who could restrict any mass participation that might cause instability during times of transition (Hertz 1982; O'Donnell and Schmitter 1986).

On the one hand, many of the democracies discussed in this volume more or less meet these criteria of wealth, civil society and a functioning state governed by democracy-minded elites. In ancient Greece and Rome, in medieval Venice and Scandinavia, and in early modern Switzerland and America, the prosperity of the citizens certainly allowed them to partake in political life, to manage the mechanisms of governance and to gradually steer towards a more equitable state. On the other hand, examples from many chapters in this collection contradict these so-called preconditions for democracy. Many of the movements recorded here emanated from among the impoverished and disenfranchised, those who could not read and write, who lived outside major cities and at a great distance from the circles of power. In fact, the emphasis on economic development as a precondition for democracy obscures the fact that it is often in the poorest circumstance that the democratic impetus emerges: the impoverished have so little to lose. Roger Southall's chapter on South Africa's gradual popular revolt against apartheid provides a clear example of an uprising of the dispossessed. The recent Arab revolutions provide further examples of the democratic initiative coming from the least wealthy: it began when a young street vendor, too poor to afford a licence or a bribe to ply his trade, set himself alight in the small rural Tunisian town of Sidi Bouzid (Isakhan *et al.* 2012).

Similarly flawed is the notion that a robust civil society must exist prior to democratisation. In many of the struggles towards democracy recounted here, communal pluralism had been quashed by the incumbent autocrats and it was the struggle itself that created a new civil society, sometimes virtually overnight as people grasped the opportunity to pursue democracy in their own way. The experience of Iraq since the US invasion of 2003 is particularly instructive. While the former Baathist state, the US occupation and then elements of the new Iraqi political elite have done much to silence dissent, limit political freedom and present a highly stage-managed version of a communal pluralism, the Iraqi people's will towards democracy is evident in the myriad of grassroots civil society organisations, political parties and media outlets that have emerged.

Finally, the notion that democracy needs a pre-functioning state ruled by more or less democratically-minded elites is also well off the mark. The urge to democracy is often a struggle against the failure of the institutions of the state to meet the needs of the people, provide the rule of law and so on. Democracy often comes about as a push from below, not above. It is often a fight against the elites and only rarely something ushered in by them. For example, Andrew Bradstock's chapter on the Diggers and Levellers during the English Civil War shows how many of the democratic rights and institutions we take for granted now can be traced back to the agitation of the poorest and most powerless members of society. Similarly, the penniless *sans culottes*, who could not afford fashionable knee-breeches (culottes), were the shock troops of the French Revolution and always strong proponents of popular democracy (Soboul 1958). Baogang He's chapter on Chinese local democratisation takes this point further when he explains that, despite the state's own authoritarianism, the people continue to practise forms of democracy at a local level.

The above analysis establishes the adaptability of democracy whatever prerequisites are theorised by academics and commentators. There is no doubt that wealth, civil society and functioning government by sympathetic elites assist democratic develop-ment and are hallmarks of recent, mature democracies, but when the people are ready to embrace democracy then they can do it on their own terms, in their own way and free of theoretical constraints. This points to the flexibility of democracy, which underlies its adaptability and thus its universal applicability. The general concept of democracy is eminently adaptable to societies regardless of their scale or the conditions of the state. While small societies provide the opportunity for direct participation in town hall meetings with decision-making clout, even large societies provide the opportunity for mass participation to produce change from well-entrenched govern-ments with unpopular policies, as was evident in India in the 1970s when the long-serving Congress government of Indira Ghandi was rejected at elections because of its authoritarian birth control policy (Frank 2001). Democracy does not need to rely on the theoretical justification – at some stage it must be done by the people – under banyan trees, in churches, mosques and temples, at town halls, meetings and assemblies, in lunchrooms, coffee shops and bars, around water-coolers and barbeques. Democracy will happen how it happens because it always relies on the people adapting their practice until they find the confidence to grasp their own sovereignty. This does not occur naturally and to achieve democracy, the people have to find a form of democracy sufficiently flexible to adapt to current conditions and overcome the problems that arise, such as the countervailing influence of oligarchy.

Problems with Democracy 1: Oligarchy and Democracy

The way of democracy is never smooth. Unlike other ideologies, democracy welcomes criticism and dissent. This book is not a hagiography for democracy and the contributors have been rigorous in alerting readers to the limitations of democracy. Recognising the universal and adaptable nature of democracy forces us to also acknowledge the universal and adaptable nature of tyranny and despotism. For all the democratic movements and moments recorded in this volume, there is also ample evidence that people everywhere are capable of bloodshed, of spreading fear and of the arbitrary domination of their fellow human beings. Just as democracy can be practised by peoples in all manner of religious and cultural settings and can defy even the best efforts to predict and control it, so too can moguls, magnates and megalomaniacs grab power with their own authoritarian agendas. Democracy's task has always been to serve as a bulwark against such events, to be the mechanism by which the collective voice of reason can emerge. But even in its best iterations, democracy is always haunted not just by the spectre of despotism, but also by the need to carefully balance the ideals of democracy against the need for pragmatic, decisive and effective leadership. This is an age-old issue, the unsteady relationship between democracy and oligarchy.

The problem of oligarchy is something internal to democracy's own make-up: while democracy is technically the rule of the people, it needs some form of leadership to be effective. Only anarchists would argue that leadership is unnecessary for democracy to flourish. While anarchism certainly remains a grand vision based on the hope that the people can manage their sovereignty by themselves, real-world experiments in Catalonia in the 1930s and the alternative movements of the 1960s and 1970s have not produced success on anything but the smallest scale and for the briefest of times. At a number of points in this book, in Rome, but also in the Greek city-states, democracy has arisen as a *concession to the lower orders* as part of a power play among the aristocracy. Aristocrats and oligarchs often use democracy, or the promise of democracy, strategically in their own battles. It was Aristotle, as M. I. Finley shows, who was the first to point out that democracy was skewed to aristocratic rather than the demotic because, whether in debate or elections, the criteria by which the 'best' argument or candidate is chosen will always be influenced by those who already have power: the elite set the terms of debate, are better at presenting compelling arguments and quicker to grab an opportunity, so they will do better in a democracy than the common people (Aristotle [350 BCE] 1962: IV:15; Finley 1973: 19). That democracy prevailed in

Athens for most of the following two centuries, despite oligarchic criticism and coups, was an early indicator of democracy's adaptability and resilience, particularly where it used the skills of the upper orders.

Inheriting the intellectual tradition of oligarchic sympathisers like Aristotle, the 'classical elitists' of the early twentieth century, such as Vilfredo Pareto, Gaetano Mosca and Robert Michels, enunciated the distance between the promise of rule by the people and the reality in any mass society of rule by elites. Michels developed a sociological theory of organisations that established 'the iron law of oligarchy' (Michels [1911] 1959: 377–92). He argued that, despite the democratic fiction that sovereignty resides in the aggregate of the people, the formal constitution never matches the real power structure which is necessarily some form of rule by a political elite: 'It is organisation which gives birth to the dominion of the elected over the electors . . . Who says organisation, says oligarchy' (Michels [1911] 1959: 401). To Michels, it is the technical necessities of organisation that produce the requirement for elitism: government of complex societies requires planning and implementation processes that need to be administered by a permanent and professional structure that in turn needs to be coordinated. Michels argues that this higher level of coordination (deciding policy goals, thematic directions and key appointments) would never be achieved by the mass of people, who would keep on arguing about alternatives. Thus, an elite is required to produce decisiveness and, while there may be some circulation of power among elites, the group with actual or potential political power is necessarily quite small.

While the 'classical elitists' subsequent accommodation of fascism did them no credit, nevertheless their work points to one of the 'the logical limits' of democracy in a mass society: when the people cede power to their representatives at elections, they then cannot regain that power because of their 'atomistic multiplicity and the inevitable gulf separating the detailed knowledge of the full-time professional from that of even the most informed amateur' (Hyland 1995: 248). The interesting question is whether democratic representation can ever escape its origins, so skilfully outlined in Ann Lyon's chapter on the development of the English Parliament as 'a device of government before ever it can be sensibly viewed as a "right" of the governed' (Crick 1962: 26). Such questions have long plagued the history of democracy and arise frequently throughout this book. For example, chapters on the American and French revolutions by Andrew Shankman and John Markoff, respectively, show how, while both these events sought democracy, they were mostly led by the middle classes who ensured that sympathetic *oligarchies were in place before the franchise was extended* to the lower orders. The battles to spread the democracy through all classes were not easily won and it took centuries of civil action – from anti-slavery movements, the suffragettes and civil rights activists of all shades – to extend the equalities and freedoms that underpinned the revolutions to the broader populace. More to the point, the extension of the franchise has done little to diffuse power beyond the wealthy and well educated. Even the world's best democracies often see authority rotate between a small circle of elites, who might govern on behalf of the masses but do so with very little consultation.

One clear indicator of the dominance of the elite is the declining share of wealth held by the middle and lower classes: in 2007, while the wealthiest 1 per cent of the US population held 35 per cent of the wealth, the bottom 80 per cent of the population owned only 15 per cent of the wealth, down from 18.7 per cent in 1983, and the bottom 40 per cent of the country controlled less than 1 per cent of the wealth (Domhoff 2011). Concentrations of wealth produce tendencies to oligarchy that do have an impact on the quality of democracy. The failure of effective campaign finance reform in the United States has produced a political environment where a small group of special interests exert an inordinate influence on the political process and can defeat policies even when those policies have broad public support. John Fisher's chapter on South America captures well how the liberally inclined, liberation movements of Bolívar and San Martín, while dedicated to democracy and remarkably successful in throwing off Spanish imperialism, nevertheless produced nations that were all too prone to oligarchy with consequential corruption, cult of personality and governments liable to overthrow by military junta. There is discussion of how democracies can manage the influence of oligarchies below, but first it is useful to consider some of the elite's most useful tools in managing populations: the threat of war and the attraction of empire.

Problems with Democracy 2: War, Empire and Democracy

This book frequently brings to the fore an issue that has long plagued democracy: the relationship between democracy, war and empire. On the whole, the preconception is that democracies are more pacifist than other regime types. There is a high-minded expectation that democracies will prefer deliberation to conflict, but the reality is that democracies too are prone to war, particularly when elites can manipulate threats from external sources and jingoistic responses from within to further their own political and economic interests. The problem for democracy is how to manage its own bellicose propensities.

There is certainly some compelling evidence that establishes that the more democratic a society, the less severe its wars have been (Rummel 1995). The claim that democracies are less prone to wars than other forms of governance is sometimes described as the Democratic Peace Theory (DPT). This theory has been limited by exceptions and clarifications, and now comes to the assertion that democracies are peaceful only in a fairly limited way: by and large they refrain from attacking other democracies (Elman 1997; Russett 1993). Proponents of DPT argue that free citizens generally prefer not to sacrifice their blood, or to use violence of any kind, especially on other free citizens. Typically, to get a democratic population to support a conflict, the cause of the war has to be just and has to be presented to the people to gain their explicit consent, ideally with the support of opposition parties and the media. Others have claimed that democracy also makes war difficult to sustain, particularly in the case of 'small wars', such as France in Algeria and the United States in Vietnam, where the larger combatants are more prone to self-inflicted defeat because their high body count and the viciousness of their counter-insurgency tactics make such wars remarkably unpopular at home (Merom 2003).

What many of the chapters in this collection draw out is that the relationship between war and democracy is actually more nuanced and diverse than preconceptions of democratic pacifism allow. War has been a central part of some democracies in which the militaristic nature of a society – like that of the ancient Assyrians or Greeks – can make war itself a democratic exercise (Pritchard 2010). In such contexts, war is subjected to popular will, decided upon by a majority in the assembly and governed by strict protocols and prescriptions. Then there is the counter-intuitive case where war sometimes leads to more democracy. In ancient China, it was the need to staff their expanding military that prompted the kings to succumb to the various demands of the people. The English Civil War, the US War of Independence, the First and Second World Wars, the Cold War and the recent interventions in Afghanistan and Iraq were all – to varying degrees of success and legitimacy – fought in the name of democracy, to defend freedom from tyranny and they all ended with at least some initial expansion of the participation of ordinary people in political life. The people will accept privation and the circumscription of rights when the case is successfully made that the survival of democracy necessitates such conditions. However, war has also destroyed many democracies: Athens succumbed first to the Spartans and then to the rise of Alexander the Great; the Roman Republic gave way to the perpetual dictatorship of Julius Caesar, civil war then the rise of Empire and its expansive military project; Napoleon came to power in the aftermath of the French Revolution; Hitler was elected and then harnessed popular resentment of the Treaty of Versailles and the Weimar Republic, among other things, to consolidate his power and trigger the Second World War.

These later examples lead us towards another element of democracy's problematic relationship with war: its equivocal attitude to empire. Perhaps the most controversial assessment of this issue was put forward by Deepak Lal's *In Praise of Empire: Globalisation and Order* in which he argues that empires have been a progressive historical force (Lal 2004). For Lal, expansive empires provide the security and stability necessary to forge a consistent system of governance which fosters trade and prosperity. He not only urges the United States to acknowledge its status as an empire, but also to do away with its supposed 'moral imperative' towards democracy, human rights and equality in order to fulfil its imperial potential. He uses the case of Iraq to argue that the United States should abandon its mission to implant democracy, as the Iraqi people are unlikely to embrace it and the US promotion of democracy will prove to be a costly failure. This raises many interesting questions. If one counters Lal's argument by asserting that empires – especially democratic ones – should seek to promulgate democracy across their territories, one is left with very few historical examples. Certainly, expansive and militant empires that have at least some democratic tendencies, like that of ancient Rome, medieval Islam or colonial France, made little effort to extend the rights and privileges of the homeland to their newest subjects. Athens' imperial adventures at the head of the Delian League not only did very little to spread democracy, but also led to massacres and other brutalities as well as bringing about the Peloponnesian War, which Athens lost almost at the cost of her democracy. In fact, as these empires expanded, more of the people with whom they came in contact were disenfranchised and/or enslaved. The alternative in recent years, however, has been 'democracy promotion', which, as Christopher Hobson's chapter demonstrates, has long served as a central pillar of US foreign policy. While this policy has met with some success, the quality of democracy so installed is often questioned in this book by Lincoln A. Mitchell and Benjamin Isakhan in their chapters on Georgia and Iraq.

What becomes apparent in consideration of democracy's relationship with war and empire is the tenuous grip of democracy when it is prescribed, installed and insisted upon by foreign powers without concern for the recipient nation's economic and social preparedness for popular government. The corollary is that where the people are ready for democracy, where they are keen to create it for themselves then it will flourish and grow regardless of external opinion. Takashi Inoguchi's chapter on Japan's transition to democracy after the Second World War is instructive in showing how the Japanese moulded the US model of democracy to their own cultural frame.

While one might argue that for democracy to flourish it is important to eliminate empires altogether, an alternative solution could be found in fresh thinking to develop ways in which democratic empires – like the United States – can move beyond mere 'democracy promotion'. Imagine, for example, if the United States were to extend the vote to any country that it occupies (such as Afghanistan today). While utopian in prospect, this idea has the virtue of a practical outcome where democracy is made real for people who have little experience of it and the US commitment to democracy is put beyond question. Similarly utopian is the notion of putting entry into a war to the popular vote – as practised in ancient Greece where the decision to go to war or not was made by the assembly. The possibilities for democracy to find new ways to limit the impact of war and manage imperial ambition should not be underestimated. It has been seen at a number of points in this book that democracy always has on offer the possibility of renewal through compromise, and nowhere is that more evident than in its ability to civilise civil wars in seemingly intractable trouble spots such as Cyprus, South Africa and Northern Ireland. If democracy could find a way though these conflicts then it has the potential to go further and make the DPT a reality.

Democratising Democracy

The final issue for this Conclusion should be a constant concern for democrats and a major challenge for the future: how to make democracy more democratic. This book shows the deep and rich history of democracy, the question now is how to ensure its future. First, it must be acknowledged that the universal applicability of democracy has a corollary in the universal possibility of despotism – the pursuit of democracy is a constant battle to overcome the human desire for the certainty and security of having someone to tell you what to do. Thinking for oneself, speaking up and arguing the issue through are all difficult to achieve, but are nevertheless necessary skills required by democrats to play a part in their own governance. As seen above, democracy is eminently adaptable, but the challenge is to improve it in any given situation. How can citizens be more egalitarian and autonomous? How can the rule of law be fairer, more compassionate and more just? How can democratic practices be more competitive, more cooperative and more participatory? Feminist scholars have taken a programmatic approach to democratising representative democracy by developing tactics that give women the experience from which they can build the skills to play a more central role in political life: 'building new pathways into politics, fostering political learning and creating new forms of articulation across and beyond existing democratic spaces'

(Cornwall and Goetz 2005: 783). It would appear that these tactics have broader applicability for anyone outside the political class.

These questions of democratising democracy take on more urgency for post-colonial scholars, who contrast the hegemony inherent in liberal democracy of the West with new experiments in participatory democracy in the South designed to open up the possibilities of citizenship rather than just easing more professionals into the political class (Santos 2005). By way of contrast, others see the democratisation project as 'the creation of new kinds of disciplined subjects who will fit into the sort of political economy required by capitalist development' (Dryzek and Dunleavy 2009: 305). Perhaps to better understand the possibilities inherent in democratising democracy it is useful to explore the potential for new forms of citizenship in emerging political environments.

As many of the chapters above show, the history of democracy is contiguous with the citizen's search for autonomy. In the classical period of Greece and Rome, the time and energy available for participation and deliberation was a product of the extra labour of women and slaves excluded from citizenship. There is still a concern that citizenship is not at all an inclusive process, but produces the solidarity of citizens on which democracy depends only by defining itself against the excluded others (Thomas and Meredyth 1996). In the early modern period the rise of the economically confident and politically creative lower classes opened the conceptual spaces to think about the potential for broader, more inclusive democracies with the vision and power to improve social conditions by alleviating poverty, improving health and spreading educational opportunity. These challenges gave democracy a purpose and prompted it to grow and develop. Democracy was understood as more than an inert system, it had become a dynamic mechanism and one of its functions was to recreate itself in ways that improved the quality of democracy by improving not just the lives of citizens but their democratic capabilities. The effect of these changes was apparent from the nineteenth century when people, rather than governments, began to use democratic tactics to improve the quality of democracy. The anti-slavery, women's suffrage and civil rights movements are all shining examples of grassroots efforts coming from the people to change government policies that were the product of deeply ingrained social beliefs.

While it may be argued that years after these successful campaigns there is still much to be done to address racial and gender injustice, nevertheless, it is now people of colour and women, many in high political office, who lead the way to a more complete egalitarianism. But, as useful as friends in high places are, the fate of democracy is always, finally in the hands of its citizens and it is from the lower classes, by far the largest section of the people to whom democracy holds out the promise of self-rule, that the potential for broad-based, grassroots movements to confront anti-democratic aspects of society come. The chapters in the final section of this book provide a selection of new ways to think about democracy as it seeks to adapt to new developments. The globalisation process, the shift of market capitalism from a national to an international focus, and the development of communications technology that allows instant access to information from people around the world have all prompted democratic theorists to move beyond a concern for popular government solely within nation-states to appreciate the potential for transnational and digital democracy with more inclusive debate and deliberation outside the hegemonical constraints of (almost) all politics to date. This offers an understanding of the unfinished nature of the democratic project and the critical importance of basing new thinking about democracy in the lived reality of ordinary people – it is their hopes and aspirations that must guide the future of democracy.

The authoritarianism that persists in places like Burma and China, and that appears to be growing in places like Russia, Iran and Venezuela is no surprise to those who appreciate the long history of interaction between democracy and autocracy, and the fragility of democracy itself. But the important lesson from history for these authoritarian situations is that gradual reformism mixed with timely, strategic interventions can develop democracy in the gaps of even the most autocratic monoliths when there is a commitment among the people to persist, to refuse martyrdom and to make their own forms of democracy in their own image. The recreation of democracy is a challenge for all democrats: democracy is not a set formula that can be applied indiscriminately in all situations, it is an invitation to participate in the unending jobs of argument and debate, of building coalitions and consensus, of the people themselves making the form of government that best responds to their needs.

So what then are potential strategies for overcoming the democratic deficit, undermining the oligarchies that arise in democracies and restoring the citizen to the centre of the political process where their sovereignty is not just theoretical as one member of the mass, but also practical in their daily lived experience? It will come as a surprise to many that recent scholars point to Niccolò Machiavelli (in *Discourses* rather than *The Prince*) as an early advocate of confronting the injustice that the elites inevitably commit and controlling them with '*ferocious populism*' not just through testing electoral mechanisms, but also 'more direct and robust modes of popular participation . . . through extra-electoral institutions and practices, such as the tribunes of the people, public accusations, and popular appeals' (McCormick 2001: 297). Some thinkers point out that democracy is already adjusting and adapting to emerging conditions. In countering the oligarchic influence of well-financed interest groups, democratically-inclined interest groups are also emerging and, for many, the important democratic moment has moved on to the post-electoral surveillance of governments through 'monitory democracy', the use of government and non-government tribunals, lobby groups and an extensive range of other bodies to check and balance the unfettered power of government against public opinion and the popular will (Keane 2011).

One extra-electoral institution that has a long tradition as a means to balance the oligarchic effects of elections and patrician style in debate has been selection by lottery. The symbolic effect of choosing key decision makers from the citizenry at large should not be underestimated. The ancient Athenians sought, and modern juries seek, to moderate the influence of the elite and establish the primacy of the individual citizen by selecting participants for key roles by lottery. Some recent scholars have gone as far as to suggest that all decision-making bodies should be chosen by lot to limit the influence of elites on electors and also to ensure that congresses and parliaments are 'statistically representative of those affected by their decisions' (Burnheim 1995: 9).

Others go even further to argue new technologies could be utilised to break down existing structures of power based on geographical seats by assigning membership of reformed constituencies by random selection (Rehfeld 2005).

Beyond these structural adjustments, however, nothing defends the integrity of democracy as much as a well-educated citizenry, who not only understand the political system in which they live, but who also appreciate the means at their disposal to participate effectively in that system: from a well-argued letter to the editor of the local paper or a timely, colourful demonstration reported on the evening news, to a mass Internet campaign focused on key legislators or a strategic electoral campaign that could even end with independents holding the balance of power. Shifting political, cultural and technological environments require citizens to be constantly learning, updating their skills and adapting to new conditions (Stockwell 2001). Even a poor democracy has much potential, but it requires a well-educated and enthusiastic citizenry to exploit that potential, close the democratic deficit and reduce the oligarch's power to that of other citizens.

Finally, one should not underestimate the opportunities provided by elections in representative democracy. Admittedly, elections will only haphazardly produce policy outcomes that exactly reflect the popular will, mass media election campaigns are dominated by repetitive, negative advertising funded by wealthy interests and the best result likely is the circulation of elites. But elections do offer a space where all citizens can confront their potential representatives, ask revealing questions and even run their own campaigns. Rather than treat elections as pointless, they are an invitation to citizens to participate in setting the democratic agenda. Elections are also very effective in preventing elites from turning into totalitarian dictatorships: first, they allow 'the law of anticipated reaction' to have effect where it is not 'the last election that exercises controlling power over the government of the day, but the anticipation of the next election' (Hyland 1995: 253); and, secondly, elections provide peaceful opportunities for citizens to dispose of bad governments. When one considers the death, injury and human cost of removing tyrannies every year, the ability to turn over governments provides as much rationale as democracy needs. So while democracy might never precisely represent social interests in proportion to the number or intensity of their supporters and even if democratic regimes do tend towards elitism, the election performs a very valuable service in allowing for peaceful change of governments.

Conclusion

Democracy is important for humanity as the primary mechanism via which people all over the world have advocated for change and improvement over the last few hundred years. To briefly return to the definition of democracy outlined at length in the Introduction, democracy is a system of governance in which the citizens are invested with the full rights and responsibilities of citizenship; governed by a set of laws or norms that both protect their citizenship and hold to account those in power; and actively encouraged to contest, cooperate and participate in political life. What this book reveals is that this definition of democracy allows one to look through history to unearth a number of different times and places where, bit by bit, people have

developed elements of this democratic ideal. There is clearly much scholarly work left
to be done to broaden the traditional narrative of democracy and to unearth a robust
vision of rule by the people and its history. The editors hope that this book might assist
in shifting the history of democracy from something exclusive, external and foreign to
most of the inhabitants of the earth, to something of which all humans feel a part, to
which they can contribute and in which they are immersed. This would not only
bolster the struggle of all peoples against tyranny, but deepen and strengthen
democracy's practice and promulgation.

The questions of how to define it and how to classify its many histories are
important questions, and not just for political science or history. For a democracy to be
democratic these are just the type of questions that people need to consider, perhaps
not in the formal terms of academia, but in the colloquial discussions between friends,
acquaintances and citizens wherever they meet. Democracy has one major attribute
that has so far gone unheralded: anyone can have a go. While professionals such as
lawyers and journalists, business people and community organisers have their contribution to make, the inspired amateur with an ear for the vernacular can come up
with the new idea, make the intervention or cause the upset that makes everyone think
in fresh ways about the nature and purpose of democracy. While that amateur's
policies and pronouncements may not be to everyone's liking, they can serve as the
inspiration required to prompt others to enter the political fray. Unlike other forms of
government, which seek to tell people what to do, in a democracy, if it really is
deserving of its name, there is some point where the people – not the politicians or the
parties or the interest groups – have their hands on the tiller and democracy's future
and fate is for the people alone.

As E. H. Carr said to the British people as they continued to suffer in the aftermath
of the Second World War while already confronting the rigours of the Cold War: 'Mass
democracy is a difficult and largely uncharted territory; and we should be nearer the
mark, and should have a far more convincing slogan, if we spoke of the need, not to
defend democracy, but to create it' (Carr 1951: 76). The editors hope that this book
and the many facts and ideas contained in it will inform not only the academic
discussion of democracy, but also, through the processes of education, libraries,
information management and chance, that it will inspire the everyday deliberations
among citizens that lead to the creation of more and better democracy.

References

Aristotle ([350 BCE] 1962), *The Politics*, trans. T. A. Sinclair, London: Penguin.
Burnheim, J. (1995), *Is Democracy Possible?*, Cambridge: Polity.
Carr, E. H. (1951), *The New Society*, London: Macmillan.
Cornwall, A. and A. M. Goetz (2005), 'Democratizing Democracy: Feminist Perspectives',
    Democratization, 12(5), 783–800.
Crick, B. (1962), *In Defence of Politics*, London: Weidenfeld & Nicolson.
Dahl, R. A. (ed.) (1966), *Political Oppositions in Western Democracies*, New Haven, CT: Yale
    University Press.
Dahl, R. A. (1971), *Polyarchy: Participation and Opposition*, New Haven, CT: Yale University
    Press.

Domhoff, G. W. (2011), *Wealth, Income, and Power*, Santa Cruz, CA: University of California.

Downs, A. (1957), *An Economic Theory of Democracy*, New York: Harper & Row.

Dryzek, J. and P. Dunleavy (2009), *Theories of the Democratic State*, London: Palgrave Macmillan.

Elman, M. F. (ed.) (1997), *Paths to Peace: Is Democracy the Answer?*, Cambridge, MA: MIT Press.

Finley, M. I. (1973), *Democracy Ancient and Modern*, New Brunswick, NJ: Rutgers University Press.

Fowler, A. (2011), 'The Storming of High Street', Foreign Correspondent, ABC-TV, 30 August.

Frank, K. (2001), *Indira: The Life of Indira Nehru Gandhi*, London: HarperCollins.

Freedom in the World: The Arab Uprisings and their Global Repercussions (2012), New York: Freedom House.

Hertz, J. (ed.) (1982), *From Dictatorship to Democracy: Coping With the Legacies of Authoritarianism and Totalitarianism*, Westwood, CT: Greenwood.

Huntington, S. P. (1968), *Political Order in Changing Societies*, New Haven, CT: Yale University Press.

Hyland, J. L. (1995), *Democratic Theory: The Philosophical Foundations*, Manchester: Manchester University Press.

Isakhan, B., F. Mansouri and S. Akbarzadeh (eds) (2012), *The Arab Revolutions in Context: Civil Society and Democracy in a Changing Middle East*, Melbourne: Melbourne University Press.

Isakhan, B. and S. Stockwell (eds) (2011), *The Secret History of Democracy*, London: Palgrave Macmillan.

Keane, J. (2009), *The Life and Death of Democracy*, New York: Simon & Schuster.

Keane, J. (2011), 'Monitory Democracy? The Secret History of Democracy since 1945', in B. Isakhan and S. Stockwell (eds), *The Secret History of Democracy*, London: Palgrave Macmillan, pp 204–18.

Lal, D. (2004), *In Praise of Empires: Globalization and Order*, New York: Palgrave Macmillan.

Lijphart, A. ([1968] 1975), *The Politics of Accommodation: Pluralism and Democracy in the Netherlands*, 2nd edn, Berkeley, CA: University of California Press.

Lijphart, A. (1977), *Democracy in Plural Societies: A Comparative Exploration*, New Haven, CT: Yale University Press.

Lipset, S. M. ([1959] 1971), *Political Man: The Social Basis of Politics*, London: Heinemann.

Marquand, D. (1979), *Parliament for Europe*, London: Jonathan Cape.

McCormick, J. P. (2001), 'Machiavellian Democracy: Controlling Elites with Ferocious Populism', *American Political Science Review*, 95(2), 297–313.

Merom, G. (2003), *How Democracies Lose Small Wars: State, Society, and the Failures of France in Algeria, Israel in Lebanon, and the United States in Vietnam*, Cambridge: Cambridge University Press.

Michels, R. ([1911] 1959), *Political Parties*, New York: Dover.

O'Donnell, G. and P. C. Schmitter (1986), *Transitions from Authoritarian Rule: Tentative Conclusions about Uncertain Democracy*, Baltimore, MD: Johns Hopkins University Press.

Pritchard, D. (ed.) (2010), *War, Democracy and Culture in Classical Athens*, Cambridge: Cambridge University Press.

Rehfeld, A. (2005), *The Concept of Constituency: Political Representation, Democratic Legitimacy, and Institutional Design*, New York: Cambridge University Press.

Rubin, E. L. (2001), 'Getting Past Democracy', *University of Pennsylvania Law Review*, 149(30), 711–92.

Rummel, R. J. (1995), 'Democracies are Less Warlike than Other Regimes', *European Journal of International Relations*, 1(4), 457–79.

Russett, B. (1993), *Grasping the Democratic Peace: Principles for a Post-Cold War World*, Princeton, NJ: Princeton University Press.

Santos, B. (ed.) (2005), *Democratizing Democracy: Beyond the Liberal Democratic Canon*, London: Verso.

Sen, A. (1999), 'Democracy as a Universal Value', *Journal of Democracy*, 10(3), 3–17

Soboul, A. (1958), *Les Sans-culottes parisiens en l'an II: mouvement populaire et gouvernement révolutionnaire, 2 Juin 1793–Thermidor an II*, Paris: Clavreuil.

Stockwell, S. (2001), 'Hacking Democracy: The Work of the Global Citizen', *Southern Review*, 34(3), 87–103.

Thomas, J. and D. Meredyth (1996), 'Pluralising Civics', *Culture and Policy*, 7(2), 5–16.

Notes on the Contributors

James Anderson is Professor Emeritus of Political Geography in the School of Geography, Archaeology and Palaeoecology at Queen's University, Belfast, Northern Ireland.

Juan Manuel Arbona is Associate Professor and Chair, Growth and Structure of Cities at Bryn Mawr College, Bryn Mawr, Pennsylvania, United States.

Christopher Boehm is Professor of Biological Sciences and Anthropology and Director of the Goodall Research Center at the University of Southern California, Los Angeles, United States.

Andrew Bradstock holds the Howard Paterson Chair in Theology and Public Issues and is Director of the Centre for Theology and Public Issues at the University of Otago, Dunedin, New Zealand.

Lincoln Dahlberg is Visiting Research Fellow at the Centre for Critical and Cultural Studies at the University of Queensland, Brisbane, Australia.

Christine Doran is Senior Lecturer in History and Political Science at Charles Darwin University, Darwin, Australia.

Seymour Drescher is Distinguished University Professor in the Department of History at the University of Pittsburgh, United States.

Conan Fischer is Professorial Fellow in the School of History at the University of St Andrews, Scotland.

John Fisher is Emeritus Professor of Latin American History at the University of Liverpool, England.

Jack Goody is Emeritus William Wyse Professor of Social Anthropology, St John's College, University of Cambridge, England.

Patricia Grimshaw is Professorial Fellow in the School of Historical and Philosophical Studies at the University of Melbourne, Australia.

Kasper M. Hansen is Professor of Political Science at the University of Copenhagen, Denmark.

Nader Hashemi is an Assistant Professor of Middle East and Islamic Politics at the Josef Korbel School of International Studies, University of Denver, United States.

Baogang He holds a Chair in International Studies in the School of International and Political Studies at Deakin University, Melbourne, Australia.

Frode Hervik is Doctoral Fellow in the Centre for Medieval Studies at the University of Bergen, Norway.

Barry Hindess is Emeritus Professor of Political Science in the Research School of Social Sciences at the Australian National University, Canberra, Australia.

John P. Hittinger is Professor of Philosophy at the Center for Thomistic Studies at the University of St Thomas, Houston, United States.

Christopher Hobson is Research Associate in the Institute for Sustainability and Peace at the United Nations University, Tokyo, Japan.

Victoria Tin-bor Hui teaches in the Department of Political Science at the University of Notre Dame, Notre Dame, Indiana, United States.

Takashi Inoguchi is Professor Emeritus, University of Tokyo and President and Chair of the Board for the University of Niigata Prefecture, Japan.

Benjamin Isakhan is Australian Research Council Discovery (DECRA) Senior Research Fellow, Centre for Citizenship and Globalization, Deakin University, Melbourne, Australia. He is also Adjunct Senior Research Associate in the Department of Politics, Faculty of Humanities at the University of Johannesburg, South Africa.

Bruce E. Johansen is Jacob J. Isaacson University Research Professor in the School of Communication at the University of Nebraska, Omaha, United States.

John Keane is Professor of Politics at the University of Sydney, Australia and at the Wissenschaftszentrum Berlin, Germany.

Thomas Lau is Professor and Maître d'Enseignement et de Recherche at the University of Fribourg, Switzerland.

Brian Loader is Senior Lecturer in the Department of Sociology and Associate Director of the Science and Technology Studies Unit at the University of York, England.

Ann Lyon is Lecturer in the Faculty of Law at the University of Plymouth, England.

John Markoff is Distinguished University Professor of Sociology at the University of Pittsburgh, United States.

Philip Matyszak teaches Ancient History at the University of Cambridge, England.

Carmen Medeiros is the Academic Director of the School for International Training La Paz, Bolivia Program.

Lincoln A. Mitchell is an Associate Research Scholar at the Harriman Institute, Columbia University, New York, United States.

Steven Muhlberger is Professor of History at Nipissing University, North Bay, Ontario, Canada.

Michael L. Ondaatje is Senior Lecturer in American History at the University of Newcastle, NSW, Australia.

Maxwell Owusu is Distinguished Professor of Anthropology at the University of Michigan, Ann Arbor, United States.

David J. Phillips is Honorary Senior Research Fellow in the Department of Ancient History at Macquarie University, Sydney, Australia.

Kurt A. Raaflaub is Emeritus Professor of Classics and History at Brown University, Providence, Rhode Island, United States.

Mike Rapport is Senior Lecturer in the School of History and Politics at the University of Stirling, Scotland.

Christian F. Rostbøll is Associate Professor of Political Science at the University of Copenhagen, Denmark.

Tim Rowse is Professorial Fellow in the School of Humanities and Communication Arts and in the Institute of Culture and Society at the University of Western Sydney, Australia.

Larbi Sadiki is Senior Lecturer in Middle East Politics at the University of Exeter, England.

Donald M. Seekins is Emeritus Professor of Southeast Asian Studies in the College of International Studies at Meio University, Nago, Japan.

Andrew Shankman is Associate Professor in the Department of History at Rutgers University, New Jersey, United States.

Roger Southall is Professor and Head of Sociology at the University of the Witwatersrand, Braamfontein, Johannesburg, South Africa.

Charles Sowerwine is Emeritus Professor in the School of Historical and Philosophical Studies at the University of Melbourne, Australia.

Stephen Stockwell is Professor of Journalism and Communication in the School of Humanities at Griffith University, Queensland, Australia

Peter M. E. Volten is founder of the Centre for European Security Studies and Emeritus Professor in International Relations and Organisation at the University of Groningen, the Netherlands.

Index